CHANGING VIEWS
ON BRITISH HISTORY

❖

Essays on Historical Writing since 1939

CHANGING VIEWS ON

BRITISH

HISTORY

Essays on Historical Writing since 1939

✧

edited for The Conference on British Studies by

ELIZABETH CHAPIN FURBER

✧

HARVARD UNIVERSITY PRESS

CAMBRIDGE, MASSACHUSETTS

1966

Preface

❖

In 1957 the Conference on British Studies decided to sponsor a series of bibliographical articles which should be *not* exhaustive bibliographies but rather essays on the most significant developments in the field of British history since about 1939, emphasizing new interpretations and indicating problems still awaiting consideration. After the articles had appeared in a number of learned journals, the sponsors felt that it would be desirable to reprint them in one volume.

A hasty reading of these essays will show that the authors have variously interpreted their mandate. Some have confined their attention largely to books published since 1939, while others have analyzed a vast amount of periodical literature. Some have treated their period in broad, sweeping strokes, while others have used a more meticulous technique. The editor did not wish to impose a rigid scheme of approach. Yet from these articles certain common lines of development in the historiography of the past twenty-five years appear.

"Revisions, revaluations, and revelations but no major revolutions in interpretation" is Margaret Hastings' appraisal of work on the later Middle Ages, while John Clive affirms that "a revolution in historical writing is being quietly accomplished. The familiar quadrivium of political, social, economic, and cultural divisions, hallowed by long usage and canonized by *The Oxford History of England,* is about to vanish . . ." This change is most evident in the essays of Clive, Roger Prouty, and Henry R. Winkler, dealing with the nineteenth and twentieth centuries, possibly because of the volume and nature of the evidence for these years, which lends itself more readily to treatment by the methods of the demographer, the statistician, the sociologist, and the economist. But the essays on earlier periods also reveal the quickening influence of these new techniques. Margaret Hastings notes, as well, "the freshening stream of Marxist interpretation of history," though her fellow medievalist, Bryce Lyon, while acknowledging the stimulus of Marxism in the study of agrarian history, deplores the fact that much research still "flows down the same old riverbeds" and that English medievalists, with some exceptions, have ignored the new patterns created by French and Belgian scholars in the study of both agrarian and town history. In post-medieval fields, the "Storm over the Gentry" in Tudor and Stuart studies, the interest of Cromwell biographers in "the movement he represented—his class and its place in society" rather than in his "character," the growing literature on the beginnings of the Industrial Revolution and on the class structure of the eighteenth, nineteenth, and twentieth centuries are indicative of recent trends.

Not surprisingly, contemporary concerns have influenced interpretation or turned historians to subjects which seem peculiarly apposite to our present situation: the ideological wars of the Tudor period, the conservatism of Edmund Burke, the wars of the French Revolution with their threats of invasion. Roger Prouty suggests that the "general broadening of the subject matter of monographs [on social history] has been encouraged (and forced) by the interests and anxieties of the present." And J. Jean Hecht remarks that many studies of the artistic creations of the eighteenth century have been inspired in part "by the progressive deepening of that romantic nostalgia, which, especially since the Second World War, has lent a new enchantment to all vestiges of those decades before the burgeoning of mass society."

These essays show that present discontents, new approaches, new questions, while not completely obliterating the old "quadrivium," have had an important impact. A relative decline in the writing of strictly political history has occurred, but "a new orthodoxy in the sphere of political history," whose "progenitor . . . was Sir Lewis Namier," characterizes much of the writing. In constitutional history, revaluation, if not total revision, has marked the work in many periods, e.g., in the debate on the Tudor constitution and in the most recent attempt at the "total obliteration of Stubbs's reputation as a historian." In religious history, Roger Walcott records a "notable revival" in the field of ecclesiastical biography and also a "tendency to cross the traditional borders . . . to treat religion both in terms of politics and of intellectual history . . ." Religious history often merges into social history, as in many studies on the Hanoverian period noted by William Bultmann and J. Jean

Hecht. Scottish historians have been busily putting forth new interpretations of the Scottish Reformation, occasioned in part by the quatercentenary in 1960 of the triumph of that movement in Scotland. While
Lacey Baldwin Smith maintains that in Reformation scholarship "there
is still almost complete inability on the part of Catholics and Protestants
to comprehend their opponents' points of view," Perez Zagorin thinks,
hopefully, that "there are signs . . . that old animosities are giving way
to mutual comprehension and greater detachment." Crossing traditional
lines and using the methods of the social sciences and the insights to
be gained from psychology and other disciplines, detailed monographs
are modifying and refining earlier generalizations on such themes as the
commutation of labor services, mercantilism, the Victorian middle class,
the working class.

Many specialized studies have appeared, but few new syntheses apart
from Sir Winston Churchill's broad canvas, or the *Oxford History* cast
largely in the old mold; such is the impression gained from reading
these essays. Maurice Lee deplores the fact that Scottish historians, too
often confining their scholarship to editing texts and reluctant to write
general interpretive works, have left the field to romancers and cranks.
Bryce Lyon pleads for a halt in piling up "minutiae" on the ground
that "enough is now known about constitutional history to warrant new
syntheses" for the earlier Middle Ages, though Margaret Hastings finds
that such is not the case for the fourteenth century or for what Lacey
Smith terms "the quagmire of the fifteenth century." To answer questions fundamental to any new synthesis, most essayists see the need
for more "grass roots" studies, local and regional. But John Clive points
out that "if . . . a contraction of the geographical horizon in terms of
concentration upon local history is called for . . . the need for an
expansion of that horizon is equally urgent . . . it [is] becoming increasingly clear that the problems of Ireland, of the Empire, and of
foreign policy cannot be dissociated from the problems of British
domestic history, social and political." The extraordinary ferment in
Irish historical studies, chronicled in Helen Mulvey's essay, should
make such an expansion easier. Yet reviewing the historiography of the
Empire and Commonwealth since he published his original essay,
Philip Curtin finds that "regional specialization, which seemed a growing tendency in 1958, has now triumphed."

An editorial in the *Times Literary Supplement* of December 10, 1964,
entitled "No Nation Is an Island," and discussing the Oxford History

"school," stated: "Its weakness, at any rate until recently, was to treat whatever was going on in England as the central theme. Events abroad were interesting for their impact or relevance in England. Its products were thus exposed to the Ptolemaic fallacy of supposing that the observation point was not subject to the same kind of laws as the phenomena observed." While the same criticism might well be directed to historians of other countries, notably to Americans writing on their own history, these essays on British history add cogency to the editorialist's comment. Apart from obvious areas, such as Anglo-Dutch relations during the Stuart period, or military, diplomatic, and Empire history, the impression gained is that the great bulk of work reflects a largely insular point of view. A notable example is the failure of medievalists to take full account of the work of their continental colleagues. In all periods there is room for more exploration of common problems awaiting solution by the comparative method.

This is only one facet of the study of British history which opens enticing prospects. The authors of these essays were asked not only to evaluate but to suggest work needing to be done. For every period they have pointed to "gaps" waiting to be filled and new "questions" waiting for an answer.

At the start of this project in 1957 the sponsors hoped, with undue optimism, that all the articles could be completed by 1959, and thus cover a tidy twenty-year period. Unavoidably, publication was not completed until 1966. A cursory glance at the table of contents reveals that the articles do not all cover the period 1939 to 1966. Paul Hardacre's essay, which was commissioned by *The Journal of Modern History* before the Conference project was full under way, reviews work done since 1929, when the last volume of the late Wilbur Cortez Abbott's bibliography of Oliver Cromwell was published. Because publication of the essays has been so long drawn out, the editor left to the judgment of the individual authors the advisability of updating their articles. Robert Walcott, Perez Zagorin, and Roger Prouty felt that, unless they were prepared to make invidious distinctions, they would have to write a whole new article, and hence chose to leave their articles as originally written. Bryce Lyon, Margaret Hastings, John Clive, Maurice Lee, and Philip Curtin have added new paragraphs or a long footnote. The others have incorporated in their text and footnotes titles of works appearing since their articles were first published. Despite such variations, these essays should be of value to all students of British history.

In conclusion, acknowledgment is made to the following journals and their publishers for permission to reprint:

The American Historical Review (The American Historical Association): essays by Perez Zagorin, Robert Walcott, John Clive, and Philip D. Curtin

The Bulletin of the New York Public Library (The New York Public Library): the essay by J. Jean Hecht

The Canadian Historical Review (The University of Toronto Press): the essay by Maurice Lee, Jr.

The Historian (Phi Alpha Theta National Honor Society in History): essays by Roger W. Prouty and Helen F. Mulvey

The Journal of Modern History (The University of Chicago Press): essays by Paul H. Hardacre, William A. Bultmann, and Henry R. Winkler

Speculum (The Mediaeval Academy of America): the essay by Margaret Hastings

Studies in the Renaissance (The Renaissance Society of America): the essay by Lacey Baldwin Smith

Tijdschrift voor Geschiedenis (P. Noordhoft, Ltd., Groningen, The Netherlands): the essay by Bryce Lyon

Elizabeth Chapin Furber

August 1965
University of Pennsylvania

Contents

✧

CHANGING VIEWS
ON BRITISH HISTORY

✧

Essays on Historical Writing since 1939

LIST OF ABBREVIATIONS

AHR	American Historical Review
BIHR	Bulletin of the Institute of Historical Research
BJRL	Bulletin of the John Rylands Library
CHJ	Cambridge Historical Journal
DNB	Dictionary of National Biography
EcHR	Economic History Review
EHR	English Historical Review
HLQ	Huntington Library Quarterly
IHS	Irish Historical Studies
JBS	Journal of British Studies
JEcH	Journal of Economic History
JMH	Journal of Modern History
LQR	Law Quarterly Review
PMLA	Publications of the Modern Language Association
PP	Past and Present
SHR	Scottish Historical Review
SPCK	Society for Promoting Christian Knowledge
Studies	Studies: An Irish Quarterly Review
TRHS	Transactions of the Royal Historical Society
UBHJ	University of Birmingham Historical Journal
VS	Victorian Studies

Place of publication of all books cited is London, unless otherwise noted.

From Hengist and Horsa to Edward of Caernarvon: Recent Writing on English History

BRYCE LYON

$\diamond$

A DECADE AGO some American scholars, deploring the status of British history in the United States, established the Eastern Conference on British Studies for an exchange of ideas and an annual listing of publications and research projects. A Midwest and a Western Conference soon followed and the three conferences now collaborate in publishing a journal devoted to British history. This attempt to stimulate the study of British history is praiseworthy but can it stem the postwar decline in interest in English history prior to 1485? The leading American universities are no longer staffed by medievalists specializing in English history as was the case in the first forty years of this century. Since World War II American Medievalists have diversified their interests and concentrated upon areas previously neglected. The effect of this trend is obvious: neither this nor the next generation will witness an era like that of Gross, Haskins, McIlwain, Adams, Cheyney, Larson, Lunt, and Willard.

At the university towns in England, however, English medieval history continues to flourish despite the recent cry of some English medievalists that modern historians are stealing the pages of learned journals. To allay this fear Denys Hay, editor of the *English Historical Review*, proved that in recent issues English medieval history had occupied its accustomed space and assured them that in the future it would not retreat a page.[1] The disaster of six war years and the period of recovery

[Reprinted from *Tijdschrift voor Geschiedenis*, 76:377–422 (no. 4, 1963).]

[1] Professor Hay made his point by noting that the 1956 volume of the *EHR* contained 177 pages of medieval history and 176 pages of modern. The 1957 volume dropped to 169 pages of medieval history but gained only one page of modern history. See editorial note in *EHR* 77:1–5 (January 1962).

seems to have made no dent in the production of, or interest in, medieval history. From 1939 to 1962 the *English Historical Review* printed roughly 210 articles and notes on English history prior to 1307. Edouard Perroy took seven articles and 237 pages in the *Revue Historique* to discuss the publications in English on medieval history that appeared between 1939 and 1958.[2]

A few years after World War II Professor V. H. Galbraith, then Director of the Institute of Historical Research at London and editor of its *Bulletin,* asked P. Grierson and G. P. Cuttino to assay the position of medieval studies in England. Both agreed that the effects of the war were temporary and that the most urgent tasks were the consolidation of public and private records in central archives and the intensified cooperation of English and American medievalists in publicizing their research and editorial projects. Both suggested fruitful areas of research that have subsequently been explored.[3] There is still need, however, for more cooperation between English and American medievalists. At present, besides the itinerant scholars who help to disseminate knowledge, there are only the annual Anglo-American Historical Conferences begun before the war and the International Commission for the History of Representative and Parliamentary Institutions in which, through the efforts of Helen Cam during her stay at Harvard, the American members became active participants and cemented ties with the British members.[4] Efforts to keep abreast of the mass of literature and to publicize research and editorial projects have come from the Continent and America. Were it not for Edouard Perroy, few medievalists, even those in England, would be *au courant* in English medieval studies. *The Bulletin for the Progress of Mediaeval and Renaissance Studies in America and Canada,* edited formerly by J. F. Willard and presently by S. H. Thomson, has provided a commentary upon English medieval studies in North America. The recent bibliographical essays sponsored by the Conference on British Studies represent an even more ambitious effort to

[2] E. Perroy, "Histoire d'Angleterre (Moyen Age). Publications des années 1940 à 1945," *Revue Historique,* 196:323–355, 443–473 (October–December 1946). See also *Revue Historique,* 203:273–320 (April–June 1950); 208:255–273 (October–December 1952); 209:65–84 (January–March 1953); 214:282–321 (October–December 1955); 220:111–155 (July–September 1958).

[3] P. Grierson, "The Present Position of Medieval Studies in England," *BIHR,* 21:101–106 (May and November 1947); G. P. Cuttino, "English Medieval History: A Survey of Needs," *ibid.,* 107–115.

[4] See, for example, the essays of American members of the Commission in *Medieval Representation in Theory and Practice* which appeared as a supplement to *Speculum,* 29 (1954).

evaluate the trends in the writing of English history. Let us hope that these efforts by American and continental scholars will stimulate medievalists in England to cooperate in the exchange of information on the work being done in English medieval history.

PUBLICATION OF AUXILIARY STUDIES, GUIDES, AND RECORDS

Most students of English medieval history have not shown the interest in historical interpretation so greatly evidenced in the works of historians writing in other areas. Books and essays dealing with historiography are scarce. D. C. Douglas has emphasized the contributions made to medieval studies between 1660 and 1730 by such antiquarians as Dugdale, Rymer, Madox, and Hearne.[5] Although admitting the biases, rigidity, and narrowness of Edward Augustus Freeman, H. A. Cronne has rightfully underlined Freeman's role as a stimulator of medieval studies and concluded that "Freeman was the Erasmus of the nineteenth-century reformation in English historiography." More recently G. Templeman, a master of the historiographical essay, has digested the writing on Edward I and shown how it has fluctuated in its appraisal of medieval England's last great ruler.[6] The hundredth anniversary in 1950 of F. W. Maitland's birth occasioned numerous expressions of appreciation. T. F. T. Plucknett, contributing a most useful essay on Maitland's view of history and law, underlined Maitland's willingness to take chances and to put himself on record. It was Maitland who labored to free the study of English law from its insularity and who pleaded for a comparative approach. Helen Cam published a collection of some of Maitland's most enduring essays, prefacing them with a sympathetic evaluation of Maitland.[7] The most spirited historiographical battle has, of course, centered about Stubbs. In 1948 Helen Cam launched a vigorous counterattack against the critics and detractors of Stubbs's *Constitutional History of England* and received support a few years later from J. G. Edwards. Such defense stirred G. O. Sayles to renewed attack in an amusingly satirical essay that no one should miss.[8] These debates emphasize that

[5] D. C. Douglas, *English Scholars* (1939).
[6] H. A. Cronne, "Edward Augustus Freeman," *History,* 28:78–92 (March 1943); G. Templeman, "Edward I and the Historians," *CHJ,* 10:16–35 (no. 1, 1950).
[7] T. F. T. Plucknett, "Maitland's View of Law and History," *LQR,* 67:179–194 (January 1951); H. Cam, *Selected Essays of F. W. Maitland* (Cambridge, Eng., 1957). See also the fine appreciation of Maitland by R. L. Schuyler, "The Historical Spirit Incarnate: Frederic William Maitland," *AHR,* 57:303–322 (January 1952).
[8] H. Cam, "Stubbs Seventy Years After," *CHJ* 9:129–147 (no. 2, 1948); J. G. Edwards, *William Stubbs,* in general series, no. 22 (1952) of Historical Association; G. O. Sayles, "The Changed Course of History: Stubbs and Renan," *Aberdeen*

Stubbs will never regain the stature he had in 1900 but that he is taken much more seriously now than he was during the 1920's and 1930's when the tide was rolling most strongly against his interpretation of English medieval institutions.

The decision of the Royal Historical Society to promote a series of manuals and bibliographical guides began to bear fruit just before the war. In 1939 appeared a handbook on chronology under the direction of F. M. Powicke. Now, after some twenty years, a second edition has appeared, thanks chiefly to the efforts of E. B. Fryde. In 1945 came C. R. Cheney's most useful book on dates.[9] For years scholars who have labored with the public records of England have been assisted by the invaluable *Record Interpreter* of C. T. Martin and the album and text on paleography and diplomatics by H. Jenkinson and C. Johnson. To these works have been added the facsimiles of royal documents by T. A. M. Bishop and P. Chaplais.[10] Work with local records has been facilitated by Eileen Gooder whose recent study explains the Latin of documents such as deeds and charters and gives sample records and transcriptions.[11] Although there has always been a surfeit of genealogical studies and guides, this genre has been profitably augmented by the work of A. R. Wagner that goes beyond the traditional genealogical study and relates the rise and fall of medieval families to political, social, and economic developments.[12]

Guides to important collections of medieval records and specialized bibliographies have appeared increasingly since the war. Published even during the war was N. R. Ker's great list of medieval libraries which noted 4,500 books in over 500 libraries. W. Bonser has collected 12,000 items on Anglo-Saxon and Celtic history; N. R. Ker has catalogued the

---

University Review, 35:235–247 (1954). Although differing with Miss Cam and Mr. Edwards on their interpretation of constitutional history, Professor Bertie Wilkinson is nevertheless a stalwart defender of much of the Stubbsian thesis.

[9] F. M. Powicke and E. B. Fryde, *Handbook of British Chronology*, 2d ed. (1962); C. R. Cheney, *Handbook of Dates for Students of British History* (1945). See also Cheney, "Rules for the Observance of Feast-Days in Medieval England," *BIHR*, 34:117–147 (November 1961).

[10] T. A. M. Bishop and P. Chaplais, *Facsimiles of English Royal Writs to A.D. 1100* (Oxford, 1957). This volume was presented to Professor V. H. Galbraith upon his retirement as Regius Professor of History at Oxford. T. A. M. Bishop, *Scriptores Regis. Facsimiles to Identify and Illustrate the Hands of Royal Scribes in Original Charters of Henry I, Stephen, and Henry II* (Oxford, 1961). See also C. E. Wright, *Early English Manuscripts in Facsimile. Bede's Leechbook* (1955); N. R. Ker, *Early English Manuscripts in Facsimile. The Pastoral Care* (1956).

[11] E. Gooder, *Latin for Local History* (1961).

[12] A. R. Wagner, *English Genealogy* (Oxford, 1960). See also L. C. Lloyd, *The Origins of Some Anglo-Norman Families* (Leeds, 1951).

Anglo-Saxon manuscripts; and G. R. C. Davis has compiled a short catalogue of medieval cartularies.[13] The Selden Society has issued a guide to its expanding list of publications.[14] The science of sigillography has been helped by H. Jenkinson's guide to the seals in the Public Record Office and by the reproductions of the seals collected by the seventeenth-century antiquarian Sir Christopher Hatton.[15] The renaissance in numismatic study is evidenced by the inventories of coins published by such scholars as D. F. Allen, P. Grierson, and J. D. A. Thompson.[16] One of the few blessings of the war was the stimulus given to archaeological work by ruins discovered beneath demolished buildings and in bomb holes. The phenomenal amount of digging and archaeological study since the war is chronicled by R. L. S. Bruce-Mitford who lists all the excavations undertaken between 1939 and 1955.[17] The patient missionary efforts of F. M. Stenton on behalf of place-name research have resulted in studies too numerous to note except for that of K. Cameron which is concerned both with word-meaning and the historical inferences to be drawn.[18]

For bulk, age, and continuity the English medieval records are without parallel on the Continent. Spared the ravages of war, revolution, and religious strife, and traditionally the object of greater veneration and care, almost all came through the last war intact. Tons and tons of the

[13] N. R. Ker, *Medieval Libraries of Great Britain, a List of Surviving Books* (1941); W. Bonser, *An Anglo-Saxon and Celtic Bibliography (450–1087)* (Oxford, 1957); G. R. C. Davis, *Medieval Cartularies of Great Britain. A Short Catalogue* (1958). See also N. R. Ker, *Catalogue of Manuscripts Containing Anglo-Saxon* (Oxford, 1957).

[14] A. K. R. Kiralfy and G. H. Jones, *General Guide to the Society's Publications* (1960).

[15] H. Jenkinson, *A Guide to Seals in the Public Record Office* (1954); L. C. Lloyd and D. M. Stenton, *Sir Christopher Hatton's Book of Seals* (Oxford, 1950).

[16] D. F. Allen, *A Catalogue of English Coins in the British Museum. The Cross-and-Crosslets ('Tealby') Type of Henry II* (1951); P. Grierson, *Sylloge of Coins of the British Isles. Fitzwilliam Museum, Cambridge* (1958), and *Sylloge of Coins of the British Isles. Hunterian and Coats Collections, University of Glasgow* (Oxford, 1961); J. D. A. Thompson, *Inventory of British Coin Hoards, A.D. 600–1500* (Oxford, 1956). See also *Anglo-Saxon Coins. Studies Presented to F. M. Stenton on the Occasion of His 80th Birthday*, ed. R. H. M. Dolley (1961).

[17] R. L. S. Bruce-Mitford, *Recent Archaeological Excavations in Britain* (1956).

[18] See, for example, the series of articles by F. M. Stenton entitled "The Historical Bearing of Place-Name Studies," *TRHS*, 4th ser., 21 (1939), pp. 1–19; 22 (1940), pp. 1–21; 23 (1941), pp. 1–24; 24 (1942), pp. 1–24; 25 (1943), pp. 1–13. See also K. Cameron, *English Place-Names* (1961); O. S. Anderson, *The English Hundred Names: The South-Western Counties* (Leipzig, 1939), and *The English Hundred Names: The South-Eastern Counties* (Leipzig, 1939); Margaret Billing and Doris M. Stenton, *The Place-Names of Oxfordshire*, 2 vols. (Cambridge, Eng., 1953–54); A. H. Smith, *English Place-Name Elements*, 2 vols. (Cambridge, Eng., 1956).

most valuable records in the Public Record Office were transported into the country for preservation. All who work with these incomparable records in the Round Room ought to realize how much they owe to the dedicated staff who labored to protect these written treasures. For these records and for those of the British Museum, county, borough, and diocese, excellent inventories, lists, and calendars abound.[19] Guides to the unpublished records continue to appear and so vast is the number of records edited and published since the war that one can discuss only a few of the editorial projects.

Those who may wonder how the hundreds of volumes in the Rolls Series began should read the delightful paper of D. Knowles given originally as a presidential address to the Royal Historical Society.[20] Those who contemplate serious work with the printed records of medieval England should consult the guide of E. L. C. Mullins that lists all the texts and calendars printed since 1901.[21] And those who would understand the public records and the tales they have to tell must read the book of V. H. Galbraith who attempts to understand medieval institutions through their records and who argues that key documents such as Domesday Book and the Letters Patent and Close of John reflect the political and administrative policies of the kings and their servants.[22] After this preliminary work the investigator may turn to the great series of government and learned society publications of documents.

For the Anglo-Saxon period the single most valuable book of documents to appear is that of Miss F. E. Harmer on Anglo-Saxon writs. In a brilliant introduction to some 121 carefully edited writs she discusses forgeries, the diplomatics of the writ, and royal Anglo-Saxon writing offices. This work not only provides material for renewed study of Anglo-Saxon institutions but forces reappraisal of traditional interpretations of Anglo-Saxon government.[23] Scarcely less valuable is A. J. Robertson's edition and translation of selected Anglo-Saxon charters, the understand-

[19] For the revision of M. S. Giuseppi's *Guide to the Public Records*, see n. 140 in the essay by Margaret Hastings, below. See H. Jenkinson, *Guide to the Public Records* (1949). For local records see R. Somerville, *British Record Association: Hand-List of Record Publications* (1951); F. G. Emmison and I. Gray, *County Records*, Historical Association (1948).

[20] D. Knowles, "Great Historical Enterprises IV. The Rolls Series," *TRHS*, 5th ser., 11 (1961), pp. 137–159.

[21] E. L. C. Mullins, *Texts and Calendars. An Analytical Guide to Serial Publications*, Royal Historical Society Guides and Handbooks, no. 7 (1958).

[22] V. H. Galbraith, *Studies in the Public Records* (Edinburgh, 1948).

[23] F. E. Harmer, *Anglo-Saxon Writs* (Manchester, Eng., 1952). For an appreciation of the value of the writ for understanding royal government see G. Barraclough, "The Anglo-Saxon Writ," *History*, 39:193–215 (October 1954).

ing of which is facilitated by F. M. Stenton who suggests a program for study and editing and pays tribute to W. H. Stevenson for the scholarly turn taken by Anglo-Saxon studies during the present century.[24] Publication of the Parker Chronicle has been a great boon to paleographers wishing to study the oldest extant version of the Anglo-Saxon Chronicle.[25] Appreciation of the Anglo-Saxon church has been increased by fine editions of Saint Guthlac and Wulfstan.[26] In addition, the numerous articles and notes on the above sources provide a critical apparatus with which to approach the Anglo-Saxon period.[27]

In 1913 when H. W. C. Davis published the first volume of the *Regesta Regum Anglo-Normannorum* it was hailed as inaugurating a new phase in the study of Norman institutions and the volumes for Henry I and Stephen were eagerly awaited. War and the death of Davis intervened. Welcome, therefore, is the recently published volume of 1,500 calendared documents from the reign of Henry I which shows how much the government of Henry I had expanded over that of his predecessors.[28] Valuable for the study of royal government and policy are the fragments of interdict documents published by the Pipe Roll Society, the Treaty Rolls by P. Chaplais, and the section on prests from the Wardrobe Book of 1294–1295.[29] In 1942 G. E. Woodbine completed a monumental edition of Bracton. Worthy of note among the numerous

[24] A. J. Robertson, *Anglo-Saxon Charters* (Cambridge, Eng., 1956); F. M. Stenton, *The Latin Charters of the Anglo-Saxon Period* (Oxford, 1955). See also C. Hart, *The Early Charters of Essex*, I, *The Saxon Period* (Leicester, 1957).

[25] R. Flower and H. Smith, *The Parker Chronicle and Laws. A Facsimile* (1941). Note also the following critical articles: I. Atkins, "The Origin of the Later Part of the Saxon Chronicle Known as D," *EHR*, 55:8–27 (January 1940); F. T. Wainwright, "The Chronology of the Mercian Register," *EHR*, 60:385–392 (September 1945); E. E. Barker, "The Cottonian Fragments of Aethelweard's Chronicle," *BIHR*, 24:46–62 (May 1951); L. Whitbread, "Aethelweard and the Anglo-Saxon Chronicle," *EHR*, 74:577–589 (October 1959). See also C. Clark's edition of the Anglo-Saxon text of *The Peterborough Chronicle, 1070–1154* (Oxford, 1958).

[26] B. Colgrave, *Felix's Life of Saint Guthlac* (Cambridge, Eng., 1956); D. Bethurum, *The Homilies of Wulfstan* (Oxford, 1957).

[27] See, for example, R. W. Southern, "The First Life of Edward the Confessor," *EHR*, 58:385–401 (September 1943); D. J. V. Fisher, "The Early Biographers of St. Ethelwold," *EHR*, 67:381–391 (July 1952).

[28] C. Johnson and H. A. Cronne, *Regesta Regum Anglo-Normannorum, 1066–1154. Regesta Henrici Primi, 1100–1135*, II (Oxford, 1956). See also H. Jenkinson, *Domesday Re-bound* (1954).

[29] P. M. Barnes and W. R. Powell, *Interdict Documents*, Pipe Roll Society, 72 (1958); P. Chaplais, *Treaty Rolls Preserved in the Public Record Office*, I (1955); E. B. Fryde, *The Book of Prests of the King's Wardrobe for 1294–1295* (Oxford, 1962). Mr. Fryde was assisted with the edition and transcription of this record by numerous students of J. G. Edwards whom they honored with the presentation of this volume.

volumes of the Selden Society is that by C. T. Flower on the Curia Regis Rolls (1199–1230) with its useful introduction and that by H. G. Richardson and G. O. Sayles on cases of procedure without writ which is accompanied by a learned preface.[30] Church sources, especially the various diocesan records, have been published in abundance by local societies. Kathleen Major's edition, for example, of the oldest register of Lincoln cathedral church is valuable for the study of cathedral lands in such areas as Holland and the polder region.[31] We also thank her for presenting us with the acts of Stephen Langton.[32] The calendar and related documents of Abbot Samson have been published by R. H. C. Davis.[33] A comparison of publication of sources in England and on the Continent shows how far ahead is the English medievalist and how efficiently organized his archives and his techniques of editing and publishing.

Although, perhaps from tradition, most medievalists complain about translations and avow they read everything in the original, many must secretly welcome the fine translations that have appeared since the war, and all must be grateful to V. H. Galbraith and R. A. B. Mynors for inaugurating the series of medieval "Loeb Classics." The new Latin texts established are in general superior to previous ones and the translations make fine reading. Fortunately, the period to 1307 has seen the largest number of translations—fifteen to date—ranging from chronicles and biographies to royal and papal correspondence and treatises on royal government.[34] In the other ambitious project of translations inaugu-

---

[30] G. E. Woodbine, *Bracton, De Legibus et Consuetudinibus Anglie,* III–IV (New Haven, Conn., 1940–42); C. T. Flower, *Introduction to the Curia Regis Rolls, 1199–1230* (1944); H. G. Richardson and G. O. Sayles, *Select Cases of Procedure without Writ under Henry III* (1941).

[31] Kathleen Major, *The Registrum Antiquissimum of the Cathedral Church of Lincoln,* Lincoln Record Society, 46 (Hereford, 1953).

[32] Kathleen Major, *Acta Stephani Langton, Cantuariensis Archiepiscopi, A.D. 1207–1228,* Canterbury and York Society, 118 (Oxford, 1950). The following articles and notes are devoted to eleventh-, twelfth-, and thirteenth-century sources: H. S. Offler, "The Tractate de Iniusta Vexacione Willelmi Episcopi Primi," *EHR,* 66:321–341 (July 1951); R. H. C. Davis, "The Authorship of the Gesta Stephani," *EHR,* 77:209–232 (April 1962); F. Barlow, "Roger of Howden," *EHR,* 65:352–360 (July 1950); R. Vaughan, "The Chronicle of John of Wallingford," *EHR,* 73:66–77 (January 1958); N. Denholm-Young, "Thomas de Wykes and His Chronicle," *EHR,* 61:157–180 (May 1946); V. H. Galbraith, "The St. Edmundsbury Chronicle, 1296–1301," *EHR,* 58:51–78 (January 1943).

[33] *The Kalendar of Abbot Samson of Bury St. Edmunds and Related Documents,* ed. R. H. C. Davis, Camden Society, 3rd ser., 84 (1954).

[34] In order of their publication these translations now include: H. E. Butler, *The Chronicle of Jocelin of Brakelond concerning the Acts of Samson Abbot of the Monastery of St. Edmund* (Edinburgh, 1949); F. M. Powicke, *The Life of Ailred*

rated after the war, *English Historical Documents* under the general editorship of D. C. Douglas, only two volumes on the Middle Ages have thus far appeared, but happily they cover the period from 500 to 1189 and include documents illustrating every facet of English medieval civilization.[35]

WORKS OF SYNTHESIS

Since 1939 attempts to write the history of medieval England have been few. Even the broadest books are limited to certain periods. These plus the hundreds of specialized monographs and articles have replaced the syntheses of the nineteenth and early twentieth centuries. This trend in historical writing is defensible, and yet one feels that in another fifty years few of the histories written between 1939 and 1962 will have the audience that Green, Stubbs, Maitland, and others have held for so long. However valuable these recent works, one lays them aside still thirsting for the grand idea and for the colorful pictures that make the permanent imprint. Is it not now time for at least a few mature historians to cease adding stones to the mosaic and, instead, to evaluate the stones already there and mold them into a new synthesis of medieval England as seen through the eyes of men of the mid-twentieth century?

---

of Rievaulx by Walter Daniel (Edinburgh, 1950); C. Johnson, *Dialogus de Scaccario: The Course of the Exchequer by Richard Son of Nigel* (Edinburgh, 1950); D. Knowles, *The Monastic Constitutions of Lanfranc* (Edinburgh, 1951); T. Symons, *The Monastic Agreement of the Monks and Nuns of the English Nation* (Edinburgh, 1953); C. R. Cheney and W. H. Semple, *Selected Letters of Pope Innocent III concerning England (1198–1216)* (Edinburgh, 1953); K. R. Potter, *The Deeds of Stephen* (Edinburgh, 1955), and *The Historia Novella by William of Malmesbury* (Edinburgh, 1955); W. J. Millor and H. E. Butler, *The Letters of John of Salisbury,* I (Edinburgh, 1955); M. Chibnall, *John of Salisbury's Memoirs of the Papal Court* (Edinburgh, 1956); D. L. Douie and H. Farmer, *The Life of St. Hugh of Lincoln,* I, (Edinburgh, 1961); C. Johnson, *Hugh the Chantor. The History of the Church of York 1066–1127* (Edinburgh, 1961); F. Barlow, *The Life of King Edward Who Rests at Westminster. Attributed to a Monk of St. Bertin* (Edinburgh, 1962).

[35] Dorothy Whitelock, *English Historical Documents c. 500–1042* (1955); D. C. Douglas and G. W. Greenaway, *English Historical Documents, 1042–1189* (1953). Note also the following important translations: the Everyman edition of *The Anglo-Saxon Chronicle* by G. N. Garmonsway (1953); Dorothy Whitelock, *The Anglo-Saxon Chronicle* (1961); the Penguin edition of *Bede. A History of the English Church and People,* trans. L. Sherley-Price (Harmondsworth, 1955); J. J. O'Meara, *The First Version of the Topography of Ireland by Giraldus Cambrensis* (Dunkald, 1951); W. Holtzmann and E. W. Kemp, *Papal Decretals Relating to the Diocese of Lincoln in the Twelfth Century,* Lincoln Record Society, 47 (Hereford, 1954); J. C. Dickinson, *The Great Charter,* Historical Association (1955); S. B. Chrimes and A. L. Brown, *Select Documents of English Constitutional History, 1307–1485* (Oxford, 1961).

Only two books have appeared since 1939 that tell the story of English history from the Roman occupation to Bosworth Field. The first, that of Winston S. Churchill, has had great success with the educated person who has no specialized knowledge of the Middle Ages and has been grudgingly read by the medievalist, if only to appreciate Churchill's incomparable style. But even the medievalist must admit that Churchill has seldom blundered in the kind of history he chooses to write; his political and military canvases have the inimitable Churchillian spirit and flair.[36] The other synthesis is by Helen Cam who sketches a succinct picture of English history from the earliest times to the reign of Elizabeth I. Oriented principally around political history, this account skillfully unfolds a story of how the habit of cooperation and a growing common spirit gave rise to self-government on both the local and central level.[37]

Other syntheses are limited in chronological coverage. G. O. Sayles has written a survey of English history from the Roman period to the reign of Edward I which, more than any other book, has spanned the gap between monograph and textbook. Primarily an institutional study, it hews to the thesis that the Norman Conquest was not a cataclysm, that it added few essentials to the pattern of the old English state.[38] While a number of specialists contributed to the new edition of *Medieval England* by A. L. Poole, most of the chapters are disappointing because they have not been sufficiently revised to incorporate the results of recent scholarship.[39]

Of books even more restricted in scope, no work has superseded that of R. G. Collingwood and J. N. L. Myres on the Roman and British period. In light of the extensive archaeological, philological, and geographical research since 1937, a revision of this work seems long overdue.[40] In a *Festschrift* for E. T. Leeds such scholars as C. H. V. Sutherland, I. A. Richmond, and T. C. Lethbridge have concentrated on the problem of Roman and Celtic survival.[41] New editions of R. H. Hodg-

---

[36] W. S. Churchill, *A History of the English-Speaking Peoples*, I, *The Birth of Britain* (1956).

[37] Helen Cam, *England Before Elizabeth* (1950).

[38] G. O. Sayles, *The Medieval Foundations of England*, rev. ed. (1950). This edition added to that of 1948 a chapter on Roman Britain. The ambitious work of D. Jerrold, *An Introduction to the History of England, from the Earliest Times to 1204* (1949), abounds in misinformation.

[39] *Medieval England*, ed. A. L. Poole, 2 vols. (Oxford, 1958). This work is a new edition of H. W. C. Davis' *Barnard's Companion to English History* (1924).

[40] R. G. Collingwood and J. N. L. Myres, *Roman Britain and the English Settlements*, 2d ed. (Oxford, 1937).

[41] *Dark Age Britain, Studies Presented to E. T. Leeds*, ed. D. B. Harden (1956).

kin's history of the Anglo-Saxons, despite incorporation of some new material, have not changed a political narrative that unduly stresses the history of Wessex.[42] Trends in Anglo-Saxon history, so well presented by Dorothy Whitelock in her inaugural lecture as Elrington and Bosworth Professor of Anglo-Saxon at Cambridge, appear in a number of recent books, especially that of F. M. Stenton who, more than any other scholar, has furthered serious study of the Anglo-Saxon period.[43] Stenton's book in the Oxford series gives major attention to social, economic, and cultural developments. Probably the most vulnerable parts of the book are those which depict early English society as resting upon the small but stalwart *ceorl* who owned his own land and carried weight in the political and economic decisions of his agrarian community. In a better but less ambitious synthesis Dorothy Whitelock weaves from her deep knowledge of the literature a compelling account of Anglo-Saxon society and culture.[44] P. H. Blair's survey of the Anglo-Saxon period has effectively used archaeological evidence.[45]

C. N. Brooke's *From Alfred to Henry III, 871–1272,* the first volume of the new Nelson series on the history of England, is well written and good on culture and religious history but not at all convincing in its treatment of social, economic, and political institutions. It suffers from the author's inability to decide whether he is writing for the scholar or the student.[46] The succeeding volume in the same series by G. Holmes and covering the period 1272 to 1485 is particularly strong in institutional history.[47] The standard work on the period from Domesday Book to Magna Carta is the Oxford volume by A. L. Poole which is the most logically organized and clearly written of the Oxford volumes on the Middle Ages. Cultural subjects suffer, but well presented is social, economic, and institutional history, especially that of Henry II and John.[48] A parallel vol-

See also the important essays by F. M. Stenton, Wainwright, Whitelock, Harmer, Turville-Petre, and Nora K. Chadwick in *The Anglo-Saxons. Studies in Some Aspects of Their History and Culture Presented to Bruce Dickins,* ed. P. Clemoes (1959).

[42] R. H. Hodgkin, *A History of the Anglo-Saxons,* 2d ed., 2 vols. (Oxford, 1939); 3d ed., 2 vols. (Oxford, 1953).

[43] Dorothy Whitelock, *Changing Currents in Anglo-Saxon Studies* (Cambridge, Eng., 1958); F. M. Stenton, *Anglo-Saxon England, c. 550–1087,* 2d ed. (Oxford, 1947). The first edition appeared in 1943.

[44] Dorothy Whitelock, *The Beginnings of English Society* (Harmondsworth, 1952).

[45] P. H. Blair, *An Introduction to Anglo-Saxon England* (Cambridge, Eng., 1956).

[46] Edinburgh, 1961.

[47] G. Holmes, *The Later Middle Ages, 1272–1485* (Edinburgh, 1962).

[48] A. L. Poole, *From Domesday Book to Magna Carta, 1087–1216,* 2d ed. (Oxford, 1955). The first edition appeared in 1950.

ume on a less ambitious scale but equally good in its treatment of social
and economic history and amazingly shrewd in its analysis of character
is that by F. Barlow.[49] Inferior by comparison is the book by G. W. S.
Barrow which goes to 1314 and that by J. Harvey on the Plantagenets
which was written without sufficient historical knowledge and tends to
advance interesting theses without supplying the evidence.[50] The thirteenth century has been the preserve of F. M. Powicke, whose life has
been devoted to fathoming the secrets of the reigns of Henry III and
Edward I. The two-volume work on Henry III and the early years of
Edward, perhaps the most important history of thirteenth-century England to appear in our century, was the first to isolate the reign of Henry
III and the early life of Edward and to treat these years as a historical
unit. Basically a political history, it centers around what to Powicke is
the essence of constitutional history—men and their personalities.
Throughout both volumes Powicke's breadth of view and mastery of
detail are remarkable as he unfolds his favorite thesis on the development of a true community of the realm in the thirteenth century.[51] His
book on the thirteenth century in the Oxford series, extending from the
death of John to that of Edward I, is broader in range and shows to
advantage the progress made in historical knowledge since comparable
volumes appeared over fifty years ago. If there are weaknesses, they are
those of difficult organization and an emphasis upon political and constitutional history often repetitive of that in the two-volume study.[52]

POLITICS AND WAR

Two recent monographs on Domesday Book remind us again that, except for feudalism and parliament, no other historical problem has so
occupied the energies of English medievalists. Although J. H. Round's

[49] F. Barlow, *The Feudal Kingdom of England, 1042–1216* (1955).
[50] G. W. S. Barrow, *Feudal Britain* (1956); J. Harvey, *The Plantagenets*, 2d ed.
(1959). The first edition appeared in 1948. The second volume in the Pelican
series on the history of England is Doris M. Stenton's *English Society in the Early
Middle Ages* (Harmondsworth, 1951) which covers the period from 1066 to 1307
but concentrates largely on social history. It gives no balanced picture of the period
and is much inferior to the volume by Dorothy Whitelock and to the one by A. R.
Myers on the fourteenth and fifteenth centuries.
[51] F. M. Powicke, *King Henry III and the Lord Edward: The Community of the
Realm in the Thirteenth Century*, 2 vols. (Oxford, 1947).
[52] F. M. Powicke, *The Thirteenth Century, 1216–1307* (Oxford, 1953). The following *Festschriften* contain important essays by able medievalists dealing largely
with the period from 1066 to 1307: *Studies in Medieval History Presented to Frederick Maurice Powicke*, ed. R. W. Hunt *et al.* (Oxford, 1948); *Studies Presented to
Sir Hilary Jenkinson*, ed J. Conway Davies (Oxford, 1957).

brilliant studies in the last decade of the nineteenth century stimulated interest in this great record of riddles, they stunted original research because his conclusions on the composition and purpose of Domesday Book were thought to be definitive.[53] It was not until 1942 that V. H. Galbraith challenged the conclusions of Round by suggesting that Domesday Book was not composed directly from local returns but was drawn up from larger regional records in which the local returns had been digested and rearranged. He also questioned the value of Domesday Book as a "geld" book and suggested that its purpose was essentially feudal.[54] Galbraith's article was as incendiary as the essays of Round for igniting Domesday study; it inspired dozens of articles and numerous books including one by Galbraith himself in 1961 which will most certainly influence the course of Domesday research for years to come. In this study Galbraith deals with the new and old hypotheses advanced on the evolution of Domesday Book, the institutional framework that made possible the great survey, the tangled question of the circuits, the relationship of the returns to the composition, and finally the influence of Domesday Book in the following ages. Here he has summarized and refined his previous studies on Domesday Book and clearly drawn the differences between his view and that of Round.[55] Also in 1961 appeared the work of R. W. Finn which is a collection and augmentation of his studies on Domesday Book. He has mainly accepted Galbraith's thesis on the composition but argues that interest in taxation greatly motivated the Conqueror to order the inquest. He demonstrates quite convincingly that Domesday Book is an incomplete and imperfect record that should not be mined too confidently for statistics.[56] Among articles grappling with these problems one by C. Stephenson strengthens the Galbraith position, especially on the question of circuits, while another by P. H. Sawyer contends that at least half of Domesday Book was compiled directly from the original returns.[57] Less interested in the

[53] Round's principal studies are found in his *Feudal England* (1895).

[54] V. H. Galbraith, "The Making of Domesday Book," *EHR*, 57:161–178 (April 1942).

[55] V. H. Galbraith, *The Making of Domesday Book* (Oxford, 1961). For more of Galbraith's views see *Herefordshire Domesday* (1950), edited with J. Tait, and "The Date of the Geld Rolls in Exon Domesday," *EHR*, 65:1–17 (January 1950).

[56] R. W. Finn, *The Domesday Inquest and the Making of Domesday Book* (1961). See also the following articles of Finn: "The Evolution of Successive Versions of Domesday Book," *EHR*, 66:561–564 (October 1951); "The Immediate Sources of the Exchequer Domesday," *BJRL*, 40:47–78 (September 1957); "The Inquisitio Eliensis Reconsidered," *EHR*, 75:385–409 (July 1960).

[57] C. Stephenson, "Notes on the Composition and Interpretation of Domesday Book," *Speculum*, 22:1–15 (January 1947); P. H. Sawyer, "The Original Returns

composition than in the purpose, D. C. Douglas sees Domesday Book as a treasure house of information for the Anglo-Norman period and believes that its purposes were mulitfarious.[58] He is to some extent correct; the *Victoria County Histories* that have appeared in such numbers since the war have tapped Domesday Book for all sorts of information. The geographical studies of H. C. Darby and his colleagues have shown that much can still be learned from Domesday Book about arable land, waste land, forests, crops, agrarian routine, and the condition of agrarian laborers.[59] We may continue to expect Domesday Book research in abundance but let us hope that some of the old furrows will cease to be plowed and that the great survey will be related to the *polyptyques* and other continental records which had similar origins and objectives.

In spite of accepting most of what Round had written on the introduction of feudalism into England by the Normans, F. M. Stenton's study of feudalism that appeared thirty years ago was the most original contribution to the subject since Round and it has not been superseded.[60] Subsequent research, which has mostly added details, has been valuable in re-examining whether feudalism was introduced by the Normans; in dealing with social, economic, and family history of the feudal aristocracy; and in tracing the evolution of the feudal system in the twelfth and thirteenth centuries. H. R. Loyn has asked why the term *gesith* disappeared in the tenth century and the term *thegn* became so prominent. He disputes H. M. Chadwick's definition of a *gesith* as one who rendered royal service and argues that *gesith* marked a man's status as a landowner. He believes, on the other hand, that a *thegn* was not a

---

and Domesday Book," *EHR*, 70:177–197 (April 1955). See also E. Miller, "The Ely Land Pleas in the Reign of William I," *EHR*, 62:438–456 (October 1947); R. Lennard, "A Neglected Domesday Satellite," *EHR*, 58:32–41 (January 1943), and "Domesday Plough-teams: The South-Western Evidence," *EHR*, 60:217–234 (May 1945); H. P. R. Finberg, "The Domesday Plough-Team," *EHR*, 66:67–71 (January 1951); R. S. Hoyt, "Farm of the Manor and Community of the Vill in Domesday Book," *Speculum*, 30:147–169 (April 1955).

[58] D. C. Douglas, *The Domesday Monachorum of Christ Church Canterbury* (1944).

[59] H. C. Darby, *The Domesday Geography of Eastern England*, 2d ed. (Cambridge, Eng., 1957); Darby and I. B. Terrett, *The Domesday Geography of Midland England* (Cambridge, Eng., 1954); Darby and E. M. J. Campbell, *The Domesday Geography of Southeast England* (Cambridge, Eng., 1961); Darby and J. S. Maxwell, *The Domesday Geography of Northern England* (Cambridge, Eng., 1961).

[60] See Stenton's second edition of *The First Century of English Feudalism* (Oxford, 1961). The book of M. Gibbs on *The Feudal Order. A Study of the Origins and Development of English Feudal Society* (1949) applies the Marxist technique to the explanation of English feudal structure but, like most such books, fails to convince and actually concerns itself with manorialism rather than feudalism.

member of a clearly defined class but rather the personal servant of a great lord, a *miles*, or a *minister;* it was the *thegn* who gradually became a royal servant in the tenth century.[61] Contrary to C. Stephenson, who because of his inability to find any fusion of fief-holding and knight service prior to 1066 supported the Round and Stenton position on the Norman introduction of feudalism, an increasing number of scholars have argued that something close to real feudalism existed before the Conquest and that the Normans appropriated a number of Anglo-Saxon customs and institutions as they further feudalized England.[62] D. C. Douglas sees considerable Anglo-Saxon influence upon Norman feudalism and contends that "the formal feudalism of mediaeval England derived from the Norman Conquest, but the revolution which marked its beginnings was neither assured nor fulfilled until the twelfth century." [63] In a recent book on land tenure E. John not only argues that "bookright" was a borrowed Roman notion of *jus perpetuum* but suggests that feudal tenure under William I was no innovation and that "military service in the Old English state was as closely bound up with landholding as ever it was after 1066." [64] In a series of articles C. W. Hollister has supported this general argument by proposing that the length of Norman knight service, scutage payment, and the five-hide unit were based on Old English precedents.[65] Marjorie Hollings has advanced a similiar argument on the five-hide unit and R. Glover contends that the Battle of Hastings shows that the Anglo-Saxons were familiar with continental military tactics, especially with mounted service.[66] Such arguments are

[61] H. R. Loyn, "Gesiths and Thegns in Anglo-Saxon England from the Seventh to the Tenth Century," *EHR*, 70:529–549 (October 1955).

[62] C. Stephenson, "Feudalism and Its Antecedents in England," *AHR*, 48:245–265 (October 1943). See also the following studies: "The Origin and Significance of Feudalism," *AHR*, 46:788–812 (July 1941), and *Mediaeval Feudalism* (Ithaca, 1942).

[63] D. C. Douglas, "The Norman Conquest and English Feudalism," *EcHR*, 1st ser., 9:128–143 (May 1939). See also M. de Bouard, "De la Neustrie Carolingienne à la Normandie féodale: continuité ou discontinuité?" *BIHR*, 28:1–14 (May 1955).

[64] E. John, *Land Tenure in Early England* (Leicester, 1960).

[65] C. W. Hollister, "The Annual Term of Military Service in Medieval England," *Medievalia et Humanistica*, 13 (1960), pp. 40–47; "The Significance of Scutage Rates in Eleventh- and Twelfth-Century England," *EHR*, 75:577–588 (October 1960); "The Five Hide Unit and Military Obligation," *Speculum*, 36:61-74 (January 1961); "The Norman Conquest and the Genesis of English Feudalism," *AHR*, 66:641–663 (April 1961); "The Knights of Peterborough and the Anglo-Saxon Fyrd," *EHR*, 77:417–436 (July 1962).

[66] M. Hollings, "The Survival of the Five Hide Unit in the Western Midlands," *EHR*, 63:453–487 (October 1948); R. Glover, "English Warfare in 1066," *EHR*, 67:1–18 (January 1952). In reference to Norman feudalism one should note the fine introduction and plates in F. M. Stenton, *The Bayeux Tapestry: A Comprehensive*

indeed evidence that the Round-Stenton-Stephenson thesis may not be as secure as ten years ago, but much more must be done on this problem, particularly in regard to the feudalism of the Continent, before we can be certain about the nature of feudalism in eleventh-century England. No English medievalist seems to be interested in relating English feudalism to the continental institution and M. Bloch, who did make a few comparisons, was primarily concerned with feudal institutions on the Continent.[67]

For the twelfth and thirteenth centuries the studies of S. Painter, I. J. Sanders, and A. L. Poole have probed deeply into the family ties of the baronage, have shown what constituted a barony, have explored the social, economic, and political resources of the feudal aristocracy, and have noted how, as feudalism became less military in the thirteenth century, the obligations, especially of the knight, became those of local political and administrative service.[68] In a number of studies B. Lyon has drawn attention to the impact of the reviving money economy upon feudal institutions and has shown how feudal custom was superimposed upon money and how the new money resources of the English kings were used to procure more knight service.[69] Recently Michael Powicke

---

Survey (1957). On the introduction of feudalism into Scotland see R. L. G. Ritchie, *The Normans in Scotland* (Edinburgh, 1954); G. W. S. Barrow, "The Beginnings of Feudalism in Scotland," *BIHR*, 29:1–31 (May 1956).

[67] An English translation of M. Bloch's *La société féodale*, 2 vols. (Paris, 1939–40) appeared in 1961 under the title *Feudal Society*. One may also find some comparisons of English and continental feudalism in F. L. Ganshof, *Feudalism* (1952).

[68] S. Painter, *Studies in the History of the English Feudal Barony* (Baltimore, Md., 1943), and "The Family and the Feudal System in Twelfth-Century England," *Speculum*, 35:1–16 (January 1960). A number of articles by Painter on baronial families and castle guard appear in the collection *Feudalism and Liberty*, ed. F. A. Cazel (Baltimore, Md., 1961). See also I. J. Sanders, *Feudal Military Service in England. A Study of the Constitutional and Military Powers of the 'Barones' in Medieval England* (1956), and *English Baronies. A Study of Their Origin and Descent, 1086–1327* (Oxford, 1961); A. L. Poole, *Obligations of Society in the XIIth and XIIIth Centuries* (Oxford, 1946); N. Denholm-Young, "Feudal Society in the Thirteenth Century," *History*, 29:107–119 (September 1944). On the tenure of knight service see J. Tait, "Knight-Service in Cheshire," *EHR*, 57:437–459 (October 1942); U. Apps, "The Muntatores—Their Relation to Other Military Tenures in the Twelfth and Thirteenth Centuries," *EHR*, 63:528–533 (October 1948); F. R. H. Du Boulay, "Gavelkind and Knight's Fee in Medieval Kent," *EHR*, 77:504–511 (October 1962).

[69] B. Lyon, "The Money Fief under the English Kings, 1066–1485," *EHR*, 66:161–193 (April 1951); "The Feudal Antecedent of the Indenture System," *Speculum*, 29:503–511 (July 1954); and *From Fief to Indenture: The Transition from Feudal to Non-Feudal Contract in Western Europe* (Cambridge, Mass., 1957). See also J. O. Prestwich, "War and Finance in the Anglo-Norman State," *TRHS*, 5th ser., 4 (1954), pp. 19–43; J. Boussard, "Les mercenaires au XIIe siècle. Henry II et les origines de l'armée de métier," *Bibliothèque de l'Ecole des Chartes*, 106:189–224 (no. 2, 1945–46).

has investigated military obligation in England with particular attention to the thirteenth and fourteenth centuries. Although examining the military obligations of all classes, he shows that nonfeudal military service superseded feudal service and that in the process the feudal aristocracy retained an important position in England's military hierarchy.[70] Finally, one should not overlook the studies on castles which show how closely the kings supervised the construction and strategic location of their castles and how they made it royal policy to restrict baronial castles and keep them under close surveillance. [71]

If one looks at the larger canvas of politics and at the figures in the forefront, he is aware of the decline of what may be properly called biographical writing. Over the past twenty-five years historians have awakened to the pitfalls of biography written chiefly from medieval chronicler and biographer and have searched out and used every sort of available record. In so doing they have had to acknowledge that the paucity of intimate sources on medieval men makes the real biography impossible and the study of a reign or of a figure's accomplishments the more satisfactory solution.

If serious writing on England's medieval people has lost those literary and stylistic characteristics of the older biography, at least it is no longer so clearly positive or negative about personal character and achievement and does not label men good or bad as dictated by the standards of some medieval monks or some proper Victorians. Most studies attempt to evaluate character and accomplishment more realistically and by more sensible standards.[72] Alfred the Great emerges about the way one would expect from the pages of Miss E. S. Duckett's book. He lacks the heroic qualities of old but retains political capacity and an essential role in the stimulation of early English culture, especially the rich accomplishment in literature.[73] No book-length study on Henry II has ap-

[70] Michael Powicke, *Military Obligation in Medieval England: A Study in Liberty and Duty* (Oxford, 1962). See also his articles "Distraint of Knighthood and Military Obligation under Henry III," *Speculum*, 25:457–470 (October 1950), and "The General Obligation to Cavalry Service under Edward I," *Speculum*, 28:814–833 (October 1953).

[71] W. Douglas Simpson, *Castles from the Air* (1949); S. Troy, *The Castles of Great Britain* (1953); R. A. Brown, *English Medieval Castles* (1954), "Royal Castle-Building in England, 1154–1216," *EHR*, 70:353–398 (April 1955), and "A List of Castles, 1154–1216," *EHR*, 74:249–280 (April 1959); J. H. Beeler, "Castles and Strategy in Norman and Early Angevin England," *Speculum*, 31:581–601 (October 1956); A. J. Taylor, "Master James of St. Georges," *EHR*, 65:433–457 (October 1950).

[72] V. H. Galbraith, "Good and Bad Kings in Medieval English History," *History*, 30:119–132 (September 1945).

[73] Eleanor S. Duckett, *Alfred the Great* (Chicago, 1956).

peared since the biography of L. F. Salzman, but Z. N. and C. N. Brooke have discussed his early life and his assumption of the titles of duke of Normandy and of Aquitaine.[74] Eleanor, the spirited wife of Henry II, has been more intriguing to scholars; she has been the subject of a number of books and articles. C. H. Walker's book reads somewhat like a Victorian biography. It relies mostly on traditional sources and adds little to our knowledge of Eleanor who, according to this modern biographer, lived among "child-like, half-barbaric people." The study by Amy Kelly is far more scholarly and successful. The result of a lifetime's work, it presents a coherent account of Eleanor's life with special emphasis upon her activity as patroness of twelfth-century culture. Some readers might ask for less romance but there is enough serious reading in Miss Kelly's book to make it the standard work on Eleanor.[75]

One reads with impatience the half-scholarly, half-popular book of P. Henderson on Richard I without learning as much as from the old study of Kate Norgate.[76] Of far more value is the work of G. V. Scammell on Hugh du Puiset, the proud bishop of Durham and justiciar for a while under Richard. Especially good are the pages on Hugh's administration of Durham and the parallels it presented with royal government.[77] The most scholarly study of an Angevin ruler has been that by S. Painter on King John. Essentially a political and administrative history of John's reign, it delineates the background and consequences of Magna Carta and deals at length with the leading baronial families in opposition to John and with their familial ties and economic and political interests. Some comments and conclusions are dubious, especially when they arise from imaginative reconstruction and from a professed intimate acquaintance with family history which the sources do not provide, but this detailed biographical approach to the understanding of John and his troubles with the barons should point the way to like investigation of the reigns of Henry III and Edward I.[78] The recent books of J. T. Appleby

[74] Z. N. and C. N. Brooke, "Henry II, Duke of Normandy and Aquitaine," *EHR*, 61:81–89 (January 1946). A. Alfred attempts in *Devil's Brood* (1957) to recount the quarrels of Henry II with Eleanor and his sons but the absence of any sense of historical criticism renders the book useless.

[75] C. H. Walker, *Eleanor of Aquitaine* (Richmond, Va., 1950); Amy Kelly, *Eleanor of Aquitaine* (Cambridge, Mass., 1950). See also H. G. Richardson, "The Letters and Charters of Eleanor of Aquitaine," *EHR*, 74:193-213 (April 1959).

[76] P. Henderson, *Richard Coeur de Lion* (1958). For a translation of the anonymous chronicler who recorded the deeds of Richard I on the Third Crusade see J. Hampden, *Crusader King. The Adventure of Richard the Lionheart on Crusade, Taken from a Chronicle of the Time* (1956).

[77] G. V. Scammell, *Hugh du Puiset, Bishop of Durham* (Cambridge, Eng., 1956).

[78] S. Painter, *The Reign of King John* (Baltimore, Md., 1950).

and W. L. Warren on John, both well written, seldom do more than summarize what has been so often said before. Appleby employs no scholarly apparatus and rarely departs from the superficial. Warren does attempt a critical evaluation of the contemporary evidence and is certainly right when he says that the popular idea of John comes largely from Matthew Paris who believed that John's presence in hell would even defile that place. To his credit Warren points up the paradox of John's repulsive character and his efficient administrative capacity.[79]

To fill in the details of Powicke's large canvases on the thirteenth century one can turn to several useful books. N. Denholm-Young's study of Richard of Cornwall portrays a cautious and shrewd adviser to whom Henry III would have done well to have given more influence. Details on the political capacity of Hubert de Burgh, another powerful figure in the government of Henry III, have been furnished by C. Ellis.[80] Margaret W. Labarge's biography of Simon de Montfort, while offering little that is new, is interesting because of her special study of Eleanor de Montfort's household rolls.[81] Though little has been written on Edward I, an excellent study of a key Edwardian adviser and official—Antony Bek, bishop of Durham and keeper of the royal wardrobe—provides good administrative history which supplements that of Tout and throws more light on the important department of the wardrobe.[82] The early years (1284–1307) of the unfortunate Edward II are the subject of a judicious study by Hilda Johnstone in which she attempts to connect Edward's inefficient performance as king to his unpleasant early years spent largely without mother or father and without suitable education for the duties of king.[83]

In turning from books on people to books on political events one

[79] J. T. Appleby, *John King of England* (1961); W. L. Warren, *King John* (1961). In a study on Isabelle of Angoulême, H. G. Richardson examines her authority as queen of England and concludes that it was much inferior to that of Eleanor of Aquitaine: "The Marriage and Coronation of Isabelle of Angoulême," *EHR*, 61:289–315 (September 1946). Subsequent volumes of the *EHR* should be seen for the debate between Richardson and Painter and F. A. Cazel engendered by this article.

[80] N. Denholm-Young, *Richard of Cornwall* (Oxford, 1947); C. Ellis, *Hubert de Burgh. A Study in Constancy* (1952).

[81] M. W. Labarge, *Simon de Montfort* (1961).

[82] C. M. Fraser, *A History of Antony Bek, Bishop of Durham, 1280-1311* (Oxford, 1957). See also C. M. Fraser, *Records of Antony Bek, Bishop and Patriarch, 1283–1311* (1953); R. S. Loomis, "Edward I, Arthurian Enthusiast," *Speculum*, 28:114–127 (January 1953); J. P. Trabut-Cussac, "Itinéraire d'Edouard Ier en France, 1286–1289," *BIHR*, 25:160–203 (November 1952).

[83] Hilda Johnstone, *Edward of Carnarvon* (Manchester, Eng., 1946). See A. M. MacKenzie, *Robert Bruce, King of the Scots*, 2d ed. (Edinburgh, 1955).

becomes acutely conscious of the current unpopularity of political history. Apparently only in articles and notes does one reshuffle political history and worry about what formerly occupied a volume or two. Welcome, therefore, is the reissue of F. M. Powicke's *Loss of Normandy* which partially recognizes some of the research done on Normandy since 1913 though it is not a fully revised study.[84] The sole political study is that of J. C. Holt on the barons of northern England who took the lead in the opposition to John. This work in the depth of its investigation of baronial families parallels that of S. Painter.[85]

The development of nationalism in medieval England has been the most important problem tackled in articles on political questions. V. H. Galbraith has been unable to discover throughout most of the Middle Ages any link between national consciousness and vernacular language; he has suggested that such a connection was relatively modern and that only in the fourteenth century did England and the Continent become vernacular conscious. B. C. Keeney has related the increased demand for public military service in the thirteenth and fourteenth centuries with a rise in national spirit and has argued that in the late thirteenth century men began to disassociate *regnum* from the idea of a great fief and associate it with the concept of a state in which the king was virtually an emperor.[86]

A number of histories have re-examined the question of the settlement of England and Scotland after the departure of the Romans. H. M. Chadwick has painstakingly traced the settlement of southern Scotland by the Picts and Scots, while G. J. Copley has skillfully employed archaeological and agronomic evidence to pinpoint the advance of the Saxons into Wessex during the sixth century.[87] The actual strength and permanence of Roman influence over the Anglo-Saxons will never be completely determined, but scholars such as Margaret Deanesly have

[84] F. M. Powicke, *The Loss of Normandy, 1189–1204* (Manchester, Eng., 1961).
[85] J. C. Holt, *The Northerners* (Oxford, 1961).
[86] V. H. Galbraith, "Nationality and Language in Medieval England," *TRHS*, 4th ser., 23 (1941), pp. 113–128; B. C. Keeney, "Military Service and the Development of Nationalism in England," *Speculum*, 22:534–549 (October 1947), and "The Medieval Idea of the State: The Great Cause, 1291–1292," *University of Toronto Law Journal*, 8:48–71 (no. 1, 1949).
[87] H. M. Chadwick, *Early Scotland. The Picts, the Scots and the Welsh of Southern Scotland* (Cambridge, Eng., 1939); G. J. Copley, *The Conquest of Wessex in the Sixth Century* (1954). See also F. T. Wainwright, *The Problem of the Picts* (Edinburgh, 1955). For an excellent discussion of the newer trends in Anglo-Saxon research see F. M. Stenton, "Early English History, 1895–1920," *TRHS*, 4th ser., 28 (1946), pp. 7–19.

assembled good arguments for the survival of some of the Roman civilization and for its influence on Anglo-Saxon culture and institutions.[88] It is enough to observe that the Germanist historians no longer hold the field unchallenged. Both Gildas and Arthur are being rehabilitated, the first as historical source and the second as authentic figure, and Bede's stature as a historian continues to grow.[89] The ties between the Franks and southern Anglo-Saxon England from the seventh to the tenth century appear to have been closer than previously thought.[90] Against Stenton, who has argued for a preponderant Danish influence in northern and eastern England, P. H. Sawyer, and F. T. Wainwright have contended that the Danes were never numerous, never erected strong or well-organized states, and exerted their temporary hegemony only by means of small bands of warriors.[91]

Historians continue to write about Duke William's claims to the throne of Edward the Confessor. D. C. Douglas, T. J. Oleson, and others are quite certain that William received some authentic promises and encouragement from Edward and Harold.[92] Douglas has also puzzled out the chronology of Norman history in the eleventh century and from a minute examination of the evidence has identified thirty-two of the men who accompanied William to England.[93] Round's studies of Nor-

[88] Margaret Deanesly, "Roman Traditionalist Influence among the Anglo-Saxons," *EHR*, 58:129–147 (April 1943).

[89] C. E. Stevens, "Gildas Sapiens," *EHR*, 56:353–374 (July 1941); A. H. Burne, "The Battle of Badon. A Military Commentary," *History*, 30:133–144 (September 1945); H. E. Walker, "Bede and the Gewissae: The Political Evolution of the Heptarchy and Its Nomenclature," *CHJ*, 12:174–186 (no. 2, 1956).

[90] Margaret Deanesly, "Canterbury and Paris in the Reign of Aethelberht," *History*, 26:97–104 (September 1941); J. M. Wallace-Hadrill, "The Franks and the English in the Ninth Century: Some Common Historical Interests," *History*, 35:202–218 (October 1950). See also P. Grierson, "The Relations between England and Flanders before the Norman Conquest," *TRHS*, 4th ser., 23 (1941), pp. 71–112.

[91] F. M. Stenton, "The Scandinavian Colonies in England and Normandy," *TRHS*, 4th ser., 27 (1945), pp. 1–12; P. H. Sawyer, "The Density of the Danish Settlement in England," *UBHJ*, 6:1–17 (no. 1, 1957); F. T. Wainwright, "Ingimund's Invasion," *EHR*, 68:145–169 (April 1948), and "The Submission to Edward the Elder," *History*, 37:114–130 (June 1952).

[92] D. C. Douglas, "Edward the Confessor, Duke William of Normandy, and the English Succession," *EHR*, 68:526–545 (October 1953); T. J. Oleson, "Edward the Confessor's Promise of the Throne to Duke William of Normandy," *EHR*, 72:221–228 (April 1957). For Edward the Confessor see E. K. Heningham, "The Genuineness of the Vita Aeduuardi Regis," *Speculum*, 21:419–456 (October 1946); B. W. Scholz, "The Canonization of Edward the Confessor," *Speculum*, 36:38–60 (January 1961).

[93] D. C. Douglas, "The Earliest Norman Counts," *EHR*, 61:129–157 (May 1946); "Some Problems of Early Norman Chronology," *EHR*, 65:289–303 (July 1950); "Companions of the Conqueror," *History*, 28:129–147 (September 1943). For in-

man genealogy have been supplemented by the research of Douglas, G. H. White, and J. H. Le Patourel.[94] Examining the motives of Henry I in arranging the marriage of Matilda to Henry V of Germany, K. Leyser sees as the principal reasons a desire to enhance the dignity of the English crown and a wish to draw closer to Henry V on policy towards the papacy.[95] Political studies on the thirteenth century range from the fortunes of the Lusignan family under Henry III to the diplomatics of the documents related to the Treaty of Paris in 1259.[96]

CONSTITUTIONAL HISTORY

As with political history, minutiae have dominated the literature on constitutional history—"the queen of the sciences" for the English medievalist. Much of the detailed and careful writing that occupies hundreds of feet on library shelves can be justified, but certainly enough is now known about constitutional history to warrant new syntheses that may halt the present waning of both scholarly and lay interest in this subject which in the past attracted many of the talented historical minds.

The most recent attempt to provide a new synthesis has been made by B. Wilkinson in three volumes on the period from 1216 to 1399. In general Professor Wilkinson's peers have not acclaimed his effort to interpret English constitutional history, particularly parliament, in neo-Stubbsian terms, nor have they concurred in his insistence upon a pattern of negotiation between king and subject that, with variations, developed under the Anglo-Saxons and slowly evolved into the fourteenth-century parliament. If Professor Wilkinson has overstressed English medieval political cooperation and negotiation until at times it becomes almost a constitutional *mystique,* he has nonetheless provided an inter-

---

terpretations of the Norman Conquest see Douglas, *The Norman Conquest and British Historians* (Glasgow, 1946).

[94] G. H. White, "The First House of Bellême," *TRHS,* 4th ser., 22 (1940), pp. 67–99; Douglas, "The Ancestors of William Fitz Osbern," *EHR,* 59:62–79 (January 1944); J. H. Le Patourel, "Geoffrey of Montbray, Bishop of Coûtances, 1049–1093," *ibid.,* 129–162 (May 1944).

[95] K. Leyser, "England and the Empire in the Early Twelfth Century," *TRHS,* 5th ser., 10 (1960), pp. 61–83. For the government of England during the absence of Richard I see B. Wilkinson, "The Government of England during the Absence of Richard on the Third Crusade," *BJRL,* 28:485–509 (December 1944).

[96] H. S. Snellgrove, *The Lusignans in England, 1247–1258* (Albuquerque, N. Mex., 1950); D. M. Williamson, "Some Aspects of the Legation of Cardinal Otto in England, 1237–41," *EHR,* 64:145–173 (April 1949); P. Chaplais, "The Making of the Treaty of Paris (1259) and the Royal Style," *EHR,* 67:235–253 (April 1952).

pretation and a good collection of translated documents that he weaves
into his discussion of the great constitutional issues. His work has a
definite viewpoint, honestly expressed, and, in doing what his carping
critics refuse to do, he has stimulated some first-class discussion. Is it not
a good book that stimulates historical debate and suggests new solutions
to old problems? [97] The recent survey of medieval constitutional and
legal history by B. Lyon has attempted no new interpretation but has
worked to incorporate, digest, and relate the mass of literature to the
principal themes of institutional development.[98] S. B. Chrimes's book on
administrative history is basically a modernized condensation of Tout's
study. T. F. T. Plucknett's eleventh edition of Taswell-Langmead's old
text has been reworked to emphasize even more the development of the
common law.[99]

Varied are the studies on royal government. While no one has written
a study of the English coronation since P. Schramm, scholars have commented upon pertinent documents.[100] H. G. Richardson finds that a
new element was added to the coronation ceremony in 1274 when Edward I swore to preserve the rights of the crown. P. L. Ward has
connected the *ordo* of Edgar with a continental version written at the
Abbey of Saint Vaast in Arras, while B. Wilkinson has derived the custom from Teutonic practice.[101] Re-examination of the structure of
Anglo-Saxon government has rendered obsolescent the conclusions of
Stubbs and Liebermann. T. J. Oleson's study of the witenagemot shows
it to have been an amoebic gathering constantly differing in number and
type of person in attendance, and thus dispels any conception of this
body as a national assembly.[102] Margaret Deanesly has found evidence

[97] B. Wilkinson, *The Constitutional History of England 1216–1399, with Select
Documents,* I‑ (1948). This volume covers the years 1216–1307.

[98] B. Lyon, *A Constitutional and Legal History of Medieval England* (New York,
1960).

[99] S. B. Chrimes, *Introduction to the Administrative History of Medieval England,*
rev. ed. (Oxford, 1958); T. F. T. Plucknett, *Taswell-Langmead's English Constitutional History* (1960). See also S. B. Chrimes and I. A. Roots, *English Constitutional
History. A Select Bibliography,* Historical Association. Helps for Students of History,
no. 58 (1958).

[100] P. Schramm, *A History of the English Coronation* (Oxford, 1937).

[101] H. G. Richardson, "The English Coronation Oath," *TRHS,* 4th ser., 23 (1941).
pp. 129–158, and "The English Coronation Oath," *Speculum,* 24:44–75 (January
1949); P. L. Ward, "The Coronation Ceremony in Medieval England," *Speculum,*
14:160–178 (April 1939), and "An Early Version of the Anglo-Saxon Coronation
Ceremony," *EHR,* 57:345–361 (July 1942); B. Wilkinson, *The Coronation in History,* Historical Association, no. 23 (1953).

[102] T. J. Oleson, *The Witenagemot in the Reign of Edward the Confessor* (Toronto, 1955). This study is marred by an imperfect understanding of Anglo-Saxon
charters and by concentration on the eleventh century.

that seems to indicate some influence of the Merovingian royal household upon that of Ethelbert of Kent. In the first of two studies on tenth-century kingship H. R. Loyn argues that the imperial titles of Athelstan, Edmund, and Edgar do not represent constitutional fact; they are but the stylistic flourishes of scribes who wished to express the great power of these rulers. In the second article he describes the role of the *thegn* in Anglo-Saxon government, suggesting that the royal commendation which bound *thegn* to king outweighed all other commendations and marked real progress towards a centralized territorial state in which the thegnly community worked for the king.[103]

Important works on royal government in the Norman and Angevin periods have appeared. G. H. White has restudied the famous *Constitutio Domus Regis* and gives a good account of the functions of each household officer.[104] R. S. Hoyt's study is pertinent to an understanding of Norman government because it argues that the ancient demesne was a creation of the Angevins and did not go back to the Normans and Anglo-Saxons.[105] Writing on Angevin kingship, J. E. A. Jolliffe shows how royal power, supreme and at times despotic, was exerted through household officers and *familiares* to dominate the realm.[106] Margaret Howell has investigated the development of regalian right with emphasis upon the twelfth century. Her account of John's seizure and administration of the bishops' lands during the conflict with Innocent III is valuable for its detail.[107] Unfortunately, J. Boussard in a lengthy work on Angevin government provides no answers to the important questions of Henry II's reign and argues unconvincingly that Henry II erected his state on a feudal plan thereby giving unity and solidity to his vast

[103] Margaret Deanesly, "The Court of King Aethelberht of Kent," *CHJ*, 7:101–114 (no. 2, 1942); H. R. Loyn, "The Imperial Style of the Tenth Century Anglo-Saxon Kings," *History*, new ser., 40:111–115 (February and June 1955), and "The King and the Structure of Society in Late Anglo-Saxon England," *History*, new ser., 42:87–100 (1957).

[104] G. H. White, "The Household of the Norman Kings," *TRHS*, 4th ser., 30 (1948), pp. 127–155.

[105] R. S. Hoyt, *The Royal Demesne in English Constitutional History: 1066–1272* (Ithaca, N.Y., 1950), and "The Nature and Origins of the Ancient Demesne," *EHR*, 65:145–175 (April 1950). See also "Representation in the Administrative Practice of Anglo-Norman England," *Album Helen Maud Cam*, II (Louvain, 1962), pp. 13–26.

[106] J. E. A. Jolliffe, *Angevin Kingship* (1955). See also Jolliffe, "The 'Camera Regis' under Henry II," *EHR*, 68:1–21, 337–363 (January and April 1953); H. G. Richardson, "The Chamber under Henry II," *EHR*, 69:596–611 (October 1954); A. C. Cramer, "The Jewish Exchequer," *AHR*, 45:327–337 (January 1940).

[107] M. Howell, *Regalian Right in Medieval England* (1962).

possessions.[108] Further studies on royal government, which include
a book by Mary C. Hill on the king's messengers, discuss such aspects
of administration as royal prisons, clerks, charters, and stannaries.[109]
Although principally interested in the diplomatics of the records, G. P.
Cuttino provides a good picture of royal diplomatic administration.[110]

When S. K. Mitchell died before completing his second volume on
royal taxation, his former student S. Painter edited and saw the unfinished manuscript through press. This volume, concentrating on the reign
of Henry III, increases our knowledge of the tallage and percentage
taxes. The material on the local assessment and collection of these taxes
is further evidence for the theme of self-government at the king's command. From this and a number of shorter studies we learn much about
the important subject of royal taxation, a subject neglected since the
work of J. F. Willard.[111]

Royal taxation leads to the larger constitutional issues of the thirteenth
century. Though it would seem that little more could be squeezed out of
Magna Carta, it remains a popular subject for critical commentary. M.
Radin and B. Lyon have investigated the myth that developed in later
centuries, and G. T. Hankin has described the influence of Magna Carta
in the United States.[112] H. G. Richardson has attempted to evaluate the
impact of Magna Carta upon the course of politics immediately after its
concession. V. H. Galbraith has seriously challenged the authority of

---

[108] J. Boussard, *Le gouvernement d'Henri II Plantagenet* (Paris, 1956). Regrettably numerous factual mistakes and unfamiliarity with important English studies
give this book an air of inaccuracy and uncertainty.

[109] M. C. Hill, *The King's Messengers 1199–1377. A Contribution to the History
of the Royal Household* (1961). See also J. C. Russell, "Attestation of Charters in
the Reign of John," *Speculum,* 15:480–498 (October 1940); F. M. Powicke,
"Master Simon the Norman," *EHR,* 59:330–344 (September 1944); R. B. Pugh,
"The King's Prisons before 1250," *TRHS,* 5th ser., 5 (1955), pp. 1–22; W. R.
Powell, "The Administration of the Navy and the Stannaries, 1189–1216," *EHR,*
71:177–188 (April 1956); G. P. Cuttino, "King's Clerks and the Community of
the Realm," *Speculum,* 29:395–409 (April, pt. 2, 1954).

[110] G. P. Cuttino, *English Diplomatic Administration, 1259–1339* (1940).

[111] S. K. Mitchell, *Taxation in Medieval England* (New Haven, Conn., 1951).
See also R. S. Hoyt, "Royal Demesne, Parliamentary Taxation, and the Realm,"
Speculum, 23:58–69 (January 1948), and "Royal Taxation and the Growth of the
Realm in Mediaeval England," *Speculum,* 25:36–48 (January 1950); F. A. Cazel,
"The Tax of 1185 in Aid of the Holy Land," *Speculum,* 30:385–392 (July 1955),
and "The Fifteenth of 1225," *BIHR,* 34:67–81 (May 1961); H. S. Deighton, "Cleri-
cal Taxation by Consent, 1279–1301," *EHR,* 68:161–192 (April 1953).

[112] M. Radin, "The Myth of Magna Carta," *Harvard Law Review,* 60:1060–1091
(no. 7, 1947); B. Lyon, "The Lawyer and Magna Carta," *Rocky Mountain Law
Review,* 23:416–433 (no. 4, 1951); G. T. Hankin, "Magna Carta in the U.S.A.,"
History, 24:318–322 (March 1940).

Roger Wendover as a primary account of the winning of Magna Carta.[113] Both J. C. Holt and C. R. Cheney have re-examined the chronology of Magna Carta. Holt argues that the *Articuli* were written and sealed before 15 June and represent an agreement made between John and the barons on 10 June, and that no formal sealed document was delivered to the barons on 19 June but that copies were made for delivery to those barons who were not present at the negotiations. Cheney argues that the *Articuli* were agreed upon on 15 June but that peace was definitely concluded by the homage of the barons to John on 19 June and the formal charter itself was delivered on 23 June. In another article Holt tries to show that the barons had a working concept of some of the ideas they tried to implement by Magna Carta, that there was a common baronial feeling upon such issues as due process, and that Magna Carta was an attempt to translate hard, practical interests into principles of law.[114] Though such studies have revised McKechnie's book, it remains the indispensable study on the subject.

On the struggle between the barons and Henry III and the events leading up to this constitutional crisis little has been added since the appearance thirty years ago of the important studies of E. F. Jacob and R. F. Treharne. Subsequent studies have worried over clarification of the issues and have worked for a more accurate presentation of detail. N. Denholm-Young would date the famous "Paper Constitution" of Matthew Paris as 1238 rather than 1244, but C. R. Cheney is certain that the date must remain 1244.[115] R. F. Treharne has continued his work on this period in a number of articles in which he has argued that the baronial reform movement was "the first deliberate and conscious politi-

[113] H. G. Richardson, "The Morrow of the Great Charter," *BJRL*, 28:422–443 (December 1944); V. H. Galbraith, *Roger Wendover and Matthew Paris* (Glasgow, 1944).

[114] J. C. Holt, "The Barons and the Great Charter," *EHR*, 70:1–24 (January 1955), "The Making of Magna Carta," *EHR*, 72:401–422 (July 1957), and "Rights and Liberties in Magna Carta," *Album Helen Maud Cam*, I, pp. 57–69; C. R. Cheney, "The Eve of Magna Carta," *BJRL*, 38:311–341 (March 1956); Naomi D. Hurnard has argued that clause thirty-four does not represent as severe a baronial feeling against expanded royal justice as has generally been thought ("Magna Carta, Clause 34," *Studies in Medieval History Presented to Frederick Maurice Powicke*, pp. 157–179).

[115] N. Denholm-Young, "The 'Paper Constitution' Attributed to 1244," *EHR*, 58:401–424 (September 1943); C. R. Cheney, "The 'Paper Constitution' Preserved by Matthew Paris," *EHR*, 65:213–221 (April 1950). See also the essays of Denholm-Young in *Collected Papers on Medieval Subjects* (Oxford, 1946). In "The Council and the Crisis of 1233–1234," *BJRL*, 27:384–393 (June 1943), B. Wilkinson has argued that baronial opposition to the Poitevins was caused by conflict over the nature of the royal council.

cal revolution in English history," that it was motivated by high political ideals, and that the knights took a decisive part in the events of 1258–1265 because experience in public affairs had prepared and united them and because as a class they were so influential that both Henry III and De Montfort felt compelled to consult them.[116] In regard to the later baronial struggle with Edward I, H. Rothwell and J. G. Edwards have jousted over that much debated *De Tallagio non Concedendo*. Edwards, whose arguments seem better supported, has relegated *De Tallagio* to the world of shadows and believes that the document known as the *Monstraunces* contains a genuine baronial petition for redress of grievances. In three long articles Rothwell has labored to prove that there was a written or unwritten supplementary baronial program whose content resembled that of *De Tallagio*. His conclusion is that "it is not yet safe to dismiss *De Tallagio non Concedendo*." [117]

Valuable essays by G. Templeman and, more recently, by J. G. Edwards, have summarized and evaluated the corpus of writing on parliament since the time of Stubbs.[118] Recent writing indicates that the judicial and political schools have little heeded Powicke's and Plucknett's calm, judicious emphasis upon parliament as a fluctuating, ill-defined assembly that disposed of all sorts of business, be it judicial, financial, political, or convivial.[119] R. F. Treharne has lately adduced evidence from the reign of Henry III to support the Wilkinson view that parliament was a political assembly.[120] Contrarily, Richardson and Sayles,

[116] R. F. Treharne, "The Significance of the Baronial Reform Movement, 1258–1267," *TRHS*, 4th ser., 25 (1943), 35–72, and "The Knights in the Period of Reform and Rebellion, 1258–67: A Critical Phase in the Rise of a New Class," *BIHR*, 21:1–12 (May and November 1946). P. Walne has edited and analyzed documents in the Archives Nationales at Paris which fill in our knowledge of the baronial argument presented at Amiens ("The Barons' Argument at Amiens, January 1264," *EHR*, 69:418–425 [July 1954], and 73:649–659 [October 1958]).

[117] J. G. Edwards, "Confirmatio Cartarum and Baronial Grievances in 1297," *EHR*, 58:147–172, 273–301 (May and September 1943); H. Rothwell, "The Confirmation of the Charters, 1297," *EHR*, 60:16–36, 177–192, 300–315 (January, May, and September 1945).

[118] G. Templeman, "The History of Parliament to 1400 in the Light of Modern Research," *UBHJ*, 1:202–231 (no. 2, 1948); J. G. Edwards, *Historians and the Medieval English Parliament* (Glasgow, 1960). See also the discussion of Helen Cam, "The Theory and Practice of Representation in Medieval England," *History*, 38:11–26 (February 1953); and R. S. Hoyt, "Recent Publications in the United States and Canada on the History of Western Representative Institutions before the French Revolution," *Speculum*, 29:356–377 (April, pt. 2, 1954).

[119] For Powicke see his Oxford volume on the thirteenth century; for Plucknett see his chapter on parliament in J. F. Willard and W. A. Morris, *The English Government at Work*, I (Cambridge, Mass., 1940).

[120] R. F. Treharne, "The Nature of Parliament in the Reign of Henry III," *EHR*,

who ignited the fierce debate with their studies in the twenties and thirties, have summarized their position as well as that of others and felt compelled to reiterate that the English parliament was an afforced session of the king's council, that there was only one kind of parliament whose essence was the dispensation of justice, and that politics and representation were unrelated to the parliament of Henry III and Edward I.[121] This thesis gains support from G. L. Haskins.[122] Ancillary to this central debate is that over the meaning of *plenum parliamentum* interpreted long ago by Pollard as meaning a "public and formal session of an assembly of the three estates." Helen Cam supports this interpretation in a study where she links *in pleno comitatu* to *in pleno parliamento* and where she connects the large assemblies of the thirteenth century to the early English folkmoots. Lately, however, T. Thorgrimisson has analyzed the famous phrase in pertinent records and has concluded that the evidence supports rendering it "in full parliament" rather than "in open parliament," and that consequently the Wilkinson political thesis on parliament is preferable to Pollard's which is strongly judicial.[123]

To say that interest in local history or that research on local institutions has declined since the war would belie the vigor of the local historical societies and belittle the many fine volumes of the *Victoria County History*. But to say that there has been a shift in research emphasis away from local political institutions, such as the hundred and the shrievalty,

---

74:590–610 (October 1959). The views of Wilkinson are found in his *Constitutional History* and numerous articles. See especially "The 'Political Revolution' of the Thirteenth and Fourteenth Centuries in England," *Speculum*, 24:502–509 (October 1949), and "English Politics and Politicians of the Thirteenth and Fourteenth Centuries," *Speculum*, 30:37–48 (January 1955).

[121] H. G. Richardson and G. O. Sayles, "Parliaments and Great Councils in Medieval England," *LQR*, 77:213–236, 401–426 (April and July 1961).

[122] G. L. Haskins, *The Growth of English Representative Government* (Philadelphia, 1948). For other stimulating essays on early English representation see J. E. A. Jolliffe, "Some Factors in the Beginnings of Parliament," *TRHS*, 4th ser., 22 (1940), pp. 101–139; R. A. Pelham, "The Provisioning of the Lincoln Parliament of 1301," *UBHJ*, 3:16–32 (no. 1, 1951); J. R. Strayer and G. Rudisill, Jr., "Taxation and Community in Wales and Ireland, 1272–1327," *Speculum*, 29:410–416 (April, pt. 2, 1954). The development of representative institutions in Ireland is covered in H. G. Richardson and G. O. Sayles, *The Irish Parliament in the Middle Ages* (Philadelphia, 1952). A comparison of parliament with representative assemblies on the Continent is made by A. R. Myers, "The English Parliament and the French Estates-General in the Middle Ages," *Album Helen Maud Cam*, II (Louvain, 1962), pp. 139–153, and by B. Lyon, "Medieval Constitutionalism: A Balance of Power," *ibid.*, pp. 155–183.

[123] Helen Cam, "From Witness of the Shire to Full Parliament," *TRHS*, 4th ser., 26 (1944) pp. 13–33; T. Thorgrimisson, "Plenum Parliamentum," *BIHR*, 32:69–82 (May 1959).

to social and economic institutions would indeed be true. Only a few scholars have followed the paths cut by Helen Cam and W. A. Morris. Happily, Helen Cam's book on the hundred has just been reissued and there appeared recently a collection of some of her most stimulating essays including those on the borough of Cambridge, the early hundred, the arrangements for reimbursing knights of the shire for their expenses in attending parliament, and the *Quo Warranto* proceedings.[124] This last and important essay goes into the details of local royal administration and justice and explains the results of the *Quo Warranto* proceedings on baronial jurisdiction, showing how strictly the royal officers supervised the baronial courts of the thirteenth century. In other studies Miss Cam has investigated society within the framework of the local community and its ties to the larger community of the realm.[125]

While the study of G. Templeman on the sheriff of thirteenth-century Warwickshire does not alter any accepted views on this office, it works out in detail the functions and powers of the sheriff and portrays him as an official of knightly rank who, as the agent of the king, had chiefly financial obligations.[126] T. F. T. Plucknett's Creighton Lecture delivered at the University of London in 1953 clearly describes the bailiff's role and function in local society.[127] We are indebted to G. Barraclough for a good picture of one of the great palatinates—Chester. Skillfully using early Cheshire charters, he recounts the immunities of the palatinate and its relations with the crown.[128]

The articles on local institutions indicate no pattern or trend in research; most simply describe the duties of officers such as keepers of

---

[124] Helen Cam, *The Hundred and the Hundred Rolls* (New York, 1960), and *Liberties and Communities in Medieval England* (Cambridge, Eng., 1944).

[125] Helen Cam, "The Community of the Vill," *Medieval Studies Presented to Rose Graham,* ed. V. Ruffer and A. J. Taylor (Oxford, 1950), pp. 1–14, and "The Evolution of the Mediaeval English Franchise," *Speculum,* 32:427–442 (July 1957).

[126] G. Templeman, *The Sheriffs of Warwickshire in the Thirteenth Century* (Oxford, 1948).

[127] T. F. T. Plucknett, *The Medieval Bailiff* (1954). For other studies on local officers see T. Lewis, "An English Serjeanty in a Welsh Setting," *History,* 31:85–99 (September 1946); C. A. F. Meekings, "Adam fitz William (d. 1238)," *BIHR,* 34:1–15 (May 1961).

[128] G. Barraclough, "The Earldom and County Palatine of Chester," *Transactions of the Historical Society of Lancashire and Cheshire,* 103 (1951), pp. 23–57, and *Early Cheshire Charters* (Chester, 1958). See also R. Stewart-Brown, "The Exchequer of Chester," *EHR,* 57:289–298 (July 1942); W. E. Wightman, "The Palatine Earldom of William fitz Osbern in Gloucestershire and Worcestershire (1066–1071)," *EHR,* 77:6–17 (January 1962); C. M. Fraser, "Edward I of England and the Regalian Franchise of Durham," *Speculum,* 31:329–342 (April 1956); A. J. Otway-Ruthven, "The Constitutional Position of the Great Lordships of South Wales," *TRHS,* 5th ser., 8 (1958), pp. 1–20.

royal buildings and escheators.[129] H. R. Loyn has studied the ealdorman and confirmed what has traditionally been accepted, that by the end of the ninth century the ealdorman was a royal servant, a noble of high birth, and the chief man of the shire, and that by the tenth century he had generally made his position and functions heritable and had become a potentate scheming to untie his bonds with the king. H. A. Cronne, investigating the office of local justiciar under the Normans, has uncovered the justiciar's link with the itinerant justices regularized by Henry II and offers new evidence that the justiciar assisted the sheriff with the administration of county justice.[130]

THE COMMON LAW

Since the classic of F. W. Maitland and the multi-volume work of W. S. Holdsworth no one has written a history of English law in the Middle Ages. When Maitland gloomily predicted that the history of England's medieval law would never be written, he did so with good reason. Most of the legal records needed for the task were unedited, many were yet unknown, and few trained historians had turned their energies to relating the common law to the institutional development of medieval England. What Maitland did for the study of legal history is known to all who work in the field of medieval England. Thanks to Maitland and his distinguished followers our knowledge of medieval law is completely different from what it was when Maitland was inspired by Vinogradoff and Stubbs to take up its study. The number of monographs and articles is legion, and legal records account for perhaps a fourth of recent publication of sources. With the possible exception of the fourteenth and fifteenth centuries the records and literature are now abundant enough to permit a new and much needed history of English medieval law. Fruitful ideas and new approaches appear in the studies of T. F. T. Plucknett, G. O. Sayles, H. G. Richardson, Doris M. Stenton, S. E. Thorne, W. H. Dunham, Jr. and others, but the broad evaluation and interpretation are found in only a few essays by Plucknett, McIlwain, and Nellie Neilson.[131] He who would study the legal history of medie-

[129] Helena M. Chew, "The Office of Escheator in the City of London during the Middle Ages," *EHR*, 58:319–330 (July 1943); C. T. Clay, "The Keepership of the Old Palace of Westminster," *EHR*, 59:1–22 (January 1944); G. A. Williams, "London and Edward I," *TRHS*, 5th ser., 11 (1961), pp. 81–99.

[130] H. R. Loyn, "The Term *Ealdorman* in the Translations Prepared at the Time of King Alfred," *EHR*, 68:513–525 (October 1953); H. A. Cronne, "The Office of Local Justiciar in England under the Norman Kings," *UBHJ* 6:18–38 (no. 1, 1957).

[131] T. F. T. Plucknett, "The Relations between Roman Law and English Common Law down to the Sixteenth Century: A General Survey," *University of Toronto*

val England must plunge into the specialized and technical monograph.

There are few studies on law in the Anglo-Saxon and Norman-Angevin periods. The one fundamental study is that on the royal writ by R. C. Van Caenegem in which he traces the origin and development of the various types of writs up to Glanville; studies the courts, the pleading, the recognitions, and the role of Glanville; and edits the most important of the different categories of writs.[132] Dorothy Whitelock has shown Bishop Wulfstan of Worcester to be the author of Canute's laws.[133] J. H. Wigmore has re-examined the evidence linking the Conqueror's Lanfranc to the Lanfranc who was professor of law in Italy and concludes that Maitland was probably correct in saying that the two Lanfrancs were the same person, but that "it is not absolutely certain." Alison Reppy has underlined the influence of William I's ordinance of 1072 upon the law of succession. R. W. Southern has questioned G. E. Woodbine's classification of the Glanville manuscripts. And H. G. Richardson has suggested that during the reign of John students were studying the common law at Oxford.[134]

Legal research on the thirteenth century has largely concentrated upon the "Bracton Problem." Before embarking upon this uncertain sea, one ought to read T. F. T. Plucknett's book on English legal literature which explains the various treatises from the *Quadripartitus* to Bracton and the Year Books.[135] In a study which W. S. Holdsworth called epochmaking, H. Kantorowicz started the debate that has raged over Bracton during the last two decades. Kantorowicz advanced a new view on the time and conditions at and under which Bracton's treatise on the common law was produced. His argument was that the treatise was begun in 1239, much earlier than Maitland had thought, and that the

---

Law Journal, 3:24–50 (no. 1, 1939); C. H. McIlwain, "The English Common Law, Barrier against Absolutism," *AHR,* 49:23–31 (October 1943); Nellie Neilson, "The Early Pattern of the Common Law," *AHR,* 49:199–212 (January 1944).

[132] R. C. Van Caenegem, *Royal Writs in England from the Conquest to Glanvill* (*Studies in the Early History of the Common Law*) (1959).

[133] Dorothy Whitelock, "Wulfstan and the Laws of Cnut," *EHR,* 63:433–452 (October 1948), and "Wulfstan's Authorship of Cnut's Laws," *EHR,* 70:72–85 (January 1955). See also her article on "Wulfstan and the So-Called Laws of Edward and Guthrum," *EHR,* 56:1–22 (January 1941).

[134] J. H. Wigmore, "Lanfranc, the Prime Minister of William the Conqueror: Was He Once an Italian Professor of Law?" *LQR,* 58:61–78 (January 1942); A. Reppy, *The Ordinance of William the Conqueror, 1072: Its Implication in the Law of Succession* (New York, 1954); R. W. Southern, "A Note on the Text of 'Glanville,' De Legibus et Consuetudinibus Regni Angliae," *EHR,* 65:81–90 (January 1950); H. G. Richardson, "Oxford Law School under John," *LQR,* 57:319–338 (July 1941).

[135] T. F. T. Plucknett, *Early English Legal Literature* (Cambridge, Eng., 1958).

work now known as Bracton's was a redaction of an original treatise after Bracton's death. It follows that, if Kantorowicz is correct, much of G. E. Woodbine's edition would be wrong and would have to be redone to remove comments and interpolations not Bracton's.[136] C. H. Mc-Ilwain seems to have been partly convinced by Kantorowicz because he has pointed out that a redaction of the Bracton original could mean that the errors in citations of Roman law were not Bracton's and that Bracton knew Roman law better than Maitland thought. McIlwain believes, however, that most of the Woodbine text is good and requires only minor revision.[137] Woodbine, who had dated Bracton's treatise between 1250 and 1259, naturally wrote a defense and was supported by F. Schulz, who stated that the true Bracton can be established only by scrupulous study of each passage. Schulz argued, for example, that Bracton derived one passage from Tancred's *Ordo Iudiciarius* rather than from Azo's *Summa* as both Maitland and Kantorowicz had believed. Schulz has seen, moreover, a stronger influence of Roman and canon law upon Bracton than of feudal law.[138] H. G. Richardson has tried to show that Bracton had an imperfect knowledge of Roman law because he did not understand the writings of such men as Azo, Drogheda, Tancred, and Raymond de Peñafort. And from one who ought to know—Doris M. Stenton—has come the prediction that "it will never be possible to produce a text of Bracton purged of all additions by other hands and containing no redundancies and confusions."[139]

Except to say that the traditional view has found more adherents than that of Kantorowicz, we shall let others decide who has the better of the Bractonian argument and turn instead to other legal treatises and compilations of the thirteenth century. Although that peculiar treatise *Fleta* has now been superbly edited and translated by G. O. Sayles and H. G.

---

[136] H. Kantorowicz, *Bractonian Problems* (Glasgow, 1941).

[137] C. H. McIlwain, "The Present Status of the Problem of the Bracton Text," *Harvard Law Review*, 57:220–240 (no. 2, 1943).

[138] See the review of Kantorowicz's book by G. E. Woodbine in *Yale Law Review*, 52:428–444 (no. 2, 1943). See also Woodbine, "The Language of English Law," *Speculum*, 18:395–436 (October 1943); F. Schulz, "Critical Studies on Bracton's Treatise," *LQR*, 59:172–180 (April 1943), "Bracton and Raymond de Peñafort," *LQR*, 61:286–292 (July 1945), and "Bracton on Kingship," *EHR*, 60:136–177 (May 1945). Cf. S. J. T. Miller, "The Position of the King in Bracton and Beaumanoir," *Speculum*, 31:263–296 (April 1956).

[139] H. G. Richardson, "Azo, Drogheda, and Bracton," *EHR*, 59:22–48 (January 1944), and "Trancred, Raymond, and Bracton," *EHR*, 59:376–384 (September 1944); Doris M. Stenton, *Rolls of the Justices in Eyre for Gloucestershire, Warwickshire and Staffordshire, 1221–1222* (1940), p. xxxv. See also G. Lapsley, "Bracton and the Authorship of the 'addicio de cartis,'" *EHR*, 62:1–29 (January 1947).

Richardson, no one is certain who wrote it, but N. Denholm-Young suggests that the author was Matthew de Scaccario, an eminent thirteenth-century lawyer, servant of the crown, and one familiar with the royal courts.[140] Our knowledge of procedure has been widened by G. J. Turner's edition of the *Brevia Placitata*, that thirteenth-century treatise in Norman-French on pleading in the royal courts, where one finds the appropriate writ, the count, further pleas, and some speeches of advocates and notes of judges' opinions.[141] The *Casus Placitorum* edited by W. H. Dunham, Jr., is a sort of annotated case book which seems to have been based on legal decisions handed down during the reign of Henry III.[142]

Scholars have investigated the learned and practical men behind the legal writing and compilation to discover something about their training, knowledge, and practice of the law. E. L. G. Stones has written on Sir Geoffrey le Scrope, a self-made man of the early fourteenth century who eventually became justice of the King's Bench.[143] F. Pegues has studied the royal clerks and presents interesting material on their social background, legal equipment, and careers; he believes it is perhaps to them we may owe the composition of the Year Books.[144] G. O. Sayles has shown the royal judges to be also legal consultants. G. L. Haskins and E. H. Kantorowicz tell of the career of Francis Accursius, learned in Roman and canon law and adviser to Edward I.[145]

On the subject of trial and procedure B. C. Keeney has traced the *judicium parium* of Magna Carta back to the early feudal court. Naomi D. Hurnard has challenged what has been taught from time out of mind, that the jury of presentment was introduced by the Assize of

---

[140] H. G. Richardson and G. O. Sayles, *Fleta*, II (1953); N. Denholm–Young, "Who Wrote 'Fleta'?" *EHR*, 58:1–13 (January 1943). See also E. H. Kantorowicz, "The Prologue to *Fleta* and the School of Petrus de Vinea," *Speculum*, 32:231–249 (April 1957); H. G. Reuschlein, "Who Wrote *The Mirror of Justices?*" *LQR* 58:265–279 (April 1942).

[141] G. J. Turner, *Brevia Placitata* (1947).

[142] W. H. Dunham, Jr., *Casus Placitorum and Reports in the King's Courts, 1272–1278* (1952). See also S. E. Thorne, "Gilbert de Thornton's Summa de Legibus," *University of Toronto Law Journal*, 7:1–26 (no. 1, 1947).

[143] E. L. G. Stones, "Sir Geoffrey le Scrope (c. 1285–1340), Chief Justice of the King's Bench," *EHR*, 69:1–17 (January 1954).

[144] F. Pegues, "The Medieval Origins of Modern Law Reporting," *Cornell Law Quarterly*, 38:491–510 (Summer 1953), and "The Clericus in the Legal Administration of Thirteen-Century England," *EHR*, 71:529–559 (October 1956).

[145] G. O. Sayles, "Medieval Judges as Legal Consultants," *LQR*, 56:247–254 (April 1940); G. L. Haskins and E. H. Kantorowicz, "A Diplomatic Mission of Francis Accursius and His Oration before Pope Nicholas III," *EHR*, 58:424–447 (October 1943).

Clarendon in 1166, and has argued that the Assize merely continued and formalized the traditional system of communal accusation common in Saxon and Norman times.[146]

T. F. T. Plucknett, the dean of English legal historians, in addition to being responsible for the edition of many legal records and assuming the leadership of the Seldon Society, has produced some of the most substantial writing on medieval law since Maitland laid down his pen. His principal achievement has been two books on the legislation of Edward I. In the first book he keenly analyzes the great statutes of Edward and their impact upon English law and stresses how essential is the combined study of law and history for the understanding of the whole historical process. He takes particular interest in explaining the historical situations that prompted legislation.[147] In the second book he concentrates upon criminal legislation and investigates such subjects as reparation and the victim, the crown and its rights, and the criminal and intention.[148]

Although the conflict of medieval spiritual and secular justice cannot be separated from the larger political, religious, and constitutional issues, the struggle had a special influence upon the development of the common law. Mary Cheney believes that the Compromise of Avranches in 1172 destroyed Henry II's plan outlined in the Constitutions of Clarendon by which he hoped to cut the English church off from the development of the continental church and to check the inflow of papalist theory and canonistic knowledge.[149] J. W. Gray, following the

---

[146] B. C. Keeney, *Judgment by Peers* (Cambridge, Mass., 1949); Naomi D. Hurnard, "The Jury of Presentment and the Assize of Clarendon," *EHR*, 56:374–411 (July 1941). See also J. H. Le Patourel, "The Date of the Trial on Penenden Heath," *EHR*, 61:378–388 (September 1946). For studies on the writ and procedure see C. Johnson, "Notes on Thirteenth-Century Judicial Procedure," *EHR*, 62:508–522 (October 1947); J. Conway Davies, "Common Law Writs and Returns: Richard I to Richard II," *BIHR*, 26:125–157 (November 1953), 27:1–34 (May 1954); R. Lennard, "Early Manorial Juries," *EHR*, 77:511–518 (July 1962); H. Wurzel, "The Origin and Development of Quo Minus," *Yale Law Review*, 49:39–64 (no. 1, 1939); G. L. Haskins, "The Development of Common Law Dower," *Harvard Law Review*, 62:42–55 (no. 1, 1948); G. D. G. Hall, "Some Early Writs of 'Trespass,'" *LQR*, 73:65–73 (January 1957); S. F. C. Milsom, "Trespass from Henry III to Edward III," *LQR*, 74:195–224, 407–436, 561–590 (April, July, October 1958).

[147] T. F. T. Plucknett, *Legislation of Edward I* (Oxford, 1949).

[148] T. F. T. Plucknett, *Edward I and Criminal Law* (Cambridge, Eng., 1960). For other studies on Edwardian law see Naomi D. Hurnard, "Did Edward I Reverse Henry II's Policy upon Seisin?" *EHR*, 69:529–553 (October 1954); A. Gwynn, "Edward I and the Proposed Purchase of English Law for the Irish, c. 1276–80," *TRHS*, 5th ser., 10 (1960), pp. 111–127.

[149] M. Cheney, "The Compromise of Avranches of 1172 and the Spread of Canon Law in England," *EHR*, 56:177–198 (April 1941).

conflict between secular and ecclesiastical jurisdiction over the right of patronage, finds that by the end of Henry III's reign the secular courts had assumed almost all the jurisdiction concerning disputes on patronage. Helena M. Chew shows how the Statute of Mortmain in 1279 conflicted with the London custom of mortmain.[150] The most significant study on the relation between royal and local justice is that of Naomi D. Hurnard who, having examined Maitland's thesis that ascribed high criminal justice to private Norman courts, argues, contrarily and convincingly, that the normal franchise court of Norman times was competent to handle only minor criminal justice and that the evidence of the Anglo-Norman law books runs against "the assumption that many lords enjoyed high powers of justice." [151] R. F. Hunnisett's study on the coroner is the first book to be written on this important official. It uses all the extant coroners' rolls to show the origin, development, and functions of this office. Of special interest is the section on the origin where, after detailed examination of the evidence, Hunnisett concludes that the date 1194 should stand and that Maitland had the better of the argument with C. Gross who preferred an earlier date.[152] In a most valuable essay A. Harding traces the history of the keeper of the peace in the twelfth and thirteenth centuries and shows how an essentially military and political official came to have judicial functions and to become the father of the justice of the peace.[153]

SOCIAL AND ECONOMIC INSTITUTIONS

Although the link between social and economic history is obvious, a reading of the literature indicates that very little social history of medieval England is being written. Most studies are more narrowly conceived and limited to such economic problems as the volume of trade, the trend in labor services, population statistics, and the physical condition and exploitation of the land. Social history, when written, concerns the people not of the towns with their urban economy of trade and industry, but of the countryside where admittedly some attempt has been made to

[150] J. W. Gray, "The Ius Praesentandi in England from the Constitutions of Clarendon to Bracton," *EHR*, 67:481–509 (July 1952). For the spread of jurisdiction of a great medieval liberty see F. Barlow, *Durham Jurisdictional Peculiars* (Oxford, 1950). Helena M. Chew, "Mortmain in Medieval London," *EHR*, 60:1–16 (January 1945).

[151] Naomi D. Hurnard, "The Anglo-Norman Franchises," *EHR*, 64:289–328 (July 1949).

[152] R. F. Hunnisett, *The Medieval Coroner* (Cambridge, Eng., 1962).

[153] A. Harding, "The Origins and Early History of the Keeper of the Peace," *TRHS*, 5th ser., 10 (1960), pp. 85–109.

relate economic trends to the social condition of the agrarian laborer. Even where there is a linking of economic and social history English medievalists have largely ignored the work of Marc Bloch and his students and disciples. In France and Belgium the studies of Ch.-E. Perrin A. Déléage, P. Dollinger, R. Boutruche, G. Duby, L. Génicot, A. E. Verhulst, A. D'Haenens, and others have created a new pattern for the study of medieval agrarian history. Sensitive to the broadest implications and interdependence of social and economic history, these studies are concerned with long-term social and economic trends. What, for example, happened to the social condition and economy of a seigniory between 800 and 1400? What were the social movements and economic cycles and developments in the regions of Namur, Flanders, Mâcon, and Burgundy from the Carolingian era to the outbreak of the Hundred Years' War? What were the social and economic differences in seigniories and agrarian regions before and after the crises of the fourteenth century? [154] In regard to the town a similar situation exists. While there has been little interest during the last quarter century in the economic and social structure of the English town, on the Continent historians are investigating the origin and development of the town and its institutions, the differences between the social and economic structure of large and small towns, and the relations between towns. Studies on English trade and industry have been limited almost exclusively to the fourteenth and fifteenth centuries. It must be said that even the good studies on English social and economic history between the fifth and early fourteenth centuries do not have the uniformly high quality found in other areas of English history and do not in general compare favorably with the writing of this kind of history on the Continent.

In the domain of social history G. C. Homans' study of English village society in the thirteenth century is original and important in concept and result. Relying on such records as manorial court rolls and accounts, royal inquests, and custumals, Homans has painted a rich picture of the thirteenth-century peasant. One is led through the yearly calendar of the peasant routine and feast and learns about the arrangement and size of peasant holdings, the agrarian techniques, inheritance, labor services, social and economic conditions, and the custom of the manor.[155] Although the nine essays recently edited by G. Barraclough are grouped

[154] For an account of what is being done with agrarian history on the Continent see A. E. Verhulst, "L'agriculture médiévale et ses problèmes," *Studi Medievali*, 3d ser., 2:691–704 (December 1961).

[155] G. C. Homans, *English Villagers of the Thirteenth Century* (Cambridge, Mass., 1941).

under the rubric of social history, most do not contain much social history. While it is indeed good to have F. M. Stenton's essay on Norman London and J. N. L. Myres's on Roman Britain so accessible, they hardly qualify as social history.[156] Doris M. Stenton's book on the English woman has some chapters on the medieval woman with interesting material on her way of life and her rights and role in Anglo-Saxon and Norman society, but it cannot be compared to Eileen Power's book on medieval people.[157] In two learned books on the Jews in medieval England C. Roth has delved into the exceptionally rich documentation and given a most complete account of the economic activities of the Jews, their life in the towns, and, especially, their intellectual accomplishments. The recent book of H. G. Richardson is confined to a study of the Jews under the Angevins. The relations between Jews and Gentiles are examined, but chiefly economic questions such as royal borrowing, the Jewish money market, taxation, and the Jewish exchequer occupy Mr. Richardson. Finally, there is the occasionally interesting but not scholarly book of M. Keen on English medieval outlaws.[158]

Throughout the 1920's and 1930's C. Stephenson and J. Tait maintained a lively debate on the nature of the Anglo-Saxon and Norman borough. English medievalists for the most part have accepted the conclusions of Tait while American and continental scholars have inclined towards those of Stephenson. Here the matter has rested. The thesis of neither has been tested in depth, as have those of Pirenne and Dopsch on the Continent. Despite what could be done and by comparison to what is being done on the Continent, there is little to report for the medieval borough. The study on Lincoln by its former mayor J. W. F. Hill is good local history quite strong on topography which seems to support Stephenson. H. A. Cronne in a short essay depicts Warwick as an Anglo-Saxon village fortified against the Danes in 914, a site chosen for a castle by the Conqueror, a place granted restricted bourgeois privileges, but never a thriving town. The topographical study of York by A. Raine, though a good idea, is unsuccessful because the chronology is faulty and the maps deficient. The somewhat more important study of W. M. MacKenzie on the development of the Scottish burghs, in spite of relying too much on legal records, proves that the Pirenne theory has

---

[156] *Social Life in Early England,* ed. G. Barraclough (1960). These essays appeared originally as Pamphlets of the Historical Association.

[157] Doris M. Stenton, *The English Woman in History* (1957).

[158] C. Roth, *A History of the Jews in England,* 2d ed. (Oxford, 1949), and *The Jews of Medieval Oxford* (Oxford, 1951); H. G. Richardson, *The English Jewry under Angevin Kings* (1960); M. Keen, *Outlaws of Medieval Legend* (1961).

some application in northern England and Scotland.[159] Of great value is Caroline Shillaber's article on the towns founded by Edward I in Wales because it makes possible a comparison of his urban policy here with that in southwestern France where he was doing much the same thing with *bastides*.[160]

It is fortunate that M. M. Postan and Miss E. M. Carus-Wilson have recently written their scholarly accounts of medieval England's trade and industry for the second volume of the *Cambridge Economic History* because there is little else to read.[161] There is, of course, Eileen Power's study on the wool trade showing the impact of this trade on English society and describing with penetrating and graceful scholarship how the wool was produced, sold, and taxed.[162] Beyond this, there are only articles of Miss Carus-Wilson dealing with the cloth and wine trade. That on the cloth trade is valuable because it concentrates on the East Anglian region during the twelfth and thirteenth centuries.[163]

Though disjointed and uneven, the survey of English agrarian history that appeared over twenty years ago in the *Cambridge Economic History* remains the most recent and scholarly.[164] Against this deficiency in surveys, however, are the many published charters, cartularies, registers, and various manorial records which form a basis for serious work on agrarian institutions. Those who deign to dirty their hands with such history have the reward of exceedingly rich source material. The published work on agrarian history groups itself about five principal prob-

[159] J. W. F. Hill, *Medieval Lincoln* (Cambridge, Eng., 1948); H. A. Cronne, *The Borough of Warwick in the Middle Ages,* Dugdale Society Occasional Papers, no. 10 (1951); A. Raine, *Medieval York: A Topographical Survey Based on Original Sources* (1955); W. M. MacKenzie, *The Scottish Burghs* (Edinburgh, 1949). The nature of the Norman commune is reviewed by S. R. Packard, "The Norman Communes Once More," *AHR,* 46:338–347 (January 1941). See also G. O. Sayles, "The Dissolution of a Gild at York in 1306," *EHR,* 55:83–99 (January 1940); and C. R. Young, *The English Borough and Royal Administration, 1130–1307* (Durham, N.C., 1961), which examines the obligations of the thirteenth-century borough to the crown.

[160] C. Shillaber, "Edward I, Builder of Towns," *Speculum,* 22:297–309 (July 1947).

[161] *The Cambridge Economic History of Europe,* II, *Trade and Industry in the Middle Ages,* ed. M. M. Postan and E. E. Rich (Cambridge, Eng., 1952).

[162] E. Power, *The Wool Trade in English Medieval History* (Oxford, 1941).

[163] E. M. Carus-Wilson, "The English Cloth Trade in the Late Twelfth and Early Thirteenth Centuries," *EcHR,* 14:32–50 (no. 1, 1944), and "The Effects of the Acquisition and the Loss of Gascony on the English Wine Trade," *BIHR,* 21: 145–154 (May and November 1947).

[164] *The Cambridge Economic History of Europe,* I, *The Agrarian Life of the Middle Ages,* ed. J. H. Clapham and E. Power (Cambridge, Eng., 1941). For a valuable discussion of research on agrarian history see J. Thirsk, "Die agrargeschichtliche Forschung in England seit 1945," *Zeitschrift für Agrargeschichte und Agrarsoziologie,* 3:54–65 (April 1955).

lems: the nature of the early Anglo-Saxon agrarian village and its inhabitants, the social and economic conditions of the late Saxon and early Norman peasant, the arrangement of fields and villages and their landed resources, the economy and administration of landed estates, and the shifting social and economic status of the peasant in the thirteenth century.

The findings of recent archaeological research on Roman villas suggest that Roman agrarian institutions may have had a more forceful influence over Anglo-Saxon agrarian routine than has been supposed. At least for some regions of England it would appear that there was continuity between the Roman villa and the Anglo-Saxon agrarian village.[165] In a number of careful studies on the ecclesiastical estates of western England, which give an excellent picture of agrarian routine, tenure, and field system, H. P. R. Finberg has uncovered evidence of Roman and Saxon agrarian links. His case for such continuity at Withington in Gloucestershire is very strong; it is the first well argued brief for the continuity of the villa and its system since the study of Seebohm.[166]

Scholarly debate continues on the social, economic, and legal condition of the Anglo-Saxon peasant, with special attention to the meaning of commendation. Maitland's conclusion that commendation was a very slender bond between lord and man retains the support of most scholars concerned with this problem. F. M. Stenton affirms a belief in a free Anglo-Saxon peasantry that began to lose its freedom only towards the end of the Saxon period. This traditional view has not, however, been acceptable to C. Stephenson who has seen in the pertinent evidence an unfree peasantry bound to lords by a commendation both permanent and personal.[167] Barbara Dodwell has replied that the East Anglian evidence supports Maitland, while T. H. Aston has questioned the Maitland-Vinogradoff-Stenton position and pointed out that much of their evidence is not contemporary and is legal rather than social and economic.[168] If the peasants of East Anglia were freer than peasants in

---

[165] See, for example, G. A. Boon, *Roman Silchester, the Archaeology of a Romano-British Town* (1957); *Roman and Native in North Britain*, ed. I. A. Richmond, (Edinburgh, 1958); W. G. Hoskins, *The Westward Expansion of Wessex*, Occasional Papers of Local History, University of Leicester (Leicester, 1960).

[166] H. P. R. Finberg, *Roman and Saxon Withington*, Occasional Papers of Local History, University of Leicester (Leicester, 1955); *Studies in Early English History* (Leicester, 1960); *Gloucestershire Studies* (Leicester, 1957); *Tavistock Abbey: A Study in the Social and Economic History of Devon* (Cambridge, Eng., 1951).

[167] C. Stephenson, "Commendation and Related Problems in Domesday," *EHR*, 59:289–310 (September 1944).

[168] B. Dodwell, "East Anglian Commendation," *EHR*, 63:289–306 (July 1948); T. H. Aston, "The Origins of the Manor in England," *TRHS*, 5th ser., 8 (1958), pp. 59–83.

other areas, it was not, according to R. H. C. Davis, because they descended from a large number of free Danish settlers, for he is convinced that the Danes were never numerous in eastern England. In the opinion of G. C. Homans the peculiar social structure of East Anglia was due to the Frisians who settled there in the fifth century.[169]

The arrangement of strips, fields, villages, and the geography and exploitation of the land have been the subjects of much valuable research stimulated in great part by the study of the Orwins on the open field system which helped to upset the classic picture of neatly arranged open fields and strips. Unfortunately, a second edition of the Orwins' book has failed to incorporate systematically the results of recent research, especially that employing aerial photography and topographical techniques.[170] M. W. Beresford has used these new methods with great success. In one study he noted 1,300 villages which disappeared during the Middle Ages and connected this phenomenon to economic trends.[171] In 1948 he surveyed and explained the results of assarting and enclosing upon the open field. And in 1958 he collaborated with J. K. S. St. Joseph to present an aerial survey of medieval fields, towns, and villages. This work, comprising a magnificent collection of photographs accompanied by a learned text, demonstrates that skillful use of aerial photography can uncover the secrets of the medieval agrarian system and suggests the lines along which such research should be pushed.[172] Other studies by H. C. Darby, H. E. Hallam, and R. Lennard have investigated the clearance of land and suggested economic reasons and results.[173] Lennard's conclusions are assembled in a book which surveys early Norman social and agrarian history.[174]

[169] R. H. C. Davis, "East Anglia and the Danelaw," *TRHS*, 5th ser., 5 (1955), pp. 23–39; G. C. Homans, "The Frisians in East Anglia," *EcHR* 2d ser., 10:189–206 (August 1957).

[170] Charles S. and Christabel S. Orwin, *The Open Fields*, 2d ed. (Oxford, 1954).

[171] M. W. Beresford, *The Lost Villages of England* (1954).

[172] M. W. Beresford, "Ridge and Furrow and the Open Fields," *EcHR*, 2d ser., 1:34–45 (no. 1, 1948); M. W. Beresford and J. K. S. St. Joseph, *Medieval England. An Aerial Survey*, 2 vols. (Cambridge, Eng., 1958). See also W. G. Hoskins, *Essays in Leicestershire History* (Liverpool, 1950), and *The Making of the English Landscape* (1954).

[173] H. C. Darby, *The Medieval Fenland and the Draining of the Fens* (Cambridge, Eng., 1940), and "Domesday Woodland," *EcHR*, 2d ser., 3:21–43 (no. 1, 1950); H. E. Hallam, *The New Lands of Elloe: A Study of Early Reclamation in Lincolnshire*, Occasional Papers of Local History, University of Leicester (Leicester, 1954); R. Lennard, "The Destruction of the Woodland in the Eastern Counties under William the Conqueror," *EcHR*, 15:36–43 (no. 1, 1945).

[174] R. Lennard, *Rural England, 1086–1135: A Study of Social and Agrarian Conditions* (1959). See also "The Composition of Demesne Plough-Teams in Twelfth-Century England," *EHR*, 75:193–201 (April 1960).

The agrarian study characteristic of the Marc Bloch school is best represented in England by the research of R. A. L. Smith, E. Miller, Marjorie Morgan, J. A. Raftis, M. M. Postan, and R. H. Hilton. These scholars have sloughed off the static approach to agrarian history and have tried to describe how the condition of land, lord, peasant, and mode of exploitation changed in response to fluctuating economic and social conditions. Some of these scholars such as Smith, Miller, and Raftis have thoroughly investigated one great landed estate such as that of Canterbury or Ely and have written their economic history with perpendicular depth. Miller's study, for example, extends from the seventh to the fourteenth century.[175] Postan and Hilton have achieved horizontal depth by spreading their investigations over several estates but limiting them to the twelfth, thirteenth, and fourteenth centuries.[176] These pioneer studies prove what can and must be done if we are eventually to have a new picture of medieval agrarian society that will furnish the information we need on the shift from an agrarian to a money economy and on the fate of landed estates of ecclesiastical and lay lords.

Much of the interest in the agrarian problems of the thirteenth century was generated by the work of E. A. Kosminsky which appeared in 1935, went through a slight Russian revision in 1947, and was translated into English in 1956. Kosminsky drew attention to the prominence of agrarian rents, the decline of labor services, the important role of hired labor, the striking social differentiation in the peasantry, and the variations in agrarian techniques of manors caused by difference in size, location, terrain, and crop.[177] These are the problems that have occu-

---

[175] R. A. L. Smith, *Canterbury Cathedral Priory: A Study in Monastic Administration* (Cambridge, Eng., 1943); E. Miller, *The Abbey and Bishopric of Ely* (Cambridge, Eng., 1951); J. A. Raftis, *The Estates of Ramsey Abbey: A Study in Economic Growth and Organization* (Toronto, 1957). See also M. Morgan, *The English Lands of the Abbey of Bec* (Oxford, 1946); M. Chibnall, *Select Documents of the English Lands of the Abbey of Bec,* Camden Series, 73 (1951).

[176] M. M. Postan, "Glastonbury Estates in the Twelfth Century," *EcHR,* 2d ser., 5:358–367 (no. 3, 1953). R. Lennard has criticized this article and denied the contraction of the Glastonbury demesne lands affirmed by Postan ("The Demesnes of Glastonbury Abbey in the Eleventh and Twelfth Centuries," *EcHR,* 2d ser., 8:355–363 [April 1956]). For Postan's reply see *EcHR,* 2d ser., 9:106–118 (August 1956). See also R. H. Hilton, "Winchcombe Abbey and the Manor of Sherborne," *UBHJ,* 2:31–52 (no. 1, 1949); "Gloucester Abbey Leases of the Late Thirteenth Century," *UBHJ,* 4:1–17 (no. 1, 1953); *Social Structure of Rural Warwickshire,* Dugdale Society Occasional Papers, no. 9 (Stratford-on-Avon, 1950); "A Thirteenth-Century Poem on Disputed Villein Services," *EHR,* 56:90–97 (January 1941).

[177] E. A. Kosminsky, *Studies in the Agrarian History of England in the Thirteenth Century* (Oxford, 1956).

pied subsequent study of the thirteenth century, but they have been approached along lines less rigid than those imposed by the Marxist methodology of Kosminsky. Typical of such work is the research of H. E. Hallam, J. Z. Titow, and J. B. Harley that probes the results of increased population upon emancipation, land clearance, and redistribution of the land.[178] M. M. Postan in a case study on the hired agrarian laborer during the twelfth and thirteenth centuries has shown that such hired labor had become common by the thirteenth century when customary services were disappearing and more land was being placed under the plow.[179] Barbara Dodwell, attempting to revise Kosminsky's picture of a rigidly structured free peasantry with uniform holdings and obligations, argues that at least for the Midlands the Hundred Rolls portray a heterogeneous and complex social structure of tenants ranging from the humble to the affluent.[180]

RELIGIOUS LIFE AND ORGANIZATION

Prior to the war scholars such as A. G. Little and A. H. Thompson had made important contributions to the history of the English medieval church but their work was almost drowned by the flood of writing on institutional history. Since the war this lopsided condition has been partially redressed. More research has been focused on the church and its history and from it have come some remarkable studies of greater originality and scope than those in the overworked area of constitutional history. Admittedly, however, one reason this writing appears more original and valuable is that church history had been neglected and there was much to be done. A history of the English medieval church has yet to appear but we do have some books that deal with important questions over a number of centuries. There are at present only two books which offer broad surveys of the church. The first by Margaret Deanesly on the Anglo-Saxon church has supplemented the literary

[178] J. Z. Titow, "Some Evidence of the Thirteenth Century Population Increase," *EcHR*, 2d ser., 14:218–223 (December 1961); H. E. Hallam, "Some Thirteenth-Century Censuses," *EcHR*, 2d ser., 10:340–361 (April 1958), and "Population Density in Medieval Fenland," *EcHR*, 2d ser., 14:71–81 (August 1961); J. B. Harley, "Population Trends and Agricultural Developments from the Warwickshire Hundred Rolls of 1279," *EcHR*, 2d ser., 11:8–18 (August 1958). See also R. A. Donkin, "Settlement and Depopulation on Cistercian Estates during the Twelfth and Thirteenth Centuries, especially in Yorkshire," *BIHR*, 33:141–157 (November 1960).

[179] M. M. Postan, *The Famulus, the Estate Labourer in the Twelfth and Thirteenth Centuries* (Cambridge, Eng., 1954).

[180] B. Dodwell, "The Free Tenantry of the Hundred Rolls," *EcHR*, 14:163–171 (no. 2, 1944). See also W. O. Ault, "By-Laws of Gleaning and the Problems of Harvest," *EcHR*, 2d ser., 14:210–217 (December 1961).

sources with archaeological evidence and the result is an intelligent account of the early church. The second by J. R. H. Moorman, though limited to the thirteenth century, weaves a rich tapestry depicting the daily life of the secular and regular clergy, the recruitment of the clergy, the attempts at reform, and the revenues.[181]

Research on the pre-Conquest church has been scattered with no emphasis on any particular theme or problem. E. G. Bowen has treated the Christian influence and activity of Celtic missionaries in Wales. In a short essay D. J. V. Fisher has indicated the salient features of decline in the church after the death of Bede and throughout the ordeal of the Danish invasions, a decline checked only by the zealous Dunstan and his reforms. Dorothy Whitelock has briefly written on the life of Wulfstan, the prominent churchman in the Canutian period, and cast more light upon his ability, character, and accomplishments as a homilist. E. John has once more investigated the *trimoda necessitas* and argues cogently for a later imposition of these burdens upon the church than the date assigned by W. H. Stevenson. He also concludes that bridge building and maintenance of fortifications were imposed by King Aethelbald about 748, while fyrd duty was exacted later by Offa.[182]

Although little attention has been given to the Norman church, much has been written on major church figures of the twelfth and thirteenth centuries and on diocesan administration.[183] The influential but neglected Theobald, archbishop of Canterbury, has finally been the subject of a study that credits him with some of the achievements formerly ascribed to Thomas Becket. A. Saltman has not only written a careful description of Theobald's ecclesiastical career and of his relations with Henry II, the monasteries, and the bishops, but he has edited over three

---

[181] Margaret Deanesly, *The Pre-Conquest Church in England* (Oxford, 1961). This book is supplemented by Miss Deanesly's special studies on architecture, literature, and administration in *Sidelights on the Anglo-Saxon Church* (Oxford, 1961). See also J. R. H. Moorman, *Church Life in England in the Thirteenth Century*, 2d ed. (Cambridge, Eng., 1946).

[182] E. G. Bowen, *The Settlements of the Celtic Saints in Wales* (Cardiff, 1954); D. J. V. Fisher, "The Church in England between the Death of Bede and the Danish Invasions," *TRHS*, 5th ser., 2 (1952), pp. 1–19; Dorothy Whitelock, "Archbishop Wulfstan, Homilist and Statesman," *TRHS*, 4th ser., 24 (1942), pp. 25–45; E. John, "The Imposition of the Common Burdens on the Lands of the English Church," *BIHR*, 31:117–129 (November 1958). See also the fine edition of Bede's prose life and the anonymous life of St. Cuthbert by B. Colgrave, *Two Lives of St. Cuthbert* (Cambridge, Eng., 1940); and E. Craster, "The Patrimony of St. Cuthbert," *EHR*, 69:177–199 (April 1954).

[183] R. A. L. Smith, "The Place of Gundulf in the Anglo-Norman Church," *EHR*, 58:257–273 (July 1943); D. C. Douglas, "The Norman Episcopate before the Norman Conquest," *CHJ*, 13:101–115 (no. 2, 1957).

hundred of Theobald's charters, including some formerly thought to have been issued by Becket.[184] C. H. Lawrence has made a study of St. Edmund of Abingdon, archbishop of Canterbury under Henry III.[185] In the first full study of Pecham, archbishop of Canterbury from 1279 to 1292, Decima L. Douie concludes that his talents were administrative ability, efficiency, and energy. Though not a great intellectual or theologian, Pecham, by his firm stand against and condemnation of the new Thomism, assured the supremacy of the Franciscans and traditional philosophy at Oxford.[186]

In the first of two studies on diocesan administration C. R. Cheney has written from episcopal *acta* between 1100 and 1250 an account of episcopal secretarial offices and of the personnel of episcopal households. In the other study he critically examines the composition and origin of a body of synodal statutes in the thirteenth century and presents a good picture of the content of diocesan legislation as well as of the organization and memberships of the synods.[187] The interest of Z. N. and C. N. Brooke in the personnel of cathedral chapters has resulted in good lists of the deans, chancellors, archdeacons, and other officers of Hereford and St. Paul's.[188] The details of diocesan and metropolitan financial administration have held the attention of R. A. L. Smith.[189] And aspects of the jurisdiction of York and Canterbury have been well discussed by R. Brentano and Marjorie Morgan.[190]

[184] A Saltman, *Theobald, Archbishop of Canterbury* (1956).

[185] C. H. Lawrence, *St. Edmund of Abingdon. A Study in Hagiography and History* (Oxford, 1960).

[186] D. L. Douie, *Archbishop Pecham* (Oxford, 1952). See also J. J. Smith, *The Attitude of John Pecham towards Monastic Houses in His Jurisdiction* (Washington, D.C., 1949); D. Knowles, "Some Aspects of the Career of Archbishop Pecham," *EHR*, 57:1–19, 178–202 (January and April 1942); Rosalind Hill, "Public Penance: Some Problems of a Thirteenth-Century Bishop," *History*, 36:213–226 (October 1951).

[187] C. R. Cheney, *English Bishops' Chanceries, 1100–1250* (Manchester, Eng., 1950), and *English Synodalia of the Thirteenth Century* (Oxford, 1941). See also "The Earliest English Diocesan Statutes," *EHR*, 75:1–29 (January 1960).

[188] Z. N. and C. N. Brooke, "Hereford Cathedral Dignitaries in the Twelfth Century," *CHJ*, 8:1–21 (no. 1, 1944); C. N. Brooke, "The Composition of the Chapter of St. Paul's, 1086–1163," *CHJ*, 10:111–132 (no. 2, 1951).

[189] R. A. L. Smith, "The Central Financial System of Christ Church, Canterbury, 1186–1512," *EHR*, 55:353–369 (July 1940); "The Financial System of Rochester Cathedral Priory," *EHR*, 56:586–595 (October 1941); "The *Regimen Scaccarii* in English Monasteries," *TRHS*, 4th ser., 24 (1942), pp. 73–94. See also Smith's *Collected Papers* (1947). See, in addition, R. W. Southern, "The Canterbury Forgeries," *EHR*, 73:193–226 (April 1958); M. Morgan, "The Organization of the Scottish Church in the Twelfth Century," *TRHS*, 4th ser., 29 (1947), pp. 135–149.

[190] R. Brentano, *York Metropolitan Jurisdiction and Papal Judges Delegate, 1279–*

This research, however meritorious, is second to the excellent series of studies on English monasticism by D. Knowles and others. In two volumes Knowles has written a definitive history of the monastic orders in England from the time of Dunstan to 1340. A superb synthesis, it describes the monks and friars in all their activities, ties English monastic development to continental trends, and delineates the temper and accomplishments of monasticism at its height. Knowles has written history characterized by fine and penetrating judgment and possessed of that all too rare quality—literary eloquence.[191] To supplement this history Knowles collaborating with R. N. Hadcock and J. K. S. St. Joseph has produced a listing and description of the religious houses of medieval England.[192] A useful accompaniment to these studies is J. C. Dickinson's recent survey of the daily life at cathedral and abbey.[193] In addition to these syntheses there are numerous short studies on various aspects of monasticism. D. J. V. Fisher has, for example, investigated the causes of the antimonastic reaction during the reign of Edward the Martyr, and Miss Raymonde Foreville has advanced the thesis that increased papal control over English monasteries in the twelfth century was due to the concordat of Avranches.[194]

While the Franciscans in England had been the subject of numerous studies before the war by A. G. Little, the other orders did not receive

1296 (Berkeley, Calif., 1959); M. Morgan, "Early Canterbury Jurisdiction," *EHR*, 60:392–399 (September 1945).

[191] D. Knowles, *The Monastic Order in England: A History of Its Development from the Time of St. Dunstan to the Fourth Lateran Council, 943–1216* (Cambridge, Eng., 1940); *The Religious Orders in England* (Cambridge, Eng., 1948). See also "Some Developments in English Monastic Life, 1216–1336," *TRHS*, 4th ser., 26 (1944), pp. 37–52.

[192] D. Knowles and R. N. Hadcock, *Medieval Religious Houses: England and Wales* (1953). This is a revised and augmented edition of Knowles's *The Religious Houses of Medieval England*, which appeared in 1940. See also D. Knowles and J. K. S. St. Joseph, *Monastic Sites from the Air* (Cambridge, Eng., 1952); G. H. Cook, *English Monasteries in the Middle Ages* (New York, 1961); D. E. Easson, *Medieval Religious Houses: Scotland* (1957).

[193] J. C. Dickinson, *Monastic Life in Medieval England* (Oxford, 1961). The study of E. S. Duckett on Dunstan and monasticism is more of a survey: *Saint Dunstan of Canterbury. A Study of Monastic Reform in the Tenth Century* (1955).

[194] D. J. V. Fisher, "The Anti-Monastic Reaction in the Reign of Edward the Martyr," *CHJ*, 10:254–270 (no. 3, 1952); R. Foreville, "La condition juridique des monastères anglais à la fin du XIIe siècle," *Revue Historique de Droit Français et Etranger*, 4th ser., 24:267–280 (July–December 1945). See also R. A. L. Smith, "The Early Community of St. Andrew at Rochester, 604-c. 1080," *EHR*, 60:289–300 (September 1945); C. J. Holdsworth, "John of Ford and English Cistercian Writing, 1167–1214," *TRHS*, 5th ser., 11 (1961), pp. 117–136; R. H. C. Davis, "The Monks of St. Edmund, 1021–1148," *History*, 40:227–239 (October 1955).

attention until after the war.[195] J. C. Dickinson has written the first good account of the Austin canons and their introduction to England.[196] A book by H. M. Colvin concerns another neglected order—the Premonstratensians—and tells especially of its foundation and its disciplinary problems.[197] Only Bede Jarret had done any significant research on the Dominicans prior to the recent work of W. A. Hinnebusch which vividly recounts the Dominicans' arrival in England, their organization, their daily routine, and their architecture. Particularly valuable is the topographical and architectural investigation of the forty-eight houses which the Dominicans established in the thirteenth century.[198] Now, sixty years after A. G. Little recorded the history of the Franciscans at Oxford, J. R. H. Moorman has written their history at Cambridge. His book, learned and pleasing in style, is a scholarly account of Franciscan intellectual and religious activity but, because Franciscan resources were concentrated at Oxford, lacks the brilliance of Little's study.[199]

Almost as good as the fine research characteristic of the work on the religious orders is that on the conflict of church and state. Though English medievalists may not have been convinced by the new interpretation of N. F. Cantor in his book on the investiture struggle during the Norman period, they must at least think over the issues of this struggle and question the traditional views of Z. N. Brooke and J. F. Whitney. Curiously, just when Thomas Becket has begun to find some supporters, Anselm is subjected to some severe criticism from Mr. Cantor.[200] To be sure, Knowles's subtle psychological study of Becket does not lend strong support to the Becket position but it suggests that after a life spent in an

[195] One should note A. G. Little's *Franciscan Papers, Lists, and Documents* (Manchester, Eng., 1943) which contains material on the relations of the Franciscans with bishops on the question of hearing confession. See also J. R. H. Moorman, "The Foreign Element among the English Franciscans," *EHR*, 62:289–304 (July 1947).

[196] J. C. Dickinson, *The Origins of the Austin Canons and Their Introduction into England* (1950). See also "English Regular Canons and the Continent in the Twelfth Century," *TRHS*, 5th ser., 1 (1951), pp. 71–89.

[197] H. M. Colvin, *The White Canons in England* (Oxford, 1951). See also C. R. Cheney, "Gervase, Abbot of Prémontré: A Medieval Letter Writer," *BJRL*, 33:25–44 (September 1950).

[198] W. A. Hinnebusch, *The Early English Friars Preachers* (Rome, 1951).

[199] J. R. H. Moorman, *The Grey Friars in Cambridge* (Cambridge, Eng., 1952). For a study of minor mendicant orders see H. F. Chettle, "The Friars of the Holy Cross in England," *History*, 34:204–220 (October 1949).

[200] N. F. Cantor, *Church, Kingship, and Lay Investiture in England, 1066–1135* (Princeton, N.J., 1958). See also C. N. Brooke, "Gregorian Reform in Action: Clerical Marriage in England, 1050–1200," *CHJ*, 12:1–21 (no. 1, 1956). This interesting article contends that as the church's doctrine on marriage became clearer the difference between marriage and concubinage became more distinct and marriage based chiefly on comfort and appetite began to find other competitors.

effort to be loved and admired, Becket finally changed and, after being abandoned by his supporters, was truly converted at Pontigny; thereafter his motives were those of an ardent churchman who sought martyrdom. In another study on the episcopal associates of Becket, Knowles indicates that the bishops offered considerably more resistance to Henry II than has been credited to them and that they by no means completely abandoned Becket. While Henry I emerges reasonably well from the study of Cantor, Henry II fares badly at the hands of Knowles, who is perhaps overly severe.[201] Miss Raymonde Foreville's massive and detailed study of the church during the reign of Henry II presents the grandest apology for the Becket position. Despite her learning Miss Foreville resembles a medieval hagiographer; she justifies practically all that Becket did and in the process manages to misinterpret some of the evidence. Arguing that Becket's stand was supported by the learning and tradition of the canon law, she has recently been supported in this interpretation by C. Duggan who has contended that Henry II had little justification in the canon law for his position on criminous clerks, that Becket's case was canonically better grounded than has been conceded, and that Becket was certainly not the innovator of the canonical doctrines often attributed to him but merely followed good canonical law.[202]

If between the towering figures of Becket and Langton the history of the church has been neglected, C. R. Cheney has rectified this omission by pointing out in his Ford Lectures the importance of this forty-year interval during which papal power developed in England and the law and administration of the church was perfected.[203] Cheney has also forced us to revise our ideas about John's struggle with Innocent III. He defends John and marshals evidence to show that the rank and file of English clergy suffered little during the interdict, that there was little violence, and that, if land and goods had been appropriated, they were easily repurchased for nominal sums. Only the bishops in exile suffered severely; only their lands and possessions had to be restored and their losses indemnified when peace was concluded. Cheney argues also that,

---

[201] D. Knowles, *Archbishop Thomas Becket: A Character Study* (1950); *The Episcopal Colleagues of Archbishop Thomas Becket* (Cambridge, Eng., 1951).

[202] R. Foreville, *L'église et la royauté en Angleterre sous Henri II Plantagenet* (1154–1189) (Paris, 1943); C. Duggan, "The Becket Dispute and the Criminous Clerks," *BIHR*, 35:1–28 (May 1962). See also G. Greenaway, "The Life and Death of Thomas Becket," *Folio Society* (1961), pp. 9–22.

[203] C. R. Cheney, *From Becket to Langton: English Church Government, 1170–1213* (Manchester, Eng., 1956).

despite what Wendover says, Innocent III never actually deposed John nor did he offer the English crown to Philip Augustus.[204]

INTELLECTUAL AND ARTISTIC HISTORY

The excellent research and synthesis characteristic of recent writing on the church is lacking in the domain of cultural history except in the fields of art and architecture. Although Anglo-Saxon culture has received more substantial research than the culture of the later periods, we still await a history of the Anglo-Saxon achievement. For the eleventh and twelfth centuries even monographic literature is extremely scarce. Then for the thirteenth century the situation improves and there are some good studies on such figures as Matthew Paris and Robert Grosseteste. Perhaps the cultural achievements of early medieval England did not equal those of France but certainly there is much yet to be done in this area. The dearth of cultural investigations suggests the need for a better balance in the research interests of scholars working on medieval England. Younger medievalists could well divert their attention from the overworked constitutional and legal fields and concentrate on the underdeveloped area of intellectual history. Perhaps both research and results would be more original and refreshing.

Available for the early period of English culture are the studies by prominent scholars on art, literature, architecture, and historical writing edited by Nora K. Chadwick.[205] One of the most valuable of these essays is that by Miss Chadwick which traces the intellectual contacts between Britain and Gaul during the fifth century. K. Jackson has written a philological study on the linguistic changes in the early English period.[206] An account of Anglo-Saxon intellectual achievements in the seventh and eighth centuries comes from the pen of Eleanor S. Duckett who, concentrating on Aldhelm, Wilfrid, Bede, and Boniface, approaches them primarily through their writings. Her section on Boniface brings to life the great drama of his missionary work in Germany.[207] Much more technical is the study by C. W. Jones on saints' lives and chronicles which focuses upon the chronology of the seventh century and, in a most original section, proves Bede's chronology to be inconsist-

---

[204] C. R. Cheney, "King John and the Papal Interdict," *BJRL*, 31:295–317 (November 1948); "King John's Reaction to the Interdict in England," *TRHS*, 4th ser., 31 (1949), pp. 129–150.

[205] *Studies in Early British History*, ed. Nora K. Chadwick (Cambridge, Eng., 1954).

[206] K. Jackson, *Language and History in Early Britain* (Edinburgh, 1953).

[207] Eleanor S. Duckett, *Anglo-Saxon Saints and Scholars* (New York, 1947).

ent.[208] The most learned study on Anglo-Saxon intellectual history is
that by W. Levison discussing the relations between England and the
Continent during the eighth century and effectively showing the important intellectual influence of England upon the Continent. Unfortunately
this book, remarkable for its erudition, is too detailed and lacks the
interpretation necessary to further our comprehension of Anglo-Saxon
culture.[209] A book by Dorothy Whitelock suggests that the audience of
Beowulf was intended to be Christian and that the great composition
comes from the eighth century.[210] In an essay Miss Whitelock emphasizes the richness of Anglo-Saxon poetry as historical evidence for such
matters as chivalrous ideals, the bonds of kinship, religious beliefs, and
the social position of women. Marie Schütt has defended Asser's life of
Alfred as a shrewd, intelligent account not at all as confused and inco-
herent as some scholars have argued. And D. Knowles has emphasized
that from Augustine to 1066 the monks provided almost the sole cultural
force on the island.[211]

Skipping the eleventh century, which scholars have neglected, and
jumping into the twelfth, one comes to the essay of R. W. Southern who
argues that there was a twelfth-century renaissance in England, though
smaller in dimensions than that in France and Italy, and that close investigation of England's less spectacular luminaries will undoubtedly
show a rich and varied cultural awakening.[212] What Southern offers
mainly as hypothesis has some support. One may point to John of Salisbury whose medieval humanism has been studied by H. Liebeschutz
and whose defense of the *trivium* in the *Metalogicon* has been translated
by D. C. McGarry.[213] C. Roth has collected material on the intellectual

[208] C. W. Jones, *Saints' Lives and Chronicles in Early England* (Ithaca, N.Y., 1947). In *A Hand-List of Bede Manuscripts* (Ithaca, N.Y., 1943) M. L. W. Laist-
ner has compiled a catalogue of all the extant Bede manuscripts and those men-
tioned in medieval catalogues.

[209] W. Levison, *England and the Continent in the Eighth Century* (Oxford, 1946).

[210] Dorothy Whitelock, *The Audience of Beowulf* (Oxford, 1951).

[211] Dorothy Whitelock, "Anglo-Saxon Poetry and the Historian," *TRHS*, 4th ser.,
31 (1949), pp. 75–94; M. Schütt, "The Literary Form of Asser's 'Vita Alfredi,'"
EHR, 72:209–220 (April 1957); D. Knowles, "The Cultural Influence of English
Mediaeval Monasticism," *CHJ*, 7:146–159 (no. 3, 1943). R. W. Hunt's *Saint Dunstan's Classbook from Glastonbury* (Amsterdam, 1961) has provided an excellent
facsimile of the various scripts composing this work. *The Sword in Anglo-Saxon
England, Its Archaeology and Literature* (New York, 1962) by H. R. E. Davidson
studies the techniques employed in the fabrication of swords and evaluates the
symbolic meaning the sword had for the Anglo-Saxons.

[212] R. W. Southern "The Place of England in the Twelfth-Century Renaissance,"
History, 45:201–216 (October 1960).

[213] H. Liebeschutz, *Medieval Humanism in the Life and Writings of John of Salis-*

activity of twelfth-century Jews at such towns as York, London, Cambridge, Lincoln, and Bristol. H. G. Richardson has discovered a community of scholars and teachers at Northampton in the twelfth century and tells how the community migrated to Oxford in the last decade of the century.[214]

Although much of the writing on the thirteenth century deals with prominent scholars and teachers and with the rise of the English universities, an article by Miriam H. Marshall suggests that we obtain a good view of thirteenth-century culture through the eyes of Matthew Paris, and a book by R. Vaughan, based largely upon extant manuscript material, surveys the whole range of Matthew Paris' interests in chronology, hagiography, domestic history, art, and cartography. Vaughan concludes that Matthew Paris was a superb writer and ardent Benedictine, but a disagreeable, fussy, and unreliable person.[215] On the problem of the French and English languages in medieval England R. M. Wilson concludes that prior to 1300 English remained the sole language of the lower classes, that the middle and upper classes were bilingual, and that the educated clergy were trilingual, and that after 1300 English became the language of the country though French was still used at the court and as a literary and legal language. The longer study of Dominica Legge points out that Anglo-Norman was used in the cloister, especially in the writing done on saints' lives, chronicles, and sermons.[216]

Since 1940 when the excellent catalogue of Grosseteste's writings by S. H. Thomson made possible intensive research on this central figure of English thirteenth-century intellectual life, many studies have appeared. Among the most valuable are those edited by D. A. Callus which include articles by A. C. Crombie on Grosseteste's interest in science, by R. W. Hunt on Grosseteste's library, and by W. A. Pantin on Grosseteste's rela-

bury (1950); D. C. McGarry, *The Metalogicon of John of Salisbury: A Twelfth-Century Defense of the Verbal and Logical Arts of the Trivium* (Berkeley, Calif., 1955).

[214] C. Roth, *The Intellectual Activities of Mediaeval English Jewry* (1950); H. G. Richardson, "The Schools of Northampton in the Twelfth Century," *EHR*, 56:595–605 (October 1941). For a brief evaluation of the author of the *History of the Kings of Britain* see J. E. Lloyd, "Geoffrey of Monmouth," *EHR*, 57:460–469 (October 1942).

[215] M. H. Marshall, "Thirteenth-Century Culture as Illustrated by Matthew Paris," *Speculum*, 14:465–477 (October 1939); R. Vaughan, *Matthew Paris* (Cambridge, Eng., 1958).

[216] R. M. Wilson, "English and French in England 1100–1300," *History*, 28:37–60 (March 1943); D. Legge, *Anglo-Norman and the Cloisters. The Influence of the Orders upon Anglo-Norman Literature* (Edinburgh, 1950).

tions with the crown and papacy.[217] Though E. Westacott's book on
the life and legend of Roger Bacon may sound interesting, its uncritical
and helter-skelter examination of the relevant sources renders it useless.[218] A. G. Little has found evidence that substantiates Roger Bacon's
assertion of the existence of thirteenth-century theological schools outside Oxford and Cambridge. In a study on Oliver Sutton, bishop of Lincoln, Miss R. M. T. Hill shows how dangerous it can be for a university
to be controlled by an intellectually inferior administrator regardless of
his solicitude for the well-being of the university.[219]

　　The history of English art and architecture between 871 and 1307 is
now superbly told and illustrated in three volumes of the *Oxford History
of English Art*. In the first, covering the period from 871 to 1100, D. Talbot Rice, unlike T. D. Kendrick who sees a decisive Viking-barbaric influence, emphasizes the original and dominant stream of English art.[220]
In the second, covering the years 1100 to 1216, T. S. R. Boase builds his
history around the architecture of the period with an insistence upon a
strong continental influence that was facilitated by the close political ties
of the twelfth century.[221] In the volume on the thirteenth century P.
Brieger makes perhaps too strong a case for English artistic individuality
but masterfully describes the three principal phases of artistic development during the century: the episcopal, the royal, and the provincial.[222] To supplement this fine history of art are other learned works.

　　[217] S. H. Thomson, *The Writings of Robert Grosseteste, Bishop of Lincoln, 1235–
1253* (Cambridge, Eng., 1940); D. A. Callus, *Robert Grosseteste: Scholar and
Bishop* (Oxford, 1955). See also the studies on Grosseteste, Pecham, and other
medieval intellectuals by Beryl Smalley, Decima Douie, and D. A. Callus in *Studies
in Medieval History Presented to Frederick Maurice Powicke* (Oxford, 1948).
　　[218] E. Westacott, *Roger Bacon in Life and Legend* (1953).
　　[219] A. G. Little, "Theological Schools in Medieval England," *EHR*, 55:624–630
(October 1940); R. M. T. Hill, "Oliver Sutton, Bishop of Lincoln, and the University of Oxford," *TRHS*, 4th ser., 31 (1949), pp. 1–16. See also G. L. Haskins, "The
University of Oxford and the 'Ius ubique docendi'," *EHR*, 56:281–292 (April
1941); Beryl Smalley, "Robert Bacon and the Early Dominican School at Oxford,"
TRHS, 4th ser., 30 (1948), pp. 1–19.
　　[220] D. Talbot Rice, *The Oxford History of English Art, 871–1100*, II (Oxford,
1952). Cf. T. D. Kendrick, *Late Saxon and Viking Art* (1949). See also Margaret
Deanesly, "Early English and Gallic Minsters," *TRHS*, 4th ser., 23 (1941), pp.
25–69. For the mass of literature that has resulted from the discovery of the Sutton Hoo Ship see F. P. Magoun, Jr., "The Sutton Hoo Ship-Burial: A Chronological
Bibliography," *Speculum*, 29:116–124 (January 1954); J. B. Bessinger, "The Sutton
Hoo Ship-Burial: A Chronological Bibliography, Part II," *Speculum*, 33:515–522
(October 1958).
　　[221] T. S. R. Boase, *The Oxford History of English Art, 1100–1216*, III (Oxford,
1953).
　　[222] P. Brieger, *The Oxford History of English Art, 1216–1307*, IV (Oxford, 1957).

L. Stone has traced the history of sculpture in medieval England for the Pelican series on the History of Art.[223] L. F. Salzman has written a survey of medieval building so detailed that it overlooks not one technique or building material.[224] F. Wormald has compiled an excellent catalogue on drawings of the tenth and eleventh centuries and has traced their origin and motif. W. Oakeshott's work in illuminated manuscripts is chiefly an album, weak in commentary. And finally, C. Woodforde has produced an excellent catalogue of stained glass windows even though he has ignored the influence of techniques and the evolution of styles.[225]

CONCLUDING IMPRESSIONS

From this *tour d'horizon* of the writing on English history between the fifth and fourteenth centuries emerge certain impressions. Research on English medieval history has been active and the production gargantuan. The excellent historical handbooks and guides, the superb published records and translations that require an expert knowledge of languages, paleography, and diplomatics as well as history command only admiration. In the fields of constitutional, legal, and political history the writing shows a need to cease the piling up of detail and to produce works of synthesis. Institutions like the crown, the council, household, parliament, the jury, common law courts, and judicial procedure should be related to the increased knowledge of medieval social and economic history, and, above all, should be compared with similar institutions on the Continent. The medievalist must learn how to write political history more perceptive of the social, economic, religious, and intellectual forces that frequently determined the course of medieval politics.

There is not enough social and economic history, especially of the kind that makes comparisons with continental institutions. Where are the histories of the English borough, the fair, the woolen industry, the trade of the eastern and southern ports, the urban social unrest caused by economic change? Such histories exist for the Continent. Think of what Henri Pirenne and Henri Sée alone have written on these subjects,

---

It may be questioned whether the chronological divisions that have been determined by political history have any relevance for phases of art and architecture.

[223] L. Stone, *Sculpture in Britain: The Middle Ages* (1955). See also F. Saxl, *English Sculptures of the Twelfth Century* (1954).

[224] L. F. Salzman, *Building in England down to 1540* (Oxford, 1952).

[225] F. Wormald, *English Drawings of the Tenth and Eleventh Centuries* (1952); W. Oakeshott, *The Sequence of English Medieval Art, Illustrated Chiefly from Illuminated MSS., 640–1450* (1950); C. Woodforde, *English Stained and Painted Glass* (Oxford, 1954).

not just their scholarly articles, but their masterful surveys abounding with interpretation and perspective!

Of all the writing during the past twenty years that on religious history has shown the greatest advance and richest accomplishment. It is too early to predict what use will be made of this writing, but eventually the fine histories of the monastic orders, the studies on church administration, the portraits of the churchmen, and the accounts of church-state conflict will have to be assimilated into a history of the English medieval church.

To ask for more from scholars working on the history of art would show enthusiasm but perhaps a lack of appreciation. Their studies in the journals are legion and from them have come the syntheses that ought always to be the final objective. One feels differently about intellectual history. Whereas in religious and art history the various streams of research have definite themes leading to broad surveys, this is not true for intellectual history. Here the research is mostly of a shotgun variety, a kind that does not seem to jell into anything larger. Time and thought must be devoted to surveying what should and can be done and what themes need to be developed. The suggestion of Southern that the intellectual achievement of the twelfth century can be assessed only after systematic study of the theologians, philosophers, and writers of the century is also applicable to most of the other centuries. We are reasonably certain how the Anglo-Saxon intellectual accomplishments compared with those of the Continent, but how about the following three centuries? We know that the English intellectual achievements of these centuries were certainly inferior to those of France, but how much inferior?

Of the writing on English medieval history during the past twenty years 80 per cent has come from English pens. It is natural the English scholars should dominate the writing in this field but they have not given enough recognition to the valuable new methods used and the work done by continental and American scholars. To be meaningful in our shrinking world writing on English medieval history must increasingly portray England, not as an island apart, but as an integral member of a western European community.

HISTORICAL WRITING SINCE 1962

For whatever reasons, since the completion of this bibliographical essay in 1962 scholarly work on English history to 1307 has so increased that a discussion here of all the articles and books to appear in this interval is impossible. This supplement includes only books and articles that have dealt with central problems, employed new concepts and methods, introduced new historical evidence, and provided valuable syntheses.

The latest study of V. H. Galbraith, who has previously expressed his ideas on the nature of medieval history and the proper approach to research, treats sensibly the use of evidence, though some historians will undoubtedly refute his interpretation of evidence which leads him to question Asser as the author of Alfred's *Life*. C. W. Hollister has examined the figure of the enigmatic John as interpreted by modern historians.[226] N. R. Ker has again placed medievalists in his debt with his excellent lists of medieval manuscripts and libraries.[227] Editions and translations of records continue to appear. Two especially fine editions are the collection of acts of the Norman dukes (911–1066) by Marie Fauroux and the *Novae Narrationes* by Elsie Shanks and S. F. C. Milsom.[228]

Outstanding among recent general surveys, which, though competent, lack the distinction and scholarly standards characteristic of such a series as the *Oxford History*, is H. R. Loyn's history of Anglo-Saxon England and the Conquest. Here is a fascinating account built around a social and economic interpretation which, contrary to a recent trend, sees no feudalism in England prior to 1066. P. H. Blair's book on early English history is too much like his previous book, and Christopher Brooke's study of the Saxon and Norman kings, though posing thoughtful problems, leans heavily toward popularization.[229]

Studies of kings run a spectrum from scholarly to unscholarly. The very recent volume on William the Conqueror by D. C. Douglas, the first in a new series on the English kings edited by Douglas, is a monument of erudition and provides a complete and up-to-date history of

---

[226] V. H. Galbraith, *An Introduction to the Study of History* (1964); C. W. Hollister, "King John and the Historians," *JBS*, 1:1–19 (May 1961).

[227] N. R. Ker, *English Manuscripts in the Century after the Norman Conquest* (Oxford, 1960), and *Medieval Libraries of Great Britain, a List of Surviving Books*, 2d ed. (1964).

[228] Marie Fauroux, *Recueil des actes des ducs de Normandie (911–1066)*, in *Mémoires de la Société des Antiquaires de Normandie*, 36 (Caen, 1961); Elsie Shanks and S. F. C. Milsom, *Novae Narrationes*, in *Publications of the Selden Society*, 80 (1963). Additional translations in the Medieval Texts are Antonia Gransden, *The Chronicle of Bury St. Edmunds, 1212–1301* (Edinburgh, 1963); J. T. Appleby, *The Chronicle of Richard of Devizes* (Edinburgh, 1963).

[229] H. R. Loyn, *Anglo-Saxon England and the Norman Conquest* (1962), the first volume of a series, *Social and Economic History of England*, ed. Asa Briggs; P. H. Blair, *Roman Britain and Early England, 55 B.C.–A.D. 871* (Edinburgh, 1963); C. Brooke, *The Saxon and Norman Kings* (1963).

William but suffers from a too enthusiastic pro-Norman bias and from repeating what has often been said before.[230] The essay of R. W. Southern investigating the kind of men serving Henry I and the techniques of his government is more suggestive and original. J. T. Appleby's biography of Henry II fails to meet professional standards of scholarship despite some good points. One hesitates to read further in this book when told in the foreword that Becket, Henry's best friend, "had been savagely hacked to death at Henry's instigation because he placed his God before his King." [231] Perhaps the moral to these three studies is that there is little more to say about most of England's medieval kings.

The massive studies of Galbraith and R. W. Finn seem to have temporarily stemmed the zeal for producing more on Domesday Book than critical notes which appear yearly and undoubtedly will until the Day of Doom.[232] On the other hand, the whole question of Norman feudalism and its introduction into England has been reopened by Hollister in his book and articles which argue for a pre-feudal period in Anglo-Saxon England, especially for a territorial system which provided the basis for a feudal army.[233]

Constitutional history has once more been catapulted to its accustomed place as "queen of the sciences" by the stimulating but exasperating book of H. G. Richardson and G. O. Sayles which aims at the total obliteration of Stubbs's reputation as a historian. While this is to be expected from Richardson and Sayles, one is aghast at a technique that debunks all English medievalists except Richardson and Sayles. Unfortunately the superb sections on Norman-Angevin central administration and revisionist ideas that deserve serious consideration are submerged by the vicious attack on Stubbs which detracts from the book and gives one the sensation of being in a boxing ring.[234]

[230] D. C. Douglas, *William the Conqueror: The Norman Impact upon England* (Berkeley, Calif., 1964). See also J. F. A. Mason, "Roger de Montgomery and His Sons (1067–1102)," *TRHS*, 5th ser., 13 (1963), pp. 1–28.

[231] R. W. Southern, "The Place of Henry I in English History," *Proceedings of the British Academy*, 48 (1962), pp. 127–169; J. T. Appleby, *Henry II, the Vanquished King* (1962).

[232] See, for example, J. S. Moore, "The Domesday Teamland: A Reconsideration," *TRHS*, 5th ser., 14 (1964), pp. 109–130.

[233] C. W. Hollister, *Anglo-Saxon Military Institutions* (Oxford, 1962), and "The Irony of English Feudalism," *JBS*, 2:1–26 (May 1963). See the comments of R. S. Hoyt on pp. 27–30 and the rejoinder of Hollister on pp. 31–32. See also Hollister and J. C. Holt, "Two Comments on the Problem of Continuity in Anglo-Norman Feudalism," *EcHR*, 2d ser., 16:104–118 (August 1963).

[234] H. G. Richardson and G. O. Sayles, *The Governance of Mediaeval England from the Conquest to Magna Carta* (Edinburgh, 1963). Other studies bearing on

Henry de Bracton would indeed chuckle if he knew of the historical and textual agonizing caused by his text which he hoped would clarify English law in the thirteenth century. What was clear to him and his contemporaries is apparently not so clear to twentieth-century historians. Brian Tierney has written a long article to support a previously advanced thesis that Bracton's mind was formed by English law and had not absorbed much Roman or canon law. Ewart Lewis has resorted to an essay to combat the suggestion of E. H. Kantorowicz that Bracton had given the king a supralegal position. Lewis convincingly argues that Bracton placed the king below the law, which was the limit and criterion of royal power, and that Bracton's professional reverence for the law could only lead to a declaration of its supremacy.[235] Another useful study of thirteenth-century law is that of D. W. Sutherland on the actual operation of the *Quo Warranto* proceedings. And the shrewd remarks of J. G. Edwards on the Welsh lawbooks deserve close reading because of what they tell us about the substance of that little-studied law.[236]

Urban history is best represented by the book of G. A. Williams which traces the government of London from Magna Carta to the Hundred Years' War. It is especially good on the aldermanic families which controlled the municipal government, providing detailed biographies of the leading city fathers. G. H. Martin examines the nature and scope of borough records previous to 1300 and discusses modern views on the thirteenth-century borough.[237] Research on rural history has concentrated upon tenures, field arrangements, and manorial accounting procedures.[238]

Historians of the church are still intrigued by the Anglo-Saxon period. Margaret Deanesly in yet another study on the Anglo-Saxon church gives special attention to its cultural and artistic achievements. Her

---

constitutional history are Helen Cam, *Law-Finders and Law-Makers in Medieval England* (1962); J. C. Holt, "The St. Albans Chroniclers and Magna Carta," *TRHS*, 5th ser., 14 (1964), pp. 67–88.

[235] B. Tierney, "Bracton on Government," *Speculum*, 38:295–317 (April 1963); E. Lewis, "King above Law? 'Quod Principi Placuit' in Bracton," *Speculum*, 39:240–269 (April 1964).

[236] D. W. Sutherland, *Quo Warranto Proceedings in the Reign of Edward I, 1278–1294* (Oxford, 1963); J. G. Edwards, "The Historical Study of the Welsh Lawbooks," *TRHS*, 5th ser., 12 (1962), pp. 141–155, and "The Royal Household and the Welsh Lawbooks," *TRHS*, 5th ser., 13 (1963), pp. 163–176.

[237] G. A. Williams, *Medieval London: From Commune to Capital* (1963); G. H. Martin, "The English Borough in the Thirteenth Century," *TRHS*, 5th ser., 13 (1963), pp. 123–144.

[238] Eleanor Searle, "Hides, Virgates and Tenant Settlement at Battle Abbey," *EcHR*, 2d ser., 16:290–300 (December 1963); H. E. Hallam, "Further Observations on the Spalding Serf Lists," *ibid.*, 338–350; A. R. H. Baker, "Open Fields and

argument strongly buttresses the views of R. R. Darlington. Contrarily, F. Barlow in a constitutional study portrays the Anglo-Saxon church as in the backwaters, out of the ecclesiastical mainstream running across eleventh-century Europe.[239] C. Duggan has studied the decretal collections of the twelfth century and shown their influence on contemporary ecclesiastical and political history, suggesting also that they stimulated similar collections of decretals on the Continent.[240]

The dearth of writing on intellectual history noted two years ago still exists and is the more unfortunate because no evidence has yet been unearthed to support the confident assertions of English historians that England played an important role in the renaissance of the twelfth century and more than contributed her share to the intellectual achievement of the thirteenth. The history of art and architecture marches healthily on. It suffices to note the massive work of R. A. Brown et al. which lists and examines all the buildings held, constructed, and maintained by the English kings down to 1485. Here is fine material for further research on military, civil, and ecclesiastical architecture.[241]

This new look at publications on English medieval history warrants no revision of the conclusions of two years ago. Quantitatively there is vigorous research activity but much of it flows down the same old riverbeds and displays a propensity to repeat and substantiate ideas long held. The one attempt to break with traditional interpretation has been too sensational and too ad hominem in its criticism. The most original work now being done is in rural social and economic history and the finest syntheses are still those on the church and artistic achievement.

Partible Inheritance on a Kent Manor," EcHR, 17:1–23 (August 1964); B. Lyon, "Encore le problème de la chronologie des corvées," Moyen Âge, 4th ser., 18:615–630 (Volume jubilaire 1963); E. Stone, "Profit-and-Loss Accountancy at Norwich Cathedral Priory," TRHS, 5th ser., 12 (1962), pp. 25-48. Valuable material on English towns, trade, and finance may be found in Cambridge Economic History of Europe, III, Economic Organization and Policies in the Middle Ages, ed. M. M. Postan et al. (Cambridge, Eng., 1963).

[239] M. Deanesly, Sidelights on the Anglo-Saxon Church (1961); F. Barlow, The English Church, 1000–1066: A Constitutional History (1963). See also C. J. Godfrey, The Church in Anglo-Saxon England (Cambridge, Eng., 1963); G. Schoebe, "The Chapters of Archbishop Oda (942/6) and the Canons of the Legatine Councils of 786," BIHR, 35:75–83 (May 1962).

[240] C. Duggan, Twelfth-Century Decretal Collections and Their Importance in English History (1963).

[241] R. A. Brown et al., The History of the King's Works. The Middle Ages, 2 vols. (1963). See also E. A. Fisher, The Greater Anglo-Saxon Churches (1962).

High History or Hack History:
England in the Later Middle Ages

✧

MARGARET HASTINGS

HE NEWEST Regius Professor of Modern History in Oxford has charged his three medievalist predecessors and their progeny of the past thirty-five years with writing useless and therefore "dead" history.[1] History, he says, should be "controversial," challenging, and therefore "useful" to the layman as well as to the professional. "Fertile error," he believes, may be more "life-giving" than "sterile accuracy."[2]

The direct answer to Professor Trevor-Roper is best left to the competent attention of the many medievalists in the colleges of Oxford, and I do not propose to challenge here the assumptions implicit in pairing the words "controversial" and "useful" or "sterile" and "accurate." But the call for a more stirring sort of historical study challenges the medievalist to take stock of the work done in the past twenty years on the history of England during the fourteenth and fifteenth centuries.

Medievalists must surely agree that the major achievement of the first half of the twentieth century has been the mining of archives for the raw materials of history and the publication of volume upon volume of texts and calendars. The output has been so great that a mere listing and indexing of the publications since 1901 fills a volume of 680 pages in the

[Reprinted from *Speculum*, 36:225–253 (April 1961).]

[1] A full and valuable bibliography will be found in May McKisack's volume in the *Oxford History, The Fourteenth Century, 1307–1399* (1959). This present essay attempts only to survey the trends in writing about the later Middle Ages for the past twenty years. From Helen Cam's store of erudition I have received invaluable criticism, especially of the sections devoted to constitutional and legal history. She is clearly not responsible for any faults of judgment or errors of fact which have crept in here, but she has saved me from a number which have not.

[2] H. Trevor-Roper, *History: Professional and Lay*, inaugural lecture (Oxford, 1957).

Royal Historical Society series of guides to historical study.[3] Understandably, the greater part of this material is medieval. Likewise, the group of distinguished archivists who in 1932 formed the British Records Association for "promoting the preservation and accessibility under the best possible conditions of Public, Semi-Public and Private Archives" was largely medieval in its scholarly interests. The question is whether these materials are useless "historical fossils" and "caddisworms" or the rich ore for a new synthesis, as editors and archivists alike have thought them to be. No sweeping answer can be given, and the real test lies in the use that is made of them in revising our knowledge and understanding of the period.

Maitland and Tout with their calls for exploration of the "tons of plea rolls" and for the "spade-work" of history are no doubt, as the Regius Professor suggests, responsible for the form and direction which medieval studies have taken in these sixty years. And some of the best fruit of their influence has been the work of Professor Trevor-Roper's two immediate predecessors. Professor Galbraith's analysis of records and chronicles has resulted in brilliant illumination of far larger areas of the medieval landscape than a mere list of titles of his published works would suggest.[4] *Studies in the Public Records* (1948), for example, turns out on examination to be a study of the emergence of institutional from personal government. What Professor Galbraith has done is to project from a study of records a developing image of the government which produced them. Similarly his Creighton Lecture for 1949, *Historical Research in Medieval England* (published in 1951) proved to be a general discussion of the philosophy and craft of the historian.

Sir Maurice Powicke's claim to respect for his achievements both as a teacher and as a historian is surely beyond challenge. To him, more than to any other single historian, we owe the advances which have been made recently in the study of ecclesiastical records, although his own published works in this field have not been quantitatively as great as in some others. He, like his successor, but rather less belligerently, has called upon historians to abandon their clubbiness and freshen the stream by bringing in knowledge and skills from other disciplines.[5] In

[3] E. L. C. Mullins, *Texts and Calendars: An Analytical Guide to Serial Publications*, Royal Historical Society Guides and Handbooks (1958).

[4] See the "Select Bibliography of the Publications, 1911–1957," of V. H. Galbraith in the presentation volume, *Facsimiles of English Royal Writs to A.D. 1100*, ed. P. Chaplais and T. A. M. Bishop (Oxford, 1957).

[5] In "After Fifty Years," *History*, 29:3–16 (March 1944), reprinted in *Modern Historians and the Study of History* (1955), pp. 225–239; his essay in *Études*

his three great volumes on the thirteenth century he has taken us further
into the lives and minds of the aristocracy than we have ever been before and thereby made more intelligible the political and constitutional
battles of the times. Applying the biographical method but without pre-
tending to be a psychologist, he has shown us believable human beings
thinking and acting in their own thirteenth-century world.

Powicke, Galbraith, the late Eileen Power, Plucknett, Helen Cam, and
their entire generation of scholars, as well as the first generation of their
students, have been aware (perhaps unduly so) of their human limitations. They have known that they did not know all the answers and have
not attempted to teach what they did not know. They have tried to discover and set down what, in fact, did happen rather than to explain the
past in terms of broad concepts. Moreover, they have concerned themselves more with the humble affairs of our fathers who begat us [6] than
with the high affairs of great men. There has been more fertile erring
and straying than Professor Trevor-Roper recognizes and much fresh
water has flowed into the channel from the "sciences of population, of
epidemics, of climate, and price-history" (if these are indeed sciences),
as well as from historical geography, archaeology, social anthropology,
sociology, psychology. Even crafts and skills, such as aerial photography
and the restoration of damaged documents, have been used to extend
our knowledge. One of the most fruitful new methods of attack has been
the biographical study of groups of men engaged in the same kind of
activity. This has been particularly effective in parliamentary and social
history, and it is worth emphasizing here that it would have been impossible without the great volume of texts and calendars noted above.

Revisions, revaluations, and revelations but no major revolutions in interpretation of the later Middle Ages have resulted from the use of new
methods and the opening up of new documentary sources. The new
"high history" [7] of the fourteenth and fifteenth centuries is yet to be
written. Those charged with the new volumes in the serial histories
have not achieved it. A. R. Myers' volume in the Pelican History [8] is not

---

présentées à la commission internationale pour l'histoire des assemblées d'états, III
(Louvain, 1939), pp. 131–140.

  [6] Readers will recognize the allusion to the introductory passages of Eileen Power's
Medieval People (1924).

  [7] See Galbraith's Creighton Lecture for 1949, *Historical Research in Medieval
England* (1951). "Philosophers, in short, divide History into two categories—High
History and Hack History."

  [8] *England in the Late Middle Ages* (1952) is painstaking but lacks the inspiration of the "high historian."

in the same class with the earlier and later volumes. No new volumes for the later Middle Ages have yet appeared in the Methuen History.[9] The two volumes by Barrow and Green [10] are surveys only and mainly political. For the new *Oxford History* May McKisack has written a masterly summary of existing knowledge about the fourteenth century.[11] She drives a straight path through the controversies among the constitutional historians over the meaning of the Statute of York, for example, and she has given us the best brief general discussion to date of English agrarian developments of the century; but she has not written an epoch-making book, as she would be the first to say. E. F. Jacob, whose fifteenth-century volume is now in the press, has allegedly "finished" it a number of times without being satisfied of its readiness for publication. No century presents greater problems of synthesis.

The truth would seem to be that the time is not yet ripe for ✱high history." For the fourteenth century the details are not yet fully assimilated. They kill the *grand ouvrage*. And about the fifteenth century we do not yet know enough. A Winston Churchill can still paint with a broad brush on a large canvas in the manner of a J. R. Green, but that is because he is writing an expression of faith, not history in the sense in which we must mean it in the twentieth century, that is, as science as well as art. For the present, science is in the ascendant, and accuracy in the accumulation, presentation, and interpretation of data is important. But perhaps there is already among us the Stubbs or the Maitland or the Macaulay who will write the great work on the later Middle Ages which will cast its long shadow over the next generation of medievalists.

II

Revision of the political and constitutional history of the later Middle Ages has meant, in the main, revision of Stubbs's *Constitutional History*.[12]

[9] K. H. Vickers' *England in the Later Middle Ages* (1913) has been reissued in its seventh edition (1950).

[10] G. W. S. Barrow, *Feudal Britain: The Completion of the Medieval Kingdoms, 1066–1314* (1956) and V. H. H. Green, *The Later Plantagenets: A Survey of English History between 1307 and 1485* (1955).

[11] See n. 1, above.

[12] For appreciation of Stubbs's work and influence, see F. W. Maitland in *Collected Papers*, III (Cambridge, Eng., 1911), pp. 495–511, reprinted in *Selected Historical Essays*, ed. Helen Cam, for the Cambridge University Press and the Selden Society (1957), pp. 266–276; J. G. Edwards, *William Stubbs*, Historical Association Pamphlet, G. 22 (1952); Helen Cam, "Stubbs Seventy Years After," *CHJ*, 9:120–147 (no. 2, 1948).

Other historical works like J. R. Green's *Short History,* C. Plummer's historical introduction to Fortescue's *Governance of England,* and Tout's and Oman's volumes in the Longmans History (all published before 1910) have influenced our conception of the period profoundly, but one need only read the debates over the meaning of the coronation oath of 1308,[13] the Statute of York,[14] the deposition of Edward II and Richard II,[15] or the work of the "Good Parliament" [16] to note that the interpretations of Trevor-Roper's nineteenth-century predecessor in the Regius chair are still central to the controversy.

Stubbs, by his own statement, expected to be revised, considering much of what he had written to be mere "hypotheses rather than facts." [17] It is safe to assume, on the other hand, that he would have rejected a mere Crocean sort of revision [18] and that he would have expected new evidence to be brought to bear on his hypotheses. Revision has come through the digging out of new sources, the re-examination of old ones, and the interpretation of both the old and the new in the light of new conceptions of the historian's task. This generation of historians wants to know about all the levels of past society, not just about rulers and leaders. We are not satisfied with mere categories of men or tags based on legal status. We want to know about functions of different sorts of people in society, their interrelationships with others of

[13] A convenient bibliography is given in B. Wilkinson, *Constitutional History of Medieval England, 1216–1399,* 3 vols. (1948–58), II, p. 85.

[14] A full and up-to-date bibliography is given in McKisack, *Fourteenth Century,* pp. 556–557. Add J. H. Trueman, "The Statute of York and the Ordinances of 1311," *Medievalia et Humanistica,* 10 (1956), pp. 64–81.

[15] See bibliography in Wilkinson, *Constitutional History,* II, pp. 157, 284, and add Kathleen Edwards, "The Political Importance of the English Bishops during the Reign of Edward II," *EHR,* 59:311–347 (September 1944) on Edward, and on Richard II, S. B. Chrimes, "Richard II's Questions to the Judges, 1387," *LQR,* 72:365–390 (July 1956).

[16] See again Wilkinson's bibliography, *Constitutional History,* II, p. 204, and add T. F. T. Plucknett, "The Impeachments of 1376," *TRHS,* 5th ser., 1 (1951), pp. 153–164; J. G. Edwards, *The Commons in Medieval English Parliaments* (1958), pp. 36–38; and McKisack, *Fourteenth Century,* pp. 387–394. Miss McKisack seems to refer less and less to Stubbs's views as she gets farther away from the thirteenth century.

[17] Edwards, *William Stubbs,* pp. 7–8, quoting C. H. Firth, *Modern History in Oxford* (Oxford, 1920), p. 24, n. 4.

[18] B. Wilkinson, in "English Politics and Politicians of the Thirteenth and Fourteenth Centuries," *Speculum,* 30:37–48 (January 1955), suggests such an approach, and his *Constitutional History,* III, p. vii, proposes "a lively common attack on the problems of the medieval constitution" on the ground that "the certainties and systems of Stubbs and Maitland are dissolving" while nothing "equally authoritative and comprehensive has been produced to take their place." "Vigorous diversity of opinion and search for new understanding" will, he thinks, produce a new synthesis.

their own sort and with other sorts. We owe these new concerns in part to the freshening stream of Marxist interpretation of history and in part, no doubt, to the challenge from our contemporary social scientists.

Whatever the cause, most of Stubbs's generalizations about the last two centuries of the medieval period have been revised or recast. His "Lancastrian experiment," like Green's "New Monarchy," is yielding place to the "Tudor Revolution" as a fertile source of controversy, but we are a long way from knowing enough about the fifteenth century to be able to dispense with Stubbs's third volume.

For the fourteenth century Stubbs's main theme, "the growth of the Commons, the mark of the period" (II, 305), has stood the test of time, but his belief that under Edward II, Edward III, and Richard II, "the third estate claimed and won its place as the foremost of the three" (II, 306) has not. He understood the importance of taxation and petition in the developing role of the Commons, but he did not fully understand the workings of petition. Moreover, he claimed prematurely for the Commons an understanding of the importance of control over expenditure and of ministerial appointments.[19]

It would be a work of supererogation to review again the great volume of recent literature on the history of parliament in the thirteenth and fourteenth centuries. It has been comprehensively surveyed a number of times, most recently by Helen Cam,[20] and has been fully worked into the texture of May McKisack's general history of the fourteenth century. From all the dust of recent controversy over its nature and functions, the fourteenth-century parliament emerges as an omnicompetent body made up of human beings, not just abstractions like lords, commons, or burgesses, and concerned more with pressing problems like the cost of the French war or the extravagance and corruption of the king's advisers than with large concepts. Precedents, like Magna Carta or the Provisions of Oxford, were called upon, to be sure, but rather in the spirit of law-

---

[19] See Cam, "Stubbs Seventy Years After," and Edwards, *William Stubbs.*

[20] Helen Cam, "Recent Work and Present Views on the Origins and Development of Representative Assemblies," in *Relazioni del X Congresso Internazionale di Scienze Storiche,* Roma 4–11 sett. 1955 (Florence, 1955), I. Cf. G. T. Lapsley, "Some Recent Advances in English Constitutional History (before 1485)," *CHJ,* 5:119–161 (no. 2, 1936), reprinted in *Crown, Community, and Parliament* (Oxford and New York, 1951); Geoffrey Templeman, "The History of Parliament to 1400 in the Light of Modern Research," *UBHJ,* 1:202–231 (no. 2, 1948), reprinted in R. L. Schuyler and H. Ausubel, *The Making of English History* (New York, 1952); R. S. Hoyt, "Recent Publications in the United States and Canada on the History of Western Representative Institutions before the French Revolution," *Etudes présentées à la commission internationale pour l'histoire des assemblées d'états,* 17, published as a special issue of *Speculum,* 29:356–377 (1954).

yers quoting precedents to support a brief than of jurists guided by an Idea of the Constitution. The constitution, such as it was, was a body of accepted notions about how a king should rule his subjects and a body of precedents, often contradictory, about what to do if a particular king failed to fulfill expectations.[21] S. B. Chrimes searched Yearbooks, treatises, and parliamentary records in order to reconstruct the practical day-to-day thoughts of members of parliament, judges, and lawyers of the Lancastrian period. He found no evidence of "a conscious constitutional experiment." His *English Constitutional Ideas in the Fifteenth Century* (Cambridge, Eng., 1936) shows that the state was not yet clearly distinguished from the royal "estate" and that even Fortescue described rather than analyzed the fifteenth-century constitution.[22]

Precedents for attempts to limit the power of fourteenth-century rulers prescribed checks on administrative officers, especially those concerned with finance and justice. T. F. Tout's massive *Chapters in the Administrative History of Mediaeval England*,[23] which described the administrative apparatus on the basis of study of the records, added greatly to the substance of our knowledge of fourteenth-century government. His work, like that of his students and disciples, supplements rather than revises the narrative which Stubbs grounded mainly on chronicles and the rather sparse record evidence in print when he wrote. The work of the Manchester school was conveniently and competently summarized in 1952 by Chrimes.[24] His chapter on the fifteenth century was necessarily thin because little work had at that date been done on fifteenth-century administration. Anthony Steel's *Receipt of the Exchequer, 1377–1485* (Cambridge, Eng., 1954) remains the one large piece of work on fifteenth-century finance, although Steel and K. B. McFarlane published brief studies of the financing of the French war and the Wars of the Roses, and J. L. Kirby a brilliant essay on the Lancastrian Exchequer.[25] Nothing as full as E. B. Fryde's studies [26] on Edward III's war finance

[21] Drawn from Helen Cam's summary in *Relazioni*.

[22] Fortescue came to the study of political thought late in life after an active career on the bench.

[23] 6 vols. (Manchester, Eng., 1920–33).

[24] *An Introduction to the Administrative History of Medieval England* (Oxford, 1952).

[25] K. B. McFarlane, "Loans to the Lancastrian Kings: The Problem of Inducement," *CHJ*, 9:51–68 (no. 1, 1947); A. Steel, "The Financial Background of the Wars of the Roses," *History*, new ser., 40:18–30 (February and June 1955); J. L. Kirby, "The Issues of the Lancastrian Exchequer and Lord Cromwell's Estimate of 1433," *BIHR*, 24:121–151 (November 1951).

[26] "Materials for the Study of Edward III's Credit Operations: 1327–48," *BIHR*, 22:105–138 (November 1949); 23:1–30 (May 1950); "The Deposits of Hugh

has yet been done for the later period. Miss J. Otway-Ruthven's study of *The King's Secretary and the Signet Office in the 15th Century* (Cambridge, Eng., 1939) is still the only study of a central executive office for this century.

The two most important contributions to administrative history since Tout's *Chapters* were published in 1953, the year after Chrimes's summary. R. Somerville's *History of the Duchy of Lancaster* (Vol. I) has greater significance and general usefulness than appears in the title because, in the words of the author (p. ix), "The Duchy is a unique blend of public administration and private estate practice." G. R. Elton's *The Tudor Revolution in Government* [27] belongs properly within the sphere of L. B. Smith's survey of recent work on the early Tudors. Yet, since Elton, in his first chapter, "The Last Phase of Medieval Government," argues that all essential features of government remained the same from 1461 to 1534, as he needs must in order to demonstrate that there was a "revolution" under Thomas Cromwell, he involves medievalists in the controversy he has roused. The test of modernity he sets up is the emergence of the state as distinct from the person of the monarch and the relegation of the household from a controlling position to that of a subordinate and narrowly specialized department. Recent work indicating that the Tudors were only following a Yorkist pattern in their use of the Council [28] supports, he believes, his argument for continuity through dynastic change. New evidence showing that feudal prerogatives were revived under Henry VII [29] demonstrates, he contends, a rejuvenation of

---

Despenser the Younger with Italian Banks," *EcHR*, 2d ser., 3:344–363 (no. 3, 1951); "Loans to the English Crown, 1328–31," *EHR*, 70:198–211 (April 1955). Some of the conclusions of his 1947 Oxford doctoral dissertation, "Edward III's War Finance, 1337–41," were presented in *History*, 37:8–24 (February 1952). See also G. L. Harriss, "Fictitious Loans," *EcHR*, 2d ser., 8:187–199 (December 1955).

[27] Second ed., reprinted (Cambridge, Eng., 1959); see also *England under the Tudors* (1955).

[28] J. R. Lander, "Council, Administration and Councillors, 1461 to 1485," *BIHR*, 32:138–180 (November 1959), and his "Administration of the Yorkist Kings," M. Litt. dissertation at Cambridge, 1949, cited by Elton in *The Tudor Revolution*, p. 19, n. 1; B. P. Wolffe, "The Management of English Royal Estates under the Yorkist Kings, *EHR*, 71:1–27 (January 1956); W. H. Dunham, Jr., "The Ellesmere Extracts from the 'Acta Consilii' of King Henry VIII," *EHR*, 58:301–318 (July 1943); "Henry VIII's Whole Council and Its Parts," *HLQ*, 7:7–46 (November 1943); "Wolsey's Rule of the King's Whole Council," *AHR*, 49:644–662 (January 1944).

[29] J. Hurstfield, "The Revival of Feudalism in Early Tudor England," *History*, 37:131–145 (June 1952), and *The Queen's Wards: Wardship and Marriage under Elizabeth I* (1958); W. C. Richardson, "The Surveyor of the King's Prerogative," *EHR*, 56:52–75 (January 1941). In his more recent work, *Tudor Chamber Administration, 1485–1547* (Baton Rouge, La., 1952), Richardson supports the traditional

personal monarchy rather than the inauguration of the traditional "New Monarchy"; Henry VII was closer in his thinking about monarchy to Edward I than to his own granddaughter. Elton's arguments on this long-mooted subject are cogent although not conclusive. Medievalists can only welcome any approach which breaks down the artificial periodization imposed by dynastic change and draws attention to the need for more knowledge of the dark fifteenth century—provided we are not required to accept the notion that the state sprang full-fledged from the brain of Thomas Cromwell.

For Stubbs the chief creator of the English state was Edward I, and the chief obstacle was feudalism. Edward completed the work begun by Henry II, delivering the *coup de grâce* to feudal institutions and thereby making possible "the growth of the nation." This interpretation, like his "Lancastrian experiment," has been revised in the light of new evidence drawn from the records. We now see that Edward's legislation and measures of judicial and military reform, far from completing its destruction, initiated a re-tooling of feudalism. T. F. T. Plucknett showed us that the famous "anti-feudal" statutes were intended to enforce the king's own landlord rights, not to destroy those of his barons.[30] Helen Cam demonstrated that the *Quo Warranto* proceedings were undertaken to clarify the distinction between public and private jurisdictions rather than to destroy the latter.[31] Edward's need for a more efficient and reliable army to fight his Welsh, Scottish, and French wars led him to abandon feudal levies in favor of indentured companies serving their leaders and the king for pay. The statute *Quia Emptores* encouraged the consolidation of larger estates among fewer families of the nobility. The ultimate consequence of these measures nearly two centuries later was the "bastard feudalism" described by Plummer.

Investigators of this "new feudalism" have approached it along three main lines. Some have studied army organization and its ramifications. Others have applied the currently popular and effective groupbiography approach to the great feudal families, their landed estates, their retinues, and their interconnections. Still others have concerned themselves with constitutional implications.

A. E. Prince's articles on the subject culminated in his essay "The

---

view that important changes were made in Henry VII's reign and that there was substantial continuity thereafter to 1547; S. E. Thorne, ed., *Prerogativa Regis* (New Haven, Conn., 1949).

[30] *Legislation of Edward I* (Oxford, 1949).

[31] *Liberties and Communities in Medieval England* (Cambridge, Eng., 1944).

Army and the Navy," in the first volume of the *English Government at Work, 1327–1336*.[32] N. B. Lewis [33] and R. A. Newhall [34] have also dealt mainly with indentured retinues and army organization. Bryce Lyon, following the lead of M. Sczaniecki,[35] has investigated the *fief-rente*.[36] He insists on a clear distinction between the indenture and its antecedent, the *fief-rente*, on the ground that the tenant of a *fief-rente* owed homage and fealty to his lord, whereas the indentured retainer did not. Yet he fails to distinguish between the limited military indenture and the more general personal indenture. M. R. Powicke of Toronto has concentrated on the relation between the obligation to military service and knighthood.[37]

The most valuable single volume on the great families is G. A. Holmes's *The Estates of the Higher Nobility in Fourteenth Century England* (Cambridge, Eng., 1957), a case study of six families: Mortimer, Bohun, Montague, Vere, Courtenay, and DeBurgh. Holmes examines the sources of their wealth, their social prestige, and their political power.[38] Only two studies carry us into the fifteenth century and only one of these into the time of the Wars of the Roses when the new feudal-

---

[32] Ed. W. F. Willard, W. A. Morris, J. R. Strayer, and W. H. Dunham, Jr., 3 vols., Publications of the Mediaeval Academy of America, Nos. 37, 48, 56 (Cambridge, Mass., 1940–50); for his articles see "The Strength of English Armies in the Reign of Edward III," *EHR*, 46:353–371 (July 1931); "The Indenture System under Edward III," in *Historical Essays in Honour of James Tait* (Manchester, Eng., 1933), pp. 283–297; "The Payment of Army Wages in Edward III's Reign," *Speculum*, 19:137–160 (April 1944).

[33] "An Early Indenture of Military Service, 27 July, 1287," *BIHR*, 13:85–89 (November 1935); "The Last Medieval Summons of the English Feudal Levy, 13 June, 1385," *EHR*, 73:1–26 (January 1958); "The Organisation of Indentured Retinues in Fourteenth Century England," *TRHS*, 4th ser., 27 (1945), pp. 29–39; "An Early Fourteenth Century Contract for Military Service," *BIHR*, 20:111–118 (May and November 1944); "English Forces in Flanders, August–November, 1297," *Studies in Medieval History Presented to F. M. Powicke* (Oxford, 1948), pp. 310–318.

[34] *Muster and Review: A Problem of English Military Administration, 1420–1440* (Cambridge, Mass., 1940).

[35] *Essai sur les fiefs-rentes*, Bibliothèque d'histoire du droit (Paris: Recueil Sirey, 1946).

[36] "The Money Fief under the English Kings, 1066–1485," *EHR*, 66:161–193 (April 1951); "The Feudal Antecedent of the Indenture System," *Speculum*, 29:503–511 (July 1954); *From Fief to Indenture* (Cambridge, Mass., 1957).

[37] "Distraint of Knighthood and Military Obligation under Henry III," *Speculum*, 25:457–470 (October 1950); "The General Obligation to Cavalry Service under Edward I," *Speculum*, 28:814–833 (October 1953); "Edward II and Military Obligation," *Speculum*, 31:92–119 (January 1956).

[38] See also Levi Fox, *The Administration of the Honor of Leicester in the Fourteenth Century* (Leicester, 1940) and A. S. Harvey, *The De La Pole Family of Kingston-upon-Hull*, East Yorkshire Historical Society (1957).

ism supposedly reached its apogee and had its most deleterious effects on society and government. C. D. Ross describes the administrative organization of an early fifteenth-century noble household in *The Estates and Finances of Richard Beauchamp, Earl of Warwick* (Stratford-on-Avon, 1956) on the basis of a few fragments of accounts. W. H. Dunham, Jr., in a study of "Lord Hastings' Indentured Retainers, 1461–83" argues that such indentured retinues as Hastings' were legal within the meaning of the statute of 1468. Moreover, despite evidence of dual loyalties and mercenary calculation, he contends that the system, far from creating social evil, was a force for stability and a more refined feudalism.[39]

Helen Cam, on the other hand, sees grave constitutional implications in the new feudalism as perpetuating the destructive political and social power of the landed aristocracy in a more virulent form than had existed under the old tenurial feudalism.[40] It worked within the framework of the national government and used and abused royal administrative machinery for its own disruptive purposes. K. B. McFarlane admits the instability and "shamelessly competitive" mercenary spirit of the new order but ascribes it to "boundless vitality and optimism" in a healthily growing society.[41] The abuses of government he blames on the weakness of kings rather than on the social order. From a constitutional point of view relations between Lords and Commons in parliament are obviously of central importance. Stubbs believed that the Commons established not only their independence but their leadership through the critical battles of the fourteenth century. Modern scholarship is more guarded in ascribing initiative to the Commons but finds little evidence of the kind of patronage through which the lower house was manipulated in Elizabeth's parliaments. N. B. Lewis, K. B. McFarlane, J. S. Roskell, and others have discovered no considerable evidence of continuity of membership from one parliament to the next, of packing, or of undue influence of great nobles in elections or in presentation of petitions.[42]

[39] *Transactions of the Connecticut Academy of Arts and Sciences*, 39 (New Haven, Conn., 1955), pp. 1–175. See also his reviews of Holmes in *AHR*, 63:387–388 (January 1958); and of Lyon, *Speculum*, 33:300–304 (April 1958).
[40] "The Decline and Fall of English Feudalism," *History*, 25:216–233 (December 1940).
[41] "Bastard Feudalism," *BIHR*, 20:161–180 (May and November 1945); "Parliament and 'Bastard Feudalism,'" *TRHS*, 4th ser., 26 (1944), pp. 53–79. So far as I know, his Ford Lectures for 1953 on "The English Nobility, 1290–1536" have not yet been published.
[42] N. B. Lewis, "Re-election to Parliament in the Reign of Richard II," *EHR*, 48:364–394 (July 1933); H. G. Richardson, "John of Gaunt and the Parliamentary

Peter de la Mare's role in the Good Parliament directs attention to the Speaker's office. J. S. Roskell has followed up his study of the *Commons in the Parliament of 1422* (Manchester, Eng., 1954) with a series of studies of fifteenth-century speakers.[43]

The official history of parliament begun nine years ago, under the leadership of the late Sir Lewis Namier, has not yet touched the medieval period. E. L. C. Mullins, the secretary and coordinator, reports that the plan is to accept J. C. Wedgwood's pioneer volumes as provisional coverage of the sixty years from 1439 to 1500 and, when funds become available, to push the history back into the earlier period. Meanwhile Roskell has set students to study some of the late medieval parliaments and is himself working on others.

Whether in sympathy with a sociological approach or not, historians have little difficulty in accepting such large generalizations as Stanislaw Andrzejewski's that "Military organization influences social structure mainly by determining the distribution of naked power." [44] Yet it is the more subtle effects, those having to do with concealed, rather than naked, power that are more interesting historically. The French war brought into being not only new patterns of personal loyalty but also new wealth and new investment of this wealth. K. B. McFarlane and D. Hay have studied this for different periods of the war, and M. M. Postan has sketched all too briefly the interconnection between the war and concurrent economic change in England.[45]

The war itself and the concomitant diplomacy have lately received some attention from historians. A. H. Burne has taken a new look at strategy and tactics, including the logistic problems faced by medieval commanders. As a responsible commander of men in World War II, he

---

Representation of Lancashire," *BJRL*, 22:175–222 (April 1938); J. C. Wedgwood, "John of Gaunt and the Packing of Parliament," *EHR*, 45:623–625 (October 1930); K. Wood-Legh, "Sheriffs, Lawyers and Belted Knights in the Parliaments of Edward III," *EHR*, 46:372–388 (July 1931); and "The Knights' Attendance in the Parliaments of Edward III," *EHR*, 47:398–413 (July 1932); J. S. Roskell, *The Knights of the Shire for the County Palatine of Lancaster, 1377–1460* (Manchester, Eng., 1937).

[43] "The Medieval Speakers for the Commons in Parliament," *BIHR*, 23:31–51 (May 1950). The articles on individual speakers, evidently preparatory to a book which will be published shortly, are too numerous to list.

[44] *Military Organization and Society* (1954), p. 1.

[45] D. Hay, "The Division of the Spoils of War in Fourteenth Century England," *TRHS*, 5th ser., 4 (1954), pp. 91–109; K. B. McFarlane, "The Investment of Sir John Fastolf's Profits of War," *TRHS*, 5th ser., 7 (1957), pp. 91–116; and "William Worcester, a Preliminary Survey," *Studies Presented to Sir Hilary Jenkinson*, ed. J. Conway Davies (1957), pp. 196–221; M. M. Postan, "Some Social Consequences of the Hundred Years War," *EcHR*, 12:1–12 (no. 1, 1942).

can bring to bear a special sympathetic insight as well as technical knowledge.[46] H. J. Hewitt's *The Black Prince's Expedition of 1355–1357* (Manchester, Eng., 1958) treats a medieval campaign on a scale not attempted before, and P. E. L. Russell's *The English Intervention in Spain and Portugal in the Time of Edward III and Richard II* (Oxford, 1955), brings chivalric extravaganza down into the context of general English objectives on the Continent.

P. Chaplais, J. H. Le Patourel, and G. P. Cuttino have re-examined the conditions preliminary to the war and Edward III's motivations and goals.[47] Cuttino has summarized the new version of the war's origins.[48] And Edouard Perroy has brought together half a century of scholarly revision into a new and readable narrative of the war.[49]

English diplomacy, its objectives and methods, as well as the administrative organization behind it, have been treated by various scholars, most notably by Joycelyne G. Dickinson and G. P. Cuttino. Cuttino's *English Diplomatic Administration, 1259–1339* (1940) studies the complex administrative coordination of Exchequer, Chancery, and Wardrobe necessitated by the Treaty of Paris of 1259. Miss Dickinson's book presents a new picture of *The Congress of Arras, 1435* (Oxford, 1955), illustrating diplomatic technique as well as the effects on English policy at the Council of Basel.

Anthony R. Wagner's cornucopia of works on heraldry can scarcely have escaped anyone's attention. As Richmond Herald he has raised the subject from the level of antiquarian dilettantism and social snobbery to

---

[46] A. H. Burne, *The Crécy War: A Military History of the Hundred Years War from 1337 to the Peace of Bretigny, 1360* (1955); *The Agincourt War: A Military History of the Latter Part of the Hundred Years War from 1369 to 1453* (Fair Lawn, N. J., 1956).

[47] P. Chaplais, "Some Documents regarding the Fulfilment and Interpretation of the Treaty of Bretigny (1361–1369)," *Camden Miscellany,* 19 (1952), pp. 1–84; J. Le Patourel, "Edward III and the Kingdom of France," *History,* 43:173–189 (October 1958), on Edward's motives. On the problems in southern France, see P. Chaplais, *The War of Saint Sardos, 1323–1325,* Camden 3d ser., 87 (1954), "Le Duché-Pairie de Guyenne," *Annales du Midi,* 69:5–38 (January 1957), "English Arguments concerning the Feudal Status of Aquitaine in the Fourteenth Century," *BIHR,* 21:203–213 (May and November 1948); G. P. Cuttino, "An Unidentified Gascon Register," *EHR,* 54:293–299 (April 1939), "The Process of Agen," *Speculum,* 19:161–178 (April 1944), and see his *The Gascon Calendar of 1322,* Camden 3d ser., 70 (1949); Eleanor C. Lodge, "Historical Revision LXX: The Relations between England and Gascony, 1152–1453," *History,* 19:131–139 (September 1934).

[48] "Historical Revision: The Causes of the Hundred Years War," *Speculum,* 31:463–477 (July 1956).

[49] *La Guerre de Cent Ans* (Paris, 1945); *The Hundred Years War,* trans. W. B. Wells, with an introduction to the English edition by D. C. Douglas (1951).

the level of serious interest for social historians.[50] *Aspilogia* is the classical name he gives to the study which he may be said to have created.
G. D. Squibb's *The High Court of Chivalry* (Oxford, 1959) distinguishes
the civil-law jurisdiction of this court from that of the Constable and
Marshal and shows that it covered far more matters than claims to bear
arms. K. B. McFarlane links heraldry with political history by identifying William Worcester, secretary to Sir John Fastolf, as the author of
the *Boke of Noblesse* and showing the importance of the conservative
chivalric outlook expressed there in perpetuating the war.[51]

Stubbs's heroes and villains have lost something both of villainy and
heroism in this post-Freudian age. His greatest hero, Edward I, belongs
mainly to a period earlier than that covered by this essay. Having run
the gauntlet of modern criticism, he comes out more human, yet a hero
still.[52] As for his son, neither the publication of a volume of his letters
nor a painstaking reconstruction of his history as Prince of Wales, by
Hilda Johnstone,[53] has done more than to add substance to Stubbs's
characterization of Edward II as a man "not so much vicious as devoid
of virtue" and his reign as a "tragedy but one that lacks in its true form
the element of pity: for there is nothing in Edward, miserable as his fate
is, that invites or deserves sympathy" (II, 314–315). This generation
may well feel more kindliness towards Edward's unaristocratic tastes
and interests, but our deeper compassion goes out to the people governed by a king and baronage unable to order their own relations well
enough to enable them to protect the north from invasion by the Scots
or to relieve the distress caused by the three years of famine between
1315 and 1318. N. Denholm-Young's new edition and translation of the
Vita Edwardi Secundi (Edinburgh, 1957), the best contemporary account of the reign, is a welcome addition to the Nelson series of medieval Latin texts and translations.

Shakespeare rather more than Stubbs determines our conception of

[50] *Heralds and Heraldry in the Middle Ages* (1939); *Historic Heraldry of Britain*
(1939). See also his King Penguin on the subject (1946), his article on the "Court
of Chivalry" in *Chambers' Encyclopedia*, IV (1959 ed.), and the one on "Heraldry"
in the new edition of *Medieval England*, ed. A. L. Poole, I (Oxford, 1958), pp.
338–381.

[51] See his article in *Studies Presented to Sir Hilary Jenkinson* (cited in n. 45,
above).

[52] In the work of Powicke, Plucknett, and Helen Cam, he emerges as a competent
feudal leader of his barons, a legislator of some vision and flexibility, yet a con-
servator rather than an innovator. See Geoffrey Templeman's "Edward I and the
Historians," *CHJ*, 10:16–35 (no. 1, 1950).

[53] *Letters of Edward, Prince of Wales, 1304–1305* (Cambridge, Eng., 1931);
Edward of Carnarvon, 1284–1307 (Manchester, Eng., 1946).

the later medieval rulers from Richard II to Henry VII. The plays transcend revision, but that does not mean that his Hall-Holinshed derived history has not been challenged both by serious historians and by amateurs. Popular success must not obscure the fact that the late Elizabeth Mackintosh, alias Gordon Daviot, alias Josephine Tey, derived her material only at second or third hand from the sources by way of professional historians to whom she failed to acknowledge her indebtedness. Her *Richard of Bordeaux* (1933) owed much of its excellence to insights borrowed from Maude Clarke and to the beauty and art of the young Gielgud, who both directed the play and acted the title role for a run of over two years. As for *Daughter of Time* (1951), her apologia for Richard III, it was launched on a ninth wave of revisionism. Beginning with Horace Walpole in 1768, many apologists have tried to right the wrong done by the Tudor historians. Miss Tey's version was largely drawn from C. R. Markham's life published in 1906. The extensive literature has been ably summarized by A. R. Myers in *History Today* (1954) and by P. M. Kendall in his recent full-scale biography, *Richard the Third* (1955). The latter has done a painstaking job of examining the evidence but has limited the usefulness of his book for historians by adopting the technique of the historical novelist in acknowledgment of his sources, presumably on the misguided assumption that precise documentation is necessarily pedantic. His second book, *Warwick the Kingmaker* (1957), adds little to our understanding of the period and subtracts something from Kendall's reputation as a biographer. He prefers Chastellain and Commynes to more substantial sources.

Anthony Steel's analysis of Richard II's character and career in terms of twentieth-century psychology has failed to convince two of the leading students of the evidence,[54] but that is not to say that his portrait of Richard as a neurotic may not be essentially sound. That psychological analysis of a historical figure is difficult would seem to be a weak reason for refusing to attempt it. It is regrettable that Maude Clarke did not live to present a full interpretation of the reign as well as to complete other work so brilliantly begun on the constitutional developments of the fourteenth century.

The two later Edwards, although not so popularly controversial, evi-

---

[54] A. Steel, *Richard II* (Cambridge, Eng., 1941). Reviewed by V. H. Galbraith in *History*, 26:223–239 (March 1942), and by E. Perroy in *Revue Historique*, 196:351–355 (July-September 1946).

dently also deserve our better opinion. May McKisack, in a skillful survey of the literature on Edward III, has made clear to us why for most of his reign, the son of Edward II was one of the most popular of medieval rulers. Like the "smoke now rising from the factory chimneys" of the Industrial Age, "the mists of a doctrinaire liberalism" have obscured his characteristically medieval virtues from our eyes.[55] J. R. Lander has gone below the surface impression of Edward IV as a sensualist and a victim of his wife's family to reveal him as a shrewd politician if not a statesman.[56]

Neither of the two new constitutional histories published within the last twenty-five years proves to be a satisfactory substitute for Stubbs. B. Wilkinson, in his three-volume history of the period from 1216 to 1399,[57] does not pretend to have made the definitive restatement. Only in his third volume has he fully enough assimilated his matter to present coherently both his views and his doubts. J. E. A. Jolliffe's "brilliant, suggestive, provocative, and provoking" *Constitutional History of Medieval England from the English Settlement to 1485* (1937) contans unscholarly errors and idiosyncratic interpretations as well as strikingly fresh treatments of familiar material.[58] The pity is that Helen Cam, the *doyenne* of English constitutional historians, has gathered together the fruits of her erudition only in the attractive little book in Hutchinsons' University Library, *England before Elizabeth* (1950).[59] More than any other constitutional historian of the present generation, she has given us the sense of a living relationship between the medieval parliament and the community life of the people.[60]

III

Economic and social historians, rather more than others, have tried to make explicit the questions they ask of their sources and to justify the particular selection of questions in terms of general concepts. When Maitland and Vinogradoff wrote, the main questions had to do with

[55] *History*, 45:1–15 (February 1960).

[56] "Edward IV: The Modern Legend: and a Revision," *History*, 41:38–52 (February–October 1956).

[57] See n. 13, above. Wilkinson evidently began this work as a revision and continuation of Stubbs's *Select Charters*, but the introductory matter, from the first, claimed as much space as the texts. Whether one accepts Wilkinson's views or not, the English translations of documents hitherto untranslated and the bibliographies are helpful for students, although some of his references contain errors.

[58] Review by Helen Cam, *EHR*, 54:483–489 (July 1939).

[59] Now available in the United States in the Harper Torchbooks paperback series.

[60] See her *Liberties and Communities in Medieval England* (cited in n. 31, above).

men's governmental relationships with one another. In this post-Marxist age historians ask and try to answer all the questions appropriate to a modern society: [61] those about growth and movements of population, increase and decrease of economic activity, nature and quantity of investment, aspirations of different social groups, power relationships, and a host of other questions only beginning to be thought of at the turn of the century (although it is hard to find any question that was not in some way in Maitland's mind). Sources for the medieval period are often inhospitable to modern questioning and obstinately resistant to handing over the facts. The results so far have been a vast array of fragmentary and often contradictory answers which have destroyed the traditional chronology and generalizations but have not yet established a new framework, especially for the later centuries of the Middle Ages. We are no longer permitted to speak of a gradual breakdown of seignorial feudalism owing to an expanding money economy and accelerated by the catastrophe of the Black Death, but we do not yet know what to say instead. Moreover, if historians stick to their métier, that is, the reconstruction of particular conditions and events, generalizing only on the basis of such particular data, we are not likely very soon to have a complete new scientific version of the changes of the later Middle Ages.

Population study, especially, is still in the realm mainly of guesswork and is likely to remain so indefinitely. J. C. Russell's attempt to construct a chronology of population growth and decline for medieval England through the use of modern statistical method has been variously criticized as unscholarly and poorly documented, nugatory, or "the best that can be achieved by the methods he uses," for the present anyhow, but no one accepts the results as definitive.[62]

[61] This statement is, in part, inspired by M. M. Postan's inaugural lecture as Professor of Economic History at Cambridge in 1939.

[62] British Medieval Population (Albuquerque, N. Mex., 1948). For a criticism of this book, see the reviews in AHR, 54:866–867 (June 1949), and in the Revue Belge de Philologie et d'Histoire, 28:600–606 (no. 2, 1950), and by M. M. Postan's article "Some Economic Evidence of Declining Population in the Later Middle Ages," EcHR, 2d ser., 2:221–246 (no. 2, 1950). For articles on the effect of the Black Death on population, see: C. E. Boucher, "The Black Death in Bristol," Transactions of the Bristol and Gloucestershire Archaeological Society, 60 (1938), pp. 31–46; J. L. Fisher, "The Black Death in Essex," Essex Review, 52:13–20 (January 1943); E. Robo, "The Black Death in the Hundred of Farnham," EHR, 44:560–572 (July 1929); A. E. Levett, Studies in Manorial History, ed. Helen Cam, Mary Coate, and Lucy Sutherland (Oxford, 1938); Yves Renouard, "Conséquences et intérêt démographiques de la peste noire de 1348," Population, 3:459–466 (July–September 1948); J. Saltmarsh, "Plague and Economic Decline in England in the Later Middle Ages," CHJ, 7:23–41 (no. 1, 1941); J. C. Russell, "The Clerical Population of Medieval England," Traditio, 2 (1944), pp. 177–212.

Population change is just one of many specific issues raised in the long and, in some ways, fruitful controversy between M. M. Postan and the late E. A. Kosminsky of the Soviet Academy of Sciences. Kosminsky's findings were presented in two books published in Russian (Moscow, 1935 and 1947), one summary of chapters from the earlier book in the *Economic History Review* in 1935,[63] a summary of his views on feudal rent in *Past and Present* in April 1955,[64] and a full-dress translation of his second book published under the editorship of R. H. Hilton in 1956.[65] Postan's criticisms and his own findings have appeared in reviews of Kosminsky's work, in a series of articles in the *Economic History Review*, in a special supplement to that journal, and in his essay on late medieval trade in the *Cambridge Economic History*.[66] It is to be hoped that Postan will soon complete the book on *Manorial Profits* which has been promised for so long,[67] and that this will present a full statement of his position.

It is difficult to sort out the issues in the controversy because both parties modified their views, and the world changed around them. Kosminsky's main contribution to a better understanding of the problems of English agrarian economy was to use the "mass-sources" available in print, that is, the *Hundred Rolls* and the *Inquisitions Post Mortem* and so to take a more than local view. English scholarship had been mainly directed towards detailed research on particular manors or groups of manors, like Ada Levett's careful but unfinished studies of the St. Albans manors. Moreover, he drew attention to the prevalence of money payments in the putatively "natural economy" of the twelfth century, and he pointed to a correlation between the size and structure of manors and the prevalence of manorial elements. For him, feudal rents were the key to changes in the later Middle Ages. Including money rents, labor rents, and rents in kind, they provided an index to the intensity of exploitation

[63] "Services and Money Rents in the Thirteenth Century," *EcHR*, 5:24–45 (April 1935.)

[64] "The Evolution of Feudal Rent in England from the XIth to the XVth Centuries," *PP*, 7 (April 1955), pp. 12–36.

[65] *Studies in the Agrarian History of England in the Thirteenth Century*, trans. Ruth Kisch (Oxford, 1956).

[66] "The Manor," review article in *EcHR*, 6:223–226 (April 1936); "The Manor in the Hundred Rolls," review article in *EcHR*, 2d ser., 3:119–125 (no. 1, 1950); "The Chronology of Labour Services," *TRHS*, 4th ser., 20 (1937), pp. 169–193; "The Fifteenth Century," *EcHR*, 9:160–167 (May 1939); *The Famulus: The Estate Labourer in the Twelfth and Thirteenth Centuries*, *EcHR*, supp. 2, Cambridge University Press, for Economic History Society (1954); *Cambridge Economic History of Europe*, II (1952).

[67] In "The Fifteenth Century," *EcHR*, 9:160–167 (May 1939).

of the peasants. Exploitation provoked peasant unrest, flight to the towns, revolt, whether against the near lord or the more distant government. And the class struggle was inevitably for him the agent of change through which the "natural economy" of the eleventh century evolved into a money economy of small producers of the fifteenth century. Capitalism is a more modern development.

Postan in 1935 welcomed Kosminsky's fresh approach to the problems of medieval agrarian economy, commending particularly the scope of his studies. With Kosminsky's failure to extend his research, Postan became increasingly critical. His main charges were that Kosminsky did not recognize sufficiently the limitations of his sources nor the need for supplementing them with local evidence, that in emphasizing size and structure of manorial units he failed to give enough attention to relative size of demesne and villein holdings within the units, and that he ignored other factors for diversity such as climate, soil, and population movements. Postan himself sees no clear pattern of evolution but rather a series of fluctuations, many of them purely local in character. The student, in trying to work out a new account of late medieval developments, must keep in mind (1) a set of relatively stable factors such as soil, climate, topography, and (2) a set of variables including population, relative size of the labor force, wages, prices, and commercial developments affecting agrarian conditions. The basic issue is obviously one of methodology. A western scholar must approach his sources with questions based on general concepts, but without predetermined answers, traditional or ideological. The interest of the controversy lies in the fact that Kosminsky, despite his ideological commitments, did succeed in throwing some light on medieval developments. Considering the obscurity of the sources, we cannot afford to shut out light from whatever direction.

Doctrinaire Marxist interpretation of the rising of 1381 and its background does not seem to have added significantly to our understanding of the event.[68] But that is not to say that a better understanding of the economic problems of the peasantry and their response to them could not yield more light. A Dutch scholar who has made a comparative study of the Flemish revolts of 1323–1328, the Jacquerie of 1358, and the English rising of 1381 has concluded that no general explanation, Marx-

[68] R. H. Hilton and H. Fagan, *The English Rising of 1381* (1950); R. H. Hilton, "Peasant Movements in England before 1381," *EcHR*, 2d ser., 2:117–136 (no. 2, 1949).

ist or otherwise, will fit all three risings. Each arose from a unique set of circumstances.[69]

Research in agrarian history in England has followed three main lines. There are perpendicular studies of particular estates over a considerable stretch of time. There are studies, both horizontal and perpendicular, of regional developments. And there are studies of particular aspects of developments over the whole of England.

The nature of the sources dictates the first line of approach. The accounts of particular landowners, most of them monastic, provide the basis for both ecclesiastical and agrarian history. The list of studies is legion, and it is hard to single out the most significant.[70] The evidence shows great diversity of agrarian organization and technique. R. A. L. Smith's *Canterbury Cathedral Priory* (Cambridge, Eng., 1943) exhibits the Benedictine monks of this house vigorously cultivating the demesne until the end of the fourteenth century, using fertilizers and opening up new land in order to increase their cash crop. Kathleen Major's volumes of the *Registrum Antiquissimum of the Cathedral Church of Lincoln*,[71] on the other hand, show small holdings in the scant arable land, vast pastures for sheep belonging both to the cathedral church and to peasant households, and a persistence of servile tenure. Edward Miller's *The Abbey and Bishopric of Ely* (Cambridge, Eng., 1951) illustrates the development from a subsistence economy in the tenth century to an economy of profit in the thirteenth and ends just after the signs of a recession begin to appear about 1325. J. A. Raftis re-examines the Ramsey Abbey material studied half a century ago by N. Neilson.[72] He concerns himself with short-term fluctuations rather than with long-term trends and carries the narrative of economic change down into the period of the Black Death and the fifteenth-century depression.

The regional historians premise that studies of individual manors or estates like the foregoing will not yield all the necessary evidence to ac-

---

[69] F. W. H. Hugenholtz, *Drie Boerenopstanden uit de veertiende Eeuw: Vlaanderen, 1323–1328; Frankrijk, 1358; Engeland, 1381* (Haarlem, 1949).

[70] Notable studies of three ecclesiastical estates are Frances May Page's *The Estates of Crowland Abbey* (Cambridge, Eng., 1934); Marjorie Chibnall (née Morgan), *English Lands of the Abbey of Bec* (Oxford, 1946), and *Select Documents of the English Lands of the Abbey of Bec*, Camden 3d ser., 73 (1951); and J. S. Drew's "Manorial Accounts of St. Swithin's Priory," *EHR*, 62:20–41 (January 1947).

[71] V (1940), VI (1950), and facsimiles of the charters in V and VI, Lincoln Record Society, 34, 41–42.

[72] J. A. Raftis, *The Estates of Ramsey Abbey* (Toronto, 1957). Nellie Neilson, *Economic Conditions on the Manors of Ramsey Abbey* (Philadelphia, 1899).

count even for internal development. Wigston Magna, the village in Leicestershire singled out for study by W. G. Hoskins, was strongly affected by the proximity of Leicester and by political, social, and economic developments in the whole midlands area. In *The Midland Peasant* (1957),[73] he has presented an up-to-date experiment in village history on the model of the study of Crawley, Hampshire, by N. S. B. and E. C. Gras.[74] As a scholar long resident in the area he discusses, he has been able to avoid some of their errors of ignorance. R. H. Tawney is alleged to have urged his students to abandon their books for their boots. Now, one would have to add surveyor's instruments, a camera, and a light airplane to the equipment for the well-outfitted student of agrarian developments. Hoskins in *The Making of the English Landscape* (1955) and Maurice Beresford in *The Lost Villages of England* (1954) have shown what can be done with the new equipment. R. H. Hilton adds a rather flexible Marxism to his tools for the study of *The Economic Development of Some Leicestershire Estates in the Fourteenth and Fifteenth Centuries* (1947).[75] In the absence of accounts and court rolls, the bulk of the material on which his analysis is based comes from terriers and inventories. In this midland area, there were few large manors, the demesne was cultivated mainly by wage-laborers and, although cereals were grown under a four-to-five culture system rather than the traditional three-field system, the more important product was wool, and the peasants' crop was added to that of the monks for sale to the merchant. His *The Social Structure of Rural Warwickshire* (Oxford, 1950) should be compared with David Douglas' *The Social Structure of Medieval East Anglia* (Oxford, 1927) for the difference in the questions asked of the sources. (It should not be otherwise compared, for the one is an "Occasional Paper" of the Dugdale Society while the other is a fully documented study for Vinogradoff's classic series, the *Oxford Studies in Social and Legal History*.)

Some specialized attacks on problems of rural economy have been made by H. C. Darby and his fellow historical geographers and by the Orwins, who have presented an ingenious explanation of the open-field

---

[73] *The Midland Peasant: The Economic and Social History of a Leicestershire Village* [Wigston Magna] (1957). For the criticism that he has not taken into sufficient account the proximity of Leicester, see Joan Thirsk's review in *EHR*, 74:682–684 (October 1959).

[74] N. S. B. and E. C. Gras, *The Economic and Social History of an English Village (Crawley, Hampshire) A.D. 909–1928* (Cambridge, Mass., 1930).

[75] See also Hilton's contribution on "Medieval Agrarian History" to the *Victoria County History* for Leicestershire, II (1954), pp. 145–198.

system.[76] The best work of both has been done for the period of Domesday Book or beyond.

George Homans' *English Villagers of the Thirteenth Century* (Cambridge, Mass., 1941) should be mentioned here because it is a new treatment of the sort of material studied by the agrarian historians referred to above. It is a worthy challenge from a sociologist to any complacency historians may feel about their method. He uses the same sources but asks a different set of questions. The family holding, not the manor, is for Homans the unit of production, and the village is the unit of decision-making. His work gives a new internal order to old facts presented in such works as N. Neilson's little book for college students on *Medieval Agrarian Economy* (New York, 1936), in G. G. Coulton's various works on village life, the most recently published being *Medieval Panorama* (Cambridge, Eng., 1938), and in the work of Coulton's student, H. S. Bennett, *Life on the English Manor* (Cambridge, Eng., 1937). The one criticism a historian might level at this challenging book is that, in his concern with change, Homans shows too little respect for chronology.

Economic history in general and the history of industry and commerce suffered a great loss in the untimely death in 1940 of Eileen Power. Her Ford Lectures for 1938–39 on *The Wool Trade* [77] display at one and the same time the scope of her learning and gifts and the importance of the subject to which she devoted the last years she had in which to work. What significant aspect of medieval history is not in some way touched upon in those six brief lectures? Production of wool and woolens affects agrarian developments, movements of population, growth of towns, taxation, monastic history, philanthropy, and sculpture, to stop with an incomplete list. Fortunately something of Miss Power's spirit and interests lives on in her students and, in turn, in their students. Eleanora Carus-Wilson has added the wool and woolen industries and trade and the Staplers to her earlier interests in Icelandic trade, the port of Bristol, and the Merchant Venturers.[78] Her essay in the second volume of the

[76] *Historical Geography of England* (Cambridge, Eng., 1936); *The Medieval Fenland* (Cambridge, Eng., 1940); C. S. and C. S. Orwin, *The Open Fields* (1938; 2d ed. Oxford, 1954).

[77] Published posthumously without documentation (1941).

[78] See her two chapters in *Studies in English Trade in the 15th Century*, ed. Eileen Power and M. M. Postan (1933), pp. 155–246; *Medieval Merchant Venturers: Collected Studies* (1954); her essay "An Industrial Revolution of the Thirteenth Century," in *Essays in Economic History*, a selection of essays from *EcHR*, ed. Eleanora Carus-Wilson (1954), reprinted 1955 and 1958. See also her articles, "Trends in the Export of English Woollens in the Fourteenth Century," *EcHR*, 2d ser., 3:162–179 (no. 2, 1950); "The Effects of the Acquisition and

Cambridge Economic History (projected and planned by Eileen Power and Sir John Clapham but continuing its arrested progress under Postan and E. E. Rich) is one of the two best in the book and provides a kind of summary of her work to date on the woolen industry. Her most helpful discovery was that a technological revolution in the process of fulling accounts in the main for the new geographical distribution and the new internal organization of the industry which characterized it in the later Middle Ages and in early modern times. Among Eleanora Carus-Wilson's students, Margery James and Nelly J. Kerling have made important contributions to the history of the wine trade between England and Gascony and the commercial relations of Holland and Zeeland with England.[79] A. R. Bridbury has, somewhat less successfully, studied the salt trade in the context of England's economic development.[80] R. L. Baker's article on "The Establishment of the English Wool Staple in 1313" is a sample only from a still unpublished doctoral dissertation on the history of the staple in the fourteenth century.[81] L. F. Salzman will need no recommendation to medievalists for his *Building in England down to 1540* (Oxford, 1952). Dorothy Burwash's *English Merchant Shipping, 1460–1540* (Toronto, 1947) was a pioneer work concerned with ships, seamen and seamanship, cargoes, the law of the sea, and other eternal factors in the history of ocean-borne commerce.

The freshening effects of Lord Beveridge's revisions of Thorold Rogers' great work on prices and wages have not yet been strongly felt for the medieval period. International collaboration on price history dictated that the first volume of the new *Prices and Wages in England from the Twelfth to the Nineteenth Century* (1939) should deal with the mercantile era rather than medieval beginnings. Other commitments have kept Lord Beveridge from making material progress on the medieval data, but there is hope that his work on wages and averages of wheat

Loss of Gascony on the English Wine Trade," *BIHR*, 21:145–154 (May and November 1947); "Evidences of Industrial Growth on Some Fifteenth Century Manors," *EcHR*, 2d ser., 12:190–205 (no. 2, 1959).

[79] "The Medieval Wine Dealer," *The Entrepreneur*, Papers presented at the Annual Conference of the Economic History Society at Cambridge, April 1957 (Cambridge, Mass., 1957); "Les activités commerciales des négociants en vins gascons en Angleterre durant la fin du moyen âge," *Annales du Midi*, 65:35–48 (January 1953); "The Fluctuations of the Anglo-Gascon Wine Trade during the Fourteenth Century," *EcHR*, 2d ser., 4:170–196 (no. 2, 1951); Nelly Kerling, *The Commercial Relations of Holland and Zeeland with England* (Leiden, 1954).

[80] *England and the Salt Trade in the Later Middle Ages* (Oxford, 1955).

[81] *Speculum*, 31:444–453 (July 1956).

prices may now proceed more rapidly. M. E. Rayner has published an article on measures,[82] an intricate subject, the study of which has revealed the extreme difficulty of preparing scientifically accurate price tables for medieval England.

A number of studies, seemingly local in scope from their titles, are far more than local in significance. Alwyn A. Ruddock's studies of Southampton trade illuminate the relations of England with the Mediterranean.[83] Alice Beardwood has followed up her earlier study of *Alien Merchants in England, 1350–1377* (Cambridge, Mass., 1935) with *The Statute Merchant Roll of Coventry, 1392–1416* (Dugdale Society, 1939), which adds not only to our information about the history of Coventry, but also to the evidence about the enforcement of the Statute of Merchants and about legal resources for creditors in collecting debts.

Martin Weinbaum has completed for the medieval period the collection and publication of borough charters begun by Adolphus Ballard and continued by James Tait.[84] He has fortunately abandoned the confusing organization of the earlier volumes. Borough history seems to be in something of a slump, although for Bristol we have had a considerable output of texts of medieval muniments, charters, and commercial documents of one sort and another published by the Bristol Record Society.[85] J. W. F. Hill's *Medieval Lincoln* (Cambridge, Eng., 1948), the one useful borough history of the past twenty years, is an enthusiastic and industrious reconstruction by a nonprofessional. Professional scholars may regret only that he did not integrate the social and economic history more fully with the topographical and give momentum to the whole.

Medieval London still lacks its biographer although the *Calendar of the Plea and Memoranda Rolls of the City of London*[86] continues its steady progress, and we have had several good books about social Lon-

[82] *Archives*, 4:154–157 (no. 23, 1960).

[83] *The Port Books or Local Customs Accounts of Southampton for the Reign of Edward IV*, ed. D. B. Quinn, with the assistance of Alwyn Ruddock, Southampton Record Society Publications, 2 vols. (1937–38); *Italian Merchants and Shipping in Southampton, 1270–1600* (Southampton, 1951); "Italian Trading Fleets in Medieval England," *History*, 29:192–202 (September 1944); "London Capitalists and the Decline of Southampton in the Early Tudor Period," *EcHR*, 2d ser., 2:137–151 (no. 2, 1949).

[84] *British Borough Charters, 1307–1660* (Cambridge, Eng., 1943).

[85] *The Staple Court Books of Bristol*, ed. E. E. Rich (Bristol, 1934); *The Great Red Book of Bristol*, ed. E. W. W. Veale, Text: Parts I–II (Bristol, 1933–50); *Bristol Charters, 1378–1499*, ed H. A. Cronne (Bristol, 1946).

[86] *1413–1437*, ed. A. H. Thomas (Cambridge, Eng., 1943); *1437–1457*, ed. P. E. Jones (1954).

don. Ruth Bird's *The Turbulent London of Richard II* (1949) is a rather too timid account of the critical conflicts of that time.[87] Eilert Ekwall's *Studies on the Population of Medieval London* (Stockholm, 1956) is a fascinating attempt to trace population movement through linguistic change. The most impressive work on London and an outstanding contribution to social and economic history in general is Sylvia Thrupp's book on *The Merchant Class of Medieval London, 1300–1500* (Chicago, 1948). A student of Eileen Power's, she has repaid her debt to her teacher by setting a new standard for social historians.

Maitland's plea for the editing of texts and calendars of the tons of unpublished medieval records has not had the widespread response he asked for. Even so, a dwindling band of faithful disciples has endeavored to maintain the flow into print of legal records and texts from the reservoir of the Public Record Office, the British Museum manuscript room, the Inns of Court libraries, and various local archives. Moreover, in some areas considerable completeness has been achieved. Bertha Putnam's *Proceedings before the Justices of the Peace in the Fourteenth and Fifteenth Centuries, Edward III to Richard III* [88] included more than half the medieval rolls, and her students or others working under her inspiration and direction edited the others. She gave us a masterly summary of the medieval history of this uniquely English office in her introduction and, in a later article, showed the importance of the records for the more general study of medieval society.[89] Her biography of Sir William Shareshull was a pioneer attempt, not altogether successful, to evoke from the shades a fourteenth-century lawyer and judge (Cambridge, Eng., 1950).[90]

G. O. Sayles, S. E. Thorne, and a small group of other scholars, under

---

[87] A bolder, more imaginative essay on a part of London's history may be found in G. A. Williams' "London and Edward I," the Alexander Prize essay for 1960, *TRHS*, 5th ser., 11 (1961), pp. 81–99.

[88] Publication of the Ames Foundation (London and Cambridge, Mass., 1938).

[89] For a list of those in print, see Elisabeth Kimball, "A Bibliography of the Printed Records of the Justices of the Peace for Counties," *University of Toronto Law Journal*, 6:401–413 (no. 2, 1946). Since Miss Kimball's article there have been published the following rolls: *Some Sessions of the Peace in Lincolnshire, 1381–1396*, I, Lincoln Record Society (1955); *The Shropshire Peace Roll, 1400–1414*, Salop County Council (Shrewsbury, 1959), both ed. Elisabeth Kimball, and *Essex Sessions of the Peace, 1351, 1377–79*, Essex Archaeological Society Occasional Publications, no. 3 (Colchester, 1953), ed. Elizabeth Chapin Furber. For potential uses of the records, see Bertha H. Putnam, "Records of Courts of Common Law, especially of the Sessions of the Justices of the Peace: Sources for the Economic History of England in the Fourteenth and Fifteenth Centuries," *Proceedings of the American Philosophical Society*, 91 (1947), pp. 258–273.

[90] See also E. L. G. Stones, "Sir Geoffrey le Scrope (c. 1285–1340) Chief Justice of the King's Bench," *EHR*, 69:1–17 (January 1954).

the editorial guidance of T. F. T. Plucknett, are extending the number of Selden Society volumes, of the *Select Cases* and of the legal treatises and Yearbooks.[91] Sayles's work on the King's Bench in the time of the first three Edwards is the most impressive single achievement. He has been particularly successful at clarifying the early relationships among the central courts. Thorne has thrown much-needed light on early legal teaching and training. Under his direction and that of the Tudor historian, S. T. Bindoff, E. W. Ives has carried through and published in summary form a study of the legal profession of Yorkist and early Tudor times.[92] Marjorie Blatcher [93] and Margaret Hastings made parallel studies of the courts of King's Bench and Common Pleas in the fifteenth century. *The Court of Common Pleas in Fifteenth Century England* (Ithaca, N.Y., 1947) did not pretend to be more than a preliminary exploration of records which by sheer bulk and quantity overwhelm the student, particularly the student who does not have easy access to the Record Office.

Plucknett, more than any other scholar, follows in Maitland's footsteps and achieves that breadth of view that seeks to think the "common thoughts about common things" of our forefathers. His Creighton Lecture for 1953, published as *The Medieval Bailiff* in 1954, insists on the need for the technical approach of the trained legal specialist in legal matters but shows Maitland's gift for making the technicalities palatable and often stirring. The list of his other works is too long to set down here, but perhaps the articles on the origin of impeachment and state trials, the essay on "Parliament" in the *English Government at Work*, and the studies of Edward I's legislation and the interpretation of statutes in the fourteenth century should be singled out for special mention.[94]

[91] G. O. Sayles, *Select Cases in the Court of King's Bench* (Edward I–Edward III), Publications of the Selden Society, Nos. 55, 57, 58, 74, 76, (1936–57); S. E. Thorne, *Readings and Moots at the Inns of Court in the Fifteenth Century*, I, Selden Society, No. 71 (1954). For a full list and guide to vols. 1–79, see the *General Guide to the Society's Publications*, compiled by A. K. R. Kiralfy and G. H. Jones (1960).

[92] "Promotion in the Legal Profession of Yorkist and Early Tudor England," *LQR*, 75:348–363 (July 1959).

[93] Marjorie Blatcher's "The Working of the Court of King's Bench in the Fifteenth Century," is an unpublished doctoral dissertation (University of London, 1936).

[94] "The Origin of Impeachment," *TRHS*, 4th ser., 24 (1942), pp. 47–71; "The Impeachments of 1376," 5th ser., 1 (1951), pp. 153–164; "The Rise of the English State Trial," *Politica*, 2:542–559 (December 1937); "State Trials under Richard II," *TRHS*, 5th ser., 2 (1952), pp. 159–171; "Parliament," *The English Government at Work*, cited above, n. 32; *Legislation of Edward I*, cited in n. 30, above; *Statutes and Their Interpretation in the First Half of the Fourteenth Century* (Cambridge, Eng., 1922).

Some of the freshening streams from the new springs of sociological and economic history have penetrated even into that canyon of past historical enterprise, the *Victoria County History*. Despite a recent reviewer's rather testy comment on the newly published Staffordshire volumes,[95] no one who has compared the latest Cambridgeshire, Leicestershire, or Wiltshire volumes with the earliest in the series can miss the more scientific, more professional, and less antiquarian direction of the latest. The improvement and greater frequency of maps, the use of sometimes brilliant aerial photographs, the introduction of indexes in individual volumes, the incorporation of new and important categories of material, the deepening of the treatment of social and economic developments both in the general sections and in the parish histories are all points of progress worth mentioning. Indeed, in looking over the publication record, on the dust jacket of the volumes currently appearing, one is torn between a feeling of satisfaction that eleven counties have been completed, six more, substantially so, and the wish that all of the early ones were now to be done under the new direction. With the enlistment of local enterprise and funds and the delegation of some of the editorial authority which has been inaugurated under R. B. Pugh's general editorship, the tempo has picked up speed. Twenty-one volumes have appeared in the last ten years, and eight new volumes are now either in the press or near completion.

No great new synthesis has brought together all the recent findings in economic history. Lipson's revisions of his medieval volume have been slight. Sir John Clapham's "lapidary" summary of the achievements of economic historians within his lifetime in the *Concise Economic History of Britain* (Cambridge, Eng., 1949) is conservative rather than adventurous in outlook. The essays in the *Cambridge Economic History of Europe* on English medieval developments, barring the exceptions already noted, are equally conservative. The bold, yet judicial, new version of the economic history of the last two centuries of the English Middle Ages remains to be written.

IV

The one common feature which informs all treatments of the cultural history of the later Middle Ages published during the last twenty years or so is a greater respect for the medieval mind and spirit than was possible to nineteenth-century historians. Believing in ourselves less arrogantly than did men of the nineteenth century, we can see more in other

[95] R. H. Hilton, *EHR*, 75:113–116 (January 1960).

ages than they did. We accept less at original value the claim of Renaissance thinkers to have revived learning and of Reformation religious leaders to have restored Christianity to its pristine purity. Having taken our own departure from naturalism in art, we understand better the transcendent spirit of medieval art. Moreover, with the increasing importance of science has come a corresponding awareness of the long medieval preparation for the scientific revolution of the sixteenth and seventeenth centuries.

More seems to have been done to date on the scientific thought of the thirteenth than on that of the fourteenth century. But A. C. Crombie has somewhat sketchily traced the origins of experimental science from 1100 through Robert Grosseteste to the beginnings of the eighteenth century.[96] Anneliese Maier has written on the fourteenth-century forerunners of Galileo and the boundaries between scholasticism and scientific learning.[97] Recently discovered in Peterhouse Library is a fourteenth-century treatise, *The Equatorie,* describing the construction and use of a predecessor to the sextant, a manuscript long lost but now published by the Cambridge University Press (1955). The editor, D. J. Price, discusses in his introduction the possibility that the text may be the work of Chaucer in his own hand.

There is a new interest in William of Occam and his fellow sceptics, on the one hand, and antisceptics like Thomas Bradwardine and Walter Burleigh, on the other. Gordon Leff's *Bradwardine and the Pelagians* (Cambridge, Eng., 1957), discusses Bradwardine's contribution, albeit indirect, to the new empiricism characteristic of the Renaissance outlook. In general we still know too little about fourteenth-century Oxford and Cambridge, although we are better off for the former than the latter. A. R. Emden has just completed an extraordinarily comprehensive and useful *Biographical Register of the University of Oxford to A.D. 1500* in three stout volumes (Oxford, 1957–59). H. G. Richardson and others have shown us that Oxford gave more practical education than had been supposed in business and legal matters.[98] Roberto Weiss's *Humanism in England during the Fifteenth Century* (Oxford, 1941)

[96] *Robert Grosseteste and the Origins of Experimental Science, 1100–1700* (Oxford, 1953). See also his *Oxford's Contribution to the Origins of Modern Science* (Oxford, 1954).

[97] *An der Grenze von Scholastik und Naturwissenschaft* (Essen, 1943); *Die Vorläufer Galileis im 14. Jahrhundert* (Rome, 1949).

[98] H. G. Richardson, "The Oxford Law School under John," *LQR,* 57:319–338 (July 1941); "Business Training in Medieval Oxford," *AHR,* 46:259–280 (January 1941); "An Oxford Teacher of the Fifteenth Century," *BJRL,* 23:436–457 (October 1939); H. E. Salter, W. A. Pantin, and H. G. Richardson, *Formularies Which Bear on the History of Oxford, c. 1204–1240* (Oxford, 1942).

adds valuable information on fifteenth-century Cambridge and Oxford to what we already had in W. F. Schirmer's *Der englische Frühhumanismus* (Leipzig, 1931), and Rosamund Mitchell and George B. Parks have each contributed some new knowledge of English contacts with Italy in the late medieval period.[99]

The literary historians have been busy. Two works are particularly worthy of mention. George Kane's, subtitled *A Critical Study of the Romances, the Religious Lyrics, Piers Plowman* (1951), is the most pertinent here. H. S. Bennett's *Chaucer and the Fifteenth Century* (Oxford, 1947), while not so stirring to historians as C. L. Kingsford's Ford Lectures for 1923–24, provides a useful general guide to the literary history of the period. Marchette Chute's *Geoffrey Chaucer of England* (1951) is a popular book but one which shows real feeling for the times. E. M. W. Tillyard, having in his earlier works emphasized the continuity between medieval and modern thought, has more recently chosen to emphasize the differences.[100]

There are a number of new editions of texts. F. N. Robinson's *The Complete Works of Geoffrey Chaucer* is in its second edition (1957), deliberately omitting the Peterhouse *Equatorie* on the ground that Chaucer's authorship, though plausible, is not proven. Kane, with others, is editing a new and definitive edition of *Piers Plowman;* the first volume (1960) gives us the A version. R. H. Robbins' *Secular Lyrics of the Fourteenth and Fifteenth Centuries* (1951) is a worthy successor to Carleton Brown's anthology of religious lyrics, and his *Historical Poems of the Fourteenth and Fifteenth Centuries* (New York, 1959) is of special interest for historians.

There is a new interest in the literacy and language of medieval Englishmen and in the books and libraries which they possessed. Galbraith's Raleigh Lecture for 1935 was entitled "The Literacy of the Medieval English Kings" and the two most important recent works on books, readers, and libraries are H. S. Bennett's *English Books and Readers, 1475–1557* (Cambridge, Eng., 1952) and N. R. Ker's guide to *Medieval Libraries of Great Britain: A List of Surviving Books* (1941), which has been published in the Royal Historical Society series of Guides and Handbooks.

[99] R. J. Mitchell, "English Law Students at Bologna in the Fifteenth Century," *EHR,* 51:270–287 (April 1936); "English Students at Padua, 1460–75," *TRHS,* 4th ser., 19 (1936), pp. 101–117; "English Students at Ferrara, 1475–1500," *Somerset and Dorset Notes and Queries,* 22:178–185 (December 1937); G. B. Parks, *The English Traveler to Italy,* I (Stanford, Calif., and Rome, 1954).
[100] *The English Renaissance—Fact or Fiction?* (1952).

Art history has taken on depth, breadth, and skill, partly through the inspiration derived from the Warburg Institute, transferred in 1933 to London (thanks to Hitler) and incorporated into the University, and partly through the development of improved techniques in photography and art reproduction. The Pelican History of Art under the editorship of Nikolaus Pevsner rivals the Oxford History of Art directed by T. S. R. Boase. The Pelican organization is topical rather than chronological, one volume each being devoted to Architecture, Painting, and Sculpture. Particularly in Lawrence Stone's volume on *Sculpture in Britain* (1955) [101] the true value of art history for other history is illustrated. Stone does not attempt to write the social history of the times. Instead, he shows sculpture as a projection of concepts and attitudes of the times, as fully as can be done in view of the scant survivals of pre-Reformation examples. Joan Evans' *English Art, 1307–1461,* appeared in the Oxford History in 1949. John Harvey's *Gothic England* (1947) would perhaps have been more valuable had the author, an archaeologist and architect, tried to be less comprehensive and confined himself to an analysis of architecture. His *English Medieval Architects: A Biographical Dictionary down to 1550* (1954) is an invaluable tool book. Although Walter Oakeshott's *The Sequence of English Medieval Art* (1950) is more an album than an analytical contribution to art history, it contains some challenging observations. Francis Wormald's main energies have gone into the study of earlier centuries, but his learned discussion of "The Wilton Diptych" [102] demonstrates the scholarly authority which accounts, in part no doubt, for his new appointment as Director of the Institute of Historical Research in the University of London.

The study of a number of other aspects of medieval English life has moved out of the circle of antiquarian interest into historical scholarship. R. Allen Brown's *English Medieval Castles* (1954) is a readable book by a trained scholar and archivist. Anthony R. Wagner's *English Genealogy* (Oxford, 1960), like his works on heraldry, raises to scholarly dignity a traditionally amateur study. Austin Lane Poole's new edition of *Medieval England* (2 vols., Oxford, 1958), the joint work of a formidable list of scholars, constitutes a useful companion to studies either of literature or history.

Church history has led the field in sheer volume of output in the last

---

[101] The other volumes are: Margaret Rickert, *Painting in Britain* (1954); Geoffrey Webb, *Architecture in Britain* (1956).

[102] *Journal of the Warburg and Courtauld Institutes,* 17:191–203 (July–December 1954).

twenty years, although history of the secular side of the church in the later Middle Ages has been neglected as compared with earlier centuries. For monastic history we have what is clearly one of the most important revisions of recent times, that is, Dom David Knowles's series of volumes on the religious orders.[103] Suffering neither from the undisciplined partisanship of Cardinal Gasquet nor from the obsessive anti-monasticism of G. G. Coulton, the Regius Professor of Modern History at Cambridge has given us a new, scholarly, balanced, and yet sympathetic view of the regular clergy in the centuries before the dissolution. Although his loyalties to his own order are clear, he can nonetheless show us calmly and dispassionately the forces at work to weaken motivations, ideals, and habits in the late medieval period. He does not pretend to have discovered new documentary material, but he has with due acknowledgment incorporated the findings of unprinted doctoral dissertations by his own and others' students. He has also used to good effect the new technique of illustration developed at Cambridge by the Department of Aerial Photography. With J. K. S. St. Joseph, he has examined from the air the leading medieval monastic sites and taken useful, sometimes spectacular, photographs of these. They have been published in a separate volume,[104] as has also his catalogue of *Medieval Religious Houses* (1953), prepared in collaboration with R. Neville Hadcock.

Knowles has also effectively used a number of monographs on individual orders of monks and friars which have appeared recently, as well as the published product of the new wave of interest in the intellectual life of the later Middle Ages.[105] On the basis of the work of Marjorie Morgan Chibnall and others,[106] he has shown that the problem of alien

---

[103] *The Religious Orders in England*, 3 vols. (Cambridge, Eng., 1948–59).

[104] *Monastic Sites from the Air* (Cambridge, Eng., 1952).

[105] H. M. Colvin, *The White Canons in England* (Oxford, 1951); F. D. S. Darwin, *The English Medieval Recluse*, S.P.C.K. (1944); Aubrey Gwynn, S.J., *The English Austin Friars in the Time of Wyclif* (1940); W. A. Hinnebusch, O.P., *The Early English Friars Preachers* (Rome, 1951); J. R. H. Moorman, *The Grey Friars in Cambridge* (Cambridge, Eng., 1952); R. A. L. Smith, *Collected Papers* (1947); A. H. Sweet, "The Apostolic See and the Heads of English Religious Houses," *Speculum*, 28:468–484 (July 1953); A. H. Thompson, *The History of the Hospital and the New College of the Annunciation of St. Mary in the Newarke* (Leicester, 1937), and *The Abbey of St. Mary of the Meadows, Leics.* (Leicester, 1949); Susan Wood, *English Monasteries and Their Patrons in the Thirteenth Century* (1955).

[106] "The Abbey of Bec-Hellouin and Its English Priories," *Journal of the British Archaeological Association*, 3d ser., 5 (1940), pp. 33–61; "The Suppression of the Alien Priories," *History*, 26:204–212 (December 1941), and the works cited in n. 70, above.

priories, although chronologically concurrent with the antimonasticism of the fourteenth century, was separate from it. In the conservative reaction which set in under Henry IV and Henry V, most of the priories were denizened rather than destroyed. Knowles's work has rendered largely nugatory for English medievalists the two hundred or so pages of Coulton's *Five Centuries of Religion* [107] which deal with the English monasteries in the last centuries before the dissolution. Coulton had an encyclopedic collection of instances to cite for any point he was making. His disconcerting habit of drawing them from enormous distances of time and space from one another makes his work difficult to use in discovering what is going on at any given time or place.

For the secular side of the church and its relation to more general European religious developments, we are somewhat better off for the fourteenth than for the fifteenth century, although the printed source material for the two centuries appears to be more or less equal. The most important addition to the already monumental but still growing list of bishops' registers in print is unquestionably E. F. Jacob's edition of the Register of Henry Chichele, archbishop of Canterbury.[108] Bishops' registers show the daily routine of diocesan work. Chichele's shows him to have been a good north countryman, "not a political prelate like Arundel or Kemp . . . at heart a man of the schools." From registers, in large part, A. Hamilton Thompson put together his account of *The English Clergy and Their Organization in the Later Middle Ages,* the Ford Lectures for 1933, published only in 1947 (Oxford). W. A. Pantin's Birkbeck Lectures for 1948 on *The English Church in the Fourteenth Century* (Cambridge, Eng., 1955), is a work rather differently conceived from J. R. H. Moorman's similar work on the thirteenth century. It is more selective, the emphasis being on the most controversial aspects of the fourteenth-century church, that is, on the caliber and background of the clergy of the period, and the relations between the hierarchy, the papacy, and the monarchy, on the intellectual controversies in the fourteenth-century church, and on the religious literature of the period. Kathleen Edwards' monograph on *The English Secular Cathedrals* (Manchester, Eng., 1949) made it unnecessary for Pantin to

[107] IV (1950), pp. 499–724.
[108] *The Register of Henry Chichele, Archbishop of Canterbury, 1414–1443*, edited for the Canterbury and York Society by E. F. Jacob (Oxford, 1937–47), and *Henry Chichele and the Ecclesiastical Politics of his Age,* Creighton Lecture in History, 1951 (pub. 1952). No mention should be made of the Canterbury-York Society without paying tribute to Rose Graham, its general editor from 1924–1958.

discuss some aspects, and her two essays on the bishops of Edward II's reign [109] were clearly helpful to him in his discussion of the early fourteenth-century bishops.

W. E. Lunt's *Financial Relations of the Papacy with England to 1327* [110] helps to clarify the three-way conflict between papal curia, royal court, and lay patrons over papal provisions in the fourteenth century, a subject earlier examined by G. Barraclough. J. R. Highfield has explored another side of this triangle.[111] We are now freed from some traditional prejudices about the fourteenth-century church. We know, for example, that the papal curia was often the best resort for the worthy applicant.[112] Pantin shows that the general level of learning and devotion to their calling among the upper clergy in the fourteenth century was not significantly lower than in the thirteenth and that Britain was not, as supposed, unaffected by the movements of lay piety which swept across the Continent in the later Middle Ages. We have two modern editions of *The Book of Margery Kempe* [113] but no really satisfactory analysis of her personality and writing. Rosalind Hill, in an article on "The Theory and Practice of Excommunication in Medieval England," [114] has shown that this weapon of the church was, like outlawry in the secular courts, overused and not taken seriously. The late B. L. Woodcock treated in vivid detail the organization and procedure of Courts Christian in his *Medieval Ecclesiastical Courts in the Diocese of Canterbury* (Oxford, 1952).

Brian Tierney's *Medieval Poor Law* (Berkeley and Los Angeles, Calif., 1959) shows the value of cross-questioning from one discipline to another. Originally a series of lectures delivered to an audience of social workers, the book presents canon law theories in terms intelligible to nonspecialists.

As in other areas, there is room for a new "high history" of the intellectual and spiritual life of the English people in the later Middle Ages,

---

[109] "Bishops and Learning in the Reign of Edward II," *Church Quarterly Review,* 138:57–86 (April–June 1944); "The Political Importance of the English Bishops during the Reign of Edward II," *EHR,* 59:311–347 (September 1944).

[110] Mediaeval Academy of America (Cambridge, Mass., 1939).

[111] "The English Hierarchy in the Reign of Edward III," *TRHS,* 5th ser., 6 (1956), pp. 115–138.

[112] E. F. Jacob, "Petitions for Benefices from English Universities during the Great Schism," *ibid.,* 4th ser., 27 (1945), pp. 41–59; "On the Promotion of English University Clerks during the Later Middle Ages," *Journal of Ecclesiastical History,* 1:172–186 (July–October 1950).

[113] By W. Butler-Bowdon (1936) and by S. B. Meech and H. E. Allen (1940).

[114] *History,* 42:1–11 (February 1957).

something to counteract the prejudice which students pick up from older textbooks which treat this period as a mere interval between the thirteenth century and the Renaissance and Reformation.

V

It should be clear that the flow of publications on England in the later Middle Ages is far from being an attenuated trickle in a lost stream-bed. It is a tidal river in full flood. There is so much output and there are so many new currents that it is hard for the reviewer to select what is important and to keep his balance in surveying it. Not sterility but fecundity is the problem.

On the other hand, it is also clear that little "high history" (in the sense in which Galbraith used the term in his Creighton Lecture) has been written. This may be, as Trevor-Roper appears to imply, because medievalists sacrifice vitality on the altar of accuracy. Yet, the truer explanation would seem to be that we are not so fortunate in respect to our sources as the modern historian. For modern history, the sources are in more nearly contemporary language and handwriting, and many more are in print. He who runs to the right library may read. For medieval history the sources are largely still in manuscript, in spite of the great volume of texts and calendars published in the past twenty years. Moreover, they need more preliminary interpretation. We are in something like the position of the Renaissance humanist who, in trying to bring to life the classical world, found that his first task was to construct grammars and dictionaries.

Essential needs are texts which can be used wherever medieval scholars may have to live and carry on their work, as well as tool books to assist them in the search for materials and in their interpretation when found. We desperately need the new edition of Gross's great bibliography. It is reported to be near publication. It is good to hear that a new and more inclusive edition of the Royal Historical Society's *Handbook of British Chronology* (1939) is to be published soon. C. R. Cheney's *Handbook of Dates* (1945) has already been reprinted once. A new edition of Ekwall's *Concise Oxford Dictionary of English Place-Names* (Oxford, 1936; 4th ed., 1960) has just been published, and A. H. Smith's *English Place-Name Elements* (2 vols., Cambridge, Eng., 1956) is a recommended companion to it. The Selden Society will publish shortly a *Glossary of Law-French*, compiled and edited by Elsie Shanks and T. F. T. Plucknett. A. R. Wagner has compiled *A Catalogue of Eng-*

lish Medieval Rolls of Arms (Oxford, 1950). There is now available *A Guide to the Records in the Corporation of London Records Office and Guildhall Library Muniment Room* (1951), compiled by P. E. Jones. G. R. C. Davis has published *Medieval Cartularies of Great Britain: A Short Catalogue* (1958). E. L. C. Mullins is preparing a guide to publications of local record societies for the Royal Historical Society Guides and Handbook series. But we have, to date, only the first and introductory volume (already out of print) of a new guide to the Public Record Office promised to supersede Giuseppi.

Regrettable from the point of view of the American teacher of medieval English history is the fact that the volumes for the later Middle Ages in the magnificent new series of *English Historical Documents* have not yet come out. Too expensive for most students to buy, they are invaluable anthologies with scholarly introductions. Only three of the medieval Latin texts with translation currently being published by Nelson under the general editorship of V. H. Galbraith and R. A. B. Mynors are texts originally written after 1300.[115]

Cooperative history, in one form or another, has been attempted as a solution to the problem of building up a competent body of basic knowledge of medieval government with which to continue and complete the work of revising Stubbs. These attempts have met with varying degrees of success. Catastrophe dogged J. F. Willard's *The English Government at Work, 1327–1336* from the start, and in the three volumes which appeared, many aspects of the subject were left untouched. The King's Bench was not treated in the volume on central administration; neither was the Exchequer nor the Exchequer of Pleas nor (strange omission) the King himself. The Privy Seal was treated only sparingly in the introduction to the first volume, a surprising neglect considering the importance of the office in the period chosen for coverage. Even without these omissions, the balance was uneven, owing simply to the different levels of current knowledge about the various governmental agencies at the time of publication. This particular cooperative project cannot be considered an outstanding success, although, because of the great value of some of the essays, no one can rightly wish that it had not been undertaken.

A broader, more institutionalized cooperation seems to have been

---

[115] *The Annals of Ghent,* ed Hilda Johnstone (Edinburgh, 1951); *The De Moneta of Nicholas Oresme,* ed. C. Johnson (Edinburgh, 1956); *The Life of Edward the Second,* ed. N. Denholm-Young (Edinburgh, 1957).

achieved by the International Commission for the History of Representative and Parliamentary Institutions. Begun in 1936, it may not have "fulfilled its ideal." Yet it survived the war, and has achieved an effective exchange of historiographical information, has sponsored the publication of some studies of more than national interest, and has at least talked about comparative studies and common problems. The English-speaking world is appropriately represented by Helen Cam and J. S. Roskell.

C. H. McIlwain's retirement in 1945 from the Eaton Professorship of Science and Government in Harvard University might be taken as a turning point in the tide away from English medieval studies in America. It is not so much that there is a dearth of good scholars and teachers as that the subject has to fight hard for a toe hold in curricula in which students are invited to study such topics as the dynamics of Soviet power, underdevelopment among the African peoples, the renascence of Moslem culture, or parliamentary institutions in Asian countries, and when English history has been dropped altogether from the curriculum of most schools.

Other studies seem more immediate and important to American students. But who shall say in the vast world of knowledge which historical scholarship claims for its own what is most immediate and pertinent. The roots of American civilization are in medieval Europe, more particularly in England. In the long perspective of history, the last days of Richard II may well be of more profound significance than the last days of Hitler.

VI

Since this article was finished five years ago, a number of important books and articles have been published, yet Professor Knowles's monumental work on the religious orders remains the one *grand oeuvre* about medieval England which has been published in the last generation. E. F. Jacob's volume of the *Oxford History* [116] is the longest and most detailed. It conveys neither the balanced summary of scholarly knowledge and interpretation which distinguished May McKisack's volume nor the original new insights of the late Sir Maurice Powicke's. On the other hand, it does present for younger students a summation of the vast store of learning accumulated by an erudite scholar in a lifetime of study of the fifteenth century. The new Nelson series is not intended to compete with the *Oxford History* but rather to fill the need for an intro-

[116] E. F. Jacob, *The Fifteenth Century, 1399–1485* (Oxford, 1961).

ductory summary. G. A. Holmes's volume on the later Middle Ages is an excellent book for the purpose.[117]

Neither Bryce Lyon's *Constitutional and Legal History of Medieval England* (New York, 1960) nor Richardson's and Sayles's *Governance of England* (Edinburgh, 1963) fill the place vacated by Stubbs's *Constitutional History*. Lyon incorporates all the major revisions of Stubbs in a clear narrative and offers a comprehensive bibliography, but his modern vocabulary achieves the effect of attributing to medieval men ideas beyond their time. *The Governance of England* concerns itself only with the period from the Conquest to Magna Carta, and the authors are so busy damning Stubbs that they make him required preliminary reading for novices. G. R. Elton's challenging thesis about the emergence of the modern state in Britain has been subjected to the criticism of able medievalists and Tudor historians and has been modified and sharpened as a consequence.[118] Mr. Elton has made the most of an opportunity to strengthen his argument by arraying the documents themselves with a lucid commentary.[119] *Select Documents of English Constitutional History, 1307–1485* (1961), edited by S. B. Chrimes and A. L. Brown, though a good collection of constitutional documents, will not replace Stephenson and Marcham's book in American universities because of its narrow basis of selection and the absence of translation or commentary. The best substitute for Stubbs's third volume is Bertie Wilkinson's *Constitutional History of England in the Fifteenth Century* (1964). Professor Wilkinson has assembled and translated an excellent collection of documents, an invaluable collection of references to recent work, and he provides the student with sensible and balanced introductory matter to help him find his way through the documents.

The most controversial work has been done in economic and social history. The central problem is one opened up by Thorold Rogers in his *Six Centuries of Work and Wages,* first published eighty years ago.[120] Rogers showed that real wages doubled in the century after the Black Death, and he believed that the English working man was better off in the later Middle Ages than he ever was again until recent times. This discovery set economic historians the task of explaining the high level of

---

[117] George Holmes, *The Later Middle Ages* (Edinburgh, 1962).
[118] See for example, *PP*, 25 (July 1963); and see *ibid.,* 29 (November 1964), "The Tudor Revolution: A Reply," by G. R. Elton.
[119] G. R. Elton, *The Tudor Constitution: Documents and Commentary* (Cambridge, Eng., 1962).
[120] Reprinted with a new preface by G. D. H. Cole (1949).

wages in relation to obvious manifestations of social unrest in the four-teenth century and the many signs of declining trade and economic decay in towns and villages in the fifteenth. Professor Postan produced an ingenious explanation in two essays cited above.[121] His hypothesis, admittedly "Malthusian" in inspiration, is that a prolonged decline in population and a consequent scarcity of labor account for high wage levels in a time of falling rents and prices. Postan's tentative chronology posited a check to growth of population early in the fourteenth century owing to pressure on the means of subsistence, a marked decline follow-ing upon the Black Death, and a continuation of this trend until past the middle of the fifteenth century when economic recovery began to make possible its reversal.

Postan's analysis has received support from studies by Cambridge colleagues and students, notably Edward Miller [122] and J. Z. Titow,[123] and has been incorporated into general works of continental scholars concerned with the period.[124] On the other hand, it has been substan-tially challenged. Dr. Barbara Harvey, in a paper delivered before the Royal Historical Society (February 1965), presented widespread evi-dence against the thesis of early fourteenth-century population decline, and J. M. W. Bean, in "Plague, Population, and Economic Decline in the Later Middle Ages," [125] has reconsidered the geographic and chrono-logical incidence of the plague and come to the conclusion that, though precise evaluation is impossible, it is open to doubt that outbreaks of endemic plague led to a continuous decline of population in the late fourteenth and fifteenth centuries.

A new challenge has recently come from the History school of the London School of Economics. A. R. Bridbury, in a book entitled *Eco-nomic Growth: England in the Later Middle Ages*,[126] attacks the whole view of the later Middle Ages as a time of decline and sets forth the claims of the fifteenth century to a higher valuation than the thirteenth.

[121] See above, n. 66.
[122] Edward Miller, "The English Economy in the Thirteenth Century," *PP*, 28 (July 1964), pp. 21–40.
[123] J. Z. Titow, "Some Evidence of Thirteenth Century Population Increase," *EcHR*, 2d ser., 14:218–223 (December 1961); "Some Differences between Manors and their Effects on the Condition of the Peasant in the Thirteenth Century," *Agricultural History Review*, 10:1–13 (pt. 1, 1962).
[124] B. H. Slicher van Bath's *The Agrarian History of Western Europe, A. D. 500–1850* (1963) and Georges Duby's *L'économie rurale et la vie des campagnes dans l'Occident médiéval* (Paris, 1962).
[125] *EcHR*, 2d ser., 15:423–437 (April 1963).
[126] Originally published in 1962 by George Allen and Unwin: London; published in the United States in 1963 by the Humanities Press: New York.

Using trade statistics compiled by himself and his colleagues, especially Professor Carus-Wilson and Miss Olive Coleman, and possibly influenced by the questions introduced into the argument by the late E. A. Kosminsky,[127] Dr. Bridbury presents the late Middle Ages as a time in which new energies were released, forces so prodigious as to change entirely England's society and economy. Production per head was higher than in the thirteenth century, and, if value rather than quantity is examined, it can be seen that England maintained her exports despite growing domestic consumption. Whether they can accept a somewhat unusual definition of the term "economic growth," economic historians should welcome a challenge which prevents Professor Postan's hypothesis from becoming canon until it has been more fully examined.

The trend in English scholarship appears to be towards what might be called "grass-roots" history. H. P. R. Finberg, editor of the *Agricultural History Review* inaugurated in 1953, promises us ultimately "a complete new social and economic history of rural England, in seven volumes, more or less." [128] R. H. Hilton, editor for the medieval volume, in "The Content and Sources of English Agrarian History before 1500," [129] warns against the application of modern concepts of economic fluctuation to a pre-industrial economy without more knowledge than we have of peasant farming. He recommends "an attempt to define regional economies of the country, and, on this basis to study the distribution of large, medium-sized and small estates, the variations in social status, the growth of local markets and specialization of production, and the changing relationships of social classes." New studies of individual estates or groups of them show the value of a wider interest in regions.[130] The

---

[127] "Peut-on considérer le XIV et le XV siècles comme l'époque de la décadence de l'économie européenne?" in *Studi in Onore di Armando Sapori* (Milan, 1957), I, pp. 553–569.

[128] *Agricultural History Review*, 4:2–3 (pt. 1, 1956).

[129] *Agricultural History Review*, 3:3–14 (pt. 1, 1955).

[130] Among the most interesting are the following: P. F. Brandon, "Arable Farming in a Sussex Scarp-Foot Parish during the late Middle Ages," *Sussex Archaelogical Collection*, 100 (1962), pp. 60–72, which shows that in 1382–1383, Alciston had the same acreage under crops as in the first quarter of the thirteenth century and that the lowest ebb was in 1470–1485; E. M. Carus-Wilson, "Evidences of Industrial Growth on Some Fifteenth Century Manors," *EcHR*, 2d ser., 12:190–205 (December 1959); R. H. Hilton, *The Stoneleigh Leger Book*, Dugdale Society, 24 (1960), which indicates an increase in large holdings but no difficulty in leasing out lands after the Black Death; K. C. Newton, *Thaxted in the Fourteenth Century* . . . , Essex County Council (1960), which illustrates the growth of a large urban settlement within the manor during the fourteenth century and the disintegration of the old manorial order by 1393; M. R. Postgate, "The Field Systems of Breckland," *Agricultural History Review*, 10:80–101 (pt. 2, 1962), which shows the variations which may occur in traditional field patterns in adapting them to local

most exciting of regional studies to date is a piece of joint research by a botanist, an engineer, and assorted archaeologists and geographers into *The Making of the Broads,* presented in book form in the Research Series of the Royal Geographical Society.[131] They discovered that intensive peat-cutting in medieval centuries followed by "a rather sudden marine transgression," created what had been assumed to be a nature-made region. This book is a triumph of interdisciplinary cooperation.

Professor Carus-Wilson has followed up her joint study (with Miss Coleman) of *England's Export Trade, 1275–1543* (Oxford, 1963) with the Ford Lectures for 1965. In these she presented a summation of her research to date with vivid pictorial illustration. Two articles of more than local interest suggest further lines of investigation of England's trade in the later Middle Ages. P. C. Jones, in a paper presented to the Cumberland and Westmoreland Antiquarian and Archaeological Society (*Transactions,* 54 [1954], pp. 65–84) cites evidence, mainly from Southampton Cloth Hall accounts, showing that Kendalmen regularly visited this port with their pack-horses from the late fifteenth to the middle of the sixteenth century to exchange north-country woolens for such foreign products as raisins, figs, oranges, dyes, alum, and canvas. And Miss G. V. Scammell makes clear the need for more study of English shipping in a brief article concluding that East coast shipping was "in a healthy condition" at the end of our period, though it is impossible to speak precisely without more knowledge of freights earned from foreign sources and other related matters.[132] Dr. R. L. Baker, in a study of English customs administration, 1307 to 1343,[133] attributes what he describes as

---

soil conditions and suggests the need for more attention to such local variations; A. H. Denney, *The Sibton Abbey Estates. Select Documents, 1325–1509,* Suffolk Records Society (1960), which illustrates a more conventional pattern. *Carte Nativorum: A Peterborough Abbey Cartulary of the Fourteenth Century,* edited by C. N. L. Brooke and M. M. Postan (Oxford, 1960) is an interesting document showing evidence of an active peasant land market in the twelfth and thirteenth centuries. Joan Thirsk's "Industries in the Countryside," in *Essays in the Economic and Social History of Tudor and Stuart England in Honour of R. H. Tawney,* edited by F. J. Fisher (Cambridge, Eng., 1961), demonstrates that types of agriculture, social organization, as well as local resources and general trends must be taken into account in studying the early growth of industry in the countryside.

[131] Joyce Lambert *et al., The Making of the Broads: A Reconsideration of Their Origin in the Light of New Evidence,* Royal Geographic Society, Research Series, no. 3 (1960).

[132] G. V. Scammell, "English Merchant Shipping at the End of the Middle Ages: Some East Coast Evidence," *EcHR,* 2d ser., 13:327–343 (April 1961).

[133] R. L. Baker, *The English Customs Service, 1307–1343: A Study of Medieval Administration,* in *Transactions of the American Philosophical Society,* new ser., 51 (Philadelphia, 1961).

the "failure of the English Customs service," to the failure of English rulers to build up a professional bureaucracy on the model of their French contemporaries.

The third volume of the *Cambridge Economic History* has finally come out (1963) lacking considerable portions of the material originally projected. The sections which deal with England are embedded in chapters by A. B. Hibbert, Sylvia Thrupp, and Edward Miller on late medieval policies with regard to economic matters. The value of seeing English developments within the larger European context is illustrated not only in this volume but also in Georges Duby's *L'économie rurale et la vie des campagnes dans l'Occident médiéval* (Paris, 1962).

The lack noted earlier of a good history for medieval London has been admirably filled in part by Gwyn A. Williams' *Medieval London: From Commune to Capital* (1963), a sound and scholarly study of the city in the critical period of its transition from communal rebellion against royal authority to national capital. For an authoritative narrative of the city's development which will incorporate the materials presented in specialized studies of late medieval London and in the calendars of London records (begun by Dr. A. H. Thomas, contributed to by Dr. Helena M. Chew, and completed for plea and memoranda rolls to 1482 by P. E. Jones) [134] we have still to wait.

The social and economic effects of war on English society from 1300 to 1600 were the subject of the fourth *Past and Present* conference at Birkbeck College in July 1961,[135] and the subject "Work and Leisure in Pre-Industrial Society" stirred some useful discussion at a more recent conference.[136] A debate between J. C. Holt and Maurice Keen as to whether Robin Hood was originally an aristocratic or a peasant hero led Keen to make a comprehensive study of *The Outlaws of Medieval Legend* (1961) but leaves Robin just about where he was before, despite Keen's thesis—that is, a popular favorite with all ages and classes of society.

The outlook in legal history is not so dim as I saw it in 1960. Although the late Professor Plucknett had, owing to progressive ill health, to give up active editorship for the Selden Society, the work carried on by younger colleagues is bearing a full harvest. Professor Milsom's edition of *Novae Narrationes* based on Miss Shanks's transcripts appeared late

[134] *Calendar of Plea and Memoranda Rolls. A.D. 1458–1482,* ed. P. E. Jones (Cambridge, Eng., 1961).

[135] *PP,* 22 (July 1962), pp. 3–35.

[136] "The Cost of the Hundred Years War," etc., *PP,* 29 (April 1964).

in 1963. Professor J. P. Collas' *Year Books of 12 Edward II* has been shipped out to the membership. Sayles's sixth volume of *Select Cases in the Court of King's Bench,* and Lady Stenton's further two volumes of *Pleas before the King or His Justices, 1203–1212,* are due to appear during the next two years. H. G. Richardson's *Bracton: The Problem of His Text* (1965) and C. H. S. Fifoot's new edition of the *Letters of F. W. Maitland* (1965) have been published in the supplementary series. Professor Thorne has made substantial progress on the new edition with translation of the full and corrected text of Bracton and is preparing a new edition of Maitland's *Collected Papers.* In the Cambridge Legal History series, two valuable recent volumes are R. F. Hunnisett's *The Medieval Coroner* (1962) and D. E. C. Yale's edition of Lord Nottingham's treatises on Chancery and Equity (1965). A. W. B. Simpson has written a clear and readable *Introduction to the History of the Land Law* (Oxford, 1961). Charles M. Gray's *Copyhold, Equity, and the Common Law* (Cambridge, Mass., 1963) explores the process whereby the courts of common law came to accept responsibility for protection of copyhold rights.

Wyclif and the Lollard movement have received some recent attention,[137] and it is clear that there is more to be understood both about the man and the movement when a balance has been struck between the adulation of earlier Protestant historians and the perhaps unduly severe reaction against it. J. C. Dickinson has given us a gentle book on *Monastic Life in Medieval England* (New York, 1962), one that is particularly useful in conveying the atmosphere of life in the cloister to American students who cannot visit the ruins of Glastonbury on their free week ends. Beryl Smalley has followed up her *Study of the Bible in the Middle Ages* (Oxford, 1941) with a witty and scholarly book about the *English Friars and Antiquity in the Early Fourteenth Century* (New York, 1960). Professor Knowles, having completed his magnum opus, has culled from it and published in a separate small volume (with two additions) twenty-five portraits of medieval saints, scholars, and ecclesiastical administrators.[138] Moreover, a group, by no means complete, of his students and admirers has presented him with the best possible tribute to so distinguished a historian, a collection of his own essays headed

[137] J. A. Robson, *Wyclif and the Oxford Schools* (Cambridge, Eng., 1961); Margaret Aston, "Lollardy and the Reformation: Survival or Revival?" *History,* 49:149–170 (June 1964). And see the early chapters of A. G. Dickens, *The English Reformation* (1964) and his "Heresy and the Origins of English Protestantism," *Britain and the Netherlands,* ed. J. S. Bromley and E. H. Kossman (Utrecht, 1962).

[138] *Saints and Scholars* (Cambridge, Eng., 1962).

by "The Historian and Character," his inaugural address as Regius Professor of Modern History in the University of Cambridge. A re-reading of this address helps the student to see that, in this historian's lifework, we have a truly distinguished fulfillment of an explicitly stated objective.[139]

The long-awaited revision of Giuseppi's *Guide to the Public Records* prepared under the editorship of H. N. Blakiston, J. R. Ede, and L. C. Hector was published late in 1963,[140] and a new edition is already expected. Her Majesty's Stationery Office has also published a handsome new volume by R. Allen Brown, H. M. Colvin, and A. J. Taylor on the medieval history of the King's Works.[141] The *Victoria County History* continues on its majestic course with ten new volumes published since 1960. There are many reprints of works long unavailable, the most valuable being without question the Record Commission edition of the *Statutes of the Realm* reprinted from the old forms by Dawson of Pall Mall, London.

Reviewing again the whole record of publication on the late Middle Ages in England for the last generation, it strikes me that, while hobnobbing with scholars in other disciplines is good for historians, useful and even distinguished work can still happily be achieved by the scholar who sets himself a limited objective but achieves it wholly and triumphantly.

[139] *The Historian and Character and Other Essays* (Cambridge, Eng., 1963).
[140] *Guide to the Contents of the Public Record Office*, in 2 vols.
[141] *The History of the King's Works. The Middle Ages*, 2 vols. (1963).

The "Taste for Tudors"
since 1940

❖

LACEY BALDWIN SMITH

$\mathbb{P}$ROFESSOR F. J. FISHER wrote in 1940
that the twentieth century has been "busily recreating the sixteenth century in its own image."[1] Historical re-evaluation is always in part narcissistic. Two world wars have left their scars on our view of history and, if nothing else, have given us insights into the Tudor age which, like our own, faced ideological wars of survival.[2] The quest for economic and military security and the dream of the welfare state have led the twentieth century to forsake not only the ethical and institutional standards of the nineteenth century but also to deny its interpretation of history. The ancient shibboleths, the familiar landmarks of Tudor history, and the comfortable generalizations about despotism, mercantilism, and "new monarchy" are all being swept aside by a generation of historians who claim greater understanding of the past.[3]

Experience with the aims, methods, and weaknesses of state planning has shifted historical interest from "Whig" reliance upon the institutional

[Reprinted from *Studies in the Renaissance*, 7 (1960), pp. 167–183].

[1] *EcHR*, 10:96 (1940).

[2] This essay deals primarily with the period from Henry VII through Mary, since a separate essay will be devoted to the reign of Elizabeth. Since the new edition of Conyers Read's *Bibliography of British History: Tudor Period, 1485–1603* (Oxford, 1959), larger than the earlier by about one-half, includes a full review of historical scholarship to date, there seems to be no particular merit in achieving completeness, and instead I have endeavored to indicate the nature and direction of Tudor scholarship throughout the last two decades. Readers who are interested in a somewhat less historically oriented bibliography should consult Elizabeth Nugent, *The Thought and Culture of the English Renaissance* (Cambridge, Eng., 1956).

[3] Much of modern scholarship has been incorporated into three fine textbooks which have appeared during the last decade. S. T. Bindoff, *Tudor England* (Harmondsworth, 1950) is a brilliant synthesis emphasizing the economic aspects of Tudor life. J. D. Mackie, *The Earlier Tudors, 1485–1558* (Oxford, 1952) is somewhat more orthodox in its approach, and G. R. Elton, *England under the Tudors* (1955) is a sparkling but controversial achievement of compression.

history of parliament to a more contemporary preoccupation with the function of government, the structure of society, and the actual operation of personality within the bureaucratic organization. The Smithfield fires which so shocked the religious and moral sensibilities of our Victorian forefathers and were viewed by them as appalling examples of bigotry and despotism have lost some of their sensationalism in a world whose sense of proportion has been warped by the knowledge of Dachau and Buchenwald. Somehow the description "despotic" no longer seems to be an adequate or even a just characterization of Tudor government and methods. Unconsciously, we associate the great "Tudor despots" with some of the more lurid examples of modern tyranny, and, in contrast, the past seems considerably more civilized than the present. Moreover, we are becoming increasingly aware that Henry VIII was a "constitutional monarch," limited and ruling by divine, natural, and common law.

More and more we see mirrored in the past the problems of the present, and the ideological convulsions of the twentieth century seem to have their prototypes in the sixteenth. More accustomed than our Edwardian grandfathers to the claims of absolute truth, we can better appreciate the strife over religious verity set loose by the Reformation. Modern wars waged in the name of secularized theologies have revealed the essential dilemma of the sixteenth century—the union of political systems with dogmatic truth and the dangerous association that can be made between heresy and treason. As E. G. Rupp has written: there was in the past a tendency "to deplore the sweat and heat of this battle for 'opinions'" until "the advent of the new Wars of (Secular) Religion" reintroduced the possibility of "truths worth dying for." [4] Our modern "taste for Tudors" is the result of a sense of rapport which has produced a new appreciation of the sixteenth century.

II

The most striking development during the last two decades has been the re-evaluation of the term "Tudor despotism." Crudely, the "Whig" view can be stated as follows: a Lancastrian parliamentary experiment, which collapsed under the impact of economic, political, and moral ineptitude, was followed by Henry VII who created the "new monarchy,"

---

[4] E. G. Rupp, *Studies in the Making of the English Protestant Tradition* (Cambridge, Eng., 1947), pp. xiv–xv.

ruled despotically, curbed the nobility, cultivated the mercantile and landed classes, and sacrificed liberty for security. Total despotism was finally achieved under Henry VIII, who destroyed the independence of the medieval Catholic church of Rome as his father had crushed the independence of the feudal baronage. Henry's ultimate act of violence to the medieval past was accomplished by purchasing the support of the "new men" of the reign by lavishing upon them the loot of the monastic lands and by making Parliament a partner to the vast social, economic, and religious revolution of the reign. Henry VIII sired a vigorous House of Commons and Elizabeth I ruled it by love and tact, but the Stuarts reaped what the Tudors had sown—the destruction of personal despotism by a parliament grown accustomed to being called upon to settle the affairs of God and man and whose members had grown fat upon the loot of the church property. Like the walls of Jericho, this "Whig" interpretation is tumbling down.

The phrase "new monarchy" was coined by John Richard Green in 1876 to signal the end of the medieval era both in England and Europe. Today, however, the Tudor period is losing most of its tidiness; medievalism persists in encroaching upon the Tudor preserve while the newness of the "new monarchy" is constantly being pushed back into the decades before 1485. Two areas of attack upon the concept of a "new monarchy" are discernible. First, there is the view that portrays Henry VII as part of the Yorkist pattern of royal development. Presumably, whatever was new under the Tudors had been inherited from Edward IV and Richard III. In this connection see R. Somerville, *History of the Duchy of Lancaster* (1953); F. W. Brooks, *The Council of the North*, Historical Association Publication G25 (1953); B. P. Wolffe, "The Management of English Royal Estates under the Yorkist Kings," *EHR*, 71 (1956); and J. R. Lander, "Edward IV: The Modern Legend: And a Revision," *History*, new ser., 41 (1956).[5] The second thesis pictures the first Tudor monarch as being essentially a medieval man who had as his model Henry II or Edward I. In his *England under the Tudors* (1955), G. R. Elton presents the medievalist's case, arguing that Henry VII's monarchy "was not essentially different" from that of Edward I and that "it fulfilled much the same ambitions and purpose with much the same

[5] J. R. Lander, "The Yorkist Council and Administration, 1461–1485," *EHR*, 73 (1958), shows how elusive the truth can be about the fifteenth century if only because of the frustrating scarcity of material. See also S. E. Lehmberg, "Star Chamber: 1485–1509," *HLQ*, 24 (1961).

instruments" (p. 11). While the Yorkists claim the newness of the Tudor monarchs for themselves, the medievalists tend to postpone any fundamental break with the past until the decade of the 1530's. Consequently, A. R. Myers (*England in the Late Middle Ages,* Harmondsworth, 1952) does not conclude the medieval period until the Reformation, and Mr. Elton (*The Tudor Revolution in Government,* Cambridge, Eng., 1953) equates the concept of a "new monarchy" with the growth of a bureaucratic administration separate from the personality of the sovereign and with a life and independence of its own—in other words, a national as opposed to a royal government. This "revolution," presumably, was originally the work of Thomas Cromwell and was further developed by the great Elizabethan statesmen. The Elton interpretation has not been without its critics, and such has been Elton's reputation that *Past and Present* (No. 25, July 1963) dedicated almost an entire issue to a critical discussion of the problem of "A Revolution in Tudor History."

In the midst of this clamor to dismiss the "new monarchy," one author has evinced a certain reluctance to throw out the baby with the bath water. W. C. Richardson (*Tudor Chamber Administration, 1485–1547,* Baton Rouge, La., 1952), detects considerable originality under Henry VII in terms of the thoroughness of Tudor administration and the development of chamber government, and he suggests that there was a "system" to Tudor chamber government long before Thomas Cromwell appeared in his rôle of administrative genius. Professor Richardson's work on the revival and extensive, almost revolutionary, use of feudal techniques on the part of the first Tudors has been further studied as it pertains to the expansion of the royal prerogative and the development of fiscal feudalism. (See particularly J. Hurstfield, "The Revival of Feudalism in Early Tudor England," *History,* new ser., 37 [1952], and S. E. Thorne's edition of Robert Constable, *Prerogativa Regis,* New Haven, Conn., 1949.) [6]

If the "new monarchy" has turned out to be somewhat less than new, we can at least say that Henry VII has recently been exposed to considerable new evaluation. The old notion of a cold, thin-lipped, Machiavellian sovereign with the mind of an actuary and the morals of an Italian banker is rapidly receding before the light spread by G. R. Elton

---

[6] Many of the works cited should be read in the light of Anthony Steel, "The Financial Background of the Wars of the Roses," *History,* new ser., 40 (1955), which is a convenient summary of his book, *The Receipt of the Exchequer, 1377–1485* (Cambridge, Eng., 1954).

("Henry VII: Rapacity and Remorse," *Historical Journal* 1 [1958]) and C. Morris (*The Tudors,* New York, 1957).[7] Though Henry has been rescued from the limbo of a dehumanized monarch, he has been the subject of current criticism ever since the fascinating thesis that Henry, not Richard III, might have murdered the little princes in the Tower hit the popular press (J. Tey, *The Daughter of Time,* 1951).[8] In this connection, Henry still awaits his apologia other than A. R. Myers's short article, "The Character of Richard III" (*History Today,* 4, 1954).

If modern historians are denying the existence of a "new monarchy" they are also casting doubt upon the existence of Tudor tyranny. The nineteenth-century image of a fully structured and despotic government does not bear scrutiny. Research into the administrative details of government and analysis of the operation of the Tudor bureaucratic system presents quite a different picture. To Elton's and Richardson's accounts of early Tudor government must be added the warning of J. R. Hooker, "Some Cautionary Notes on Henry VII's Household and Chamber 'System'" (*Speculum,* 33, 1958), in which the author observes that it is extraordinarily difficult to generalize about the nature of Tudor government since the question of office is often a matter of the personality of the officeholder and "the performer becomes inseparable from the performance" (p. 75).[9] Finally, law enforcement and law effectiveness, those two most elusive topics, have been in part touched upon by two important and pioneer articles: M. W. Beresford, "The Common Informer, the Penal Statutes, and Economic Regulation" (*EcHR,* 2d ser., 10, 1957),[10] and Elton, "Informing for Profit: A Sidelight on Tudor Methods of Law-enforcement" (*CHJ,* 11, 1954).[11]

Though much of the testimony being gleaned by Messrs. Elton, Wolffe, Hooker, *et al.* pictures a random, undirected mechanism simply evolving out of expediency and the actions of "individuals working in a

[7] Elton's view of Henry VII has been criticized by J. P. Cooper, "Henry VII's Last Years Reconsidered," *Historical Journal,* 2 (1959). See Elton's answer: "Henry VII: A Restatement," *ibid.,* 4 (1961).

[8] A more scholarly analysis and indictment of Henry VII can be found in P. M. Kendall, *Richard the Third* (1955), Appendix I, "Who Murdered the 'Little Princes'?" See also W. G. Zeeveld, "A Tudor Defense of Richard III," *PMLA,* 55 (1940).

[9] See Sybil Jack and R. S. Schofield, "Four Early Tudor Financial Memoranda," *BIHR,* 36 (1963).

[10] Another aspect of the Tudors' difficulties with law corruption, evasion and enforcement is treated by G. D. Ramsay, "The Smuggler's Trade: A Neglected Aspect of English Commercial Development," *TRHS,* 5th ser., 2 (1952).

[11] More of the same can be found in G. R. Elton, *Star Chamber Stories* (1958).

somewhat unorganized and haphazard manner," [12] certain broad outlines are still discernible, especially in matters of finance. W. C. Richardson ("Some Financial Expedients of Henry VIII," *EcHR*, 2d ser., 7, 1954), emphasizes the opportunistic aspects of Henry's government,[13] but two other groups of studies show that possibly there was considerably more system than previously thought.[14] There is growing evidence that the sale of monastic lands was somewhat more rational, businesslike, and profitable than heretofore suspected, and that Henry VIII was a more astute businessman than many historians are willing to credit. (See J. A. Youings, "The Terms of the Disposal of the Devon Monastic Lands, 1536–58," *EHR*, 60, 1954, and H. J. Habakkuk, "The Market for Monastic Property, 1539–1603," *EcHR*, 2d ser., 10, 1958). It is also becoming apparent that there was a concerted effort on the part of the government to increase its feudal revenues, especially those from wardship. (See three articles by J. Hurstfield, "Revival of Feudalism in Early Tudor England," *History*, new ser., 37, 1952; "The Profits of Fiscal Feudalism, 1541–1602," *EcHR*, 2d ser., 8, 1955; "Corruption and Reform under Edward VI and Mary: The Example of Wardship," *EHR*, 68, 1953; also H. E. Bell, *An Introduction to the History and Records of the Court of Wards and Liveries,* Cambridge, Eng., 1953.)

The results of more careful inspection of the realities of Tudor government has tended to confuse the picture. On one subject, however, there is substantial agreement; the description "despotic" no longer is considered an accurate or an adequate term to apply to the Tudor governmental process either in fact or in theory. It may have been personal government but it certainly was not tyrannical or absolute.[15] Exactly what the Tudor system was is still a matter of conjecture and dispute,

---

[12] G. R. Elton, *The Tudor Revolution in Government* (Cambridge, Eng., 1953), p. 9.

[13] See also G. Hammersley, "The Crown Woods and Their Exploitation in the Sixteenth and Seventeenth Centuries," *BIHR*, 30 (1957).

[14] B. P. Wolffe, "Henry VII's Land Revenues and Chamber Finance," *EHR*, 79 (1964), has destroyed one of the most persistent myths about the first Tudor: the vast surplus and Treasure Trove which he bequeathed his sons. Instead of the legendary £1,800,000 it now appears to be closer to £200,000 in jewels and plate and possibly an actual deficit in hard cash.

[15] W. O. Williams, *Tudor Gwynedd* (1958), shows how little effect Henry VIII's legislation really had upon social change in Wales or how little the Act of Union actually modified the ancient administrative methods. This work is the result of and was originally the introduction to Mr. Williams' *Calendar of the Caernarvonshire Quarter Sessions Records, 1541–58,* 1 (Caernarvonshire Historical Society, 1956).

and on the theoretical side the subject has received some, but certainly not sufficient, investigation.[16] As usual, Mr. Elton has decided views as to the constitutional and medieval nature of Tudor political theory and the structure of sixteenth-century kingship. (See his "Political Creed of Thomas Cromwell," *TRHS*, 5th ser., 6, 1956.) Besides Elton's work there is F. Le Van Baumer, *The Early Tudor Theory of Kingship* (New Haven, Conn., 1940); W. G. Zeeveld, *Foundations of Tudor Policy* (Cambridge, Mass., 1948); E. H. Kantorowicz's controversial and at times brilliant account, *The King's Two Bodies: A Study in Mediaeval Political Theology* (Princeton, N.J., 1957); and finally, C. Morris' sparkling and concise *Political Thought in England: Tyndale to Hooker* (1953). In the opposite camp are L. B. Smith, "English Treason Trials and Confessions in the Sixteenth Century" (*Journal of the History of Ideas*, 15, 1954), who suggests that Tudor England manifests some of the less pleasant mental aspects of modern totalitarianism, and L. Stone, "Political Programme of Thomas Cromwell" (*BIHR*, 24, 1951), who argues that both the common law and Parliament were in very real danger "of extinction by the armed autocracy of the efficient despot" (p. 9).[17]

The questions of Tudor despotism, state policy, and governmental efficiency have also been handled from the standpoint of economics in a series of important articles by Fisher, Stone, and Nef.[18] The opinions of these three historians represent a major revision of the Edwardian and Victorian picture of Tudor England as a highly organized, paternalistic, and despotic state in which mercantilistic laws and governmental regulation of most aspects of life effectually produced what the nineteenth century regarded as a regimented society. The idea of mercantilism as an effective economic force was under attack long before 1940 by those who pointed out that law enforcement and government policy are two quite different things.[19] Professor F. J. Fisher in his "Commercial Trends and Policy in Sixteenth-Century England" (*EcHR*, 10, 1940) fur-

[16] The best discussions of the operation of early Tudor government and the balance between statute, precedent, and prerogative are W. H. Dunham's articles: "Wolsey's Rule of the King's Whole Council," *AHR*, 49 (1944); "Henry VIII's Whole Council and Its Parts," *HLQ*, 7 (1943); and "Regal Power and the Rule of Law: A Tudor Paradox," *JBS*, 4 (1964).

[17] See G. R. Elton's "Parliamentary Drafts, 1529–1540," *BIHR*, 25 (1952).

[18] J. U. Nef, "War and Economic Progress, 1540–1640," *EcHR*, 12 (1942).

[19] For example, see A. Marshall, *Industry and Trade* (1919), pp. 719–720. For more recent works see: P. Ramsey, "Overseas Trade in the Reign of Henry VIII:

ther modified the orthodox belief by indicating that state control of economic life was in direct proportion to the condition of the overseas trade
and the general state of prosperity; boom periods produced liberal government policy and free trade while depression years brought forth state
control of exports, imports, and exchange in much the same fashion as
the great depression of the 1930's produced economic nationalism in almost every nation in the world. Professor Fisher's theories have in part
been challenged by L. Stone, "State Control in Sixteenth-Century England" (*EcHR*, 17, 1947), who argues that Tudor economic laws were
more effective than is sometimes thought, and that the motive for government regulation was the quest for security both from social revolution at home and military attack from abroad and was not merely a
matter of economic prosperity.

The position of Tudor economic theory, purpose of state regulation,
and manipulation of the economic and social impulses of life are intimately associated with political theory while the gulf that existed between theoretical aims and actual law enforcement was constantly miti-
gating and distorting the realities of Tudor planned economy. Both
problems deserve further study.[20] An interesting start, however, has
been made by Mr. Elton in "An Early Tudor Poor Law" (*EcHR*, 2d ser.,
6, 1953), which reveals both the modernity and the extent of welfare
legislation under Henry VIII.

In the area of state organization, operation, and theory, one problem
remains—that of personality and responsibility. Most writers emphasize
the personal nature of Tudor government, but the question arises:
whose personality dominated, king's or minister's? More specifically, was
it Cromwell or Henry VIII who initiated and guided the policies that
underlay the Reformation? Only Mr. Elton ("King or Minister?: The
Man behind the Henrician Reformation," *History*, 39, 1954), in league
with Messrs. Parker, Ogle, and Zeeveld,[21] has dared to suggest that

---

The Evidence of Customs Accounts," *EcHR*, 2d ser., 6 (1953), and R. de Roover,
Gresham on Foreign Exchange: An Essay on Early English Mercantilism (Cambridge, Mass., 1949).

[20] See two articles by A. A. Ruddock, "London Capitalists and the Decline of
Southampton in the Early Tudor Period," *EcHR*, 2d ser., 2 (1949), and "The
Earliest Records of the High Court of Admiralty, 1515–1558," *BIHR*, 22 (1949);
also G. Connell-Smith, *Forerunners of Drake* (1954), which is the story of Anglo-
Spanish trade relations and their connection with foreign policy, 1485–1558.

[21] T. M. Parker, "Was Thomas Cromwell a Machiavellian?" *Journal of Ecclesias-
tical History*, 1 (1950) (Parker says yes); A. Ogle, *The Tragedy of the Lollards'
Tower* (Oxford, 1949); W. G. Zeeveld, "Thomas Starkey and the Cromwellian
Polity," *JMH*, 15 (1943).

Pollard's classic account of Henry as the determined intelligence direct-
ing the Reformation may be wrong.[22] This is a controversy only recently
joined; the returns are not yet all in, and we must wait for further arguments such as Elton's "The Evolution of a Reformation Statute" (*EHR*,
64, 1949).

III

Reformation scholarship is approximately where it was four hundred
years ago; there is still almost complete inability on the part of Catholics
and Protestants to comprehend their opponents' points of view. The controversy is less intense than in the past and we no longer burn the participants. Though time may have mellowed the protagonists, it has not,
however, changed the issues.[23] For Catholics the Reformation remains a
bad thing and Henry VIII a bad man; conversely, Protestants, though
somewhat uncertain on the subject of Henry, are unanimous in their ap-
proval of the break with Rome. One thing that both faiths have in
common is a growing interest in the religious problems of the century,
and, as Conyers Read's new edition of his bibliography of Tudor history
indicates, the field of religion is growing considerably faster than most.
During the last fifteen years ecclesiastical affairs have lagged behind cultural and social subjects, which have risen 115 per cent, but religious
topics have increased at almost twice the rate of economic history, which
has risen only 30 per cent.

The most judicious recent accounts of the religious revolution in England are by clerics. E. G. Rupp (*The English Protestant Tradition*,
Cambridge, Eng., 1947) is sympathetic to the reformers and their aims,
and, along with A. Ogle (*The Tragedy of the Lollards' Tower*, Oxford,
1949),[24] emphasizes the Lollard and indigenous nature of the religious
protest. H. Maynard Smith, *Henry VIII and the Reformation* (1948) is
a straightforward Anglican approach, and Philip Hughes, *The Reformation in England* (1950–54) is by far the best work on the subject and at
the same time the fairest Catholic account of the whole Reformation
period.[25] To these general narratives should be added two briefer stud-

---

[22] For the opposite view see R. Koebner, " 'The Imperial Crown of This Realm':
Henry VIII, Constantine the Great, and Polydore Vergil," *BIHR*, 26 (1953).

[23] K. Booth, "The Problem of the Breach with Rome, 1529–34," *The Month*,
new ser., 10 (1953).

[24] See also H. G. Russell, "Lollard Opposition to Oaths by Creatures," *AHR*, 51
(1946).

[25] See also Dom David Knowles's monumental third volume of his *Religious
Orders in England: The Tudor Age* (1961).

ies by laymen—F. M. Powicke, *The Reformation in England* (1941), which is the work of a fine medievalist who sees the Reformation as an act of state, and L. B. Smith, "The Reformation and the Decay of Medieval Ideals" (*Church History*, 24, 1955), which views the religious revolution as part of the spiritual collapse of medieval Christendom. A. G. Dickens, *Lollards and Protestants in the Diocese of York 1509–1558* (1959) is a detailed and penetrating study of indigenous religious protest in the north of England.[26]

The lessons and experiences of the twentieth century have also had their impact upon the religious field of history. For better or worse, modern historians have imposed the present upon the past. The association between heresy and treason, and the interplay between religious ideologies and social and economic grievances are scarcely new topics. Recently, however, there has been renewed interest in the Tudor efforts to curb and control the wave of socially and religiously disturbing ideas set loose by the Reformation. H. C. White, *Social Criticism in Popular Religious Literature in the Sixteenth Century* (New York, 1944) is a useful and suggestive compilation of quotations; L. B. Smith, *Tudor Prelates and Politics* (Princeton, N.J., 1953) discusses the government's fear that religious revolution in the church would produce social revolution in the state; M. MacLure, *The Paul's Cross Sermons, 1534–1642* (Toronto, 1958) studies the official sermon as an instrument of indoctrination and control of the popular mind; and C. C. Butterworth, *The English Primers (1529–1545)* (Philadelphia, 1953) is a detailed analysis of the English primer as one of the forces that shaped the public mind and as one of the means by which the government hoped to mold and guide the religious upheaval of the age.

IV

The twentieth century's conception of Tudor England may be in the process of fundamental change but one fact remains constant—the popularity of Tudor biography. If anything, the "taste for Tudors" is on the increase and so is the number of amateur historians who see in the splendor and vitality of Tudor personality a ready sale for their books. The two most prolific of the popular authors in current years have been Philip Lindsay [27] and Theodore Maynard.[28] A relative newcomer is Sir

[26] Cf. Margaret Aston, "Lollardy and the Reformation: Survival or Revival," *History*, 49 (1964).

[27] *The Secret of Henry the Eighth* (1953); *The Queen Maker: A Portrait of John Dudley* (1951).

[28] *Henry the Eighth* (Milwaukee, Wis., 1949); *Humanist as Hero: The Life of*

Arthur MacNalty [29] who has revived a favorite question: medically speaking, what was wrong with Henry VIII? The thesis that he sustained a brain injury as a consequence of a fall from his horse is considerably more convincing than the older argument that the king had syphilis. More recently, two other works have appeared: C. F. Ferguson, *Naked to Mine Enemies: The Life of Cardinal Wolsey* (Boston, Mass., 1958) and H. W. Chapman, *The Last Tudor King: A Study of Edward VI* (1958), both of which are biographies by nonprofessionals. [30]

Strangely enough the professional historians have been noticeably inactive in the field of biography, and by and large the giants of a generation ago have remained unchallenged. Pollard's *Henry VIII* (1905), *Thomas Cranmer* (New York, 1904), and *Wolsey* (1929), continue to be the classic accounts. R. W. Chambers, *Thomas More* (1935) and J. A. Muller, *Stephen Gardiner and the Tudor Reaction* (1926) remain unrivaled. Only the lesser figures have attracted revisionist biographies and we must add to the list of old masters the names of H. F. M. Prescott, *A Spanish Tudor: The Life of 'Bloody Mary'* (1940), P. M. Kendall, *Richard the Third* (1955), G. Mattingly, *Catherine of Aragon* (Boston, Mass., 1941), W. Schenk, *Reginald Pole, Cardinal of England* (1950), and L. B. Smith, *A Tudor Tragedy, the Life and Times of Catherine Howard* (1961).

Clerical figures continue to receive relatively greater attention than lay, and recently Cranmer, [31] Latimer, [32] Ridley, [33] Ponet, [34] and Bucer [35] have all found their biographers. The man, however, who continues to exercise the greatest fascination is Sir Thomas More, who is burdened with an ever-increasing bibliography. [36] The enigma of More the hu-

---

Sir Thomas More (New York, 1947); *The Crown and the Cross: A Biography of Thomas Cromwell* (New York, 1950); *The Life of Thomas Cranmer* (Chicago, 1956); *Bloody Mary* (Milwaukee, Wis., 1958). Mr. Maynard espouses the liberal Catholic view.

[29] *Henry VIII, a Difficult Patient* (1953).

[30] See also E. Read, *Catherine, Duchess of Suffolk* (1962).

[31] G. W. Bromiley, *Thomas Cranmer, Theologian* (New York, 1956); E. G. Rupp, *Six Makers of English Religion, 1500–1700* (New York, 1957) has excellent chapters on Cranmer, Tyndale, and Foxe. The best and most recent biography of Cranmer is Jasper G. Ridley, *Thomas Cranmer* (Oxford, 1962).

[32] A. G. Chester, *Hugh Latimer, Apostle to the English* (Philadelphia, 1954); H. S. Darby, *Hugh Latimer* (1953).

[33] J. G. Ridley, *Nicholas Ridley, a Biography* (1957). Compare G. W. Bromiley's 32-page pamphlet: *Nicholas Ridley*, Church Book Room Press, Great Churchmen Series, no. 19 (1950).

[34] W. S. Hudson, *John Ponet, Advocate of Limited Monarchy* (Chicago, 1942).

[35] C. Hopf, *Martin Bucer and the English Reformation* (Oxford, 1946).

[36] To name but a few of the better works: Maynard, *Humanist as Hero*; E. E. Reynolds, *St. Thomas More* (New York, 1953); J. Farrow, *The Story of Thomas*

manist, the statesman, the martyr, and the Utopian still baffles and at-
tracts the twentieth century which has had sufficient experience of
martyrdom to recognize the uniqueness of the humanistic martyr.[37]
Chambers' *More* with its insistence upon the medieval orientation of the
Utopia remains the standard interpretation, but recently two other
theses have been offered. R. Ames, *Citizen Thomas More and His
Utopia* (Princeton, N.J., 1949) argues a sophisticated version of the
Kautsky hypothesis—that More and his *Utopia* were products of a
capitalistic attack upon feudalism and a middle-class humanistic criticism of a decaying social order. J. H. Hexter, *More's Utopia: The Biography of an Idea* (Princeton, N.J., 1952) portrays More as both the real-
ist and the idealist: the astute lawyer who regarded the sin of pride as
the cancer that eats at the heart of the commonwealth and who endeavored to construct his Utopia so as to limit and control the evil effects of
pride; and the religious dreamer who sought "to remould human society
into a holy community, to bring it into closer conformity to God's law by
the imposition of a firm but just and righteous discipline on the daily life
and doings of all citizens" (p. 94).[38]

V

If the popularity of things Tudor has retained its vigor and the lessons
of the twentieth century have modified our view of the sixteenth century, then it might be said that a new discipline in historical research has
been the handmaid, or, more correctly, the scullery maid, who has sustained and complemented the other two. Tudor history, ever since
Tawney and Pollard pioneered the way, has been rewritten on the basis
of more exacting standards. The truth, or what passes for the truth, is
today being sought in the slow, meticulous, and dispassionate review of
the sources.

We are picking away at the details—administrative, local, personal,
and economic—and under the impact of such investigation the ancient
legends are fading away. A case in point is two studies of the Commons'
supplication of 1532 by Elton (*EHR*, 66, 1951) and J. P. Cooper (*ibid.*,

More (New York, 1954). E. L. Surtz, "Interpretations of Utopia," *Catholic Historical Review*, 38 (1952), has a convenient summary of modern scholarship.
[37] The publication of Ro. Ba., *Lyfe of Syr Thomas More, sometymes Lord Chancellor of England*, ed. E. V. Hitchcock and P. E. Hallett, Early English Text
Society, old ser., no. 222 (1950), and E. F. Rogers, *The Correspondence of Sir
Thomas More* (Princeton, N.J., 1947), have added to our understanding of More.
[38] See also his "Thomas More: on the Margins of Modernity," *JBS*, 1 (1961),
and J. D. M. Derrett, "The Trial of Sir Thomas More," *EHR*, 79 (1964).

72, 1957) in which the multitude of drafts and fragments which preceded the final supplication are scrutinized with loving devotion. Whether the uninitiated will be any clearer in his own mind after reading these two articles is beside the point. He will at least be closer to the truth that things are not as simple as previous historians have sometimes imagined.[39] In economics there is what W. G. Hoskins has described as the "laundry bill" approach to history.[40] It is on this level—the careful inspection and accumulation of minutiae—that major advances in scholarship and comprehension are being made. E. Kerridge, "The Movement of Rents, 1540–1640" (*EcHR*, 2d ser., 6, 1953) has taken a long and careful look at a limited number of estate records and has succeeded in seriously questioning the notion that rents lagged behind prices throughout most of the century. W. K. Jordan has likewise worked on the accumulated evidence of minutiae—a fascinating study of philanthropy as revealed in hundreds of Tudor wills.[41] Another example of the same process is the time-honored controversy over enclosure which has lost none of its fervor [42] by having most of its facts and figures swept aside by E. Kerridge's questioning article, "The Returns of the Inquisitions of Depopulation" (*EHR*, 70, 1955), and P. J. Bowden, "Movement in Wool Prices, 1490–1610" (*Yorkshire Bulletin of Economic and Social Research*, 4, 1952). The present state of the enclosure controversy is, like most Tudor topics, in a state of flux. As Joan Thirsk has pointed out in her admirable review of the subject: "the truth is that enclosures took many forms," and neither were caused solely by sheep nor were they always acts of unmitigated ruthlessness.[43]

The efforts to impose a new rigor upon Tudor scholarship has been helped by the continued publication of original sources. The *Calendar of State Papers, Spanish* is now available through Mary's reign; the *Calendar of Inquisitions Post Mortem* is complete for Henry VII; volume one of *The Close Rolls, 1485–1500* has recently been printed, and Bishop Cuthbert Tunstall's register (1530–1559) for Durham was edited and

---

[39] For still another example see Elton, "The Quondam of Rievaulx," *Journal of Ecclesiastical History*, 7 (1956), in which the author deprives Abbot Edward Kirkby of any claim to a martyr's crown.

[40] W. G. Hoskins, "English Provincial Towns in the Early Sixteenth Century," *TRHS*, 5th ser., 6 (1956).

[41] W. K. Jordan, *Philanthrophy in England, 1480–1660* (New York, 1959).

[42] See also F. V. Semenov, *Enclosures and Peasants' Revolts in England in the Sixteenth Century* (in Russian, Moscow, 1949) and C. Hill's review *JEcH*, 2d ser., 3 (1950); W. G. Hoskins, *Essays in Leicestershire History* (Liverpool, 1950); M. Beresford, *The Lost Villages of England* (1954.)

[43] J. Thirsk, *Tudor Enclosures*, Historical Association Publication G41 (1959), p. 3.

calendared by Gladys Hinde in 1952. The county and historical societies have been equally busy. The Catholic Record Society (vol. 45, 1950) published Archdeacon Nicholas Harpsfield's visitation of Canterbury in 1557; the Sussex Record Society (vol. 56, 1957) brought out *The Lay Subsidy Rolls for the County of Sussex, 1524–25*, edited by Julian Cornwall; the Lincoln Record Society has published in three volumes the *Visitations of the Diocese of Lincoln, 1517–31*, edited by A. Hamilton Thompson (1940–47); and L. S. Snell has compiled a series of *Documents towards a History of the Reformation in Cornwall*, no. 1: *The Chantry Certificates for Cornwall* (Exeter, Eng., 1953). Not only has the level of scholarship risen, but the scope of professional interest has broadened. It is true that group biography has not yet been utilized extensively in the early Tudor period and Henry VIII's parliaments await their Neale. Some work, however, has been done along these lines. Using the term "group biography" with considerable latitude we might include such studies as J. S. Roskell, "The Social Composition of the Commons in a Fifteenth-Century Parliament" (*BIHR*, 24, 1951); B. Winchester, *Tudor Family Portrait* (1955), which is the story of the Johnson brothers and their friends and relations; M. L. Loane, *Masters of the English Reformation* (1954); and E. Auerbach, *Tudor Artists: A Study of Painters in the Royal Service and of Portraiture on Illuminated Documents* (1954), which is as much a source book as a group analysis.

To date the early Tudor period has escaped the worst of the "Storm over the Gentry."[44] All the signs, however, point to a full-scale reevaluation of the notion of "new men," who commenced their "rise" under the economic and social tutelage of Henry VII and who fortified their position with the loot of the monastic lands during the Reformation years. The vital parts of the anatomy of the Elizabethan aristocracy, anatomized or otherwise, were formed during the twilight years of the "new monarchy." (See in this connection: L. Stone, "The Anatomy of the Elizabethan Aristocracy," *EcHR*, 18, 1948; F. Caspari, *Humanism and the Social Order in Tudor England* [Chicago, Ill., 1954]; J. H. Hexter, "The Education of the Aristocracy in the Renaissance," *JMH*, 22, 1950; P. N. Siegel, "English Humanism and the New Tudor Aristocracy," *Journal of the History of Ideas*, 13, 1952.) The complete story of the gentry and titled nobility in the sixteenth century has yet to be written;

[44] J. H. Hexter, *Reappraisals in History* (Evanston, Ill., 1961), especially the chapters, "The Myth of the Middle Class in Tudor England" and "Storm over the Gentry."

however, a number of suggestive starts have been made, such as H. J. Habakkuk, "The Market for Monastic Property, 1539–1603" (*EcHR*, 2d ser., 10, 1958), which questions whether the "new men" actually got the new land; T. B. Pugh and C. D. Ross, "Materials for the Study of Baronial Incomes in Fifteenth-Century England" (*EcHR*, 2d ser., 6, 1953); and two studies by Helen Miller, "Subsidy Assessments of the Peerage in the Sixteenth Century" (*BIHR*, 28, 1955), and "The Early Tudor Peerage, 1485–1547", a London University thesis, a summary of which is given in the *Bulletin of the Institute of Historical Research* (24, 1951).

VI

The historian of early Tudor England has constantly operated under a twofold disadvantage which his colleagues in Elizabethan history have escaped. Statistically speaking, the great divide in Tudor history is the year 1538, when Thomas Cromwell ordered all parishes to keep vital statistics as an act of state (in actual fact most parish records and other biographical data such as visitation figures do not really become complete until the latter half of the century). Consequently, the study of the House of Commons in terms of its members and research into any individual or group not sufficiently distinguished to have been included in the *DNB* become extremely difficult for the pre-Elizabethan period. Moreover, most early Tudor scholarship is grounded upon the quagmire of the fifteenth century, which of all eras is the least understood or studied. The Tudor historian is suddenly brought up short by the year 1485 which, if it has lost most of its meaning as a date of historical significance, still represents in Tudor historiography a curtain through which we see only dimly. In many ways, we have gone just about as far as it is possible to go in the study of the "new monarchy," the "new gentry," and the "new parliament," without vastly more investigation into the Lancastrian-Yorkist crown, aristocracy, social order, and parliamentary system.

Not only is such research perplexing, but there still remains much to be accomplished. For an age that abounds in the clash and vitality of personality, it is somewhat surprising that a number of the major luminaries either have no biography or a highly inferior one. The Howards, father and son, William Paget,[45] the Dukes of Somerset and

[45] An exception is S. R. Gammon, "Master of Practises: A Life of William, Lord Paget of Beaudesert, 1506–63" (doctoral thesis, Princeton University, 1953).

Northumberland, and Thomas Cromwell [46] all deserve biographies of major proportions. Besides the laymen, there are the ecclesiastics who still lack adequate narratives of their careers. Certainly Bonner, Heath, Morton, Thirlby, and Richard Fox warrant full-scale accounts.

The area, however, that remains most obscure is that of the little Tudors. Here is a decade in which the scholar can perceive the Henrician system of government operating under unique conditions—when it came close to collapsing entirely—and those who would learn more of the artistry of Henry VIII and Elizabeth might do well to turn to those dreary years which, though plagued by economic, social, and religious misfortune, deserve a better epithet than "sterile."

Some headway has, in fact, been made. The older image of a neurotic, bigoted, and bloody Mary has been softened by H. F. M. Prescott, *A Spanish Tudor* (1940); E. H. Harbison, *Rival Ambassadors at the Court of Queen Mary* (Princeton, N.J., 1940); P. Hughes, *The Reformation in England* (1950–54); [47] S. R. Gammon, "Mary Tudor's Tragedy of Conscience" (*Emory University Quarterly,* 9, 1953); and W. Schenk, *Reginald Pole, Cardinal of England* (1950). A reversion to the less charitable picture of Mary and evidence that the issue is anything but dead can be found in M. Barrington, "Queen Mary" (*Notes and Queries,* 195 [1950], pp. 4, 173).

Edward's reign remains equally barren, [48] and, except for H. W. Chapman's *The Last Tudor King* (1958), no full-length work has appeared during the last twenty years dealing specifically with the problems of the reign. A splendid and pioneering work on the *History of the Court of Augmentations* (1961) by W. C. Richardson is the authoritative study on the subject and goes far in helping us trace the collapse of political and governmental morality under Edward VI. Ket's Rebellion has received useful but brief attention by S. T. Bindoff; [49] the commonwealth men are the subject of an article by A. B. Ferguson. [50] F. G. Emmison has recently produced a fine study of Sir William Petre both as

[46] Elton has, in fact, made a start; see besides his other works already mentioned in this essay, "Thomas Cromwell," *History Today,* 6 (1956), and "Thomas Cromwell's Decline and Fall," *CHJ,* 10 (1951). See also A. G. Dickens, *Thomas Cromwell and the English Reformation* (1959).

[47] See especially his criticism of Pollard's conclusions about Mary's responsibility for the Smithfield fires, pt. III, ch. II.

[48] The same can be said for the last years of Henry VIII. See L. B. Smith, "The Last Will and Testament of Henry VIII: a Question of Perspective," *JBS,* 2 (1962).

[49] *Ket's Rebellion,* Historical Association Publication G12 (1949).

[50] "Renaissance Realism in the 'Commonwealth' Literature of Early Tudor England," *Journal of the History of Ideas,* 16 (1955).

a country gentleman and as a government official;[51] and three new documents have recently thrown light upon the nefarious operations of Northumberland and his ingenious efforts to seize and retain power under Edward and Lady Jane Grey.[52]

The problems still remaining in early Tudor historiography are legion. New techniques, new questions, and new facts are only beginning to open up a renaissance of Tudor studies. The horizons are still unmapped and the full impact of much of the research being done in the decades immediately adjacent to the early Tudor era has not yet been felt. Not only is our ignorance massive, but the magnitude of that ignorance is constantly increasing as the old answers no longer suffice in the face of new questions. Even the broad outlines of Tudor government are uncertain and shadowy; queries involving the chain of command, initiative, patronage, factionalism, economic and political influence both at court and in the shires, bribery and corruption, and government influence over local administration[53] and electoral procedure are only just beginning to be raised.

Probably no area of research is in greater need of investigation than the Reformation Parliament. All the balanced and tidy answers of the nineteenth century have been swept aside, and today we are again faced with such trying problems as who controlled the commons; was it a rubber stamp; did Henry or Cromwell or someone else conceive of and engineer the break with Rome; was Parliament a medieval high court or can we say that by 1536 it had evolved into something discernibly different from the past; what was the social composition of the lower house; who controlled it and how; what was the rôle and influence of the lords; and finally what were the precise function and organization of such administrative organs as the Council of the West, the Court of First Fruits and Tenths, and the Exchequer? On every front the questions cry out for answer, but the responses stubbornly elude us. What was the truth about enclosure; how important was it either in myth or in fact; what

---

[51] *Tudor Secretary: Sir William Petre at Court and Home* (Cambridge, Mass., 1961). See also Emmison's "A Plan of Edward VI and Secretary Petre for Reorganizing the Privy Council's Work, 1552–1553," *BIHR*, 31 (1958).

[52] S. T. Bindoff, "A Kingdom at Stake, 1553," *History Today*, 3 (1953); D. Hayes, "The 'Narratio Historica' of P. Vincentius, 1553," *EHR*, 63 (1948); A. J. A. Malkiewicz, "Eye-witness's Account of the Coup d'Etat of October, 1549," *EHR*, 70 (1955).

[53] A highly suggestive start has been made by W. T. MacCaffrey, *Exeter, 1540–1640* (Cambridge, Mass., 1958). However, the bulk of this work lies outside of the scope of this essay. See also W. G. Hoskins, "English Provincial Towns in the Early Sixteenth Century," *TRHS*, 5th ser., 6 (1956).

was the extent and effect of the price rise; who actually got the monastic lands both in an immediate and ultimate sense; how new was the "new gentry" and how old was the feudal nobility? [54]

Possibly the only conclusion that can honestly be maintained is that the last twenty years has set aside the standard interpretation of Tudor England. The process of reconstruction is only just commencing, and it will probably be another generation before we again establish an "orthodox" synthesis of early Tudor England.

[54] A significant, if to the mere historian still confusing, start has been made. See Y. S. Brenner, "The Inflation of Prices in Early Sixteenth-Century England," *EcHR*, 2d ser., 14 (1961–62); "The Inflation of Prices in England 1551–1650," *ibid.*, 15 (1962–63); and J. D. Gould, "Y. S. Brenner on Prices: A Comment," *ibid.*, 16 (1963).

English History, 1558–1640:

A Bibliographical Survey

❖

PEREZ ZAGORIN

M Y PURPOSE in the following pages is to take a selective view of the writings on Elizabethan and early Stuart history which have appeared within the past two decades or so. Brief as this period is, and despite the interruption to historical scholarship caused by almost six years of war, there can be no doubt that the study of the age lying between the accession of Queen Elizabeth I and the meeting of the Long Parliament has never been in so flourishing a state.[1] It seems likely that more research is now devoted to it, in proportion to other parts of English history, than ever before. Unfamiliar areas have been explored, fresh problems propounded, and new methods of investigation applied. Established views, hallowed for years by an apostolic succession of clichés, have been deprived of orthodoxy. While an increasing number of younger scholars have dedicated themselves to profitable work in the field, the fundamental contributions resulting from the researches of some of our veteran historians show that there are still giants in the land.[2]

I shall begin with political and constitutional history, as it is here that some of the outstanding advances have been achieved. For the reign of

[Reprinted from *AHR*, 68:364–384 (January 1963).]

[1] An estimate of the trends and opportunities in Tudor and Stuart scholarship is contained in the report of a conference held at the Folger Shakespeare Library, Washington, D.C., to commemorate the fourth centenary of Queen Elizabeth's accession. (See *Tudor and Stuart History* [Washington, D.C., 1959].)

[2] A full listing of works on the Tudor period up to 1957, with a brief sampling of a few that appeared thereafter, will be found in *Bibliography of British History: Tudor Period, 1485–1603*, ed. Conyers Read, 2d ed. (New York, 1959). About 2,500 titles have been added to this new edition over the first, which appeared in 1933. A second edition of *Bibliography of British History: Stuart Period, 1603–1714*, ed. Godfrey Davies (Oxford, 1928), is announced and will appear under the editorship of Professor Mary F. Keeler.

Elizabeth, no work of recent years stands higher in importance than the masterly volumes in which Professor Sir John Neale first told the full story of the Elizabethan Commons. The first, *The Elizabethan House of Commons* (1949), anatomizes the lower house as an institution. The types and quality of members are depicted, a number of elections in county and borough described, and procedure explained. Neale conclusively answers in the negative the question whether the government packed the House, and he shows how the normal processes of election operated without much deliberate intervention to assure the court a substantial representation in Parliament. The remaining two volumes, *Elizabeth I and Her Parliaments, 1559–1581* (1953), and *Elizabeth I and Her Parliaments, 1584–1601* (1957), form a consecutive narrative of the parliamentary history of the reign. Neale used a large quantity of new material in constructing his great study. He assembled fresh data on Elizabethan M.P.'s. New speeches and private members' journals of proceedings have come to light, so that Sir Simonds D'Ewes's *Journal* has ceased to be the source par excellence for the parliamentary transactions of these years.[3] It is very much to be hoped that the most important of these journals, such as those for 1572, will be published *in extenso*.[4]

The picture of Parliament that Neale has painted is not only far richer in detail and more dense with life than any before; it also materially alters the conception previously held respecting the development of the Commons. Most significant, it has revealed that the extent of organized opposition to the government's measures was very much stronger in the earlier years of the reign than had been realized. The notion that Parliament raised itself to defy the Queen only when the country had been released from the Spanish danger after 1588 must be definitely discarded. As the new evidence makes plain, apprehension over the succession, patriotic wrath against Mary Stuart, and dislike of Elizabeth's politique policy led members into frequent collision with the Queen from the 1560's onward. Neale finds the mainspring of this opposition in the Puritan members. It was they, he says, who "taught the House of Commons . . . the art of opposition, which might be considered the

[3] Sir Simonds D'Ewes, *The Journals of All the Parliaments during the Reign of Queen Elizabeth* (1682).

[4] Neale describes the journal of this Parliament kept by Thomas Cromwell as rivaling in interest and importance that of Heywood Townshend (Heywood Townshend, *Historical Collections, An Exact Account of the Last Four Parliaments of Elizabeth* [1680]) for the Parliament of 1601 and remarks that another anonymous journal for 1572 is almost as valuable as Cromwell's. (See Neale, *Elizabeth I and Her Parliaments, 1559–1581*, p. 243.)

outstanding contribution of the Elizabethan period to Parliamentary history . . ." [5]

Despite the breadth of Neale's synthesis and the firmness of many of his conclusions, numerous aspects of parliamentary history still await investigation, and certain problems continue to perplex. Some important statutes of the reign, for example, are barely touched upon in his work, though one may surmise that new information could now be presented on their passage in the House. The description of the composition of the Commons, trenchant and artful as it is, is only an outline. By means of the biographical approach, much more can be done to analyze the characteristics of the members socially, economically, and in other ways. Here we shall have to await the appearance of the great history of Parliament now in progress. Neale is himself the director of the Elizabethan section and has said that his period will contain the biographies of about 2,700 members, most of them not included in the *Dictionary of National Biography*.[6] Finally, there is the crucial question of opposition in the House. Neale's emphasis on the role of the Puritan members is undoubtedly justified. They must be regarded as the prototype of the Country opposition which took shape in the next reign, the germ of the first political movement in modern English history, which was to be more than a faction because it was founded not as the following of a great man but on the basis of policy and principles. But when the Elizabethan opposition is considered in the perspective of the sixteenth century as a whole, the question necessarily arises as to the basis of the resistance to the crown so manifest at times before Elizabeth's accession. Neale has referred, for instance, to several remarkable episodes in Mary's Parliaments as very important in this respect.[7] What, since it was presumably not Puritanism, had the leaders of this resistance in common with their fellows in Elizabeth's Parliaments? Was it mainly a concern for their purses that produced such a crossing of the government's will? Does the gentry members' independence of the court, as well as Puritanism, help to explain the opposition to Elizabeth, as earlier to Mary? The whole subject, it would seem, must be considered further before we can feel that we have all the clues.

For the reigns of James I and Charles I, nothing exists comparable to Neale's work, and a history of the Parliaments between 1604 and 1629,

[5] Neale, *Elizabeth I and Her Parliaments, 1584–1601*, p. 436.
[6] See *Tudor and Stuart History*, p. 9.
[7] Neale, *Elizabeth I and Her Parliaments, 1559–1581*, pp. 21–26.

in which the themes are the evolution of the Commons as an institution and the formation of the opposition movement, has still to be written. In the meantime one must continue to refer for a general picture mainly to Professor Wallace Notestein's famous paper, "The Winning of the Initiative by the House of Commons" (*Proceedings of the British Academy* [1924–25], pp. 125–175), eked out by several recent monographs on individual Parliaments and particular aspects of parliamentary development. David H. Willson's invaluable *The Privy Councillors in the House of Commons, 1604–1629* (Minneapolis, Minn., 1940), is a definitive description of the role of the councilors and the decline of their influence over proceedings as leadership in the House passed from them to private members in the opposition. Harold Hulme, *Sir John Eliot, 1592 to 1632: Struggle for Parliamentary Freedom* (New York, 1957), gives much detail on parliamentary transactions in the 1620's. Thomas L. Moir, *The Addled Parliament of 1614* (Oxford, 1958), presents a good account of that abortive two-month meeting and sets it in the context of more long-range parliamentary development. He also provides informative appendices on the membership of both houses. Williams M. Mitchell's *The Rise of the Revolutionary Party in the English House of Commons, 1603–1629* (New York, 1957), bears a most tantalizing title, but is unfortunately marked by serious inadequacies. It offers some interesting remarks on the continuity of opposition members from Parliament to Parliament and raises some fundamental questions that it does little to answer.

A few recent articles relating to the parliamentary aspect of this period may also be noticed. An excellent study of Wiltshire members and elections is Stanley T. Bindoff's "Parliamentary History 1529–1688" in *Victoria County History, Wiltshire*.[8] Hulme has shown how the Commons extended its privilege of freedom of speech in the earlier seventeenth century.[9] On the basis of newly found evidence, I. H. C. Fraser effects a revision of the traditional narrative of the tumultuous scene in the Commons on March 2, 1629. His story makes clear that the conduct of Sir John Eliot, Denzil Holles, and their friends on that memorable day was even more audacious than had been thought.[10] Eliza-

---

[8] *The Victoria History of the Counties of England: A History of Wiltshire*, ed. R. B. Pugh and Elizabeth Crittall, 7 vols. (1953–57), V, pp. 111–170.

[9] Harold Hulme, "The Winning of Freedom of Speech by the House of Commons," *AHR*, 61:825–853 (July 1956).

[10] I. H. C. Fraser, "The Agitation in the Commons, 2 March 1629, and the Interrogation of the Leaders of the Anti-Court Group," *BIHR*, 30:86–95 (May 1957).

beth R. Foster describes the way in which the Commons brought the provocative subject of monopolies within the scope of its attack on grievances.[11] The restoration of representation to certain boroughs by action of the Commons is carefully considered by Evangeline de Villiers. As earlier under Elizabeth, so also this increase in borough representation after 1621 was a result of the desire of local patrons and gentry for seats.[12] Lawrence Stone has analyzed well the influence exercised in parliamentary elections by the second Earl of Salisbury.[13] With this may be compared an earlier account of the electoral influence of two other great peers, the third and the fourth Earls of Pembroke.[14]

Little progress has been made in recent years in the editing of original materials pertaining to transactions in early Stuart Parliaments. A large number of manuscript diaries of proceedings of the Commons kept by private members is known, and the publication of the more important of these is an urgent requirement of scholarship. They ought to be printed even if they cannot be provided with the copious apparatus and notes that distinguish the great edition of the Commons' debates of 1621 by Notestein and his collaborators.[15] For the House of Lords—one of the really neglected topics in the writings on parliamentary history—Evangeline de Villiers has published some fragments of a journal of the Parliament of 1621 kept by the fifth Earl of Huntingdon. This includes the only known firsthand account of an important speech delivered by King James to the upper house.[16]

The discussion of the literature for the period after 1640 belongs to the bibliography of the English Revolution and is beyond our present scope. Two works, however, dealing with members of the Long Parliament happily fall within our province. They are Mary F. Keeler, *The Long Parliament, 1640–1641: A Biographical Study of Its Members* (Philadelphia, 1954), and Douglas D. Brunton and Donald H. Penning-

---

[11] Elizabeth R. Foster, "The Procedure of the House of Commons against Patents and Monopolies, 1621–1624," in *Conflict in Stuart England: Essays in Honour of Wallace Notestein*, ed. William A. Aiken and Basil D. Henning (New York, 1960).

[12] Evangeline de Villiers, "Parliamentary Boroughs Restored by the House of Commons, 1621–1641," *EHR*, 67:175–202 (April 1952); see Neale, *Elizabethan House of Commons*, chap. vii.

[13] Lawrence Stone, "The Electoral Influence of the Second Earl of Salisbury, 1614–68," *EHR*, 71:384–400 (July 1956).

[14] Violet A. Rowe, "The Influence of the Earls of Pembroke on Parliamentary Elections, 1625–1641," *EHR*, 50:242–256 (April 1935).

[15] *Commons Debates 1621*, ed. Wallace Notestein *et al.*, 7 vols. (New Haven, Conn., 1935).

[16] *The Hastings Journal of the Parliament of 1621*, ed. Evangeline de Villiers, *Camden Miscellany*, 20 (1953).

ton, *Members of the Long Parliament* (1954). Though these two books in part cover the same ground, they also usefully supplement each other and together form the indispensable basis for all future study of this great Parliament. Mrs. Keeler's book is a detailed portrait of the original members of the Commons and contains much information on their political experience and allegiance, their economic and social position, and their family connections. It provides a biographical article on each member and includes a brief account of the elections in every county and borough. Brunton and Pennington extend their study to the men elected over the entire thirteen years of the Long Parliament and concentrate more strongly on their social and occupational character. Appendices that list the members both alphabetically and by constituency and analyze some of their main features in statistical form constitute an extremely useful part of their work. By means of these writings, we are able at last to see many members of the Long Parliament as individuals. The whole story has thus become fuller and far more interesting. At the same time, the main conclusion that emerges is the substantial social similarity, if not identity, of the members who opposed the King and those who supported him.

In other departments of political and constitutional history than the parliamentary, a number of publications should be mentioned. Additions have been made to various collections of state papers and other sources. The *Acts of the Privy Council* have been augmented by a further installment covering July 1628–April 1629.[17] An interval of eighteen years separates this volume from its predecessor in the series.[18] Surely the Public Record Office and other authorities who have shown such deplorable slowness in printing the chief records in their care might find some means of accelerating their present glacial rate of publication. A new volume, the first and only one since 1936, was published in 1950 in the calendar of foreign state papers for Elizabeth's reign with an informative introduction by the editor, Professor Richard B. Wernham.[19] There have also been a few—a very few—additions to the publications of the Historical Manuscripts Commission relating to this period. These, and most of the other serial publications of texts pertaining to English his-

---

[17] *Acts of the Privy Council of England 1628 July–1629 April* (1958).

[18] *Acts of the Privy Council of England 1627 Sept.–1628 June* (1940).

[19] *Calendar of State Papers Foreign . . .* , vol. XXIII, *January–July, 1589*, ed. Richard B. Wernham (1950). The preface to this volume contains an announcement that the foreign calendar is to be discontinued and replaced by a series of "descriptive lists."

torical subjects, can now best be found by consulting E. L. C. Mullins' invaluable analytical guide to such works, which the Royal Historical Society has recently issued.[20]

As regards constitutional documents, a new selection covering the Tudor age has been edited with commentary by Geoffrey R. Elton.[21] This work will probably take the place held in the past by Joseph R. Tanner's *Tudor Constitutional Documents, 1485–1603* (2d ed., Cambridge, Eng., 1930), as the principal collection for purposes of teaching and reference. Although it omits certain documents for which Tanner will still be consulted, it also contains important new ones and is better arranged. The vigorous and incisive commentary, often controversial, brings the discussion of outstanding questions up to date. Among other texts recently published are William Lambarde's *Archeion: Or, A Discourse upon the High Courts of Justice in England,* edited by Charles H. McIlwain and Paul L. Ward (Cambridge, Mass., 1957), and the historian William Camden's brief "Discourse concerning the Prerogative of the Crown," edited by Frank S. Fussner.[22]

No modern scholar has tried to write the history of Elizabeth's reign or that of her two successors in anything like the fullness of detail of James Anthony Froude or Samuel Gardiner. While such an undertaking would doubtless be a work of supererogation, there is a pressing need for histories of these periods, composed on a smaller and more selective scale, that will reflect the present state of learning and present-day interests, correct old errors, and give attention to important problems neglected in the earlier literature. Perhaps the time will not come for a synthesis of this kind, however, until the analytical preoccupation that presently dominates most historical work provides the material for it in a fuller harvest of monographs and special studies. There has been a strong tendency recently to blame historians for excessive specialization and narrowness of interest. If some measure of justice must be conceded to this charge, it must also be pointed out, first, that in the best research the sense of the whole, and of the relation of the part to the whole, is always present, and, second, that this concentration on the analysis of particular topics is really an expression of the conscience of the historian

[20] *Texts and Calendars: An Analytical Guide to Serial Publications* (1958).
[21] *The Tudor Constitution,* ed. Geoffrey R. Elton (Cambridge, Eng., 1960).
[22] William Camden, "Discourse concerning the Prerogative of the Crown," ed. Frank S. Fussner, *Proceedings of the American Philosophical Society,* 101:204–215 (April 1957).

revolting against superficial answers and trite opinions and determined by painstaking labor to get at the truth of things.

An intimation of the sort of synthesis in political history we may hope for in the future is provided in Neale's lecture, "The Elizabethan Political Scene" (*Proceedings of the British Academy*, 34 [1948], pp. 97–117). This, despite its brevity, is one of the most penetrating treatments of political institutions and the nature of power at this time that has been written. Its discussion of the court, patronage, and the factional character of politics suggests fruitful lines of research and points the way to a profounder conception of state and society in the sixteenth century. An interesting paper exemplifying a similar approach is Arthur H. Dodd, "North Wales in the Essex Revolt of 1601" (*EHR*, 59:348–370 [September 1944]).

Several recent monographs on administration are also of importance. Henry E. Bell's *An Introduction to the History and Records of the Court of Wards and Liveries* (Cambridge, Eng., 1953), is a model account of the great institution whose exactions so deeply affected the governing class. It should be studied in conjunction with Joel Hurstfield, *The Queen's Wards: Wardship and Marriage under Elizabeth I* (1958), a good analysis of wardship and of the role of the Court of Wards under Elizabeth. For the reign of Charles I, Gerald E. Aylmer, *The King's Servants: The Civil Service of Charles I, 1625–42* (1961), is indispensable. It describes in almost superabundant detail the nature of service under the crown, the social origins and character of the official body, and the political significance of officeholding. Its implications for the better understanding of politics before and during the Civil War are far-reaching. One of the important prerogative instruments of the crown is treated in Penry Williams, *The Council in the Marches of Wales under Elizabeth I* (Cardiff, 1958). Allegra Woodworth, *Purveyance for the Royal Household in the Reign of Queen Elizabeth* (Philadelphia, 1945), offers a scholarly picture of the administrative and financial aspects of the provisioning of the court and describes the attempt to devise solutions for the grievances to which purveyance gave rise. Geoffrey R. Elton's article on the Elizabethan Exchequer also has useful bearings on politics and institutions.[23]

---

[23] Geoffrey R. Elton, "The Elizabethan Exchequer: War in the Receipt," in *Elizabethan Government and Society: Essays Presented to Sir John Neale* ed. S. T. Bindoff *et al.* (1961). Except for Elton's essay, I have seen none of the papers in this volume, which was not available to me when the present article was written in May 1961.

Of general works concerned principally with political and constitutional matters, one of the best-known, John B. Black's *The Reign of Elizabeth, 1558–1603* (*The Oxford History of England,* VIII [Oxford, 1936]), has appeared with some important alterations in a second edition (Oxford, 1959). Stanley T. Bindoff's brief *Tudor England* (Harmondsworth, 1950) contains several sparkling chapters on the Elizabethan period. The companion volume on the Stuart period by Maurice P. Ashley is somewhat dull and prosaic.[24] The same must be said for Godfrey Davies' *The Early Stuarts, 1603–1660* (*The Oxford History of England,* IX [Oxford, 1937; 2d ed., Oxford, 1959]). C. Veronica Wedgwood, *The King's Peace, 1637–1641* (1955), is a well-written account of the last years of Charles I's reign before the Civil War. Alfred L. Rowse, *The England of Elizabeth: The Structure of Society* (1951), discusses politics and much else. Full of learning and informed by a deep poetic responsiveness to the vanished glories of the sixteenth century, it is the best picture of the Elizabethan age. Conyers Read's life of Lord Burghley, the last work of a great scholar recently passed from our midst, centers almost wholly on political history and foreign affairs and has copious citations from documents.[25] For foreign affairs, Garrett Mattingly, *The Defeat of the Armada* (1959), gives a brilliant account of international relations during the Anglo-Spanish war and shrewdly describes the European context and ramifications of the great struggle. Another useful but much less detailed treatment is that of Gaston Zeller, *Histoire des relations internationales,* II, *Les temps modernes: De Christophe Colomb à Cromwell* (Paris, 1953). No modern works exist that concentrate exclusively on foreign affairs and present a full and connected narrative of English relations, or the conditions governing them, with other European states.[26] The history, for instance, of Anglo-Netherlands relations under Elizabeth and James I has not yet been written, despite the abundant documents that are available and the importance of the subject. One hopes that future scholarship will turn its attention to this undeservedly neglected topic.

Military history is another subject deserving of more attention. The Armada naturally still remains the focus of interest, and Mattingly

---

[24] Maurice P. Ashley, *England in the Seventeenth Century* (Harmondsworth, 1952).

[25] Conyers Read, *Mr. Secretary Cecil and Queen Elizabeth* (1955), *Lord Burghley and Queen Elizabeth* (1960).

[26] Such writings as there are in this field are listed in *Bibliography of British History: Tudor Period,* ed. Read, pp. 65–85.

has a fresh description of the battle in *The Defeat of the Armada*. Charles G. Cruickshank, *Elizabeth's Army* (Oxford, 1946), is a valuable study of military organization. Cyril Falls, *Elizabeth's Irish Wars* (1950), provides an excellent account of the campaigns connected with the Irish rebellion. An illuminating presentation of the difficulties that governed strategy and a defense of the Queen's policy in the operations of the Anglo-Spanish war is given in Richard B. Wernham, "Queen Elizabeth and the Portugal Expedition of 1589" (*EHR*, 66:1–26, 194–218 [January and April 1951]).

From things earthly, we pass to things heavenly and of the spirit, although this may seem to be an infelicitous description of the religious history of a period that has been as bitterly fought over by scholars as have the preceding reigns of Henry VIII, Edward, and Mary. Perhaps there are signs, however, that old animosities are giving way to mutual comprehension and greater detachment. There is surely no reason why historians should wish to wage again the struggle of enraged generations three and a half centuries ago. Let us be thankful that the past, whose protagonists have long lain mingled with dust, is over and done. The essence of tragedy is the conflict, not of right against wrong, but of right against right. No one can gaze on the confessional strife of the sixteenth and seventeenth centuries and not recognize it as a tragic conflict in which compelling moral claims were to be found on all sides. No one can contemplate the pretensions of the churches of that unhappy age to religious infallibility without an ironical awareness of the delusions that gain an empire over men. The historian may, indeed he must, stigmatize persecution and cruelty, guilt and injustice. Yet before the terrible hatreds of denominations and creeds, nothing will suffice him for understanding but charity and irony, the twin talismans he must take with him as he passes through the scenes of anger and carnage that mark the course of religion in Tudor and Stuart times.

The only recent work offering a detailed ecclesiastical history of Elizabeth's reign is the third volume of Philip Hughes's excellent *The Reformation in England: "True Religion Now Established"* (3 vols., 1950–54). This is a judicious and objective narrative, written from a Catholic standpoint and based on wide study of the printed materials. His *Rome and the Counter-Reformation in England* (1942) is also valuable and makes use of fresh manuscript evidence from the Vatican Library and the Roman Congregation *De Propaganda Fide*. The great obscurity surrounding the statutory settlement of religion in 1559 has been largely cleared away in Neale's article, "The Elizabethan Acts of Supremacy and Uniformity" (*EHR*, 65:304–332 [July 1950]). On the institutional side of the Established Church, the outstanding contribution is Christopher Hill's learned *Economic Problems of the Church from Archbishop Whitgift to the Long Parliament* (Oxford, 1956). Following to some extent the fruitful path of investigation opened by Roland G. Usher, *The Reconstruction of the English Church* (2 vols., New York, 1910), Hill describes with admirable clarity the economic difficulties of the clergy, the forms of clerical income and the lay depredations made upon them, and shows how Laud's effort to restore the status of the clergy helped to provoke revolution. A few other writings also treat the institutional functioning of the church. F. Douglas Price has pictured the decline of ecclesiastical discipline in the diocese of Gloucester and also has discussed at length the work of the ecclesiastical commission both there and in Bristol diocese.[27] The Laudian church in Buckinghamshire is described with the aid of visitation records by E. R. C. Brinkworth.[28] Various documents pertaining to the working of church institutions have been published: episcopal registers, dean and chapter records, and archidiaconal and consistory court proceedings.[29] Henry I. Longden has compiled biographies of hundreds of clergy in Northamptonshire and Rutland.[30]

Much attention has been directed to Puritanism in this period and to the argument over church government between the defenders and the enemies of episcopacy. The best general survey of sixteenth-century

[27] F. Douglas Price, "The Abuses of Excommunication and the Decline of Ecclesiastical Discipline under Queen Elizabeth," *EHR*, 57: 106–115 (January 1942), and "The Commission for Ecclesiastical Causes for the Dioceses of Bristol and Gloucester, 1574," *Transactions of the Bristol and Gloucestershire Archaeological Society*, 59 (1937), pp. 51–151.

[28] E. R. C. Brinkworth, "The Laudian Church in Buckinghamshire," *UBHJ*, 5:31–59 (no. 1, 1955).

[29] Some examples are: *The Registers of . . . James Pilkington, Bishop of Durham, 1561–76*, ed. Gladys Hinde, Surtees Society, 161 (1952); *Peterborough Local Administration . . . the Dean and Chapter as Lord of the City*, ed. William T. Mellows and Daphne H. Gifford, Northamptonshire Record Society, 18 (1956); *The Archdeacon's Court: Liber Actorum, 1584*, ed. E. R. C. Brinkworth, Oxfordshire Record Society, 20, 21 (1942–46); *Select 16th Century Causes in Tithe from York Diocesan Registry*, ed. John S. Purvis, Yorkshire Archaelogical Society, 114 (1949); *Tudor Parish Documents of the Diocese of York*, ed. Purvis (Cambridge, Eng., 1948); *Winchester Consistory Court Depositions 1561–1602*, ed. Arthur J. Willis (Lyminge, 1960).

[30] Henry I. Longden, *Northampton and Rutland Clergy, A.D. 1500–1900*, Northamptonshire Record Society, 16 vols. (1939–52).

Puritanism is Marshall M. Knappen, *Tudor Puritanism: A Chapter in the History of Idealism* (Chicago, 1939). William Haller's valuable *The Rise of Puritanism, or The Way to the New Jerusalem as Set Forth in Pulpit and Press from Thomas Cartwright to John Lilburne and John Milton, 1570–1643* (New York, 1938), deals mainly with the early seventeenth century and concentrates on the teachings of the clerical brotherhood of Puritan preachers. Neither of these works has much to say about Puritanism as an organized movement or about its lay patrons and adherents. This continues to be the most neglected aspect of the subject and is a very serious lack that ought to be filled. A lively account of the Puritans and their critics in Cambridge University is presented in Harry C. Porter, *Reformation and Reaction in Tudor Cambridge* (Cambridge, Eng., 1958). Among the useful material in this book is a long summary of the theology of William Perkins, which shows plainly how very much Calvinism was a doctrine of assurance rather than despair.[31] On Puritan theology and ideas generally, Perry Miller, *The New England Mind: The Seventeenth Century* (New York, 1939), is fundamental. Other writings concerned with Puritan thought are Leonard J. Trinterud, "The Origins of Puritanism" (*Church History*, 20:37–51 [March 1951]), which stresses the non-Calvinist sources of the covenant theology, and Alan Simpson, *Puritanism in Old and New England* (Chicago, 1955), a work that appears to exaggerate the importance of the apocalyptic and enthusiast element in Puritan belief. A treatment of the debate on episcopacy containing a fine analysis of the attitude of the authorities of the Established Church is Norman Sykes, *Old Priest and New Presbyter* (Cambridge, Eng., 1956). Ebenezer T. Davies, *Episcopacy and the Royal Supremacy in the Church of England in the XVI Century* (Oxford, 1950), summarizes the teachings of the Anglican formularies on episcopacy and discusses the status of the episcopal order. The sermons delivered at Paul's Cross, some of the most famous of which, such as Richard Bancroft's in 1589, were attacks on the Puritans, are dealt with in Millar MacLure, *The Paul's Cross Sermons, 1534–1642* (Toronto, 1958). William P. Holden has surveyed some of the contemporary literature critical of the Puritans in *Anti-Puritan Sa-*

---

[31] Perkins is also discussed in Louis B. Wright, "William Perkins: Elizabethan Apostle of Practical Divinity," *HLQ*, 3:171–196 (January 1940); Rosemary A. Sisson, "William Perkins, Apologist for the Elizabethan Church of England," *Modern Language Review*, 47:495–502 (October 1952); and Christopher Hill, "William Perkins and the Poor," *Puritanism and Revolution* (1958). Hill's volume also contains an essay on another great Puritan clergyman, "The Political Sermons of John Preston."

tire, 1572–1642 (New Haven, Conn., 1954). The points of similarity between the Puritan and the common lawyers' opposition to the Stuarts are discussed in familiar terms by John D. Eusden, *Puritans, Lawyers, and Politics in Early Seventeenth-Century England* (New Haven, Conn., 1958).

The last years have seen the publication of many important texts relating to Puritanism. Donald J. McGinn, *The Admonition Controversy* (New Brunswick, N.J., 1949), offers a most useful abridgment of the chief tracts in the debate between John Whitgift and Thomas Cartwright. One of the principal collections of documents, *Puritan Manifestoes*, edited by Walter H. Frere and Charles E. Douglas (1907), has been reprinted with a preface by Sykes (1954). The late Dr. Albert Peel and Leland H. Carlson have edited two volumes of texts in the series "Elizabethan Nonconformist Texts": *Cartwrightiana* (1951) and *The Writings of Robert Harrison and Robert Browne* (1953). Among works promised in this series for the future is the indispensable *A Parte of a Register*. Some manuscript pamphlets written by Bancroft against the Puritans have appeared: *Tracts Ascribed to Richard Bancroft*, edited by Peel (Cambridge, Eng., 1953). One of the last of Peel's many services to Puritan studies was *The Notebook of John Penry, 1593* (1944), the introduction to which considers the question of the authorship of the Marprelate tracts without reaching a definite conclusion. In 1943 they were ascribed to Penry by Donald J. McGinn, "The Real Martin Marprelate" (*PMLA*, 58:84–107 [March 1943]), and, more recently, to Job Throckmorton by Neale.[32] The main documents in the government's successful move in 1633 against the feoffees for impropriations—the Puritan effort to infiltrate the Established Church by buying up rights of patronage—are printed in *Activities of the Puritan Faction of the Church of England 1625–33*, edited by Isabel Calder (1957). They should be read in connection with Professor Calder's article, "A Seventeenth Century Attempt to Purify the Anglican Church" (*AHR*, 53:760–775 [July 1948]), and with E. W. Kirby's "The Lay Feoffees: A Study in Militant Puritanism" (*JMH*, 14:1–25 [March 1942]).

Roman Catholicism, too, has been the subject of important publication in the last years. On Catholic writings in the reigns of Elizabeth, James, and Charles, there are now two indispensable guides: A. C.

---

[32] Neale, *Elizabeth I and Her Parliaments, 1584–1601*, p. 220. Neale does not give much evidence for this identification, and it must still remain an open question.

Southern, *Elizabethan Recusant Prose 1559–1582* (London and Glasgow, 1950), which contains a richly annotated bibliography, and Antony F. Allison and David M. Rogers, "A Catalogue of Catholic Books in English, Printed Abroad or Secretly in England, 1558–1640" (*Biographical Studies*, 3:1–187 [Jan.–Apr. 1956]). A new journal, *Biographical Studies*, was founded in 1951 for the study of English Catholic history and has continued since 1957 under the title *Recusant History*. Many articles on sixteenth- and early seventeenth-century Catholics have appeared both in this periodical and in *The Month*. Father Leo Hicks, the author of several of these, has edited documents relating to one of the most extraordinary personalities of the time, the Jesuit, Robert Persons.[33] The Latin autobiographies of two Elizabethan priests, John Gerard and William Weston, have been translated afresh by Philip Caraman.[34]

No aspect of Elizabethan and early Stuart history has been more diligently cultivated recently than the social and economic. Here some of the liveliest discussion has ensued, and some of the most solid results have been achieved. Most provocative of debate has been the question of the rise of the gentry, which is, of course, related to the whole problem of the evolution of the social and economic order between 1540 and 1640 and, beyond that, to the nature of the English revolution. Professor Richard H. Tawney's famous article, "The Rise of the Gentry, 1558–1640," appeared in 1941 (*EcHR*, 11:1–38 [no. 1, 1941]) and was followed in 1948 by Lawrence Stone's account of the financial straits of the Elizabethan aristocracy ("The Anatomy of the Elizabethan Aristocracy," *EcHR*, 18:1–53 [nos. 1–2, 1948]). Professor Hugh R. Trevor-Roper's attacks on their views are contained in "The Elizabethan Aristocracy: An Anatomy Anatomized" (*EcHR*, 2d ser. 3:279–298 [no. 3, 1951]) and *The Gentry, 1540–1640* (Cambridge, Eng., 1953). The whole controversial literature of criticism, reply, counter-reply, and commentary is surveyed and appraised with full references in two articles by Perez Zagorin.[35] Other papers that review the debate in trenchant terms are Jack H. Hexter's "Storm over the Gentry" (*Encounter*, 10:22–34 [May

[33] *Letters and Memorials of Robert Persons, S.J.*, ed. Leo Hicks, Catholic Record Society, 39 (1942).

[34] *John Gerard*, trans. Philip Caraman (1951), and *William Weston*, trans. P. Caraman (1955).

[35] Perez Zagorin, "The English Revolution," *Journal of World History*, 2:668–681 (pts. 3–4, 1955), and "The Social Interpretation of the English Revolution," *JEcH*, 19:376–401 (September 1959).

1958]), Willson H. Coates, "An Analysis of Major Conflicts in Seventeenth-Century England" (*Conflict in Stuart England,* ed. Aiken and Henning), and Christopher Hill, "Recent Interpretations of the Civil War" (*Puritanism and Revolution*).

While it is too soon for any definitive conclusions on the major questions at issue, even in the present state of the discussion three points may confidently be ventured. First, no economic historian has concurred with Trevor-Roper's opinion that the gentry as an order was in difficulties in the later sixteenth and early seventeenth centuries. Indeed, recent studies of landownership such as Mary E. Finch's important monograph, *The Wealth of Five Northamptonshire Families 1540–1640* (Oxford, 1956), suggest precisely the contrary. Second, Trevor-Roper has certainly exposed some errors of Tawney and Stone. Third, his emphasis on the significance of court office has opened an important area of inquiry, and the political origin of the English revolution is likely to be found, as he has proposed, in the conflict between the court and the Country opposition formed largely of nonofficial peers and gentry, though his conception of the latter as an economically declining body of "outsiders" is surely mistaken.

Other writings of a less controversial character pertaining to social classes also have been published. Mildred Campbell, *The English Yeoman under Elizabeth and the Early Stuarts* (New Haven, Conn., 1942), is an outstanding description of the economic position, status, and culture of one of the main strata in English society. On the nobility, there have been several important papers by Lawrence Stone, particularly "The Inflation of Honours 1558–1641." [36] *The Social Structure in Caroline England* (Oxford, 1948) and *The Age of Charles I* (1951), by David Mathew, survey the early seventeenth-century social order interestingly and often with deep insight, but are spotty and incomplete. Wallace Notestein, *The English People on the Eve of Colonization, 1603–1630* (New York, 1954), contains interesting material and a good bibliography of social history. Mark H. Curtis, *Oxford and Cambridge in Transition 1558–1642* (Oxford, 1959), traces the changing functions of the university in English society and depicts the new relation between

---

[36] Lawrence Stone, "The Inflation of Honours 1558–1641," *PP,* 14 (November 1958), pp. 43–65; see also L. Stone, "The Nobility in Business," *The Entrepreneur* (Cambridge, Mass., 1957), pp. 14–21, and "Marriage among the English Nobility in the 16th and 17th Centuries," *Comparative Studies in Society and History,* 3:182–206 (January 1961). On the inflation of honors, see also Charles R. Mayes, "The Sale of Peerages in Early Stuart England," *JMH,* 29:21–37 (March 1957).

them which came into being. On the same topic, Jack H. Hexter, "The Education of the Aristocracy in the Renaissance" (*JMH*, 22:1–20 [March 1950]), should also be read, as well as Fritz Caspari, *Humanism and the Social Order in Tudor England* (Chicago, 1954). On the milieu, taste, and interests of citizens and the "middle sort of people," Louis B. Wright's extraordinarily full *Middle-Class Culture in Elizabethan England* (Chapel Hill, N.C., 1935) has recently been reprinted (Ithaca, N.Y., 1958). Walter L. Woodfill, *Musicians in English Society from Elizabeth to Charles I* (Princeton, N.J., 1953), is a definitive account of the musical profession in all its aspects: in London, the provinces, the church, and the court. In *The Professional Writer in Elizabethan England* (Cambridge, Mass., 1959), Edwin H. Miller deals with the literary profession. The nature and motives of the patronage extended to literature by a great nobleman are analyzed in Eleanor Rosenberg, *Leicester: Patron of Letters* (New York, 1955). Among texts valuable for the study of social life and much else besides, the chief recent publication is the complete and well-annotated collection—479 in all—of *The Letters of John Chamberlain*, the busy gossip who knew so much of what was happening or rumored in the city, the court, and among the governing class.[37] English domestic relations are depicted in two works that have good illustrations and useful bibliographies: Carroll Camden, *The Elizabethan Woman: A Panorama of English Womanhood, 1540 to 1640* (1952), and Lu E. Pearson, *Elizabethans at Home* (Stanford, Calif., 1957).

Of works relating to the social order, special mention must be made of Wilbur K. Jordan's *Philanthropy in England, 1480–1660: A Study of the Changing Pattern of English Social Aspirations* (New York, 1959) and its tributary volumes, *The Charities of London, 1480–1660: The Aspirations and the Achievements of the Urban Society* (New York, 1960) and *The Forming of the Charitable Institutions of the West of England: A Study of the Changing Pattern of Social Aspirations in Bristol and Somerset, 1480–1660* (Philadelphia, 1960).[38] The scope of this monumental study is much wider than its title implies, and both its innovations in method and its conclusions establish it as the chief contribution in this century to English social history. The method is to use as

[37] *The Letters of John Chamberlain*, ed. Norman E. McClure (Philadelphia, 1939). A new and hitherto unknown letter of Chamberlain dating from 1587 has been published by John W. Stoye in *EHR*, 62:522–532 (October 1947).

[38] A concluding volume in this study on the charitable institutions of Buckinghamshire, Norfolk, and Yorkshire is promised.

evidence the wills of charitable donors on so massive a scale as to render feasible a detailed investigation of the transition from one state of society to another. The gifts and benefactions of nearly 35,000 men and women of all classes and ranks have been studied for the years 1480–1660 in ten counties that comprised perhaps one-third the population and over half the wealth of the nation. A careful analysis of this huge number of gifts by decade intervals, by social rank, and according to their many different objects—church, poor relief, social rehabilitation, education, and other—has enabled Jordan to demonstrate the changing pattern of aspirations of the various sorts and conditions of men during this long period. He has thus been able to show how, and in what proportions, the provision of wealth for secular purposes supplanted gifts to the church, and how men set themselves to create with their benefactions new institutions of social assistance and betterment, removed from the supervision of the traditional ecclesiastical authorities. The examination of the pace of this process in different regions and classes, illustrated by numerous statistical tables, is one of the most fascinating aspects of the work. Jordan is aware of the limitations and problematic features of his method, the most serious of these being the inability to make allowance in the data for the steady rise in prices over the epoch treated. Despite this, the main lines of the work stand firm, and its depiction of the earlier stages in the transition to a liberal society, as well as the quantities of information it contains on many other subjects, will have to be pondered by all students of the period.

An aspect of social history that is increasingly pursued with the most promising results is the study of particular towns, counties, and regions. At one time the preserve mainly of antiquarians and of warmhearted amateurs engaged in celebrating their own *lares* and *penates*, local history is today more and more a subject of research by professional scholars. By means of their investigations, grandiose generalizations can be tested and brought down to earth, the perspective that sees all events from London and the center of government can be corrected and enlarged, and the experience of local communities, whose life before the appearance of the present metropolitan age was so vivid and embracing, can be integrated into the general history of the nation. What may be done in local history is to be seen in Alfred L. Rowse's rich and detailed book, *Tudor Cornwall* (1941), an outstanding example of the synthesis between local and national history, which is to be looked for from such work. Many distinguished contributions have also been made by William G. Hoskins, a master in this field of study. Some of the best are in *Essays in Leicestershire History* (Liverpool, 1950) and in *Devonshire Studies* (the latter written in collaboration with H. P. R. Finberg [1952]). His "An Elizabethan Provincial Town: Leicester," in *Studies in Social History,* edited by John H. Plumb (1955), should also be read. William B. Willcox, *Gloucestershire: A Study in Local Government, 1590–1640* (New Haven, Conn., 1940), gives a valuable picture of this county. Several chapters in Arthur H. Dodd, *Studies in Stuart Wales* (Cardiff, 1952), deal illuminatingly with this period. Wallace T. Mac-Caffrey, *Exeter, 1540–1640: The Growth of an English County Town* (Cambridge, Mass., 1958), is an able account of an important town, which shows the cohesive and protectionist spirit that prevailed in the community and its dominant merchant group. James W. F. Hill, *Tudor and Stuart Lincoln* (Cambridge, Eng., 1956), has interesting material, but leaves important topics untouched. Large quantities of documents relating to local history are being published by British record and antiquarian societies. Most of these are listed in Edward L. C. Mullins' guide, already mentioned. Charles Gross's indispensable *A Bibliography of British Municipal History* (Cambridge, Mass., 1915) should be reissued in a new and up-to-date edition.

We come finally to economic history, whose connections with both social and local history are so multifarious and on which so much of importance has been done in recent years. Most of the principal contributions have appeared in articles in the *Economic History Review* and should be sought there. Owing no doubt to the controversial character of some of the problems and to the conviction that more monographic material is necessary, no new detailed economic history of the sixteenth and seventeenth centuries has appeared. However, the second and third volumes of Ephraim Lipson's great *Economic History of England* (1931), which treat this period, were reprinted in a fifth edition with fresh information (1948–56).[39] A brief but useful survey is George N. Clark's *The Wealth of England from 1496 to 1760* (Oxford, 1946). Among more specialized works the chief one is Richard H. Tawney, *Business and Politics under James I: Lionel Cranfield as Merchant and Minister* (Cambridge, Eng., 1958), which describes with inimitable style and scholarship Cranfield's career in business and government and gives a masterly account of commerce at this time. Another valuable study, out-

[39] This fifth edition seems little changed from the third enlarged edition of 1943 which contains much additional material in both text and notes.

standing for its scope and its analytical trenchancy, is Barry E. Supple, *Commercial Crisis and Change in England, 1600–1642: A Study in the Instability of a Mercantile Economy* (Cambridge, Eng., 1959). John U. Nef's *Industry and Government in France and England, 1540–1640* (Philadelphia, 1940), is a suggestive attempt to relate political and constitutional factors to economic growth. Its assertion that English economic development in this century was so great in some fields as to have constituted a "first industrial revolution" is perhaps questionable. Robert K. Ashton, *The Crown and the Money Market, 1603–1640* (Oxford, 1960), presents a penetrating account of royal borrowing and its political implications under the early Stuarts. Foreign trade is discussed in Thomas S. Willan, *The Early History of the Russia Company, 1553–1603* (Manchester, Eng., 1956), and *Studies in Elizabethan Foreign Trade* (Manchester, Eng., 1959), and in George D. Ramsay, *English Overseas Trade during the Centuries of Emergence* (1957), and Raymond W. K. Hinton, *The Eastland Trade and the Commonweal in the Seventeenth Century* (Cambridge, Eng., 1959). An important work relating to industrial regulation is Margaret G. Davies, *The Enforcement of English Apprenticeship: A Study in Applied Mercantilism, 1563–1642* (Cambridge, Mass., 1956). The wool trade is treated in George D. Ramsay, *The Wiltshire Woollen Industry in the Sixteenth and Seventeenth Centuries* (Oxford, 1943), and Thomas C. Mendenhall, *The Shrewsbury Drapers and the Welsh Wool Trade in the XVIth and XVIIth Centuries* (Oxford, 1953). On agrarian life, Joan Thirsk, *English Peasant Farming: The Agrarian History of Lincolnshire from Tudor to Recent Times* (1957) and *Fenland Farming in the Sixteenth Century* (Leicester, 1953), should be noted. The same writer has given a serviceable summary of the enclosure problem in *Tudor Enclosures* (1959).

Turning briefly to cultural history and the history of ideas (from which literary history proper is excluded as beyond our purview), we may notice a few important works. Two learned and detailed treatments of the sixteenth and early seventeenth centuries respectively, containing much material on thought, both written with distinction and compendiously supplied with bibliographies, are: Clive S. Lewis, *English Literature in the Sixteenth Century, Excluding Drama* (*The Oxford History of English Literature*, III [Oxford, 1954]), and Douglas Bush, *English Literature in the Earlier Seventeenth Century* (*The Oxford History of English Literature*, V [Oxford, 1945]). Eustace M. W. Tillyard, *The*

Elizabethan World Picture (1943), is a stimulating presentation of the presuppositions of sixteenth-century thought and its basis in the idea of cosmic order. It should be read together with James Winny, *The Frame of Order: An Outline of Elizabethan Belief* (1957), a brief anthology of texts. Paul H. Kocher also deals with significant aspects of intellectual history in *Science and Religion in Elizabethan England* (San Marino, Calif., 1953). A rather pedestrian treatment of Bacon as a thinker is Fulton H. Anderson, *The Philosophy of Francis Bacon* (Chicago, 1948).[40] On political ideas in the sixteenth century, the outstanding recent work is Christopher Morris, *Political Thought in England: Tyndale to Hooker* (1953), a brilliant essay. There are several books devoted to Richard Hooker, among them Peter Munz, *The Place of Hooker in the History of Thought* (1952), and F. J. Shirley, *Richard Hooker and Contemporary Political Ideas* (1949). Interesting and valuable studies on special aspects of political thought are John G. A. Pocock, *The Ancient Constitution and the Feudal Law: A Study of English Historical Thought in the Seventeenth Century* (Cambridge, Eng., 1957), and J. H. M. Salmon, *The French Religious Wars in English Political Thought* (Oxford, 1959). Margaret Judson's scholarly *The Crisis of the Constitution* (New Brunswick, N.J., 1949) is a full and careful analysis of constitutional and political ideas from 1603 to 1645. George L. Mosse, *The Struggle for Sovereignty in England from the Reign of Queen Elizabeth to the Petition of Right* (East Lansing, Mich., 1950), deals usefully with the same subject. A good short essay on James I's political philosophy is W. H. Greenleaf, "James I and the Divine Right of Kings" (*Political Studies,* 5:36–48 [February 1957]).

Many biographies of both greater and lesser luminaries in the Elizabethan and early Stuart worlds have appeared during the years under review, though some notable personalities still remain inadequately treated or completely unchronicled. The outstanding recent work of biography is Read's history of Lord Burghley, already referred to, which definitively fills the longstanding need for a life of the great Tudor statesman. An account of the earlier years of his son, Sir Robert Cecil, has been written by Phyllis M. Handover, *The Second Cecil* (1959), but more and deeper work needs to be done on this important individual.

---

[40] On Bacon, see also Benjamin Farrington, *Francis Bacon, Philosopher of Industrial Science* (New York, 1949), and James G. Crowther, *Francis Bacon, The First Statesman of Science* (1960).

Catherine D. Bowen, *The Lion and the Throne: The Life and Times of Sir Edward Coke (1552–1634)* (Boston, 1957), has no new material, but does partial justice to Coke's extraordinary and many-sided career. Two lives of Raleigh have appeared: Ernest A. Strathmann, *Sir Walter Ralegh: A Study in Elizabethan Skepticism* (New York, 1951), and Willard M. Wallace, *Sir Walter Raleigh* (Princeton, N.J., 1959). Yet this protean man of genius still defies definition, and some mysteries still lurk about his career. David B. Quinn, *Raleigh and the British Empire* (1947), is a good study of Raleigh's activities as an explorer and colonizer. Cyril Falls has written the biography of the Earl of Essex' successor in the Irish command—*Mountjoy: Elizabethan General* (1955). A major biographical contribution is David H. Willson, *King James VI and I* (1956). There have been lives of Archbishop Whitgift by Powel M. Dawley (*John Whitgift and the English Reformation* [New York, 1954]) and Victor J. K. Brook (*Whitgift and the English Church* [1957]). Paul A. Welsby wrote a biographical account of another great ecclesiastic: *Lancelot Andrewes 1555–1626* (1958). The most recent life of William Laud is now Hugh R. Trevor-Roper, *Archbishovp Laud* (1940). Irvonwy Morgan, *Prince Charles's Puritan Chaplain* (1958), describes the political career of the influential Puritan clergyman, John Preston, and has a suggestive though not always accurate analysis of Puritan-court relations. A most interesting life of a financial magnate, which displays the seamier side of Elizabethan politics, is Lawrence Stone's *An Elizabethan: Sir Horatio Palavicino* (Oxford, 1956). James A. Williamson, *Hawkins of Plymouth: A New History of Sir John Hawkins and of the Other Members of His Family Prominent in Tudor England* (1949), presents new facts about this great sailor and his relations.

There are many gaps in our portrait gallery of these wonderful years. The careers of Elizabeth's favorites, Leicester and Essex, have never yet been fully related and their political roles traced through all their ramifications. There is no satisfactory life of Sir Christopher Hatton, nor any at all of Archbishop Bancroft, Nicholas Bacon, Elizabeth's Lord Keeper, his son, Anthony Bacon, who was Essex' intimate, nor of Lord Chancellor Ellesmere. Neither have the two famous Catholic activists, William Cardinal Allen and the Jesuit, Robert Persons, found a biographer. The life of Sir Edwin Sandys, the colonizer and parliamentary opposition leader, remains to be written, as does that of another notable oppositionist, Sir Robert Phelips. Hugh F. Kearney's *Strafford in Ireland, 1633–41: A Study in Absolutism* (Manchester, Eng., 1957) is probably a definitive treatment of the Irish phase of the great Lord Lieutenant's career, yet his life as a whole must now be reconsidered on the basis of the vast collection of Wentworth Woodhouse manuscripts at Sheffield, first made available to historians in 1948.[41]

The last topic to be noticed is exploration and empire—one of the greatest themes in Elizabethan historiography. Alfred L. Rowse has risen finely to the occasion in *The Expansion of Elizabethan England* (1955) and *The Elizabethans and America* (1959). Scientific history has not banished the moist eye and the patriotic swelling from these evocative narratives in which the mighty transatlantic destiny of the English people is prefigured. A survey of voyages and exploration by the leading authority on the subject has appeared in a revised edition: James A. Williamson, *The Age of Drake* (2d ed., 1946). Rayner Unwin has given an engrossing account of a famous episode in Hawkins' career in *The Defeat of John Hawkins: A Biography of His First Slaving Voyage* (1960). Louis B. Wright's *Religion and Empire: The Alliance between Piety and Commerce in English Expansion, 1558–1625* (Chapel Hill, N.C., 1943), discusses the support given by piety to expansion. A number of important texts have been edited by David B. Quinn for the Hakluyt Society: *The Roanoke Voyages, 1584–1590: Documents to Illustrate the English Voyages to North America under the Patent Granted to Walter Raleigh in 1584* (2 vols., 1955), and *The Voyages and Colonising Enterprises of Sir Humphrey Gilbert* (2 vols., 1940).

Taking a retrospective glance at the many writings listed in this survey, one sees that much has been done and that much more remains to be done. As the great French historian, Georges Lefèbvre, used to say, "Il faut travailler." For those who live under Clio's bracing influence, there is ever the prospect of "Tomorrow to fresh Woods, and Pastures new."

[41] The financial side of Strafford's career and his resourceful use of the opportunities of crown office are well described by J. P. Cooper, "The Fortune of Thomas Wentworth, Earl of Strafford," *EcHR* 2d ser., 11:227–248 (December 1958).

Writings on Oliver Cromwell
since 1929

❖

PAUL H. HARDACRE

I N *A Bibliography of Oliver Cromwell* the late Wilbur Cortez Abbott enumerated 3,520 principal items, together with
many pieces of subordinate or related interest.[1] There is no sign of
slackening interest in the great Puritan's life. To describe the chief contributions to Cromwell research in the last generation is the purpose of
this paper. A discussion of Abbott's contribution is followed by a description of the major narrative histories of the time. The stages in
Cromwell's career to 1653 are then considered bibliographically. The
Protectorate is treated topically, and a number of studies are mentioned
which in some way elucidate his policy, even though Cromwell is not
the central theme. A concluding section is devoted to recent biographies
of Cromwell. Discussion of theories explaining the revolution in social
terms is deliberately eschewed on the ground that adequate summaries
exist.[2]

It is natural to begin with Abbott's own magnum opus, *The Writings
and Speeches of Oliver Cromwell, with an Introduction, Notes and a
Sketch of His Life* (4 vols., Cambridge, Mass., 1937–47). Abbott was

[Reprinted from *JMH*, 33:1–14 (March 1961).]

[1] (Cambridge, Mass., 1929). Addenda through 1944 raised the total to 3,692
(*The Writings and Speeches of Oliver Cromwell*, IV, pp. 957–972).

[2] H. R. Trevor-Roper, "La révolution anglaise de Cromwell: une nouvelle inter-
prétation," *Annales: Économies-Sociétés-Civilisations*, 10:331–340 (July–September
1955); C. Hill, "À propos d'un article récent sur Cromwell," *ibid.*, 11:490–494
(October–December 1956); Hill, "Recent Interpretations of the Civil War," *History*,
41:67–87 (February–October 1956), reprinted in his *Puritanism and Revolution*
(1958); Hill, "La révolution anglaise du XVIIᵉ siècle," *Revue Historique*, 221:5–32
(January–March 1959); P. Zagorin, "The Social Interpretation of the English
Revolution," *JEcH*, 19:376–401 (September 1959); W. H. Coates, "An Analysis of
Major Conflicts in Seventeenth-century England," in *Conflict in Stuart England:
Essays in Honour of Wallace Notestein*, ed. W. A. Aiken and B. D. Henning
(1960), pp. 15–39.

able to add more than seven hundred items to the corpus of Cromwelliana as provided in the last edition of Thomas Carlyle's *Letters and Speeches of Oliver Cromwell*.[3] Many of these had been previously published in out-of-the-way places, but about 150 appeared for the first time. That many significant additions can be made seems improbable.[4] Abbott's presentation of the documents has been criticized in both plan and execution,[5] but the greatness of his achievement cannot be denied. In addition to collecting the letters and speeches, Abbott systematically recorded for the first time accounts of Cromwell's conversation as reported by Englishmen and foreigners. These add depth and conviction to his portrait. Like Carlyle, Abbott interspersed surveys of events among the letters, but his comments are fuller, more accurate, and less biased than those of his predecessor. Abbott was not wholly an admirer of Cromwell, whose actions and whose cause he criticized freely and forcefully. It is in his sympathetic attitude toward the royal cause that Abbott differed chiefly from S. R. Gardiner and C. H. Firth.

These two had related the history of England in detail down to 1658. In 1935 Sir Charles Firth expressed the hope that Godfrey Davies would write the history of England from Cromwell's death to the Restoration, on a large scale, to complete the series. Davies, whose volume *The Early Stuarts* supplied a general account of the civil war and interregnum,[6] had long been collecting materials and intensively studying the period. In *The Restoration of Charles II* (San Marino, Calif., 1955) he provided a detailed history of politics under Richard Cromwell and the republic until May 1660. Regret has been expressed that the author adhered so strictly to the political and chronological structure adopted by Gardiner and Firth. No one knew more keenly than Davies the desirability of a full economic and social history of the revolution. To furnish it within the framework of the history begun by his predecessors was impossible. Even so, in analyzing many hundreds of contemporary tracts which appeared after the relaxation of the Cromwellian censorship he expressed a larger outlook than they on the aspirations of the age and on the true character of Puritanism, and the completion of the history of the inter-

[3] Ed. S. C. Lomas, 3 vols. (1904).
[4] The letter to Valentine Walton sold at Sotheby's in October 1959 and described as unpublished (*Times Literary Supplement,* Nov. 20, 1959) has been printed at least five times.
[5] E. S. De Beer, in *History,* 23:120–129 (September 1938); examples of transcribing slips are given in *JMH,* 13:241–243 (June 1941).
[6] *The Oxford History of England,* IX (Oxford, 1937; 2d ed., 1959).

regnum made it possible more fully to appreciate the achievement of Oliver Cromwell.[7]

Another general account of major importance is Miss C. V. Wedgwood's *The Great Rebellion,* of which two volumes have now appeared.[8] The happy union of lively style and intimate knowledge of the sources promises a long future for the series. Miss Wedgwood employs a purely narrative approach, integrating Scottish and Irish history with the domestic, and on many topics the interrelationships are accordingly more apparent and "the immediate pressures and confusions" are better brought out.

Concerning the stages of Cromwell's life, much interest has been expressed in his prewar economic position, and Abbott collected a number of documents illustrating property transactions to which he was party. While it seems to be impossible to determine whether his condition was improving or worsening, his subscription in 1642 of £2,050 for raising a force for Ireland does not suggest serious decline.[9] Another aspect which has been studied is his advocacy of the cause of the fen-dwellers during the drainage disputes of 1637.[10]

Cromwell's religious development during the formative years, and its expression in his only recorded speech in the parliament of 1628–29 have, of course, been commented on by all his biographers. There is no trace of his activity in the Short Parliament. For the proceedings in the Long Parliament the main new source is the published continuation of D'Ewes's diary.[11] Cromwell was not a frequent speaker, but details illustrating his diligence in committees show him to have been an influential member, and it seems probable that he was one of those who met with Pym, Hampden, and others to organize an opposition strategy. It is

[7] A bibliography of the works of Godfrey Davies is appended to his *Essays on the Later Stuarts* (San Marino, Calif., 1958); see also his posthumous "Oliver Cromwell," *Encyclopaedia Britannica* (1960), VI, pp. 739–745.

[8] *The King's Peace, 1637–1641* (1955); *The King's War, 1641–1647* (1958).

[9] J. R. MacCormack, "The Irish Adventurers and the English Civil War," *IHS,* 10:21–58 (March 1956), a valuable article.

[10] Margaret Albright, "The Entrepreneurs of Fen-draining in England under James I and Charles I," *Explorations in Entrepreneurial History,* 8:51–65 (no. 2, 1955).

[11] *The Journal of Sir Simonds D'Ewes* [Oct. 12, 1641—Jan. 8, 1642], ed. W. H. Coates (New Haven, Conn., 1942). The completion of this series is devoutly to be wished, and will be facilitated by two works on the personnel: D. Brunton and D. H. Pennington, *Members of the Long Parliament* (1954), and Mary Frear Keeler, *The Long Parliament, 1640–41: A Biographical Study of Its Members* (Philadelphia, 1954).

not known why he took no share in the proceedings against Strafford.

Cromwell's first military service was in the army of the Earl of Essex.[12] In 1643 he converted his troop into a regiment which was soon put under the Earl of Manchester.[13] The main source for the new details adduced on this period is the collection of Commonwealth Exchequer papers (S.P. 28) in the Public Record Office. On the organization and administration of parliament's army they are of the utmost value, and contain a mass of details still awaiting exploration. They furnished the skeleton for a full account of the New Model—Sir Charles Firth and Godfrey Davies, *The Regimental History of Cromwell's Army* (2 vols., Oxford, 1940). The work provides copious information on literally hundreds of major and minor figures, as well as making a substantial contribution to general history. The Cromwellian army was an estate of the nation, and each regiment in a sense a constituency. From 1653 until 1659 the army was England's real government. National changes in religious and political sentiment found full expression in the army. In turn the character of the commanders, and especially of Cromwell, is thrown into striking light by military decisions such as the purging and replacement of individuals and the attempts to mold the opinion of rank and file.

Cromwell's quarrel with Manchester in 1643 is the subject of some correspondence of the Committee of the Eastern Association in a collection edited by A. M. Everitt, *Suffolk and the Great Rebellion* (Suffolk Record Society, 1961). He also figures prominently in another fine volume, *The Letter Books, 1644–45, of Sir Samuel Luke, Parliamentary Governor of Newport Pagnell,* edited by H. G. Tibbutt (Historical Manuscripts Commission, Joint Publication No. 4, 1963), where one new Cromwell letter appears, relating to the convoy of money in 1645.

Cromwell's commander from 1645 to 1649 has found a sympathetic biographer in M. A. Gibb, *The Lord General: A Life of Thomas Fairfax* (1938). Among other military lives the most important is W. H. Dawson, *Cromwell's Understudy: The Life and Times of General John Lambert* (1938), which occasionally debases Cromwell without justification.

---

[12] Godfrey Davies, "The Parliamentary Army under the Earl of Essex, 1642–5," *EHR,* 49:32–55 (January 1934); *Journal of Sir Samuel Luke, Scoutmaster-general to the Earl of Essex, 1643–4,* ed. I. G. Philip, 3 vols., Oxfordshire Record Society (1950–53).

[13] Godfrey Davies, "The Army of the Eastern Association, 1644–5," *EHR,* 46:88–96 (January 1931).

Sir James Berry and S. G. Lee, *A Cromwellian Major General: The Career of Colonel James Berry* (Oxford, 1938), depicts the scene through the eyes of a commander of horse; H. G. Tibbutt, *Colonel John Okey, 1606–1662* (Bedfordshire Historical Society, Streatley, 1955), through those of a colonel of dragoons. Lambert and Skippon are included in C. E. Lucas Phillips, *Cromwell's Captains* (1938), and an even more generous selection is M. P. Ashley, *Cromwell's Generals* (1954).

The operations of the civil war received relatively little attention after Gardiner. A. H. Burne and Peter Young, *The Great Civil War* (1959), is a summary of campaigns down to 1646 which amply demonstrates the growth of Cromwell's ability to control his men on the battlefield. His skill as a strategist and tactician did not become so apparent until 1648 and 1651. Three of the principal engagements in which Cromwell took part (Marston Moor, Naseby, and Preston) are examined by Austin Woolrych, *Battles of the Civil War* (1961). Other recent military publications are discussed by the present writer, in the introduction to C. H. Firth, *Cromwell's Army* (4th ed., 1962). Among a host of local studies, the following treat campaigns in which he participated: F. J. Varley, *Cambridge during the Civil War, 1642–1646* (Cambridge, Eng., 1935); F. J. Varley, *The Siege of Oxford* (Oxford, 1932; Supplement, 1935); [14] A. C. Wood, *Nottingham in the Civil War* (Oxford, 1937); and D. R. Guttery, *The Great Civil War in the Midland Parishes* (Birmingham, 1951). R. M. Dore, "Sir William Brereton's Siege of Chester and the Campaign of Naseby," calls for special mention in that it includes two hitherto unpublished Cromwell letters of 1645.[15]

Perhaps no comparable period of English history has received more attention than the crisis of 1647–48. The quarrels between parliament and the army, and between Presbyterians and Independents, and the radical political and social doctrines which were then enunciated have all been intensively studied. The publication of new texts of old sources has also been a marked advance. A good selection is provided in *Tracts on Liberty in the Puritan Revolution, 1638–1647*, edited by William Haller (3 vols., New York, 1933–34), and Professor Haller has also written a vigorous account of *The Rise of Puritanism* (New York, 1938), followed by his *Liberty and Reformation in the Puritan Revolution*

[14] Cf. *Mercurius Aulicus*, comp. F. J. Varley (Oxford, 1948), consisting of extracts from Birkenhead's newspaper published at Oxford, 1643–1645.

[15] *Transactions of the Lancashire and Cheshire Antiquarian Society*, 67 (1957), pp. 17–44.

(New York, 1955).[16] A related work is W. Schenk, *The Concern for Social Justice in the Puritan Revolution* (1948), which affords a general exploration of the roots of social unrest. A penetrating treatment of the nontheological aspect of Puritanism is Christopher Hill, *Society and Puritanism in Pre-revolutionary England* (New York, 1964). George Yule, *The Independents in the English Civil War* (Cambridge, Eng., 1958), is a convincing account of Cromwell's party and its goal, a state church with toleration. A similar analysis of the Presbyterians would be most useful.[17]

A fresh discussion of religion in the army is L. F. Solt, *Saints in Arms* (Stanford, Calif., 1959), while the army's most famous preacher is the subject of Raymond P. Stearns, *The Strenuous Puritan: Hugh Peter, 1598–1660* (Urbana, Ill., 1954). The political views of the army are set forth with great fullness in *Puritanism and Liberty, Being the Army Debates (1647–9) from the Clarke Manuscripts*, edited by A. S. P. Woodhouse (1938), which is fortified with numerous extracts from the pamphlets of the day. The foremost conservative spokesman in these debates, and Cromwell's son-in-law, is portrayed by R. W. Ramsey, *Henry Ireton* (1949).[18] For the Levellers there is an excellent bibliographical review, O. Lutaud, "Le Parti 'Niveleur' et la première révolution anglaise" (*Revue Historique*, 227:77–115, 377–414 [January–March, April–June 1962]), and two good collections which do not significantly duplicate each other, *The Leveller Tracts, 1647–1653*, edited by William Haller and Godfrey Davies (New York, 1944), and *Leveller Manifestoes of the Puritan Revolution*, edited by Don M. Wolfe (New York, 1944). A general account is Joseph Frank, *The Levellers* (Cambridge, Mass., 1955). Special studies include D. B. Robertson, *The Religious Foundations of Leveller Democracy* (New York, 1951); M. A. Gibb, *John Lilburne the Leveller* (1948); Pauline Gregg, *Free-born John* (1961); and M. P. Ashley, *John Wildman, Plotter and Postmaster* (1947), which is also useful for the Commonwealth and Protectorate. The communist movement may be studied in: *The Works of Gerrard Winstanley*, edited by G. H. Sabine (Ithaca, N.Y., 1941); *Selections from the Works of Gerrard Winstanley*, edited by Leonard Hamilton (1944); and D. W.

---

[16] A shorter treatment written with great insight is Alan Simpson, *Puritanism in Old and New England* (Chicago, 1955).

[17] See Vernon F. Snow, "Attendance Trends and Absenteeism in the Long Parliament," *HLQ*, 18:301–306 (April 1955).

[18] He also wrote *Studies in Cromwell's Family Circle* (1930), *Henry Cromwell* (1933), and *Richard Cromwell* (1935).

Petegorsky, *Left-wing Democracy in the English Civil War* (1940).[19] A convenient guide to all these movements, together with the later doctrines of the interregnum, is P. Zagorin, *A History of Political Thought in the English Revolution* (1954).

Cromwell is a principal figure in all the writings on 1647–1649. He was denounced by parliamentarians and Levellers alike. The first charged him with persuading the soldiers to refuse parliament's terms for disbandment; the second with betraying the soldiers' cause by setting aside the council of the army. A review of the evidence suggests that while Cromwell was hesitant and inconsistent, he was not the hypocrite excoriated by Holles and Lilburne, but that he changed his course from time to time as the situation seemed to demand. Thus the danger of mutiny in the army caused him to incline steadily toward the conservative side.

In the second civil war Cromwell was employed in Wales,[20] and then struck north to meet the Scottish invasion. The campaign of Preston and the siege of Pontefract occupied him until November 1648, and thus he was absent from the momentous debates at St. Albans and Westminster on the settlement of the kingdom. At this juncture more than ever his outlook defies analysis. He returned to London on December 6, 1648, but appears to have attended only two of the meetings of the council of officers held between then and February 1649. Although he declared that he was unacquainted with the plan to purge parliament, he approved it once it was accomplished. Thereafter the picture becomes clearer, and Cromwell was the moving spirit in bringing the king to trial. The details are set forth by J. G. Muddiman, *Trial of King Charles the First* (n.d. [c. 1928]), who prints the text of Bradshawe's journal and collects the evidence taken at the trials of the regicides after the Restoration.[21]

In March 1649 Cromwell was nominated to command in Ireland, but before he departed he was called on to suppress the Leveller mutiny of

[19] See also W. S. Hudson, "Economic and Social Thought of Gerrard Winstanley," *JMH*, 18:1–21 (March 1946). *Puritanesimo e Libertà: Dibattiti e Libelli*, ed. Vittorio Gabrieli (Turin, 1956) has independent value because of the editor's excellent introduction.

[20] A. L. Leach, *The History of the Civil War (1642–49) in Pembrokeshire and on Its Borders* (1937).

[21] The credibility of Herbert, whose *Memoirs* were long accepted with respect to the captivity of the king, and whom Gardiner followed, "though with grave misgivings," has now been convincingly demolished by N. H. Mackenzie, "Sir Thomas Herbert of Tintern, a Parliamentary 'Royalist,'" *BIHR*, 29:32–86 (May 1956).

the soldiers at Burford.[22] He arrived in Ireland in August 1649. The state of that kingdom may be studied in Thomas L. Coonan, *The Irish Catholic Confederacy and the Puritan Revolution* (Dublin and New York, 1954), which naturally deals mainly with the period before 1649, but which also has material on the Cromwellian period. Two notable additions to the sources on Ireland have been edited by Charles McNeill, "Reports on the Rawlinson Collection of Manuscripts Preserved in the Bodleian Library, Oxford," [23] and *The Tanner Letters* (Dublin 1943), consisting of Irish material from that collection, also in the Bodleian. The former includes a number of documents which Thomas Birch omitted from his edition of the Thurloe papers.

Although Cromwell was not its architect, he acquiesced in the Commonwealth settlement of Ireland and originated the policy of transplantation as finally adopted. The basis on which lands were confiscated and reassigned is *The Civil Survey, A.D. 1654–1656,* edited by R. C. Simington (9 vols., Dublin, 1931–53).[24]

Cromwell's Scottish campaigns were so thoroughly studied by Gardiner and Firth that there was not much to be gleaned by their successors.[25] When he returned to London after the victory at Worcester his position was somewhat ambiguous. Although nominally subordinate to parliament his power was unbounded if he chose to use the army. Yet despite charges of ambition brought against him many years later he showed no signs of personal motives, and in fact was defeated in parliament on issues in which he was interested. Together with the army leaders he wanted reconciliation, toleration, reform, and a general election, and the failure of the Rump to gratify any of these desires explains his decision to terminate its sittings.[26] Then, with complete inconsistency, after having dispersed the Rump for its refusal to dissolve in favor of a

---

[22] As Abbott did not include it in his *Bibliography,* or refer to it in the *Writings,* mention should be made of R. H. Gretton, *The Burford Records* (Oxford, 1920), pp. 233–256, where details are given.

[23] *Analecta Hibernica,* no. 1 (March 1930), pp. 12–178; no. 2 (January 1931), pp. 1–92.

[24] See J. G. Simms, "The Civil Survey, 1654–6," *IHS,* 9:253–263 (March 1955), and E. Strauss, *Sir William Petty* (1954). I have not seen *Books of Survey and Distribution,* ed. R. C. Simington (Dublin, 1949——), which shows the position regarding landownership in each parish and barony prior and subsequent to the Cromwellian forfeitures. [See below, essay by H. Mulvey, n. 25.]

[25] Kenneth C. Corsar, "The Surrender of Edinburgh Castle, December 1650," *SHR,* 28:43–54 (April 1949), suggests the commander abandoned his trust with only a token resistance.

[26] L. H. Carlson, "A History of the Presbyterian Party from Pride's Purge to the Dissolution of the Long Parliament," *Church History,* 11:83–122 (June 1942).

more representative body, the army leaders called into being the Nominated Parliament, whose members were hand-picked from lists forwarded by the gathered churches.[27] These abdicated on December 12, 1653, and four days later Cromwell was installed as Protector.

The history of the Protectorate is the history of the attempt to put into effect the ideas of the army. Although not their originator, Cromwell shared these ideas, but in attempting to implement them he had to take into account other forces and pressures, foreign and domestic. The machinery of government which he inherited was a mixture of old and new. The Instrument of Government (1653) and the Humble Petition and Advice (1657) embodied certain fundamental principles,[28] but having been imposed on the nation these constitutions had no popular sanction or support in national loyalty. H. R. Trevor-Roper, "Oliver Cromwell and His Parliaments," [29] argues vigorously that Cromwell's attempt to govern through parliament failed abjectly for want of management along the lines employed by Elizabeth. Whether any amount of such management could have overcome basic disagreement over the perpetuation of military rule is, however, problematical.

Except as regards the financial side, the administrative history of the Protectorate has hardly been touched, and even here the problems are obscure and the figures often contradictory. In a most useful volume, M. P. Ashley, *Financial and Commercial Policy under the Cromwellian Protectorate* (Oxford, 1934) discussed the revenue system, and advanced some suggestions about the relationship between politics and the state of the public debt.[30] The history of the excise was treated by Edward Hughes, *Studies in Administration and Finance, 1558–1825* (Manchester, Eng., 1934), the sale of royal estates by Sidney J. Madge, *The Domesday of Crown Lands* (1938), and the sale of the lands of delinquents by Joan Thirsk, "The Sales of Royalist Land during the Interregnum." [31] By 1653 a multiplicity of committees had grown up to

[27] In a very significant article, Margaret James rehabilitates to some extent this much-maligned body: "The Political Importance of the Tithes Controversy in the English Revolution, 1640–60," *History*, 26:1–18 (June 1941).

[28] J. W. Gough, *Fundamental Law in English Constitutional History* (Oxford, 1955); Vernon F. Snow, "Parliamentary Reapportionment Proposals in the Puritan Revolution," *EHR*, 74:409–442 (July 1959).

[29] *Essays Presented to Sir Lewis Namier*, ed. R. Pares and A. J. P. Taylor (1956), pp. 1–48.

[30] Cf. R. D. Richards, "The Exchequer in Cromwellian Times," *Economic History*, 2:213–233 (January 1931).

[31] *EcHR*, 2d ser., 5:188–207 (December 1952); cf. H. J. Habakkuk, "Public Finance and the Sale of Confiscated Property during the Interregnum," *ibid.*, 2d ser., 15:70–88 (August 1962).

administer these and related matters, some exercising almost plenary powers, often so as to give rise to great complaint. It has been suggested that the reform of these, and the training of competent and honest administrators, constituted Cromwell's "most lasting achievement." [32] In the absence of detailed studies of the Protectorate councils and bureaucracy, generalization is risky, but the great attention which Cromwell devoted to detail gives the impression that government was more personal and centralized under him than under Charles I or Charles II. [33]

The enforcement of policy depended largely on local bodies and individuals, some representing the prewar political machine, others inherited from the period of the civil war. Judging from the surviving records the Protector did not interfere much with the traditional forms of county government until 1655. Of the civil war innovations the most important was the county committee, [34] on which, for the Protectorate, there are accounts in Mary Coate, *Cornwall in the Great Civil War and Interregnum, 1642–1660* (Oxford, 1933) (a model local history), and A. H. Dodd, *Studies in Stuart Wales* (Cardiff, 1952). For about two years, 1655–1656, local government was largely administered by the major generals. Thus the lives of Lambert, Berry, Okey, and others, cited above, supply many details. [35] At the municipal level the most important aspect of Cromwell's rule was the inquisition into borough charters, which in many cases were eventually surrendered. [36] C. G. Parsloe dealt with some examples of this in "The Growth of a Borough Constitution: Newark-on-Trent, 1549–1688," [37] "The Corporation of Bedford, 1647–64," [38] and in his edition of *The Minute Book of Bedford Corporation, 1647–1664.* [39]

One of the most useful collections for the Protectorate which has ap-

[32] A. H. Dodd, *The Growth of Responsible Government* (1956), p. 45, quoting W. Cunningham, *The Growth of English Industry and Commerce*, II, 182–184. For one example of conspicuous improvement see Howard Robinson, *The British Post Office* (Princeton, N.J., 1948).

[33] See Godfrey Davies, in *The Yale Review*, 37:376 (winter 1948).

[34] A fresh general account is the introduction to *The Committee at Stafford, 1643–1645*, ed. D. H. Pennington and I. A. Roots (Manchester Eng., 1957); see also A. M. Everitt, *The County Committee of Kent in the Civil War* (Leicester, 1957).

[35] Cf. P. H. Hardacre, "William Boteler: A Cromwellian Oligarch," *HLQ*, 11:1–11 (October 1947).

[36] For a survey of the older literature on this subject, together with some additional references, see G. D. Ramsay, "Industrial *laisser-faire* and the Policy of Cromwell," *EcHR*, 16:93–110 (no. 2, 1946), especially pp. 97–99.

[37] *TRHS*, 4th ser., 22 (1940).

[38] *Ibid.*, 29 (1947).

[39] Bedfordshire Historical Record Society (Streatley, 1949).

peared in recent years is royalist in origin. The *Calendar of the Clarendon State Papers,* IV, edited by F. J. Routledge (Oxford, 1932), covers the period 1657–1660, and includes much information on the state of politics and many side lights on Cromwell. Royalist correspondence was largely connected with plans for risings against the interlopers, a subject which has been treated in detail by David Underdown, *Royalist Conspiracy in England, 1649–1660* (New Haven, Conn., 1960). The book sheds much light on the Protector's security system, as well as on the suppression of the few risings which took place.[40] Cromwell's rule is viewed through royalist eyes in *The Diary of John Evelyn,* edited by E. S. De Beer (6 vols., Oxford, 1955), and *The Oxinden and Peyton Letters, 1642–1670,* edited by Dorothy Gardiner (1937), while the Protector's moderation toward peaceable royalists is discussed in P. H. Hardacre, *The Royalists during the Puritan Revolution* (The Hague, 1956).[41]

The ideas of the Commonwealthmen, another dissident group, are discussed by Zera S. Fink, *The Classical Republicans* (Evanston, Ill., 1945). A leading pamphleteer against Cromwell's tyranny is portrayed by William Lamont, *Marginal Prynne, 1600–1669* (1963).[42]

A very profound explication of the Protector's religious outlook is G. F. Nuttall, *The Holy Spirit in Puritan Faith and Experience* (Oxford, 1946; 2d ed., 1947). There is a fine account of the Cromwellian church in volume III of W. K. Jordan, *The Development of Religious Toleration in England* (4 vols., Cambridge, Mass., 1932–40).[43] This can be supplemented fruitfully through local history: an example is Harold Smith, *The Ecclesiastical History of Essex under the Long Parliament and Commonwealth* (Colchester, 1932), where information is collected on the triers and ejectors, presentations by the Protector, augmentations, etc. The lives of intruding ministers during the interregnum should be approached through A. G. Matthews, *Calamy Revised* (Oxford, 1934).

The waning under the Protectorate of the classical Presbyterian system erected in 1645 is illustrated by *The Register-Booke of the Fourth Classis in the Province of London, 1646–59,* edited by C. E. Surnam

---

[40] See also A. H. Woolrych, *Penruddock's Rising, 1655,* Historical Association (1955).

[41] Cf. C. H. Firth, "The Royalists under the Protectorate," *EHR,* 52:634–648 (October 1937).

[42] For a full list of Prynne's writings see Godfrey Davies and Mary Isabel Frye, "William Prynne in the Huntington Library," *HLQ,* 20:53–93 (October 1956).

[43] Cf. E. W. Kirby, "The Cromwellian Establishment," *Church History,* 10:144–158 (June 1941).

(1953): meetings after 1650 were never as frequent as provided by law, and a quorum was never present at any meeting from 1654 to 1659.

The literature of sectarianism is fully explored in Jordan's *Development of Religious Toleration*.[44] Among recent works which shed particular light on Cromwell and his policy, the following are valuable: G. F. Nuttall, *Visible Saints: The Congregational Way, 1640–1660* (Oxford, 1957);[45] E. Fogelkou, *James Nayler* (1931); Isabel Ross, *Margaret Fell, Mother of Quakerism* (1949); and new editions of *The Journal of George Fox*,[46] and of W. C. Braithwaite's *The Beginnings of Quakerism*.[47]

For the ejected Anglican ministers, A. G. Matthews, *Walker Revised* (Oxford, 1948), is the best guide. Robert S. Bosher, *The Making of the Restoration Settlement* (Westminster, 1951), brings out the extent of Anglican conformity to the Cromwellian church in addition to showing the continuity of Laudian thought among a minority. The relative absence of political expressions on the part of a displaced bishop is striking in *The Correspondence of Bishop Brian Duppa and Sir Justinian Isham, 1650–1660,* edited by Sir Gyles Isham.[48]

A comprehensive account of the Roman Catholics under the Commonwealth and Protectorate is sorely needed. The enforcement against them of the act of abjuration (1657) can be traced in *London Sessions Records, 1605–1685,* edited by Dom Hugh Bowler (Catholic Record Society, 1934); probably Cromwell prevented the severe enforcement of the law. A perennial problem is treated by W. R. Trimble, "The Embassy Chapel Question, 1625–1660."[49] Cromwell's alleged Catholic favorite is the subject of two recent biographies: R. T. Petersson, *Sir Kenelm Digby, the Ornament of England* (1956), and Vittorio Gabrieli, *Sir Kenelm Digby, un Inglese italianato* (Rome, 1957).

Probably the best introduction to the resettlement of the Jews is Cecil Roth, *Life of Menasseh ben Israel* (Philadelphia, 1934). Documents are printed in *Bevis Marks Records,* edited by L. D. Barnett (2 vols., Ox-

[44] A number of addresses to Cromwell are analyzed by W. K. Jordan, "Sectarian Thought and Its Relation to the Development of Religious Toleration, 1640–1660," *HLQ*, 3 (1940), in three parts. The standard histories and collections are listed in W. R. Powell, "The Sources for the History of Protestant Nonconformist Churches in England," *BIHR*, 25:213–227 (November 1952).
[45] He also wrote *The Welsh Saints, 1640–1660* (Cardiff, 1957), a valuable contribution on millenarianism.
[46] Ed. J. L. Nickalls (Cambridge, Eng., 1952).
[47] Ed. H. J. Cadbury (1955).
[48] Northamptonshire Record Society (1955).
[49] *JMH*, 18:97–107 (March 1946).

ford, 1940), and in *Three Hundred Years: A Volume to Commemorate the Tercentenary of the Resettlement of the Jews* (1957).

Cromwell's religious policy with respect to Scotland, and his attempt to mediate between the principal parties there, are elucidated by two modern collections, *The Register of the Consultations of the Ministers of Edinburgh and Some Other Brethren of the Ministry, II, 1657–1660*, edited by William Stephen, and *The Diary of Sir Archibald Johnston of Wariston, III, 1655–1660*, edited by J. D. Ogilvie.[50] James Sharp, spokesman for the Resolutioners, copiously described these meetings in letters to the ministers at Edinburgh, as well as reporting the conversation of the Protector in some fullness. Wariston, who represented the Remonstrants, was more laconic but nevertheless is valuable for the characters of all the English leaders he met. A striking article by H. R. Trevor-Roper, "Scotland and the Puritan Revolution," in *Historical Essays, 1600–1750, Presented to David Ogg*, edited by H. E. Bell and R. L. Ollard (1963), is novel in its departure from the purely ecclesiastical terms in which English policy is usually described, maintaining that the Puritans attempted to carry out a social revolution in Scotland.

A miscellaneous collection, illustrating *inter alia* Cromwell's interest in Protestant unity and the relief of persecuted groups, is G. H. Turnbull, *Hartlib, Dury and Comenius* (Liverpool, 1947).[51]

The economic history of the Protectorate clearly reveals Cromwell's conservatism, although probably the dislocation caused by the civil war made it impossible for his government to revive the authoritarian tradition of state regulation which had prevailed down to 1642.[52] An important study of the industrial policy of the Protectorate is by G. D. Ramsay, who evaluated the evidence relative to corporations and the regulation of wages, prices, and apprenticeship, concluding that while an imperceptible movement away from statism was taking place in the seventeenth century, the crucial period was around 1700, and that the Protectorate was conservative rather than revolutionary in economic matters.[53]

[50] Scottish History Society (1930, 1940).

[51] For the relief of the Vaudois there are articles by B. Gagnebin, "Oliver Cromwell, Genève et les Vaudois du Piémont (1655–1656)," *Bollettino della Società di Studi Valdesi*, 58:237–254 (September 1939); "Cromwell and the Republic of Geneva," *Proceedings of the Huguenot Society of London*, 18 (1948).

[52] E. Lipson, *The Economic History of England*, II–III (1931; 2d ed., 1934), is more useful for this period than E. F. Heckscher, *Mercantilism*, 2 vols. (1935; 2d ed., 1955).

[53] See article by Ramsay, cited above, n. 36; see also the references to Cromwell's policy in J. U. Nef, *The Rise of the British Coal Industry*, 2 vols. (1932).

The same author has provided a useful collection of studies in *English Overseas Trade during the Centuries of Emergence* (1957), which deals with the main areas of commerce during the seventeenth century. The Protestant interest has long been regarded as dominating Cromwell's policy. In its economic aspects this policy has generally been described as contrary to the interests of the English trading element. This is the argument of Menna Prestwich, who found Cromwell neglectful and unrealistic, and insensitive to the City.[54] Others have regarded Cromwell's continual insistence on religion as a camouflage for worldly motives. Perhaps he believed that religion benefited by English expansion, but recent scholarship brings out clearly his judicious and well-founded striving for solid mercantile advantages in more than one region. "Prudent idealism" is the description of the period 1654–1660 in Charles Wilson, *Profit and Power: A Study of England and the Dutch Wars* (1957).[55] For the Baltic, there is an important revision by Michael Roberts, "Cromwell and the Baltic," *EHR*, 76:402–446 (July 1961), who argues from a host of English, Dutch, and Swedish evidence that the Protector's policy was "sound in its objectives, appropriate in its choice of means, and (by and large) correctly calculated." R. W. K. Hinton, *The Eastland Trade and the Common Weal in the Seventeenth Century* (Cambridge, Eng., 1959), is a very learned work, incorporating the results of recent Scandinavian research and fortified with tables and documents shedding much light on Cromwell's northern policy.[56] The same work contains a new examination of the Navigation Act, supplementing the standard account, L. A. Harper, *The English Navigation Laws* (New York, 1939). M. P. Ashley, *Financial and Commercial Policy*, is useful here too, as are lives of those who influenced Cromwell's measures, such as Anthony Ashley Cooper.[57]

Although Cromwell possessed an imperial outlook, his colonial ideas were only dimly expressed in his writings and speeches, and here as else-

[54] "Diplomacy and Trade in the Protectorate," *JMH*, 22:103–121 (March 1950). That the Protector did not consult the merchant classes on policy is confirmed in the case of Henry Robinson: W. K. Jordan, *Men of Substance: A Study of the Thought of Two English Revolutionaries* (Chicago, 1942).

[55] See Michael Roberts, in *Journal of Ecclesiastical History*, 8:112–115 (April 1957), reviewing Sven Göransson, *Den europeiska Konfessionspolitikens Upplösning. Religion och Utrikespolitik under Karl X Gustav 1654–1660* [The Decline of Confessional Motives in International Affairs] (Uppsala, 1955).

[56] Cf. R. Przezdziecki, *Diplomatic Ventures and Adventures: Some Experiences of British Envoys at the Court of Poland* (1953), chap. v, where reference is also made to Cromwell's corresponding with Chmielnicki, leader of the Cossack insurrection in the Ukraine (unknown to Abbott).

[57] Louise Fargo Brown, *The First Earl of Shaftesbury* (New York, 1933).

where he must be judged on the basis of actions rather than words. Standard works include the *Cambridge History of the British Empire,* I (Cambridge, Eng., 1929); C. M. Andrews, *The Colonial Period of American History* (4 vols., New Haven, Conn., 1934–38); and W. F. Craven, *The Southern Colonies in the Seventeenth Century* (Baton Rouge, La., 1949). K. E. Knorr, *British Colonial Theories, 1570–1850* (Toronto, 1944), is rather thin on the interregnum, but one practical aspect of Cromwell's policy, the peopling of the colonies with political and military prisoners, is described fully by A. E. Smith, *Colonists in Bondage* (Chapel Hill, N.C., 1947). The propagation of the gospel in the colonies is the subject of William Kellaway, *The New England Company, 1649–1776* (1961), and the same movement in Wales, so dear to Cromwell's heart, is discussed by Christopher Hill in a notable essay.[58]

Cromwell's use of sea power, which became so terrible an instrument in his hands, is summarized by Sir Herbert Richmond, *Statesmen and Sea Power* (Oxford, 1946).[59] For the Western Design against the Spanish in the West Indies there is an appreciation in James A. Williamson, *The Ocean in English History* (Oxford, 1941). Operations in the Mediterranean are traced in *The Letters of Robert Blake,* edited by J. R. Powell,[60] in C. D. Curtis, *Blake, General-at-Sea* (Taunton, Eng., 1934), and in Sir Godfrey Fisher, *Barbary Legend: War, Trade and Piracy in North Africa* (Oxford, 1957).

On the diplomatic side the great desideratum is the publication of calendars of the State Papers, Foreign, in the Public Record Office and the further publication, or at least the systematic examination, of the correspondence of the foreign representatives at Cromwell's court. The dimensions of these tasks can be studied in *Repertorium der diplomatischen Vertreter aller Länder,* I, edited by L. Bittner and L. Gross (Oldenburg, 1936), where details are set forth under national headings. Among contributions since 1929 the following may be cited. For Brandenburg-Prussia, the dispatches of Schlezer were employed by Abbott. Those of the Oldenburg envoy are printed by Herman Oncken, *Cromwell: vier Essays* (Berlin, 1935). The *Receuil des instructions données aux ambassadeurs et ministres de France: Angleterre,* edited

[58] "Propagating the Gospel," in *Historical Essays Presented to David Ogg,* ed. Bell and Ollard, pp. 35–59.

[59] He also wrote *The Navy as an Instrument of Policy, 1558–1727,* ed. E. A. Hughes (Cambridge, Eng., 1953). The great collection begun by Gardiner has now been completed: *Letters and Papers relating to the First Dutch War,* VI, ed. C. T. Atkinson, Navy Records Society (1930).

[60] Navy Records Society (1937).

by J. J. Jusserand (2 vols., Paris, 1929), includes the embassy of Bordeaux (1652–1660).[61] The Genoese ambassador's reports were used by E. Momigliano, *Cromwell* (English trans. by L. E. Marshall, 1930), and there is a full account of the mission (1654–1655) of Ugo Fiesco by O. Pàstine, "Genova e Inghilterra da Cromwell a Carlo II." [62] The great contribution of the Venetian envoys' reports for the Protectorate lies in the addition of countless details about the political scene and public opinion.[63]

Clarendon remarked of Cromwell that "his greatness at home was but a shadow of the glory he had abroad." Although often quoted, this dictum has never been fully tested. The foreign impact of the revolution might well repay further study. R. B. Merriman, *Six Contemporaneous Revolutions* (Oxford, 1938), traced the parallels and crosscurrents between the risings in Catalonia, Portugal, Naples, Britain, France, and the Netherlands, but concluded that the revolutionists did not do much to join forces. Suggestive views were expressed in a symposium in London on "Seventeenth Century Revolutions," [64] and there is a useful article by Christopher Hill which explores the sentiments of internationalism expressed during the English revolution.[65] Cromwell's reputation in France can be traced in numerous verse and prose publications: they are generously quoted by Georges Ascoli, *La Grande-Bretagne devant l'opinion française au XVIIe siècle* (2 vols., Paris, 1930). For Holland there is Daniel Grosheide, *Cromwell naar het Oordeel van zijn Nederlandse Tijdgenoten* (Amsterdam, 1951).[66]

The accounts of foreigners are especially useful because the English press was so highly restricted during the Protectorate, particularly after 1655. The Cromwellian censorship has been much studied. The fullest treatment is by W. M. Clyde, *The Struggle for the Freedom of the Press from Caxton to Cromwell* (1934), which is almost entirely devoted to the period of the revolution and which is very good on journalism as

[61] Cromwell's negotiations with D'Estrades, 1651–1652, are examined in C. L. Grose, "England and Dunkirk," *AHR*, 39:1–27 (October 1933).

[62] *Revista Storica Italiana*, 66:309–347 (no. 3, 1954).

[63] *Calendar of State Papers and Manuscripts, Relating to English Affairs, Existing in the Archives and Collections of Venice*, vols. 29–31, *1653–59*, ed. A. B. Hinds (1929–31).

[64] *PP*, no. 13 (April 1958), pp. 63–72.

[65] "The English Revolution and the Brotherhood of Man," *Science & Society*, 18:289–309 (fall 1954), reprinted in his *Puritanism and Revolution* (1958).

[66] On Cromwell in Germany see the introduction to Andreas Gryphius, *Carolus Stuardus*, ed. H. Powell (Leicester, 1955).

well as government restriction.[67] The related topic of government propaganda has received inadequate attention, although there are suggestive
articles.[68] Further investigation of this field would contribute to a more
satisfactory estimate of the state of public opinion toward the rule of
Cromwell. Outside his own circle, published expressions were almost
universally hostile.[69]

Whether Cromwell deserved this opprobrium will, presumably, ever
be a controversial issue. The age produced projects for social betterment
in great number and variety,[70] but the only ones Cromwell wholeheartedly espoused fell far short of hopes. In law reform his ordinance to reg-
ulate Chancery is deemed a failure, and his bill to decentralize the administration of wills, etc., came to nothing.[71] Efforts to enforce morality
not only met with small success but converted men who cared nothing
for royalism into the Puritans' bitterest enemies. Except insofar as he
enjoyed religious toleration the common man probably derived very little benefit from Cromwell's rule. The trifling gains made by individuals
during the civil war [72] were surely outweighed by the heavy burden of
taxation and the oppression of military rule in the years which followed.
The lot of the poor appears to have worsened. For example, the scattered details in E. M. Hampson, *The Treatment of Poverty in Cambridgeshire, 1597–1834* (Cambridge, Eng., 1934), confirm earlier hypotheses about the breakdown of the administration of the poor law during the war and reveal that town governments were negligent, work in
bridewells was abandoned, and that at least one workhouse fell into private hands.

A brighter side exists in Cromwell's labors on behalf of education.
W. A. L. Vincent, *The State and School Education, 1640–1660* (1950),
shows that the Protector continued the Long Parliament's program of

[67] See also C. R. Gillett, *Burned Books*, 2 vols. (New York, 1932), and F. S.
Siebert, *Freedom of the Press in England, 1476–1776* (Urbana, Ill., 1952).
[68] P. S. Havens, "A Tract Long Attributed to Milton," *Huntington Library Bulletin*, no. 6 (1934), pp. 109–114 (on John Hall, employed as a propagandist by
the Commonwealth); Kermit Roosevelt, Jr., "Propaganda Techniques of the English
Civil Wars—and the Propaganda Psychosis of Today," *Pacific Historical Review*,
12:369–379 (December 1943).
[69] M. Dorothy George, *English Political Caricature to 1792: A Study of Opinion
and Propaganda*, 2 vols. (Oxford, 1959), a sumptuous and valuable work.
[70] Margaret James, *Social Problems and Policy during the Puritan Revolution*
(1930).
[71] The most recent of several surveys is G. B. Nourse, "Law Reform under the
Commonwealth and Protectorate," *LQR*, 75:512–529 (October 1959).
[72] C. V. Wedgwood, *The Common Man in the Great Civil War* (Leicester, 1958).

grants and augmentations for schools and pursued a vigorous policy of educational supervision and encouragement in general. No doubt there was a political motive in the examination of schoolmasters, and preaching ministers seem to have been aided far more frequently than teachers, but the record of Cromwell in this area compares very favorably with those of the governments before and after the revolution.[73]

From all the foregoing it seems amply evident that the task of Cromwell's biographer has become yearly more complicated. It goes without saying that each age has given rise to a new evaluation. It will always be a matter of regret that Abbott did not attempt his own in a systematic way. Instead he appended to his book a revised essay, "The Fame of Cromwell," [74] which may serve as the starting point for a very brief survey of the interpretations of Cromwell which have appeared in the period covered by this paper. After tracing Cromwell's reputation down to the twentieth century Abbott pointed out that the thirties had transformed Cromwell into a dictator in the eyes of biographers.[75] Correctives to this interpretation soon appeared, notably in John Buchan, *Oliver Cromwell* (1934), F. H. Hayward, *The Unknown Cromwell* (1934), Ernest Barker, *Oliver Cromwell and the English People* (Cambridge, Eng., 1937), and C. V. Wedgwood, *Oliver Cromwell* (1939). If these now seem dated, it is because, as D. H. Pennington has observed, academic historians are no longer so concerned with the "character" of Cromwell as with the movement he represented—his class and its place in society.[76] To Trevor-Roper he is the representative of a declining gentry, an Independent without constructive policies. R. S. Paul, *The Lord Protector* (1955), sees religious conscience as the centrally important feature of his character and policy. Christopher Hill holds that any

---

[73] On the general subject of education and learning the following are useful: R. Schlatter, "The Higher Learning in Puritan England," *Historical Magazine of the Protestant Episcopal Church*, 23:167–187 (June 1954); L. F. Solt, "Anti-intellectualism in the Puritan Revolution," *Church History*, 25:306–316 (December 1956); and D. J. Maitland, "Puritan Attitudes towards Learning," *Christian Scholar*, 40:101–108 (June 1957). The argument of J. B. Conant, "The Advancement of Learning during the Puritan Commonwealth," *Proceedings of the Massachusetts Historical Society*, 66 (1942), pp. 3–31, cannot, it seems to me, be sustained.

[74] First published in 1913, and reprinted in Abbott's *Conflicts with Oblivion* (New Haven, Conn., 1924). Abbott also wrote "The Historic Cromwell," reprinted in his *Adventures in Reputation* (Cambridge, Mass., 1935).

[75] M. P. Ashley, *Oliver Cromwell, the Conservative Dictator* (1937); Mary T. Blauvelt, *Oliver Cromwell, A Dictator's Tragedy* (New York, 1937); H. Oncken, *Cromwell: vier Essays über die Führung einer Nation* (Berlin, 1935).

[76] "Cromwell and the Historians," *History Today*, 8:598–605 (September 1958).

verdict is doubtful until there is more agreement on the relation of economics to the English revolution, and goes on, in a summary account of the problem of interpretation, to point out how much Cromwell's career is characterized by paradoxes: revolutionism versus conservatism, constitutionalism versus dictatorship, egalitarianism versus class-consciousness, toleration versus anti-Romanism, idealism versus practicality, hesitancy versus violent action.[77]

In his second biography, *The Greatness of Oliver Cromwell* (1957), M. P. Ashley attempts with considerable success to explain such paradoxes and to take into consideration the new materials which have become available. Cromwell's greatness he found to be the struggle for religious toleration. As a general verdict this may well be true, but curiously this insistence on toleration, like other achievements for which Cromwell is remembered today (union with Scotland, administrative reorganization, military leadership, imperialism, etc.) lies outside the bounds of that Puritanism of which he has so long been regarded as the representative par excellence.

[77] *Oliver Cromwell, 1658–1958*, Historical Association (1958).

The Later Stuarts (1660–1714):
Significant Work of the
Last Twenty Years (1939–1959)

✧

ROBERT WALCOTT

A STRIKING FACT about recent historical work on later seventeenth-century English history is the continuing importance of historians who were already doing major work in the thirties.[1] Work from the pen of G. M. Trevelyan at Cambridge, although not his greatest, was appearing as late as 1949.[2] Norman Sykes, also at Cambridge until very lately, has made more important recent contributions, particularly in the field of ecclesiastical biography, where he has inspired a notable revival.[3] At Oxford two of the leading figures of the thirties are still active. A volume by Sir George Clark on Dutch history appeared in 1947 and was followed two years later by his *Science and Social Welfare in the Age of Newton* (1949). Together they are evidence of Sir George's continued interest in Anglo-Dutch themes and in the fields of intellectual and social history. His colleague David Ogg, whose two volumes on *England in the Reign of Charles II* (Oxford, 1934) first appeared over twenty-five years ago, completed the trilogy recently with a third volume that gives a continuous narrative from the

[Reprinted from *AHR*, 67:352–370 (January 1962).]

[1] This article does not include all works in the field of later Stuart history published during the years 1939–1959; new editions of source material and articles in periodicals were considered beyond its scope. It is confined to extended historical treatments, but does not profess to be exhaustive even in this category.

[2] Namely, G. M. Trevelyan, *An Autobiography and Other Essays* (1949) which, however, includes for the later Stuart period only a brief address on Jonathan Swift and the 1926 Romanes Lecture on "The Two-Party System in English Political History." His *English Social History* (1942), which appeared seven years earlier, includes a chapter on England in the later Stuart period, but it is drawn almost entirely from the earlier *England under Queen Anne*, 3 vols. (1931–34).

[3] See below, nn. 26 and 28.

Restoration to the accession of Anne.[4] On this side of the Atlantic Godfrey Davies, late of the Huntington Library, takes us back not only to the thirties but to Sir Charles Firth. Two years before his death in 1957 Davies published his *Restoration of Charles II: 1658–1660* (San Marino, Calif., 1955) fulfilling a promise once made to Firth that he would carry on Firth's continuation of Gardiner down to 1660.[5] It is good news that Davies' useful *Bibliography of British History: Stuart Period, 1603–1714* (Oxford, 1928), is to be revised, brought up to date, and reissued.

No native American enjoyed as important a place in later Stuart studies as Davies, but a number of British writers prominent in the thirties were still doing significant work in the fifties. At Glasgow Professor Andrew Browning, whose Stanhope essay on Thomas Osborne, Earl of Danby, appeared many years ago, in 1951 completed the most solid recent biography of a later Stuart figure, his three-volume study of his first love, Danby.[6] Among nonacademic historians, Sir Winston Churchill found time during the thirties to do a massive biography of his ancestor the Duke of Marlborough, and his recent *History of the English-Speaking Peoples* (3 vols., New York and London, 1956–57) gives considerable space to the later Stuarts.[7] There is finally Esmond S. De Beer, "the uncrowned king of 17th century historical research," [8] whose edition of John Evelyn's *Diary* (6 vols., Oxford, 1955) is an enormous labor of devoted and meticulous scholarship. Unfortunately, the time and energy given to this project have meant the abandonment of De Beer's promising work on Restoration parliamentary politics.[9]

The considerable proportion of major work in later Stuart history accounted for by the foregoing suggests not so much the mature productivity of these historians as a rather surprising paucity of work by younger scholars, at least in the field of general political history. For example, when Sir George Clark brought out a new edition of *The Later*

[4] David Ogg, *England in the Reigns of James II and William III* (Oxford, 1957).

[5] *The Restoration of Charles II*, of course, falls just outside the boundaries of the field covered in this essay. Davies' work in the later Stuart period proper was in the form of articles, many of them in the *Huntington Library Quarterly*. None of them is sufficiently extensive to be included in this article.

[6] Andrew Browning, *Thomas Osborne, Earl of Danby and Duke of Leeds, 1632–1712*, 3 vols. (Glasgow, 1944–51), and see below.

[7] The last part of volume II and the first part of volume III give considerable space to the later Stuarts, but students of that period will read the work more because Churchill wrote it than for any new insights or reinterpretation.

[8] Review of F. C. Turner's *James II*, in *Times Literary Supplement*, Aug. 21, 1948.

[9] The only article to appear within the last twenty years is De Beer's "The House of Lords in the Parliament of 1680," *BIHR*, 20:22–37 (November 1943).

Stuarts, and David Ogg, a second edition of *England in the Reign of Charles II* (2 vols., 1955), in neither case despite the lapse of over twenty years was it necessary to make any major modifications.[10] Similarly, Ogg's third volume, on the reigns of James II and William III, could have appeared twenty years ago as far as any essentially new interpretation of political developments is concerned. On two specific constitutional matters—the legality of James II's ecclesiastical commission and the significance of the coronation oath of 1689—there are some interesting new verdicts, and the sections on social and economic conditions reflect the useful recent work being done in these fields. However, on basic questions of interpretation, such as the character of James II or of William III or the ultimate nature and significance of the Revolution of 1688, the treatment is unflinchingly orthodox. The volume's chief originality lies in the analytical essays, particularly those on "Freehold and Status" (in chapter iii), which stand apart from the main narrative.

The same essential orthodoxy appears in the chief political biographies published during the past twenty years. Browning's *Danby,* for all its three volumes, is a single-volume biography, volumes II and III consisting respectively of a selection of Danby's correspondence and of materials (chiefly lists of members of Parliament with contemporary annotations) for the thorough analysis of party politics that Browning never really completed. Whether biography is the form of historical writing best calculated to advance our knowledge of the period is doubtful. Special investigation of exactly how Danby put together and managed a new "Court Party" and how effective he was as finance minister are what is needed. Browning presumably found that the exigencies of a narrative treatment prevented any definitive analysis of either problem. Browning's *Danby* is the best biography we have of that nobleman and a very useful work, but it cannot take the place of the thorough spadework still needed on late seventeenth-century parliamentary history and public finance.

Biography remains the most popular form of historical writing, but for

[10] Ogg did not find it necessary to make any changes. Browning, reviewing the revised edition of Clark's *The Later Stuarts,* mentions "substantial modifications," but a careful comparison shows that few of the changes were major. The new edition notes forty-two previously unnoticed works: twenty new titles are listed in the bibliography; twelve additional monographs and nine articles are mentioned in footnotes. Of the textual changes only two go beyond the change of a word, a phrase, or at most a sentence: namely, the addition of a new paragraph and other lesser changes to take account of Robert S. Bosher's work on the Restoration religious settlement (see below); and the same, to take account of my 1941 essay on party politics (see below).

the later Stuart period most of the biographical work has unfortunately
been unimportant. Besides Browning's *Danby* there have been only two
biographies of any significance: Francis C. Turner's *James II* (1948)
and John P. Kenyon's *Robert Spencer, Earl of Sunderland, 1641–1702*
(1958). The remainder of the better biographies have been pedestrian
treatments of major figures or adequate accounts of distinctly minor
ones. Such important political personalities as John Lord Somers,
Charles Montagu Lord Halifax, Sidney Earl Godolphin, Robert Harley,
and Henry St. John still lack adequate modern treatment.

Biographies of monarchs form a somewhat specialized class, since
they are difficult to dissociate from histories of their reign. In this respect
Turner's *James II* compares unfavorably with Ogg's latest volume.
Turner is no more sympathetic with James and in his general interpretation comes to much the same conclusions, but he seems to lack the indispensable foundation of solid historical knowledge. He even perpetuates,
with no adequate documentation, the story that in the crisis of 1688
James's virtual paralysis of will and action was due to a long history of
syphilis. Hester W. Chapman's biography of James's daughter Mary [11]
is less bulky and pretentious, but again most of her conclusions are
essentially orthodox. The judgment on Mary is of course favorable. She
is unique among the later Stuarts in escaping the general condemnation
of recent writers.

This was not always so. In the thirties Arthur Bryant led a movement
to rehabilitate Charles II, a movement aided, curiously enough, by William A. Shaw, the learned editor of the *Calendar of Treasury Books*. Not
content simply to edit the documents, in a series of long prefaces Shaw
delivered some remarkable obiter dicta.[12] A man of strong opinions, he
had a pronounced distaste for the niggardliness of Stuart Parliaments,
which he believed to have intentionally starved the Restoration government and to have been guilty of complete financial incompetence. In his
clever *Charles II* (London and New York, 1931) Bryant built on this
foundation to construct a new Charles II, sympathetic, able, a genius at

[11] Hester W. Chapman, *Mary II, Queen of England* (1953). Mrs. Chapman has
also done biographies of Buckingham (*Great Villiers: A Study of George Villiers
Second Duke of Buckingham, 1628–1687* [1949]) and of the young Duke of
Gloucester, who died at eleven (*Queen Anne's Son: A Memoir of William Henry,
Duke of Gloucester, 1689–1700* [1954]). Neither is important.

[12] William A. Shaw's most recent preface was sent to the press in 1940 and appeared posthumously in 1952 in *Calendar of Treasury Books, 1685–, Preserved in
Her Majesty's Public Record Office*, 25 vols. (1904———), XXV, *January–December,
1711*, pt. I.

foreign relations, in contrast with a bumbling legislature. This work has recently been reissued. Sir Arthur's other work during the past twenty years has lain outside the Stuart period.

Bryant's justification of the later Stuarts has been continued by disciples like Cyril Hughes Hartmann. Hartmann's *The King My Brother* (1954) relies on Charles II's sympathetic relationship with his favorite sister, the Duchess of Orleans, for its favorable view of the King, and on Hartmann's earlier works for its documentation. *The King's Friend: A Life of Charles Berkeley, Viscount Fitzhardinge, Earl of Falmouth (1630–1665)* (1951), makes use of fragmentary Berkeley papers for the rehabilitation of an essentially minor figure. Hartmann's work is more respectable than the recent work of such a familiar Stuart champion as Sir Charles Petrie. Petrie's *The Marshal Duke of Berwick* (1953) does little more than paraphrase Berwick's own memoirs,[13] and in similar fashion Lord Cardigan's *Life and Loyalties of Thomas Bruce: A Biography of Thomas, Earl of Ailesbury and Elgin, Gentleman of the Bedchamber to King Charles II and to King James II, 1656–1741* (1951) does not go far beyond the memoirs of the author's ancestor, the Jacobite Earl of Ailesbury. Most students would prefer to read the original memoirs in both cases.[14]

John P. Kenyon's recent life of the second Earl of Sunderland shows that biography can make a real contribution. A major figure during three reigns, Spencer was involved under William III in some tricky maneuverings with party groups, which Kenyon takes great pains to elucidate.[15] The chapters on this topic are overburdened with detail and a bit hard to follow, but Kenyon makes good use of hitherto unused letters between Sunderland and William's Dutch favorite, the Earl of Portland. The picture of Sunderland and his countess is sharply etched, and our knowledge of the man and his period is advanced; this is a great deal to have accomplished.

Sunderland has been more fortunate in his biographer than another of

[13] Petrie's volume on the Jacobite movement is discussed below.

[14] Other recent biographies rate only a footnote. Maurice Ashley's *John Wildman, Plotter and Postmaster* (1947) is the poorest of his works. It is nonetheless better than the following: Jane Lane, *Titus Oates: The First Biography* (1949); Dorothy Middleton, *The Life of Charles, 2nd Earl of Middleton, 1680–1719* (1957); and Cecil Price, *Cold Caleb: The Scandalous Life of Ford Grey, 1st Earl of Tankerville, 1655–1701* (1956), which is not as bad as its title.

[15] Reference should also be made to Kenyon's detailed articles: "The Earl of Sunderland and the Revolution of 1688," *CHJ*, 11:272–296 (no. 3, 1955), and "The Earl of Sunderland and the King's Administration, 1693–95," *EHR*, 71:576–602 (October 1956).

the "three chits" of James II's reign. The most recent life of Godolphin is a disappointment. In *Godolphin: His Life and Times* (1952) Sir Tresham Lever includes enough new material on Godolphin's family (culled from the Blenheim Manuscripts and chiefly about the family after Godolphin's death) to fill an article, but there is little else that is new. Lever relies almost entirely on Churchill's *Marlborough* for Godolphin's politics, and of his important work in public finance there is nothing. Similarly, Harford Montgomery Hyde's *Judge Jeffreys* (1940) provides some new information on the personal side and is a better life than any previous one, but, as De Beer has said, that is "not much of a compliment." [16] Lord Wharton of the Junto was sketched in John Carswell's *The Old Cause: Three Biographical Studies in Whiggism* (1954) which does a little to fill the gap on Junto biography, but Charles H. Collins Baker and Muriel I. Baker missed an opportunity in their *Life and Circumstances of James Brydges, 1st Duke of Chandos, Patron of the Liberal Arts* (Oxford, 1949). A long series of accounts and letters dating from Brydges' tenure of the Pay Office during the War of the Spanish Succession still awaits the efforts of an intelligent and persistent investigator to yield an explanation of the enormous wealth accumulated by Brydges and some of his successors in that office. Instead, the Bakers provide a rather thin diet of social history.

Lack of solid background in political history seems to be true of other biographers who have tried to do justice to the political activities of what to them were essentially literary figures. Homer E. Woodbridge's *Sir William Temple: The Man and His Work* (New York, 1940) is better on Temple's writings than on his public and diplomatic career; Charles K. Eves's *Matthew Prior: Poet and Diplomatist* (New York, 1939) does more justice to Prior's verse than to his political and diplomatic activities, the importance of which Eves greatly exaggerates; while John R. Moore's *Daniel Defoe, Citizen of the Modern World* (Chicago, 1958), though done by a lifelong student of Defoe's writings, gives a highly inflated estimate of his standing in the world of politics, picturing him as William III's trusted friend and political mentor.

In the field of political biography there is finally John H. Plumb's *Robert Walpole: The Making of a Statesman* (1956), the first of several projected volumes on Walpole. Plumb, Tutor of Christ's College, Cambridge, has directed some fine theses in the later Stuart period (notably Kenyon's study of Sunderland), continuing the work of Trevelyan, of

[16] In a review in *History*, 26:157 (September 1941).

whom Plumb is a disciple. As befits a follower of Trevelyan, Plumb includes in his biography a long section on social history. The volume deals chiefly with the period from 1714 to 1722, but it also covers Walpole's apprenticeship under Queen Anne. Here Plumb has been able to add very little to Archdeacon William Coxe's account, at least on the public side. The work's chief merits are its readability and some new, mostly negative verdicts on Walpole's rise to power at the time of the Bubble.

Turning to the monographic material on later Stuart political history, one is struck by the concentration on Anglo-Dutch themes, naturally pivoting on William III. There have been four Dutch studies in this area and nearly as many English and American. The most important Dutch work has been the publication of Marlborough's correspondence with the Pensionary Anthony Heinsius.[17]

The most ambitious attempt at reinterpretation in English is Lucile Pinkham's *William III and the Respectable Revolution: The Part Played by William of Orange in the Revolution of 1688* (Cambridge, Mass., 1954). Miss Pinkham, a student of Wilbur C. Abbott, has turned a fresh eye on the familiar sources and has seen there justification for a radical revision of the "old myths." William III, she finds, came to England in 1688 not to preserve English liberties and Protestantism (many have doubted this) or even "to save Holland and Europe from the aggression of Louis XIV" (the usual view), but simply because he was ambitious for the English throne and had been for many years. There is much to be said for this point, but Miss Pinkham unfortunately feels that she must revise many other verdicts. She allows no public spirit to the English governing class; she vigorously takes up the cudgels for James II (who she feels would have settled his difficulties with his subjects had it not been for William's intervention); and her tone tends to be shrill, putting the reader off so that he is apt to lose sight of some worthwhile questioning of the accepted canons.[18]

---

[17] *The Correspondence of John Churchill and Anthony Heinsius, 1701–1711*, ed. Bert Van't Hoff (The Hague, 1951). The Dutch monographs are Pieter Geyl, *Oranje en Stuart, 1641–1672* (Utrecht, 1939); Augustus J. Veenendaal, *Het Engels-Nederlands Condominium in de Zuiderlijke Nederlanden tijdens de Spaanse Successieoorlog* (Utrecht, 1945); and Johanna K. Oudendijk, *Willem III Stadhouder van Holland, Koning van Engeland* (Amsterdam, 1954).

[18] I think this last fact explains why the reviewers, with the exception of Kenneth H. D. Haley in the *EHR*, 70:330 (April 1955), generally failed to do the book justice.

At the opposite extreme is Kenneth H. D. Haley's *William of Orange and the English Opposition, 1672–1674* (Oxford, 1953),[19] which draws on the Dutch archives to describe the activities of William's principal agent in England during the 1670's. Though an interesting story in itself, it lacks general significance. The English opposition appears only dimly, and William's "secret weapon" turns out to be pamphlets, something of an anticlimax for the reader who hoped for some substantiation of the persistent rumors of Dutch gold going to leading Country politicians. The year 1672, where Haley begins, is where Charles H. Wilson breaks off in *Profit and Power: A Study of England and the Dutch Wars* (1957), a stimulating synthesis of the economic, diplomatic, and political elements in Anglo-Dutch relations. The remaining monographs in the Anglo-Dutch field are Douglas Coombs's *The Conduct of the Dutch: British Opinion and the Dutch Alliance during the War of the Spanish Succession* (The Hague, 1958), and Rosalie L. Colie's *Light and Enlightenment: A Study of the Cambridge Platonists and the Dutch Arminians* (Cambridge, Eng., 1957), an essay in intellectual history.[20]

Aside from the Anglo-Dutch theme, there have been a half dozen monographs on specifically political topics. William R. Emerson's *Monmouth's Rebellion* (New Haven, Conn., 1951) attempts in painstaking fashion to show (with little success) that Monmouth might well have been successful. Abbie T. Scudi's *The Sacheverell Affair* (New York, 1939) is a routine study useful chiefly for its bibliography. Sir Charles Petrie's *The Jacobite Movement: The First Phase, 1699–1716* (1948), is marred by many inaccuracies. Robert Walcott's application of the so-called "Namier method" to the party politics of the reigns of William III and Anne, first sketched in an essay that appeared in 1941,[21] was presented more elaborately in *English Politics in the Early Eighteenth Century* (Cambridge, Mass., and Oxford, 1956).

In this last work it was suggested that the Whig versus Tory interpretation of parliamentary politics needed to be revised to take account of distinct Court and Country groups, which with the more familiar his-

[19] Reference should also be made to Haley's article, "The Anglo-Dutch Rapprochement of 1677," *EHR*, 73:614–648 (October 1958).

[20] Miss Colie's work is included here as an example of the strong Dutch emphasis rather than in the discussion of intellectual history where it might seem more properly to belong.

[21] In *Essays in Modern English History in Honor of Wilbur Cortez Abbott* (Cambridge, Mass., 1941), pp. 81–132. Two other essays in this volume on the Stuart period should be mentioned: Ethyn Williams Kirby's "The Reconcilers and the Restoration, 1660–1662," and Dorothy K. Clark's "A Restoration Banking House."

toric parties would constitute a four-way party framework. It was suggested, further, that within the traditional parties there were separate "connections" (three Tory and two Whig), which should also be taken into account. Case studies of William III's last Parliament, of the election of 1702, and of the parliamentary session of 1707–1708 were used to illustrate this multiparty hypothesis.

More restricted geographically, though less so chronologically, Millicent B. Rex's *University Representation in England, 1604–1690* (1954) draws on the archives of both universities to illuminate a previously obscure corridor of the English representative system—one that was closed in 1948. About a third of the book deals with the period after 1660, and the treatment is as much political as constitutional. It may be classed with recent works in constitutional and administrative history. These include, among general works, Betty Kemp's *King and Commons 1660–1832* (1957). Miss Kemp's brief study is a synthesis of recent work on the developing relations between monarch and legislature, and her interpretation owes much to Sir Lewis Namier.

In the field of administrative history five monographs should be listed. Peter Fraser's *The Intelligence of the Secretaries and Their Monopoly of Licensed News, 1660–1688* (Cambridge, Eng., 1956), explains in detail the mechanism in the Secretary's office for the gathering and dissemination of news and illuminates the relationship of government to the emerging popular press.[22] More strictly administrative are Stephen B. Baxter's *Development of the Treasury, 1660–1702* (Cambridge, Mass., 1957), William R. Ward's *English Land Tax in the 18th Century* (Oxford, 1953), and Orlando C. Williams' *Clerical Organization of the House of Commons, 1661–1850* (Oxford, 1954).[23] Archibald P. Thornton's fine monograph on *West India Policy under the Restoration* (Oxford, 1956) is partly administrative, partly imperial or colonial history.

Of political history on the local level there has been very little in the past twenty years. Recent volumes of the *Victoria County History* have included sections on political and parliamentary history that are use-

---

[22] Fraser goes much deeper than does Frederick S. Siebert in *Freedom of the Press in England, 1476–1776* (Urbana, Ill., 1952). See also John Johnson and Strickland Gibson, *Print and Privilege at Oxford to the Year* 1700 (Oxford, 1946) for the history of the Oxford Press's privileged exemption from the printing monopoly of the Stationers' Company.

[23] An article in this field that deserves mention is Edward Hughes's "The English Stamp Duties, 1664–1764," *EHR*, 56:234–264 (April 1941).

ful,[24] but most of the work in local history has been topographical or has consisted of editions of local records. Specifically political contributions such as Philip Styles's excellent "The Corporation of Bewdley under the Later Stuarts," *UBHJ*, 1:92–133 (no. 1, 1947) are quite exceptional.[25]

Unlike political, ecclesiastical history has seen considerable activity during the past two decades. In part this has been owing to Sykes. His recent two-volume biography of Archbishop Wake [26] is the latest and most distinguished in a gallery of episcopal portraits of the later Stuart and early Hanoverian periods, the product of a fruitful collaboration between the Church Historical Society and the Society for Promoting Christian Knowledge on the one hand, and a group of able clerical biographers on the other. Arthur Tindal Hart's *Life and Times of John Sharp: Archbishop of York* (1949) [27] and his *William Lloyd, 1627–1717* (1952), Edward F. Carpenter's *Thomas Tenison, Archbishop of Canterbury: His Life and Times* (1948) and the more recent *The Protestant Bishop: Being the Life of Henry Compton, 1632–1713, Bishop of London* (1956), and Gareth V. Bennett's *White Kennett, 1660–1728, Bishop of Peterborough: A Study in the Political and Ecclesiastical History of the Early Eighteenth Century* (1957) together with Sykes's work have corrected the old view of a secular-minded, worldly episcopate, which neglected its episcopal duties. On the contrary, these men were faithful, hard-working administrators, and many of them were notable scholars as well. Naturally they were involved in politics, and to the secular historian the most interesting sections of these biographies are usually those on politics.

Not all the recent biographies of bishops are by English clergymen. Francis G. James's *North Country Bishop: A Biography of William Nicolson* (New Haven, Conn., 1956), the work of an American scholar,

[24] Namely, *Cambridgeshire and the Isle of Ely*, 4 vols. (1938–59), II–III, *Leicestershire*, 4 vols. (1907, 1955–58), III–IV, *Oxfordshire* (I–III, V–VI, 1907, 1954), I, III, and *Wiltshire* (I–V, VII, 1953, 1957), V.

[25] Reddaway's *Rebuilding of London* and Darby's *Draining of the Fens*, which can both be classed as local history, are included below under social and economic history, since that is their chief emphasis.

[26] Norman Sykes, *William Wake, Archbishop of Canterbury, 1657–1737*, 2 vols. (Cambridge, Eng., 1957).

[27] All of the biographies in this and the following paragraph, except those of F. G. James and Carpenter's *Protestant Bishop*, were published by the Society for Promoting Christian Knowledge for the Church Historical Society, London.

compares very favorably with those of Hart and Carpenter. It is superior to Charles E. Whiting's *Nathaniel Lord Crewe, Bishop of Durham (1674–1721) and His Diocese* (1940), which is adequate on the diocese and its palatine jurisdiction, but which in its uncritical attempt to rehabilitate Crewe is marked by some notable historical inaccuracies and omissions. Henry P. Thompson's *Thomas Bray* (1954) does not deal with a bishop, but is a good short account of one of the founders of the SPCK.

Besides his life of Wake, Sykes has published a number of lectures on nonbiographical subjects [28] and has directed some very able monographs. The most important of these is Robert S. Bosher's *The Making of the Restoration Settlement: The Influence of the Laudians, 1649–1662* (1951). An American scholar at General Theological Seminary, Bosher shows convincingly that the uncompromising nature of the religious (in contrast to the political) restoration was due to the efforts of a highly organized and capably led group of Laudians (including George Morley, Gilbert Sheldon, and John Cosin), who completely outmaneuvered the Presbyterians.

Sykes's interest in the relations between the English and continental "reformed churches" finds echoes in Joseph Minton Batten's *John Dury, Advocate of Christian Reunion* (1944) and George H. Turnbull's *Hartlib, Dury, and Comenius: Gleanings from Hartlib's Papers* (1947), which focus chiefly on the years just prior to 1660. For the later period George Every's *The High Church Party, 1688–1718* (1956), treats such important issues as comprehension, Convocation, and occasional conformity in terms of principles rather than politics; Dudley W. R. Bahlman's *Moral Revolution of 1688* (New Haven, Conn., 1957) discusses the societies for the reformation of manners; while Alan Savidge deals with *The Foundation and Early Years of Queen Anne's Bounty* (1955), mostly for the years after 1714.

In Quaker historiography, three books require mention. Henry J. Cadbury's long introduction to his edition of *George Fox's Book of Miracles* (Cambridge, Eng., 1948) relates Quaker theology to medicine and is more "social history" than Arnold Lloyd's *Quaker Social History,*

---

[28] Namely, *The Study of Ecclesiastical History* (Cambridge, Eng., 1954), *The Church of England and Non-Episcopal Churches in the Sixteenth and Seventeenth Centuries* (Cambridge, Eng., 1948), *Daniel Ernest Jablonski and the Church of England* (Cambridge, Eng., 1950), *Old Priest and New Presbyter* (Cambridge, Eng., 1956), and *From Sheldon to Secker: Aspects of English Church History, 1660–1768* (Cambridge, Eng., 1959).

1669–1738 (1950), which deals chiefly with the growth of Quaker organization as reflected in Fox's papers. Isabel Ross's *Margaret Fell, Mother of Quakerism* (London and New York, 1949), a sound biography of Fox's wife, is also virtually a history of the Society of Friends during the last half of the seventeenth century.

On Restoration Puritanism there have been a number of studies in recent years. Harry G. Plum's *Restoration Puritanism: A Study of the Growth of English Liberty* (Chapel Hill, N.C., 1943) is brief and inaccurate. Gerald R. Cragg, a Canadian scholar who has worked with Sykes, has done two studies: *From Puritanism to the Age of Reason: A Study of Changes in Religious Thought within the Church of England, 1660 to 1700* (Cambridge, Eng., 1950), and *Puritanism in the Period of the Great Persecution, 1660–1688* (Cambridge, Eng., 1957). The latter retells chiefly from Nonconformist sources the familiar story of the "sufferings of the clergy" and of their flocks, and while eloquent does not add materially to Calamy. The earlier work lies less in the field of ecclesiastical than of intellectual history. It is an interpretation of that basic change in the climate of opinion which divides the England of Milton and Bunyan from that of Newton and Locke.

It is not easy to distinguish the history of religion from the history of ideas, since the two obviously overlap. In any case, much of the activity in the field of later Stuart intellectual history during the past two decades has been concerned with the relation between religion and the "new science." The inspiration for many of these treatments comes from three influential prewar books: Edwin A. Burtt's *The Metaphysics of Sir Isaac Newton: An Essay on the Metaphysical Foundations of Modern Science* (1925), Basil Willey's *Seventeenth-Century Background: Studies in the Thought of the Age in Relation to Poetry and Religion* (1935), and Arthur O. Lovejoy's *The Great Chain of Being: A Study of the History of an Idea* (1936). The two most stimulating recent studies of "the cultural revolution of the seventeenth century" are Samuel L. Bethell's essay of that title (1951) and Richard S. Westfall's *Science and Religion in Seventeenth-Century England* (New Haven, Conn., 1958). The two chapters on the later Stuart period in Meyrick H. Carré's *Phases of Thought in England* (Oxford, 1949) are a much more pedestrian synthesis.

On the philosophical side of the cultural revolution the Cambridge Platonists continue to receive attention. Ernst Cassirer's fine 1932 German study appeared in English translation in 1953; John A. Passmore's

Ralph Cudworth: An Interpretation (Cambridge, Eng., 1951) was published two years earlier; while Miss Colie's study of the Cambridge Platonists and the Dutch Arminians has already been noticed.[29] On the religious side is Richard B. Schlatter's *Social Ideas of Religious Leaders, 1660–1688* (Oxford, 1940), which emphasizes the low-keyed social morality advocated both by the Anglican and Nonconformist clergy, signalizing the shift away from Calvinist soul searching toward the comfortably "reasonable" ethical religion of the early eighteenth century.[30] How radical "reasonable Christianity" could become is suggested in Herbert McLachlan's *Religious Opinions of Milton, Locke, and Newton* (Manchester, Eng., 1941) and his son H. John McLachlan's *Socinianism in 17th-Century England* (Oxford, 1951). As Unitarians, the McLachlans have little difficulty in showing that Locke and Newton (Milton is another matter) would certainly be classed as "Unitarians" today, as would many of their contemporaries like Thomas Firmin, who managed to propagate Socinian doctrines without ever leaving the Church of England.

On the scientific side of the cultural revolution, Locke, Newton, and Newton's predecessors and associates have received much attention. Marie Boas' *Robert Boyle and Seventeenth-Century Chemistry* (Cambridge, Eng., 1958) is a far more original work than Louis T. More's *The Life and Works of the Honourable Robert Boyle* (London and New York, 1944). Miss Boas shows that Boyle's achievement in sweeping aside Aristotelian debris and thus clearing the way for Lavoisier and the other notable eighteenth-century chemists was far greater than previously recognized; nor was seventeenth-century chemistry generally "backward" as compared to the physics and astronomy of the same period. Margaret 'Espinasse's *Robert Hooke* (Berkeley, Calif. and London, 1956) is a more polemical work. She is naturally determined to buttress Hooke's reputation, and this leads her to some rather doubtful criticism of Newton (who quarreled violently with Hooke). It is a stimulating book, more so than either of Edward N. Da C. Andrade's brief accounts of Newton.[31]

[29] See above.

[30] George N. Clark's *Science and Social Welfare in the Age of Newton* (1949) places the same emphasis on the social side of intellectual history, but this emphasis has been uncommon in recent years.

[31] The most original recent comments on Newton are by John Maynard Keynes in *Essays in Biography*, ed. Geoffrey Keynes, new ed. (1951), pp. 310–323. Keynes was instrumental in acquiring for Cambridge the great mass of Newton's mathematical, religious, and "magical" papers known as the Portsmouth Collection.

Newton, Hooke, and Boyle were all closely connected with the Royal Society, the origins of which receive fresh treatment by Miss Rosemary H. Syfret in "The Origins of the Royal Society" (*Notes and Records of the Royal Society of London*, 5 [Apr. 1948], pp. 75–137). She finds an interesting connection with Hartlib and the interchurch movement of the later interregnum. A relatively minor member of the society is noticed in Montague F. Ashley Montagu's *Edward Tyson, M.D., F.R.S., 1650–1708, and the Rise of Human and Comparative Anatomy in England* (Philadelphia, 1943). A physician and naturalist, Tyson was a less important figure than the great Cambridge naturalist, John Ray, to whom the former Master of Christ's College has devoted a scholarly labor of love.[32]

Interest in the history of science and of scientists has been paralleled by an upsurge of interest in Locke, aided by the deposit in Bodley's Library of the great Lovelace Collection of the philosopher's letters and papers.[33] Two of the recent Locke studies are independent of this new material. Willmoor Kendall's *John Locke and the Doctrine of Majority Rule* (Urbana, Ill., 1941) is a clever attempt to revise the orthodox view of Locke as a father of individualism, making him instead a precursor of Rousseau in establishing the metaphysical foundations for the all-powerful state of the future. John W. Gough, in *John Locke's Political Philosophy: Eight Studies* (1950), a series of essays written considerably earlier than the date of publication, is at pains to refute Kendall and to re-establish the conventional interpretation.

Maurice Cranston's *John Locke: A Biography* (1957) is the most substantial work based on material in the Lovelace Collection. As straight biography, this life may be called "definitive." On a number of points previous ideas must now definitely be revised. No longer, for example, can it be said that the *Treatises on Civil Government* were "written to justify the Glorious Revolution." Cranston shows that they were actually composed during the height of the Exclusion controversy to justify the "attempted Whig revolution" and only afterward were published to buttress the successful Revolution of 1688. Cranston also demonstrates that Locke's influence at the Board of Trade was much greater than is generally realized.

[32] Charles E. Raven, *John Ray, Naturalist, His Life and Works* (Cambridge, Eng., 1942).
[33] Wolfgang Von Leyden, who catalogued it, describes the collection in his introduction to *John Locke: Essays on the Law of Nature* (Oxford, 1954), pp. 1–10.

On this last point and on Locke's relations with his patron, Lord Shaftesbury, Cranston needs to be corrected and supplemented by Peter Laslett's work. From a defense of Sir Robert Filmer [34] (Locke's target in the First Treatise), Laslett has moved on to studies of Locke's political career, which are more detailed and informative than the material in Cranston.[35] Nor is Cranston adequate on Locke's thought. For this aspect of Locke's career one should take into account such recent work as Daniel J. O'Connor's *John Locke* (London and Baltimore, 1952), Von Leyden's study of Locke's early work on natural law,[36] and John W. Yolton's *John Locke and the Way of Ideas* (Oxford, 1956). The last emphasizes in interesting fashion the essential radicalism of Locke's philosophical doctrines in the *Essay*, showing how violent was the contemporary reaction to Locke's skepticism. Theologians and moralists had no doubt that Locke's ideas were ultimately subversive of the traditional religion—and who can say they were wrong?

Aside from the work on Locke [37] there has been little on the political thought of the later Stuart period. John Bowle's lively *Hobbes and His Critics: A Study in Seventeenth-Century Constitutionalism* (1951) [38] and A. H. MacLean's very concise "George Lawson and John Locke" (*CHJ*, 9:69–77 [no. 1, 1947]) deal with some of Locke's predecessors primarily in terms of their relationship to him. Locke figures also in Caroline Robbins' interesting *The Eighteenth-Century Commonwealth Man: Studies in the Transmission, Development, and Circumstances of English Liberal Thought from the Restoration of Charles II until the War with the Thirteen Colonies* (Cambridge, Mass., 1959), a study of the transmission of left-wing Whiggism from the interregnum trio of John Milton, James Harrington, and Algernon Sidney [39] to the genera-

---

[34] In his introduction to the Blackwell edition of *Patriarcha and Other Political Works of Sir Robert Filmer* (Oxford, 1949).

[35] In addition to lesser articles in *History Today* and *The Listener,* these include "Locke and the First Earl of Shaftesbury," *Mind*, 61:89–92 (January 1952), "The English Revolution and Locke's *Two Treatises on Government*," *CHJ*, 12:40–55 (no. 1, 1956), and "John Locke, the Great Recoinage and the Origins of the Board of Trade, 1695–98," *William and Mary Quarterly*, 3d. ser., 14:370–402 (July 1957).

[36] Von Leyden, *John Locke.*

[37] To complete the list of recent work on Locke, one should include Gabriel Bonno, *Les relations intellectuelles de Locke avec la France* (Berkeley, Calif., 1955) and John Lough's *Locke's Travels in France, 1675–1679* (Cambridge, Eng., 1953).

[38] Although studies of Hobbes fall outside the limits of this essay, Bowle's work is included because it deals primarily with later criticism of that philosopher.

[39] See also Zera S. Fink's *The Classical Republicans: An Essay in the Recovery of a Pattern of Thought in Seventeenth Century England* (Evanston, Ill., 1945),

tion of the American Revolution. This study's principal emphasis is on Robert Molesworth and his group of friends and disciples in England, Ireland, and Scotland. Edward C. O. Beatty's *William Penn as a Social Philosopher* (New York, 1939) is a less important essay.

Scholarship, literature, and the arts are other fields of intellectual activity during the period of the later Stuarts that have come in for treatment in the last twenty years. David C. Douglas' *English Scholars* (1939) is an attractive work, being at once a history of later seventeenth-century medieval scholarship and a lively group biography of the remarkable scholars from William Dugdale to Thomas Madox who made that period a memorable one. In literary history the most important publication has been Bonamy Dobrée's *English Literature in the Early Eighteenth Century, 1700–1740*, in *The Oxford History of English Literature*, VII (Oxford, 1959).[40] The field of literature is too large, and much of the work in it is of too specialized a nature, to be dealt with here except briefly. Useful general treatments are George W. Sherburn's section on the Restoration and eighteenth-century literature in *A Literary History of England*, edited by Albert C. Baugh (New York, 1948), and John E. Butt's *The Augustan Age* (1950).

Of literary biographies the best recent example is Peter Smithers' *Life of Joseph Addison* (Oxford, 1954), a scholarly and thorough treatment. Lives of Temple, Prior, and Defoe have already been discussed.[41] Two attractive but relatively minor figures who have come in for recent discussion are John Evelyn and John Aubrey. Walter G. Hiscock has tried "to remove the halo" and "reveal the real John Evelyn" in *John Evelyn and Mrs. Godolphin* (1951) and *John Evelyn and His Family Circle* (1955). Taken with De Beer's new edition of the *Diary*, this amounts to an Evelyn "movement." Anthony Powell, the novelist, has accompanied his attractive new edition of *Aubrey's "Brief Lives" and Other Selected Writings* (1949) with a pleasant biography of *John Aubrey and His Friends* (1948).

The art and architecture of the later Stuart period have received recent treatment both in the Oxford and Pelican Histories of English Art. Margaret D. Whinney and Oliver Miller, in *English Art, 1625–1714*, in *The Oxford History of English Art*, VIII (Oxford, 1957) devote too

---

most of which is devoted to the interregnum work of Milton and Harrington, but which also includes some later material on Sidney and Moyle.

[40] The volume on the later seventeenth century has yet to be published.

[41] See above.

much space perhaps to Christopher Wren and concentrate rather heavily on architecture, but, supplemented by the relevant sections of Ellis K. Waterhouse's *Painting in Britain, 1530–1790* (London and Baltimore, 1953), John N. Summerson's *Architecture in Britain, 1530–1830* (London and Baltimore, 1953), and his *Sir Christopher Wren* (London and New York, 1953), and Marcus Whiffen's *Stuart and Georgian Churches: The Architecture of the Church of England outside London 1603–1837* (1948), it gives a good picture of this aspect of Stuart England.

With education one comes to a bridge between intellectual and social history. Mary G. Jones's *The Charity School Movement: A Study of Eighteenth Century Puritanism in Action* (Cambridge, Eng., 1938) is rooted firmly in the society of its period. Emphasis is on the period after 1714, but this important study of middle-class piety and benevolence in action also looks back to the origins of the movement in the late seventeenth century. Aytoun Ellis' *The Penny Universities, A History of the Coffeehouses* (1956), which is not about education, but is a chatty history of the coffeehouses, belongs obviously in the field of social history.

Considering the vogue for social history, it is surprising how little has been done in that field during the past two decades. Trevelyan, the master of this genre, has not inspired a school.[42] The two most significant recent studies in social history have both been on a local scale: Thomas F. Reddaway's *The Rebuilding of London after the Great Fire* (1940) and Henry C. Darby's *The Draining of the Fens* (Cambridge, Eng., 1940). Darby's volume, a sequel to his *Medieval Fenland* (Cambridge, Eng., 1940) and, like its predecessor, a combination of history, geography, and economics, gives a good picture of the development of the area from 1500 to 1900, with some three chapters on the later Stuart period. Reddaway's book is also an interesting combination of economic and social history. A well-balanced and fully documented treatment, it shows mastery in the varied fields of local government, social history, business, and finance. Reddaway thinks little of Wren's famous plan for London, in contrast to Jane Lane's worship of Wren in her conscientious, but romanticized *Rebuilding of St. Paul's after the Great Fire of London* (1956).

---

[42] One might expect evidences of such a school in *Studies in English Social History: A Tribute to G. M. Trevelyan*, ed. John H. Plumb (1955). Of the two contributors dealing with later Stuart themes, H. J. Habakkuk has done his work in economic history, particularly landholding, while Plumb has done political biography, though with considerable attention to the social background (see above).

Social history in the more familiar sense is attractively presented in Gladys Scott Thomson's volumes drawn from the domestic records of the Russell family. The first half of *The Russells in Bloomsbury, 1669–1771* (1940), and parts of *Family Background* (1949) deal with the later Stuart period. These illuminate such diverse topics as family genealogy, the topography of London, social customs, and domestic economy.[43] Alfred L. Rowse's *The Early Churchills: An English Family* (1956) is also family history of the same period, but while lively and readable, it breaks no new ground. Other recent volumes in social history are remarkably miscellaneous. Charles F. Mullett has written of *Public Baths and Health in England, Sixteenth-Seventeenth Centuries* (Baltimore, Md., 1946); Campbell R. Hone's *Life of Dr. John Radcliffe 1652–1714, Benefactor of the University of Oxford* (1950) tells much about London society and the state of the medical profession, while Christopher Morris has edited with an informative introduction a fine edition of *The Journeys of Celia Fiennes* (1947).

In economic history there has been much more activity than in social history. Books specifically or exclusively on the later Stuart period have been rare, but a number of recent works have devoted useful sections to this period. On the subject of trade and commerce George D. Ramsay's *English Overseas Trade during the Centuries of Emergence: Studies in Some Modern Origins of the English-speaking World* (1957) is a useful synthesis of recent work, valuable for its emphasis on non-English sources. It is much fuller for the sixteenth and early seventeenth centuries than for the later Stuart period. Lawrence A. Harper's *The English Navigation Laws: A Seventeenth-Century Experiment in Social Engineering* (New York, 1939) is an important description of a complicated subject.[44] Jean O. McLachlan's *Trade and Peace with Old Spain, 1667–1750* (Cambridge, Eng., 1940), furnishes valuable economic background for the War of the Spanish Succession and the Peace of Utrecht. It is an original combination of commercial and diplomatic history; the same can be said for Harold A. Innis' *The Cod Fisheries: The History of an International Economy* (Oxford, 1940), which might be described as

---

[43] Mention should also be made of Miss Thomson's *Life in a Noble Household: 1641–1700* (1937), the first of this trilogy, published two years before the earlier limit of this essay.

[44] Some of Harper's conclusions concerning the benefits of the system have been questioned as being derived from unreliable commercial statistics. See Edward Hughes's long review in *EHR*, 55:660 (October 1940).

a fish's eye view of the political and economic relations of the "North Atlantic Triangle."

Recent similar studies of particular areas of trade have stressed this same combination of the political and the economic, often reassessing some of the usual views of mercantilism. Raymond W. K. Hinton, in *The Eastland Trade and the Common Weal in the Seventeenth Century* (Cambridge, Eng., 1959), studies the Baltic trade and government policy toward it, concluding that government economic policy was not nearly so influenced by mercantile "pressure groups" as has been generally believed. Kenneth G. Davies' *The Royal African Company* (1957) is a fine study of the "Triangular Trade" from the standpoint of the London Company's monopoly of the slave trade. It is useful on all three sides: English, African, and West Indian. The fur trade, both in America and Europe, is treated by Edwin E. Rich in *Hudson's Bay Company, 1670–1870* (1958), the first volume of which has just been published.[45]

On industry and finance there have been somewhat fewer books. George D. Ramsay has written on *The Wiltshire Woollen Industry in the Sixteenth and Seventeenth Centuries* (Oxford, 1943), emphasizing the earlier part of the period, and William H. B. Court has studied *The Rise of the Midland Industries, 1600–1828* (Oxford, 1953), stressing the period after 1714. Sir John Clapham's *The Bank of England: A History* (2 vols., Cambridge, Eng., 1944) does not supersede Richard D. Richards' *Early History of Banking in England* (1929), but it does include in an appendix a useful analysis of the original subscribers. Sir John Craig's *Newton at the Mint* (Cambridge, Eng., 1946) should perhaps be classed as administrative rather than financial history. It shows the great scientist performing adequately as a civil servant in a comfortably respectable and responsible position.

Of recent work in naval and military history it is to be observed that there has been nothing worth mentioning in the latter field save possibly Churchill's set battle pieces in his *History of the English-Speaking Peoples*. By contrast the field of naval history has seen considerable activity. The most comprehensive work is that of the late Admiral Sir Herbert Richmond. His Ford Lectures, first published as *Statesmen and Sea Power* (Oxford, 1946) and later partially expanded and documented in

[45] There is no documentation but the numerous published volumes of company records, many of which Rich edited, partially supply this deficiency.

The Navy as an Instrument of Policy, 1558–1727 (Cambridge, Eng., 1953), is an important contribution not only to naval history, but also to the history of British foreign policy.[46]

An outstanding monograph is John Ehrman's *The Navy in the War of William III, 1689–1697* (Cambridge, Eng., 1953), which again is not strictly confined to naval history. Ehrman emphasizes the administrative, financial, and economic problems connected with the rapid naval expansion of the reign, and his book is equally valuable on naval administration, public finance, and economic history.[47] A much more specialized topic is *The Walker Expedition to Quebec, 1711* (1953), discussed by Gerald S. Graham in his long introduction to a collection of documents on that subject. Similar historical introductions by Roger C. Anderson to collections of documents on the Second and Third Dutch Wars [48] illuminate the earlier period.

A summary of recent work in the later Stuart field is not easy. As might be expected in this age of specialization, monographs and other detailed studies predominate in most fields, with biography running a close second. Large works of synthesis are the exception, the only example being Ogg's volume on the period 1685–1702. Even in the field of biography there has been little of a broadly interpretive character. Browning's life of Danby and Turner's *James II* both have a broad sweep that covers virtually all of the period, but while neither biographer eschews judgment, their verdicts on men and events are very closely in line with the accepted traditions. New interpretations and lively debate have been lacking in recent political treatments of the later Stuart period.

In fields other than political, the picture is somewhat different. There has been an encouraging tendency to cross the traditional borders between various aspects of history: to treat religion both in terms of politics and of intellectual history (witness the amount of investigation of the impact of later seventeenth-century science on the thought and religion of that period); to explore the relationship of politics and econom-

---

[46] The history of foreign policy, 1660–1714, has received no treatment during the past twenty years except in two or three articles by Professor Mark A. Thomson.

[47] Some of the material used by Ehrman is published by the Navy Records Society in *The Sergison Papers*, ed. Reginald D. Merriman (1940).

[48] *The Journals of Sir Thomas Allin, 1660–1668*, ed. Roger C. Anderson, 2 vols. (1939–40) and *Journals and Narratives of the Third Dutch War*, ed. R. C. Anderson (1946).

ics with a critical eye toward the familiar generalizations about mercantilism; or to discuss naval history in broad terms of economics and
politics.

Explorations of this nature provide a basis for reinterpretations and
reassessments that can inspire fruitful synthesis during the next generation of historical writing on the later Stuart period.

Early Hanoverian
England (1714–1760):
Some Recent Writings

❖

WILLIAM A. BULTMANN

D URING the past two decades the early Han-
overian period has proved a rewarding field for historical research. Specialists in political history, drawing upon such rich collections as the
Newcastle, Hardwicke, and Cholmondeley papers, have applied the
method of the late Lewis B. Namier with considerable success in an
effort to delineate more closely the constitutional development of the
age. The new approach has brought to light a wealth of information
about elections, party structure, the sovereign's role in politics, and the
power and tactics of ministers of the crown. At the same time, the findings of these revisionists have created a dilemma for the writers of general accounts of Hanoverian history. For while the work of revision
progresses with due speed, much still remains to be accomplished; a life
of the Duke of Newcastle is needed, for example, a few key families
such as the Bedfords call for closer study, and certain parts of the period
require deeper investigation. The result is that any general account must
necessarily be based upon a difficult and often irreconcilable combination of still-to-be-superseded older, orthodox works on the one hand and
an incomplete patchwork of revisionist literature on the other.

Basil Williams' highly reputed volume in the *Oxford History of England* series remains a more useful general study of the age than any produced during the past two decades,[1] but it suffers from having been
written at a time when the Whig view was not sufficiently discredited,
nor revisionist accounts sufficiently numerous, to make necessary a clear

[Reprinted from *JMH*, 35:46–61 (March 1963).]

[1] Basil Williams, *The Whig Supremacy: 1714–1760* (Oxford, 1939; 2d ed. revised
and edited by C. H. Stuart, 1962).

choice between the two. Consequently it perpetuates older concepts now known to require careful qualification. The 1962 revision leaves Williams' presentation intact, but it does indicate corrections and new findings through the judicious use of editorial footnotes. A more successful effort to synthesize recent views into a general text is Dorothy Marshall's *Eighteenth Century England* (1962), in which economic, social, and intellectual matters have been subordinated to a careful, up-to-date elucidation of political trends. Useful as a quick, critical review of ideas put forward by the revisionists since 1929 is W. R. Fryer's incisive essay, "The Study of British Politics between the Revolution and the Reform Act." [2] Vivian H. H. Green's *The Hanoverians, 1714–1815* (1948), a survey of political history written for undergraduates and the general reader, presents the traditional Whig view of the constitution together with a smattering of ideas on politics gleaned from recent monographs. The result is an account which is unconvincing and to some degree confusing. *The Eighteenth-Century Constitution, 1688–1815*, edited by E. Neville Williams (1960), is a well-organized selection of documents chosen to give the nonspecialist an idea of Hanoverian political institutions as seen by present-day historians. Williams' brief introductory essays at the opening of each section contain valuable comments.

In the field of political biography some of the longest strides have been taken toward definition of the Hanoverian political system. J. H. Plumb's *Sir Robert Walpole: The Making of a Statesman* (1956) affords an excellent example of critical writing in which traditional legends surrounding a subject are dismissed. The first of a projected three-volume set, it traces Walpole's career through 1722, disclosing an astute, forceful personality with an unrivaled mastery of parliamentary methods, a man greedy for wealth and power and without strong scruples, a politician skillful in the handling of people. It disposes of the theory that Walpole demonstrated financial acumen in the South Sea Bubble crisis, attributing his rise instead to the fortuitous end of his struggle with the Earl of Sunderland. Perhaps the most illuminating passage is the introductory essay on Walpole's world, where the author analyzes with skill and insight the structure of Hanoverian society and government. Throughout, Plumb traces the shifting patterns of party alignment, demonstrating the lack of fixed party lines and the important role played in parliament by independent members. He shows that the monarch was far from weak, and indicates that personal feelings between political figures sometimes

[2] *Renaissance and Modern Studies*, 1 (1957), pp. 91–114.

held a determining position in the solution of national problems. In his second volume, *Sir Robert Walpole: The King's Minister* (1961), Plumb moves into the years of Walpole's greatest influence and power. He traces the complexities of foreign relations after 1722, showing the minister's increasing ability at handling the details of diplomacy. Turning to domestic issues, the author reconstructs the whole political milieu in which Walpole maneuvered for the twelve years following 1722. Excellent descriptions of the conduct of Newcastle, Horatio Walpole, and the first Earl of Egmont, and a fresh appraisal of the character of George II, serve to set Walpole's abilities in perspective. But it is in describing Walpole's use of the machinery of government, his management of patronage, and his tactics at court and in the House of Commons, that the author's skill is most in evidence. Throughout the two volumes Plumb has thrown substantial light upon the art of political management as it was understood by the Hanoverians. This first biography of Walpole to appear in recent times will replace the standard work by Archdeacon William Coxe published in 1798.

Lewis M. Wiggin, *The Faction of Cousins: A Political Account of the Grenvilles, 1733–1763* (New Haven, Conn., 1958), is a family biography written to test the thesis that party organization in the eighteenth century revolved around family centers. The author traces the rise of the Grenvilles from county prominence to great influence in national affairs. He has examined every available source, amassing a great body of detail upon the cousinhood. His finding is that the Grenvilles did not always stick together on critical issues and therefore cannot be classed as a party. Whatever the value of this conclusion, Wiggin's book contains abundant information upon the Grenvilles in Buckinghamshire affairs, their family quarrels, their keen ability to obtain honors, promotions, and sinecures, and their support of Pitt. As a discussion of Hanoverian politics the volume reveals little, but as a reference book of biographical detail it will have its use.

The public career of John Carteret is sympathetically presented in Basil Williams' *Carteret and Newcastle: A Contrast in Contemporaries* (Cambridge, Eng., 1943), a work painstakingly constructed from the findings of lifelong research. Carteret was at his best in the give and take of diplomacy, where he could believe himself instrumental in setting the course of kings and states. Skillful, daring, arrogant, and blessed with personal charm, he offers an attractive subject for the biographer. Williams has made the most of these characteristics as he describes Car-

teret's lord lieutenancy in Ireland and his ambitious foreign policy while
secretary of state. Since Carteret's practice was to permit the dispersal of
his private papers, his biographer had to search very widely for information, a task which Williams' vast knowledge of the period equipped him
to undertake. The account of Carteret's role as head of the 1742 ministry
is brilliant in the area of diplomacy, much less lucid in home affairs and
in the management of parliament. His relations with the Pelhams, especially after 1742, are presented without sufficient clarity to enable the
reader to distinguish lines of division between political groups. The difficulty here springs as much from Carteret's own disdain of parties as
from Williams' preoccupation with the more heroic side of his subject's
career; consequently, this study is more useful to students of foreign
affairs than to those interested in parliamentary government in the
1740's. Precisely because this is true, the portrait of the Duke of Newcastle which emerges is more that of the fussy plodder of tradition than of
the manager of government majorities and the skilled dispenser of
favors and offices. Although Williams has used the massive Newcastle
correspondence, the Duke comes off second best. Newcastle's understanding of men and politics does not receive due space, nor does the
author present much that is fresh upon the political techniques of the
period. But Williams' study shows that the Hanoverian political world
contained space enough to accommodate men of widely varying talents
and interests who were able to pursue the goals of statecraft for similar
purposes along dissimilar paths.

A work which should be read along with the one by Williams is John
B. Owen's *The Rise of the Pelhams* (1957). This meticulously written
account provides a detailed analysis of political alignments in parliament
between 1741 and 1747. Owen examines the biography of every member
who sat in the Commons during these years, for the purpose of identifying and describing precisely the membership and program of each faction. Tories are found to exist in fact as well as in name, comprising a
group of country gentlemen interested in retaining control over county
affairs and willing to eschew proffered places and pensions. Independent
members and those tied only nominally to factions are discovered to be
more numerous than has been thought and of critical importance to ministries whenever sharply contested issues were up for decision. Owen
holds that too much emphasis has been placed upon the use of patronage and too little upon the personal popularity, the powers of persua-
sion, and the public record of individual ministers in the winning of in-

dependent votes. The successful ministry was one which recognized the need to persuade independents, to win backing from sources of potential opposition, and to dispense patronage skillfully. At the same time it was necessary to retain the sovereign's confidence and to present his views faithfully before the Commons. Henry Pelham, Newcastle, and Lord Hardwicke understood these requirements and so were able to perpetuate their ascendancy. Carteret, on the other hand, never grasped the realities of parliamentary management and was therefore unable to maintain his position of leadership.

Other features in Owen's volume include a reappraisal of the sovereign's role, in which George II is found to be more active and independent than had been supposed, an analysis of parliamentary opposition which disposes of the idea that reversionary interest was the sole base for an opposition rally, and a close examination of the constitutional crisis of 1746. The Duke of Newcastle is seen in a new perspective in this work. As a study of Hanoverian parliamentary politics Owen's work will rival that of Namier for the fresh light which it throws on a period hitherto not very well known; no student of the reign of George II will be able to bypass it. Donald Grove Barnes's recent article on Henry Pelham and Newcastle includes some worthwhile observations upon the contrasting personalities and changing political situations of the two brothers, and takes the view that Newcastle ultimately became little more than a handicap to Pelham.[3] Philip Haffenden's "Colonial Appointments and Patronage under the Duke of Newcastle, 1724–1739," is a brief defense of Newcastle's actions in the nomination of colonial officials.[4]

A biography written in an older style than is currently fashionable, and intended for the general student of history, is O. A. Sherrard's *Lord Chatham* (3 vols., 1952–58). This work, the product of detailed research in the Chatham, Newcastle, and Hardwicke papers, covers Pitt's political career from 1735 until his death in 1778. Unfortunately, Sherrard is so much the champion of Pitt that he fails to provide an adequate analysis of the political stage upon which his subject appeared. A tendency to view politics as an elaborate series of intrigues and deceptions has prevented him from discerning much pattern in the activities of Walpole, Henry Fox, and Newcastle, and from providing a clear picture of their relations with Pitt. More successful is Sherrard's description of the care-

[3] "Henry Pelham and the Duke of Newcastle," *JBS*, 1:62–77 (no. 2, 1962).
[4] *EHR*, 78:417–435 (July 1963).

ful direction of affairs which Pitt assumed during the Seven Years' War. But here the reader is led to believe that the fall of the Pitt ministry in 1761 was more the result of a willful opposition than of shortcomings in Pitt's statecraft. The author's heroic view of his subject robs these volumes of any semblance of balance. A slim, sprightly, popular book based upon recent studies of the period is Charles Grant Robertson's *Chatham and the British Empire* (1948), which presents in a few pages an unusually lucid, brief account of constitutional practice in the time of George II and carefully describes Pitt's rise to power. Robertson takes the position that imperial affairs formed the paramount concern of Britain and Europe throughout Pitt's political life, and that Pitt's own imperial policies, successful before 1761, failed to keep pace with basic changes in the Empire after that date. Romney Sedgwick's "Letters from William Pitt to Lord Bute, 1755–1758," consists of ninety-one letters which illuminate Pitt's connection with the Leicester House faction.[5]

Recent works on the royal family between 1714 and 1760 have been few. Averyl Edwards' *Frederick Louis, Prince of Wales* (1947) is a well-written, brief account of this rather pathetic personality, while Betty Kemp's essay "Frederick, Prince of Wales," explains for the general reader the reasons for Frederick's unpopularity with his father and for the vilification he received in the writings of Horace Walpole and Lord Hervey.[6] A. N. Newman's article on Frederick lists and describes the household posts and other offices in the disposition of the Prince of Wales and concludes that the funds attached to these offices were greater than has generally been realized and may have accounted for the size of the Prince's following.[7] J. H. Plumb's *The First Four Georges* (1956) is a pleasant, small volume for the nonspecialist, containing attractive personality sketches of the Hanoverians as well as a brief, succinct portrait of the Georgian political and social world. *Lord Hervey's Memoirs*, edited by Romney Sedgwick (1952), is a much-abridged version of Sedgwick's well-known 1931 edition. The editor has singled out Hervey's candid comments upon the royal family and other figures at the palace, excluding the extensive material on parliamentary debates and foreign affairs to be found in the earlier edition. The sordid

[5] See *Essays Presented to Sir Lewis Namier*, ed. Richard Pares and A. J. P. Taylor (1956), pp. 108–166.
[6] See *Silver Renaissance: Essays in Eighteenth-century English History*, ed. Alex Natan (1961), pp. 38–56.
[7] "The Political Patronage of Frederick Louis, Prince of Wales," *Historical Journal*, 1:68–75 (no. 1, 1958).

quarrels between the Prince of Wales and his father form the central theme of this edition. Alvin Redman's *The House of Hanover* (1960) adds little that is new.

The composition of the eighteenth-century House of Commons is analyzed with the aid of a computing machine in Gerrit P. Judd IV, *Members of Parliament, 1734–1832* (New Haven, Conn., 1955). Judd presents, in tabular form, information about the age, length of tenure in parliament, social and economic status, education, and vocation of the 5,034 men elected to the Commons during the ninety-eight-year period. Unfortunately this work is marred by omissions and errors and must be used with caution. Some personalities have been placed in social or vocational classifications where they do not belong; for others the author has been unable to collect sufficient data. An obvious drawback to the method of classification employed is that significant differences between particular individuals may be lost, so that all who are tagged as bankers, for example, are equated in the tables, while in fact the interests which they represented may have been quite widely divergent. The purpose of the volume was to demonstrate that the statistician's methods can be applied to the historian's problem in sorting and classifying unwieldy masses of data. *The Parliamentary Diary of Sir Edward Knatchbull, 1722–1730*, edited by A. N. Newman (1963), illustrates the pattern whereby Tory country gentlemen of George I's day gradually adjusted to the new dynasty and in some instances came to hold great respect for the Walpole ministry. Lewis B. Namier's essay on country gentlemen in parliament briefly notes the essential independence of these rural members, explains their apparent view of parliament's proper function, and speculates upon the extent of their political influence.[8]

The evolution of parliamentary opposition from the condition of unstable faction to relative permanence and acceptance as a necessary feature of the constitution is the theme of Archibald S. Foord in *His Majesty's Opposition, 1714–1830* (Oxford, 1964). This study is a first-rate addition to historical literature. It concentrates largely upon early Hanoverian times, where the author analyzes with great care the composition of successive opposition groups and the *raison d'être* of each, the development of political theories concerning opposition, the means used by ministers to weaken and eliminate opposing factions, the gradual formation of quasi-permanent opposition parties, and the fashioning of

---

[8] "Country Gentlemen in Parliament, 1750–84," in his *Crossroads of Power: Essays on Eighteenth-century England* (1962), pp. 30–45.

opposition methods and techniques. In *The Old Cause: Three Biographical Studies in Whiggism* (1954) John Carswell chooses for examination in the early Hanoverian period the ideas of George Bubb Dodington, and credits Dodington with having developed the concept of an opposition party permanently organized as an alternate ministry awaiting the sovereign's call. A. N. Newman's article "Leicester House Politics, 1748–1751" takes issue with the view that Dodington was the leader of Prince Frederick's faction and contends that it was instead the second Earl of Egmont who held the party together and advised the Prince during the years under consideration.[9] Bolingbroke's view of opposition is explored at some length in Kurt Kluxen's *Das Problem der politischen Opposition: Entwicklung und Wesen der englischen Zweiparteien Politik im 18 Jahrhundert* (Freiburg, 1956). Bolingbroke believed that the tendency of any ministry to degenerate into corruption could be curbed by the continuous activity of a viable opposition party. Thomas W. Perry's *Public Opinion, Propaganda, and Politics in Eighteenth-Century England* (Cambridge, Mass., 1962) is a brief study, based on wide research, of the techniques employed by opposition groups to raise a public clamor and embarrass the Pelham ministry over the Jewish Naturalization Act of 1753.

A field which offers considerable opportunity for fresh scholarship is administrative history. Too little is known about the precise functions of individual departments, boards, and commissions, about relationships between local units of government and national, and about government personnel of the early eighteenth century. The works which have been completed in this field during the last two decades serve to indicate how much is still to be learned. Dora Mae Clark's *The Rise of the British Treasury: Colonial Administration in the Eighteenth Century* (New Haven, Conn., 1960) is an excellent account of the ways whereby the treasury came to wield steadily increasing authority in colonial affairs between the reign of Queen Anne and the American Revolution. John A. Schutz's *William Shirley: King's Governor of Massachusetts* (Chapel Hill, N.C., 1961) is a masterful statement of the difficulties of colonial administration which confronted even an unusually able politician. Shirley is seen building up a governor's party within the legislature, using patronage to the utmost advantage in recruiting his following, attempting to reconcile British policy and American interests in many areas of disagreement, and being required to defend himself to the home administration when attacks were made against his regime. Kenneth

[9] *EHR*, 76:577–589 (October 1961).

Ellis' *The Post Office in the Eighteenth Century: A Study in Administrative History* (1958) provides a useful account of the operations, problems, and organization of this department from 1738 to the end of the century. Rex Whitworth's *Field Marshal Lord Ligonier: A Story of the British Army, 1702–1770* (Oxford, 1958) contains a wealth of detail upon military organization and the efforts of Ligonier to bring efficiency into the service at the time of the Seven Years' War. Ligonier's struggle against inadequate supply and transport systems is depicted in terms that reveal the cumbersome administrative procedures which stalled the Hanoverian armies. Military historians will find useful the careful description of Ligonier's strategy for the winning of Canada in 1759, and his concern over French plans for an invasion of England in the same year. *The Vernon Papers*, edited by B. M. Ranft (1958), provides a view into naval administration between 1739 and 1745, the years covered by Admiral Edward Vernon's correspondence preserved in the National Maritime Museum. In *At Twelve Mr. Byng Was Shot* (1962), a book written for a popular audience, Dudley Pope indicts Lord Anson of the Admiralty and the Duke of Newcastle for sacrificing Byng in order to cover up the ministry's poor administration of the war. Pope has used a wide range of documentary material which was not available when W. B. Tunstall prepared his definitive biography of Byng, and states his case convincingly that the Admiral was less to blame for failure at Minorca than was the general incompetence of military and naval management.

In a short, lucid article upon the window tax of the eighteenth century, William R. Ward recounts the administrative problems connected with tax collection and shows that no effective means existed in times of peace whereby the government could impose its demands for revenue upon the English community and expect full compliance.[10] His *The English Land Tax in the Eighteenth Century* (Oxford, 1953) elaborates upon the inability of assessment and collection machinery to cope adequately with the administration of a great national tax.

The influence which the City of London brought to bear upon Walpole's ministry is appraised in Alfred James Henderson's *London and the National Government, 1721–1742* (Durham, N.C., 1945). Based upon the Guildhall records, this work provides a comprehensive account of London's complex political institutions, although Henderson fails to explain why the City steadily opposed the government despite the economic

[10] "The Administration of the Window and Assessed Taxes, 1696–1798," *EHR*, 67:522–542 (October 1952).

growth which London was enjoying. He does point out the extent to which national policies had an immediate effect upon the City, and shows that failure to gain London support could be critical for a government. Lucy S. Sutherland probes into the question of London's almost constant opposition to the government after 1720 and suggests that a social struggle within the City, a pervasive feeling that London was a distinctive entity entitled to special treatment, and a series of temporary alliances between City members and opposition factions contributed to the position.[11]

The most serious political crises of early Hanoverian times, Jacobite rebellions, have continued to attract historians who are drawn by the charm and pathos of the Stuarts and their followers into presenting accounts which emphasize the heroic elements of this ill-fated cause. Charles Petrie's *The Jacobite Movement* (2 vols., 1948–50) is a well-written, heavily partisan work that surveys the whole period from 1688 to 1807 in a spirit of sympathy which builds toward a crescendo as the Stuarts' chances become more hopeless. Petrie's writing is graphic, his descriptions of military operations in the Fifteen and the Forty-five are dramatic, and his bias toward the Jacobites is so obvious as to make it unlikely that one could be misled into mistaking his volumes for works of objective scholarship. Before a definitive general account can be published, additional basic research must still be completed in the extensive Stuart papers at Windsor. George Hilton Jones's *The Main Stream of Jacobitism* (Cambridge, Mass., 1954) is a careful study in which the exiled Stuarts are followed as they bid for support from continental statesmen and monarchs. Based upon materials at the British Museum and in the Bodleian Library, this volume exemplifies the kind of close examination of Stuart policies and personalities that is needed. Jones is more interested in presenting an accurate account of the negotiations pursued by the pretenders than in lamenting the outcome of the Fifteen, and his study is an illuminating catalogue of intrigue, mistakes, and sinking morale as the diplomatic moves of the Stuarts failed of their purpose. Two interesting articles by John J. Murray add a sidelight on Stuart diplomacy by recounting negotiations conducted with Swedish agents in 1716 and 1717.[12]

Henrietta Tayler has edited another volume in her series of published

---

[11] "The City of London in Eighteenth-century Politics," in *Essays Presented to Namier*, ed. Pares and Taylor, pp. 49–74.

[12] "Sweden and the Jacobites in 1716," *HLQ*, 8:259–276 (April 1945); and "An Eighteenth-Century Whitebook," *HLQ*, 13:371–382 (July 1950).

Jacobite papers, *Jacobite Epilogue* (1941). Included is correspondence between Jacobite leaders covering the years from 1716 to 1759. Local records bearing upon Jacobitism in northern England are published in *The Jacobite Risings of 1715 and 1745,* edited by Rupert C. Jarvis (Carlisle, 1954). These papers from the County Record Office at Carlisle document the collapse of the militia and trainband defenses at the time when they were needed most. Donald Nicholas, *The Young Adventurer* (1949), is a light, highly sympathetic, but unrevealing, account of Prince Charles Edward during the Forty-five. Katherine Tomasson's *The Jacobite General* (Edinburgh, 1958), describes the role of Lord George Murray in the Forty-five and provides a vivid picture of the Pretender's military moves from the time of his landing to the Culloden defeat.

The local political scene in Hanoverian times has been described in several works, but among the most revealing is Ralph John Robson's *The Oxfordshire Election of 1754* (1949). Robson examines the strength of the contending interests in this disputed election, the role of the university and its colleges, and the behavior of the voters, election officials, and the House of Commons; in the course of his study he presents a clear description of election procedures. William R. Ward's *Georgian Oxford: University Politics in the Eighteenth Century* (Oxford, 1958) covers the entire period from 1689 to 1780 in great detail, including within its scope university and church matters as well as those purely political. Ward believes that the university has been unjustly accused of Jacobite sympathy during the half century following the Glorious Revolution; in fact the majority accepted the Protestant Succession but frequently disagreed with the crown's ministers. Party alignments, the election machinery, the Jacobite risings, and the pressures brought to bear upon the community by the court are examined. These two studies of Oxford demonstrate convincingly that local records and the workings of community politics would amply repay the attention of scholars interested in the relationship between local and national political institutions. For the north of England Brian Bonsall's *Sir James Lowther and the Cumberland and Westmorland Elections, 1754–1775* (Manchester, Eng., 1960) reveals a powerful local family in the process of extending its political influence, by means of electioneering, over two counties. Bonsall describes Lowther's elaborate program of election management, and makes the point that freeholders were independent enough in that area to vote as they wished during critical elections, despite the pressures which might be placed upon them.

Among recent contributions to Hanoverian diplomatic history the most valuable general study is David Bayne Horn's *The British Diplomatic Service, 1689–1789* (Oxford, 1961). Horn inquires carefully into the organization of the service, the privileges, difficulties, and background of English diplomats, the increasing tendency toward professionalism, some of the problems of diplomatic activity, and the relationship between policy formulation and the service. This well-written volume will prove a welcome and useful reference work. Still needed is an account of the course of events in Hanoverian diplomatic history. In the meantime several works bearing upon specific problems have appeared. Two volumes, which should be read together for the light they throw on Anglo-Dutch relations, are Ragnhild Hatton, *Diplomatic Relations between Great Britain and the Dutch Republic, 1714–1721* (1950), and *An Honest Diplomat at The Hague: The Private Letters of Horatio Walpole, 1715–1716,* edited by John J. Murray (Bloomington, Ind., 1955). The Hatton account makes use of material in Dutch as well as in British archives to explain the highly complex diplomatic problems which followed in the train of the Peace of Utrecht. Charles Viscount Townshend emerges as an underrated statesman whose perception of Dutch affairs was keener than that of Lord Stanhope. Murray's volume covers the critical period when Stanhope's foreign policy was beginning to predominate and Walpole at The Hague found himself increasingly reluctant to endorse the changes in action required of him. Taken together these two studies provide a broad view of a specific change in course which British foreign relations experienced as a result of the Hanoverian accession. Graham C. Gibbs's article on the 1725 treaty with Hanover is a carefully written short account of the reasoning involved in reaching the decision in England that such a treaty was essential.[13] In a second article Gibbs examines the various means which ministers of the crown used in the early eighteenth century to present and explain foreign policy questions in parliament.[14] Richard Pares's essay "American versus Continental Warfare, 1739–63," reveals the dilemma faced in the reign of George II over whether England's interests would be better served by concentrating diplomatic and military efforts upon a continental policy of support-

[13] "Britain and the Alliance of Hanover, April 1725–February 1726," *EHR,* 73:404–430 (July 1958).

[14] "Parliament and Foreign Policy in the Age of Stanhope and Walpole," *EHR,* 77:18–37 (January 1962).

ing her allies and protecting Hanover, or upon a program of building maritime and imperial strength.[15]

Stetson Conn's *Gibraltar in British Diplomacy in the Eighteenth Century* (New Haven, Conn., 1942) sees in the possession of Gibraltar and the question of retrocession a central issue in Spanish-English-French relations. The book covers the diplomatic activities which revolved around the Gibraltar question but suffers from the fact that Spanish records were not available to the author. Jean O. McLachlan's *Trade and Peace with Old Spain, 1667–1750* (Cambridge, Eng., 1940), based both upon Spanish and English records, points up the great value of the Spanish trade to eighteenth-century British merchants, and describes the complexities which this exchange introduced into diplomatic relations. Allan Christelow's essay, "Economic Background of the Anglo-Spanish War of 1762," complements the McLachlan work by analyzing the trade between British merchants and Spain's American colonies prior to hostilities, and by disclosing Madrid's apprehensions over Britain's growing commercial power in the Spanish empire.[16] An illuminating article by Lawrence Henry Gipson examines Anglo-Spanish diplomacy between 1750 and 1757 and concludes that the Pelham-Newcastle ministries displayed great skill in regaining Spanish friendship in 1750 and retaining it until the coming of Pitt's ministry.[17]

Max Savelle's *The Diplomatic History of the Canadian Boundary, 1749–1763* (New Haven, Conn., 1940) is the most useful analysis of relations between England and France in the crucial years following the Peace of Aix-la-Chapelle. Attempts to solve by diplomatic means the problems of imperial rivalry which had been left untouched by the peace of 1748 are placed in perspective in the main course of European diplomacy, and the reader is left convinced that colonial causes loomed larger than European ones in setting off the Seven Years' War.

While the field of imperial history in the eighteenth century is so vast as to call for its own bibliographical essay, space may be found for comment upon a few of the most significant works. Since 1940 Lawrence Henry Gipson has added three more volumes dealing with the early Hanoverian period to his great work *The British Empire before the*

---

[15] See *The Historian's Business and Other Essays*, ed. R. A. and Elisabeth Humphreys (Oxford, 1961), pp. 429–465.

[16] *JMH*, 18:22–36 (March 1946).

[17] "British Diplomacy in the Light of Anglo-Spanish New World Issues, 1750–1757," *AHR*, 51:627–648 (January 1946).

American Revolution, and has moved on into the age of George III, re-turning long enough to revise the first three volumes in the series. Volume V, *Zones of International Friction: The Great Lakes Frontier, Canada, the West Indies, India 1748–1754* (New York, 1942) completes the survey begun in Volume IV of all points of contact between the British Empire and other imperial systems. Taken together, these two volumes provide an excellent account of the contrasts between French and English colonial society prior to the Seven Years' War. Volume V also describes Anglo-French negotiations on imperial problems between 1749 and 1755 and closes with a comparison of French and British colonial policies. Volume VI, *The Great War for the Empire: The Years of Defeat, 1754–1757* (New York, 1946) shows how dependent the colonies were upon England for defense measures, recounts the train of military disasters which befell the British, and traces the domestic and diplomatic policies of George II and his ministers. Volume VII, *The Great War for the Empire: The Victorious Years, 1758–1760* (New York, 1949) continues the narrative from Pitt's rise to power to the fall of French Canada, focusing almost entirely upon the prosecution of the war. Gipson's writing reaches a dramatic climax when he describes the defeat of Montcalm's forces at Quebec, but throughout the volume questions of military strategy are treated with such penetrating clarity that the work is unlikely to be surpassed as a definitive account. The revision of Volume I, *The British Isles and the American Colonies: Great Britain and Ireland, 1748–1754* (2d ed., New York, 1958) was required in the light of recent scholarship upon Hanoverian government and society. New sections on Ireland, Scotland, and Wales are included as well as an up-to-date account of British colonial institutions. The revised edition of Volume II is little changed from the original except in style, while Volume III has been rewritten to include new material on the Delaware settlements and a chapter which describes the British colonial system at mid-century.[18] The majestic breadth of Gipson's work, the formidable task of research which it involves, and the definitive picture that it affords of the Empire, assure its place among the century's great contributions to the field of historical writing.[19]

[18] Vol. II: *The British Isles and the American Colonies: The Southern Plantations, 1748–1754;* III: *The British Isles and the American Colonies: The Northern Plantations, 1748–1754,* 2d ed. (New York, 1960).

[19] A first-rate critical analysis of Gipson's great undertaking is Arthur R. M. Lower, "Lawrence H. Gipson and the First British Empire: An Evaluation," *JBS,* 3:57–78 (no. 1, 1963).

James Isham's Observations on Hudson's Bay, 1743, edited by E. E. Rich (1949), includes a long and useful introductory essay upon the Hudson's Bay Company's policies in America in the 1730's and 1740's. Although Isham's observations, based upon years of experience in company territory, are diverting and informative, it is the editor's account of the company's servants overseas and its struggle to preserve a territorial monopoly from incursion by English merchants that will be found most valuable. Glyndwr Williams' *The British Search for the Northwest Passage in the Eighteenth Century* (1962) traces the attempts of English seafarers between 1719 and 1795 to locate an all-water route across Canada, and chronicles the efforts of commercial speculators in England to keep the search alive. Arthur H. Buffington's article on the Canadian expedition of 1746 demonstrates how closely imperial policies were subject to the shifting balance of strength among factions in parliament during the 1740s.[20] Buffington believes that the expedition was responsible for first rousing the interest of Pitt and the Duke of Bedford in America.

Henry Campbell Wilkinson's excellent *Bermuda in the Old Empire: A History of the Island from the Dissolution of the Somer's Island Company until the End of the American Revolutionary War, 1684–1784* (1959) supplies an abundance of information about problems of imperial administration in war and peace in Bermuda and provides data on economic and social conditions in the island colony. Marshall Smelser's *The Campaign for the Sugar Islands, 1759* (Chapel Hill, N.C., 1955) relates the British military and naval operations at Guadeloupe and Martinique to West Indian economic conditions and to the other military activities throughout the empire in the same year.

In economic history the years since 1940 have demonstrated the enormous value of records preserved by families, business houses, plantation owners, local boards and commissions, municipal authorities, and customs collectors. Through the careful use of such records specialists have revealed much about the Hanoverian economic scene that cannot be gained from the older standard works of E. Lipson and William Cunningham. Local developments, regional economic change, and specific features of agriculture, commerce, manufacturing, and monetary movements have replaced broad economic trends as the focal points for study. Out of this new emphasis upon the particular, a fresh interpreta-

[20] "The Canada Expedition of 1746: Its Relation to British Politics," *AHR,* 45:552–580 (April 1940).

tion of the period may evolve, but a prodigious amount of close research is still called for in special subjects.

T. S. Ashton's *An Economic History of England: The Eighteenth Century* (1955) is a first-rate volume which points the direction the new research is taking. In successive chapters Ashton analyzes long-term trends in agriculture, internal trade, overseas trade, manufacturing, money, and labor, making the point that in each area those shifts which took place through the century were gradual rather than revolutionary. His contention is that writers have overstressed the disruptive forces of economic change in the period, thereby missing the basic continuity which characterized most aspects of English economic life. In a complementary work, *Economic Fluctuations in England, 1700–1800* (Oxford, 1959), Ashton probes closely into the causes of fluctuating poverty and prosperity and presents statistical evidence which reveals periodic price and production changes.

Studies in the Industrial Revolution, edited by L. S. Pressnell (1960), is a collection of twelve essays published in Ashton's honor by his friends and former students. Eight of the essays deal with Hanoverian times; all of them illustrate the current trend to seek out and exploit forms of economic endeavor previously overlooked by historians. The subjects are: early canal-building projects, the industrial operations of an ambitious ironmaster, the effect of British iron production upon Swedish exports, industrial unrest in Wiltshire, population shifts in Nottingham, agricultural changes, the effects of warfare on eighteenth-century London banks, and changes in interest rates.

Douglas Vickers' *Studies in the Theory of Money, 1690–1776* (Philadelphia, 1959) provides the only available analysis of English monetary theories for the century preceding the publication of *The Wealth of Nations.* Vickers examines the ideas of nine eighteenth-century theorists concerning the precise function and value of money and its relation to prices, interest rates, and employment. Two brief articles by A. W. Coats points out that by 1750 the attitudes in England toward the laboring classes and the poor were changing as social and economic theorists began to advocate general improvements in the living conditions of depressed groups.[21]

Several studies have appeared to illustrate regional economic change. Thomas Stuart Willan's *The Navigation of the River Weaver during the*

---

[21] "Changing Attitudes to Labour in the Mid-eighteenth Century," *EcHR,* 2d ser., 11:35–51 (August 1958); "Economic Thought and Poor Law Policy in the Eighteenth Century," *ibid.,* 13:39–51 (August 1960).

Eighteenth Century (Manchester, Eng., 1951) traces the involved struggle to develop a Cheshire waterway and estimates the effect of increased navigation upon local government and the economic setting. W. H. B. Court has published an illuminating essay upon industrial organization in the Midlands, demonstrating that a pattern of diversified industrial production was well-established by the early years of the century.[22] The growth of Birmingham's trade and manufactures is described in two articles which should be read together.[23] Port operations, shipping procedures, and the problems of trade at Liverpool, are chronicled in *The Customs Letter-books of the Port of Liverpool, 1711–1813,* edited by Rupert C. Jarvis (Manchester, 1954). In *The Trade of Bristol in the Eighteenth Century* (Bristol, 1957), Walter E. Minchinton edits selected documents which illustrate the activities of that port. The same editor's *Politics and the Port of Bristol in the Eighteenth Century* (Bristol, 1963) consists of petitions sent by Bristol merchants to parliament and the crown between 1698 and 1803. These petitions quite dramatically disclose the shift from a dynamic, aggressive trading community at the beginning of the century to a rather fearful, protective group of shippers and traders at the century's end. Minchinton's "Bristol—Metropolis of the West in the Eighteenth Century," suggests some of the influences which brought about the rise and decline of this commercial center.[24]

The London sugar trade has been closely studied by Richard Pares through the ledgers and correspondence of a leading eighteenth-century sugar importer.[25] Richard B. Sheridan considers the role of British sugar planters in promoting passage of the Molasses Act of 1733.[26] In an article upon banking practices after 1720, D. M. Joslin points out that the importance of London's private banks to the economy of England has generally been underestimated.[27] A. H. John has analyzed the economic effects of war upon eighteenth-century England and concludes that the

[22] "Industrial Organisation and Economic Progress in the Eighteenth-century Midlands," *TRHS*, 4th ser., 28 (1946), pp. 85–99.

[23] Michael J. Wise, "Birmingham and Its Trade Relations in the Early Eighteenth Century," *UBHJ*, 2:53–79 (no. 1, 1949); and R. A. Pelham, "The West Midland Iron Industry and the American Market in the Eighteenth Century," *UBHJ*, 2:141–162 (no. 2, 1950).

[24] *TRHS*, 5th ser., 4 (1954), pp. 69–89.

[25] "A London West-India Merchant House, 1740–1769," in *Essays Presented to Namier,* ed. Pares and Taylor, pp. 75–107; see also Richard Pares, "The London Sugar Market, 1740–1769," *EcHR*, 2d ser., 9:254–270 (December 1956).

[26] "The Molasses Act and the Market Strategy of the British Sugar Planters," *JEcH*, 17:62–83 (March 1957).

[27] "London Private Bankers, 1720–1785," *EcHR*, 2d ser., 7:167–186 (December 1954).

losses have been stressed out of reason while the stimulating effects of a successful war have been overlooked.[28] An excellent study of a great eighteenth-century industrial complex is Michael Flinn's *Men of Iron: The Crowleys in the Early Iron Industry* (Edinburgh, 1962). Based upon family papers, a wide selection of local records, and Admiralty documents, this work affords a close view of the century's largest iron-fabricating firm and its unusually enlightened management.

Agricultural economics has attracted less study than might be expected for a period in which experimentation with new farming methods and enclosure were significant features. H. C. Pawson's *Robert Bakewell, Pioneer Livestock Breeder* (1957) adds only some details to the available literature upon this experimenter. In an article based upon research in the Duke of Kingston's records, G. E. Mingay examines the effects of the agricultural depression which began in 1730.[29] Edward Hughes has charted the rise of the estate agent in sections of northern England which were undergoing dramatic change.[30]

A significant reappraisal of the colonial fur trade is found in Murray G. Lawson's *Fur: A Study in English Mercantilism, 1700–1775* (Toronto, 1943), where it is established that fur played only a minor role during this period in the economy of England and her colonies, the commodity being used chiefly by the hatters of London. The author illustrates the operation of mercantilist policy by examining the laws, customs, and conditions which governed the fur trade.

The East India Company is the subject of an essay by Lucy S. Sutherland in which the author describes, for early Hanoverian times, the relationship which existed between the company and the government through the company's connections in the House of Commons.[31] Sukumar Bhattacharya's *The East India Company and the Economy of Bengal from 1704 to 1740* (1954) offers a detailed analysis of the company's trading operations and connections in the Ganges basin. Brijen K. Gupta's *Sirajuddaullah and the East India Company, 1756–1757* (Leiden, 1962) treats the company's increasing involvement in the economics and politics of Bengal in the 1750's, and recounts the drift into warfare and the events which led up to Plassey.

---

[28] "War and the English Economy, 1700–1763," *ibid.*, 7:329–344 (April 1955).
[29] "The Agricultural Depression, 1730–1750," *ibid.*, 8:323–338 (April 1956).
[30] "The Eighteenth-century Estate Agent," in *Essays in British and Irish History in Honour of James Eadie Todd*, ed. H. A. Cronne, T. W. Moody, and D. B. Quinn (1949), pp. 185–199.
[31] "The East India Company in Eighteenth-century Politics," *EcHR*, 17:15–26 (no. 1, 1947).

John Carswell's *The South Sea Bubble* (1960) provides a survey of events leading to the South Sea Company's formation, gives a step-by-step account of company activity in the period of the Bubble, and supplies valuable biographical information relative to lesser-known figures associated with the company. John J. Sperling's *The South Sea Company, an Historical Essay and Bibliographical Finding List* (Boston, Mass., 1962) supplements Carswell's work, being especially informative as to the origins and early years of the company.

Charles Henry Wilson's *Anglo-Dutch Commerce and Finance in the Eighteenth Century* (Cambridge, Eng., 1941) is based upon study of both Dutch and English archives. Wilson finds that the nature of Dutch enterprise in England shifted about 1730, with Dutch family firms in London gradually moving into the lucrative field of public and private lending, where their resources were in demand owing to England's expanding economy. The result was that relations between the two countries came to be shaped to some extent by the needs of financiers. Wilson's volume provides so much information about the nature of England's foreign trade that it points out the need for further studies of a similar kind.

A useful manual for the study of British import-export trade is Elizabeth B. Schumpeter's *English Overseas Trade Statistics, 1697–1808* (Oxford, 1960). Based upon records of the Inspector-General's office, this is a set of tables listing the annual value and quantity of each commodity which passed through English and Welsh ports. Ralph Davis' recent article on foreign trade identifies the dynamic, the more stationary, and the declining elements in eighteenth-century England's export trade,[32] while H. E. S. Fisher's brief account of Anglo-Portuguese trade illuminates the nature and significance of trade between London and Lisbon, and gives reason for its eventual deterioration.[33] Conrad Gill's *Merchants and Mariners of the 18th Century* (1961) is a brief biography of Thomas Hall, who traded successively in the Baltic, the East Indies, and along the China coast during the reign of George I. Hall's papers constitute the principal source for the volume, which contains a smattering of information about the problems and practices of sea traders to the Orient as well as the personal adventures of Hall.

Writings in the field of social history have been diverse in type and purpose but have not resulted in the recasting of many fundamental

[32] "English Foreign Trade, 1700–1774," *ibid.*, 2d. ser., 15:285–301 (December 1962).
[33] "Anglo-Portuguese Trade, 1700–1770," *ibid.*, 16:219–233 (December 1963).

concepts. Additional data have been brought forward about each class in the social system, while regional differences of a social nature have been discussed in some studies. Perhaps the most significant finding has been the discovery that humanitarian activity existed in larger measure in Hanoverian times than had been realized. Dorothy Marshall's *English People in the Eighteenth Century* (1956) provides a welcome fresh survey of prevailing social conditions. The author has sifted through monographs on economic and social history and has added the results of her own researches to arrive at a well-balanced treatment which takes into account the changes in society occurring in the course of the century. Edward William Hughes's *North Country Life in the Eighteenth Century: The North-East, 1700–1750* (1952) is an excellent example of regional social history based almost entirely upon the use of local records. Hughes portrays a society of businessmen, professional people, industrialists, and landlords engaged in altering profoundly the social and economic conditions of a part of England which had traditionally lagged behind, but at last was making an effort to catch up with, the rest of the nation. He ranges so widely through subjects of social, political, and economic interest that the volume will prove useful as a general reference work on the north country. G. E. Mingay's *English Landed Society in the Eighteenth Century* (1963) reassesses the organization and activities of the landholding class and concludes that the small-scale landholder did not disappear from the scene as completely as had been thought, nor did enclosures disrupt the countryside as thoroughly as had previously been suggested. Especially valuable is Mingay's account of involvement by the landholding class in commercial and industrial developments.

Local records, family papers, and diaries have been published to illustrate, with varying degrees of success, the daily social intercourse of Hanoverian England. Among the more revealing of such published documents is *Blundell's Diary and Letter Book, 1702–1728*, edited by Margaret Blundell (Liverpool, 1952), the daily record of a Lancashire squire who participated wholeheartedly in the political and social life of the county and left an unusually complete diary containing the details of his career and times. *The Letters and Papers of the Banks Family of Revesby Abbey*, edited by James W. F. Hill (Lincoln, Eng., 1952), includes entertaining accounts of estate management, family relationships, and the social practices of a prosperous family in eighteenth-century Lincolnshire. Nesta G. Evans' informative *Religion and Politics in Mid-*

Eighteenth-Century Anglesey (Cardiff, 1953) is based upon the diary of a squire who was deeply interested in the Welsh church as well as in local politics and social life. *The Diary of Benjamin Rogers,* edited by C. D. Linnell (1950), shows the wide range of social responsibilities which fell to the country parson in rural England. Village life is depicted with unusual clarity in two small studies based upon diaries: Dean K. Worcester, Jr., *The Life and Times of Thomas Turner of East Hoathly* (New Haven, Conn., 1948), and Ralph Arnold, *A Yeoman of Kent* (1949). William Byrd of Virginia, *The London Diary, 1717–1721, and Other Writings,* edited by Louis B. Wright and Marion Tinling (New York, 1958), illustrates the day-to-day concerns of an American who was as much at home in Hanoverian London as he was in Virginia and who was accepted in intellectual circles and in good society.

The changing status of professional classes in the eighteenth century has begun to attract the scholarly attention which it deserves. Bernice Hamilton's article on the medical profession provides general information upon the struggle of apothecaries, surgeons, and physicians to raise their professional competence and social standing through the mastery of new techniques and the formation of specialists' societies.[34] One doctor's efforts to reform the practices in his profession are traced in *The Letters of Doctor George Cheyne to Samuel Richardson (1733–1743),* edited by Charles F. Mullett (Columbia, Mo., 1943). The rising status of the legal profession is described in Robert Robson's *The Attorney in Eighteenth Century England* (1959). In this careful account Robson shows the range of activities undertaken by members of the profession and concludes that the enhanced status enjoyed by attorneys was brought about partly by demands within the complex and expanding business and political world for trained minds and partly by movements within the profession directed at improved recruitment and training.

Social historians of the past two decades have disposed of the myth that Hanoverian England was devoid of a social conscience. Betsy Rodgers' *Cloak of Charity: Studies in Eighteenth Century Philanthropy* (1949) surveys the humanitarian impulse as it appeared in the careers of Thomas Coram, Jonas Hanaway, John Howard, Robert Raikes, and other reformers. Her volume is pleasantly written but makes little attempt to be profound. More scholarly is John Harold Hutchins' *Jonas Hanaway, 1712–1786,* (1940), a satisfactory account of Hanaway's efforts

---

[34] "The Medical Profession in the Eighteenth Century," *ibid.,* 4:141–169 (December 1951).

in behalf of England's foundlings. J. Jean Hecht's *The Domestic Servant Class in Eighteenth Century England* (1956) is an excellent and lively study of the recruitment, living conditions, responsibilities, ambitions, and rewards of the servant class, the relationship between servant and master, the hierarchy within the servant class, and the relation of the class to the rest of English society. Frank J. Klingberg's *Anglican Humanitarianism in Colonial New York* (Philadelphia, 1940) examines the efforts of the Society for the Propagation of the Gospel and the Society for Promoting Christian Knowledge to bring England's social institutions to the colonies where they would be shared by English colonists, Negro slaves, and Amerinds. Leonard W. Cowie's *Henry Newman, An American in London, 1708–1743* (1956) describes the wide-ranging programs of the S.P.C.K. in aiding distressed European Protestants, distributing religious and educational publications throughout England and the colonies, and encouraging the establishment of charity schools and foreign missions during the thirty-five-year period in which Newman served as the society's secretary.

In a unique study, J. Harry Bennett's *Bondsmen and Bishops* (Berkeley and Los Angeles, Calif., 1958), social and economic history are blended in a discussion of conditions on two West Indian plantations which came by bequest in 1710 to the Society for the Propagation of the Gospel and remained under the Society's care for over a century. The Society's rich records chronicle the details of plantation management and economics as well as the provisions of a program for the social and moral betterment of the Negro slaves. From these sources the author has produced this vital account of an unusual West Indian enterprise. Mary Clement's *The S.P.C.K. and Wales, 1699–1740* (1954) traces the efforts of Anglican reformers to bring schools, improved churches, books, and employment to the poverty-ridden Welsh dioceses.

In religious history Norman Sykes and his students have attacked the myth that the Hanoverian church was somnolent and unproductive. Sykes's *William Wake, Archbishop of Canterbury, 1657–1737* (2 vols., Cambridge, Eng., 1957) is the product of a quarter-century's research in the massive Wake manuscripts at Oxford. The study is exhaustive; the Bangorian controversy, the convocation quarrels, Wake's long-sustained attempt to secure closer relations with the Gallican church and the Protestants of Switzerland and Germany, and the broad range of diocesan responsibilities of eighteenth-century bishops are each treated in such complete detail that earlier works on these subjects have been superseded. Sykes demonstrates that the Hanoverian bishops were more often overworked than neglectful of their duties, and that the archbishop of Canterbury was expected to back the views of the king's ministers in ecclesiastical legislation under threat of being discarded as the king's adviser in religious matters. A second study by Sykes, *From Sheldon to Secker: Aspects of English Church History, 1660–1768* (Cambridge, Eng., 1959) singles out several phenomena that militated against the church. The failure of efforts at comprehension, the cessation of regular sittings of the convocation, the growth of Erastianism and anticlericalism among political leaders, and the intellectual revolution of the eighteenth century are examined as causes for the diminishing prestige and authority of the church. Despite the obvious difficulties of the period, Sykes finds that the church possessed a vitality that has too often been disregarded. Spencer C. Carpenter's *Eighteenth-century Church and People* (1959) incorporates the main conclusions of recent research in a text aimed at general readers interested in the Church of England.

The Letters of Spencer Cowper, Dean of Durham, 1746–74, edited by Edward Hughes (Durham, 1956), consists of 231 revealing letters written by an ecclesiastic who represents the time-serving, disinterested cleric so often associated with the Hanoverian church. Spencer Cowper resented taking holy orders, regretted his appointment to Durham, and found northern England and the cares of his office wholly disagreeable. Roland N. Stromberg's *Religious Liberalism in Eighteenth-Century England* (1954) is concerned with departures from orthodox religious thought in the century following 1688. The doctrinal teachings of Anthony Collins, John Toland, Samuel Clarke, Thomas Sherlock, and others are carefully presented. Stromberg's interest is more in religious ideas than in their application; his study provides an effective analysis of the impact which rationalism made upon doctrinal interpretation and development in the eighteenth century. Walter McIntosh Merrill's *From Statesman to Philosopher: A Study in Bolingbroke's Deism* (New York, 1949) compares Bolingbroke's deism with the ideas of other deist thinkers and gives a good brief summary of deism in Hanoverian England.

Nonconformists in the eighteenth century have not received the attention which they merit although source materials are abundant. Duncan Coomer's *English Dissent under the Early Hanoverians* (1946) offers a brief, simple guide to the activities of Presbyterians, Independents, Baptists, and others, showing how these groups reacted to deism, unitarianism, and evangelism, but makes no attempt to measure the relative strength of each or to estimate the influence of nonconformity upon the nation's life. The Methodist movement in its beginning stages is described in Leslie Frederic Church's *The Early Methodist People* (1948), a sympathetic but shallow account which undertakes to explain the Methodist spirit and its effect upon the daily lives of those who subscribed to Wesley's teachings. *Selected Letters of John Wesley,* edited by Frederick C. Gill (New York, 1956), is a selection of representative letters taken from the eight-volume Telford edition. It includes the lengthy letter to Vincent Perronet in which Wesley outlined the Methodist program, as well as letters to political figures and members of Wesley's family. Perhaps the best work yet to appear on Wesley's evolving religious ideas is Martin Schmidt's *John Wesley, a Theological Biography,* volume I translated by Norman P. Goldhawk (1962), which emphasizes especially the influence of the Moravian Brethren upon his thinking. George C. B. Davies' *The Early Cornish Evangelicals, 1735–1760* (1951) describes the efforts at religious revival made by Samuel Walker of Truro and points out essential differences between the Methodists and the Anglican evangelicals. Norman C. Hunt's *Two Early Political Associations: The Quakers and the Dissenting Deputies in the Age of Sir Robert Walpole* (1961) traces the activities of the Friends in later Stuart and early Hanoverian times in urging the government to repeal the Test and Corporation Acts, and shows how the Quaker example in political affairs was followed by Presbyterians, Baptists, and Independents in 1732 with the establishment of a committee of dissenters whose purpose was to bring effective pressure upon parliament and the king's ministers to remove the remaining civil disabilities. Richard B. Barlow's *Citizenship and Conscience: A Study in the Theory and Practice of Religious Toleration in England during the Eighteenth Century* (Philadelphia, 1962) also elucidates the long struggle of Nonconformists to gain public acceptance first of the principle of toleration and later of civil equality. This is a dramatic account of the frustrations encountered in overcoming apathy and inertia. Carl Bridenbaugh's *Mitre and Sceptre: Transatlantic Faiths, Ideas, Personalities and Politics, 1689–1775* (New York, 1962) supplements A. L. Cross's volume of sixty years ago on the Anglican episcopate in the colonies. Bridenbaugh stresses the existence of strong bonds between English dissenters and their American counterparts and discusses the ties between colonial Anglicans and the English church. He holds that continuous and increasing controversy over the church-state relationship in the colonies, and the fear of an

Anglican establishment, created tensions which grew into a major cause of the American Revolution.

The Augustan age is viewed as a vehicle for the transmission and development of ideas in Caroline Robbins' *The Eighteenth-Century Commonwealthman: Studies in the Transmission, Development and Circumstances of English Liberal Thought from the Restoration of Charles II until the War with the Thirteen Colonies* (Cambridge, Mass., 1959). The author shows that radical ideas of the seventeenth century concerning political forms and organization, the rights of individuals, freedom from thought control, and many other subjects were handed down through successive generations of teachers, pamphleteers, lawyers, clergymen, and the spokesmen of minority groups, until they were grasped at the time of the American Revolution and used first to supply the philosophic basis for revolt and later as a guide for the construction of a new American government.

During the two decades under review valuable studies on the early Hanoverian period have appeared in the fields of literary history, art history, historical geography, biography, and bibliography. In addition, eighteenth-century source material ranging in kind and purpose from the records printed in volumes of the *Calendar of State Papers,* through documents of purely local interest published by county historical societies, to the great edition of Horace Walpole's correspondence under production at Yale University, have been made available. A discussion of these many contributions to the historian's craft is precluded by considerations of space, but one distinguished work which will be useful to the reader desiring an idea of the breadth of materials available for the Hanoverian period is the *Bibliography of British History: The Eighteenth Century,* edited by Stanley Pargellis and D. J. Medley (Oxford and New York, 1951). This notable example of Anglo-American cooperation in historical bibliography is the most comprehensive guide obtainable to each of the fields omitted from consideration in this essay. One quick perusal of the Pargellis and Medley volume will serve to demonstrate the vitality which has characterized recent historical writings upon early Hanoverian England.

The Reign of George III
in Recent Historiography

❖

J. JEAN HECHT

P ERHAPS no period of English history has been
the subject of more intensive examination in recent years than the reign
of George III. Its art, architecture, and literature, its economic and political life, its moral and religious values, have been the preoccupation of a
host of scholars; and when the lucubrations of these specialists are considered together, the aggregate appears enormous. A superficial explanation of this activity is easy to adduce. The reign of George III compre-
hended a variety of phenomena to which a standard set of constructs has
been applied. It was the "Age of Johnson"; it was the "Age of Adam." It
experienced the "Agricultural Revolution" and the "Industrial Revolution." It brought maturity to the "Romantic Movement," the "Evangelical Movement," the "Humanitarian Movement," *cum multis aliis.* Each
of these constructs has itself become a focus of specialization, inviting
fresh investigation, reappraisal, and revision. But there is also a more
fundamental explanation. The greater part of the reign of George III
shared the long-standing proscription that prejudice and revulsion imposed on the whole eighteenth century: it was a segment of the "neglected period" of English history. Only in the early decades of the present century was serious investigation begun; only in the years after the
First World War did this new interest quicken and produce a substantial
corpus of significant work. In consequence, during the past two decades
much remained to be done; and scholars, attracted by the broad range
of possibilities, took up the task in considerable numbers.

No really adequate attempt has yet been made to incorporate the vast
accretions of this recent work into a general synthesis. But three broad
surveys of major significance have lately appeared. The early chapters of

[Reprinted from *The Bulletin of the New York Public Library,* 70:279–304 (May
1966).]

Asa Briggs's *The Age of Improvement, 1783–1867* (1959) treat with singular freshness and perspicuity all but the first two decades of the reign. They are almost entirely concerned, however, with its economic, political, and constitutional aspects. Very much more comprehensive is J. Steven Watson's *The Reign of George III, 1760–1815* (Oxford, 1960), which constitutes an essentially sound and richly informative manual of the period, although marred by a number of minor inaccuracies. Originally assigned to George S. Veitch and then to Richard Pares, whose successive deaths long postponed its advent, this volume of the *Oxford History of England* compensates for the protracted delay by the modernity of much of its interpretation. The same virtue characterizes Dorothy Marshall's excellent *Eighteenth Century England* (1962), the last six chapters of which cover the period 1760–1784. As in the case of Watson's work, the principal strength of this survey is the degree to which it utilizes those findings and formulations that have latterly assumed the status of a new orthodoxy in the sphere of political history.

The progenitor of this new orthodoxy was Sir Lewis Namier. The twin pillars of his achievement were erected between 1911 and 1930. Their completion inaugurated a revisionary era in the historiography of the period, for the innovations they introduced were manifold and diverse. They destroyed the view that political conflict was a contest between two organized and disciplined parties; they demonstrated that the politicians of the day were motivated by interest and ambition rather than by ideology; they showed that the monarch retained considerable constitutional powers and that George III was guilty of no nefarious usurpation when he exercised them; they discredited the notion that the ministers of the Crown dispensed large sums of secret service money in order to control elections; they made it clear that the "King's Friends" were not merely a phalanx of venal placemen; and much else besides. But the revision of old interpretations was by no means their sole contribution. They also introduced a new method, a novel approach. The new method entailed a careful and precise anatomy of the political organism. It identified the major lines of structure; it isolated and examined the component elements. The basic units scrutinized in this analysis were the biographies of many different men; the principal objective sought was the disclosure of motivations and interrelationships. The enduring importance of these innovations is attested by the recent republication of Sir Lewis' *The Structure of Politics at the Accession of George III* (1957) in a second edition that is virtually identical with the original, except for minor changes in phraseology. Although Sir Lewis did not see fit to revise his early work, he amplified it in two important essays that appear in *Personalities and Powers* (1955). In "Monarchy and the Party System" he presents a brilliant explication of the political role of the eighteenth-century King, and demonstrates anew the absence of organized parties. In "Country Gentlemen in Parliament, 1750–84" he analyzes the part played in the House of Commons by the apostles of "independency," showing their responsiveness to public opinion and their power when united against the government of the day. Several posthumous volumes significantly augment his *oeuvre*. One of these is a slender but by no means inconsequential collection of miscellaneous pieces, *Crossroads of Power* (1962). Along with essays on Daniel Pulteney, a typical rank and file member of Parliament whose mediocrity recommended him as a suitable subject, and on the procedures and techniques of imposing political discipline in the House of Commons, it includes three early lectures on "The King and His Ministers," "The Cabinet," and "The Prime Minister," which are of interest because they reveal certain positions that Sir Lewis either modified or abandoned as his research proceeded and his formulations developed. Far more substantial in size as well as more important in content are the three volumes of *The House of Commons, 1754–1790* (1964), which constitute the first installment of *The History of Parliament*. Sir Lewis, assisted by a team of collaborators, labored on them steadily from 1951 until his death in 1960; and they were subsequently brought to completion by John Brooke. Seen by Sir Lewis' disciples as the capstone of his work on the eighteenth century, these volumes form a mammoth compendium of socio-political data. The first of them contains an introductory survey, embodying the conclusions drawn by Sir Lewis from that material; it also includes capsule histories of all the parliamentary constituencies. The second and third volumes are devoted to miniature biographical sketches of the 1,964 members who sat between 1754 and 1790.

But the most important of Sir Lewis' later contributions was made indirectly. Unable to complete the ambitious project he began with the publication of his second and greatest work, *England in the Age of the American Revolution* (1930), he delegated the task to a band of young disciples. He gave them a plan and a method; he provided them with inspiration and direction. Even the title of the enterprise was supplied by Sir Lewis; the original name of the parent work, which in due course will take its place with the other studies as *Newcastle and Bute,* was adopted for the whole series. Three volumes in the series have already appeared. In *The Chatham Administration, 1766–1768* (1956) John Brooke, Sir Lewis' "closest collaborator," details the abortive attempt of the great statesman to establish a stable government. The formation and disintegration of the administration are painstakingly described; so, too, are the growth and development of the opposition. The permutations of the various political alignments are minutely examined throughout the study, but two sections in particular are devoted to a thorough analysis of the coteries of the day. Ian R. Christie's *The End of the North Ministry* (1958) treats a very different theme. It is concerned with the maneuvers of Lord North and his colleagues to maintain themselves in office and with the failure of these efforts in the face of the American disaster. It pays more attention than does its predecessor to the impact of events and public opinion on the fluctuating strength of government and opposition. But like its predecessor, it also contains two sections in which political structure is carefully analyzed. Bernard Donoughue's *British Politics and the American Revolution* (1964) deals with an earlier phase of Lord North's administration, "The Path to War, 1773–75." It relates with exceptional clarity how the King and his ministers, with the enthusiastic backing of the general public, took steps to reduce the recalcitrant colonists to submission. At the same time, it includes excellent analyses of the opposition coteries led by Rockingham and Chatham, and of the election of 1774.

Sir Lewis' influence has by no means been confined to this cooperative undertaking. Betty Kemp, another of his disciples, has drawn heavily on his work in her *King and Commons, 1660–1832* (1957), a valuable survey of the changing relationship of the monarch and legislature between the Restoration and the Great Reform Bill. Although in no sense a disciple, Richard Pares likewise borrowed extensively from Sir Lewis for his *George III and the Politicians* (Oxford, 1953), which is the most lucid and precise delineation available of the mechanics of the late eighteenth-century constitutional and political system. Similarly, Archibald S. Foord has taken much from Sir Lewis for the later sections of *His Majesty's Opposition, 1714–1830* (Oxford, 1964), a study that charts the metamorphosis of disreputable coterie faction into legitimate party dissent.

The pervasive influence of Sir Lewis has been sharply challenged by Herbert Butterfield in *George III and the Historians* (1957), an essentially polemical work that contrives to combine much ill-tempered and irrelevant criticism with some perceptive suggestions and a highly useful body of historiographical data. Its basic approach was foreshadowed some twenty years ago by the late Gerda R. Crosby in her excellent essay on George III, "Historians and a Royal Reputation." [1] But whereas her objective was to demonstrate the vagaries of historical relativism, Butterfield's is to erect a platform from which to assail Namier. By surveying the interpretations that were made from the time of Adolphus and Bisset to that of Winstanley, Butterfield attempts to show that the innovations usually credited to Sir Lewis were anticipated by his precursors. He then carries forward the attack by indicting Sir Lewis and his followers for the fallaciousness of their preconceptions and the limitations of their method. One of their most egregious errors, he holds, is the assumption that categorizes as irrelevant the rationalizations and professed ideological commitments of historical *personae*. Another is their dilation upon structure and their unconcern with issues and events. Such views and attitudes, Butterfield contends, are highly pernicious; and for this reason he decries the existence of the Namier school.

Outside the ambit of Namier's influence, the political and constitutional history of the reign has received a substantial amount of attention. George H. Guttridge's *English Whiggism and the American Revolution* (Berkeley and Los Angeles, Calif., 1963), which was first published in 1942, attempts to trace the complex interrelationship of practical politics, popular movements, and ideological currents during the conflict with the colonies; and although now so obsolete as to be scarcely worthy of a second edition, it contains some suggestive notions. But Charles R. Ritcheson's *British Politics and the American Revolution* (Norman, Okla., 1954) provides a much sounder treatment and clearly demonstrates the influence of the colonial issue on the general course of political development. The most crucial phase of the subject is provocatively examined in Herbert Butterfield's *George III, Lord North and the People, 1779–1780* (1950), which traces the crisis with which the government was ultimately confronted to a convergence of the movements for Irish autonomy, parliamentary reform, and diminished executive power. Understanding of a later critical juncture is markedly extended by John W. Derry's authoritative *The Regency Crisis and the Whigs, 1788–89* (Cambridge, Eng., 1963), which explores the interplay of regal psychosis, constitutional theory, and the machinations of parliamentary

[1] *Essays in English History in Honor of Wilbur Cortez Abbott* (Cambridge, Mass., 1941), pp. 295–313.

coteries. The genesis of the principal opposition coterie is portrayed in George H. Guttridge's *The Early Political Career of Lord Rockingham* (Berkeley, Calif., 1954), an uninspired study that fails to say much that is new or revise much that is old. The objectives and maneuvers of another opposition coterie are expertly explored in John Norris' *Shelburne and Reform* (1963), a work remarkable for its thoroughness. Even more remarkable is Lewis M. Wiggin's *The Faction of Cousins* (New Haven, Conn., 1958), which depicts the growth and disintegration of that typical family coterie the Grenvilles. The means whereby a landed magnate might create and maintain such a parliamentary group are made manifest by Brian Bonsall's *Sir James Lowther and Cumberland and Westmorland Elections, 1754–1775* (Manchester, Eng., 1960). The interests and influence of a very different sort of magnate are exposed by Lucy Sutherland in her *East India Company in Eighteenth-Century Politics* (Oxford, 1952), which skillfully reconstructs the intricate web of relations that subsisted between directors, ministers, and party henchmen. And W. R. Ward's *Georgian Oxford* (Oxford, 1958) depicts the political role of the universities.

The opening decades of the reign, with which most of these studies are concerned, witnessed the birth of radicalism, a movement that has been explored with some care in recent years. Simon Maccoby has provided a comprehensive and detailed treatment of the subject in his magisterial volumes, *English Radicalism, 1762–1785* (1955) and *English Radicalism, 1785–1832* (1955). One of the earliest phases of the movement that Maccoby surveys is very deftly anatomized in George Rudé's *Wilkes and Liberty* (Oxford, 1962), which carefully considers the social milieu in which the demagogue played his part, the nature of his appeal, the provenance and interests of his supporters, and the manner in which current economic conditions abetted his rise and maintained his popularity. The initial section of Ian R. Christie's *Wilkes, Wyvill, and Reform* (1962) covers some of the same ground, but with a deplorable superficiality and a fundamental incomprehension of the protagonist, who is characterized with prissy censoriousness; the section on the moderate Christopher Wyvill and his Yorkshire Association, which is executed with inordinate precision and in great detail, is much better. Later phases of the movement are given competent if somewhat prejudiced treatment in E. P. Thompson's *The Making of the English Working Class* (1963), a massive work written very much in the spirit of G. D. H. Cole. Some aspects of these later phases are also examined intensively in more specialized studies. The influence of Jacobinism on the radical movement as well as on its opponents is incisively probed in Jules Dechamps, *Les Îles Britanniques et la Révolution Française, 1789–1803* (Brussels, 1949), a book worthy of translation. François Crouzet, *L'économie britannique et le blocus continental, 1806–1813* (Paris, 1959) shows how the economic dislocations produced by the Napoleonic Wars contributed to the movement's development in the early years of the nineteenth century. The culmination of the discontent, tension, and conflict of those years is reviewed in Reginald J. White's light and literate, yet scholarly, study, *From Waterloo to Peterloo* (1957). White's account of the tragic events in St. Peter's Fields is somewhat shallow, but they are analyzed with great thoroughness and penetration in Donald Read's *Peterloo: The 'Massacre' and Its Background* (1958).

The antipodal position in politics during the latter part of the reign has likewise been re-examined. W. R. Brock's *Lord Liverpool and Liberal Toryism* (Cambridge, Eng., 1941) is a judicious appraisal of a regime whose essential character and policies have often been grossly distorted. C. R. Fay's *Huskisson and His Age* (1951) contains a useful sketch of one of the major political groupings that supported the regime. The strength and weaknesses characterizing the citadel of that regime and the partisan warfare in which it figured are admirably portrayed in Arthur S. Turberville's *The House of Lords in the Age of Reform, 1784–1837* (1958), a posthumously published continuation of his earlier work that was put into final form by Reginald J. White.

Like political practice, political theory has not been neglected. The reassessment of several radical thinkers has been recently undertaken. Carl B. Cone's *Torchbearer of Freedom, the Influence of Richard Price on Eighteenth-Century Thought* (Lexington, Ky., 1951), although essentially biographical, contains a certain amount of commentary and exegesis. Some cogent suggestions concerning the thought of a more important figure are included in the prefatory essay of Harry H. Clark's *Thomas Paine: Representative Selections, with Introduction, Bibliography, and Notes* (New York, 1944). The basic postulates to be found in these sample passages are carefully tabulated and classified in Dominic Elder's *The Common Man Philosophy of Thomas Paine* (Notre Dame, South Bend, Ind., 1951). Less methodical treatment is accorded the views of another radical thinker in the expository section of George Woodcock's *William Godwin: A Biographical Study* (1946). A more discriminating and detailed analysis is provided by David Fleischer's *Wil-*

liam Godwin: A Study in Liberalism (New York, 1951), which places
the archadvocate of revolution in the tradition of Lockean empiricism,
explains why he abandoned certain of his early convictions, and indicates the current significance of his thought. David H. Monro's *Godwin's
Moral Philosophy: An Interpretation of William Godwin* (1953) offers
an equally sympathetic but somewhat more compelling defense, stressing, like Fleischer's work, the Lockean element in Godwin's thinking,
arguing that he entertained no naïve optimism about natural goodness,
and maintaining that he was not primarily a political reformer but a
moralist. On the conservative side attention has been focused primarily
on Edmund Burke. Annie M. Osborn's *Rousseau and Burke* (New York,
1940) attempts to demonstrate an affinity between some aspects of his
thought and the theories of Rousseau. But it is largely as an antilibertar-
ian prophet and philosopher whose ideas have considerable contemporary relevance that he has inspired the current "Burke Revival." Some
very valuable hints towards an interpretation of his thought are supplied
by Ross J. S. Hoffman, one of the leaders of the "Revival," in a discerning essay that introduces *Burke's Politics* (New York, 1949), a volume of
selections. A more thorough attempt at interpretation is Charles Parkin's
The Moral Basis of Burke's Political Thought (Cambridge, Eng., 1956),
which carefully examines his views on the contract theory, government
and society, natural rights, and abstract idealism. It exonerates him of
the charges of inconsistency and expediency, and maintains that he saw
politics as under a divine and immutable moral law. Another comprehensive analysis is Peter J. Stanlis' *Edmund Burke and the Natural Law*
(Ann Arbor, Mich., 1958), which seeks to refute the conventional view
that he was antagonistic to the concept of natural law. Pointing out that
Burke adopted the classical and medieval versions of the concept, this
penetrating and closely reasoned study establishes how fully and deeply
he was committed to it. Some of the same terrain is traversed in Francis
P. Canavan's *The Political Reason of Edmund Burke* (Durham, N.C.,
1960), a work notable for its clarity of argument. Identifying practical
political reason as the key to the mode of thinking about politics peculiar
to Burke, it attempts to show how he understood the concept to function
in actual practice and how that concept determined the structure of his
whole philosophy. An entirely different type of analysis is essayed in
Stephen R. Graubard's *Burke, Disraeli, and Churchill* (Cambridge,
Mass., 1961). Appraising Burke's thought in its historical context, this
facile and provocative study considers the degree to which it was critical

of contemporary practice as well as the extent to which it contributed to English conservative doctrine. In addition to Burke, two other conservative thinkers have lately aroused interest. John Colmer's *Coleridge, Critic of Society* (Oxford, 1960) laboriously traces the development of the poet's views, discusses fully all their ramifications, and subjects them to careful evaluation. Much the same sort of thing is done by Geoffrey Carnall in *Robert Southey and His Age* (Oxford, 1960), which is especially enlightening in its treatment of the conflicts and tensions that characterized the evolution of Southey's conservatism.

Even more substantial than this concern with political theory has been the interest shown in the various actors who peopled the political scene. The King himself has been the subject of several biographical studies. None of these, however, is a full-length portrait with serious scholarly pretensions. Guy M. Boustead's *The Lone Monarch* (1940) is a popular life that perpetuates some antiquated misconceptions. Although no better in its treatment of politics, Manfred Guttmacher's *America's Last King* (New York, 1941), an intensive examination of George III's psychosis, is valuable for the medical data that it brings together; at least in part, however, it has been superseded as a diagnostic study by Charles Chenevix Trench's *The Royal Malady* (1964), which displays a much firmer grasp of eighteenth-century political realities. Perhaps the best recent biographical treatment of the King is Sir Lewis Namier's brief but discerning "George III: A Study in Personality," which appears in *Personalities and Powers* (1955). A sparkling but somewhat superficial essay in J. H. Plumb's *The First Four Georges* (1956) treats George III at considerable length, retailing for the common reader a number of interpretations that have recently achieved the status of truths. Yet another popular life is John C. Long's sympathetic *George III: The Story of a Complex Man* (1961), which, like Namier's little essay, is more concerned with personality than politics. The same quasi-journalistic approach has been employed in recent biographies of the King's sons. Roger Fulford's attempt to rehabilitate those princes, *Royal Dukes: The Father and Uncles of Queen Victoria* (1949), which was originally published in 1933 and first republished in 1940, is an excellent example; so is his life of the Regent, *George IV* (1949), which initially appeared in 1935. Another example is the overly favorable and rather slapdash sketch of that prince in J. H. Plumb's volume on the Hanoverian Georges. Several of the King's ministers have been dealt with in such biographies; others have been given more sober treatment. John C.

Long's *Mr. Pitt and America's Birthright* (New York, 1940), an infor-
mally written life of the greatest of those ministers, is markedly lacking
in detachment and excessively adulatory. A more discriminating discussion of Chatham's career is to be found in Erich Eyck's singular attempt
at quadripartite biography, *Pitt versus Fox: Father and Son, 1735–1806*
(1950). Ignorance of Namierite doctrine, however, permits Eyck to embrace the traditional view that Chatham was a paladin who sought to
frustrate the tyrannical aspirations of George III. Considering the brevity of its compass, J. H. Plumb's *Chatham* (1953) is remarkably successful in its comprehension of the man and his historical role. No such success can be credited to Owen A. Sherrard's trilogy on Chatham, a highly
detailed narrative account that indiscriminately lauds its hero, vigorously defends him against well-deserved criticism, and presents only surface explanations for the perplexities of his behavior. The second volume, *Pitt and the Seven Years' War* (1955), covers the first two years of
the reign of George III; the third, *Lord Chatham and America* (1958),
carries the story through the statesman's years of failure and decline.
The career of Chatham's son is fully outlined in Eyck's work; it is interpreted with much greater astuteness in John W. Derry's *William Pitt*
(1962). The political life of Chatham's stanchest follower, with all its
shifts and tergiversations, is admirably described in John Norris' *Shelburne and Reform* (1963), which, regrettably, is little concerned with
that enigmatic man's character and personality. Besides these major figures, a number of lesser ministers have been resurrected in biographies.
Combining profound psychological insight with unrivaled mastery of
political fact, Sir Lewis Namier has provided what is easily the most
notable of such works. His superb *Charles Townshend* (1964), which
was revised and completed by John Brooke after the author's death, is
not only a highly successful study of a brilliant and erratic politician; it
is also a paradigm for small-scale biography. Far inferior in quality is
Louis Marlow's *Sackville of Drayton* (1948), which does its best to res-
cue from obloquy the man who directed the American War, absolving
him from the charge of misconduct at Minden and palliating the ineptitude with which he managed the struggle with the colonies. But Alan
Valentine's definitive life, *Lord George Germain* (Oxford, 1962), which
is the product of vast, if not always careful, labor, clearly indicates that
the traditional indictment is well deserved, although Gerald S. Brown's
impressively solid and erudite monograph, *The American Secretary:
The Colonial Policy of Lord George Germain, 1775–1778* (Ann Arbor,

Mich., 1963), offers effective rebuttal on several interpretive points. Another effort to cleanse a tarnished reputation is Robert Gore-Browne's *Chancellor Thurlow, the Life and Times of an XVIIIth Century Lawyer* (1953), which, despite its jaunty tenor, contains much worthwhile information. The very reverse of jaunty, Alison G. Olson's *The Radical Duke* (Oxford, 1961) unconvincingly seeks to endow with consequence the career of that unstable political maverick the third Duke of Richmond. And yet another endeavor at rehabilitation, George Martelli's *Jemmy Twitcher* (1962), strives to present the fourth Earl of Sandwich as essentially meritorious, exaggerating his undoubted abilities and excusing his undeniable frailties. Resuscitation rather than rehabilitation is the objective of Denis Gray's *Spencer Perceval: The Evangelical Prime Minister* (1963), although this able pioneer study makes a strenuous effort to picture its not untalented subject in flattering terms. Two politicians who were primarily opposition leaders rather than ministers also have been treated in biographies. One of these is Charles Fox, the other Burke. Christopher Hobhouse's *Fox* (1947) which was first issued in 1934, although outdated in its political interpretation, is still of value as a vivid portrait of the man. Erich Eyck's *Pitt versus Fox* (1950), as already mentioned, suffers largely from the same defect. A sounder treatment is to be found in the last third of John Carswell's *The Old Cause: Three Biographical Studies in Whiggism* (1954). The "Burke Revival" has inspired much more solid work on Fox's onetime colleague. Thomas W. Copeland's *Our Eminent Friend Edmund Burke* (New Haven, Conn., 1949) resolves some of the many perplexities that have long beset students of the statesman's life. The superb introductory essay to Ross J. S. Hoffman's *Edmund Burke: New York Agent* (Philadelphia, 1956) illuminates a hitherto little-known aspect of his career. Carl B. Cone's *Burke and the Nature of Politics* (Lexington, Ky., 1957–64) is an ambitious general biography in two volumes, which bear the subtitles, *The Age of the American Revolution* and *The Age of the French Revolution;* although a careful and detailed piece of scholarship, it is marred by an obstinate determination to present Burke the politician in a highly favorable light, despite the overwhelming contrary evidence brought forward by the followers of Namier. And Thomas H. D. Mahoney's *Edmund Burke and Ireland* (Cambridge, Mass., 1960) competently surveys Burke's life from the perspective of his abiding relationship with his native land. An opposition politician of a lesser order is treated in Charles Chenevix Trench's *Portrait of a Patriot* (1962), an engaging full-length life of John Wilkes, which, although it adds little to Bleackley's account and is often less incisive than Postgate's, is, on the whole, based on sound premises and respectable research. Another opposition figure is rescued from obscurity in James N. M. Maclean's *Reward Is Secondary* (1963), an overblown biography of the unsavory Lauchlin Macleane, which suggests that he was one of a group of collaborators who produced the letters of Junius.

While diverse aspects of internal politics have thus been examined from various points of view, the intricacies of foreign relations have been subjected to only limited scrutiny. Some of the works in which that scrutiny is undertaken, however, make valuable contributions. Zenab E. Rashed's *The Peace of Paris* (Liverpool, 1951), which is based on both British and French archival data, examines with great thoroughness the negotiations that ended the Seven Years' War. Frank Spencer's introduction to *The Fourth Earl of Sandwich: Diplomatic Correspondence, 1763–1765* (Manchester, Eng., 1961) treats with acute perception England's enduring phobia of French control of the Netherlands, which he argues was unwarranted, and offers an exceedingly lucid exposition of the tangled Swedish and Polish problems of 1763–1765. S. T. Bindoff's *The Scheldt Question to 1839* (1945) includes a chapter that describes how in 1780–1785 England, sharply reversing her traditional attitude, conducted an effective campaign for the opening of the strategically important river to navigation. Isabel de Madariaga's *Britain, Russia, and the Armed Neutrality of 1780* (New Haven, Conn., 1962), centering its attention on Lord Malmesbury's mission to St. Petersburg, successfully attempts to chart the course of Anglo-Russian relations during the American War. Alfred Cobban's *Ambassadors and Secret Agents* (1954) details with signal clarity Lord Malmesbury's work in the Netherlands, where, between 1785 and 1788, he effectively combatted French influence by building up a pro-English party and by subsidizing individual provinces; so that he was finally able to bring the Dutch into a triple alliance with England and Prussia. John Ehrman's *The British Government and Commercial Negotiations with Europe, 1783–1793* (Cambridge, Eng., 1963) traces the diplomatic efforts of the Younger Pitt to secure advantageous trade treaties with seven continental states and thereby compensate for the supposed loss of the American market. Bradford Perkins' *The First Rapprochement: England and the United States, 1795–1805* (Philadelphia, 1956) sketches the course of Anglo-American relations during the early years of the French Wars; its sequel,

Prologue to War: England and the United States, 1805–1812 (Berkeley and Los Angeles, Calif., 1961), chronicles the progress of their deterioration; and the final volume of the trilogy, *Castlereagh and Adams: England and the United States, 1812–1823* (Berkeley and Los Angeles, Calif., 1964), describes the gradual restoration of harmony between the two nations. And Stetson Conn's able if tedious *Gibraltar in British Diplomacy in the Eighteenth Century* (New Haven, Conn., 1942) shows how after 1763, as earlier, the rock was "the principal European focus of Anglo-Spanish enmity," reviving and maintaining the Bourbon Family Compact.

There are also several works on diplomatic history that treat less conventional themes. D. B. Horn's brief *British Public Opinion and the First Partition of Poland* (Edinburgh, 1945) demonstrates how popular sentiment supported government inaction between 1772 and 1775, when the continental powers embarked on the dismemberment of Poland. The beginning of A. J. P. Taylor's originally conceived *The Trouble Makers, Dissent over Foreign Policy, 1792–1939* (1957) discusses with acumen the Foxite advocacy of "appeasement." And D. B. Horn's *The British Diplomatic Service, 1689–1789* (Oxford, 1961) includes data on such matters as the recruitment, training, emoluments, and ranks in the diplomatic corps.

If, as this recapitulation attests, diplomatic history has been illuminated by little sustained and significant research, administrative history has been almost totally neglected, despite the consequence that the followers of Namier have attributed to it by implication. Very few sectors of the governmental apparatus and its adjuncts have been analyzed or even described. The postal service is a notable exception. Howard Robinson's general survey, *The British Post Office* (Princeton, N.J., 1948), includes a sketch of its development under George III. Kenneth Ellis's *The Post Office in the Eighteenth Century* (Oxford, 1958) subjects it to intensive study, fully exposing in the process such aspects of public administration as nepotism, the nature of a civil service career, and the relationship between civil servants and politicians. The machinery for formulating and executing fiscal policy has also been carefully examined. J. E. D. Binney's excellent *Public Finance and Administration, 1774–92* (Oxford, 1958), although concerned only with a brief period, explores in detail the beginnings of administrative reform, the organization of the treasury and the exchequer, the sources of revenue and the means by which it was collected and expended, and the influence exerted by outstanding finance ministers on the operation of their department. Likewise pertinent is D. M. Clark's *The Rise of the British Treasury* (New Haven, Conn., 1960), which, despite its preoccupation with the influence of financial officials on colonial policy, affords insight into the workings of various fiscal agencies. Another governmental office that has been seriously investigated is the third secretaryship of state. Margaret M. Spector's *The American Department of the British Government, 1768–1782* (New York, 1940) skillfully depicts its personnel, problems, and performance, and is especially enlightening on the influence wielded by the under secretaries.

In strong contrast to this dearth is the abundance of work, much of it important, that has been produced in the sphere of economic history. A great deal of that work is synthesized in T. S. Ashton's *An Economic History of England: The Eighteenth Century* (1955), which, maintaining a fresh point of view throughout and using statistics wherever possible, seeks to interpret anew the growth of population and the changes in manufacture, agriculture, trade, finance, and conditions of labor. The companion piece to this survey, Ashton's *Economic Fluctuations in England, 1700–1800* (Oxford, 1959), which is the fruit of immense labor and profound learning, assembles a mass of statistical data in a remarkably systematic and coherent fashion. But perhaps the most outstanding of Ashton's many contributions is his *Industrial Revolution, 1760 to 1830* (1948), the best treatment of the subject since Mantoux. A miracle of compression, this little volume, which brings together much new material, brilliantly portrays the transformation of the system of production and the concomitant social effects. Its most significant feature, however, is the revisionist interpretation that it incorporates. It stresses the importance of entrepreneurship, currency conditions, and interest rates in the process of economic change; shows that war, political maladministration, and ineptitude contributed to the bad lot of the workers during the crucial decades 1790–1820; argues that for many operatives living standards actually improved; contends that the conflicts and strains of the period have been greatly exaggerated by romantic leftists; and, in general, views industrialization as a triumph of social cooperation.

The recent literature on industrialization runs to many volumes. Some of it is polemical. Colin Clark's *The Conditions of Economic Progress* (1940) and Jürgen Kuczynski's *A Short History of Labour Conditions under Industrial Capitalism* (1942) advance the traditional view that the plight of the lower classes deteriorated between 1760 and 1830. This belief is vigorously assailed by T. S. Ashton in two essays that appear in F. A. Hayek's *Capitalism and the Historians* (Chicago, Ill., 1954). In the first he exposes the gross distortions erected into dogma by the Webbs, the Hammonds, and G. D. H. Cole, all of whom drew heavily on Engels' propagandistic treatise, *The Condition of the Working Classes in England in 1844;* in the second he endeavors to destroy the myth that industrialization worsened the living conditions of the poor. The animus of Sir George Clark's *The Idea of the Industrial Revolution* (Glasgow, 1953) is similarly corrective. Maintaining that the new machinery effected no violent disruption of the patterns of living inherited from the past, it points out that such evils as child labor, lengthy hours, bad housing, and malnutrition long antedated the factory system. Other studies are concerned with the effects of industrialization on particular areas. These include A. H. John's *The Industrial Development of South Wales, 1750–1850* (Cardiff, 1950), John Rowe's *Cornwall in the Age of the Industrial Revolution* (Liverpool, 1953), and T. C. Barker's and J. R. Harris' *A Merseyside Town in the Industrial Revolution: St. Helens, 1750–1900* (1954). There are works, too, devoted to individual industries, such as G. W. Armitage, *The Lancashire Cotton Industry from the Great Inventions to the Great Disaster* (Manchester, Eng., 1951), G. A. Turnbull, *A History of the Calico Printing Industry* (Altrincham, 1951), and A. and N. L. Clow, *The Chemical Revolution* (1952). Several worthwhile monographs also deal with particular firms. Among the best of these essays in business history are John P. Addis, *The Crawshay Dynasty: A Study in Industrial Organization and Development, 1765–1867* (Cardiff, 1957), R. S. Fitton and A. P. Wadsworth, *The Strutts and the Arkwrights, 1758–1830* (Manchester, Eng., 1958), and W. G. Rimmer, *Marshalls of Leeds, Flax-Spinners, 1788–1886* (Cambridge, Eng., 1960). Perhaps none of this literature is as genuinely creative as those studies that assess the effects of industrial change from a sociological point of view. Their approach is well illustrated by Reinhard Bendix' *Work and Authority in Industry: Ideologies of Management in the Course of Industrialization* (New York, 1956), which suggests that the factory system gradually produced a new type of person. Another, more impressive, example is Neil J. Smelser's ingenious *Social Change in the Industrial Revolution: An Application of Theory to the Lancashire Cotton Industry, 1770–1840* (Chicago, Ill., 1959). Systematically employing the formulations of Talcott Parsons in analyzing a multitude of historical data, Smelser cogently depicts the transformation wrought by the factory system on the lower-class family in the new industrial areas.

There are also a considerable number of writings on other facets of economic life. In some instances these bear titles suggesting that their contents are more closely related to industrialization than is actually the case. L. S. Pressnell's *Country Banking in the Industrial Revolution* (Oxford, 1956) is an example. Based on original records, it is really concerned with the origins of provincial bankers, the volume of notes issued, and the loans made to turnpikes, canals, and local authorities. So, too, a superb summary of present-day demographic knowledge pertaining to the period in William Petersen's *Population* (New York, 1961) is denominated "Population during the Industrial Revolution," although what it is concerned with is the conclusions of Thomas McKeown and R. G. Brown, whose "Medical Evidence Related to English Population Changes in the Eighteenth Century," *Population Studies* (1955), attributes the great growth in numbers to improved diet rather than to advances in therapy. But such misleading labels are fortunately rare amongst the wide assortment of works on different aspects of the economy. That assortment includes monographs on taxation. W. R. Ward's *The English Land Tax in the Eighteenth Century* (1953) is a definitive treatment of the principal source of revenue. A lesser work, A. Farnsworth's *Addington, Author of the Modern Income Tax* (1951) adjusts the record by depriving the Younger Pitt of some of his fiscal glory. Internal transportation is another area that is canvassed in recent studies. Thomas S. Willan, with his usual industry, describes the development of a waterway in his *Navigation of the River Weaver during the Eighteenth Century* (Manchester, Eng., 1951). The contribution of the third Duke of Bridgewater to the establishment of routes of this kind is retailed for the common reader in Bernard Falk's breezy *The Bridgewater Millions: A Candid Family History* (London, 1942). A better account of the Duke's achievement is Hugh Malet's *The Canal Duke* (1961). Overseas commerce is likewise the subject of several books. G. D. Ramsay's *English Overseas Trade during the Centuries of Emergence: Studies in Some Origins of the English-speaking World* (1957) provides an excellent synoptic view of both foreign and colonial commerce. The content, volume, and value of that traffic are set forth with exemplary precision in Elizabeth B. Schumpeter's *Overseas Trade Statistics, 1697–1808* (Oxford, 1961), a highly ambitious venture carried through in part by the author before her death, and then, happily, completed by T. S. Ashton. Consisting of numerous tables of figures, for imports, exports, and re-exports, it constitutes a singularly rich and informative body of economic data. The growth of one center for such imports and exports is expertly described in C. Northcote Parkinson's *The Rise of the Port of Liverpool* (Liverpool, 1952). A more succinct discussion of Liverpool, as well as good short accounts of the ports of London and Bristol, appears in the collection of essays by eight scholars that Parkinson edited as *The Trade Winds: A Study of British Overseas Trade during the French Wars, 1793–1815* (1948). The volume likewise contains sketches of certain major branches of commerce, such as the West Indian trade and the slave trade. But the former is probed to much better effect in a chapter of Richard Pares's *A West-India Fortune* (1950). Few attempts have been made to treat such trades at greater length. One effort to do so is Averil Mackenzie-Grieve's *The Last Years of the English Slave Trade, 1750–1807* (1941), which, concentrating on the human rather than the purely economic aspects of the traffic, sharply portrays the merchants and sea captains by whom it was carried on and interestingly describes the system of barter by which they secured their cargoes. Another is Murray G. Lawson's *Fur: A Study in English Mercantilism, 1770–1775* (Toronto, 1943), wherein the interconnection of vested interest, government regulation, and changing fashions in hats, for which the imported pelts were used, is adroitly elucidated. And a less esoteric variety of trade is investigated in Charles Wilson's *Anglo-Dutch Commerce and Finance in the Eighteenth Century* (Cambridge, Eng., 1941), a work characterized both in conception and execution by unusual originality.

Agriculture, the basic sector of the economy, has likewise attracted scholars whose labors have produced rewarding results. Since none of them has ventured to offer a general history of the period, the relevant sections of Lord Ernle's venerable *English Farming, Past and Present* (1961) remain the best survey. First published in 1912 and later revised by Sir David Hall, that classic work has recently achieved a new edition, which is prefaced by an exceedingly useful critical and bibliographical introduction for the era before 1815 by G. E. Fussell. A much more concise account occurs in C. S. Orwin's brief though well-written *A History of English Farming* (1949). But the most solid contributions are the fruit of research that has been concentrated on a particular locality. Replete with patiently assembled data, these studies exhibit agrarian continuity and change in a communal setting. Outstanding amongst them are: Olga Wilkinson, *The Agrarian Revolution in the East Riding of Yorkshire* (York, 1956); Joan Thirsk, *English Peasant Farming: The Agrarian History of Lincolnshire* (1957), in which are five pertinent chapters entitled "Population and Prosperity," "The Fenland," "The Marshland," "The Uplands," and "The Clays and Miscellaneous Soils"; W. G. Hoskins, *The Midland Peasant: The Economic History of a Leicestershire Village* (1957), which covers the period in two sections, called "Wigston on the Eve of the Revolution" and "The Enclosure, 1764–5"; C. S. Davies, *The Agricultural History of Cheshire, 1750–1850* (Manchester, Eng., 1960); and Alan Harris, *The Rural Landscape of the East Riding of Yorkshire, 1700–1850* (Oxford, 1962). One of the cardinal changes recorded in these volumes is given novel treatment in V. M. Lavrovsky's *Parliamentary Enclosures of Common Lands in England in the Late Eighteenth and Early Nineteenth Centuries* (Moscow and Leningrad, 1940 [in Russian]), which is Marxist in orientation and statistical in method. Arthur H. Johnson's classic study of the subject, *The Disappearance of the Small Landowner* (1963), which was first published in 1909, devotes three chapters to the reign of George III; it is argued therein that enclosures did not by themselves destroy what Joan Thirsk terms the "peasant proprietor" and that by 1760 his numbers had already drastically declined. A major change of another kind, the improvement of herds and flocks through scientific breeding, is expounded with model clarity in R. Trow-Smith's *A History of British Livestock Husbandry, 1700–1900* (1959), which pictures Bakewell as the pivotal figure. The same consequence is attributed to him in H. C. Pawson's *Robert Bakewell, Pioneer Livestock Breeder* (1957). The life story of Sir John Sinclair, who played a leading role in the dissemination of the new techniques in husbandry that were devised by such innovators as Bakewell, is well told in Rosalind Mitchison's *Agricultural Sir John* (1962), which also presents important details of the whole movement for agrarian "improvement." Some of the less momentous details of the agricultural history of the period are catalogued and discussed in those unpretentious but eminently reliable works of G. E. Fussell, *More Old English Farming Books: From Tull to the Board of Agriculture, 1731 to 1793* (1950) and *The Farmer's Tools, 1500–1900* (1952).

While the quantity of recent work on social history is equal to that dealing with these different aspects of the economy, its quality is, on the whole, decidedly inferior. The blame rests largely on the belletristic tradition that has long exerted a peculiarly potent influence on the genre. That influence has fostered the production of work more endowed with entertainment value than with power to augment or explain the historical record. Moreover, it has discountenanced analysis and favored description, an historiographical mode that has an inevitable appeal for those who nostalgically view the period as the last vital phase of F. R. Leavis' "organic society." Finally, it has sanctioned relaxed and unrigorous discipline both in research and interpretation.

When the worthless has been dismissed, however, much remains that is of value to a greater or lesser degree. A very good comprehensive treatment of the epoch is provided in Dorothy Marshall's *English People in the Eighteenth Century* (1956), whose essence is a dissection of class structure and the patterns of living of the major social strata. Although lauded by J. H. Plumb because of its Trevelyanesque character, E. Neville Williams' *Life in Georgian England* (1962) is much less worthy of esteem. Wholly devoid of theme or thesis, it is essentially an evocative pastiche that seeks to recreate sights, sounds, smells, and "color." Rural society, which, of course, figures extensively in these surveys, is also considered separately in several recent works. E. W. Bovill's *English Country Life, 1780–1830* (1962) is an attempt to give a broad-scale portrayal of that milieu. It fails, on the whole, being merely another pictorial piece, wherein the components are ill selected, ill evaluated, and ill assembled. Essentially the same faults render almost worthless Reginald J. White's *Life in Regency England* (1964). More serious and therefore more valuable is the analysis undertaken in G. E. Mingay's *English Landed Society in the Eighteenth Century* (1963) and in the first eight chapters of F. M. L. Thompson's *English Landed Society in the Nineteenth Century* (1963). But Mingay's volume is not without major defects. Throughout its course, fanciful reconstructions and questionable assertions are interspersed amongst the gobbets of hard historical fact. No such charge can be made against two modest works on specialized aspects of rural society, G. E. Fussell's *Village Life in the Eighteenth Century* (Worcester, Eng., 1947) and his *The English Rural Labourer: His Home, Furniture, and Clothing from Tudor to Victorian Times* (1949), which are excellent of their kind. Much concerning the status, mores, and values possessed by the urban counterparts of Fussell's rural proletarians is to be found scattered through the early chapters of E. P. Thompson's *The Making of the English Working Class* (1963), a turgid synthesis pervaded by leftist bias, but a work commended by Asa Briggs for its successful explication of "new social forces and new social relationships." In addition to these broad surveys and studies concerned with particular social classes, there are monographs in which occupational groups are fully examined. One of the largest of such groups is thoroughly investigated in J. Jean Hecht's *The Domestic Servant Class in Eighteenth-Century England* (1956), which demonstrates the potentialities of the sociological approach. Less consciously sociological but more dynamic is Robert Robson's *The Attorney in Eighteenth-Century England* (Cambridge, Eng., 1959), which describes in detail the recruitment, training, and major roles of an important profession and also traces its gradual rise in status.

The comprehensive character of social history is strongly reflected in the diversity of other subjects on which significant works have appeared. Clothing is one of them. Iris Brooke and James Laver depict it most engagingly in their *English Costume of the Eighteenth Century* (1945). Much more erudite and authoritative is C. W. and Phyllis Cunnington's *Handbook of English Costume in the Eighteenth Century* (1957), a work notable for its encyclopedic scope. Diet is another subject that has been studied to good effect. Sir John Drummond and A. C. Wilbraham, equipped with both a knowledge of nutrition and a firm grasp of the eating habits of the period, provide a good account in *The Englishman's Food* (1957), which was first issued in 1939. Important addenda to that account appear in R. N. Salaman's remarkable *The History and Social Influence of the Potato* (Cambridge, Eng., 1949). Moral deviance is yet another subject into which inquiry has profitably been made. The most deviant coteries of the era are reviewed in Louis C. Jones's *The Clubs of the Georgian Rakes* (New York, 1942), which, regrettably, is studded with inaccuracies. How one of these coteries acquired a legendary infamy is recounted in Donald McCormick's *The Hell-Fire Club* (1958), which, although the product of sound research, disappoints because of its jejune, unimaginative interpretation. Interesting attempts have been made to trace the shift in attitude that gradually brought such coteries into total disrepute. The most convincing of these attempts is Maurice Quinlan's *Victorian Prelude: A History of English Manners, 1700–1830* (New York, 1941). Muriel Jaeger's *Before Victoria* (1956) is much more superficial, although not devoid of merit. And G. Rattray Taylor's *The Angel-Makers* (1958), a courageous effort to discover the psychological roots of historical change, fails dismally because of grossly defective scholarship, extreme tendentiousness, and too rigid adherence to a preconceived theory.

These probings of moral standards naturally involve some scrutiny of religion; it is also dealt with on its own account in a voluminous literature. The orthodox core of the established church, the dissident Evangelical and Methodist sectors, and the various segments of Nonconformity are all represented.

The reinterpretation of the state of the established church that was inaugurated two decades ago by Norman Sykes is continued in recent writings. Sykes supplements his magnum opus with *From Sheldon to Secker: Aspects of English Church History, 1660–1768* (Cambridge, Eng., 1959), wherein, while explaining why the Anglican church did not possess greater vigor, he once again indicates that it was far from moribund. His influence pervades S. C. Carpenter's *Eighteenth-Century Church and People* (1959), an informal account of religious life. It is also manifest throughout A. Tindal Hart's *The Eighteenth-Century Country Parson* (Shrewsbury, 1955), which, although conspicuously amateurish and woefully imprecise, contains a good many useful details.

The Evangelicals, too, are reappraised in new studies, which at the same time considerably extend existing knowledge of that group. Easily the most important of these works is L. E. Eliott Binns's *The Early Evangelicals* (1953), which, although primarily intent on showing that Evangelicalism was from the beginning a phenomenon distinct from Methodism, allocates much space to the development of the movement; its progress in different regions; its methods, doctrines, literature, and achievement. Binns also includes a sketch of Evangelicalism in the universities. The subject is explored more fully by Marcus L. Loane in two series of biographical essays on the leaders produced by those seminaries, *Oxford and the Evangelical Succession* (1950) and *Cambridge and the Evangelical Succession* (1952). The most celebrated group of Evangelicals, whose philanthropy and moral vigilance were impugned by the Hammonds and their followers, is strongly defended by Ernest M. Howse in *Saints in Politics: The "Clapham Sect" and the Growth of Freedom* (Toronto, 1952). A savage renewal of the old attack is to be found in Ford K. Brown's *Fathers of the Victorians* (Cambridge, Eng., 1962), which, while making some telling points, rather overstates its case. The meliorative efforts of the Evangelicals overseas are likewise treated in recent studies. Kenneth Ingham's *Reformers in India, 1793–1833* (Cambridge, Eng., 1956) describes the "remarkable resurgence of missionary activity" after 1793 and the various improvements effected by the Evangelical Anglicans as well as by the missionaries of other denominations who went out to the subcontinent in the early nineteenth century. The influence of a fervent Evangelical in opening up the subcontinent to such missionaries is well portrayed in Ainslie T. Embree's *Charles Grant and British Rule in India* (New York, 1962).

More numerous but less uniformly satisfactory are the volumes produced by students of the early Methodists, abetted by the highly receptive Epworth Press. Some are vital; others are little better than hack work. None of them forms the authoritative introduction to the Methodist movement and its influence that is so badly needed. But taken together, the motley assortment of specialized works provides a fairly full account. They include T. D. Shepherd, *Methodism and the Literature of the Eighteenth Century* (1940), a dull, insipid study but an informative one; Robert F. Wearmouth, *Methodism and the Common People of the Eighteenth Century* (1945), which, like the exasperatingly shoddy works of Bready and Whitely earlier, greatly exaggerates both the degradation of the lower classes and the reformative effects of the Wesleyan Revival; H. F. Mathews, *Methodism and the Education of the People* (1950), a solid study that painstakingly traces the effects of Wesleyanism on the diffusion of learning amongst the masses; Frederick C. Gill, *The Romantic Movement and Methodism* (1954), a work first published in 1937, which, unlike Shepherd's study, maintains that Wesleyanism exerted a strong influence on the Romantics; and Albert M. Lyles, *Methodism Mocked* (1961), which presents a mass of well-ordered evidence on the hostility that beset Wesleyan tenets, practices, and personalities.

There are fewer works in which the Nonconformists are investigated. Two that scrutinize them with care and competence are R. Tudur Jones, *Congregationalism in England, 1662–1962* (1962) and Allan Brockett, *Nonconformity in Exeter, 1650–1875* (Manchester, Eng., 1962). The vicissitudes of their struggle to remove the disabilities under which they labored are expertly described in Richard B. Barlow, *Citizenship and Conscience: A Study in the Theory and Practice of Religious Toleration in England during the Eighteenth Century* (Philadelphia, 1962), which devotes four chapters to the futile agitation in the period 1760–1800 to extend "the limited indulgence granted in 1689 and confirmed in

1718." Ursula Henriques, *Religious Toleration in England, 1787–1833* (1962), continues the account through the later stages of the campaign and its ultimate triumph.

Military and naval history are almost as well represented as religious history, due largely to a special cause. The Second World War aroused a strong and seemingly abiding interest in those historiographical genres concerned with armed conflict.

As a consequence, the warfare that accompanied the American Revolution has been completely reassessed. The lead was supplied by Eric Robson, whose *The American Revolution in Its Political and Military Aspects, 1763–1783* (1955) inquires "Why British Defeat?" "Why American Victory?" and then considers the changes in strategy necessitated after Saratoga by the transformation of a colonial rebellion into a global war. Robson's point of view is Anglocentric; he sees the American Revolutionary War as an episode in England's long struggle with France. Piers Mackesy likewise adopts this point of view in *The War for America, 1775–1783* (Cambridge, Mass., 1964), a full-length treatment of general policy, over-all strategy, and particular campaigns. The most competent examination of British strategy and campaigns in America, however, is to be found in William B. Willcox' superb biography of Sir Henry Clinton, *Portrait of a General* (New York, 1964), a masterly piece of scholarship and writing. A good account of British action in another theater is T. H. McGuffie's *The Siege of Gibraltar, 1779–1783* (1964).

But if the Second World War revived interest in military history, it was the apparent parallels between that struggle and the French Wars that served as the most powerful stimulus. The force of that stimulus is perhaps most obvious in the vivid narrative of Sir Arthur Bryant's trilogy, *The Years of Endurance, 1793–1802* (1942), *Years of Victory, 1802–1812* (1944), and *The Age of Elegance, 1812–1822* (1950), whose central theme is the military and naval contest with Gallic tyranny. From the same source of inspiration derive such works as Sir Herbert Richmond's *The Invasion of Britain* (1941); Carola Oman's *Britain against Napoleon* (1942); E. H. Stuart Jones's *An Invasion That Failed* (Oxford, 1950), an account of an attempt to land at Bantry Bay in 1796; Jones's *The Last Invasion of Britain* (Cardiff, 1950), which describes a landing in Pembrokeshire in 1797; and A. Temple Patterson's *The Other Armada* (1961), a full-scale investigation of the Franco-Spanish expedition that threatened the English coast in 1779.

The subject of counterinvasion likewise held a great appeal, making the victorious Peninsular War and the climactic Waterloo campaign prime foci of attention. These celebrated exploits are lightly sketched in a chapter of Godfrey Davies' *Wellington and His Army* (Oxford, 1954), which also comments on the character and abilities of the great soldier and, considering the expeditionary forces, discusses such topics as "officers and men," "amusements and recreations," "wives and children." The Iberian incursion is likewise covered in Christopher Hibbert's *Corunna* (1961) and Michael Glover's *Wellington's Peninsular Victories* (1963). A rich fund of new information on the methods used in this struggle and elsewhere to secure intelligence, train officers, maintain communications, and transport men and impedimenta is brought together in S. P. G. Ward's *Wellington's Headquarters* (1957). Much the same sort of subject matter is to be found in Richard Glover's *Peninsular Preparation: The Reform of the British Army, 1795–1809* (Cambridge, Eng., 1963).

There is a like assortment of works on the naval history of the period. The fundamentals of the subject are adeptly outlined by Sir Herbert Richmond in four chapters of his *Statesmen and Seapower* (Oxford, 1946). More specialized are two good monographs that depict the naval warfare on certain stations, C. Northcote Parkinson's *War in the Eastern Seas, 1793–1815* (1954) and Piers Mackesy's *War in the Mediterranean, 1803–1810* (Cambridge, Mass., 1957). Operations in the Mediterranean are also considered in Carola Oman's *Nelson* (New York, 1946), undoubtedly the best recent life of the admiral. Notable biographies of other commanders of the epoch include Dorothy Hood, *The Admirals Hood* (1942) and two books on St. Vincent, Sir William James, *Old Oak* (New York, 1950) and E. Berckman, *Nelson's Dear Lord* (1962), better on the personal side. The provenance, promotions, emoluments, and casualties of those who served under such commanders are examined by Michael Lewis in his massive *A Social History of the Navy, 1793–1815* (1960). A less orthodox subject is handled with consummate proficiency by Christopher Lloyd and Jack L. S. Coulter in the third volume of their *Medicine and the Navy, 1200–1900* (Edinburgh, 1962). Novel, too, is the topic of Michael Lewis' *Napoleon and His British Captives* (1962). A counterweight to those volumes that describe the naval glories of the epoch, it details the fate of the seamen taken prisoner by the French.

Just as the reign of George III was an epoch of naval glories, so too it witnessed a brilliant efflorescence of the arts. Indeed, it was the age in which British painting and architecture reached their apogee. Very naturally, then, scholars have devoted much attention to its artistic creations. They have been attracted to them, moreover, by the progressive deepening of that romantic nostalgia, which, especially since the Second World War, has lent a new enchantment to all vestiges of those decades before the burgeoning of mass society.

As a consequence of this appeal, the volumes on painting are numerous. Unrivaled as a broad-scale commentary on much of the period are the sections of E. Waterhouse's *Painting in Britain, 1530–1790* (1953) labeled "Hogarth and the Precursors of the Classical Age" and "The Classical Age," which trace the emergence of a native style, an "English School." The foremost portraitist of the "Classical Age" is justly limned in Derek Hudson's *Sir Joshua Reynolds* (1958). A *catalogue raisonné* of his work and a magnificent set of illustrations compose Ellis K. Waterhouse's *Reynolds* (1941). Mary Woodall's *Thomas Gainsborough* (1948) is the best recent life of Reynolds' great rival. His pictures are catalogued and many reproduced in Ellis K. Waterhouse's *Gainsborough* (1958). Another rival of Reynolds is thoroughly studied in Alastair Smart's *The Life and Art of Allan Ramsay* (1952). Reynolds' successor as president of the Academy is considered with equal thoroughness in Evans Grose's *Benjamin West and the Taste of His Times* (Carbondale, Ill., 1959). A perceptive biography of another of the later portraitists is supplied by Douglas Goldring in his *Regency Portrait Painter: The Life of Sir Thomas Lawrence* (1951). It is supplemented by Kenneth Garlick's critique, *Sir Thomas Lawrence* (1954). There are works on landscape painters too. Among those that make at least a modest contribution are Rotha M. Clay's *Samuel Hieronymous Grimm* (1941) and her *Julius Caesar Ibbetson, 1759–1817* (1948), in which all that is known of two minor artists is painstakingly collected; Jonathan Mayne's *Thomas Girtin* (Leigh-on-Sea, 1949), which does the same thing for a pivotal figure who stands between the topographical landscape painters and the more imaginative Norwich School; Thomas Girtin's and David Loshak's much more complete treatment of the artist, *The Art of Thomas Girtin* (1954), which includes a life, critique, and *catalogue raisonné;* Victor Rienaecker's *John Sell Cotman, 1782–1842* (Leigh-on-Sea, 1949), a somewhat superficial assessment of one of the leaders of the Norwich School that does not replace Kitson's life; Sidney J. Key's *John Constable: His Life and Work* (1948), a reliable short account of the pioneer impressionist; and A. J. Finberg's *The Life of J. M. W. Turner, R.A.* (Oxford, 1963), which, first published in 1937 and lately reissued, remains the only satisfactory life of the greatest landscape painter of the period.

Caricature is another variety of graphic art on which there are good recent studies. F. D. Klingender's entertaining picture book, *Hogarth and English Caricature* (1944), displays the whole gamut of its achievement. M. Dorothy George has diligently compiled the particulars of that achievement for the years 1771–1819 in five volumes of her *Catalogue of Political and Personal Satires* (1935–52), an annotated register of prints in the British Museum. A synthesis of those of the prints that are concerned with politics forms the basis of her extremely erudite *English Political Caricature* (Oxford, 1959), which traces "the shifting pictorial pattern of national life." The most talented pictorial satirist of the period scarcely comes within her purview, but he is the subject of several recent volumes. Edward C. J. Wolf's *Rowlandson and His Illustrations to Eighteenth-Century Literature* (Copenhagen, 1947) exposes a neglected side of the artist's activity. Arthur W. Heintzelman's *The Water Color Drawings of Thomas Rowlandson* (New York, 1947) and Adrian Bury's *Rowlandson's Drawings* (1950) are picture books that present more familiar aspects. Bernard Falk's *Thomas Rowlandson: His Life and Art* (1950), the most ambitious of the lot, incorporates some new information and rectifies some old errors. The only contemporary satirist who approached Rowlandson in ability is at last adequately treated in Draper Hill's *Mr. Gillray: The Caricaturist* (1965), the first study of him since Joseph Grego's work.

This profusion of works on painting and drawing is not matched by the number on architecture. But if the number is smaller, the quality is equally high. The most satisfactory description of the main lines along which architecture developed is the section entitled "Neo-classicism and the Picturesque (1750–1830)" in Sir John Summerson's *Architecture in Britain, 1530–1830* (1953). They are also well delineated in a pair of volumes that possess considerable propaedeutic value, James Lees-Milne's *The Age of Adam* (1947) and Donald Pilcher's *The Regency Style* (1948). The architecture of the countryside, which figures so prominently in these studies, is given definitive treatment in Christopher Hussey's sumptuous *English Country Houses: Mid-Georgian, 1760–1800* (1956) and *English Country Houses: Late Georgian, 1800–1830* (1958), which combine broad coverage and scrupulous accuracy of detail. Urban architecture is likewise scrutinized in general works. Sir John Summerson's *Georgian London* (1946) contains some nine chapters that touch informatively on the multifarious activities of architects, patrons, and speculative builders in the metropolitan area. Walter Ison's lavish annotated albums, *The Georgian Buildings of Bath* (1949) and *The Georgian Buildings of Bristol* (1951), and Anthony Dale's more modest *The History and Architecture of Brighton* (1950) treat the fruits of comparable activities in lesser centers. There are, moreover, excellent brief monographs on some of the leading architects: Dorothy Stroud's *Henry Holland* (1950), Reginald Turnor's *James Wyatt* (1950), and Sir John Summerson's *Sir John Soane, 1753–1837* (1952) which has recently been superseded by Dorothy Stroud's much fuller *The Architecture of Sir John Soane* (1961).

The number of volumes produced by recent editorial work exceeds that indited or compiled in any of these scholarly genres. Virtually all of them are utile; many are of high quality. Among the best are those assembled by Wilmarth S. Lewis and his assistants in *Horace Walpole's Correspondence* (New Haven, Conn., 1937——). There are now twenty-nine; when the enterprise is brought to completion in 1973, there will be fifty. Edited with meticulous care, they preserve the uncorrupted text of all Walpole's remains. The extraordinary copious annotations with which they are embellished, moreover, make them a vast thesaurus of social history. Another superb editorial enterprise is Thomas W. Copeland's *Correspondence of Edmund Burke* (Chicago, Ill., and Cambridge, Eng., 1958——). Designed to run to ten volumes, five of which are already in print, it will comprehend some two thousand letters, both to and from the statesman. A third editorial venture of distinction is Arthur Aspinall's *The Later Correspondence of George III* (Cambridge, Eng., 1962——), of which two volumes have appeared and three are yet to come. A continuation of the work begun by Sir John Fortescue and abandoned after Sir Lewis Namier had demonstrated its inaccuracies, it presents a multitude of new data of various kinds. Besides these major editorial projects, there is a host of lesser publications that make available a wide diversity of manuscript material.[2] Their collective contribution to the historical record of the period is a substantial one.

[2] Typical products of the multiferous editorial work of the past two decades are *Hary-o: The Letters of Lady Harriet Cavendish*, ed. George Leveson-Gower (1940); *Lady Bessborough and Her Circle*, ed. Lord Bessborough (1940); *Elizabeth Ham by Herself, 1783–1820*, ed. Eric Gillet (1945); *The Jenkinson Papers, 1760–1766*, ed. Ninetta S. Jucker (1949); Richard Hays, *A Yeoman of Kent*, ed. Ralph Arnold (1949); *Letters of the Princess Charlotte, 1811–1817*, ed. Arthur Aspinall (1949); *Correspondence of Emily, Duchess of Leinster*, ed. Brian Fitzgerald (Dublin, 1949–57); *The Diary of Sylas Neville, 1765–1785*, ed. Basil Cozens-Hardy

The manifold titles enumerated in the foregoing critique indicate the extent to which scholars have recently investigated the reign of George III. In an epoch like the present, which has long since made what F. R. Leavis terms "the transition from quality to quantity," it is gratifying to find that so much of their work is endowed with merit.

(1950); *The Heber Letters, 1783–1832,* ed. R. H. Cholmondeley (1950); *Pembroke Papers, 1780–1794,* ed. Lord Sidney Charles Herbert (1951); *The Correspondence of John Wilkes and Charles Churchill,* ed. Edward Weatherly (New York, 1954); *Georgiana,* ed. Lord Bessborough (1955); *Portrait of a Whig Peer,* ed. Brian Connell (1957); *The Banks Letters,* ed. Warren R. Dawson (1959); and *The Correspondence of George, Prince of Wales, 1770–1812,* ed. Arthur Aspinall (1963–65).

England and Wales, 1820–1870,
in Recent Historiography:
A Selective Bibliography

❖

ROGER W. PROUTY

$\mathcal{S}$YDNEY SMITH once remarked that his idea of heaven was eating *pâté de foie gras* to the sound of trumpets. A historian's idea of hell could well be the task of preparing a bibliographical terrine to the inaudible but anticipated cacophony of his learned colleagues' reactions. A usable bibliography like a palatable menu must select and combine many ingredients in accordance with the too often neglected distinction between satisfaction and satiety. The present selection thus makes no pretence to completeness. A necessary editorial ukase has restricted it to books about England relating to the period 1820–1870 and published since 1938. I have attempted, within these limits, to illustrate and to assess only the main trends in historical writing. My canvas avoids the detail of Frith in the hope of achieving the atmospherics of Whistler.[1]

The work of economic historians and of economists who write history is fundamental to the understanding of a period which, opening with railway building and closing with the establishment of a functionally specialized capital market, coincides with the second phase of English industrial growth. Before 1938 the writing of economic history had concentrated on the period of the so-called Industrial Revolution, and economic histories, though insistent on the irrelevance of dates, conformed

[Reprinted from *The Historian*, 24:270–307 (May 1962).]

[1] Readers are asked to note that the structure and balance of this bibliography reflect the material available when it was composed early in 1960. Some more recent publications have been added subsequently; others have been excluded because an adequate assessment would have necessitated a radical rewriting.

in practice to a period as rigid as that adopted by the older Toynbee. These histories usually stopped *ca.* 1830 and the histories of the present century started ca. 1870. The period 1820–1870 remained largely terra incognita. The only outstanding work which offered a sustained narrative throughout the century was the trilogy of J. H. Clapham, *An Economic History of Modern Britain* (Cambridge, Eng., 1926–38).[2] Useful as this large work always is, it was based too narrowly upon and reflected too closely the interests of *The Economist*. Because of the lacunae due to the older dating of "The Revolution" and the kinds of problems raised by critiques of Clapham, most of the best economic history written since 1938 has accepted the view of T. S. Ashton's inaugural lecture of 1946: that the conception of *Zeitgeist* together with the teleological use of such a word as *capitalism* has no useful meaning for the historian whose main concern ought to be "detailed work on the records of some one merchant, manufacturing concern, banking house, trade union, or other organisation"—thus making economic history an empirical test of economic theory and a bridgehead between it and the practice of the real world.[3]

In economic history the older interests continue to dominate. For example there have been some excellent recent histories of business firms and of businessmen. T. C. Barker, *Pilkington Brothers and the Glass Industry* (1960), covering the history of this important (but, as a private company, atypical) firm down to the present, offers a very detailed history of a neglected industry, the problems of competition at home and

---

[2] The best brief review of the period is W. H. B. Court, *A Concise Economic History of Britain from 1750 to Recent Times* (Cambridge, Eng., 1954).

[3] T. S. Ashton, "The Relation of Economic History to Economic Theory," *Economica*, n. s. 13:81–96 (May 1946), p. 95, delivered at the London School of Economics. This new trend in English economic historiography is likely to be temporary for the reasons authoritatively developed by H. L. Beales in the new introductory essay to the 1958 reprint of his *Industrial Revolution*, first published in 1928. They include the undue Anglicization of the story; the stressing of fluctuations in economic development as a major factor therein as against a longer social perspective which sees in them kinks on the graph of development rather than its main determinant; a far from credible, because Cobdenite, assessment of the effects of war upon a changing economy; and an unwillingness to believe that humble people are better judges of their contemporary and transitional miseries than the later reconstructors of the conditions of life as computed from dubious, imperfect, and misleading interpretations of very incomplete and capricious statistical survivals. Like the Hammonds, Beales insists that a reconstruction of the past in the terms of neoclassical economic theory is as imperfect as history as Marxism with its false prophecies or Whiggism with its distorted values. A succinct statement of Beales's views is printed in *The Listener* (February 21, 1957) under the title "Was There an Industrial Revolution?"

abroad, of finance, and of the family who ran it. It is a model of what business history can yield in the hands of a historian who never forgets that the firm is part of the national economy. R. S. Fitton and A. P. Wadsworth, *The Strutts and the Arkwrights 1758–1830: A Study of the Early Factory System* (Manchester, Eng., 1958) is factually interesting business history which consistently underplays the interpretation of materials that do not quite fit in with the conventionally fashionable interpretation of incipient industrialism. The important study of L. F. Haber, *The Chemical Industry during the Nineteenth Century: A Study of the Economic Aspect of Applied Chemistry in Europe and North America* (Oxford, 1958) examines, *inter alia,* the industrial manufacture of chemicals in England and the scientific context from which it emerged. W. E. Minchinton, *The British Tinplate Industry* (Oxford, 1957) traces the history of this small but significant export industry and shows the effects on its organization when faced with the economic problems of the latter part of the century. D. C. Coleman, *The British Paper Industry, 1495–1860* (New York, 1958) provides a clear analysis of the economic and technical problems which faced paper makers in the long period before the final abolition of the "taxes on knowledge," the utilization of wood pulp as raw material, and the development of new machinery. Another addition to industrial history is W. G. Rimmer, *Marshalls of Leeds, Flax-Spinners, 1788–1886* (Cambridge, Eng., 1960). Three generations are spanned in the history of the rise, greatness, and decline of the firm founded in 1788 by John Marshall who became a millionaire, a member of parliament, a landowner, and a utilitarian agent of his employees' educational welfare. Other branches of textile history are usefully surveyed in *The Memoir of a Nottingham Lace Merchant, William Cripps* (ed. J. D. Chambers, *Bulletin of Business Historical Society,* 1950) and J. Thomas, *History of the Leeds Clothing Industry,* in *Yorkshire Bulletin of Economic and Social Research* (1955), an interesting example of the penetration of British manufacture by American machines. There is, finally, a life of *Sir George Cayley: The Inventor of the Aeroplane* (1961) by J. L. Pritchard; Cayley was a "born" inventor in many fields as well as a benevolent and efficient manager of his estates—a characteristic though long-forgotten figure of the age of individualistic technological adventure.[4]

---

[4] Other good studies are S. Taylor, *A History of Industrial Chemistry* (New York, 1958); W. Woodruff, *The Rise of the British Rubber Industry during the Nineteenth Century* (Liverpool, 1958); and J. H. Morris and L. J. Williams, *The South Wales Coal Industry* (Cardiff, 1958).

Although the half century following 1820 was characterized by urban growth of a cataclysmic character, only a few of the many histories of regions or towns maintain the acceptable standards of scholarship evidenced in T. C. Barker and J. R. Harris, *A Merseyside Town in the Industrial Revolution: St. Helens 1750–1900* (Liverpool, 1954). W. H. Chaloner, *The Social and Economic Development of Crewe, 1780–1923* (Manchester, Eng., 1950) traces in meticulous detail the planned growth of a typical railway town. If this study lacks the imaginative insight capable of recreating a living community, it delineates the dreary quality of urban development controlled by railway companies only too evident today to passengers on the Midland Region of British Railways. C. Gill, *History of Birmingham*, I: *Manor and Borough to 1865* (Oxford, 1952) should be read with the second volume written by A. Briggs. Gill looks backwards; Briggs looks forward from the mid-sixties with the result that the vitality of Victorian Birmingham is neither explained nor fully treated. A recent study by J. Prest, *The Industrial Revolution in Coventry* (Oxford, 1960), has a wider ambience than is usual in such studies and does something in brief compass to utilize the writings of George Eliot and to show how public policies and land enclosure conditioned the industrialization of a small town with a medieval background and the thinking as well as the enterprise of its inhabitants. M. Rose, *The East End of London* (1951), in covering the years of its greatest expansion, again shows how valuable a range of interests that includes literature and architecture as well as economic development is to the writer of urban history. It is noteworthy and regrettable that even now there is no satisfactory or even reasonably adequate summary of the material collected by the Municipal Corporations Commission which reported in 1835 or any substantial study of urbanization since the pathbreaking nineteenth-century book of A. Weber, *Growth of Cities* (New York, 1899).[5]

Since W. T. Jackman's *The Development of Transportation in Modern England* (2 vols., 1916), there has been no synthesizing history of communications and transport. This is all the more regrettable because dramatic changes in the industry between 1820 and 1870 were determining factors in the growth of industrialism. There are a few good particu-

---

[5] Others are D. T. Williams, *The Economic Development of Swansea and of the Swansea District to 1921* (Swansea, 1940); and A. H. John, *The Industrial Development of South Wales, 1750–1850* (Cardiff, 1950). Few books have such interesting chapter headings as the last and few so lamentably fail to fulfill their stated intention.

lar studies. The heyday of coaching has been well described in E. W. Bovill, *The England of Nimrod and Surtees, 1815–1854* (1959), but there has been no general study of horse transportation. The best accounts of the vital railway industry are the first volume of H. Ellis, *British Railway History: An Outline from the Accession of William IV to the Nationalization of Railways 1830–1876* (1954), which serves as a good introduction but neglects the crucial problem of finance, and E. F. Carter, *An Historical Geography of the Railways of the British Isles* (1959). Some of the consequences of railway development are indicated in J. B. Jefferys, *Retail Trading in Britain 1850–1950: A Study of Trends in Retailing with Special Reference to the Development of Co-operative, Multiple Shop and Department Store Methods of Trading* (Cambridge, Eng., 1954). Canals remained important during this period but have received scanty attention. The best history of merchant shipping is still the fourth volume of W. S. Lindsay, *History of Merchant Shipping and Ancient Commerce* (4 vols., 1874–76), despite his bias as a shipowning M. P. There have been numerous centenary histories of companies but they attest more to the importance of the industry in general than they contribute to the history of the flags they were written to honor. The whole field of parliamentary lobbies, local societies, and governmental regulation remains to be explored. The best recent biographies of men responsible for the great progress in the transport industry are those of L. T. C. Rolt, *Isambard Kingdom Brunel: A Biography* (1957), *Thomas Telford* (1958), and *George and Robert Stephenson* (1960).

One of the distinctive British contributions to industrial civilization was the development of adequate financial procedures and institutions. These now have had their political and social importance and their national and international interrelationships laid bare by D. S. Landes, *Bankers and Pashas: International Finance and Economic Imperialism in Egypt* (1958) in a brilliant exposition of the penetration of the Middle East by a new kind of imperialist, neither soldier nor proconsul but banker. Here, as in no other study, are delineated the crosscurrents of the cotton famine resulting from the American Civil War, the new resources for expansion of credit, the European bulls and bears, the speculative journalists, and the new zeal for expanded communications. The Victorians exploited with a clear conscience and in their wake left financial institutions of impeccable reputations. P. H. Emden, *Money Powers of Europe in the Nineteenth and Twentieth Centuries* (ca. 1945) serves to recall Alfred Marshall's dictum that insular economic history is impossible after 1880 and to give some approaches to the developing world economy. Valuable insular histories include J. H. Clapham, *The Bank of England* (2 vols., Cambridge, Eng., 1945); R. S. Sayers, *Lloyds Bank in the History of English Banking* (Oxford, 1957); and R. Hidy, *The House of Baring in American Trade and Finance 1763–1861* (Cambridge, Mass., 1949). *The Works and Correspondence of David Ricardo* (Cambridge, Eng., 1951–55), edited by P. Sraffa in ten volumes, do not strictly belong to this period, for Ricardo died in 1823, but he remained persistently influential. Ricardo, however, did not grasp the importance of the technical transformation of industry which was proceeding in his lifetime, so his corpus of writings remains more revealing to economists than to historians.

There has been a growing interest in recent years in the problems of "economic growth," particularly in the economic growth of "backward" and "new" countries. These terms have not yet acquired anything like finality of definition; they are still in fact baffling in their vagueness. While the historians' interests have stemmed largely from the theorists' activities, there has been a quick growth of historical or quasi-historical studies of great interest which will stimulate discussion in this field. Some of these studies are devised avowedly to provide a defense of the "old" economic order in the capitalist countries or as a counterargument to Marxist interpretations of the defects of the "old" or the superior dynamics of the "new" planned civilizations. Outstanding among such writings are the books of W. W. Rostow. The latest of these, *The Stages of Economic Growth* (Cambridge, Eng., 1960), is a "non-communist manifesto" based on "the whole span of modern history" and aimed at the prediction of political and economic trends. It is a stimulating (or, to some, irritating) anti-Marxist interpretation of the rival economic worlds of today. No doubt much quantitative material that passed under Rostow's hand in the making of A. D. Gayer, W. W. Rostow, and A. J. Schwartz, *The Growth and Fluctuation of the British Economy, 1790–1850: An Historical, Statistical and Theoretical Study of Britain's Development* (2 vols., Oxford, 1953) went into the crystallization of Rostow's theories in his latest book. Yet there are false quantities in this indispensable survey; there is, too, the inevitable elusiveness which a historical study of development based on quantitative data must reflect because so much of that development left no reliable quantitative data behind or was merely nonquantitative. In the same way, C. Clark, *The Conditions of Economic Progress* (3d ed., 1957) analyzes production and income over the world at large in order to show the consequent changes of economic structure. It stimulates economists more than historians because basically historians are more interested in the roots of the present in the past, while most economists are lukewarm about anything but the present. Historians feel uneasy, for the same reason, with W. Hoffman, *British Industry 1700–1950* (Oxford, 1955) and with such wage-series as E. H. Phelps Brown and S. V. Hopkins, *The Course of Wage Rates in Five Countries, 1860–1939* (Oxford, 1950). Two important fluctuation studies stand out: R. C. O. Matthews, *A Study in Trade Cycle History: Economic Fluctuations in Great Britain, 1833–1842* (Cambridge, Eng., 1954) and J. R. T. Hughes, *Fluctuations in Trade, Industry and Finance: A Study of British Economic Development 1850–1860* (1960). These provide not merely studies of their decades in terms of economic conditions but the essential background of much that was important in politics and policy making. W. W. Rostow, *British Economy of the Nineteenth Century* (Oxford, 1948) is still useful and suggestive, and a recent study by A. J. Youngson, *Possibilities of Economic Progress* (Cambridge, Eng., 1959) gives comparative material for some other countries. W. Ashworth, *A Short History of the International Economy, 1850–1950* (1952), as its title promises, has much of value about Great Britain. Substantial studies of the history of foreign trade have been made in recent years. W. Schlote, *British Overseas Trade from 1700 to the 1930's* (Oxford, 1952) translated by W. O. Henderson and W. H. Chaloner, and A. H. Imlah, *Economic Elements in the Pax Britannica: Studies in British Foreign Trade in the Nineteenth Century* (Cambridge, Mass., 1958) are the most valuable of these.

In the tradition of the older histories, the social consequences of industrialism have been seen very much in Fabian terms and largely through the spectacles supplied by the Webbs and the late G. D. H. Cole. The latter set the pattern for much work in the history of socialist thought, the conditions of labour, and the politics of labour. *Essays in Labour History,* edited by A. Briggs and J. Saville (1960), as well as the newly-founded Labour History Society attest to Cole's contributions and to the continued interest in this field.[6]

---

[6] Some of the works by Cole are, *inter alia, A Short History of the British Working-Class Movement 1789–1947* originally published in 1925–1927, revised and reprinted in one volume in 1948; *Attempts at General Union, A Study in British Trade Union History, 1818–1834* (1953); *Chartist Portraits* (1941); *British Working Class Politics 1832–1914* (1941); *A Century of Cooperation* (1945); and I and II of *A*

The best of the studies describing conditions of labour is D. Williams, *The Rebecca Riots: A Study in Agrarian Discontent* (Cardiff, 1955), which shows vividly the response to the new economy in one area. Most books about the working classes are more interested in their attempts to organize or to exert political pressure than in their condition. R. F. Wearmouth, *Methodism and the Working-Class Movements of England 1800–1850* (1937) and *Methodism and the Struggle of the Working Classes 1850–1900* (Leicester, 1955) offer detailed commentaries on Halévy's famous generalization, although they assume too easily the alleged intimacy between Nonconformity and the self-helpful organization of labour. *Democracy and the Labour Movement*, edited by J. Saville (1954), a symposium by Marxists, contains some interesting and relevant essays, especially that of the editor on the Christian Socialists. A. T. Patterson, *Radical Leicester: A History of Leicester, 1780–1850* (Leicester, 1954) is concerned with the growth of radicalism in this important Chartist center.[7]

Chartism continues to attract more sentimental attention than its importance warrants. But D. Williams, *John Frost: A Study in Chartism* (Cardiff, 1939) is a brilliant account of the movement in Wales. A. R. Schoyen, *The Chartist Challenge: A Portrait of George Julian Harney* (1958) is a very good and fresh study which looks outward from its subject while *Chartist Studies*, edited by A. Briggs (1959), helps to fill out the regional picture. D. Read and E. Glasgow, *Feargus O'Connor: Irishman and Chartist* (1961) is a painstaking if rather less than illuminating account of O'Connor's work in the Chartist movement because the historical background is too narrow. F. C. Mather, *Public Order in the Age of the Chartists* (Manchester, Eng., 1960) gives a clear picture both of the response of the governing classes and the limitations of the means to safeguard public order at that time. He establishes a substantial differ-

---

History of Socialist Thought, The Forerunners 1789–1850 (1953) and *Marxism and Anarchism* (1954). In recent years many documents relating to the labour movement have been made easily accessible in the collection of G. D. H. Cole and A. W. Filson, *British Working Class Movements* (1951); M. Morris, *From Cobbett to the Chartists* (1948); and J. B. Jefferys, *Labour's Formative Years* (1948).

[7] There have been some improved, but still largely unreadable, trade union histories: for example, J. B. Jefferys, *The Story of the Engineers* (1946); R. P. Arnot, *The Miners* (1949); E. Howe and J. Child, *The Society of London Bookbinders* (1952); and A. E. Musson, *The Typographical Association* (1954). Trade unions' sponsored histories, like the histories of business firms, are more conspicuous for piety than veracity. An exception is the disciplined and readable book of B. V. Humphreys, *Clerical Unions in the Civil Service* (1958). A. Aspinall, *The Early English Trade Unions* (1949) is a collection of extracts from Home Office Papers, uninterestingly edited, covering the years 1791–1825.

ence between the liberalism of Whigs and the repressive fundamental-
ism of Tories and shows how the experience of Chartism led to the establishment of provincial police forces in the fifties.

Good biographies of the men concerned with the interests of the
working classes are few. C. Driver, *Tory Radical: The Life of Richard
Oastler* (New York, 1946) is a lively and authoritative account of the
factory reform movement, of the struggle against the new poor law, and
of one of the chief fighters for factory regulation. Furthermore it lays
bare the origins of Disraeli's "Young England" doctrines. J. Saville,
Ernest Jones (1952) and E. P. Thompson, *William Morris: Romantic to
Revolutionary* (1955) are admirable and scholarly portraits by leading
exponents of latter-day Marxism.[8] R. K. Webb, *Harriet Martineau:
Radical Victorian* (1960) is a distinguished contribution to the development and content of early- and mid-Victorian radical thought as well as
to that increasing list of studies which Victorian historiography owes to
American scholars.

Since 1938 the content of social history has been greatly extended by
the work of noneconomic social scientists busily developing new interests of research and techniques of analysis. Furthermore this general
broadening of the subject matter of monographs has been encouraged
(and forced) by the interests and anxieties of the present. The major
changes in British society in this century—the impact of war, of organized science, the development of social policy, the rapid growth of collective responsibility and public administration, and the changing structure and functions of the family—have all raised questions and issues
which dominate present political discussion and increasingly determine
the subjects for historical investigation. But the labors of demographers,
sociologists, criminologists, lawyers, and others have as yet made little
impact on the institutional structure of professional history in England
where, today, only two university posts carry "social history" in their
titles.

The new sociologists' history has been strongly influenced by the work
of a long line of demographers, of whom the most recent is D. V. Glass,
Population Policies and Movements in Europe (1940), which contains
the authoritative account of the birth control movement in England, and
by the widening interests of natural scientists, notably evidenced by
R. N. Salaman in his brilliant *The History and Social Influence of the*

[8] R. K. P. Pankhurst, *William Thompson* (1954) and *The Saint Simonians Mill
and Carlyle* (1957) are useful scholarly studies in the minor key.

Potato (Cambridge, Eng., 1949). Fears of a declining population during the 1930's led to the appointment of a Royal Commission on Population. Its *Report* (Cmd. 7695, 1949) contains a useful historical retrospect that can now be supplemented by the work of D. V. Glass and E. Grebenik, *The Trend and Pattern of Fertility in Great Britain (Papers of the Royal Commission on Population, VI*, 1954). The study splices the fertility data collected in 1911 with modern data and provides a detailed statistical measure of the decline in family size since the 1870's, stemming from the earlier middle class experience surveyed in the suggestive but too narrowly conceived J. A. Banks, *Prosperity and Parenthood, A Study of Family Planning among the Victorian Middle Classes* (1954). It surveys the circumstances that led in the seventies to a sharp conflict between the Christian parents' duty to be fruitful and multiply and the middle class parents' duty to secure his children's future social status and concludes that the rising cost of maintaining social appearances was one of the chief factors in the adoption of the birth control habit. A fresh and penetrating analysis of this and other views of the relation between standards of living and population growth is provided in the scholarly D. E. C. Eversley, *Social Theories of Fertility and the Malthusian Debate* (Oxford, 1959). *Introduction to Malthus*, edited by D. V. Glass (1953), includes a fairly complete bibliography of the literature, and K. Smith, *The Malthusian Controversy* (1951) usefully documents the range of contemporary opinion in the early decades of the century. B. Thomas, *Migration and Economic Growth: A Study of Great Britain and the Atlantic Economy* (Cambridge, Eng., 1954) examines the westward aspects of the emetic solution for overpopulation.[9]

Sociological interests have led to the examination by C. Erickson, *British Industrialists: Steel and Hosiery 1850–1950* (Cambridge, Eng., 1959) of the social origins and career patterns of leaders in those industries. N. J. Smelser, an American disciple of Talcott Parsons, bravely and impressively attempts to demonstrate the validity of the theory of social action through a detailed examination of the history of the textile industry in his thoroughly workmanlike *Social Change in the Industrial Revolution: An Application of Theory to the Lancashire Cotton Industry 1770–1840* (Chicago, Ill., 1959).

Current British anxieties about the health and stability of the family have been responsible for new historical explorations. O. R. McGregor,

[9] No. 2 in the series of *Guides to Official Sources* helpfully covers *Census Reports of Great Britain 1810–1931* (1951).

"The Social Position of Women in England, 1850–1914: A Bibliography," *The British Journal of Sociology*, 6 (1955) provides a sane perspective upon this important but hitherto emotionally treated topic. R. Haw, *The State of Matrimony* (1952) is an Anglican theologian's history. O. R. McGregor, *Divorce in England* (1957) gives a present-minded social historian's inescapable conclusion on the adaptation of family structure and function to the conditions of industrial society. A lawyer's history is to be found in the symposium of R. H. Graveson and F. R. Crane, *A Century of Family Law 1857–1957* (1957). The related book of M. Hewitt, *Wives and Mothers in Victorian Industry* (1958) judiciously subjects a topic of mid-twentieth-century anxiety to historical examination.

The growth of urban sociology is reflected in such studies as R. Glass, *Urban Sociology in Great Britain: A Trend Report and Bibliography*, *Current Sociology*, 4 (UNESCO, Paris, 1955) and W. Ashworth, *The Genesis of Modern British Town Planning* (1954), worthwhile despite its puzzling inconsequential conclusions. The unshakeably realistic British belief in the significance of social class is echoed in the learned bibliography of D. G. MacRae, *Social Stratification: A Trend Report*, *Current Sociology*, 2 (UNESCO, Paris, 1953–54). G. D. H. Cole, *Studies in Class Structure* (1955) brings together and clarifies much scattered statistical material.

The pervasive influence of the sociologists may also be seen in the widening range of interests exemplified by the books, for example, of A. F. Young and E. T. Ashton, *British Social Work in the Nineteenth Century* (1957); K. Jones, *Lunacy Law, and Conscience 1744–1845: The Social History of the Care of the Insane* (1955); R. S. E. Hinde, *The British Penal System, 1773–1950* (1951); C. Reith, *British Police and the Democratic Ideal* (Oxford, 1943); J. M. Hart, *The British Police* (1951); and the continuing series of massively erudite volumes, already three in number, on the social history of the criminal law by L. Radzinowicz, *A History of English Criminal Law and Its Administration from 1750*, I (1948), II and III (1958). In its emphasis upon the development of social investigation and social policy, such writing has reinforced the current reinterpretations of the history of public administration in this period.

Current interest in the social anxieties and threatened stability of the growing urban and industrial society in the decades before 1848 has produced a slow trickle of books. The intractable difficulties of rural indigence were freshly considered in the light of the anthropological inter-

ests of K. Polanyi, *Origins of Our Time: The Great Transformation*
(1945). The public health movement was surveyed in G. Newman, *The
Building of a Nation's Health* (1939). The work of *Some British Pio-
neers of Social Medicine* (1948) was assessed by M. Greenwood; to this
should be added the pamphlet biography of Thomas Wakley, founder of
The Lancet, by C. Brook, *Battling Surgeon* (Glasgow, 1945) and C. F.
Brockington, *Medical Officers of Health, 1848–1855* (1957). The studies
of M. B. Simey, *Charitable Effort in Liverpool* (Liverpool, 1951) and
J. F. C. Harrison, *Social Reform in Victorian Leeds: The Work of James
Hole 1820–1895* (Leeds, 1954) are models for future local histories.
M. W. Thomas, *The Early Factory Legislation* (Leigh-on-Sea, 1948) is
important for the light it sheds both on its main subject and on the establishment and growth of a new department of state. Apologists for the
doctrinal purities of the classical economists might with advantage
assimilate the experience embedded in this work; one doubts, sometimes, whether it has been read by the neo-Manchester defenders of the
early factory system.[10] The important and very useful study of D.
Roberts, *Victorian Origins of the British Welfare State* (New Haven,
Conn., 1960) assembles biographical and social information about the
remarkable group of men who, as civil servants, inspectors, commissioners, and the like, harried and badgered the first reform parliaments by
their measurements of the cost of social wastage inherent in unregulated
industrialism.

The history of education in Britain between 1820 and 1870 has been
pursued mainly in specialized fields of inquiry. One exception is the
admirable research of L. J. Saunders, *Scottish Democracy, 1815–1840*
(Edinburgh, 1950) in which the development of the Scottish system
of schools and universities is set firmly in its brilliantly drawn context of
social and intellectual transformation. In this context, seminal for Britain
as a whole, the Scottish character is seen to be hardened as well as
adapted and the distinctively Scottish contribution to educational
thought and practice is rendered luminous. It is tragic that Saunders did
not live to compose the second volume of his valuable study.
    One other general study may be mentioned. B. Simon, *Studies in the*

---

[10] For example, W. H. Chaloner and W. O. Henderson in their new translation of
Friedrich Engels' *The Condition of the Working Class in England* (Oxford, 1958)
have no difficulty in showing that his account of conditions in Manchester in 1844
was, in some details, inaccurate. They make it clear that his classic would not have
satisfied the examiners for a Ph.D. in the University of Manchester, but they altogether fail to explain why his doctrines moved men to action.

History of Education, 1780–1870 (1960) has both the value and the values of a Marxist approach to educational history. His book shows unfairness of judgment and an imperfect appreciation of the sincerity and the costs of the commitment to education of religious sectarians. Yet this study is necessary because it stresses with a wealth of documentation the distorting effects upon educational development—most urgently needed in an educationally backward area like England between 1820 and 1870—of the sectarian wrangling and the Anglican "monopoly." These effects involved the withering of scientific education, the impoverishment of the old universities scholastically, and the segregation of science and the newer nonclassical disciplines in the parvenu institutions of London and the other civic universities. Simon may overwork his class struggle interpretation of the last fifty years in his study, but he makes educational history readable and much of the existing historiography incredible.

Attention may be drawn also to W. H. G. Armytage, *The Civic Universities: Aspects of a British Tradition* (1955), which deals with the "new" universities of Britain. The subtitle is not too happy because these institutions could never have been established if older elements in the British tradition had not been displaced, modified, or reoriented. These "new" institutions were the urban educational institutions of an urban civilization and served to develop in "red brick" institutions the necessary educational activities and pursuits of the sciences and techniques as well as the arts which, in the years before 1870, were not adequately provided for in Oxford and Cambridge.[11]

The public schools figure very largely in British educational history and have included the best and some of the worst institutions in the British school system. E. C. Mack, *Public Schools and British Opinion: An Examination of the Relationship between Contemporary Ideas and the Evolution of an English Institution*, 2 vols. (1938–41) includes one hundred pages devoted to the decade of the sixties when many of these schools were still important institutions. Public school development owed much to Arnold of Rugby, but Strachey's famous denigratory essay raised doubts as to the nature of the debt. T. Bamford, *Thomas Arnold* (1960) enables a firm answer to be given. Strachey's detractors may, like the rest of us, read it with profit.

Clerical control of English education has been much discussed but lit-

---

[11] One of the best studies of the "old" universities is D. A. Winstanley, *Early Victorian Cambridge* (Cambridge, Eng., 1940).

tle studied apart from J. Murphy, *The Religious Problem in English Education* (Liverpool, 1959). Another specialized study is A. Tropp, *The School-teachers: The Growth of the Teaching Profession in England and Wales from 1800 to the Present Day* (1957). It stems from the current interest of some English sociologists in social mobility, traces the growth of the numerically most important profession, corrects some persistent misconceptions about the quality of working class schooling in the period when this was controlled by private religious enterprise, but has too much the character of an apologia for the National Union of Teachers for its later findings to be accepted without reserve. No attempt can here be made to list the many histories of separate institutions. Mention may be made, though, of J. Kamm, *How Different from Us* (1958) on the educational lives and work of Miss Buss of the North London Girls' Collegiate Schools and Miss Beale of Cheltenham Ladies' College. These masterful ladies did a work of wide influence upon the foundations of which much in current girls' education still rests.

Adult education has a long history in England. It includes the self-helpful education of the educationally underprivileged and the upper class educational conditioning of the lower ranks, analyzed in illuminating detail in the scholarly but regrettably mistitled work of R. K. Webb, *The British Working Class Reader, 1790–1848: Literary and Social Tension* (1955), whose theme is less the working class reader than the middle class author of books for the working class. Webb includes also the efforts of sensitive academic consciences to help their undereducated but humbler fellow citizens to acquire the necessary intellectual equipment to become effective citizens. There have been two recent studies of Mechanics' Institutes which were the outstanding development in the conditioning process: T. Kelly, *George Birkbeck: Pioneer of Adult Education* (Liverpool, 1957) and M. Tylecote, *The Mechanics' Institutes of Lancashire and Yorkshire before 1851* (Manchester, Eng., 1957). D. Read, *Press and People, 1790–1850: Opinion in Three English Cities* (n.d. [1961]) opens up a neglected area of inquiry by using scissors and paste upon the newspapers of Manchester, Leeds, and Sheffield. Early industrialization was not effected without the collaboration of the artisans and the workers who required technical as well as general understanding of the nature of the dynamics of change and who had to be weaned away from the "dangerous thoughts" of "revolutionary" radicalism. J. F. C. Harrison, *A History of the Working Men's College, 1854–1954* (1954) traces carefully, in all its limitation and its generous idealism, the mid-century adult educational foundations in London of F. D. Maurice and his Christian Socialist collaborators who regarded the college as the natural educational successor to the Mechanics' Institutes.

These institutions made their main contribution to the slow development of technical education in Britain. That, too, has a disappointing history. There is more than hindsight in a historical criticism of the halting development in Britain of an educational system appropriate to an industrializing society. Something can be learned of the reasons for this and of the influences working for improvements from G. Haines, *German Influence upon English Education and Science 1800–1866* (New London, Conn., 1957) and D. S. L. Cardwell, *The Organisation of Science in England* (1957), which deals with many aspects of the subject but has gaps including, for example, the formation in 1840 of the Rothamsted Experimental Station for agriculture. A useful but not impressive book in this field is S. F. Cotgrove, *Technical Education and Social Change* (1958), and to this may be added much of value in C. Bibby, *T. H. Huxley* (1959), which makes excellent use, for the first time, of the Huxley papers at Imperial College, London.[12]

It is ironical that science and technology in this the first period of their great efflorescence have as yet attracted less attention than has been devoted to their growth in the seventeenth century. The historian must still attempt to fit together a jigsaw puzzle which lacks many essential pieces. There are, for example, no modern biographies of giants like Faraday or Kelvin (save those written for schoolchildren), or of minor but inescapable figures like Charles Babbage from whose work the calculating machine has grown to electronic maturity, or even of Lyon Playfair, the progenitor of Sir Charles Snow's scientific civil servants, who established himself as the leading interpreter of science to the governments of his

[12] The diffusion of ideas among the educated classes may be traced in the many histories of periodicals, newspapers, and publishing houses. Among them are M. M. Bevington, *The Saturday Review* (New York, 1941); L. G. Johnson, *General T. Perronet Thompson* (1957); H. Kogan, *The Great E. B.: The Story of the Encyclopaedia Britannica* (Chicago, 1958); L. A. Marchand, *The Athenaenum* (Chapel Hill, N.C., 1941); R. G. G. Price, *A History of "Punch"* (1957); H. Shine and H. C. Shine, *The Quarterly Review under Gifford* (Chapel Hill, N.C., 1949); J. C. Trewin and E. M. King, *Printer to the House: The Story of Hansard* (1952), vol. II of *The History of the Times* (1939); F. Beckwith, *Account of the Leeds Intelligencer* (Leeds, 1954), *Adam and Charles Black* (1957); A. Blackie, *Blackie and Son* (1959); and C. Morgan, *The House of Macmillan* (1943). Among the biographies are M. F. Brightfield, *John Wilson Croker* (Berkeley, Calif., 1940); D. Hudson, *Thomas Barnes of "The Times"* (Cambridge, Eng., 1943); and R. Straus, *Sala* (1942).

day. The two final volumes of the recently published monumental *A History of Technology*, IV: *The Industrial Revolution c. 1750–c. 1850*, and V: *The Late Nineteenth Century* (Oxford, 1958), edited by C. Singer *et al.*, are likely to suffer the fate of many monuments and to enjoy a respectful neglect. Both provide massive documentation of technological changes, chronologically arranged; both are written without that constant reference to changing economic circumstances which alone can preserve technological history from the dullness and irrelevance of mechanical antiquarianism. The historian must still rely on the skilled and readable popularizers such as L. Hogben, *Science for the Citizen* (1938), F. S. Taylor, *The Century of Science* (1941), and H. C. Cameron, *Joseph Lister* (1948) as guides to his use of contemporary sources.

The central importance as well as the centenary of *The Origin of Species* has occasioned many books as well as reviving old controversies in new guises. The historian enters this labyrinth at his peril, though many qualified guides offer their services. The sweep of evolutionary ideas in the eighteenth and nineteenth centuries is surveyed by L. Eiseley, *Darwin's Century* (Garden City, N.Y., 1958) and in the symposium, *Forerunners of Darwin*, edited by B. Glass, O. Temkin, and W. Strauss (Baltimore, Md., 1959). The ecological orientation of Darwin's work is emphasized by P. Sears, *Charles Darwin* (New York, 1950); the debt that he owed to Malthus as well as the disastrous history of natural selection as it came to be embodied in some social theories are considered by D. G. MacRae, "Darwinism and the Social Sciences," in *A Century of Darwin*, edited by S. A. Barnett (1958).[13]

The library of polemical and hagiographical books about Victorian religious beliefs and personalities is now a formidable barrier to the understanding of the role and influence of religion in the period. Personalities obscure the institution. Such books as those of B. Willey, *Nineteenth Century Studies* (1949) and *More Nineteenth Century Studies* (1956), and J. S. Reynolds, *The Evangelicals at Oxford 1735–1871: A Record of an Unchronicled Movement* (Oxford, 1953), and the many studies of Newman buttress the myth of the Victorian age as a deeply religious era.[14] The corrective provided by E. R. Wickham, *Church and People*

---

[13] VS, 3 (1959) is devoted to Darwin scholarship. For an excellent analysis of the debate over the development hypothesis in geology 1830–1850 see W. F. Cannon, "The Uniformitarian-Catastrophist Debate," *Isis*, 51 (1960).

[14] For example see L. Bouyer, *Newman: His Life and Spirituality* (1958); O. Chadwick, *From Bossuet to Newman: The Idea of Doctrinal Development* (New

in an Industrial City (1957) a sociological study of the churches' negligible influence on the working class written by a suffragan bishop of the Church of England, is thus especially significant. V. D. Lipman, *Social History of the Jews in England 1850–1950* (1954) studies the adaptation of religious institutions to the varied problems of social control and assimilation resulting from the mass immigration of poverty-stricken foreigners. A cool historical assessment of a period when religious belief was largely a middle class habit except in the Celtic fringe and in isolated mining communities must await studies of the clergy as a profession, of the institutional influence of organized religion, and of the bases of working class morality. The influence of religion on the rich and powerful can best be assessed in biographies and memoirs. The limitations of a primarily religious biography are illustrated by a comparison between the admirable books: G. C. B. Davies, *Henry Phillpotts: Bishop of Exeter 1778–1869* (1954) and R. S. Lambert, *The Cobbett of the West: A Study of Thomas Latimer and the Struggle between the Pulpit and Press at Exeter* (1939).

Of the many books published about writers and literature, some are particularly useful to historians.[15] Letters and memoirs often help the historian to overhear the conversation of sensitive minds as in the superb editions of the letters of Eliot, Thackeray, Swinburne, Smith, and Dickens.[16] Of the many biographies the following are likely to become

York, 1957); C. F. Harrold, *John Henry Newman* (New York, 1945); J. Moody, *John Henry Newman* (New York, 1945); E. E. Reynolds, *Three Cardinals: Newman, Wiseman, Manning* (New York, 1958); *Autobiographical Writings of John Henry Newman*, ed. H. Tristram (1956); and M. Ward, *Young Henry Newman* (1948).

[15] In intellectual and cultural history there are a few helpful bibliographical aids. The thorough compilations of W. Matthews, *British Diaries, An Annotated Bibliography of British Diaries Written between 1442 and 1942* (Berkeley, Calif., 1950) and *British Autobiographies, An Annotated Bibliography of British Autobiographies Published or Written before 1851* (Berkeley, Calif., 1955) have admirable indexes. M. Sadleir, a dedicated bibliographer of great erudition, has left us his *XIX Century Fiction, A Bibliographical Record Based on His Own Collection*, 2 vols. (1951). The forthcoming (eight or nine years hence, alas) *Wellesley Index of Victorian Periodicals*, now in preparation under the direction of W. E. Houghton, promises to be a magnificent addition to nineteenth-century bibliographical equipment. There is also the annual Victorian bibliography prepared for the Modern Language Association and published each June in *Victorian Studies*.

[16] They are *George Eliot, pseud., 1819–80, Letters*, ed. G. S. Haight, 7 vols. (New Haven, Conn., 1954–56); *The Letters and Private Papers of William Makepeace Thackeray*, ed. G. N. Ray, 4 vols. (Cambridge, Mass., 1945–46); *The Swinburne Letters*, ed. C. Y. Lang, I and II (1959); *Sidney Smith, Selected Letters*, ed. N. C. Smith, 2 vols. (Oxford, 1953); *Letters from Charles Dickens to Angela Burdett-Coutts*, ed. E. Johnson (1955); and *The Diaries of John Ruskin*, ed. J. Evans and J. H. Whitehouse, I and II (1958).

standard works. J. Evans, *John Ruskin* (1954) is the best biography of Ruskin and excuses if it does not fully explain his sexual and personal difficulties. E. Johnson, *Charles Dickens: His Tragedy and Triumph* (2 vols., 1953) valuably assembles much contemporary material on this inescapable novelist and editor [17] but lacks the compelling authority of G. N. Ray, *Thackeray* (2 vols., 1956–57). J. Simmons, *Southey* (1945) introduces and makes intelligible for modern readers this previously enigmatic figure. L. Trilling, *Matthew Arnold* (New York, 1939) must rank as the foremost study of his political and social thought.[18] M. Packe, *The Life of John Stuart Mill* (1954) is, astonishingly, the only large-scale secondary study. It adds biographical flesh to the intellectual bones of the *Autobiography* which, paradoxically, is the major lion in Packe's path. F. A. Hayek has put all students in his debt by collecting the documentary *John Stuart Mill and Harriet Taylor: Their Correspondence and Subsequent Marriage* (Chicago, 1951). Readers are under no obligation to accept Hayek's curious gloss that Mill's apparently unaccountable though wicked decline into socialism was the result, not of Benthamite sin, but of the masterfulness of Harriet Taylor.

There have been some good analyses of the social and religious outlook of the Victorian literati. A. W. Brown, *The Metaphysical Society: Victorian Minds in Crisis 1869–1880* (New York, 1947) helps to explain the failure of Christian belief to retain intellectual loyalties in the later decades of the century. J. H. Buckley, *The Victorian Temper: A Study in Literary Culture* (1952) traces the rise and decline of the "moral aesthetic," mostly in literary sources. J. Holloway, *The Victorian Sage: Studies in Argument* (1953) examines a particular phase of the Victorian *Zeitgeist*. B. N. Schilling, *Human Dignity and the Great Victorians* (New York, 1946) exposes the mental attitudes of people who, a generation ago, were considered unimportant. K. Tillotson, *Four Early Victorian Novelists* (Oxford, 1954) is one of the most mature and penetrating commentaries on this constantly discussed group. F. J. Woodward, *The Doctor's Disciples: A Study of Four Pupils of Arnold of Rugby—Stanley, Gell, Clough and William Arnold* (1954) portrays men whose intellectual promise exceeded their achievement but whose comparative failures throw a necessary light on the Victorian world. *Studies*

[17] Those who like to explore the sexual proclivities of great Victorians should, in Ruskin's case, refer to the devotional exercise of Admiral James, *The Order of Release* (1947); and, for Dickens, alias Tringham, to F. Aylmer, *Dickens Incognito* (1959). The best account of Ruskin as a social critic remains J. A. Hobson, *John Ruskin, Social Reformer* (1898).

[18] W. F. Connell provides the best account of *The Educational Thought and Influence of Matthew Arnold* (1950).

in Social History: A Tribute to G. M. Trevelyan, edited by J. H. Plumb (1955) contains the essay of G. S. R. Kitson Clark on "The Romantic Element, 1830 to 1850" and the excellent delineation of the familial basis of the intellectual aristocracy by N. G. Annan, "The Intellectual Aristocracy." J. Marlow, *The Puritan Tradition in English Life* (1957) is a study of the effect of the Puritan tradition in the nineteenth century concluding with two examples of its flowering: Gladstone and Gordon.

In addition to the traditional interest in literary history, there has been a growth of work in this field with a sociological bias. Marxist writers followed a path first cut by Hippolyte Taine and came under blistering attack in the cogent but neglected R. C. Churchill, *Disagreements: A Polemic on Culture in the English Democracy* (1950). Too often sociology has seemed to contribute to this particular approach little more than its often pretentious language and not very much of its method. However such criticism does not apply to the perceptive reassessment of M. J. Quinlan, *Victorian Prelude: A History of English Manners, 1700–1830* (New York, 1941).[19] W. E. Houghton, *The Victorian Frame of Mind, 1830–1870* (New Haven, Conn., 1957) is a wide-ranging display of erudition which raises, for the historian, the legitimacy of the literary identification of the Victorian frame of mind with the minds of the clerisy. Houghton's assumptions and conclusions may usefully be compared with those of R. Williams, *Culture and Society, 1780–1950* (New York, 1958) and *The Long Revolution* (1961).

Not all may agree with J. Betjeman and the *Architectural Review* in their enthusiasm for Victorian architecture, but there has been a growing appreciation, if not for the taste of the Victorians, certainly for their creative energy, their vigor and imagination, and their organizational ability. The best general review of this fertile period is H. Hitchcock, *Early Victorian Architecture in Britain* (2 vols., New Haven, Conn., 1955), which catalogues admirably the buildings and style which make this period so appealing or appalling according to taste.[20]

For Victorian engineering and organizational skill few have anything but admiration. The centenary of the Great Exhibition of 1851 served to

[19] M. Jaeger, *Before Victoria* (1956) lacks the scholarship but covers the same ground, and reaches the same conclusions, without once referring to Quinlan.

[20] The interplay of romanticism, religion, and architecture which is the essence of the Gothic revival is well recounted in K. Clark, *The Gothic Revival,* 2d ed. (1950); and D. Gwynn, *Lord Shrewsbury, Pugin and the Catholic Revival* (1946). Astonishingly, we still lack a biography of the greatest of the architectural entrepreneurs, Scott.

remind a later generation how skillfully Paxton responded to that unique challenge.[21] But it was the railways which occasioned so much of the best in architecture and engineering. C. Barman, *Early British Railroads: An Introduction to Railway Architecture* (1950) and C. L. V. Meeks, *The Railroad Station: An Architectural History* (New Haven, Conn., 1956) show the confusions of styles and of engineering and architecture which mark the period. E. de Mare, *The Bridges of Britain* (1954) describes another kind of building in which the Victorians excelled. J. Gloag and D. Bridgewater, *A History of Cast Iron in Architecture* (1948) includes a good and well illustrated chapter on this period when utilitarian uses of cast iron achieved the standards of fine art.[22]

There has also been evident for some time a more favorable view of Victorian taste, as well as ingenuity, in furniture and the decorative arts. The various catalogues of the Great Exhibition have been supplemented by some worthwhile books but few offer a fresh point of view.[23] W. Gaunt, *The Pre-Raphaelite Tragedy* (1942) shows how the most talented group of painters and creative artists of the period, rejecting industrialism, sought other solutions and made of art an escape from their society. His *Victorian Olympus* (1952) is an account of the classical revival, particularly in painting, which triumphed in the seventies and eighties. J. Steegman, *Consort of Taste, 1830–1870* (1950) explores this theme and discusses what artists, connoisseurs, and collectors considered good taste in painting and architecture and the reasons which led them to break with the past and to develop new canons of taste. And F. D. Klingender, *Art and the Industrial Revolution* (1947) is a brief but well illustrated Marxist account of how artists were conditioned by industrial development.[24]

[21] They are Y. French, *The Great Exhibition* (1951); C. H. Gibbs-Smith, *The Great Exhibition of 1851* (1950); C. Hobhouse, *1851 and the Crystal Palace* (1937); N. Pevsner, *High Victorian Design* (1951); and K. W. Luckhurst, *The Story of Exhibitions* (New York, 1951).

[22] N. Pevsner's county guides currently being produced by Penguin Books can be read with profit by the historian as well as by the tourist. New volumes are being added to the old *Victoria County History* series. The quality of the contributions is so variable as to defeat critical review.

[23] See also T. S. R. Boase, *English Art 1800–1870* (Oxford, 1950), vol. X of *The Oxford History of English Art; The Early Victorian Period*, ed. R. Edwards and L. G. G. Ramsey (1958), vol. VI in *The Connoisseur Period Guides;* and the many books on dress by C. W. Cunnington. The many pamphlets published by H.M.S.O. and The Victoria and Albert Museum are excellent.

[24] Among biographies are E. George, *The Life and Death of B. R. Haydon* (Oxford, 1948); T. Balston, *John Martin* (1947); and to these may be added the recent publication of an abridged version of W. P. Frith's three volume autobiography by N. Wallis called *A Victorian Canvas* (1957).

J. Laver, *Taste and Fashion: From the French Revolution to the Present Day* (new and revised ed., 1946) develops a famous Freudian theory which links changes in fashion of dress with changes in taste in interior decoration and architecture. R. Dutton, *The Victorian Home: Some Aspects of Nineteenth-Century Taste and Manners* (1955) shows well how important it was in that society so concerned for status that the household should be large and impressive. H. Gernsheim, *Masterpieces of Victorian Photography* (1951) is the first thorough account of this new technique for recording history and provides a visual review of changing taste.

The great importance of sports and games in English society is often recognized but there is no good general account of what they were, who enjoyed them, and what their relationship was to other aspects of Victorian life. There are some rewarding studies of particular activities. The elegant and charming study of R. Clark, *The Victorian Mountaineers* (1953) opens up the history, still insufficiently explored, of the way in which the interrelated pressures of geology and agnosticism drove Victorian intellectuals to the top of Swiss mountains and helped to establish the most thriving tourist industry in Europe today. It may, incidentally, be confidently expected that those who specialize in mining best sellers from rich Victorian veins will soon discover the as yet untapped deposit of early- and mid-Victorian literature relating to sports dependent upon the horse. L. Cooper, *R. S. Surtees* (1952) and A. Noakes, *The World of Henry Alken* (1952) give an indication of, though they do not fully exploit, the available resources. While the variety of sports is suggested in C. Hole, *English Sports and Pastimes* (1949), few have been documented, and the kind of analysis developed by J. Huizinga in *Homo Ludens: A Study of the Play-Element in Culture* (1949) suggests a fruitful line for further research.

In political history a new pattern of ideas was suggested by J. B. Brebner in his seminal article of 1948, "Laissez Faire and State Intervention in Nineteenth-Century Britain." [25] Liberal historians of an earlier generation taught, in the too readily accepted tradition of Dicey, that the period 1820–1870 was the "heyday of *laissez faire*." Brebner related the thought of Bentham to the growth of government during this period, exposed the confusions, and destroyed the authority of Dicey's Harvard lectures. Thus *laissez faire* must now be viewed not as a system but as an

[25] *JEcH Supplement,* 8 (1948).

attitude of mind and as an ideal which could not be realized. Furthermore, as L. Robbins has argued in his *Theory of Economic Policy in
English Classical Political Economy* (1952), the classical economists
were often advocates of regulation to ensure fair and free competition
rather than proponents of noninterference. His survey—by ignoring
both the popularizers of classical doctrines, Mrs. Marcet, Miss Martineau, Charles Knight *et hoc genus omne,* and the economists' post-1848
revision of their earlier attitudes—fails to draw the essential historical
distinction between the thought of the books and the far cruder and un-
qualified notions that influenced policy makers. Nevertheless, *laissez
faire* has come to mean "let us by" rather than "let us alone." The agency
of its realization was the free trade movement which secured not only
final reform but also, through the administrative devices of the "new"
poor law and the companies acts, the "transferability of labour and capital" which Bagehot described as "the fundamental postulates of English
political economy." [26]

The best general account of governmental growth is K. B. Smellie, *A
Hundred Years of English Government* (2d ed., 1951). Most histories,
however, have been concerned with the *ad hoc* accretion of duties and
the periodic reorganization of particular departments of government.
There have been too few of these studies. The Whitehall Series of
"house histories" is no substitute for the extended historical treatment
urgently necessary to establish the main outlines of public administration in this period. However R. Prouty does something to document *The
Transformation of the Board of Trade, 1830–1855* (1957), and the consequences of the need for free trade in the transmission of information
upon one public service are ably drawn out in H. Robinson, *The British
Post Office, A History* (Princeton, N.J., 1948). S. E. Finer, *The Life and
Times of Sir Edwin Chadwick* (1952) provides no more than the chronologically arranged materials from which a biography might be written.
R. A. Lewis, *Edwin Chadwick and the Public Health Movement
1832–1854* (1952) shows, through its very able examination of one phase

---

[26] For a discussion of *laissez faire* and the dating of the "Industrial Revolution"
see the penetrating lecture of G. N. Clark, *The Idea of the Industrial Revolution*
(Glasgow, 1953). The quotation from Bagehot is taken from his posthumously published *Economic Studies,* ed. R. H. Hutton (1880). Bagehot's ironical, empirical,
and fundamentally pessimistic view of politics is particularly agreeable to the present
day English outlook, and his reputation is again growing. The most recent study is
A. Buchan, *The Spare Chancellor* (1959). This odd title derives from Gladstone's
remark that Bagehot was for many years "a sort of supplementary Chancellor of
the Exchequer."

of Chadwick's activity, how valuable a functional study might be of his other multifarious activities. P. Knaplund, *James Stephen and the British Colonial System 1813–1847* (Madison, Wis., 1953) shows the process of reform in another department.[27] O. Brose, *Church and Parliament* (Stanford, Calif., 1959) discusses the reshaping of the Church of England, 1828–1860, in response to the changing society and contains a good appraisal of the importance of Charles Blomfield, Bishop of London.

The work of the only postwar historian who commands the sales (on both sides of the Atlantic) of a best-selling novelist has been directed to an explanation of the intractable difficulties of reform in those social areas controlled by the aristocracy. *The Reason Why* (1953) leads logically to Mrs. Woodham-Smith's forthcoming study of the Irish Famine.[28] H. Morris in her charming *Portrait of a Chef: The Life of Alexis Soyer, Sometime Chef to the Reform Club* (Cambridge, Eng., 1938) shows how an inventive mind was harnessed to social purposes never dreamed of by his patrons at the Club. Indeed, there were many men and women who similarly secured the reform or adaptation of institutions and who still await biographers.

The expansion and reform of the civil service in the heyday of *laissez faire* reveal the extent and nature of the redefinition of the functions of government in this period of industrial expansion and social reconstruction. Of the general histories, H. R. G. Greaves, *The Civil Service in the Changing State* (1947) and J. D. Kingsley, *Representative Bureaucracy: An Interpretation of the British Civil Service* (Yellow Springs, Ohio, 1944) relate bureaucratic past and present. The two pamphlets of W. Griffith, *A Hundred Years: The Board of Inland Revenue 1849–1949* (1949) and *The British Civil Service 1854–1954* (1954) are representative of the high quality of much of the writing published for the centenary of the Northcote-Trevelyan Report. Nevertheless the best work has been reported in articles.[29]

[27] An excellent collection of documents is *The Law and Working of the Constitution*, II, *1784–1914*, ed. W. C. Costin and J. S. Watson (1952).

[28] For criticisms of Mrs. Woodham-Smith see W. H. Greenleaf, "Biography and the 'Amateur' Historian: Mrs. Woodham-Smith's 'Florence Nightingale,'" *VS*, 2 (1959); and B. D. Gooch, "The Crimean War in Selected Documents and Secondary Works since 1940," *VS*, 1 (1958). I think the virtues of Mrs. Woodham-Smith's histories far outweigh their faults. [See Miss Mulvey's article below for Mrs. Woodham-Smith's study of the famine, published in 1962.]

[29] Among the better articles are E. Hughes, "Civil Service Reform 1853–5," *History*, 27 (1942); and "Sir Charles Trevelyan and Civil Service Reform, 1853–5," *EHR*, 64 (1949); O. R. McGregor, "Civil Servants and the Civil Service: 1850–1950," *The Political Quarterly*, 22 (1951); and K. C. Wheare, *The Civil Service in the Constitution* (1954). *Public Administration* conveniently reprinted the Northcote-Trevelyan Report in the spring issue, 1954.

The many-volumed barrier erected by the Webbs still discourages new general explorations in the political history of local government. The direction of future studies has been pointed by B. D. White in *A History of the Corporation of Liverpool 1835–1914* (Liverpool, 1951) and S. D. Simon, *A Century of City Government: Manchester 1838–1938* (1938), enriched by her own long and distinguished experience in Manchester.

The character of Parliament was largely determined by the persistent attack of the urban middle class upon the entrenched power and privileges of the territorial aristocracy. Land in this period was not only the "mountain backbone" of English society but also the main source of food to sustain a rapidly growing urban population. The conflict between these two functions of land is the central theme of O. R. McGregor's long, bibliographical introduction to the modern section of the new sixth edition, G. E. Fussell and O. R. McGregor, eds., of Lord Ernle's classic *English Farming Past and Present* (1961). His exhaustive survey of contemporary and secondary sources is designed both to destroy the authority of Ernle's account of the nineteenth and twentieth centuries and to demonstrate the irrelevance of agrarian history limited to agricultural themes and ignoring their social and political, and hence tenurial, setting. This approach illustrates the new perspectives which disciplined social history can extract from sterile specialisms and helps towards the functional understanding of early- and mid-Victorian government that will emerge from the increasing exploration of aspects of political structure and behavior.[30] A. S. Turberville, *The House of Lords in the Age of Reform, 1784–1837, with an Epilogue on Aristocracy and the Advent of Democracy* (1958) suggestively describes the inert weight of the upper house. J. A. Thomas, *The House of Commons, 1832–1901: A Study of Its Economic and Functional Character* (Cardiff, 1939), reflecting sociological interests, examines briefly the economic connections of individuals and party groups in the lower house.

N. Gash in his careful and detailed *Politics in the Age of Peel: A*

---

[30] There are few bibliographical aids in political history such as appear in specialist research publications. The work of P. and G. Ford is in a class apart. Their invaluable *Hansard's Catalogue and Breviate of Parliamentary Papers 1696–1834* (Oxford, 1953) and *Select List of British Parliamentary Papers 1833–1899* (Oxford, 1953) are most useful. *A Breviate of Parliamentary Papers 1900–1916* (Oxford, 1957) and *A Breviate of Parliamentary Papers 1917–1939* (Oxford, 1951) are also helpful because so often the recent reports draw on those published before 1870 and therefore serve as a good starting point for research in this period. Of a more strictly political nature the two volumes in the *English Historical Documents* series, those edited by A. Aspinall and E. Anthony-Smith, *1783–1832* (1959) and G. M. Young and W. D. Handcock, *1833–1874* (1957) include a preface to each section with a bibliographical survey.

Study in the Technique of Parliamentary Representation 1830–1850 (1953), responding to the growing interest in the details of electoral processes, analyzes the local basis of the power of Members and shows how much of pre-1832 habit persisted in the constituencies despite the formal changes at Westminster. H. J. Hanham, *Elections and Party Management: Politics in the Time of Disraeli and Gladstone* (1959) carries this kind of study into the later period. H. B. Witmer, *The Property Qualifications of Members of Parliament* (New York, 1943) recounts the background of the repeal in 1858 of the Qualifications Act of 1710 and illustrates the redefinition of the functions of property in the political system of the industrial state. Sir I. Jennings, a constitutional lawyer with the practical experience of a proconsular constitution maker, has published two of the projected three volumes of his *Party Politics*. The first volume, *Appeal to the People* (Cambridge, Eng., 1960), surveys the electoral system; the second analyzes *The Growth of Parties* (Cambridge, Eng., 1961); and the third, *Politics*, yet to be published, will treat the history of English political ideas.

O. C. Williams, *The Historical Development of Private Bill Procedure and Standing Orders in the House of Commons* (2 vols., 1948–49) describes an aspect of reform little noticed by historians but crucial to the efficiency of Parliament and thus to subsequent reforms. His *The Clerical Organisation of the House of Commons 1661–1850* (Oxford, 1955) is the definitive work on another equally vital reform. G. Campion, *Introduction to the Procedure of the House of Commons* (1947) and B. Chubb, *The Control of Public Expenditure* (Oxford, 1952) are essential works of reference.

There are several studies of the relations of government and public opinion but none which attempts a definition of this convenient, elusive, and dangerous concept. A. Aspinall, *Politics and the Press, c. 1780–1850* (1949) demonstrates that the government failed to control the press. L. S. Marshall, *The Development of Public Opinion in Manchester* (Syracuse, N.Y., 1946) is a useful but carelessly edited compilation. That most important force for reform, the parliamentary lobby, long recognized by historians but seldom documented because it often worked in the dark, has been well exposed in two cases only: L. Brown, *The Board of Trade and the Free-Trade Movement, 1830–1842* (Oxford, 1958) shows the relentless pressure exerted on Parliament in the area of fiscal reform; N. McCord, *The Anti-Corn Law League 1838–1846* (1958) outlines fully for the first time the many-sided and sometimes discreditable efforts of the League to rally opinion out-of-doors and to pressure Parliament. Many fascinating aspects of reform and of lobbying still await historians with a capacity for detection and a liking for muckraking.

The legal history of the nineteenth century has not yet found its Pollock and Maitland, but some lawyers' histories are rewarding sources as well as skillful summaries. The thirteenth volume of Sir W. Holdsworth's great *A History of English Law* has been edited by A. L. Goodhart and H. C. Hanbury (1953). T. F. T. Plucknett, *A Concise History of the Common Law* (1948) gives the background for the reforms of this period. There have been some good monographs. N. St. John-Stevas, *Obscenity and the Law* (1956) traces the history of one of the more curious Victorian legacies. C. A. Cooke, *Corporation, Trust and Company: An Essay in Legal History* (Manchester, Eng., 1950) is a clear account of the legal ideas and economic purposes behind the reforms in corporation law, very usefully summarized in L. C. B. Gower, *Modern Principles of Company Law* (1954). *Jeremy Bentham and the Law: A Symposium,* edited by G. Keeton and G. Schwarzenberger (1948), is a contribution to a surprisingly neglected field. Benthamite studies will be enriched by the forthcoming edition of *The Constitutional Code* from C. Everett and the subsequent volumes to be issued under the auspices of a committee entrusted to supervise the publication of a definitive edition of Bentham's major writings and correspondence under the chairmanship of Lord Cohen. What can be done in the revealing of Bentham's thought was admirably foreshadowed in the article of T. W. Hutchison, "Bentham as an Economist," based upon a new but not altogether satisfactory edition of *Jeremy Bentham's Economic Writings* (edited by W. Stark, 3 vols., 1952–54).[31]

While these monographs have helped the understanding of the polity of the period, there is no adequate history of the functioning of the government. There are the outlines of the new regulatory responsibilities of government, of the growing civil service, together with the contributions of many of the very able men responsible for *ad hoc* reforms, but there is still much to be learned about its actual functioning. New and unexplained relationships between industry and the government are indicated in A. R. Ilersic and P. F. B. Liddle, *Parliament of Commerce: The Story of the Association of British Chambers of Commerce 1860–1960* (1960). How effective were lobbies and how did they operate? How effectively, and by whom, were regulatory acts enforced? How did class

[31] T. W. Hutchison, "Bentham as an Economist," *The Economic Journal,* 66 (1956).

conflicts promote or obstruct the making of social policy? These and many other questions invite a continued re-examination of the period despite the great amount already published. Contemporary interest in the definition of social policy, notably evidenced by the work of R. M. Titmuss and his collaborators, is stimulating historical investigation along lines first marked out in the seminal Hobhouse Memorial Lecture of H. L. Beales, *The Making of Social Policy* (Oxford, 1946) and more recently followed up by O. R. McGregor in "Social Research and Social Policy in the Nineteenth Century." [32]

Biographies and memoirs frequently offer the best insight into the lives of the rich and powerful and also suggest unexpected social and political relationships. But good biography is rarely achieved. The subject must be significant either in what he did or at least in those whom he knew and influenced, and the biographer must combine breadth of knowledge with balance of interpretation. J. Pope-Hennessy, *Monckton-Milnes* (2 vols., 1949–51) is a gracefully written professional literary biographer's account of the life of an upper class Victorian intellectual who had a passion both for Florence Nightingale and for pornography. Edith, Marchioness of Londonderry, *Frances Anne: The Life and Times of Frances Anne, Marchioness of Londonderry and Her Husband, Charles, Third Marquess of Londonderry* (1958) tells the story of an unusual woman who combined marriage to a diplomat with the personal direction of the Vane-Tempest mines in Northumberland. O. W. Hewett, *Strawberry Fair: A Biography of Frances, Countess Waldegrave* (1956) recounts the career of a leading hostess in the London of the mid-century. E. M. Forster, *Marianne Thornton 1797–1887: A Domestic Biography* (1956) is an elegantly written, revealing, but over-long sketch of a member of the Clapham Sect. Of the many biographies of political figures, one of the best is L. Cooper, *Radical Jack* (1959), a life of Lord Durham. One of the most revealing is B. R. Jerman, *The Young Disraeli* (1961) with its frank disclosure of the unscrupulous diplomacy which reconciled embarrassing sexual and financial transactions with political ambition, and undoubtedly one of the most important is N. Gash, *Mr. Secretary Peel* (1961). This, the first volume of Gash's

[32] *The British Journal of Sociology,* 8 (1957). See also R. M. Titmuss, *Essays on 'The Welfare State'* (1958) and B. Abel-Smith, *A History of the Nursing Profession* (1960).

projected two-volume biography, is conceived on the heroic, Victorian scale and carries Peel's political life to its first minor crisis over Catholic emancipation. Final judgment must be deferred until the second volume can be assimilated: but this study will be indispensable for the next generation of students.[33]

There are a few workmanlike and historically useful editions of journals and letters and these challenge in interest the work of the best biographers: Lord Bessborough's two volumes of extracts from the Journal of *Lady Charlotte Guest 1833–1852* (1950) whose first marriage provided the ferruginous wealth which, as *Lady Charlotte Schreiber, 1853–1891* (1952) she later converted into porcelain; *Three Howard Sisters: Selections from the Writings of Lady Caroline Lascelles, Lady Dover and Countess Gower 1825–1833*, edited by Maud, Lady Leconfield and J. Gore (1955); *Elizabeth, Lady Holland to Her Son, 1821–1845*, edited by Lord Ilchester (1946); and *"My Dear Duchess," Social and Political Letters of the Duchess of Manchester, 1858–1869*, edited by A. L. Kennedy (1956) are entertaining and informative. The new edition of G. E. C., *The Complete Peerage*, by H. A. Doubleday, G. H. White, and Lord Howard de Walden, of which volume ten was published in 1945, retains its impeccable high standard as it advances through the decades.

The Correspondence of Charles Arbuthnot, edited by A. Aspinall (1941) is of particular interest politically, for it characterizes high Tory circles around 1830. His *Diary of Henry Hobhouse, 1820–1827* (1947) throws light on the working of the cabinet, and *Three Early Nineteenth Century Diaries* (1952) delineates the role of Edward Littleton (Lord Hatherton), Sir Denis Marchant, and Lord Ellenborough in the crisis of 1832. *The Journal of Mrs. Arbuthnot 1820–1832*, edited by F. Bamford and the Duke of Wellington (2 vols., 1950) makes available further information about the Iron Duke's circle. A. Ramm has edited *The Politi-*

---

[33] See J. Clive, "More or Less Eminent Victorians: Some Trends in Recent Victorian Bibliography," VS, 2 (1958). For a list of biographies and other works on literature see *From Dickens to Hardy*, ed. B. Ford (1958), vol. VI in *The Pelican Guide to English Literature*. The relatively small number of biographies of politicians published in recent years is itself evidence of a marked trend. Among the major biographies are W. D. Jones, *Lord Derby and Victorian Conservatism* (Oxford, 1956); C. Roth, *Benjamin Disraeli* (New York, 1952); E. Eyck, *Gladstone* (1938); G. Battiscombe, *Mrs. Gladstone* (1956); P. Magnus, *Gladstone* (1954); A. B. Erickson, *The Public Career of Sir James Graham* (Oxford, 1952); W. R. Brock, *Lord Liverpool and Liberal Toryism* (Cambridge, Eng., 1941); D. Cecil, *The Young Melbourne* (1939) and *Lord M* (1954); and the Marquess of Anglesey, *One-leg* (1961).

cal Correspondence of Mr. Gladstone and Lord Granville 1868–1876 (2 vols., 1952). S. A. Wallace and F. E. Gillespie, *The Journal of Benjamin Moran, 1857–1865* (2 vols., Chicago, 1949) provides a picture of life in London through the eyes of a secretary of the United States Legation.

The history of a country house or of a family is seldom well done. Perhaps the two best, for this period, are Lord Ilchester, *Chronicles of Holland House, 1820–1900* (New York, 1938) and J. Wake, *The Brudenells of Deane* (1953).

Only two continuous narratives attempt a textbook synthesis of this period. E. L. Woodward, *The Age of Reform* (Oxford, 1938) contains everything that is necessary for a history in the grand manner save an organizing principle to give coherence and purposive unity to the many sections. If Woodward is an example, perhaps the last, of country house history, A. Briggs, *The Age of Improvement* (1959) is an exponent of the common people school. But wide social sympathies here result in surprisingly narrow historical interests. The sad conclusion to this bibliography must be that nothing here cited approaches in quality G. M. Young's *Victorian England: Portrait of an Age* (1936). Brilliant, elusive, and allusive, his *Portrait,* like those of the greatest painters, captures the character of his subject. Young once remarked that historians should go on reading until they could hear contemporaries talking. His *Portrait* remains the greatest piece of historical writing of his generation because it was written from the inside. He would have insisted that a bibliography of secondary writing about his period is useful only in so far as it stimulates its readers to immerse themselves in the inexhaustible resources of contemporary comment.

What, it may finally be asked, will be the subject and approach of future histories of England and Wales 1820–1870? Inevitably, the postwar demonstration of the unexpected strength of political conservatism, nourished, as it now seems, by the social policies of labour governments, will be reflected in new historical explorations and interests. It is a safe prediction that such developments will be reflected in a historical reexamination of the history of the labour movement in the nineteenth century and in particular in studies which will seek to explain the failure of late nineteenth-century liberalism to assimilate and to provide for the political aspirations of labour. Sociological interests will certainly lead to examinations of problems so far ignored by conventional historians: the histories of the family, of crime—its treatment and control—of the growth of the professions, and of interests and pressure groups. Studies of the growth of social policy in the context of the elaboration of new techniques of social investigation and of the history and functioning, as distinct from the structure, of public administration may provide a perspective leading to a recognition that the old emphasis on an "age of reform" conceals the distinctiveness of an "age of construction."

British History, 1870–1914,
Reconsidered: Recent Trends in
the Historiography of the Period

❖

JOHN CLIVE

O SURVEY the important historical litera-
ture that has appeared about the period under review since World War II
is to be brought up sharply against the realization that a revolution in historical writing is being quietly accomplished. The familiar quadrivium
of political, social, economic, and cultural divisions, hallowed by long
usage and canonized by *The Oxford History of England,* is about to vanish, "into air, into thin air," but not without leaving many a bookrack
behind. An approach to recent British history that takes account of the
interconnectedness of these spheres and does not attempt the increasingly unrewarding task of compartmentalizing them is replacing it.
More and more historians of the recent period have come to see their
work as part of an endeavor to understand the structure and articulation
of the various parts of modern British society as a whole, a society existing at a particular stage of advanced industrial development and subject
to the stresses characteristic of such a stage.

This does not mean, however, that all good books dealing with this
period necessarily embrace all aspects of British life. In fact, R. C. K.
Ensor, *England, 1870–1914* (Vol. XIV of *The Oxford History of England* [15 vols., Oxford, 1934–65]) has not yet been replaced as the best
work on the period as a whole. It does mean that the best writing about
the period shows an awareness of the impossibility of separating a particular problem or investigation from its wider ramifications, relationships, and repercussions. "What probably in the long run determines the
shape of politics are the social movements, the groupings and regroup-
ings in the mass of the community, which are beyond the reach of politi-

[Reprinted from *AHR*, 68: 987–1009 (July 1963).]

cians," writes George Kitson Clark.[1] What politicians, and even statesmen, do or say may not be the most important part of history. As far as
the historian is concerned, the dramatic events that supply newspaper
headlines should often defer to the slow and silent changes in the way of
life of a country's population, or of particular segments of it. To study
the movements and groupings of society is to study the habits, traditions, unexpressed assumptions, instincts, and feelings that are part of
those movements and groupings, and thus part of the new stuff of history.

In their intimate linking of the political scene with society as a whole,
Kitson Clark's lectures reflect the general trend of historical writing during the last twenty years or so. To say that the importance of social history has been in the historian's consciousness since Voltaire and Macaulay and that the relation of political programs, postures, and platforms
to the forces exerted by economic tendencies and class situation has
been a commonplace since Marx would be to miss the point of this
trend. For what has happened is also an expansion of the term "social
history," from its original position as residuary legatee for those aspects
of history which would not fit the traditional categories of politics, great
men, and battles to a new position where the history of society is history,
and a contraction of the extent to which the hidden underpinnings of
the visible superstructure of words and ideas can be held to be primarily
economic. Any living society is marked by the continuous interplay of
diverse forces: some rational, others irrational; some ideological, others
instinctive; some institutional, yet others the result of individual action.
These forces mesh into each other so that to isolate one or the other in
the search for a single or even a principal "cause" of events is to do injustice to the rest. Doing such injustice is, of course, built into the very
process of writing history:

> Like following life through creatures you dissect,
> You lose it in the moment you detect.[2]

The best one can hope for is a consciousness on the part of the historian
of the sins of omission he is inevitably committing, and an endeavor on
his part to mitigate them, if only by the very fact of such awareness.

[1] George S. R. Kitson Clark, *The Making of Victorian England: Being the Ford
Lectures Delivered before the University of Oxford* (1962), p. 240.
[2] Alexander Pope, *Epistles to Several Persons* (*Moral Essays*), ed. F. W. Bateson
(1961), p. 18.

An excellent example both of the interconnectedness of historical tissue and of the historian's attempt to take account of it in his search for explanation is Joseph A. Banks's *Prosperity and Parenthood: A Study of Family Planning among the Victorian Middle Classes* (1954). Here the problem was to account for the reduction in the size of families which, before becoming general during the twentieth century, took place first in business and professional families during the final decades of the nineteenth century. This had momentous consequences, in terms of the changing role of women, the standard of living, the income spending priorities of a great number of people, and even, as Richard M. Titmuss points out in his *Essays on 'the Welfare State'* (New Haven, Conn., 1959), in terms of changing mutual relationships between husbands and wives. H. J. Habakkuk has suggested that the initial period of falling fertility was associated with the deferment of marriage and that only later did the increased use of birth control within marriage begin to play an important role.[3] But what accounts for this increased use? Contraceptive techniques were certainly nothing new. Why did people adopt them more widely at a particular time? Part of the answer is to be found in the rise of the feminist movement.[4] Another part, dealt with as a general problem in Herbert Wood, *Belief and Unbelief since 1850* (Cambridge, Eng., 1955), lies in the decline of religious faith with its corollary that Providence alone was to determine family size. Also to be taken into account is the increasingly pervasive scientific attitude that came to regard natural processes as susceptible of human, in the absence of divine, control.[5]

[3] H. J. Habakkuk, "The Economic History of Modern Britain," *JEcH*, 18:486–501 (December 1958).

[4] See Joseph A. and Olive Banks, *Feminism and Family Planning in Victorian England* (Liverpool, 1964), and "The Bradlaugh-Besant Trial and the English Newspapers," *Population Studies*, 8:22–34 (July 1954). On the changing status of women in general, see the indispensable bibliographical article by Oliver R. McGregor, "The Social Position of Women in Victorian England, 1850–1914," *British Journal of Sociology*, 6:48–60 (January 1955). The same author's *Divorce in England: A Centenary Study* (1957) contains a brilliant chapter on "The Victorian Family: Illusion and Reality," which makes clear how limited a view we have been getting by excluding the working classes from our consideration of the Victorian family. Margaret Hewitt, *Wives and Mothers in Victorian Industry* (1958), is useful in this connection. For statistical material, see David V. Glass and E. Grebenik, *The Trend and Pattern of Fertility in Great Britain: A Report on the Family Census of 1946*, 2 vols. (1954), issued as vol. VI of *Papers* of the British Royal Commission on Population. For a breezy account of the political aspects, see Roger Fulford, *Votes for Women: The Story of a Struggle* (1957).

[5] See, in this connection, Noel G. Annan, *Leslie Stephen: His Thought and Character in Relation to His Time* (1951), and Harold C. Bibby, *T. H. Huxley: Scientist, Humanist, and Educator* (New York, 1960).

Meanwhile, public school and university education was becoming both more necessary and more expensive for the children of those who had prospered: more necessary since the major professions, with ever higher standards of admission and advancement, and the civil service, now thrown open to competition, favored the best educated; [6] more expensive because the supply of first-rate education lagged behind the demand for it.[7] Education of a high order was not, however, merely a means toward professional advancement. It was also one way of staving off the potential threat to status and security represented by the growing number of those in white-collar occupations.[8] David Lockwood, in *The Blackcoated Worker: A Study in Class Consciousness* (1958), has well described the affectation, mannerisms, and status aping that were part of the ambitious clerk's striving after the gentlemanly ideal in the late nineteenth century.

Material standards of comfort, no less than status, stood in need of preservation. As far as Londoners were concerned, this may often have meant a house in the outer suburbs, properly distant from the rapidly growing new suburban working-class habitations.[9] Such a house was expensive. Servants, then an essential mark of privilege, were increasingly difficult to acquire, partly as a consequence of the Education Act of 1870, which made it possible for many young people to seek other avenues of employment.[10] While the Great Depression of the 1880's probably did not reduce incomes, it helped to undermine the sense of expan-

[6] See Roger K. Kelsall, *Higher Civil Servants in Britain from 1870 to the Present Day* (1955), for a discussion of the myth that the immediate effects of civil service reform were democratic.

[7] See F. Musgrove, "Middle Class Education and Employment in the Nineteenth Century," *EcHR*, 2d ser., 12:99–111 (August 1959); Harold J. Perkin's "Critical Note" on that article, *ibid.*, 14:122–130 (August 1961); and Musgrove's "Rejoinder," *ibid.*, 14:320–339 (December 1961). On the public schools, old and new, in this period, the best book is still Edward C. Mack, *Public Schools and British Opinion since 1860* (New York, 1941).

[8] See Moses Abramovitz and Vera F. Eliasberg, *The Growth of Public Employment in Great Britain* (Princeton, N.J., 1957).

[9] The way in which these communities grew, thanks largely to newly available cheap means of transport, is brilliantly described in Harold J. Dyos, *Victorian Suburb: A Study of the Growth of Camberwell* (Leicester, Eng., 1961). See also Thomas W. Freeman, *The Conurbations of Great Britain* (Manchester, Eng., 1959), and William Ashworth, *The Genesis of Modern British Town Planning: A Study in the Economic and Social History of the Nineteenth and Twentieth Centuries* (1954).

[10] Richard D. Altick, *The English Common Reader: A Social History of the Mass Reading Public, 1800–1900* (Chicago, 1957), while holding that Forster's Act maintained rather than significantly accelerated the rate of increase in the spread of literacy, calls it a mopping-up operation for the children of the very poor. For the story of the workers' education movement, see John F. C. Harrison, *Learning and Living, 1790–1960: A Study in the History of the English Adult Education Movement* (1961).

siveness and security so characteristic of mid-Victorian prosperity. Thus, if accustomed economic standards were to be maintained, some sort of cutting down of expenditure was essential. Reducing the number of children per family would, of course, effect this. Banks deliberately resists the temptation to give primacy to the economic factor as a causative force behind the changing pattern of family size among the business and professional classes. We simply do not know enough yet to be able to judge with absolute certainty. Taking up such a problem is like throwing a pebble into a pond; the ever-widening ripples reflect the complex, interlocking network of forces that move human beings living in society to action. He is foolhardy indeed who, at this stage of our knowledge, would make bold to assign priority to any one factor.

An investigation of the phenomenon of family limitation in the late Victorian period illustrates the necessity for taking account of the mutual involvement of different levels of human activity and motivation. We have seen that one of these levels was economic. More specifically, it might be labeled "Decline of Mid-Victorian Prosperity." The historical problems arising out of this decline, many of them related to the so-called Great Depression, do more than merely reinforce the need for this awareness of interconnection within a given society. They point up the advantages of another methodological approach that has yielded rich fruit in recent years: the substitution of precise detail for shopworn historical clichés, the desirability of piercing the veil of language in order to get at the actual historical reality, the attempt to use exact methods of quantification wherever possible and appropriate. Apparently simple and self-explanatory terms such as "middle class" and "working class" turn out much of the time to be bad shorthand for a multitude of variables, including regional and occupational differences not readily amenable to such summary treatment by the historian.[11] The difficulties increased with the use of catchwords like "Great Depression" to characterize the last quarter of the nineteenth century, catchwords all too often employed in the past as a substitute for historical explanation.

Not that there is any doubt that this period was one of social crisis. A combination of factors—Britain's changing position in the world, a succession of short-term slumps that underlined the plight of unskilled labor, the problem of Ireland and its English repercussions, the expan-

---

[11] On the difficulties associated with the words "middle class," see Peter Laslett, "The Solid Middle Class," *Listener*, 67 (January 4, 1962), pp. 13–15; on those associated with "working class," see Richard Hoggart, *The Uses of Literacy* (1957).

sion of literacy and of political democracy—produced much heart searching as well as fact finding on the part of the privileged, and of action in the form of a struggle for social justice on the part of the underprivileged classes.[12] Helen M. Lynd, in her *England in the Eighteen Eighties: Toward a Social Basis for Freedom* (New York, 1945), interprets that decade in these terms, and though her approach is at various points open to question, her book still repays close reading. Several recent volumes and articles supplement her treatment of unionism, old and new. Benjamin C. Roberts, *The Trades Union Congress, 1868–1921* (1958), has become the standard work on that subject. Both A. E. P. Duffy and John Saville de-emphasize the novelty of New Unionism and see the organization of unskilled labor antedating the dock strike, which thus becomes less of a critical landmark than it has been considered heretofore.[13] On the other hand, Eric J. Hobsbawm stresses the significance of the sharp distinction made in the 1890's between skilled and unskilled labor. Both sides kept to their proper stations and were thereby able to avoid serious clashes.[14] But the distinction between skilled and unskilled labor is by no means the sole distinction worthy of notice and study. In treating *A History of Labour in Sheffield* (Liverpool, 1959), Sidney Pollard demonstrates the importance of distinguishing between the traditional outlook of workers in the "light" (cutlery and silver) trades, and the more forward-looking attitude of workers in the "heavy" (steel and engineering) trades. The entire history of Sheffield labor during the latter part of the nineteenth century seems to have been very largely determined by fundamental differences of this sort.

The story of organized agricultural labor is told by George E. Fussell in *From Tolpuddle to T.U.C.: A Century of Farm Labourers' Politics*

[12] Charles L. Mowat, *The Charity Organisation Society, 1869–1913: Its Ideas and Work* (1961), and Thomas S. and Margaret B. Simey, *Charles Booth, Social Scientist* (1960), contain good accounts of notable attempts made respectively to mitigate and to publicize the worst conditions. See also David Owen, "The City Parochial Charities: The 'Dead Hand' in Late Victorian London," *JBS*, 1:115–135 (May 1962); Kathleen Woodroofe, *From Charity to Social Work in England and the United States* (1962); Herman Ausubel, *In Hard Times: Reformers among the Late Victorians* (New York, 1960).

[13] A. E. P. Duffy, "New Unionism in Britain, 1889–1890: A Reappraisal," *EcHR*, 2d ser., 14:306–319 (December 1961); John Saville, "Trade Unions and Free Labour: The Background of the Taff Vale Decision," *Essays in Labour History*, ed. Asa Briggs and John Saville (1960). On the dock strike itself, see Ann Stafford, *A Match to Fire the Thames* (1961).

[14] Eric J. Hobsbawm, "General Labour Unions in Britain, 1889–1914," *EcHR*, 2d ser., 1:123–142 (August 1948).

(Slough, Eng., 1948). But by far the most vivid picture of what life was really like for farm laborers two generations ago is to be found in that masterpiece of the art of biography, Mabel K. Ashby's *Joseph Ashby of Tysoe: A Study of English Village Life* (Cambridge, Eng., 1961). Here one is brought close not only to the concrete, local manifestations of movements one usually reads about only in general terms—Primitive Methodism, agricultural unionism, depopulation [15]—but also to the even more important truth that many of the events that made headlines in London and, later, chapter headings in textbooks, bore little relevance to the daily concerns of country dwellers.

Can one really ascribe all the social tensions of the final decades of the nineteenth century to one great lowering black cloud labeled "Great Depression"? Taking nothing for granted, historians and economists have again asked such basic questions as "Just who was depressed when and where?" And they have obtained some illuminating answers. For one thing, given general deflation throughout the world and a generally undiminished demand for labor in Britain, it appears clear that so far as at least a substantial number of workers were concerned, conditions improved rather than deteriorated. Real wages rose; the number of working hours per week fell. If there was a decline, it occurred in the returns from investments made by the more affluent classes, especially now that Britain's task as the world's railroad builder was finished, and savings were forced to move into other, less profitable channels.[16] For another thing, British industry as a whole was not so hard hit by the sudden influx of cheap materials and goods from abroad as has sometimes been assumed. A loss of strength, a check to industrial productivity, certainly took place toward the end of the century, but it was a relative rather than an absolute loss of strength. Furthermore, as Keith Hutchison points out in his useful and eminently readable *Decline and Fall of British Capitalism* (1951), one must not omit the invisible items in Britain's international accounts. The dumping of cheap steel on Britain, for in-

---

[15] On the general problem of depopulation, see John Saville, *Rural Depopulation in England and Wales, 1851–1951* (1957).

[16] For the clearest exposition of this view, see Walt W. Rostow, *The British Economy of the Nineteenth Century* (Oxford, 1948). For a critique of Rostow's views, see John Saville, "A Comment on Professor Rostow's *British Economy of the Nineteenth Century,*" *PP*, 6 (November 1954), pp. 66–81. For the view that the British rate of growth in this period was closely related to economic conditions in the United States, see Brinley Thomas, *Migration and Economic Growth: A Study of Great Britain and the Atlantic Economy* (Cambridge, Eng., 1954).

stance, proved to be a boon to the engineering trades, just as the dumping of beet sugar helped biscuit and preserve manufacturers.

In this, as in so many other spheres, the precise state of affairs is best established by means of local and regional studies, such as John D. Marshall's *Furness and the Industrial Revolution* (Barrow-in-Furness, Eng., 1958). Here, in terms of production and new construction, there was progress of a sort in the local steel industry. At the same time, the Great Depression "stalks through the Duke of Devonshire's diary," in the guise of falling profits, wage reductions, and unemployment. It is only by eventually assembling the evidence gleaned by many such studies— hopefully still to come—that we shall arrive at any kind of definitive conclusions about the effects of the Great Depression on British industry.[17]

What is true of industry applies in some measure to agriculture.[18] In the late 1870's bad weather, poor harvests, and cheap grain from the United States combined to create a major crisis for growers of cereals. Yet what proved disastrous for arable farming turned out to be something of a windfall for livestock farming, which benefited by cheaper feed prices. Furthermore, every fall in the price of bread brought with it a greater demand for dairy products and meats from the cities and the new suburbs.

All in all, we may agree with the judgment of William Ashworth in his solid and reliable *Economic History of England, 1870–1939* (1960), that the late Victorians met the problems of the Great Depression far more successfully than has usually been thought. In fact, both Albert H. Imlah, in his *Economic Elements in the Pax Britannica: Studies in Brit-*

[17] For an interim stocktaking, see Alfred E. Musson, "The Great Depression in Britain, 1873–1896: A Reappraisal," *JEcH*, 19:199–228 (June 1959); for other regional studies, see William H. Chaloner, *The Social and Economic Development of Crewe, 1780–1923* (Manchester, Eng., 1950), and Theodore C. Barker and John R. Harris, *A Merseyside Town in the Industrial Revolution: St. Helens, 1750–1900* (Liverpool, Eng., 1954); for other studies of specific industries, see Walter E. Minchinton, *The British Tinplate Industry: A History* (Oxford, 1957), Ludwig F. Haber, *The Chemical Industry during the Nineteenth Century: A Study of the Economic Aspect of Applied Chemistry in Europe and North America* (Oxford, 1958), and Peter G. Hall, *The Industries of London since 1861* (1962).
[18] This was shown by T. W. Fletcher, "The Great Depression of English Agriculture, 1873–1896," *EcHR*, 2d ser., 13:417–432 (April 1960). This view is one of several modifications of Lord Ernle's account of the subject. A sixth edition of his classic work has recently appeared, with new introductions, which are in fact bibliographical essays of great scope: Lord Ernle, *English Farming, Past and Present*, ed. George E. Fussell and Oliver R. McGregor (1961).

ish Foreign Trade in the Nineteenth Century (Cambridge, Mass., 1958), and Samuel B. Saul, in his *Studies in British Overseas Trade, 1870–1914* (Liverpool, 1960), emphasize the resilience of the British economy during the last decades of the nineteenth century and see the continuation of free-trading policies justified by their success.[19]

If, in the sphere of economic history, studies of detail, whether of particular industries or of local conditions, have helped to clarify the picture, this does not mean that wider implications are lacking. Some of these are technological. For information on these one can refer to John Jewkes *et al.*, *The Sources of Invention* (1958), to Charles Singer *et al.*, *A History of Technology, V: The Late Nineteenth Century* (Oxford, 1958), and to the articles in the controversy concerning the check to industrial production in the 1890's. Is this check to be ascribed to the fact that steam and steel techniques were becoming increasingly obsolescent at this time, while the new techniques of electricity, the internal combustion engine, and novel chemical processes did not attain massive application until during and after World War I? Or were technical improvements in iron rather than in steel production more significant in this connection? [20]

The attempt to explain signs of backwardness in British industry takes the historian far beyond the realm of technology and once again into the realms of social structure and psychological attitudes. Habakkuk concludes in his *American and British Technology in the Nineteenth Century: The Search for Labour-Saving Inventions* (Cambridge, Eng., 1962) that what was basically responsible for the lagging of British behind American technological and entrepreneurial performance between 1874 and 1914 was a slower rate of expansion. His analysis touches on the following related factors: the "hemorrhage" of capital and ability from industry and trade into landownership and politics; the loss of drive among the second and third generations of entrepreneurs during the later stages of industrialization; persisting habits and attitudes, engendered by a reliably abundant labor supply, which militated against easy adjustment to mechanization and mass production; the giving way

[19] For a general history of economic growth, see Phyllis Deane and W. A. Cole, *British Economic Growth: Trends and Structure, 1688–1959* (Cambridge, Eng., 1962).

[20] For the former position, see Ernest H. Phelps Brown and S. J. H. Jones, "The Climacteric of the 1890's: A Study in the Expanding Economy," *Oxford Economic Papers*, 4 (October 1952), pp. 266–307; for the latter, see Dennis J. Coppock, "The Climacteric of the 1890's: A Critical Note," *Manchester School of Economic and Social Studies*, 24 (January 1956), pp. 1–31.

of mid-Victorian optimism before the doubts and uncertainties of the final decades of the century; and the prestige value of the professions in siphoning off talent that might otherwise have found a place in industry. Habukkuk does not adhere to the argument that British entrepreneurs were hampered by the absence of scientific skills, but emphasizes instead that recruitment of outstanding and adventurous entrepreneurial talent becomes more difficult in periods of slow growth.

For an assessment of industrial personnel in terms both of scientific education on the one hand and boldness on the other, Charlotte Erickson's *British Industrialists: Steel and Hosiery: 1850–1950* (Cambridge, Eng., 1959) is invaluable. One of her conclusions is that the steel industry lacked bold, young men during a revolutionary phase of its development, between the 1860's and the 1880's. Prior to World War I few men with technical training or a university education were to be found in it.[21] On the other hand, the hosiery industry during this same period showed a greater response to changing industrial circumstances in the matter of social recruitment, successfully casting a much wider net for new talent. In the course of her investigation she shows one of the striking phenomena of social mobility in modern British society, perennially remarked on, but hitherto statistically undocumented: the ascent in social status by means of the appropriate kind of marriage. Steel men, unlike their counterparts in the hosiery industry, sought social prestige rather than wealth in their wives. Many more detailed studies are needed before any sociological generalizations about British society can be scientifically supported. Mrs. Erickson's book, nonetheless, is a good start; its very existence demonstrates the impossibility of putting significant pieces of historical research into neatly labeled boxes, with one or the other "subject" marked on them. For this is not merely a book about two particular industries. It presents essential raw material for anyone wanting to trace the history of the shifting patterns of social class in Britain.

Industrialists not only married into the aristocracy; they increasingly became part of it.[22] Yet, if the composition of the British aristocracy un-

[21] On the general subject, see Stephen F. Cotgrove, *Technical Education and Social Change* (1958).

[22] See Ralph E. Pumphrey, "The Introduction of Industrialists into the British Peerage: A Study in the Adaptation of a Social Institution," *AHR*, 65:1–16 (October 1959); William L. Guttsman, "The Changing Social Structure of the British Political Elite, 1886–1935," *British Journal of Sociology*, 2:122–134 (April 1951); and Harold J. Hanham, "The Sale of Honours in Late Victorian England," *VS*, 3:277–289 (March 1960).

derwent change through the greater frequency of commercial, industrial, and professional creations, and if, as David Spring has pointed out,[23] one can note a change of tone and manners in the 1880's and 1890's from those of the old nobility and gentry to those of the mess, the club, and the stock exchange, it would still be rash to speak too glibly of aristocratic decline in the period under consideration. True, the social and political advantages of landownership declined along with land market values as a result of the agricultural depression.[24] But for at least some landowners the reorganization of county government between 1888 and 1902 meant more rather than less administrative responsibility, and for them the traditional aristocratic ethic of service to the community remained undiminished.[25] Harold J. Hanham, in his *Elections and Party Management: Politics in the Time of Disraeli and Gladstone* (1959), points to the persistence of the local political influence exerted by knights of the shire and by landed and industrial proprietors considerably beyond the second Reform Act and the introduction of the secret ballot. Late nineteenth-century politics, we learn from Hanham's book, should not be too readily postdated according to twentieth-century usages, even though the origins of modern party organization can be found in this period.[26] Many seats remained uncontested in elections. Electoral corruption had by no means disappeared.[27] Local party machinery was on the whole still quite weak, and individual personalities still tended to play the decisive role in local politics.

In turning from the machinery to the substance of politics in this period, we find once again that conventional formulas and old-fashioned

[23] David Spring, "The Role of the Aristocracy in the Late Nineteenth Century," *ibid.*, 4:55–64 (September 1960).

[24] See Francis M. L. Thompson, "The Land Market in the Nineteenth Century," *Oxford Economic Papers*, 9 (October 1957), pp. 285–308; and D. A. Reeder, "The Politics of Urban Leasehold in Late Victorian England," *International Review of Social History*, 6:413–430 (pt. 3, 1961).

[25] See, e.g., Lord Percy of Newcastle, *Some Memories* (1958).

[26] See Robert T. McKenzie, *British Political Parties: The Distribution of Power within the Conservative and Labour Parties* (New York, 1955; 2d ed., New York, 1963), for a good account of the growth of modern party structures. On the caucus, see Trygve R. Tholfsen, "The Origins of the Birmingham Caucus," *Historical Journal*, 2:161–184 (no. 2, 1959). For Liberal organizations, see Barry McGill, "Francis Schnadhorst and Liberal Party Organization," *JMH*, 34:19–39 (March 1962); and Francis H. Herrick, "The Origins of the National Liberal Federation," *ibid.*, 17:116–129 (June 1945). On Conservative political organizations, see E. J. Feuchtwanger, "J. E. Gorst and the Central Organisation of the Conservative Party, 1870–1882," *BIHR*, 32:192–208 (November 1959).

[27] See Cornelius O'Leary, *The Elimination of Corrupt Practices in British Elections, 1868–1911* (Oxford, 1962), for a detailed study of the effects of the Corrupt and Illegal Practices Act of 1883.

lines of investigation have been giving way to fresh approaches. To be sure, there can be no politics without politicians. Biography, therefore, remains one well-traveled road to historical understanding. Some important biographies of major figures have appeared in recent years. Sir Philip Magnus, in *Gladstone: A Biography* (1954; 4th impression with corrections, 1960), treats his subject sympathetically, but does not gloss over Gladstone's errors of judgment. Aubrey L. Kennedy's *Salisbury, 1830–1903: Portrait of a Statesman* (1953) gives us not merely the man of public affairs; it contains an illuminating discussion of Salisbury's religious views and of other important aspects of his character and personality. Roy Jenkins' *Sir Charles Dilke: A Victorian Tragedy* (1958) centers around a thorough treatment of the famous divorce case and raises the possibility that Joseph Chamberlain may have played a sinister role. Robert Rhodes James disposes of "forgetting Goschen" and other legends and does justice both to the emotional and the political appeal of his subject in *Lord Randolph Churchill* (1959). Robert Blake's *Unrepentant Tory: The Life and Times of Andrew Bonar Law, 1858–1923* (New York, 1956) is a brilliant study of the "gilded tradesman," with especially revealing sections on Bonar Law's succession to the leadership of the party and on Tory tariff and Irish policies in the years before World War I. Thomas Jones's *Lloyd George* (Cambridge, Mass., 1951) is both more modest in scope and more reliable than Frank Owen's *Tempestuous Journey: Lloyd George, His Life and Times* (1954). The first volume of Alan Bullock's *The Life and Times of Ernest Bevin, I: Trade Union Leader, 1881–1940* (1960), is particularly good on Bevin's youth and on the conditions that drove him into politics.

Occasionally, a minor but significant figure is also well served. Such is the case with Aretas Akers-Douglas, Tory Chief Whip from 1885, whose role is well described in Eric Alexander, Third Viscount Chilston, *Chief Whip: The Political Life and Times of Aretas Akers-Douglas 1st Viscount Chilston* (1961), and with that "Fabian before the Fabians," A. J. Mundella, in Walter H. G. Armytage, *A. J. Mundella, 1825–1897: The Liberal Background to the Labour Movement* (1951). New source material sometimes comes to light in printed form, as in *The Political Correspondence of Mr. Gladstone and Lord Granville, 1868–1886*, edited by Agatha Ramm (4 vols., Oxford, 1952–61), and in Joseph Chamberlain, *A Political Memoir, 1880–1892*, edited by Christopher H. D. Howard (1953). Good, brief accounts of nineteenth-century Liberalism and Conservatism are to be found, respectively, in John L. Hammond and

Michael R. D. Foot, *Gladstone and Liberalism* (1952), and in Robert B. McDowell, *British Conservatism, 1832–1914* (1959).[28]

Very little political history in the grand manner is being written at the present time, but as long as the political scene contains personalities as enigmatic as those of Disraeli, Herbert Asquith, and Lloyd George, there will be attempts to probe their motives and characters and to analyze their quarrels and friendships. And as long as secrets and mysteries remain a part of politics, it is the historian's job to try to probe them. It is, after all, important for us to know the details of the 1906 election deal between the Liberal party and the Labour Representation Committee [29] just as it is important to learn the inside story of the cabinet resignations of Joseph Chamberlain and the Duke of Devonshire, in 1903.[30] No general analysis of, say, the relationship of political parties to social structure would ever reveal that the Budget of 1909 was in all likelihood not intended deliberately to provoke the House of Lords to reject it, though Lloyd George was by no means unhappy over the prospect of a showdown fight with the upper chamber.[31] No amount of statistical research would tell us that it was Lord Knollys who played a crucial role in the royal involvement in the constitutional crisis of 1910 [32] or that it was Balfour, on his own, who turned down the proposed federalist solution of the Irish problem during the conference held that same year.[33] History may lean on the social sciences; it will never become one.

Without unduly minimizing the significance of "straight" political his-

[28] On the Radicals, see Simon Maccoby, *English Radicalism, 1886–1914* (1953), and *English Radicalism: The End?* (1961). On the Whigs, see Donald Southgate, *The Passing of the Whigs, 1832–1886* (1962).

[29] Frank Bealey, "The Electoral Arrangement between the Labour Representation Committee and the Liberal Party," *JMH*, 28:353–373 (December 1956). For the historical background of this arrangement, see Royden Harrison, "The British Working Class and the General Election of 1868," *International Review of Social History*, 5:424–455 (pt. 3, 1960), and 6:74–109 (pt. 1, 1961).

[30] In Randolph S. Churchill, *Lord Derby, "King of Lancashire": The Official Life of Edward, 17th Earl of Derby, 1865–1948* (1959).

[31] See Roy Jenkins, *Mr. Balfour's Poodle: An Account of the Struggle between the House of Lords and the Government of Mr. Asquith* (1954), for a thorough and lively account of the entire constitutional crisis.

[32] See Harold Nicolson, *King George the Fifth: His Life and Reign* (1952), which is especially good on all constitutional issues. See also Lucy Masterman's lively and revealing "Recollections of David Lloyd George," *History Today*, 9:160–169, 274–281 (March, April 1959); and James Pope-Hennessy, *Lord Crewe, 1858–1945: The Likeness of a Liberal* (1955), for some essential glimpses of the Parliament Act controversy.

[33] See Alfred M. Gollin, *The Observer and J. L. Garvin, 1908–1914: A Study in Great Editorship* (1960). This book is particularly revealing in its treatment of the close political relationship between Balfour and Garvin; it contains a good account of the tariff reformers and their policies, 1911–1912.

tory, it still remains true that the principal questions historians have recently been asking about the politics of this period do seem to be variations upon themes already sounded in this essay: the lag between traditional customs, attitudes, and habits of thought, and changing historical circumstances; the need for regional and local historical investigation as one major means of doing justice to the richness and variety of concrete historical experience; the importance of quantification as a method for breaking down the easy clichés of both social and economic history; and, above all, the way in which historians of this period have been driven to study it, not in terms of isolated and compartmentalized topics, but rather in terms of the changing structure of British society as a whole. The best means of showing these trends in political history is to pose some of the questions that appear to have been of the most urgent concern to recent historians of late nineteenth- and early twentieth-century Britain.

What forces besides the Irish troubles led to the Liberal breakup of the late 1880's? What role, for example, did issues such as the railway rates and land purchase questions play in alarming the propertied classes about the intentions of the Gladstone government, thereby driving them into the Conservative fold? [34] What was the nature of Conservative strength in the country at large? Did workingmen really vote Conservative in large numbers? If so, in what regions? To what extent was it rather the growing numbers of the middle and lower middle classes in the new conurbations that supplied Conservative voting strength? [35] Is the key to the long period of working-class acceptance of middle-class leadership and ideology to be found in the way in which individual industrial towns had dealt with the problem of class relations inherited from the Chartist era? [36] Are there significantly consistent

[34] On this, see Walter H. G. Armytage, A. J. Mundella, 1825–1897: The Liberal Background to the Labour Movement (1951), and "The Railway Rates Question and the Fall of the Third Gladstone Ministry," EHR, 65:18–51 (January 1950), as well as the devastating reply by Philip M. Williams, "Public Opinion and the Railway Rates Question in 1886," EHR, 67:37–73 (January 1952). On the Irish issue as an important factor in driving the propertied classes toward Conservatism, see Robert C. K. Ensor, "Some Political and Economic Interactions in Later Victorian England," TRHS, 4th ser., 31 (1949), pp. 17–28. Asa Briggs, in The History of Birmingham, II: Borough and City, 1865–1938 (1952), a superlative example of urban historiography, shows that even before 1886 several Birmingham businessmen anticipated Chamberlain's break from Radicalism, passing from the offensive to the defensive in politics.

[35] These questions are raised by Gordon L. Goodman, "Liberal Unionism: The Revolt of the Whigs," VS, 3:173–189 (December 1959).

[36] For this view, see Trygve R. Tholfsen, "The Transition to Democracy in Victorian England," International Review of Social History, 6:226–248 (pt. 2, 1961).

differences in the political as well as the economic and cultural atmosphere of two cities such as Manchester and Birmingham?

Just how "socialist" was British socialism? In exploring the intellectual origins of the Labour party, should we assign greater importance to the "socialism of the heart," as represented by Ruskin, Carlyle, and Dickens, and later by William Morris, Robert Blatchford, and Edward Bellamy, than to the "socialism of the head" of H. M. Hyndman and the Fabians? [37] What of the role here of the trade-union movement, both nationally and locally? [38] And that of religion, either directly exerted in the Labour Churches and in the strong Nonconformist influences on the Labour movement, or indirectly, in the way in which this movement fulfilled emotional needs no longer adequately satisfied by institutional religion, especially in the larger industrial cities? [39]

What was the real meaning of the Liberal triumph in the general election of 1906? Was it a triumph for the principle of social reform, or, as Balfour thought, international socialism? Or was it not rather that the voters condemned the new, not the traditional, elements of Conservatism and demanded a return to nineteenth-century Liberal policies of the Gladstonian type? [40] How clearly, in this and other elections of the period, did the electorate perceive the issues supposedly involved? Can one speak of 1906 as a victory for Nonconformity? [41] How many apparently large-scale changes of mind were in fact the result of population shifts and of varying polls? [42] To what extent was the social legislation

[37] The contrasting phrases from R. H. Tawney, *The Webbs in Perspective* (1953); on Hyndman, see Chūshichi Tsuzuki, *H. M. Hyndman and British Socialism*, ed. Henry Pelling (1961); on the Fabians, see A. M. McBriar, *Fabian Socialism and English Politics, 1884–1918* (Cambridge, Eng., 1962), and Margaret Cole, *The Story of Fabian Socialism* (1961). For an appeal for a multiform interpretation, see Hugh L. Beales, "Three Octogenarians," *Political Quarterly*, 32:62–70 (March 1961).

[38] On this aspect, see especially Philip Poirier, *The Advent of the British Labour Party* (New York, 1958).

[39] For this approach, see especially Henry Pelling, *The Origins of the Labour Party, 1880–1900* (New York, 1954), and K. S. Inglis, "The Labour Church Movement," *International Review of Social History*, 3:445–460 (pt. 3, 1958); see also the study of Sheffield by Edward R. Wickham, *Church and People in an Industrial City* (1957).

[40] Frank Bealey and Henry Pelling also stress the importance of regional factors in the results of the 1906 election, for example, Lancashire's particular aversion to tariff reform as a threat to the cotton industry, in their *Labour and Politics, 1900–1906* (1958).

[41] On Liberalism and Nonconformity, see John F. Glaser, "English Nonconformity and the Decline of Liberalism," *AHR*, 63:352–363 (January 1958); see also K. S. Inglis, "English Nonconformity and Social Reform, 1880–1900," *PP*, 10 (April 1958), pp. 73–88.

[42] James Cornford, "The Transformation of Conservatism in the Late Nineteenth Century," *VS*, 7:35–66 (September 1963).

sponsored by the Liberals in the decade before the First World War, in spite of its "socialist" undertones, still in some significant ways imbued with the individualistic premises of the Victorian age? [43] To what extent was it, like the other social legislation of the period under review, not so much a matter of "concession," but rather a social imperative, an essential response exacted by the social consequences of advanced industrialism? [44]

These are only some of the questions that are being asked about recent British political history. It will take some time to find satisfactory answers to them, in large part because many of the detailed regional and statistical studies required for such answers have yet to be undertaken. But if, in one sense, a contraction of the geographical horizon in terms of concentration upon local history is called for, in another and equally important sense the need for an expansion of that horizon is equally urgent. Just as historians are finding the various components of British society to be inextricably involved, one with the other, so also is it becoming increasingly clear that the problems of Ireland, of the Empire, and of foreign policy cannot be dissociated from the problems of British domestic history, social and political. It was Gladstone's Irish land legislation that, even before his conversion to Home Rule, was regarded as capable of future English application—and therefore as a possible threat—by British property owners, whom it helped to unite in defense of Britain's imperial position. It was the Irish issue that brought leading intellectuals such as Henry Sidgwick, Albert Venn Dicey, and Sir Richard Jebb into the Unionist camp.[45] And it was the Irish issue that played the principal role in splitting the Liberal party. Protests against coercion in Ireland were important factors in the rise of the socialist movement in the 1880's. The group of Irish nationalist members of Parliament, acting as a disciplined body under Parnell's brilliant leadership,

---

[43] For a most perceptive discussion of this problem, see Richard M. Titmuss, *Essays on 'the Welfare State'* (New Haven, Conn., 1959) and the same author's introduction to *Lloyd George's Ambulance Wagon: Being the Memoirs of William J. Braithwaite, 1911–1912*, ed. Henry N. Bunbury (1957). See also Brian Abel-Smith, "Social Security," in *Law and Opinion in England in the Twentieth Century*, ed. Morris Ginsberg (1959). In the same volume, G. D. H. Cole, in an essay entitled "The Growth of Socialism," points out that while Lloyd George's reforms were antisocialist, so was the labour movement itself at the time. For a guide to sources, see Percy and Grace Ford, *Breviate of Parliamentary Papers, 1900–1916: The Foundation of the Welfare State* (Oxford, 1957).

[44] H. L. Beales, in *The Making of Social Policy* (1946), puts forth this viewpoint.

[45] John Roach, "Liberalism and the Victorian Intelligentsia," *CHJ*, 13:58–81 (no. 1, 1957).

served as a living example, crying out for imitation by an independent Labour party.[46]

Parnell was able to steer his party into a position in which for some years it controlled the political balance of the House of Commons. Lord Morley remarks in his *Recollections* (2 vols., New York, 1917) that it would require the pen of Tacitus or Sallust or Cardinal de Retz to do justice to such a remarkable character. None of these worthies has been able to heed the call. But Conor Cruise O'Brien's *Parnell and His Party, 1880–90* (Oxford, 1957), succeeds for the first time in penetrating behind the clichés of "mystery" and "inscrutability" to show how Parnell's chameleonlike role was quite consciously adopted by him, under the pressure of political necessity. The book contains a most illuminating discussion of the social composition of the Parnellite parliamentary party and disposes of many legends, including the one immortalized by William Butler Yeats that it was the bishops who caused the great man's fall. Francis S. L. Lyons, in *The Fall of Parnell, 1890–1891* (1960), illuminates that tawdry last act of the tragedy by showing, for instance, that Parnell's overconfidence before the divorce trial was owing to his certainty that William Henry O'Shea was a conniving husband rather than a deceived innocent. Parnell's fall was not the end of the Irish story and its fatal interplay with English politics. The Irish Parliamentary party continued to operate at Westminster, though after the fall of its great leader it lost the unity, the discipline, and, above all, the masterly direction that had made it such a potent force in Westminster politics.[47] For the Unionists, Ulster remained a holy cause, and the lengths to which some of them were prepared to go on its behalf are graphically depicted in Alfred P. Ryan's *Mutiny at the Curragh* (1956).

Lord Salisbury observed that it was Gladstone's fight for Home Rule that awakened the slumbering genius of imperialism.[48] The Irish question was part of the imperial problem as a whole, and the two realms are dramatically linked by that catalytic agent who, more than any other figure, seems to incorporate the principal currents and tendencies of the

[46] See Theodore W. Moody, "Michael Davitt and the British Labour Movement, 1882–1906," *TRHS*, 5th ser., 3 (1953), pp. 53–76.

[47] See Francis S. L. Lyons, *The Irish Parliamentary Party, 1890–1910* (1951), and Eric Strauss, *Irish Nationalism and British Democracy* (New York, 1951).

[48] On the question of the involvement of imperial and domestic issues, see Ronald E. Robinson, "Imperial Problems in British Politics, 1880–1895," *The Cambridge History of the British Empire*, III, *The Empire-Commonwealth, 1870–1919*, ed. Ernest A. Benians *et al.*, 8 vols. (Cambridge, Eng., 1929–59). This volume contains a useful bibliography compiled by A. Taylor Milne.

period within himself—Joseph Chamberlain.[49] For it was he who helped to split the Liberal party over Ireland. And it was he who when, in his attempt to push his more radical domestic policies, he saw himself frustrated by his new Conservative colleagues and outflanked by the growing Labour movement, made the imperial issue his own upon becoming Colonial Secretary in 1895.[50] Through Chamberlain, South Africa became a dominant factor in British politics—a channel, as one writer puts it, through which the mounting tide of British imperialist sentiment could pour.[51] It is now certain that Chamberlain was at the very least an accessory before the fact of the Jameson Raid,[52] that tragicomic prelude to the unexpectedly grim war so vividly depicted in Rayne Kruger's *Good-Bye, Dolly Gray: The Story of the Boer War* (Cambridge, Eng., 1959). If any, it is these years, from the beginning of Chamberlain's tenure at the Colonial Office to the end of the Boer War, that might justly be described as witnessing a "new" imperialism, expansionist in nature and sustained by some popular fervor. Yet, even then, Colonial Office policy was still basically consolidationist. It was Alfred Milner's belligerence rather than any waves of mass enthusiasm that drove Britain into the Boer War.[53]

Behind the imperialism of the 1890's lay a complex web of causation, ranging from economic slumps to the exigencies of European power politics. We now know that it is certainly wrong to speak, as John A. Hobson and Lenin did, of ineluctable pressures for new fields of investment exerted by monopoly capitalism as a primary causal factor.[54] As

[49] On Chamberlain, see James L. Garvin, *The Life of Joseph Chamberlain*, 4 vols. (1932–51), especially IV, *1901–1903: At the Height of His Power*, completed by Julian Amery. For an important corrective to Garvin's summary of the Unauthorized Programme, see Christopher H. D. Howard, "Joseph Chamberlain and the 'Unauthorized Programme,'" *EHR*, 65:477–491 (October 1950).

[50] See Peter Fraser, "The Liberal Unionist Alliance: Chamberlain, Hartington, and the Conservatives, 1886–1904," *EHR*, 77:53–75 (January 1962), on how lengthy the process was before Chamberlain actually made up his mind to throw in his lot with the Conservatives, after his secession.

[51] Eric Stokes, "Great Britain and Africa: The Myth of Imperialism," *History Today*, 10:554–563 (August 1960).

[52] On this complex question, see Ethel Drus, "The Question of Complicity in the Jameson Raid," *EHR*, 68:582–593 (October 1953), and "A Report on the Papers of Joseph Chamberlain Relating to the Jameson Raid and the Inquiry," *BIHR*, 25:33–62 (May 1952); also Jean van der Poel, *The Jameson Raid* (Cape Town, 1951), and C. M. Woodhouse, "The Missing Telegrams and the Jameson Raid," *History Today*, 12:395–404, 506–514 (June, July 1962).

[53] See Eric Stokes, "Milnerism," *Historical Journal*, 5:47–60 (no. 1, 1962).

[54] See D. K. Fieldhouse, "Imperialism: An Historical Revision," *EcHR*, 2d ser., 14:187–209 (December 1961); Richard Koebner, "The Concept of Economic Imperialism," *ibid.*, 2:1–29 (August 1949); Koebner and Helmut D. Schmidt, *Im-*

opposed to some long-accepted interpretations of the genesis of Victorian imperialism, we also know that its "new" version was both late in coming and short lived. In convincing fashion, John Gallagher and Ronald Robinson, in "The Imperialism of Free Trade" (*EcHR*, 2d ser., 6:1–15 [August 1953]), have argued that rather than looking at British imperial policy in the course of the nineteenth century in terms of a long period of "anti-imperialism," followed in due course from about 1870 by a period of "imperialism," we ought to regard that policy throughout as a function of the need for integrating new regions into an expanding economy. This was to be accomplished preferably without force and without occupation. Yet, if circumstances required it, the use of either or both was sanctioned. The same two authors point out elsewhere [55] the paradox that the true founder of the British African Empire was none other than the so-called "little Englander," William Ewart Gladstone, who stumbled into Egypt in 1882 and remained there in bondage, unable to get out. A weakening Turkey and an increasingly powerful Russian threat to the Dardanelles meant that Cairo inevitably replaced Constantinople as the key to the vital route to India. As a corollary, Britain had to stay in Egypt, since the old and tried policy of leaving stable and trusted native governments in charge would no longer work in an age of burgeoning African nationalism. This meant that the entire Nile Basin had to be protected against any threatened encroachments by the other European powers. From 1888 on this need began to dominate British policy in Africa.

By the subtitle of Robinson and Gallagher's *Africa and the Victorians, The Official Mind of Imperialism,* the authors point out that what

---

perialism: The Story and Significance of a Political Word, 1840–1960 (Cambridge, Eng., 1964). Nicholas Mansergh's essay on "Imperialism: The Years of European Ascendancy," in Chapters in Western Civilization, edited by the Contemporary Civilization Staff of Columbia College, Columbia University, 3d ed., 2 vols. in 3 (New York, 1961–62), is excellent. On the specific problem of investments, see J. H. Lenfant, "Great Britain's Capital Formation, 1865–1914," Economica, 18:151–168 (May 1951), and Alexander K. Cairncross, Home and Foreign Investment, 1870–1913: Studies in Capital Accumulation (Cambridge, Eng., 1953), which shows that most of exported capital went to countries like the United States, Canada, Australia, India, and Argentina, rather than to the new possessions. For a critically modified restatement of the Hobson-Lenin thesis, see John Strachey, The End of Empire (1959); see also Bernard Semmel, Imperialism and Social Reform: English Social-Imperial Thought, 1895–1914 (Cambridge, Mass., 1960), for an illuminating study, especially good on the Fabians and the Liberal Imperialists, of social imperialist ideas and their influence in Britain.

[55] Ronald Robinson and John Gallagher, with Alice Denny, *Africa and the Victorians: The Official Mind of Imperialism* (1961).

moved statesmen to act in one way or the other in Africa were not necessarily the realities of the situation there, but rather the analysis of that situation made in Whitehall. Thus an understanding of the workings of the "official mind," the mind of the British ruling class, with its prejudices and traditions, its notions of duty and of the national interest, is crucial in any attempt to comprehend imperial policy during the late nineteenth century. In spite of the much-touted arrival of democracy in the shape of mass electorates and the beginnings of modern party organization, that policy was still formulated in the main by an inner circle at the top, whose views of what was best for Britain transcended party differences and public opinion. Archibald P. Thornton, in his trenchant and witty *The Imperial Idea and Its Enemies: A Study in British Power* (1959), supplies a vivid account not only of the bylaws and membership of this "club," but also of the sources from which the loyalties of those who actually built the Empire derived. These men were individualists and men of strong character. Yet one should not underestimate the enormous influence of the institutions and groups that helped to cement their beliefs, attitudes, and prejudices: the public schools, Balliol under Benjamin Jowett, Garnet Wolseley's staff ring, Milner's "Kindergarten." [56]

What was true of the making of imperial policy was true of the making of foreign policy. Whether the substantive problem at hand was charting a "new course" for Britain away from the Triple Alliance and toward the *Entente*,[57] or, subsequently, engaging in military staff talks with the French, policy making remained for a surprisingly long time the preserve of a small group of aristocratic statesmen, not, on the whole, subject to party controversy or to popular control by means of the House of Commons.[58] Foreign Secretaries became very discreet in-

[56] Some proconsuls and generals have been well served by recent biographers, others less well. In the first category belong Godfrey Elton, *General Gordon* (1954); Philip Magnus, *Kitchener: Portrait of an Imperialist* (1958); Leonard Moseley, *Curzon: The End of an Epoch* (1960); and David James, *Lord Roberts* (1954). Milner still awaits an impartial biographer, though he has lately received much sympathetic appreciation from Evelyn Wrench, *Alfred Lord Milner: The Man of No Illusions, 1854–1925* (1958); Vladimir Halperin, *Lord Milner and the Empire* (1952); and Edward Crankshaw, *The Forsaken Idea: A Study of Viscount Milner* (1952). The singer of Empire has been more fortunate; see Charles E. Carrington, *Rudyard Kipling: His Life and Work* (1955), and Noel Annan, "Kipling's Place in the History of Ideas," *VS*, 3:323–348 (June 1960).

[57] See Lillian M. Penson, "The New Course in English Foreign Policy, 1892–1902," *TRHS*, 4th ser., 25 (1943), pp. 121–138, and "Obligations by Treaty: Their Place in British Foreign Policy, 1898–1914," in *Studies in Diplomatic History and Historiography, in Honour of G. P. Gooch, C.H.*, ed. A. O. Sarkissian (1961); see also Christopher Howard, "Splendid Isolation," *History*, 47:32–41 (February 1962).

[58] See Frans Gosses, *The Management of British Foreign Policy before the First*

deed at question time, conceiving of their role as representing the national interest, immune from domestic political controversy. Independent members became less powerful as party machines became more so, and with a great many Radical members of Parliament swallowing their distaste for the drift of foreign policy in the decade before the First World War for the sake of domestic legislation in which they had a bigger stake, a decided lessening of the tradition of dissent in matters of foreign policy took place.[59] Furthermore, fewer Blue Books on foreign affairs were published. Thus, somewhat paradoxically, as Parliament became increasingly democratic, it exerted less rather than more control over foreign policy.

On the one hand, this trend formed part of a general tendency that saw a decline of the power of Parliament in relation to that of the cabinet and the bureaucracy,[60] and, within the House of Commons, greater control by ministers in the interests of a dominant parliamentary majority, with the rights and powers of private members reduced to relative insignificance.[61] On the other hand, selected members of the press often found themselves better informed on vital matters of policy than the House of Commons: witness Grey's irregular channel to John Alfred Spender of the *Westminster Gazette*, or Fisher's feeding of cabinet secrets to James Louis Garvin of *The Observer*.[62]

Whether any of the foregoing factors really played a decisive role in

World War, Especially during the Period 1880–1914 (Leiden, 1948), for an excellent treatment. Gosses, by the way, exonerates Edward Grey from any intentional deception of his cabinet colleagues in the matter of Anglo-French staff talks, of which the cabinet did not learn until 1912. For a vivid popular account of Britain's entry into the war in 1914, see Barbara Tuchman, *The Guns of August* (New York, 1962).

[59] See A. J. P. Taylor, *The Trouble Makers: Dissent over Foreign Policy, 1792–1939* (1957).

[60] Gosses, *Management of Foreign Policy*, is especially good on this. On the specific question of defense and war policy making, see John Ehrman, *Cabinet Government and War, 1890–1940* (Cambridge, Eng., 1958), and Franklyn A. Johnson, *Defence by Committee: The British Committee of Imperial Defence, 1885–1959* (New York, 1960).

[61] See Peter Fraser, "The Growth of Ministerial Control in the Nineteenth Century House of Commons," *EHR*, 75:444–463 (July 1960).

[62] See Gollin, *The Observer and Garvin*. On Spender and the *Westminster Gazette*, see Michael R. D. Foot, *British Foreign Policy since 1898* (1956). On other aspects of the press, see *The History of the Times: The Twentieth Century Test, 1884–1912*, 4 vols. (1935–52), III; and Reginald Pound and Geoffrey Harmsworth, *Northcliffe* (1959). On Fisher and the navy, see the following works by Arthur J. Marder: *Fear God and Dread Nought: The Correspondence of Admiral of the Fleet Lord Fisher of Kilverstone*, 3 vols. (Cambridge, Mass., 1952–59) and *From the Dreadnought to Scapa Flow: The Royal Navy in the Fisher Era, 1904–1919*, I, *The Road to War, 1904–1914*, 2 vols. (New York, 1961).

bringing Britain into the First World War remains open to doubt. So does George Dangerfield's conjecture, put forward in what is still the most readable book about the period, *The Strange Death of Liberal England* (1935), that the combination of suffragette violence, Unionist intransigence over Ulster, and labour unrest might have produced some sort of internal explosion had not the outbreak of war come when it did. One must remember, for instance, that, as Ernest Phelps Brown points out in his important book, *The Growth of British Industrial Relations: A Study from the Standpoint of 1906–1914* (1959), labour strife during the years just before the war was confined to the unskilled and to the miners and railway workers, while other sectors of labour remained undisturbed to a remarkable degree.[63] It may well be that, as Raymond W. Postgate remarks in his *Life of George Lansbury* (1951), it was the very security of the period that made its extravagant aspects possible: "When the ice is many inches thick, skaters may caper as wildly as they will" (pp. 106–107).

Yet we might well ask: security for whom? A great gulf yawned between the brilliant life of the court, of society, of London literary coteries—the world of Sergei Diaghilev, "the Souls," the *Merry Widow*, John Singer Sargent and sables and ten-course dinners, of Eddie Marsh and the Georgians—and the world of Joseph Ashby and his fellow villagers at Tysoe, or the world of that third of the population of York whom Seebohm Rowntree's survey had found to be living in poverty.[64] And in between lay other worlds, movingly recalled in some recent memorable recollections. There was the leisurely world of university life, of friendships and gossip and ideas, conjured up in Sir Lawrence Jones's *An Edwardian Youth*, (1956), in Leonard Woolf's *Sowing: An Autobiography of the Years 1880–1904* (1960), and in Gwen Raverat's minor classic, *Period Piece: A Cambridge Childhood* (1952). And there was

---

[63] See also Eric J. Hobsbawm's point in "Twentieth Century British Politics: A Review Article," *PP*, 9 (April 1957), pp. 100–108, to the effect that the biographies and memoirs of middle-class politicians in this period (1910–1914) show them surprisingly unpreoccupied by dangers from this side of labour.

[64] On the court, see Virginia Cowles, *Edward VII and His Circle* (1956); and also James Pope-Hennessy's evocative, *Queen Mary, 1867–1953* (1960); Frederick Ponsonby, *Recollections of Three Reigns* (1951). On London literary and cultural life in the years before the First World War, see Osbert Sitwell's classic treatment in *Left Hand, Right Hand!* (Boston, Mass., 1944), *The Scarlet Tree* (Boston, Mass., 1946), and *Great Morning!* (Boston, Mass., 1947); see also Christopher Hassall, *Edward Marsh, Patron of the Arts: A Biography* (1959); on Rowntree, see Asa Briggs, *Social Thought and Social Action: A Study of the Work of Seebohm Rowntree, 1871–1954* (1961).

the world of the Manchester "cottontots," their ideas rigidly set into the mold of economic individualism, their way of life combining hard work, charitable effort, and cultivated leisure, a world unforgettably re-created in Lady Katharine Chorley's *Manchester Made Them* (1950).[65] Here once again, as in so many other realms of historical investigation, easy generalizations and sacrosanct clichés tend to lose their force when confronted with the concrete variety of life actually experienced. At the risk of underlining the obvious, it should also be stressed that contemporary source materials, especially when they are of high literary quality, are still the best means of transport into the midst of the period. We cannot afford to do without Beatrice Webb's *My Apprenticeship* (1926), George and Weedon Grossmith's *Diary of a Nobody* (1892), Charles F. G. Masterman's *Condition of England* (1909), or the novels of H. G. Wells, particularly *The New Machiavelli* (1911), *Ann Veronica* (1909), and *Tono Bungay* (1909).

Only by steeping ourselves in the actual life of the period will we be able to avoid the treacherous pitfalls of glib categorizations. Terms like "Late Victorian" and "Edwardian," for instance, inevitably set off chain reactions of associations in our minds, destined in the end to mislead rather than to guide us.[66] The late 1880's and the early 1890's certainly mark a major watershed of modern British history. One may draw the line at the first Home Rule Bill, at Keir Hardie's entry into Parliament, or at the Local Government Act of 1894. Or one may draw it at the introduction of electricity, the gas engine, and the telephone. But value judgments, too, are involved. The word "late" bespeaks autumn and dusk, ripeness and decay. And one thinks of dandyism, decadence, and the Yellow Book [67] or of that decline from godliness and good learning to militant athleticism in the public schools which David Newsome has delineated,[68] forgetting the fact that this was also the period which, in the sphere of public morality, saw considerable improvements in the

[65] For some very different aspects of Manchester life in this period, see Neville Cardus, *Autobiography* (1947).

[66] On periodization, see Maurice B. Reckitt, "When Did Victorianism End?" *VS*, 1:268–271 (June 1958). On manners and fashions, see John Gloag, *Victorian Comfort: A Social History of Design from 1830 to 1900* (1961), and Alison Adburgham, *A "Punch" History of Manners and Modes, 1841–1940* (1961). Also James Laver, *Victorian Vista* (1954), and *Edwardian Promenade* (1958).

[67] See Ellen Moers, *The Dandy: Brummell to Beerbohm* (1960), and Katherine L. Mix, *A Study in Yellow: The "Yellow Book" and Its Contributors* (Lawrence, Kan., 1960).

[68] David Newsome, *Godliness and Good Learning: Four Studies on a Victorian Ideal* (1961).

conduct of elections, and in which there was an increasing awareness that society as a whole rather than individuals bore collective responsibility for social ills.

One's judgment of decline, just as one's judgment of the entire period under review, depends on one's angle of vision. Thus, on the one hand, it makes just as much (if not more) sense for us to regard that period not so much in terms of a partial triumph of democracy, but in terms of the remarkably successful defense in depth put up against its total triumph by the governing classes and groups. On the other hand, it now seems eminently reasonable to regard the *fin de siècle* as a beginning rather than as an end.[69] Walter E. Houghton's *The Victorian Frame of Mind, 1830–1870* (New Haven, Conn., 1957) has recently taught us how much struggle and heart searching lay even behind the so-called normalcy of the Victorian intellectual equilibrium. Yet, granted that in Europe, as well as in Britain, the closing years of the century witnessed an inordinate amount of skepticism about heretofore widely accepted shibboleths—social, moral, and scientific—this fact in itself should give that "decadent" period a standing far more important than that of merely constituting the tag end of a heroic age. In those doubts and questions of traditional values we can now see the seedbed of our own problems and concerns. Those decades are closer to us in spirit than the ones that went before.

This, admittedly, is looking at the past with the eyes of the present—a perilous practice, we are told. But it is one that holds rewards as well as perils. The judicious historian should be able to guard against the latter, while garnering the former. It is because the British working classes today are no longer regarded as useful, dangerous, or charitable objects, but as an integral part of their society, that the study of labour history is flourishing, that no self-respecting historian would dream of writing the history of nineteenth-century Britain without devoting proper attention to the struggles and aspirations, the way of life and the culture of the laboring population.[70] It is because we are currently concerned about the successes and failures of the welfare state and of mass communications that we have become particularly interested in the origins of

[69] On the 1890's, see *Edwardians and Late Victorians*, ed. Richard Ellman (New York, 1960), and Ian Fletcher, "The 1890's: A Lost Decade," *VS*, 4:345–354 (June 1961).

[70] On the cultural aspects, see Hoggart, *Uses of Literacy*. On the history of the working classes in general, see the *Bulletin* of the Society for the Study of Labour History (Sheffield), of which the first issue appeared in the autumn of 1960.

both.[71] The social scientists have taught us that in the study of an advanced industrial society, phenomena such as the growth of a white-collar class, of conurbations, of bureaucracy, and of a consumer oriented economy cut across both capitalist and socialist conceptions of property, and, even more important, political party differences.[72] It is because we have learned this that we tend today to be less concerned with speeches, slogans, and manifestoes, and more with changes in demographic patterns and in the structure of industries and occupations, and with the relationship of these changes to value systems, moral attitudes, and social habits.[73]

[71] See, e.g., David Roberts, *Victorian Origins of the British Welfare State* (New Haven, Conn., 1960), and Charles L. Mowat, "The Approach to the Welfare State in Great Britain," *AHR*, 58:55–63 (October 1952); above all, see Asa Briggs, "The Welfare State in Historical Perspective," *Archives Européennes de Sociologie*, 2:221–258 (no. 2, 1961). On mass culture and communications, see Raymond Williams, *Culture and Society, 1780–1950* (1958) and *The Long Revolution* (1961); see also Richard D. Altick, "The Sociology of Authorship: The Social Origins, Education, and Occupations of 1,100 British Writers, 1800–1935," *Bulletin of the New York Public Library*, 66:389–404 (June 1962).

[72] See H. Stuart Hughes, "The Historian and the Social Scientist," *AHR*, 66:20–46 (October 1960).

[73] The following books, which have appeared since the publication of the above article in 1963, are of special interest. They are listed alphabetically: Philip Bagwell, *The Railwaymen: The History of the National Union of Railwaymen* (1963); Asa Briggs, *Victorian Cities* (1963); Violet Bonham Carter, *Winston Churchill: An Intimate Portrait* (New York, 1965); H. A. C. Clegg, Alan Fox, and A. F. Thompson, *A History of British Trade Unions since 1889*, I, *1889–1910* (Oxford, 1964); A. O. J. Cockshut, *The Unbelievers* (1964); L. P. Curtis, Jr., *Coercion and Conciliation in Ireland, 1880–1892* (Princeton, N.J., 1963); Frances Donaldson, *The Marconi Scandal* (1962); *Edwardian England, 1901–1914*, ed. Simon Nowell-Smith (1964); James Fergusson, *The Curragh Incident* (New York and London, 1964); Alfred M. Gollin, *Proconsul in Politics: A Study of Lord Milner in Opposition and in Power* (1964); J. A. S. Grenville, *Lord Salisbury and Foreign Policy: The Close of the Nineteenth Century* (1964); W. L. Guttsman, *The British Political Elite* (1963); Christopher Hassall, *Rupert Brooke* (1964); R. F. V. Heuston, *Lives of the Lord Chancellors, 1885–1940* (Oxford, 1964); K. S. Inglis, *Churches and the Working Classes in Victorian England* (1963); Robert Rhodes James, *Rosebery: A Biography of Archibald Philip, Fifth Earl of Rosebery* (1963); Roy Jenkins, *Asquith* (1964): Royston Lambert, *Sir John Simon, 1816–1904* (1963); Joseph Lehmann, *The Model Major-General: A Biography of Field-Marshal Lord Wolseley* (Boston, Mass., 1964); J. G. Lockhart and C. M. Woodhouse, *Rhodes* (1963): Elizabeth Longford, *Victoria R.I.* (1964); A. M. McBriar, *Fabian Socialism and English Politics, 1884–1918* (Cambridge, Eng., 1962); Philip Magnus, *Edward VII* (1964); G. W. Monger, *The End of Isolation: British Foreign Policy, 1900–1907* (1963); Kenneth Morgan, *Wales in British Politics* (Cardiff, 1963); Donald Read, *The English Provinces* (1964); Melvin Richter, *The Politics of Conscience: T. H. Green and His Age* (1964); Giles St. Aubyn, *The Royal George, 1819–1904: The Life of H. R. H. Prince George Duke of Cambridge* (New York, 1964); R. T. Shannon, *Gladstone and the Bulgarian Agitation, 1876* (1963); Peter Stansky, *Ambitions and Strategies: The Struggle for the Leadership of the Liberal Party in the 1890's* (Oxford, 1964); and F. M. L. Thompson, *English Landed Society in the Nineteenth Century* (1963).

Some Recent Writings
on Twentieth-Century Britain

✧

HENRY R. WINKLER

MOST OF the twentieth-century history of Great Britain is still too recent for any but the most tentative of assessments. Yet much that is of value is being published and many of the guide lines for further inquiry are being suggested in the works which ceaselessly pour from the presses. The contemporary historian makes up in part for what he lacks in perspective by his opportunity to sense and even to test the atmosphere of the times about which he writes. Often he can identify the issues and developments which men of his period considered significant and, while the passage of time may prove their judgments to have been mistaken, he can at least offer future scholars something of a self-portrait of the generations with whom he is concerned.

For Britain in the twentieth century, certain major trends stand out. The transformation of the machinery of government, particularly as it is revealed in the history of the monarchy, the civil service, and the political parties, is clearly a prime area for study. The development of the cabinet system, the nature of British elections, and the shifting structure of local government are likewise fundamental to an understanding of government in this period. Parallel with changes in the structure of government have gone, of course, changes in its role. Above all, the emergence of the welfare state has required a thorough reassessment of the history of social conditions, the expansion of the social services, and the changing patterns of social reforms. Still another phenomenon of the most marked significance has been the rise of Labour and the decline of Liberalism as a major force in British political life.

In a period when much of what has transpired in Britain has been the result of two major wars, the civil and military impact of conflict on the

[Reprinted from JMH, 32:32–47 (March 1960).]

nation looms large. Equally vital, and closely connected with the impact of war, are the problems raised by the varying pattern and scale of the economic life of the country. Beyond this, the position of a Britain which until 1945 remained at the very center of international affairs has made imperative the analysis of the foreign policies and diplomacy pursued by successive governments over the years. And finally, since Britain's recent history, like that of any other nation, has been shaped by the men who directed her destinies, evaluation of her leaders has, of course, attracted the attention of observers who seek to understand that history.

For the student of these various aspects of twentieth-century history, certain problems are posed. The researcher into constitutional and economic questions has the great advantage that his basic sources are largely public, but for the student of diplomatic or military history—unless he be an "official" historian—the archives remain closed. The publication of massive collections of documents, while indispensable, hardly serves as a substitute for access to all the materials. Beyond this, the sheer volume of the outpourings of the printing presses makes the physical task of the historian backbreaking indeed. He confronts an overwhelming mass of memoirs, reports, special monographs, and, even more, special apologia, and must, presumably, examine the mountains of press and periodical materials which have not yet disappeared into the limbo of the ephemeral. In brief, his problem is often that of a scarcity of certain basic sources in a vast sea of white paper and printer's ink.

Of prime importance in the overwhelming flood of printed materials are the Parliamentary Papers. Students of contemporary Britain have at times been seriously inconvenienced and sometimes frustrated by their enormous bulk and range of subjects. Accordingly they will be more than grateful for the two guides prepared by a team of scholars at the University College, Southampton, under the editorship of P. and G. Ford.[1] While all papers dealing with foreign and diplomatic questions have been excluded, these "breviates" of the Parliamentary Papers, along with other departmental materials, are an indispensable key to the reports of royal commissions and other committees of inquiry in the fields of constitutional, economic, financial, and social policy, and of legal administration.

For the entire first half of the century, Alfred F. Havighurst's *Twentieth Century Britain* (New York and Evanston, 1962) is a most useful

---

[1] *A Breviate of Parliamentary Papers, 1917–1939* (Oxford, 1951); *A Breviate of Parliamentary Papers, 1900–1916* (Oxford, 1957).

introduction. For the first time we have a succinct and balanced general account through which to approach the study of Britain in the present century. Havighurst has reflected on his materials and presents his conclusions with imagination and intelligence. His central thread is political, but he is as convincing in analyzing the economic environment as he is informative in discussing literary trends. No other book published in the last half decade will be quite as useful in introducing students to the main outlines of British history in the recent past. D. C. Somervell's *British Politics since 1900* (New York, 1950) is an informal, sprightly assessment of parties and political leaders, heavily weighted against the Labour party. Since it shows little evidence of any wrestling with the voluminous sources available for exploitation, the serious student is not likely to learn anything new from its entertaining pages. Written from almost a diametrically opposite viewpoint, Keith Hutchison's *Decline and Fall of British Capitalism* (New York, 1950) serves as an excellent journalistic supplement to Somervell. Hutchison attempts unassumingly to examine the transformation of British social life over a span of some seventy years. His political judgments, like those of Somervell, tend to color his treatment of the historical sweep of events, but he is markedly effective in outlining the economic tangles of the 1920's and 1930's.

For the years before 1914, no outstanding synthesis has gathered together the fruits of recent special studies. The works of Élie Halévy [2] and R. C. K. Ensor,[3] both published before 1940, continue as the standard accounts. Halévy's predominantly political survey of the period from 1895 to 1914—a period with which he had little sympathy—is perhaps disappointing in comparison with his seminal treatment of early nineteenth-century England, but Ensor's contribution to the *Oxford History* stands out as a model description of a rapidly changing society.

By all odds the most useful single volume for the period after World War I is C. L. Mowat's *Britain between the Wars, 1918–1940* (1955). Thorough and meticulous, it is a most knowledgeable summary of the findings of the first generation of scholars—economists, sociologists, political scientists, as well as historians—to deal with the years of disap-

---

[2] *Histoire du peuple anglais au xixe siècle: Epilogue, 1895–1914*, I, *Les impérialistes au pouvoir, 1895–1905* (Paris, 1926) and II, *Vers la démocratie sociale et vers la guerre, 1905–1914* (Paris, 1932). There is a penetrating assessment of Halévy in C. C. Gillispie, "The Work of Elie Halévy; a Critical Appreciation," *JMH*, 22: 232–249 (September 1950). See also J. B. Brebner, "Elie Halévy" in *Some Modern Historians of Britain*, ed. H. Ausubel, J. B. Brebner, and E. M. Hunt (New York, 1951), pp. 235–254.

[3] *England, 1870–1914* (Oxford, 1936).

pointment which terminated in the achievement of 1940. Mowat does not conceal his tendency to be more critical of the Tories, particularly in matters of foreign policy, than of their Labour opponents. Yet his sympathies do not interfere with a balanced and consistent presentation which must take its place with Halévy and Ensor until the lengthening perspective of time and the appearance of additional documentation prepare the way for the revisionist accounts of the future. Mowat's full-dress study may now be supplemented by A. J. P. Taylor's brilliant addition to the *Oxford History of England*. Written with Taylor's familiar flair for the telling epigram and the unexpected conclusion, *English History 1914–1945* (Oxford, 1965) is a masterly account of the steady decline of British fortunes in the bitter years that began and ended in the two world wars. As disrespectful as ever of the sacred cows of popular wisdom, he has nevertheless produced a sound, occasionally uneven, but often exciting, history, which is, moreover, fun to read as many such surveys distinctly are not. And he has added a bibliographical essay which is a model of informed selectivity, marred only by a number of misspelled names. To these major works should be added Robert Graves's and Alan Hodge's *The Long Week-end* (1940). Dealing with the period between 1918 and 1939, it still offers, despite the too frequent flippancy of its tone, the best general insight currently available into the social history of the times. Covering much the same ground are three volumes, each of which attempts an impressionistic survey of the 1920's and 1930's. *The Baldwin Age*, edited by John Raymond (1960), consists of a series of essays on various phases of English life, some of them provocative but thin, as in the case of A. J. P. Taylor's discussion of "Confusion on the Left," others disappointingly dull as in Robert Blake's unsuccessful special pleading in "Baldwin and the Right." More interesting, if sometimes a bit idiosyncratic, is Ronald Blythe's *The Age of Illusion*,[4] which looks at such diverse phenomena as the notorious gambols of the Rector of Stiffkey and the tortured legend-building of T. E. Lawrence with sophisticated penetration and a light, but revealing, wit. In the same genre, but somewhat more restricted—and less satisfactory—is William McElwee's *Britain's Locust Years 1918–1940* (1962), which concentrates largely on major political and economic developments in the interwar years.

The monarchy, the civil service, and the system of political parties are the major bulwarks of continuity and stability in Britain's twentieth-

---

[4] *The Age of Illusion. England in the Twenties and Thirties, 1919–1940* (1963).

century parliamentary government. Yet each has undergone considerable change since the beginning of the century. For the monarchy, that change is perhaps best symbolized by the contrast between the public personality of Edward VII at the start and of George VI at the end of our period. Some additions have been made in recent years to the studies of Edward VII by Lee and Benson. Virginia Cowles's light-hearted *Edward VII and His Circle* (1956) is an intelligent and lively though rather limited popular work, and Sir Philip Magnus has succeeded admirably in doing what Miss Cowles did not really attempt. He makes his study of the king [5] interesting not only because of the peccadilloes of Edward's not-so-private life, but also because of the significance of Edward's public career. Avoiding the official reticences of Lee and Benson, Magnus manages to tell not quite all with taste and with a reasonably modern search for the psychological clues to his protagonist's behavior. While "angry young men" have lately fulminated against the "Establishment," the monarchy as an institution has hardly been affected by the criticism. Two recent lives, of George V by Harold Nicolson and of George VI by J. W. Wheeler-Bennett, tend to demonstrate why. Both Nicolson and Wheeler-Bennett have used the royal archives to the full and both have made solid contributions. Wheeler-Bennett's account,[6] generally speaking, reflects the solid, if somewhat dull, virtues of his subject. Nicolson's study,[7] on the other hand, while it is not concerned primarily with the personality of George V, as is John Gore's memoir,[8] is an absorbing evaluation of a public career which strengthened the monarchy and established its importance in the parliamentary system more firmly than ever before. Altogether, this is one of the outstanding political biographies of the century, not the least because it is written with wit and grace.

The rapid development of effective and disciplined party machines is perhaps the distinguishing characteristic of Britain's recent political life. The party system has been examined in some detail by an ex-M.P., Ivor Bulmer-Thomas.[9] In an attempt to do what Moisei Ostrogorski did for British parties a half century ago, Bulmer-Thomas surveys their history, analyzes party machinery, and then takes up the relations of the parties with such institutions as the press and the churches. Systematic, clear,

[5] *King Edward the Seventh* (1964).
[6] *The Life of George VI* (1958).
[7] *King George the Fifth; His Life and Reign* (1952).
[8] *King George V* (1949).
[9] *The Party System in Great Britain* (1953).

and up-to-date, this work tends somehow to be formal and dull. If any recent volume can be compared with Ostrogorski or Abbott Lawrence Lowell it is rather R. T. McKenzie's *British Political Parties*.[10] Although contemporary in its focus and sometimes unsatisfactory in its treatment of historical details, McKenzie's pioneer study uses the historical experience of Conservative and Labour parties effectively in developing his theme that though the two parties appear so radically different in their makeup their practical working is very similar. His conclusion that authority is more complete in the Labour party, and less in the Conservative, than either claims is somewhat exaggerated, but it finds some confirmation in a monograph by Byrum E. Carter [11] which, while not so politically sophisticated as McKenzie's, nevertheless is a fresh approach to the recent evolution of the office of prime minister.

As for the civil service, it is noteworthy that so little was written about it before 1940. The centenary of the Northcote-Trevelyan report in 1953 brought out a rash of popular discussions, few of them as informative as O. R. McGregor's earlier *Political Quarterly* article [12] which analyzed changes in the civil service since the report. Even before this, in the forties, two substantial studies appeared. Miss E. W. Cohen's *Growth of the British Civil Service* (1940) is the best all-round survey, clear and informative on the historical development of the civil service from 1780 to 1939. *The Higher Civil Service of Great Britain* by H. E. Dale (Oxford, 1941) contains a good deal of material, but is marred by an uncritical complacency which tends to underestimate the nature of the problems confronted by this group. In addition, a contemporary sociological inquiry, R. K. Kelsall's *Higher Civil Servants in Britain* (1955) is of real value to historians in working out the origins and characteristics of this occupational stratum.

The shifting pattern of parliamentary power has elicited a cry of alarm [13] from G. W. Keeton of the London Institute of World Affairs. Pointing to the growing ascendancy of the executive over parliament and the regular courts in the twentieth century, Keeton views the development as threatening an approach to "despotism." Unrestrained and overstated, Keeton's analysis nevertheless raises an issue of paramount

---

[10] *British Political Parties: The Distribution of Power within the Conservative and Labour Parties* (N.Y. 1955; 2d ed., 1963).

[11] *The Office of Prime Minister* (Princeton, N.J., 1956).

[12] "Civil Servants and the Civil Service: 1850–1950," *Political Quarterly*, 22:154–163 (April–June 1951).

[13] *The Passing of Parliament* (1952).

importance. Its Cassandra-like warnings may usefully be tempered by consulting John Eaves's *Emergency Power and the Parliamentary Watchdog*.[14] This well-balanced and thoughtful American study of the years after 1939 thoroughly documents Commons' important employment of questioning to control the legislative activities of the executive and its use of vast emergency powers. Equally fundamental is Herbert Morrison's *Government and Parliament* (Oxford, 1954) the considered judgment of a veteran House of Commons man who loves parliament and sees little reason for significant change. The standard manual is Sir Ivor Jennings' erudite *Parliament*,[15] which is descriptive rather than comparative and critical, although from time to time the author's anti-Conservative bias shows through. Also authoritative, if not nearly so interesting to read, is P. A. Bromhead's study of *The House of Lords and Contemporary Politics, 1911–1957* (1958). In contrast is the colorfully titled *Mr. Balfour's Poodle*,[16] Roy Jenkins' well-told story of the struggle between the House of Lords and the Liberal government before 1914.

The vast expansion of central government since 1900 has been a historical fact of prime importance. The sheer growth in the number of persons employed by government agencies is the most obvious measure of this expansion and a magnificent job of collating and analyzing the statistics which document this growth has been done by Moses Abramowitz and Vera Eliasberg.[17] Somewhat more literary in its approach is an essay by W. A. Robson [18] which concentrates on the period after 1939, while a later article by H. R. G. Greaves [19] discusses the significant changes in central government, including the increasing number of officials, the improvement of centralized coordination, the expansion of economic activities, and the impact of science on the conduct of government. A parallel survey by a study group of the Royal Institute of Public Administration [20] concentrates especially on the organization of central government after 1914.

[14] John W. Eaves, Jr., *Emergency Power and the Parliamentary Watchdog: Parliament and the Executive in Great Britain, 1939–1951* (1957).
[15] Cambridge, Eng., 1940; 2d ed., 1957.
[16] *Mr. Balfour's Poodle: An Account of the Struggle between the House of Lords and the Government of Mr. Asquith* (1954).
[17] *The Growth of Public Employment in Great Britain* (Princeton, N.J., 1957).
[18] "The Machinery of Government, 1939–1947," *Political Quarterly*, 19:1–14 (January–March 1948).
[19] "British Central Government, 1914–1956," *Political Quarterly*, 28:383–389 (October–December 1957).
[20] F. M. G. Willson, *The Organization of British Central Government, 1914–1956: A Survey by a Study Group of the Royal Institute of Public Administration*, ed. D. N. Chester (1957).

Of considerable interest in this complex development has been the role played by the cabinet. Several investigations have addressed themselves to this issue, notably D. N. Chester's informative account of the transformation of the cabinet since 1914, which appeared in a series of essays edited by Sir Gilbert Campion,[21] and a first-rate study of the role of the cabinet minister in relation to the administrative aspects of his post. In this latter article,[22] R. McGregor Dawson outlines the very dissimilar methods employed by Herbert Asquith, Lloyd George, and Lord Curzon to deal with administrative difficulties and in so doing underlines the complexity of the cabinet minister's role in the twentieth century. Finally, for a half century dominated by conflict and the fear of conflict, there is a thorough demonstration by John Ehrman [23] of how the cabinet adjusted itself to cope with the many and complex problems of war between 1890 and 1940. The latest edition of Sir Ivor Jennings' *Cabinet Government* (3d ed., Cambridge, Eng., 1959) parallels his *Parliament* as a standard description of the functioning of the cabinet in the twentieth-century political framework.

The electoral system upon which this structure of government rests has been exposed to serious study since 1945. Each of the elections since that year has elicited a detailed statistical and analytical monograph. As a pioneer effort, *The British General Election of 1945*, by R. B. McCallum and Alison Readman (Oxford, 1947), has earned considerable praise, although critics have pointed out that the authors, in explaining their data, have tended occasionally to confuse unverified opinion with checked observation. Nevertheless, subsequent observers, particularly D. E. Butler for the elections of 1951 and 1955, have benefited markedly from the highlighting by McCallum and Readman of pitfalls to be avoided in analyzing election results. Butler has written an excellent work on the electoral system from 1918 to 1951.[24] His comparative analysis crystallizes the materials relating to trends over the period, above all the steady decline of the Liberal vote, and he has added much that is

---

[21] D. N. Chester, "Development of the Cabinet, 1914–49," in Sir Gilbert Campion *et al., British Government since 1918* (1950).

[22] "The Cabinet Minister and Administration: Asquith, Lloyd George, Curzon," *Political Science Quarterly*, 55:348–377 (September 1940).

[23] *Cabinet Government and War, 1890–1940* (Cambridge, Eng., 1958). This may be usefully supplemented by Herman Finer, "The British Cabinet, the House of Commons and the War," *Political Science Quarterly*, 56:321–360 (September 1941), which is devoted to the years 1939–1941.

[24] *The Electoral System in Britain, 1918–1951* (Oxford, 1953).

useful by way of surveys of proposals for electoral reform, assessments of by-election results, and a miscellany of other matters.

Finally, to round out the picture of the machinery of government, changes on the local level have been studied in a series of essays [25] by a group of research assistants at Nuffield College and especially in K. B. Smellie's concise and fresh *History of Local Government* (1958). The twentieth-century material in Smellie's work includes discussions of the Housing and Town Planning Acts of 1919 and 1925, the Local Government Act of 1933, and the Education Act of 1944, along with a separate chapter on the complex government of London.

The advent of the welfare state has merely underscored the British government's growing absorption with the provision of various social services during the twentieth century. For an understanding of the social environment out of which such services emerged three works stand out. *A Survey of Social Conditions in England and Wales* [26] by A. M. Carr-Saunders, D. Carradog-Jones, and C. A. Moser, brings up to date a study which has long been standard. B. Seebohm Rowntree's *Poverty and Progress: A Second Social Survey of York* (1941) follows in the path of Rowntree's epochal house-to-house study of the town in 1901. To these should be added R. M. Titmuss' *Birth, Poverty and Wealth* (1943), whose stress on the apparent increase in inequality from 1911 to the early forties rests heavily on data relating to infant mortality among various classes in society. And to put these investigations into perspective, a massive survey of the contemporary scene is almost indispensable. *Social Mobility in Britain,* ed. D. V. Glass, appears to indicate that there has been much less shift in the pattern of social mobility after 1945—a period of presumed acceleration—than has generally been assumed (Glencoe, Ill., 1954).

Social conditions need to be studied in conjunction with the social action they elicited. While a number of valuable general studies of the social services have appeared, attention should be called to a few specialized studies. To sample them, R. W. Harris, a former civil servant, has studied national health insurance from 1911 to 1946 in an awkwardly written account which is nevertheless packed with information.[27] For

---

[25] *Essays on Local Government,* ed. C. H. Wilson (Oxford, 1948).

[26] *A Survey of Social Conditions in England and Wales as Illustrated by Statistics* (Oxford, 1958). See also D. C. Marsh, *The Changing Social Structure of England and Wales, 1871–1951* (1958).

[27] *National Health Insurance in Great Britain, 1911–1946* (1946).

old age pensions, Sir Arnold Wilson's and G. S. Mackay's historical and critical survey [28] is of utmost importance, not only from a descriptive view but also for its comparisons with other countries and its proposals for reform. Unemployment insurance is covered by Sir Frank Tillyard and F. N. Ball in a detailed history of legislation from the National Insurance Act of 1911 through the reports of royal commissions and other committees to the implementation of the National Insurance Act of 1946.[29] All of these works, important in their own right, are also valuable background for the famous Beveridge Report, published in 1944 as *Full Employment in a Free Society*.[30] An impressive piece of economic diagnosis, the report is the single most important statement of the policy upon which the whole structure of the contemporary welfare state rests. It has justly been termed one of the few recent books likely to be of lasting historical significance.

Somewhat different from the ubiquitous social services noted is the provision of housing under the auspices of government and of private enterprise. In a book which is a model of economic history, Marian Bowley [31] has surveyed and analyzed housing policy in the interwar years. She demonstrates that at least down to the Housing Act of 1933 not the working class but other groups benefited mainly from the course pursued by British governments. From another point of view, A. P. Becker [32] has called attention to the unprecedented building expansion of the thirties and argues that it played a great role—perhaps the greatest—in economic recovery from the slump of 1931. There is still much controversy over the implications of housing policy between the wars, but these studies are an excellent start toward clearing away some of the distortions of party polemics. Even more broadly conceived is W. Ashworth's *The Genesis of Modern British Town Planning* (1954). Subtitled *A Study in Economic and Social History of the Nineteenth and Twentieth Centuries*, this useful work does much to illuminate the broader changes of which housing policy was only a part.

The portrait which emerges from this mass of material on legislation and policy is that of a society more than ordinarily a society in transition. The character of that change is difficult to summarize, but a few

[28] *Old Age Pensions: A Historical and Critical Survey* (1941).
[29] *Unemployment Insurance in Great Britain, 1911–48* (Leigh-on-Sea, 1949).
[30] 1944. The report itself was issued in 1942.
[31] *Housing and the State, 1919–1944* (1945).
[32] "Housing in England and Wales during the Business Depression of the 1930's," *EcHR*, 2d ser., 3:321–341 (no. 3, 1951).

outstanding works will help to point the way. In his brilliant and evocative five-volume autobiography,[33] Sir Osbert Sitwell has brought vividly to life the patrician world of country houses and Edwardian manners. No less effective is his intimate description of the transformation of the "lost age of peace" before 1914 in the shattering changes resulting from two world wars.

The decline of the middle classes rather than the upper classes is the theme of a persuasive tract for the times written by R. Lewis and A. Maude.[34] Urbane and learned, this little volume surveys the development of the middle classes, outlines their functions and place in English society, and bewails their contemporary frustrations and difficulties. Lewis and Maude see in this development a significant weakening of the "natural ladder" by which most of England's talent has emerged and been able to make its fullest contribution to society.

Finally, there is the working class. While the examination of social patterns in works of fiction—John Galsworthy, George Bernard Shaw, H. G. Wells, G. K. Chesterton, Hilaire Belloc come first to mind—has been deliberately omitted from this survey, one recent novel should be mentioned. Walter Allen's *All in a Lifetime* (1959) does more to capture the temper and the feel of working-class life between 1885 and 1950 than a host of admittedly important special studies. It is well worth the attention of any student of twentieth-century Britain.

The rise of Labour has been the key political development in British history since 1900 and the literature devoted to this phenomenon has reflected its importance.[35] Labour's outstanding historian was the late G. D. H. Cole; his *History of the Labour Party from 1914* (1948), which can be supplemented by the last part of his *British Working Class Politics, 1832–1914* (1941), is a full-scale study such as neither Tory nor Liberal party has as yet received. Authoritative and detailed, Cole's *History* is virtually a year-by-year account of the Labour party's fortunes, described against the broader background of the labour movement as a whole. It is especially effective in analyzing the controversy over foreign policy in the late 1930's and always informative on issues of economic and financial significance. Perhaps its one major weakness, as has been

[33] *Left Hand, Right Hand!* (1944); *The Scarlet Tree* (1946); *Great Morning!* (1947); *Laughter in the Next Room* (1948); *Noble Essences* (1950). All first published in Boston, Mass.

[34] *The English Middle Classes* (1949).

[35] C. L. Mowat, "Some Recent Books on the British Labour Movement," *JMH*, 17: 356–366 (December 1945), and "The History of the Labour Party: The Webbs, and Some Others," *ibid.*, 23:146–153 (June 1951).

pointed out by C. L. Mowat, is that nowhere in the book do the leaders of Labour come to life as individual personalities. That particular shortcoming is remedied in Francis Williams' *Fifty Years' March: The Rise of the Labour Party* (1949). Williams deals mainly with the years down to 1918 and in his frank expression of partisan support he manages to project a warm and living picture of the men who made the Labour party a reality.

To supplement Cole we now have Carl F. Brand's *The British Labour Party: A Short History* (Stanford, Calif., 1964), a conventional narrative which tends to play down the crucial tensions among various elements in the party, yet represents the summing up of a life's study by the dean of American analysts of British Labour. For Labour between the wars and after the relevant chapters of Henry Pelling's brief history [36] are useful, but much more penetrating is Ralph Miliband's critical evaluation of the tactics of parliamentary labour over the years of its history.[37] Miliband argues, in effect, that the Labour party's dogmatic and consistent devotion to the parliamentary system militated against any fullfledged implementation of its drive toward "socialism." Instead, he declares, the party was committed to what he calls "Labourism," sinking, despite temporary success, into a decline only to be halted by a genuinely socialist policy. To these studies should perhaps be added Catherine Cline's monograph dealing with the recruits, mainly Liberals, who came over to the Labour party in the years after 1914.[38] More specialized, because less in the main current, are works by Pelling and by Colin Cross on the British Communists [39] and Fascists [40] who tried, in their respective fashions, to contest the growth of Labour's support in the interwar years. The former book should be consulted in conjunction with Neal Wood's *Communism and British Intellectuals* (New York, 1959), whose title indicates the nature of its investigation.

Recently, a number of other scholarly studies have tackled the issues and forces involved in the rise of Labour to national prominence. Henry Pelling has written a notable analysis of the origins of the Labour party. Based on meticulous research in the published and unpublished papers of late nineteenth-century socialist organizations, his *Origins of the La-*

---

[36] *A Short History of the Labour Party* (1961).
[37] *Parliamentary Socialism: A Study in the Politics of Labour* (1961).
[38] *Recruits to Labour: The British Labour Party, 1914–1931* (Syracuse, N.Y., 1963).
[39] *The British Communist Party: A Historical Profile* (New York, 1958).
[40] *The Fascists in Britain* (New York, 1963).

bour Party (1954) is extremely suggestive in working out their contribution to the emergence of Labour as a political force. A Canadian scholar, J. H. Stewart Reid, has treated the same subject in a volume [41] not nearly as penetrating as that of Pelling. Reid's book nevertheless adds substantially to our grasp of the period between 1906 and 1914, when frustration and controversy, particularly over relations with the Liberals, threatened to split the fledgling party wide apart—until perhaps it was "saved," ironically enough, by the eruption of war and the electoral truce.

Relations with the Liberals, then, were crucial in the early years of the Labour party. The excellent monograph by Philip Poirier [42] and another by Pelling in collaboration with Frank Bealey [43] have thrown much light on the history of the Labour Representation Committee and particularly on the arrangement which permitted Labour to contest a number of seats without Liberal opposition in the election of 1906. Pelling and Bealey were able to use the Labour party letter files for 1900 to 1906 and as a result their account of the bargain struck by Ramsay MacDonald with Herbert Gladstone, the Liberal chief whip, is probably a bit more thorough. In the main, however, the findings of both books run side by side and both make a real contribution to the understanding of Keir Hardie and Ramsay MacDonald. Hardie is revealed as much more politically flexible than the public figure of speeches and newspaper articles or indeed than the hero of a recent work of hagiography by his son-in-law, the Labour M. P. Emrys Hughes.[44] And MacDonald stands out as a patient, skillful negotiator, carefully organizing the victory of 1906 from which subsequent triumphs eventually flowed.

Once an independent Labour group became established in the House of Commons, the decline of the Liberal party was assured. So at least goes the conventional explanation and H. L. Beales has given it a most illuminating reading in the *Political Quarterly* for January–March 1947.[45] Beales accepts the thesis that the Liberals after 1914 suffered the fate of a Center party not rooted in working-class support. In particular, he

[41] *The Origins of the British Labour Party* (Minneapolis, Minn., 1955).
[42] *The Advent of the Labour Party* (1958).
[43] *Labour and Politics, 1900–1906: A History of the Labour Representation Committee* (1958). See also Frank Bealey, "The Electoral Arrangement between the Labor Representation Committee and the Liberal Party," *JMH*, 28:353–373 (December 1956).
[44] *Keir Hardie* (1957).
[45] "Has Labour Come to Stay?" *Political Quarterly*, 18:48–60 (January–March 1947).

traces briefly but persuasively the intellectual and emotional currents which combined with events finally to convince a reluctant trade union leadership that it could be politically independent of the Liberals. Rather more general is the recent conclusion of a young American scholar, John F. Glaser, who sees in the decline of Nonconformity before 1914 the explanation for the Liberal party's loss of political strength and, above all, for the loss of the "religious ethos and moral passion" which had distinguished Liberalism in its most creative period.[46] This brief article in some ways tells us more than Colin Cross's useful, but disappointingly superficial, account of the Liberal party in office before the first World War.[47]

Central to an understanding of the early Labour party are analyses of certain of its key leaders. Keir Hardie, as we have noted, still awaits a thoughtful biographer and Ramsay MacDonald needs to be freed of the myths of adulation and vituperation which have clustered about his career and personality. A huge and somewhat undigested mass of his writings and utterances has been gathered together by Benjamin Sachs,[48] but the enigma of MacDonald remains to be solved. What appears to be the most balanced view yet available is offered by Mary Agnes Hamilton, author of several earlier works of hero-worship, in *Remembering My Good Friends* (1944), a brilliant account of inner party politics in the twenties. Arthur Henderson, the architect of the party machine, has fared better at her hands than MacDonald, but her 1938 biography leaves ample room for further investigation.[49]

Possibly more important for the Labour party and for Britain as a whole than any of these Labour leaders were Sidney and Beatrice Webb. Their contribution to the transformation of the social services and to the whole concept of public administration was so all-pervasive that it has led one observer to compare the revolutionary content of the "age of the Webbs" with the impact of Benthamism on earlier British institutions.[50] As early as 1926 Beatrice's *My Apprenticeship* had revealed the Webbs as something quite different from the cold automata caricatured by H. G. Wells in *The New Machiavelli*. Two decades later

[46] "English Nonconformity and the Decline of Liberalism," *AHR*, 63:352–363 (January 1958).

[47] *The Liberals in Power (1905–1914)* (1963).

[48] *J. Ramsay MacDonald in Thought and Action: An Architect for a Better World* (Albuquerque, N. Mex., 1952).

[49] *Arthur Henderson* (1938).

[50] Donald G. MacRae, "The Webbs and Their Work," *Political Quarterly*, 19:14–23 (January–March 1948).

Our Partnership (1948) covered the period when their behind-the-scenes influence was at its height. In these volumes and in the *Diaries* edited by Margaret Cole,[51] the warmth and shrewdness as well as the limitations of Beatrice and Sidney are made fascinatingly evident. No student of twentieth-century Britain can neglect these volumes even though he must approach their judgments with great caution. They may be supplemented by a sympathetic, though not entirely uncritical, short study of Beatrice Webb by Mrs. Cole [52] and finally by the incisive and revealing summary given by R. H. Tawney in the Webb Memorial Lecture for 1952.[53]

Edward Pease's long-outdated history of the Fabian Society has finally been superseded by two first-rate works. Margaret Cole, *The Story of Fabian Socialism* (Stanford, Calif., 1961), is perhaps weak in her analysis of Fabian limitations, particularly on international issues, but she is excellent in her exegesis of the development of the Society itself. And to make up for her lacunae, there is *Fabian Socialism and English Politics, 1884–1918* (Cambridge, Eng., 1962), in which A. M. McBriar assesses Fabian ideas and attitudes, whether in the Society's posture toward Marxism in its early days or in its work on the London County Council or in other municipal bodies thereafter. Along with these two studies one should put the final installment of S. Maccoby's exhaustive description of English radicalism, whose title indicates the gist of its sweeping coverage of the period from 1906 to 1951.[54]

A number of special studies have scrutinized particular aspects of Labour's history since 1914. In *British Labour's Rise to Power* (Stanford, Calif., 1941), Carl Brand has collected a group of eight articles, most of them dealing with the period between 1914 and 1919. These essays, covering a wide range of topics from the conversion of the trade unions to political action to Labour's reactions to Woodrow Wilson, are exploratory analyses, suggesting avenues for further investigation. Of particular importance are two monographs originally prepared under the supervision of David Owen at Harvard University. Stephen Graubard's *British Labour and the Russian Revolution, 1917–1924* (Cambridge, Mass., 1956) convincingly demonstrates that in the years between 1919 and

---

[51] *Beatrice Webb's Diaries, 1912–1924* (1952), and *Beatrice Webb's Diaries, 1924–1932* (1956).

[52] 1945. See also *The Webbs and Their Work*, ed. Margaret Cole (1949), a series of critical judgments on the Webbs, including assessments of their dogmatism and rigidity by Leonard Woolf and R. C. K. Ensor.

[53] *The Webbs in Perspective* (1953).

[54] *English Radicalism: The End?* (1961).

1924 the labour movement forged an attitude toward Russia that was never seriously modified despite frequent disagreement over its application. Graubard's volume supplements Richard W. Lyman's sensitive and well-written study of the 1924 Labour government.[55] This latter work contains a revealing analysis of the general election of 1923 which thoroughly documents the difficulties of the Liberal party, and proceeds to give creditable marks to Labour for its first performance as His Majesty's Government.

International issues are of course prominent in each of the publications just noted, but thus far there has appeared only one full-dress study of Labour's foreign policy over the sweep of the half century. Elaine Windrich's contention that Labour consistently followed a "socialist" foreign policy is not at all convincing, but her didactic account has the minor merit of gathering together a great deal of information.[56] The present writer, in two brief articles, has attempted to probe more deeply into how a relatively new party, faced for the first time with the imminence of office, went about substituting a supposedly realistic program of action for the propaganda of a minority movement.[57]

The much debated fall of Labour in 1931 and the subsequent formation of the National government has recently received an exhaustive airing by R. S. Bassett. *1931 Political Crisis* (1958) is an uncompromising defense of Ramsay MacDonald which should bury forever the familiar "plot" theory of the crisis. It is indispensable in straightening out the chronology of events, but Bassett's implication that all who differ from him are either fools or knaves makes for uncomfortable reading. Despite the appearance of this big book, C. L. Mowat's brief account which appeared in the *Huntington Library Quarterly*[58] is still worth consulting.

A few biographies of figures who were particularly prominent after World War I deserve mention. Raymond Postgate has published an informative, though uncritical, study of his father-in-law, George Lansbury,[59] the most interesting part of which is Postgate's description in a foreword of how Lansbury's official papers from the period of the second Labour government were "seized" by the 1944 government and not

---

[55] *The First Labour Government, 1924* (1958).
[56] *British Labour's Foreign Policy* (Stanford, Calif., 1952).
[57] "The Emergence of a Labor Foreign Policy in Great Britain, 1918–1929," *JMH*, 28:247–258 (September 1956), and "Arthur Henderson," in *The Diplomats, 1919–1939*, ed. G. Craig and F. Gilbert (Princeton, N.J., 1953), pp. 311–343.
[58] "The Fall of the Labour Government in Great Britain, August, 1931," *HLQ*, 7:353–386 (August 1944).
[59] *The Life of George Lansbury* (1951).

made available for study. Eric Estorick, the author of a somewhat un-critical panegyric of Stafford Cripps,[60] has printed some useful excerpts from Cripps's correspondence, while Colin Cooke, in his quasi-official study,[61] has added a thorough description of the gradual development of Cripps as a significant political figure. Both biographies are particu-larly disappointing in their reserved handling of Cripps's mercurial shifts in position during the years immediately preceding World War II. Equally unsatisfactory, although pleasant enough to read, is the cautious portrayal of Clement Attlee by Roy Jenkins, a Labour M.P.[62] Much more revealing than any of these biographies are a trio of sketches con-cerned with the Buxton brothers and Josiah Wedgwood. Ex-Liberals contributed greatly to the maturation of the Labour party, especially on international questions, during the interwar years, and the modest ac-counts by M. Anderson, Victoria de Bunsen, and C. V. Wedgwood help to explain the influence in the Labour party of this most interesting group of Radicals.[63] Equally valuable is the study of F. W. Jowett, one of the founders of the Independent Labour party, by Fenner Brockway, whose *Inside the Left* (1942) is an intriguing autobiographical account of left-wing politics. The Jowett biography [64] is most revealing on the differences between the I. L. P. and the Labour party between 1922 and 1932 when the I. L. P. withdrew from the party. More important than any of the above is what promises to be the outstanding British biogra-phy of recent years. Alan Bullock's admiring but critical study of Ernest Bevin,[65] which brings the story down to 1940 when Bevin became Min-ister of Labour in the coalition government of Winston Churchill, illumi-nates also major issues in the history of British trade unionism. And while Aneurin Bevan has already attracted a number of biographers,[66] only one study, the first volume of Michael Foot's adulatory but reveal-ing memoir, merits serious notice.

Finally, three autobiographies require comment. Clement Attlee's *As It Happened* (1954) does not fulfill the promise of its title. It is rather one of the most reticent and therefore disappointing memoirs to appear

[60] *Stafford Cripps* (1949).
[61] *The Life of Sir Richard Stafford Cripps* (1957).
[62] *Mr. Attlee: An Interim Biography* (1948).
[63] M. Anderson, *Noel Buxton: A Life* (1952); Victoria de Bunsen, *Charles Roden Buxton: A Memoir* (1947); C. V. Wedgwood, *The Last of the Radicals: Josiah Wedgwood, M.P.* (1951).
[64] *Socialism over Sixty Years: The Life of Jowett of Bradford (1864–1944)* (1947).
[65] *The Life and Times of Ernest Bevin*, I, *Trade Union Leader, 1881–1940* (1960).
[66] Mark M. Krug, *Aneurin Bevan: Cautious Rebel* (New York, 1961); Michael Foot, *Aneurin Bevan*, I, *1897–1945* (1962).

in recent years, rivaled in this respect, however, by the autobiography of Herbert Morrison.[67] Few of the major issues which the Labour party debated during Attlee's political career are really probed and the reader constantly finds himself frustrated by the veil of understatement and good taste skillfully lowered by the author. In sharp contrast, Hugh Dalton has published a three-volume account of his career.[68] Based largely on diaries which Dalton appears to have kept systematically, these volumes go down to 1960. Refreshingly unconventional, they are strikingly uninhibited and as a result add up to one of the three or four most important British political autobiographies in the past few decades.

Closely associated with the history of the Labour party is of course that of the trade union movement. Thus far B. C. Roberts has brought his history of the Trade Union Congress [69] down to 1921 and his second volume should complete a scholarly and standard work which will please neither enthusiasts nor critics, but will be indispensable to serious students. Two works of contemporary analysis, while they deal with the present, throw much light on twentieth-century trade unionism in general. J. Goldstein's *Government of British Trade Unions* (1952) created a furor at Transport House when it appeared in 1952. Studying the gigantic Transport and General Workers' Union, Goldstein pointed up the high rate of membership turnover, which in turn left a tiny minority of "activists" to control affairs. The implication that the trade union membership was therefore less "democratic" than appeared on the surface was exaggerated, particularly since the T. and G.W.U. was not necessarily typical of British trade unionism in its entirety. Goldstein's work needs to be used in conjunction with V. L. Allen's *Trade Union Leadership* (Cambridge, Mass., 1958), on the whole, a more balanced treatment, based on a study of Arthur Deakin. Of the histories of individual unions, the most ambitious is R. P. Arnot's three-volume study of the Miners' Federation.[70] Arnot, using Marxism as his tool of analysis, distorts the issues involved in the story of the miners, especially in his huge second volume. For the period before 1910 the first volume has greater perspective and stands up as a fair general account of developments.

Since the foreign office records are as yet available only until 1902, the student of twentieth-century foreign policy is still heavily dependent on

[67] *An Autobiography* (1960).
[68] *Call Back Yesterday: Memoirs, 1887–1931* (1953); *The Fateful Years: Memoirs, 1931–1945* (1957); and *High Tide and After: Memoirs, 1945–1960* (1962).
[69] *The Trades Union Congress, 1868–1921* (1958).
[70] *The Miners: A History of the Miners' Federation of Great Britain, 1889–1910* (1949); *From 1910 Onwards* (1953); *From 1930 Onwards* (1961).

the two major collections of documents published under government auspices. A comparison [71] of the materials in the early volumes of the *British Documents on the Origins of the War* with the recently opened archives for 1898 to 1902 shows that the G. P. Gooch and Harold W. Temperley selections bear no trace of major omissions or deliberate distortions. The very structure of the series may sometimes have dictated the choice of documents, but the skill and integrity of the editors are clearly confirmed. Despite the natural suspicion of historians toward any prior selection of the documents they wish to consult, it seems likely that the same verdict will one day be returned for the *Documents on British Foreign Policy, 1919–1939*, edited by Sir Llewelyn Woodward and Rohan Butler (1946). Thus far, Series III, dealing with the years 1938 and 1939, has been completed, but it will be some time before all the volumes of Series I, for the early period, and Series II, for the years 1929 to 1937, are available.

There has been little significant revision of the great works of the 1920's and 1930's dealing with prewar diplomacy. One exception is A. J. P. Taylor's careful account of British policy in Morocco from 1886 to 1902.[72] Making thorough use of the newly opened archival material, Taylor argues that skillful French exploitation of the Morocco situation forced Britain out of her "feeble dependence" on Germany and brought into being the Anglo-French Entente. Rather different is the claim of E. W. Edwards,[73] who sees in the Far Eastern situation, with its danger of a general war resulting from the alliance system, the catalyst of British policy leading to the acceptance of negotiations with France. A few other studies, notably by A. F. Pribram on relations with Austria-Hungary,[74] J. D. Hargreaves on the Anglo-French military conversations,[75] M. K. Chapman on the Bagdad Railway,[76] and a sympathetic biography of Sir Edward Grey by G. M. Trevelyan,[77] add some matters of detail but do not change the picture of the main outlines of British policy.

Questions of war aims and peacemaking in the World War I period

[71] J. D. Hargreaves, "Some Critical Notes on Gooch and Temperley," *History*, n.s., 39:68–75 (February–June 1954).

[72] "British Policy in Morocco, 1886–1902," *EHR*, 66:342–374 (July 1951).

[73] "The Japanese Alliance and the Anglo-French Agreement of 1904," *History*, n.s., 42:19–27 (February 1957).

[74] *Austria-Hungary and Great Britain, 1908–1914* (New York, 1951).

[75] "The Origin of the Anglo-French Military Conversations in 1905," *History*, n.s., 36:244–248 (October 1951).

[76] *Great Britain and the Bagdad Railway, 1888–1914*, Smith College Studies in History, 31 (Northampton, Mass., 1948).

[77] *Grey of Fallodon* (1940).

have attracted some recent attention. The present writer,[78] for example, has studied the currents of opinion, both official and public, which produced the British attitude toward the League of Nations, while A. J. P. Taylor [79] has argued, in effect, that not the secret treaties, but the "idealistic" statements of war aims really indicated the goals of the allied and associated powers once the war was well under way. In contrast, Gerda Crosby, in an uncompleted essay published posthumously,[80] has developed the implied argument that those who sought arms limitation, both at the peace conference and subsequently, were considerably more realistic than the opponents who looked upon them as visionaries. R. B. McCallum's *Public Opinion and the Last Peace* (Oxford, 1944) defends the Treaty of Versailles with great vigor if not with sober historical judgment.

For World War I itself, Lord Hankey's massive and intimately informed study of the Supreme Command is indispensable.[81] Of another order of magnitude, but interesting as an example of the monograph material now emerging, is Trumbull Higgins' *Winston Churchill and the Dardanelles* (New York and London, 1963), an essay in which the author's chip on the shoulder concerning Churchill and overly sanguine assessment of the wisdom of military leaders mar an otherwise thoroughly researched and searching performance. To these should be added a completely different kind of work, *The Deluge, British Society and the First World War* (1965), a fascinating account of the social changes that took place during the course of the war written by a young Scottish scholar who has also given us among other things a good study of Clifford Allen of the Independent Labour party.[82]

The years between 1919 and 1939 are still so fresh in memory that it is somewhat surprising to find three temperate and balanced accounts of the general pattern of British diplomacy. W. N. Medlicott's *British Foreign Policy since Versailles* (1940) is something of a tour de force. Emphasizing the dilemmas rather than the failures of strategy, this cool analysis by one of Britain's leading diplomatic historians is all the more noteworthy when one remembers that it was published in 1940. An ex-

---

[78] *The League of Nations Movement in Great Britain, 1914–1919* (New Brunswick, N.J., 1952).
[79] "The War Aims of the Allies in the First World War," in *Essays Presented to Sir Lewis Namier,* ed. Richard Pares and A. J. P. Taylor (1956).
[80] *Disarmament and Peace in British Politics, 1914–1919* (Cambridge, Mass., 1957).
[81] *The Supreme Command, 1914–1918,* 2 vols. (London, 1961).
[82] Arthur H. Marwick, *Clifford Allen: The Open Conspirator* (1964).

cellent contrasting volume is P. A. Reynolds' *British Foreign Policy in the Inter-war Years* (1954), a sensible and convincing topical survey. He assesses the causes of British failure and concludes that it resulted from the attempt to pursue traditional policies "when British power was no longer sufficient and world conditions were no longer wholly suitable," and to practice "conciliation and tolerance to the point of failure to recognize evil, and in evil danger." Reynolds' attack on conciliation refers, of course, to the 1930's, but a wartime address by G. P. Gooch, subsequently expanded into an important article,[83] argues that the tragedy of that decade might have been averted if the Locarno agreements had been implemented by broader conciliation of the Weimar Republic. Whether any conciliation which was practicable in the twenties would have long satisfied the new Germany is debatable, but Gooch's contention that too little firmness was displayed when Hitler came to the helm is clearly tenable.

Two impressive special studies are necessary supplements to these general volumes. In *Britain and France between Two Wars* (New York, 1940), Arnold Wolfers has concentrated on the forces which went into the making of British policy. Although it was completed before many of the relevant documents were yet public, this volume is particularly suggestive in its discussion of the differences between "traditionalists" and "internationalists" in their approach to the issues of the period. Even more important is W. M. Jordan's *Great Britain, France and the German Problem, 1919–1939* (1943). This sound and objective study of reparations, security, and disarmament draws the lesson that the failures of Anglo-French policy stemmed directly from the inability of British and French statesmen to agree, before the peacemaking, on the principles upon which they were to try to build the peace and rebuild Europe. It is in many ways the most satisfactory monograph that we have for the diplomatic history of the interwar period.

A more narrowly restricted line of investigation into problems of security and disarmament has been opened by the appearance of some of the volumes of the *Foreign Relations of the United States* as well as the *British Documents on Foreign Policy*. Conyers Read[84] has outlined the importance of these materials for the London Naval Conference of 1930

---

[83] "British Foreign Policy, 1919–1939," in *Studies in Diplomacy and Statecraft* (1942).

[84] "Recent United States and British Government Publications on the London Naval Conference of 1930," *AHR*, 54:307–314 (January 1949).

and J. L. Godfrey [85] has begun their exploitation in a study of Anglo-American naval conversations prior to the conference. Nevertheless, the availability of additional data, notably in the Henry L. Stimson Papers now at the Sterling Memorial Library at Yale University, makes it clear that much remains to be done on this subject as on other aspects of British relations with the United States.

The collapse of the international order under the hammer blows of totalitarian aggression has resulted in a rash of explanations, some of them tendentious, some politically inspired, most of them impassioned. Failure to deal adequately with the Far Eastern crisis of 1931 to 1933 has often been cited as the first step in a deepening spiral of British surrender to force and the threat of force. R. Bassett, in his *Democracy and Foreign Policy*,[86] has taken sharp issue with this view. Arguing in effect that British foreign policy between the wars has been unfairly maligned, he uses the Sino-Japanese dispute as a case history to illustrate. He demonstrates rather convincingly that neither the Labour party nor the Left in general categorically proposed any program for dealing with the crisis according to League of Nations principles, but his assertions that the policy of the National government was wise are strikingly unpersuasive.

Even more than "Manchuria," "Munich" has become a term of opprobrium or of defense, as the case may be, but very few studies— quite understandably perhaps—have yet been able to free the recent past from the involvements of the present. Of those which try to make the case for the policy pursued by Neville Chamberlain from 1937 to 1939, W. W. Hadley [87] has argued that Chamberlain is to be praised for accepting a diplomatic defeat in order to gain time for vital military preparations. Viscount Maugham [88] likewise takes this position, but he combines it with a series of other claims, including a defense of Munich as a workable compromise if it had been honored, which are in mutual contradiction. And Keith Feiling, in his important biography of Chamberlain,[89] uses extensive quotations from Chamberlain's diaries and letters in a defensive analysis of the "appeasement" policy which hardly succeeds in acquitting his subject.

[85] "Anglo-American Conversations Preliminary to the London Naval Conference of 1930," *South Atlantic Quarterly*, 49:303–316 (July 1950).
[86] *Democracy and Foreign Policy: A Case History: The Sino-Japanese Dispute, 1931–33* (1952).
[87] *Munich, Before and After* (1944).
[88] *The Truth about the Munich Crisis* (1944).
[89] *Life of Neville Chamberlain* (1946).

On the other side is a full-scale study of the background, chronology, and aftermath of the Czechoslovak crisis by J. W. Wheeler-Bennett.[90] Written before the British or German documents had been published, this study is still useful, despite occasional lapses, as a detailed condemnation of the weaknesses and follies of Anglo-French policy in the late thirties. Even more important are two volumes by Sir Lewis Namier which lay bare the frightening errors of that policy with a controlled contempt only equaled by the author's brilliant command of his materials. Consisting largely of a series of essays reviewing the documents, memoirs, and apologia as they appeared, Namier's *Diplomatic Prelude*[91] and *Europe in Decay*[92] together are a most telling scholarly indictment of the appeasement policy and the men who were responsible for it. He is particularly scathing in his comments on Nevile Henderson, whose *Failure of a Mission: Berlin, 1937–1939* (New York, 1940) is surely one of the most self-condemnatory documents to be published in recent years. Equally harsh in its judgment of Henderson is Felix Gilbert's study of "Two British Ambassadors,"[93] in which the Earl of Perth, who also supported Chamberlain's general approach from his post at Rome, is contrasted with Henderson at Berlin. But the most controversial recent volume has been A. J. P. Taylor's *The Origins of the Second World War* (1961), which in effect purports to show that Hitler did not deliberately seek war and indicts the National Government not for trying to appease Hitler but for failing to appease him sufficiently or effectively. Taylor's clever but perverse reading of the evidence has been challenged by a number of able scholars, but the clearest and most detailed monograph to conclude that the policy of appeasement was a disaster is the work of two young men in their twenties, Martin Gilbert and Richard Gott, whose somewhat oversimplified sorting out of men and policies into blacks and whites is nevertheless a revealing indication of how a new generation is now beginning to try to understand the prewar era.[94] Another young man, K. W. Watkins, has studied the effect of the Spanish Civil War on British public opinion in a book whose important information is too often concealed by the sententiousness of the author's obiter dicta.[95] And there is a peculiar and highly personal little essay by

[90] *Munich: Prologue to Tragedy* 1948).
[91] *Diplomatic Prelude, 1938–1939* (1948).
[92] *Europe in Decay: A Study in Disintegration, 1936–1940* (1950).
[93] In *The Diplomats, 1919–1939*, ed. Craig and Gilbert, pp. 537–554.
[94] *The Appeasers* (1963).
[95] *Britain Divided: The Effect of the Spanish Civil War on British Public Opinion* (1961).

A. L. Rowse,[96] which indicts the Conservative leadership of the thirties within the framework of a slightly strained memoir of Rowse's confrontations with some of the high priests of appeasement at the dinner table of All Souls. Finally, the British and German documents of the Munich era are surveyed in two revealing bibliographical articles by Gordon Craig [97] and Bernadotte E. Schmitt,[98] while work in the international field after 1918 will be made considerably more convenient by the appearance of Robert Vogel's *A Breviate of British Blue Books, 1919–1939* (Montreal, 1963), which supplements the work of H. W. V. Temperley and L. M. Penson for the nineteenth century.

One of the most important commentaries on the prewar decade of tragedy is the first volume of Sir Winston Churchill's magisterial *Second World War* (London and New York, 1948–1953). *The Gathering Storm* is a deeply felt account of disaster, not particularly concerned with subtle niceties of policy, but profoundly evocative of the agony of a great and sensitive man witnessing his country's descent into the abyss. It has little to offer in the way of new materials, yet as the literary expression of Churchill's deepest feelings it is the most effective of the series. The five wartime volumes, on the other hand, are filled with messages, orders, memoranda that will be invaluable to historians for years to come. These documents are rather loosely strung together in a narrative which conceals as much as it reveals. Perhaps the best judgment of the work is that it is a highly conscious and artful memoir in which Churchill consistently presents his admittedly magnificent achievement in the light he wishes posterity to remember.

Already Churchill's account is being challenged by other interpretations of the war years. Thus Arthur Bryant,[99] in a peculiar book based on Lord Alanbrooke's diary, tends to play up Alanbrooke's very important contribution at the expense of Churchill as well as of the Americans. By giving Alanbrooks's postwar recollections equal weight with selected diary entries, themselves often revelatory of the exasperations of dealing with a man of Churchill's mercurial temperament, Bryant has succeeded in overstating his case and vitiating the force of some well-founded criticisms. Trumbull Higgins,[100] has castigated Churchill for his resistance

---

[96] *All Souls and Appeasement* (1961).
[97] "High Tide of Appeasement: The Road to Munich, 1937–38," *Political Science Quarterly*, 65:20–37 (March 1950).
[98] "Munich," *JMH*, 25:166–180 (June 1953).
[99] *The Turn of the Tide* (1957).
[100] *Winston Churchill and the Second Front* (New York, 1957).

to the idea of a second front in Western Europe. Higgins underestimates Churchill's practical reasons for interest in the Mediterranean just as he minimizes the real problems of a 1943 cross-channel operation. Rather more balanced is the argument in John Ehrman's *Grand Strategy* (vol. V),[101] which explains the British viewpoint, as compared with that of the Americans, in terms of Britain's geographic position, military experience, and limitations of manpower. Ehrman's study is one of the military series, edited by J. R. M. Butler as part of the official *History of the Second World War,* which is setting a high standard of thorough yet readable scholarship in this field.[102]

As valuable and even more impressive in scope are the studies so far published in the civil series of the official history. Under the general editorship of Sir Keith Hancock, the volumes range from studies of agriculture and civil defense to accounts of financial policy and war production. Two contributions merit a particular word of comment. In their *British War Economy,*[103] Hancock and Mrs. M. M. Gowing have set the stage for the special studies that follow in a brilliant and thorough description of the dilemmas, problems, and crises which had to be faced as Britain geared her economy for war. A second synoptic volume by R. M. Titmuss, entitled *Problems of Social Policy,*[104] in similar fashion opens up the whole question of the war's impact on a civil society and suggests countless lines of inquiry which can be followed in the more

[101] *Grand Strategy,* V, *August 1943–Sept. 1944* (*History of the Second World War,* military ser., ed. J. R. M. Butler [London, 1956]). An interesting article dealing with the earlier part of the war is J. C. Cairns, "Great Britain and the Fall of France: A Study in Allied Disunity," *JMH,* 27:365–409 (December 1955). See also W. H. McNeill, *America, Britain and Russia: Their Co-operation and Conflict, 1941–1946* (1953) based on printed sources but well balanced and clear.

[102] Some of the volumes in the military series with dates of publication follow: J. R. M. Butler, *Grand Strategy,* II, *Sept. 1939–June 1941* (1957); L. F. Ellis, *The War in Flanders, 1939–40* (1954); C. I. Savage, *Inland Transport* (1957); B. Collier, *The Defence of the United Kingdom* (1957); Maj. Gen. I. S. O. Playfair et al., *The Mediterranean and Middle East* (1956); T. K. Derry, *The Campaign in Norway* (1952); and Capt. S. W. Roskill, *The War at Sea, 1939–1945,* I, *The Defensive* (1954). For more recent volumes, see R. Higham, "The History of the Second World War: British Official Series," *The Library Quarterly,* 34:240–248 (July 1964).

[103] Published in 1949. Among the volumes are J. Hurstfield, *The Control of Raw Materials* (1953); H. D. Hall, *North American Supply* (1955); H. D. Hall and C. C. Wrigley, *Studies of Overseas Supply* (1956); M. M. Postan, *British War Production* (1952); W. N. Medlicott, *The Economic Blockade,* I, *1939–41* (1952); R. S. Sayers, *Financial Policy, 1939–45* (1956); Sir Keith Murray, *Agriculture* (1956); R. J. Hammond, *Food,* I, *The Growth of Policy* (1951); J. D. Scott and R. Hughes, *Administration of War Production* (1956).

[104] Published in 1950. See also S. M. Ferguson and H. Fitzgerald, *Studies in the Social Services* (1954).

specialized volumes on social policy. Space precludes any further comment on individual contributions, but taken as a whole the official histories are a monumental and indispensable record of the British war experience.

While many of the materials on foreign policy in the twentieth century are still hidden in the archives, the student of economic history is favored by the fact that his data are in large measure available. The result is an imposing volume of publications, so that a general commentary can only give a hint of what has been done. Since 1940 attention has been concentrated on the interwar period, but two works on the 1914 war should be noted. Samuel J. Hurwitz,[105] in what is essentially a series of disparate essays, has examined state intervention in terms of the administration of economic controls and the public response to it. In the field of war finances, E. V. Morgan[106] covers the period from 1914 to 1925 in a group of solid essays concerned with such questions as the economic environment, governmental finances, and relations between debt operations and the Bank of England.

The growth of wartime economic controls suggests the problem of their relaxation, a subject to which two penetrating articles turned during the early forties. Both Albert Lauterbach, writing in the *Political Science Quarterly*,[107] and R. H. Tawney, in the *Economic History Review*,[108] have assessed the experience of economic demobilization after World War I and both have concluded that the government erred in yielding to the demand for a rapid and impossible return to prewar conditions. Their findings are confirmed by Stephen Graubard's study of military demobilization[109] which documents the enormous pressure built up against a cautious government plan designed to prevent mass unemployment.

Other scholars have concentrated on a variety of economic matters. An excellent account of the tariff controversy in the early twenties is given by R. K. Snyder,[110] while for the same period the distinguished

[105] *State Intervention in Great Britain: A Study of Economic Control and Social Response, 1914–19* (New York, 1948).

[106] *Studies in British Financial Policy, 1914–1925* (1952).

[107] "Economic Demobilization in Great Britain after the First World War," *Political Science Quarterly*, 67:376–393 (September 1942).

[108] "The Abolition of Economic Controls, 1918–1921," *EcHR*, 13:1–30 (nos. 1 and 2, 1943).

[109] "Military Demobilization in Great Britain Following the First World War," *JMH*, 19:297–311 (December 1947).

[110] *The Tariff Problems in Great Britain, 1918–1923* (Stanford, Calif., 1944). See also F. C. Benham, *Great Britain under Protection* (1941).

economist, A. C. Pigou,[111] has surveyed the economy in fields such as employment, production, monetary questions, and government intervention in industry. Pigou concludes with a useful analysis of the movement of real income and real wages which may profitably be compared with Dudley Seers's studies in the cost of living and distribution of incomes after 1938.[112] W. A. Morton's *British Finance* (Madison, Wis., 1943), which deals largely with the thirties, is especially helpful in sketching the effect of monetary and banking policy on Britain's foreign and domestic trade and on economic conditions in general. And W. A. Lewis,[113] to cite only one other work, has made available a compact, simple survey of economic developments, not entirely devoted to Britain, but containing an excellent synthesis of a good deal of information.

The recent literature on individual industries has been especially good in the fields of coal and steel. For the coal-mining industry, J. H. Jones's careful general survey [114] appeared just before World War II, while at the end of the war W. H. B. Court [115] put his finger on its major problems. The loss of foreign markets, the poor state of industrial relations, and the difficulties of capital accumulation interacted disastrously between the wars and paved the way for postwar nationalization. As for steel, the most authoritative work has been done by D. L. Burn, whose *Economic History of Steelmaking* [116] is critical of the weaknesses displayed by the industry but balanced in describing its development. In particular, Burn has illuminated the ways in which British steelmakers reacted—or did not react—to the impact of competition over the years. His survey may be brought up to date by his brief article in the *Economic History Review* [117] assessing recent trends in the industry.

Finally, there are three general works on economic history to which reference should be made. William Ashworth's *An Economic History of England, 1870–1939* (1960) is virtually a model of its kind, a balanced, informative, and clearly presented survey of the period. Somewhat more limited, but almost a manual for the area of its concern is Sidney Pol-

---

[111] *Aspects of British Economic History, 1918–1925* (1947).

[112] *The Levelling of Incomes since 1938* (Oxford, 1951). See also A. L. Bowley, *Studies in National Income, 1924–1938* (Cambridge, Eng., 1942).

[113] *Economic Survey, 1919–1939* (1949).

[114] *The Coal-mining Industry* (1939).

[115] "Problems of the British Coal Industry between the Wars," *EcHR*, 15:1–24 (nos. 1 and 2, 1945).

[116] *The Economic History of Steelmaking, 1867–1939: A Study in Competition* (Cambridge, Eng., 1940).

[117] Recent Trends in the History of the Steel Industry," *EcHR*, 17:95–102 (no. 2, 1947).

lard's study of the development of the British economy after 1914.[118] And to round out this useful trilogy there is S. B. Saul's *Studies in British Overseas Trade, 1870–1914* (Liverpool, 1960), which treats a most important period with deep understanding and lucid presentation.

Government and politics, social and economic change are often incomprehensible except in terms of the personalities most intimately involved. For the twentieth century, in addition to such studies as the Neville Chamberlain biography and those of the Labour leaders already noted, there have recently been a number of important additions to the literature. Winston Churchill, indeed, has yet to be captured by a scholarly biographer and must be sought in the memoirs and official documents. Most biographies, like that by Philip Guedalla,[119] are wartime Churchilliads, but Lewis Broad[120] has written a fairly satisfactory account of Churchill's career down to 1951. If not very critical, it does sketch in the surface events of a remarkable career. It will probably be some time before we have a fully rounded picture though Peter de Mendelssohn has combed through mountains of secondary material before spinning out the first volume of a projected three-volume biography.[121] If the author can control his compulsion to speak with bated breath on every page and occasionally permit the record to speak for itself, we may have more successful second and third volumes of this massive undertaking. Lady Violet Bonham Carter's *Winston Churchill: An Intimate Portrait* (New York, 1965) affords a view of Churchill's early career that, while occasionally revealing in its intimate details, nevertheless adds relatively little to our general knowledge of his development.

The passage of time, perhaps, explains why there is at least one outstanding study among the numerous biographies of Lloyd George. The "official" life by Malcolm Thomson[122] is no better nor worse than many such efforts, and a long, loose, high-pitched melodrama entitled *Tempestuous Journey: Lloyd George, His Life and Times* (1954) is grievously disappointing. Its author, Frank Owen, had access to the Lloyd George Archives owned by Lord Beaverbrook, but instead of an analytical study he has presented a breathless and repetitive exposition of the obvious. Fortunately, Thomas Jones's brief biography[123] is a masterpiece

---

[118] *The Development of the British Economy, 1914–1950* (New York, 1962).
[119] *Mr. Churchill* (New York, 1942).
[120] *Winston Churchill, 1874–1951*, rev. and enl. (1951).
[121] *The Age of Churchill*, I, *Heritage and Adventure, 1874–1911* (1961).
[122] *David Lloyd George* (1948).
[123] *Lloyd George* (Cambridge, Mass., 1951).

of compression and analysis. Offering little new material, Jones brings the complex, mercurial, weak greatness of Lloyd George to life with sympathy, yet with mature judgment—altogether one of the best political biographies of the past two decades.

Jones is also indispensable for insights into Ramsay MacDonald, Neville Chamberlain, and, above all, Stanley Baldwin. As a leading figure in the cabinet secretariat from 1916 to 1931 and as a close friend of many of Britain's leaders thereafter, he was in an exceptional position to observe and privately to record his impressions. His *Diary with Letters, 1931–1950* (Oxford, 1954) is packed with valuable information and astute judgments, such as his clear demonstration that there was no "Cliveden set" plotting appeasement at the Astors' country home. He describes Baldwin as "ruminant" rather than lazy, and well informed, not ignorant, on foreign affairs. He is especially good in describing Baldwin's alertness and skill in dealing with the abdication crisis in 1936.

These comments highlight the fact that Baldwin, more perhaps than any recent prime minister except MacDonald, has occasioned conflicting responses from observers of his career. As early as 1941, A. L. Rowse pictured Baldwin as a sham democrat, soothing the people with platitudes, failing to rearm because he feared it would hurt the Tories' prospects at the polls.[124] This assessment, which was substantially repeated by Winston Churchill in *The Gathering Storm* as late as 1948, was challenged after the war by R. Bassett who, in a penetrating article in the *Cambridge Journal*,[125] showed that Baldwin's so-called "confession" on the rearmament issue must not be taken to mean that Baldwin put his party before the defense of Britain. Despite Bassett's exegesis, the myth has been repeated in G. M. Young's *Stanley Baldwin* (1952), surely one of the most curious "official" memoirs ever to be published. This brief and confused account, as one reviewer has put it, virtually makes a plea of *nolo contendere* to Rowse's charges and belittles Baldwin in a framework which emphasizes his dullness and indolence even when praising him. As a result, both D. C. Somervell and Baldwin's son have risen to the defense in volumes [126] which answer some of the charges but do not succeed in acquitting Baldwin of serious mistakes of judgment and pol-

[124] "Reflections on Lord Baldwin," *Political Quarterly*, 12:305–317 (July–September 1941).

[125] "Telling the Truth to the People: The Myth of the Baldwin 'Confession,' " *Cambridge Journal*, 2:84–95 (November 1948).

[126] D. C. Somervell, *Stanley Baldwin: An Examination of Some Features of Mr. G. M. Young's Biography* (1953); A. W. Baldwin, *My Father: The True Story* (1956).

icy. The whole controversy is summed up by Charles Mowat in an excellent review article published in the *Journal of Modern History*.[127]

In sharp contrast to the tone of the Baldwin literature is that of Robert Blake's substantial biography of Andrew Bonar Law.[128] Based on private papers, this reasonable and detailed picture of Bonar Law's role in the transformation of the Conservative party is too kind to its subject on the Ulster issue but generally it is one of the better political biographies. Deserving to stand with it is Roy Harrod's sympathetic but completely honest portrait of John Maynard Keynes.[129] This massive work, rooted largely in private papers and official documents, is of tremendous value, not simply because it so reveals one of the most influential minds of the century, but because it illuminates many facets of the times in which Keynes lived and worked.

By way of contrast, two professional historians have given us thoroughly solid, if somewhat less than exciting, studies of two professional, if somewhat less than exciting, politicians. John W. Wheeler-Bennett makes out a good case [130] for the vital services of Sir John Anderson, particularly during the second World War, while J. R. M. Butler deals sympathetically with Philip Kerr,[131] who was so brilliant as a young adviser to David Lloyd George and so much less so as adviser to certain of his successors. To these may be added Robert Rhodes James's competent biography of Lord Rosebery,[132] Kenneth Young's rather more penetrating study of the complex intellectual who became prime minister, Arthur Balfour,[133] and Roy Jenkins' shrewd and extremely well-written though somewhat defensive assessment of H. H. Asquith (1964).

Of utmost interest, because of what is said rather than how it is said, is Sir Anthony Eden's three-volume memoir of his professional career.[134] Flat and tedious in their presentation, these volumes are of course as much a case of special pleading as Winston Churchill's "history" of the second World War. But whether concerned with Eden's

[127] "Baldwin Restored?" *JMH*, 27:169–174 (June 1955).
[128] *The Unknown Prime Minister: The Life and Times of Andrew Bonar Law* (1955).
[129] *The Life of John Maynard Keynes* (1951).
[130] *John Anderson, Viscount Waverley* (New York, 1962).
[131] *Lord Lothian (Philip Kerr), 1882–1940* (New York, 1962).
[132] *Rosebery: A Biography of Archibald Philip, Fifth Earl of Rosebery* (1963).
[133] *Arthur James Balfour: The Happy Life of the Politician, Prime Minister, Statesman and Philosopher, 1848–1930* (1963).
[134] *The Memoirs of Anthony Eden, Earl of Avon. Full Circle* (Boston, Mass., 1960); *Facing the Dictators* (Boston, Mass., 1962); *The Reckoning* (Boston, Mass., 1965).

hardheaded assessment of Hitler and Mussolini during the thirties or his much less hardheaded conduct during the Suez crisis of the fifties, his recollections are marred by a note of querulous self-justification which may go far to explain how the politician of such promise became a failure as a statesman when he took on the burdens of the prime ministership. It is a relief to turn to the three installments so far published of the autobiography of Leonard Woolf,[135] a sensitive and civilized human being equally at home in the Bloomsbury of his wife's circle or in the shabby offices of the Labour party's Transport House. Written with honesty and with grace, this promises to be one of the outstanding autobiographies of the past few decades.

Altogether, then, this brief survey has attempted to select some of the main contributions to contemporary scholarship dealing with Britain's very recent past. Much has been omitted, including excellent commentaries on such subjects as education, religion, and the press, but only because of the pressure of space. Virtually all the works noted have inevitably been pioneer reconnaissances, outlining some features of twentieth-century Britain which deserve comment, offering tentative judgments, but hardly presuming to have the perspective for more than contingent assertions. Most will have to be revised, but meanwhile the foundations are being laid for the continuing task of reassessment which is one of the major functions of the historical scholar.

[135] Leonard Woolf, *Sowing* (1960); *Growing* (1961); *Beginning Again* (1963).

Scottish History since 1940

❖

MAURICE LEE, JR.

EVER SINCE Queen Victoria built Balmoral, Scotland has been, for non-Scots, a place to visit on vacations, a land of grouse and deer and salmon and striking scenery. For Scots and non-Scots alike, the history of Scotland has been thought of, for the most part, in equally picturesque terms. The historical figures that everyone knows about are almost all highly romantic figures, and, with the notable exception of the unromantic John Knox, they are associated with lost causes: Wallace, Queen Mary, Montrose, Bonnie Prince Charlie. Even Robert Bruce is best remembered for the spider, and for the slaying of Bohun rather than John Comyn.[1]

The consequence of all this is that a great deal of Scottish history has been written in a fashion worthy of a seaside lending-library. Scotland, of course, is not the only country which suffers from this complaint. But in the case of Scotland matters are made very much worse by two factors which have combined to leave the field to the romancers almost by default. In the first place, there are very few academic positions in the field of Scottish history; they exist only at Scottish universities. Consequently, the bright young graduate student is warned off the field by his professor, because of the difficulty of placing him when he has finished his graduate work. In the second place, there has been a general and unhappy reluctance on the part of the present generation of Scottish historians to write general interpretive works. Their scholarship is generally excellent, but it is too often confined to the editing of texts. This sort of work has been, and will continue to be, of very great value, but it is,

[Reprinted from *The Canadian Historical Review*, 40:319–332 (December 1959).]

[1] In this article no attempt has been made to deal with Scottish history before the eleventh century, since the writer is not competent to judge the literature dealing with that period. Also omitted are all works on English history which discuss Scotland, for example, C. V. Wedgwood's recent work on the civil war, since these books will be discussed in other articles in this series.

after all, the mere quarrying of stones. The building remains to be built. One of the abler of the younger generation of Scottish historians has put it this way: "The divorce of *oeuvres de vulgarisation* from scholarship has been the greatest obstacle to an intelligent interest by layman or teacher in Scottish history. Scholars have become the victims of the cranks—who misspell their names and misrepresent their words— because scholars see the gaps in our knowledge and only cranks dare to essay comprehensive studies in Scottish history. Perhaps the scholars should have greater courage." [2]

The most important book on medieval Scotland to appear since 1940 is R. L. G. Ritchie's *The Normans in Scotland* (Edinburgh, 1954). Ritchie sets out to demonstrate that there was a "Norman Conquest" of Scotland, none the less thorough for not being military, that from the reign of Malcolm III (1057–1093) the institutions and ideals of the Normans—their zeal for religious and social reform, their legal-minded-ness, their talent for organization—became more and more pervasive, the culmination of the process coming in the time of David I (1124– 1153). Some of Ritchie's judgments are rather extreme, but his work represents one of the few attempts by Scottish historians to present a comprehensive interpretation of a long period of Scottish history. Since Ritchie's work appeared, two important modifications have been sug-gested. G. W. S. Barrow has pointed out that the feudalization of Scot-land was far from complete by the death of David I, that it penetrated north of the Forth only in the second half of the twelfth century, and that a more suitable terminal date would be the death of William the Lion (1214).[3] A. A. M. Duncan argues much more strongly than Ritchie for the view that, for the period 1097–1124 at least, the kings of Scotland were in fact vassals of Rufus and Henry I for the whole of the king-dom.[4]

The records of the period of the War of Independence have been re-studied by E. L. G. Stones, whose most important discoveries are sum-marized in "The Treaty of Northampton, 1328" [5] in which he points out, among other things, that the treaty was negotiated at Edinburgh rather than Northampton, and that the question of the forfeited estates was not dealt with in the treaty at all.[6] A. A. M. Duncan has examined in some

[2] A. A. M. Duncan, *SHR*, 35:150 (October 1956).
[3] "The Beginnings of Feudalism in Scotland," *BIHR*, 29:1–31 (May 1956).
[4] "The Earliest Scottish Charters," *SHR*, 37:103–135 (October 1958).
[5] *History*, n.s., 38:54–61 (February 1953).
[6] Stones has published a series of articles and documents on this period in the

detail the administrative records of Bruce's reign and has concluded that chancery no longer itinerated with the King. Since Bruce was almost constantly on the move, the consequence was the greatly extended use of the privy seal, which, in Duncan's phrase, now became "a necessary instrument of government." [7] The relations of Bruce's distressingly inept son with Edward III have been the subject of a brief pamphlet by E. W. M. Balfour-Melville, who has done a great deal with scanty materials.[8]

The political history of the period of the Scottish Renaissance has come in for a certain amount of exposition, if no radical revision, at the hands of A. I. Dunlop in her massive *Life and Times of James Kennedy, Bishop of St. Andrews* (Edinburgh, 1950) and of R. L. Mackie in his *King James IV of Scotland* (Edinburgh, 1958). This latter work is based in part on Mackie's completion of R. K. Hannay's calendar of James's correspondence,[9] which he supplied with an introduction containing an excellent account of Scottish foreign policy in the eight years before Flodden.[10] With respect to the political side of the Reformation period, there has been a welcome decline in the output of sentimental maunderings about Mary. W. C. Dickinson has supplied us with a modernized two-volume edition of John Knox's *History of the Reformation in Scotland* (New York, 1950) copiously annotated and preceded by a lengthy introduction which summarizes well the standard facts about the Reformation and Knox's life. J. H. Burns has shown that Knox came to his celebrated advocacy of rebellion against a godless magistrate later than has commonly been supposed—not, in fact, until early in 1558.[11] M.

Scottish Historical Review between 1949 and 1956. See also G. G. Simpson, "The Claim of Florence, Count of Holland, to the Scottish Throne, 1291–92," *SHR*, 36:111–123 (October 1957), and R. Nicholson, "The Franco-Scottish and Franco-Norwegian Treaties of 1295," *ibid.*, 38:114–132 (October 1959).

[7] The *Acta* of Robert I," *ibid.*, 32:1–39 (April 1953).

[8] *Edward III and David II* (1954).

[9] *The Letters of James the Fourth 1505–1513*, Scottish History Society (Edinburgh, 1953). D. Hay similarly completed Hannay's calendar of *The Letters of James V* (Edinburgh, 1954).

[10] Some of the same ground is covered in J. D. Mackie, "Henry VIII and Scotland," *TRHS*, 4th ser., 29 (1947), pp. 93–114, which despite its title deals almost exclusively with the Flodden crisis. W. M. Mackenzie, "The Debateable Land," *SHR*, 30:109–125 (October 1951), has provided a convenient summary of one of the chief points at issue between the two countries in Henry's reign.

[11] "The Political Ideas of the Scottish Reformation," *Aberdeen University Review*, 36:251–268 (spring 1956). The ideas of Samuel Rutherford, who pushed the anti-monarchical tendencies in Reformation thought to their extreme in the Covenanting period, have been analyzed by W. M. Campbell, "Lex Rex and Its Author," *Records of the Scottish Church History Society*, 7 (1941), pp. 204–228.

Lee, Jr.'s *James Stewart, Earl of Moray* (New York, 1953) is an attempt to reassess the history of the Reformation from the point of view of the aristocracy.

Of all Scotland's kings, James VI has been the most extensively scrutinized by historians in recent years, and judgments have varied according to the author's interests. The traditional unflattering picture of James, stemming largely from Gardiner, is supported by those scholars whose primary interest lies south of the Tweed, such as G. Davies,[12] and, more moderately, C. V. Wedgwood [13] and D. H. Willson, whose biography, *King James VI and I* (1956) is a splendid piece of work, the culmination of a lifetime of research. Much more favorable to James are those scholars who have concentrated on James as King of Scots, such as H. G. Stafford [14] and M. Lee, Jr.[15]—a situation doubtless explained by the fact that James was far more successful in his native land than he ever was in England.[16]

The main lines of historical opinion on the union have not altered since the work of Mackinnon, Hume Brown, Dicey and Rait, and G. M. Trevelyan was done, most of it more than a generation ago; but G. S. Pryde has edited the text of *The Treaty of Union of England and Scotland* (Edinburgh, 1950) and supplied a concise and informative introduction dealing with the making of the treaty and its effects. Another general survey of the consequences of the union in the eighteenth century is given by R. Pares.[17] S. M. F. Johnston [18] has shown how the Scottish army was employed as a patronage device to help achieve union; virtually all Scots nobles with military connections favored the

---

[12] "The Character of James VI and I," *HLQ*, 5:33–63 (October 1941).

[13] "Anglo-Scottish Relations, 1603–40," *TRHS*, 4th ser., 32 (1950), pp. 31–48.

[14] *James VI of Scotland and the Throne of England* (New York, 1940). M. Lee, Jr., has dealt with a somewhat earlier problem in Anglo-Scottish relations in James's reign, "The Fall of the Regent Morton," *JMH*, 28:111–129 (June 1956).

[15] "James VI, King of Scots," *History Today*, 6:155–163 (March 1956); *John Maitland of Thirlestane and the Foundation of the Stewart Despotism in Scotland* (Princeton, N.J., 1959).

[16] A review of the evidence in the still-mysterious Gowrie conspiracy, on the whole favorable to James, has been made by W. F. Arbuckle, *SHR*, 36:1–24, 89–110 (April and October 1957). Students of the sixteenth century have benefited by the continuation of the publication of two important series of state papers: *Calendar of State Papers Relating to Scotland and Mary Queen of Scots*, XII, 1595–7, ed. M. S. Giuseppi (1952); *The Register of the Privy Seal of Scotland*, IV, 1548–56, ed. J. Beveridge (1952); *ibid.*, V, 1556–67, ed. J. Beveridge and G. Donaldson (1957); *ibid.*, VI, 1567–74, ed. G. Donaldson (1963).

[17] "A Quarter of a Millennium of Anglo-Scottish Union," *History*, n.s., 39:233–248 (October 1954).

[18] "The Scots Army in the Reign of Anne," *TRHS*, 5th ser., 3 (1953), pp. 1–21.

treaty. Douglas Nobbs is at his best in *England and Scotland 1560–1707* (1952) on the problem of the union; his general conclusion is that after 1688, owing to the complete change in the character of the Scottish Parliament, the only alternatives were union or total separation.

If the tide of Marian literature has receded somewhat, the same cannot be said for the Jacobites. Amid the waves of sentimental claptrap and antiquarianism, a few works stand out. C. H. Hartmann's *The Quest Forlorn: The Story of the 'Forty-Five'* (1952) is a straightforward narrative, admittedly unoriginal, written from the sensible point of view that Prince Charles was doomed to failure from the start. Hartmann stresses the importance of the government's command of the sea, a point also made by J. Fergusson in *Argyll in the Forty Five* (1951), an account based largely on the manuscripts of various branches of the Campbell family and centering on the loyalist major general John Campbell of Mamore. Also worth mentioning is the monograph by G. H. Jones, *The Main Stream of Jacobitism* (Cambridge, Mass., 1954), a fully documented account of the negotiations of the exiled court with other governments and with its agents in Great Britain from 1688 to 1746. Jones is rather sympathetic to the Old Pretender, but in the end he agrees with the prevalent verdict that he was a "decent failure."

Other aspects of eighteenth-century politics have received sporadic attention at best. There has been a flurry of interest in the Appin Murder, touched off by J. Fergusson's challenge to the long-standing opinion that Stewart was an innocent man condemned after an outrageously unfair trial. The challenge is partly successful: the trial was not as unfair as has been alleged; but obstacles were certainly put in the way of the defense.[19] Fergusson has also presented us with a "Namier's-eye-view" of eighteenth-century electoral practices in Ayrshire, in which he concludes that personal relationships, rather than the conferring of favors, formed the basis for electoral success.[20] This is a valuable pioneer article and much more work of this kind on Scottish elections needs to be done. It is well known that Scottish politics were dominated by a series of political

[19] The important articles are J. Fergusson, "The Appin Murder Case," *SHR*, 31:116–130 (October 1952); J. Cameron, "The Appin Murder," *ibid.*, 33:89–99 (October 1954); W. P. MacArthur, "The Appin Murder," *ibid.*, 34:183–188 (October 1955).

[20] "'Making Interest' in Scottish County Elections," *ibid.*, 26:119–133 (October 1947). See also on this subject W. Ferguson, "Dingwall Burgh Politics and the Parliamentary Franchise in the Eighteenth Century," *ibid.*, 38:89–108 (October 1959).

bosses in the eighteenth century; less well known is the fact that, as time went on, more and more people became discontented with this state of affairs. D. I. Fagerstrom has shown that one cause of that discontent was the American Revolution.[21] Many leading Scots, including David Hume and Adam Smith, felt some sympathy for the American position; the automatic support of the government—any government—by almost all Scottish M.P.'s caused a good deal of annoyance. One result of the discontent was a movement for reform of the governments of the Scottish burghs which has been described by R. C. Primrose.[22]

Scottish political history after the French Revolution has not attracted the attention of historians.[23] It has either been treated as part of the history of England or, more commonly, not treated at all. The almost total neglect of Scotland in such standard modern works as the volumes by E. L. Woodward and R. C. K. Ensor in the *Oxford History of England* series is deplorable but not unusual. The one exception to this prevalent neglect is the vexed question of the Scottish nationalist movement. Here it seems likely that the silence of serious historians has permitted the enthusiasts to take even greater liberties with the truth than usual. It would be beyond the scope of this essay to attempt any account of the nationalist question; the work of R. Coupland, *Welsh and Scottish Nationalism* (1954) can be recommended as a judicious account of the origins of the movement, particularly useful for the nineteenth century.

T. B. Franklin's *A History of Scottish Farming* (Edinburgh, 1952), an expansion of the work which won him the David Berry Prize, is an important addition to our knowledge of medieval economic history. About half the book deals with the contributions of the Scottish monasteries to agriculture; this is genuinely original work. Aside from this volume, the only significant contribution to medieval economic history is an article by W. S. Reid, which argues that a major cause of the eventual Scottish success in the War of Independence was England's inability to cut off Scottish trade with the Continent and Ireland, whence came the food

[21] "Scottish Opinion and the American Revolution," *William and Mary Quarterly*, 3d ser., 11:252–275 (April 1954).
[22] "The Scottish Burgh Reform Movement, 1783–1793," *Aberdeen University Review*, 37:27–41 (spring 1957).
[23] Two exceptions may be noted: B. L. Crapster, "Scotland and the Conservative Party in 1876," *JMH*, 29:355–360 (December 1957); D. W. Crowley, "The 'Crofters' Party,' 1885–1892," *SHR*, 35:110–126 (October 1956), the latter is of some importance for the problem of the origins of the Labour party.

and weapons the Scots needed to keep the resistance going.[24] This article suggests one direction which future research into the period of the War of Independence might profitably take.

Many of the political works already mentioned have a good deal to say about Scottish economic and social life, especially Mrs. Dunlop's biography of Bishop Kennedy, but not until we get to the eighteenth century do we find large numbers of works devoted exclusively to this topic. Then, the trickle becomes a flood, and small wonder. For there is general agreement that the eighteenth century, particularly the last two-thirds of it, was the decisive era in the transformation of a backward country into an economically advanced and prosperous one. In the past twenty years particular attention has been paid to Scottish agriculture. The most comprehensive treatment is J. E. Handley's *Scottish Farming in the Eighteenth Century* (1953), a book written with a lightness of touch unusual among economic historians. Handley has been criticized, and rightly, for neglecting important manuscript sources and for drawing the traditional overly gloomy picture of conditions in the first half of the century; but his account of the changes in the second half of the century is thorough and informative. The part played by the landowners in the agricultural improvements of this century has been skillfully described in the most interesting chapter of J. Fergusson's *Lowland Lairds* (1949). An important case study of the efforts of a particular improving landlord, Grant of Monymusk, much drawn on by Handley and others, has been supplied by H. Hamilton, who has published two volumes of selections of papers, with introductions and notes.[25] The papers have been selected to illustrate not only the changes in farming methods which took place on Grant's estate, but also the social consequences flowing from them. The editor is careful to warn us that Grant was far from a typical landlord. Much more material of this sort will have to be digested before the definitive agricultural history of the eighteenth century can be written.

Whenever the improving movement may have started in the lowlands, there is no doubt that the great changes in the highlands began after

---

[24] "Trade, Traders, and Scottish Independence," *Speculum,* 29:210–222 (April 1954). Further evidence on this point is in J. W. Dilley, "German Merchants in Scotland 1297–1327," *SHR,* 27:142–155 (October 1948).
[25] *Selections from the Monymusk Papers 1713–1755,* Scottish History Society (Edinburgh, 1945); *Life and Labour on an Aberdeenshire Estate 1735–1750,* Spalding Club (Aberdeen, 1946). Also of interest along the same line is *Powis Papers 1507–1894,* ed. J. G. Burnett, Spalding Club (Aberdeen, 1951), most of which deals with the eighteenth and nineteenth centuries.

1745. The importance of the Commissioners of Forfeited Estates in this connection has long been recognized, and their work has been conveniently summarized by J. Mason.[26] M. Gray has described the necessary first step in the improvement of highland agriculture, the abolition of runrig,[27] and A. McKerral has discussed the contemporaneous weakening of the class of tacksmen.[28] Gray's recent study, *The Highland Economy 1750–1850* (Edinburgh, 1956), deals with the entire economic structure of the highlands, not just agriculture, and carries the story further, through the era of progress in the period 1785–1815 to the period of decline in the 1820's and 1830's which led to real dearth by the 1840's.[29] One important reason for this decline was the fact that the highlands were still overpopulated, in spite of a fairly steady emigration. One phase of that emigration has been dealt with by I. C. C. Graham in *Colonists from Scotland: Emigration to North America, 1707–1783* (Ithaca, N.Y., 1957). Graham draws a sharp line between Scots and Scots-Irish, a line often blurred by American historians; he points out the communal nature of highland emigration, by contrast with that of the solitary lowlander, and he also argues much more strongly than, for instance, Handley, that rising rents, rather than the clearing of arable land to turn it into pasture, were the key factor in highland emigration. This last point is also made by D. M. Sinclair who points out, however, that the highland clearings became a major factor in emigration after 1783.[30]

In the wake of H. Hamilton's great work on the Industrial Revolution in Scotland, which appeared in 1932, most of the work on Scottish industrial, commercial, and financial history has dealt with individual industries and specific, and rather narrow, problems. A few articles of more general interest may be mentioned. Hamilton himself has contributed two articles on financial questions, which help to elucidate a subject not fully covered in his book, and an interesting account of the founding of

[26] "Conditions in the Highlands after the 'Forty-five,'" *SHR*, 26:134–146 (October 1947).
[27] "The Abolition of Runrig in the Highlands of Scotland," *EcHR*, 2d ser., 5:46–57 (no. 1, 1952). Runrig was the Scots term for land held and worked in intermixed strips.
[28] "The Tacksman and His Holding in the South-West Highlands," *SHR*, 26:10–25 (April 1947). A tacksman, in this sense, was a large leaseholder who divided up his holding among subtenants.
[29] A. Collar, *The Crofting Problem* (Cambridge, Eng., 1953), though dealing mostly with current questions, has some information on the changes in the economic and social structure of the highlands since 1880.
[30] "Highland Emigration to Nova Scotia," *Dalhousie Review*, 23:207–220 (July 1943).

the Glasgow Chamber of Commerce.[31] Scottish commercial connections
with America have also come in for some attention. Especially important
is M. L. Robertson's analysis of the impact of the American Revolution
on the Scottish economy; his conclusion is that it was the Revolution
which shifted the focus of the economy from commerce to industry.[32]

Hamilton concentrated on a discussion of things in his book, and
rather neglected people. One consequence has been a series of important
works on Scottish social history in the period of industrialization. Pride
of place should go to L. J. Saunders for his *Scottish Democracy,
1815–1840: The Social and Intellectual Background* (Edinburgh, 1950),
a splendid and comprehensive discussion of the social impact of the new
technology. M. Plant's *The Domestic Life of Scotland in the Eighteenth
Century* (Edinburgh, 1952) is a careful and thorough description of all
aspects of domestic life in the period just before industrialization, written mostly from account books, diaries, and so on; within its narrow
compass it is extremely valuable. Many of the social problems of industrialization, and some of the solutions, are discussed by T. Ferguson in
The Dawn of Scottish Social Welfare (Edinburgh, 1948). This book
covers the period from the Middle Ages to 1863, but the emphasis is on
the nineteenth century; as the title suggests, Ferguson deals only with
those fields in which the state has assumed responsibility for solutions to
social problems, for example, poor relief, and control of infectious dis-
ease.

A number of recent works have dealt with the problems of the new
working class produced by the industrialization. L. C. Wright's *Scottish
Chartism* (Edinburgh, 1953) is a pioneer work of great importance, the
first study of Chartism in Scotland as a distinct movement, different
from that of England. R. K. Webb has discussed the problem of working-
class literacy.[33] The work of A. J. Y. Brown,[34] G. Evans,[35] and K. D.

---

[31] "Scotland's Balance of Payments Problem in 1762," *EcHR*, 2d ser., 5:344–357
(no. 3, 1953); "The Failure of the Ayr Bank, 1772," *ibid.*, 8:405–417 (April 1956);
"The Founding of the Glasgow Chamber of Commerce, 1783," *Scottish Journal of
Political Economy*, 1:33–48 (March 1954).

[32] "Scottish Commerce and the American War of Independence," *EcHR*, 2d ser.,
9:123–131 (August 1956). See also J. M. Price, "The Rise of Glasgow in the
Chesapeake Tobacco Trade, 1707–1775," *William and Mary Quarterly*, 3d ser.,
11:179–199 (April 1954).

[33] "Literacy among the Working Classes in Nineteenth Century Scotland," *SHR*,
33:100–114 (October 1954).

[34] "Trade Union Policy in the Scots Coalfields 1855–1885," *EcHR*, 2d ser.,
6:35–50 (August 1953).

[35] "Farm Servants' Unions in Aberdeenshire from 1870–1900," *SHR*, 31:29–40
(April 1952).

Buckley [36] on Scottish unions all points in the same direction, namely that Scottish unionism was unsuccessful in satisfying the demands of its constituents by economic action alone, and that the inevitable result was the creation of a workingman's political party.

Finally, two books of a rather disparate nature might be mentioned before we leave this area. J. D. Kyd in an introduction to Webster's census of 1755, analyzes the trends in Scottish population from that time to the present.[37] J. Prebble's *Disaster at Dundee* (New York, 1957) is the work of a newspaperman, an account of the collapse of the railroad bridge over the Tay in 1879. It suffers from the defects of journalese, but, for all that, is a lively and skillful account of the seamy side of Victorian material progress.

The most ambitious recent undertaking in Scottish legal and constitutional history is the Stair Society's *An Introduction to Scottish Legal History* (Edinburgh, 1958), a large-scale piece of cooperative scholarship which attempts partially to fill the yawning gap in Scottish historiography resulting from the absence of a Scottish Holdsworth. The attempt is only partially successful, since the book covers far too much ground. The opening section, on the general development of Scots law from David I, contains only sixty-one pages; the resulting compression is so extreme that the value of these chapters is seriously diminished. Some of the later chapters are much better. In a generally excellent section on courts and procedure, graced by contributions from some of the most important Scottish historians now writing, there is a particularly fine chapter on the central courts before 1532 by A. A. M. Duncan.

Other work in Scottish constitutional and legal history since 1940 has for the most part taken the form of the editing of documents, with learned introductions. There are some exceptions. One of the most notable is a brilliant lecture by W. C. Dickinson, given on the occasion of the inauguration of legal studies at Aberdeen.[38] Dickinson gives an admirable survey of the judicial structure of Scotland as it existed in the reign of Alexander III, its subsequent deterioration, and the revival of the judicial authority of the central government in the later fifteenth century. In this latter connection he makes the suggestion, heartily

[36] *Trade Unionism in Aberdeen, 1878 to 1900* (Edinburgh, 1955).

[37] J. D. Kyd, ed., *Scottish Population Statistics,* Scottish History Society (Edinburgh, 1952).

[38] "The Administration of Justice in Medieval Scotland," *Aberdeen University Review,* 34:338–351 (autumn 1952).

endorsed by the present writer, that the reign of James III needs re-studying.

A second exception is the splendid David Murray Lecture by T. M. Cooper, *The Dark Age of Scottish Legal History 1350–1650* (Glasgow, 1952). The age was dark (or rather, dim), Lord Cooper concluded, be-cause of faulty administration and a weak executive, not because of in-adequate laws or inadequate knowledge of the law. In this lecture Lord Cooper was straying a bit from his specialized field of research, which was the legal history of the thirteenth century. In this area he published *Selected Scottish Cases of the Thirteenth Century* (Edinburgh, 1944) and two volumes edited for the Stair Society, *Regiam Majestatem and Quoniam Attachiamenta* (Edinburgh, 1947) and *The Register of Brieves* (Edinburgh, 1946). His general conclusion was that no period prior to the late seventeenth century had had a greater effect on Scottish law than this one (he argues convincingly for dating the writing of *Regiam Majestatem* around the year 1230), and that Scottish law was essentially derivative, borrowing not only from Anglo-Norman law but also from canon law, the influence of which was greater than has been commonly supposed. Since his death in 1955, Lord Cooper's work has been superseded on one point. H. McKechnie's *Judicial Process upon Brieves, 1219–1532* (Glasgow, 1956), another David Murray Lecture, has shown that, contrary to Lord Cooper's belief, the register of brieves did not fall into decay in the later Middle Ages. Taken as a whole, how-ever, Lord Cooper's work was a most valuable pioneering effort in a neg-lected area of Scottish history.

Among the numerous collections of documents, mostly published by the Stair Society, three stand out. One is the Stair Society's edition by J. D. Mackie of *Thomas Thomson's Memorial on Old Extent* (Edinburgh, 1946), which has an extremely interesting and valuable introduction summarizing the case which prompted Thomson's memorial and discuss-ing the whole complicated problem of the representation of shires in the Scottish Parliament and its connection with tax questions.[39] The second, *Regality of Dunfermline Court Book, 1531–1538* (Dunfermline, 1953), is edited by J. M. Webster and A. A. M. Duncan. This work contains a really brilliant introduction on the development of regalian rights, which demonstrates that grants of regality were originally given, not as conces-

---

[39] The review of this book by Lord Carmont, in *SHR* 26:178–188 (October 1947), should be read in connection with Mackie's introduction.

sions to a too powerful baronage, but in order to further the administration of justice—something they were certainly not doing by the sixteenth century. The third, an entirely different sort of work, is the Stair Society's six-volume edition of *Baron David Hume's Lectures, 1786–1822* edited by G. C. H. Paton (Edinburgh, 1939–58), which includes a biography of Hume by the editor in volume VI. Hume was professor of Scots law at the University of Edinburgh for thirty-five years, and was undoubtedly the greatest authority on the subject in his day. Two other figures in Scottish legal history have also found biographers. D. E. Easson's *Gavin Dunbar* (Edinburgh, 1947) concerns James V's chancellor, who was instrumental in the erection of the College of Justice. J. Fergusson has contributed a lively and amusing biographical sketch of Lord Hermand, in the Stair Society's *Lord Hermand's Consistorial Decisions 1689–1777*, edited by F. P. Walton (Edinburgh, 1940).

Some important work has been done on the constitutional history of the Scottish burghs. W. M. Mackenzie's *The Scottish Burghs* (Edinburgh, 1949) deals largely with the medieval period; it is an expansion of a series of lectures, and therefore deals in generalizations and trends. Mackenzie was not afraid of generalizations; some of them seem a little too sweeping; but the book is nevertheless an important contribution to constitutional history, in the sense that it should stimulate further research. An entirely different sort of work is *Early Records of the Burgh of Aberdeen*, Scottish History Society (Edinburgh, 1957), edited by W. C. Dickinson with an introduction of 150 pages, which is an exhaustive and minute study of the constitutional, legal, and administrative position of the royal burgh in medieval Scotland to the end of the fourteenth century. This is a remarkable piece of scholarship, worthy of a position beside Dickinson's earlier work on the sheriff court and the baron court.[40] One of the few subjects neither Mackenzie nor Dickinson touched on is that of the burghs' representation in Parliament. E. W. M. Balfour-Melville has returned to the vexed question of the earliest date at which burgh representatives can be shown to have been present in Parliament. The great authorities of the last generation, R. S. Rait and R. K. Hannay, abandoned the traditional date of 1326, and put off the appearance of the burgh representatives to 1357. Balfour-Melville has

---

[40] *The Sheriff Court Book of Fife 1515–1522*, Scottish History Society (Edinburgh, 1928); *Barony Court Book of Carnwath 1492–1525*, Scottish History Society (Edinburgh, 1937).

shown that they were present in 1341, and he is inclined to accept the traditional date.[41]

The outstanding work which has appeared on the medieval Church is D. E. Easson's *Medieval Religious Houses, Scotland* (1957), detailed and immensely scholarly, and representing a real breaking of ground, since there is no real Scottish equivalent to Dugdale. This is likely to remain the indisputable reference work for the medieval Church in Scotland for many years. While this work was in progress, Easson published a number of articles on the medieval Church, the most suggestive of which points out that during the Wars of Independence the Scottish abbots were far more prone to collaborate with Edward I than were the bishops, largely for reasons of self-defense.[42] Easson closes his article with the observation that the ecclesiastical history of the period needs rewriting, by someone with the skill and patience to work through the sources.

A good deal of writing has been done on the medieval Church, and has been published by organizations like the Scottish Church History Society, but most of it is of little more than antiquarian interest. There are a few important exceptions, notably two articles by G. W. S. Barrow, which demonstrate the virtually exclusive responsibility of the Scottish royal family for the foundation of religious houses of the western European type, and the connection between Canterbury and the first of these houses, the abbey of Dunfermline.[43] M. Morgan has undertaken the difficult task of delineating the social and economic structure of the twelfth century through a study of church organization.[44] An occasional pre-Reformation ecclesiastic has found a biographer; in addition to Bishop Kennedy and Archbishop Dunbar, already mentioned, a life of *Adam of Dryburgh* (1958), written by J. Bulloch, has appeared. It is a solid, if unoriginal, account.

The antecedents of the Reformation have occasioned a series of articles by W. S. Reid. He has shown that Scottish anticlerical legislation in

[41] "Burgh Representation in Early Scottish Parliaments," *EHR*, 59:79–87 (January 1944).
[42] "The Scottish Abbeys and the War of Independence," *Records of the Scottish Church History Society*, 11 (1955), pp. 63–81.
[43] "Scottish Rulers and the Religious Orders, 1070–1153," *TRHS*, 5th ser., 3 (1953), pp. 77–100; "A Scottish Collection at Canterbury," *SHR*, 31:10–28 (April 1952).
[44] "The Organization of the Scottish Church in the Twelfth Century," *TRHS*, 4th ser., 29 (1947) pp. 135–149.

the fifteenth century was owing, not to the English example, but to the desire of the Crown (or the ruling faction of nobles, as the case may be) to control appointments to ecclesiastical benefices; once such control was obtained, this legislation ceased.[45] Reid has also explored further a problem discussed by Hannay in his work on the founding of the College of Justice. Reid has shown that heavy taxation of the clergy continued after the death of James V; in his view, it was this continuous tax burden, rather than the "Great Tax" of the 1530's, which prompted the extensive feuing of church lands in the pre-Reformation period.[46]

The outstanding figure in recent Reformation research has been G. Donaldson. He is the first scholar systematically to examine the records dealing with the administration of church property—the strictly financial records, such as the *Accounts of the Collectors of the Thirds of Benefices,* Scottish History Society (Edinburgh, 1949), as well as the more general records, such as the register of presentation to benefices.[47] His major conclusions chiefly concern administration, and are three in number—first, that in the days of John Knox the Kirk had no objection to the office of bishop as such, and that the attack on episcopacy was the work of Andrew Melvill; second, that the office of superintendent, as established in the First Book of Discipline,[48] was intended to be permanent; third, that by 1592 the presbyteries had already engrossed the powers of presentation to, and deprivation of, benefices, so that the so-called Golden Act of 1592, far from being revolutionary, simply recognized a *fait accompli.*[49]

J. H. S. Burleigh has summarized the melancholy story of too little and too late that represented the efforts of the old church to reform itself in the last decade before the triumph of Protestantism,[50] and H. Chadwick has explored the origins of the seminary which was expected to bring a rejuvenated Catholicism back to Scotland from France.[51] The

[45] "The Origins of Anti-Papal Legislation in Fifteenth-Century Scotland," *Catholic Historical Review,* 29:445–469 (January 1944).

[46] "Clerical Taxation: the Scottish Alternative to Dissolution of the Monasteries, 1530–1560," *ibid.,* 34:129–153 (July 1948).

[47] "Sources for the Study of Scottish Ecclesiastical Organization and Personnel, 1560–1600," *BIHR,* 19:188–203 (May 1943).

[48] Donaldson has also suggested that the First Book of Discipline may be modeled in part on the Danish *Ordinatio:* " 'The Example of Denmark' in the Scottish Reformation," *SHR,* 27:57–64 (April 1948).

[49] "The Scottish Episcopate at the Reformation," *EHR,* 60:349–364 (September 1945); "The Polity of the Scottish Church, 1560–1600," *Records of the Scottish Church History Society,* 11 (1955), pp. 212–226.

[50] "The Scottish Reforming Councils, 1549–1559," *ibid.,* pp. 189–211.

[51] "The Scots College, Douai, 1580–1613," *EHR,* 56:571–585 (October 1941).

efforts of the Roman Church in both cases proved futile; much more important to the future of the Kirk was the attitude of the Anglicans. Here again Donaldson is the leading authority. He has pointed out the consistent hostility of the Anglican leaders to Presbyterianism;[52] after 1603, and especially after 1625, they were able to make that influence felt. The eventual result was the Prayer Book of 1637. Donaldson has edited the text of this book,[53] and contributed a long and valuable introduction which shows, first, that the Prayer Book did not represent so startling a departure from the customary Scottish service as has been thought, and, second, that the original plan of Charles and Laud had been to impose the English liturgy without alteration, and that the text of the liturgy was revised in a serious effort to meet Scottish objections. Donaldson's conclusion is that the greater part of the Prayer Book might well have been acceptable, if it had been considered on its merits. The implications of this view are rejected by S. A. Burrell, who has forcibly restated the traditional view that the Scottish revolt was primarily inspired by religious discontent.[54]

Work on religious history after 1660 has been scattered and rather meager of late. F. Goldie's A Short History of the Episcopal Church of Scotland (1951), is a useful unoriginal summary. James Gordon's Diary, 1692–1710, Spalding Club (Aberdeen, 1949), edited by G. D. Henderson and H. H. Porter, is a nice illustration of the tribulations of an episcopal minister in the post-Revolutionary period. The centennial of the disruption produced a flurry of work, the best of which is the summary of the controversy provided by A. B. Erickson,[55] who is sympathetic to Chalmers. Finally, one should mention G. D. Henderson's The Claims of the Church of Scotland (1951), a book which ranges widely, if not systematically, over the whole history of the Church since the Reformation.

The Scottish educational system and particularly higher education, has come in for a good deal of attention. D. E. R. Watt has discussed the situation of Scots students at Paris in the days before there was any Scottish university, by an examination of the minute books of the Proctor of

[52] "The attitude of Whitgift and Bancroft to the Scottish Church," TRHS, 4th ser., 24 (1942), pp. 95–115.
[53] The Making of the Scottish Prayer Book of 1637 (Edinburgh, 1954).
[54] "The Covenant Idea as a Revolutionary Symbol: Scotland, 1596–1637," Church History, 27:338–350 (December 1958).
[55] "The Non-intrusion Controversy in Scotland, 1832–1843," ibid., 11:302–325 (December 1942).

the English Nation there.[56] The five hundredth anniversary of the founding of the college of St. Salvator in 1450 brought forth, not only A. I. Dunlop's biography of the founder, Bishop Kennedy, mentioned above, but also R. G. Cant's history of the college.[57] In this book Cant's chief concern is with the constitutional form of the college as it was set up by Kennedy, and with its first hundred years. Its development after the Reformation is dealt with very briefly indeed. G. D. Henderson's *The Founding of Marischal College, Aberdeen* (Aberdeen, 1947) provides a careful description of the state of higher education in the 1590's, in the first generation after the Reformation, as well as a useful account of the educational ideas of Andrew Melvill. The five hundredth anniversary of the founding of the University of Glasgow produced an admirable short history by J. D. Mackie, a book which, fittingly, is at its best in dealing with the eighteenth century, the time of the university's greatest influence.[58] Of special interest to American historians of the colonial period is G. S. Pryde's pamphlet, *The Scottish Universities and the Colleges of Colonial America* (Glasgow, 1951), a brief summary of the Scottish influence, with a good bibliography. As for the most important part of any university, the students, their life at St. Andrews in the fifteenth century has been described by A. I. Dunlop.[59] *Two Students at St. Andrews (1711–1716)* (Edinburgh, 1952), edited by W. C. Dickinson, is an extremely interesting book drawn from the contents of the Delvine Papers at the National Library of Scotland. The documents published are mostly letters from the tutor of the two sons of a member of the Faculty of Advocates to their father, letters which illustrate the curriculum, expenses, and diversions of what seem to have been a pair of typical undergraduates. The boys were enthusiastic golfers; among the many references to the game Dickinson believes he has discovered the earliest known mention of an iron!

Education below the university level has been much less well served. J. Mason has described the laudable but not particularly successful effort to provide some religious education in the highlands in the eighteenth century.[60] An interesting and valuable regional study by I. J. Simpson,

[56] "Scottish Masters and Students at Paris in the Fourteenth Century," *Aberdeen University Review*, 36:169–180 (autumn 1955).

[57] *The College of St. Salvator* (Edinburgh, 1950).

[58] *The University of Glasgow 1451–1951: A Short History* (Glasgow, 1954).

[59] "Scottish Student Life in the Fifteenth Century," *SHR*, 26:47–63 (April 1947).

[60] "Scottish Charity Schools of the Eighteenth Century," *ibid.*, 33:1–13 (April 1954).

Education in Aberdeenshire before 1872 (1947), shows that there was virtually no public education before the seventeenth century, and that even in the eighteenth century the mortality rate among schools was very high. This book is full of detail, and has a good deal of material for the social historian.

With respect to intellectual history, the focus has been on the so-called Scottish enlightenment. H. W. Meikle's David Murray Lecture, *Some Aspects of Later Seventeenth Century Scotland* (Glasgow, 1947), has suggested that it is time to get below the surface political and religious quarrels of this period and restudy its intellectual history. This was, after all, the age of Stair, Sir Robert Moray, the Gregorys, and the founding of the Advocates' Library. As for the eighteenth century itself, there is an important book by G. Bryson, *Man and Society: The Scottish Inquiry of the Eighteenth Century* (Princeton, N.J., 1945). This work is an exposition of the intellectual assumptions of the most important Scottish writers of this period, and of their analysis of human nature, society in general, and various social institutions in particular. The author's stress is on the empirical nature of their approach to "moral philosophy"; she demonstrates their connection with each other and with France. Eighteenth-century Scottish connections with America, a popular subject these days, have received some attention in their intellectual aspects. C. Robbins has analyzed the political philosophy of Francis Hutcheson, Adam Smith's predecessor in the chair of moral philosophy at Glasgow,[61] and R. A. Humphreys has discussed Principal Robertson's history of America.[62]

Literary history is beyond the scope of this paper, but the continuing series of publications of the Scottish Text Society must be mentioned. The Society's emphasis in recent years has been heavily on the later sixteenth century, and to a lesser extent on the eighteenth. Of special interest to historians are J. Craigie's excellent two-volume edition of *Basilicon Doron* (Edinburgh, 1944, 1950), and G. Watson's edition of the Mar Lodge translation of the first part of Boece's *History* (Edinburgh, 1946). The poet William Dunbar and the odd Jacobite writer Ramsay have found biographers.[63] Finally, E. C. Mossner has produced a massive

[61] " 'When It Is That Colonies May Turn Independent': An Analysis of the Environment and Politics of Francis Hutcheson (1694–1746)," *William and Mary Quarterly,* 3d ser., 11:214–251 (April 1954).
[62] *William Robertson and His History of America,* Canning House Lecture (1954).
[63] J. W. Baxter, *William Dunbar* (1952); G. D. Henderson, *Chevalier Ramsay* (1952).

and learned *Life of David Hume* (Edinburgh, 1954), a work of more interest to the historian than the philosopher, since Mossner's concern is with his subject's life, and he discusses Hume's writings only where necessary to illuminate some biographical fact.

The writing of local and family history, and the publishing of local and family records, have been flourishing in Scotland for a long time. Much of this work is of very little general interest, but there are some exceptions. W. R. Kermack's *The Scottish Highlands: A Short History* (Edinburgh, 1957) is a good brief survey especially on economic and military questions; it is unfortunately without scholarly apparatus. C. M. MacDonald's *The History of Argyll, up to the Beginning of the Sixteenth Century* (Glasgow, 1950) is just the reverse; it is scholarly, and almost entirely political. It contains nothing startling, but it does pull together a good deal of widely scattered material. The northern islands have come in for a good deal of attention of late. A conference of British and Scandinavian scholars was held in Lerwick in 1950 to discuss all aspects of the Norse occupation of the islands. The papers delivered have been collected and edited by W. D. Simpson under the title *The Viking Congress* (Edinburgh, 1954). The work of J. Mooney,[64] an amateur scholar who lived in Kirkwall, has shed a good deal of light on the marriage treaty of 1468, especially in the matter of the distinction between the power of the Crown in the islands and that of the earl. What James III acquired by the marriage treaty were the royal rights; by an exchange with the then earl in 1470, James also became earl. The fact that the earl's powers in the island were much greater than those of the Crown goes far to explain the Danish failure to redeem the pledge and resume sovereignty over the islands. G. Donaldson's *Shetland Life under Earl Patrick* (1958) has re-created conditions as they existed under perhaps the most hated of all the many rulers of the northern islands, a ruler whose tyranny eventually led James VI to have him executed. Donaldson's conclusion is that the earl's regime was extortionate and oppressive, but not illegal—a pattern followed by many another autocrat, both before and since.[65]

One new series of documents should be mentioned, the *Aberdeen*

[64] *The Cathedral and Royal Burgh of Kirkwall* (Kirkwall, 1943); *Charters and Other Records of the City and Royal Burgh of Kirkwall*, Spalding Club (Kirkwall, 1950).

[65] Donaldson has edited one of the sources on which this study is based: *The Court Book of Shetland, 1602–4* (Edinburgh, 1954).

Council Letters, edited by L. M. Taylor, five volumes of which have appeared since 1942, covering the years 1552–1675. They contain a great
deal of information for the economic historian and are interesting as an
illustration of how the great national convulsions of these years affected
local interests in one of Scotland's largest burghs.

What is shown least well in a survey of this kind is the enormous
amount of work in Scottish history that remains to be done. Scottish historians have tended to "bunch," to walk along the well-beaten paths,
while whole areas lie untouched—a sin of which the present writer is as
guilty as any other. The area most strikingly neglected is the last hundred years; perhaps the Scottish nationalists, if they accomplish nothing
else, will succeed in creating some interest in Scotland's recent past.
Scotland also badly needs a new general history. Only one attempt has
been made in the past twenty years by an historian to look at Scottish
history as a whole other than on the textbook level. This was W.
Notestein in *The Scot in History* (New Haven, Conn., 1946). This work
is an attempt to trace the historical evolution of the Scottish national
character; like most such attempts by serious historians, it is full of statements which are open to challenge, and of others which are extraordinarily stimulating. But, of course, it is not a general history. It is something of a scandal that the work which must still be referred to as the
"standard" history of Scotland first appeared in 1900. Hume Brown's
volumes have done service long enough; it is high time for them to be
replaced, by something on the order of the *Oxford History of England.*
The completing of such a project would be the greatest possible contribution to the next twenty years of Scottish historiography.

Since the original publication of this article in 1959, several important
books on Scottish history have appeared.[66] Perhaps the most encourag-

---

[66] In the interest of brevity articles appearing in scholarly journals since 1959
will not be mentioned in this supplement. This omission makes less difference now
than it might have in the past, because in 1960 the *Scottish Historical Review* began
the very useful practice of listing in its October issue all such articles on Scottish
history which appeared the previous year.

It has been pointed out to me that in my original survey I failed to mention any
of the contributions to scholarship which appeared in the *Proceedings of the Society
of Antiquaries of Scotland* and the *Innes Review.* These were unaccountable over-
sights. The former deals mostly with problems which pre-date the eleventh century,
but there are some useful medieval articles in it. The *Innes Review* is a journal
of Catholic historical studies, and has a wide range of articles, not all by Catholic
scholars, dealing with the Roman Church in Scotland.

ing news is the projected four-volume *Edinburgh History of Scotland,* under the general editorship of G. Donaldson, which, when it appears, will, hopefully, make obsolete the most serious of the strictures contained in the last paragraph above.[67] In the meantime, *A New History of Scotland,* in two volumes, has appeared, the first volume, to 1603 by W. C. Dickinson (Edinburgh, 1961) and the second by G. S. Pryde (Edinburgh, 1962). It is a sound textbook survey, with some weak spots, notably the sketchy treatment of seventeenth-century political history, and some very fine chapters, especially those on medieval institutions and on social and economic change in the recent period. Another promising development is the decision of a group of medievalists to collect and publish the written acts of the Scottish kings from 1153 to 1424, under the general title, *Regesta Regum Scottorum.* If the first volume to appear, *The Acts of Malcolm IV, King of Scots, 1153–1165,* edited by G. W. S. Barrow (Edinburgh, 1960), is any criterion, this will be much more than just another collection of documents. Professor Barrow has supplied an excellent account of Malcolm's reign and a brilliant description of the governmental structure of the twelfth century as well as a careful analysis of the texts themselves. If the rest of the series maintains Professor Barrow's standards, this will be a very distinguished contribution indeed to our knowledge of medieval Scotland. Professor Barrow has also written a stunning biography of *Robert Bruce* (Berkeley, Calif., 1965), a really magnificent reassessment of the significance of the greatest of Scotland's medieval kings.

Another interesting piece of editing is by W. A. Gatherer, *The Tyrannous Reign of Mary Stewart: George Buchanan's Account* (Edinburgh, 1958). The editor has done a skillful piece of historical detective work on Buchanan's narrative, and, rather unsurprisingly, concludes in his preface that Buchanan was a liar. In fact, Mr. Gatherer's animus against his subject leads him to a somewhat over-critical opinion of Buchanan's historical work as a whole.

Three contributions to *Festschrifts* should be mentioned. Two of them, oddly enough, deal with different aspects of the same subject. G. Donaldson, "Foundations of Anglo-Scottish Union," in *Elizabethan Government and Society, Essays Presented to Sir John Neale,* edited by S. T. Bindoff *et al.* (1961), deals with the cultural and economic as well as the

---

[67] The third volume, the first to appear, has just been published: *Scotland, James V to James VII* (Edinburgh, 1965) written by Professor Donaldson himself. Like all of his work, it is excellent.

more obvious religious connection between the two countries in the six-
teenth century with his customary skill. D. H. Willson, the king's biogra-
pher, supplies a careful account of "King James I and Anglo-Scottish
Unity" in *Conflict in Stuart England: Essays in Honor of Wallace
Notestein,* edited by W. A. Aiken and B. D. Henning (1960). H. R.
Trevor-Roper, "Scotland and the Puritan Revolution," in *Historical
Essays 1600–1750 Presented to David Ogg,* edited by H. E. Bell and
R. L. Ollard (1963), is concerned with two major points. The Scottish
effort to impose Presbyterianism on England in the 1640's was a failure,
says Professor Trevor-Roper, because there were no real Presbyterians in
England with whom the Scots could ally. Similarly, Cromwell's efforts to
impose his religious and legal ideas on the Scots in the 1650's came to
nothing because there were no Scottish "backbench gentry" on whom he
could depend to carry out his policy. Professor Trevor-Roper's arguments are not entirely convincing, and he has some odd views respecting
Scottish affairs in the two generations or so before 1640, but he is, as
always, plausible and stimulating.

In economic history the last few years have seen the publication of a
comprehensive study of Scottish agriculture in the modern period, J. A.
Symon, *Scottish Farming: Past and Present* (Edinburgh, 1959). The
first two-thirds of the book constitute a historical account, with particular attention to the period since the eighteenth century; the medieval
section is a bit thin. The last third of the book deals with a series of special subjects such as horticulture. Our knowledge of sixteenth-century
economic history has been increased by two very different works, each
important in its own way. One is *Accounts of the Masters of Works for
Building and Repairing Royal Palaces and Castles, I, 1529–1615,* edited
by H. M. Paton (Edinburgh, 1957). These accounts tell us a good deal
about social as well as economic history; the editor's introduction deals
with the various classes of people who worked on the buildings and the
conditions under which they worked, which evidently were not very
good—real wages, for instance, apparently did not rise at all in the
course of the century. The other work is a monograph by S. G. E. Lythe,
The Economy of Scotland in Its European Setting 1550–1625 (Edinburgh, 1960), a book whose chief value lies in its careful study of foreign trade, for which the author has made good use of manuscript
sources. His conclusion is that trade expanded and Scotland prospered
under James VI, not because the king was a skillful economist, but
rather because he provided internal order and peace abroad. And, in-

deed, James did recognize the economic value of peace. Lythe also takes a passing glance at the Weber-Tawney thesis and concludes that religious changes had no discernible direct effect on economic life before 1625.

In another thorough monograph T. C. Smout, *Scottish Trade on the Eve of Union, 1660–1707* (Edinburgh, 1963), has shown that the economic results of the union were in some sense anticipated in the two preceding generations. Trade with England was growing, and the traditional trade with France and the Dutch was declining owing to the wars and Colbert's tariff policy. H. Hamilton, *An Economic History of Scotland in the Eighteenth Century* (Oxford, 1963), makes it clear that the economic expectations aroused by the union were not immediately fulfilled, and that in some respects the terms of the treaty itself were violated by the English majority in Parliament. It was not until the last quarter of the century that a soundly based economic expansion began. This is a splendid and detailed description of Scottish economic life; it would have been still better if it had analyzed the causes of economic change more thoroughly. For a later period T. Ferguson, *Scottish Social Welfare 1864–1914* (Edinburgh, 1958) has continued his studies of that important subject, with a rather pronounced medical bias. On the topics he covers, such matters as population growth, mortality rates, and water supply, he is extremely thorough.

In legal and constitutional history two important works have appeared. One is J. Fergusson, *The Sixteen Peers of Scotland* (Oxford, 1960). This witty and urbane book is both a description of present constitutional practice written by a man who, in his capacity as Keeper of the Records, plays an important part in the conduct of elections of Scotland's representative peers, and a historical account of past elections, especially in connection with the problems of the right to vote and electoral canvassing. The other is *The Court Book of the Burgh of Kirkintilloch 1658–1694*, edited by G. S. Pryde, Scottish History Society (Edinburgh, 1963), which contains a splendid introductory essay on the history of ecclesiastical and baronial burghs from the twelfth century on.

The story of one of Scotland's great families has been written by I. F. Grant, *The MacLeods: The History of a Clan, 1200–1956* (1959), a book based on the records preserved in the MacLeod muniment room at Dunvegan. The dates in the title are misleading. The book really ends with the eighteenth century, but for the six hundred years which Miss Grant covers, she has written much more than a clan history. This book is really a social and economic history of the Highlands, and, barring some slips in detail, is very well done. Another contribution to the history of the Highlands in the eighteenth century, which also is chiefly interesting for what it has to say about social and economic questions, is contained in R. J. Adam's introduction to *John Home's Survey of Assynt*, Scottish History Society (Edinburgh, 1960). A different sort of regional history is provided by R. C. Reid's introduction to his edition of *Wigtownshire Charters*, Scottish History Society (Edinburgh, 1960), which contains an account of the institutions of medieval Galloway, especially the feudal courts and the church. The documents themselves are mostly of the fifteenth and sixteenth centuries.

Three works in intellectual history are worth mention. *Acta Facultatis Artium Universitatis Sanctiandree, 1413–1588*, edited by A. I. Dunlop, Scottish History Society (Edinburgh, 1964), in addition to the *acta*, contains an excellent introduction by Mrs. Dunlop which discusses the history of the university in its early years and the life and organization of its faculty. W. C. Lehmann, *John Millar of Glasgow* (Cambridge, Eng., 1960), is an important study of a man who was a kind of pioneering sociologist who had a very considerable impact on eighteenth-century social thought. G. E. Davie, *The Democratic Intellect: Scotland and Her Universities in the 19th Century* (Edinburgh, 1961) is a book by an angry young philosopher. It is an account of the effort to force Scottish universities to conform to the Oxbridge pattern in the nineteenth century, an effort which was largely successful and which the author bitterly regrets. Mr. Davie's book has several serious shortcomings as history, but it is highly interesting and very provocative.

The year 1960 marked the quatercentenary of the triumph of the Reformation in Scotland, and so a good many works on religious history have been published recently, some of them of the first importance. Pride of place must go to G. Donaldson, *The Scottish Reformation* (Cambridge, Eng., 1960). Professor Donaldson's concern in this book is with the church as an institution, not with theological questions or Scottish religious life. In addition to providing further support for the views he has previously advocated, the author points out that the question in 1559 was not whether there would be reform in the church—the Catholic hierarchy itself had accepted the need for reform—but whether there would be reform or revolution. He also contends that, just as the superintendent was a substitute for a nonexistent Godly bishop, the General

Assembly was a substitute for a nonexistent Godly magistrate. The whole tendency of Professor Donaldson's approach is to lay stress on continuity rather than change in the development of the Scottish church as an institution before and after 1560, which he regards as a date of no great importance; the really radical change, he says, comes in the next generation, with Andrew Melvill. This is not the place to argue the merits of Professor Donaldson's views; suffice it to say that this is the most important book on the Reformation to appear for many years.

A rather different approach to the Reformation is apparent in *Essays on the Scottish Reformation 1513–1625*, edited by D. McRoberts (Glasgow, 1962). All but one of these essays appeared in the two numbers of the *Innes Review* for 1959, and virtually all of them are written by Catholics. The viewpoint which emerges is that the faults of the ancient church were grievous, although not so grievous as has been supposed; the hierarchy was to blame for these faults; the crown was to blame for the faults of the hierarchy; the Reformation triumphed in Scotland, not for religious reasons, but owing to English intervention, the greed of the aristocracy, and the collapse of the authority of the Crown. James V emerges as one of the major villains of the piece, on account of his cynical exploitation of the church for his own ends. The essays are interesting and supply some useful corrections in detail; many are extremely learned; but the main line of argument leaves this (non-Catholic) writer unconvinced.

Some other works on religious history may be more briefly noted. J. S. MacEwen, *The Faith of John Knox* (1961) has filled an important gap by refusing to accept the common assumption that Knox was simply a disciple of Calvin; he has shown that the Scottish reformer differed from his great contemporary in several significant ways. G. Hay, *The Architecture of Scottish Post-Reformation Churches* (Oxford, 1957) is far broader in scope than its title would suggest, and contains a good deal of social and economic history. W. R. Foster, *Bishop and Presbytery: The Church of Scotland 1661–1688* (1958) effectively demolishes the old notion that almost everyone in Restoration Scotland hated bishops with Covenanting fervor. Genuine disaffection was confined largely to the southwest; in many areas the bishops and their subordinates got on well together; and episcopacy might well have been successfully integrated with the Presbyterian structure if the government of Charles II had behaved more intelligently. H. Escott, *A History of Scottish Congregation-*

alism(Glasgow, 1960), has produced a definitive work on that subject. Finally, J. H. S. Burleigh, *A Church History of Scotland* (Oxford, 1960), has written an excellent one-volume survey, fair and impartial, by far the best book to use to introduce a newcomer to the study of Scottish religious history.

Modern Irish History since 1940: A Bibliographical Survey (1600–1922)

❖

HELEN F. MULVEY

THE HISTORY of Ireland, it is probably fair to say, has not yet been adequately written.[1] The past twenty-five years have seen the publication of useful general works, valuable source materials, several distinguished books, and numerous monographs and articles which have answered significant questions or suggested new ones. Works of broad interpretation which raise questions about the deeper meanings of Irish history have, with some exceptions, been missing. There are, it hardly needs saying, stages in the understanding of any nation's history, and on the scholarly foundations laid in the past generation more intricate structures should arise. In some very recent observations on the study of Irish history, J. C. Beckett comments on the special difficulties of the Irish historical framework, and on the ways in which the tasks of the Irish and English historian differ. The stable element in Irish history, Beckett suggests, has been the land, the place, the country itself; the unstable element, the people, who arriving at different times, make impossible the reduction of the history of the country to a simple formula of native against foreigner. All the Irish people must be the concern of the historian, but any historical survey might better be called *The History of Ireland* rather than *The History of the Irish People*.[2]

[Reprinted from *The Historian*, 27:516–559 (August 1965).]

[1] No article on medieval Ireland will appear in this series but see *Historical Studies*: I, *Papers Read to the Second Irish Conference of Historians* (1958): Eric St. John Brooks, "The Sources of Mediaeval Anglo-Irish History," pp. 86–92; and Aubrey Gwynn, "Bibliographical Note on Mediaeval Anglo-Irish History," pp. 93–99.

[2] James C. Beckett, *The Study of Irish History*, An Inaugural Lecture delivered before The Queen's University of Belfast on 13 March 1963 (Belfast, 1963).

At the center of much of the scholarly work of the past quarter of a century is the outstanding journal, *Irish Historical Studies*,[3] founded in 1938, under the editorship of R. Dudley Edwards and Theodore W. Moody. It contains critical articles and historical revisions, reviews which have often been contributions to Irish historiography, and a yearly comprehensive list of all publications in Irish history. The founders of *Irish Historical Studies* have also shared in the establishment of the series, Studies in Irish History, in which, beginning in 1944, a number of original contributions to Irish history have been published.[4] For new viewpoints and interpretations there is another series, *Historical Studies*, begun in 1958, which has now (1965) reached four volumes. It contains the papers read before the biennial Irish conferences of historians. A number of new journals devoted to special aspects of Irish history have appeared.[5] One of these, easily overlooked, is the small yearly, *Proceedings of the Irish Catholic Historical Committee*, 1955——, which contains brief scholarly statements on significant research in Irish ecclesiastical history.[6] Another annual journal, *Studia Hibernica*, appeared in 1961 (Dublin). It carries articles in both English and Gaelic, on both historical and literary subjects.

Important source materials have been appearing under the auspices of the Irish Manuscripts Commission, founded in 1928.[7] The materials so far published are most significant for the period before 1700.[8] The Com-

[3] The journal appears twice yearly under the auspices of the Irish Historical Society in the Republic and the Ulster Society for Irish Historical Studies. A mimeographed *Bulletin of the Irish Committee of Historical Sciences*, sent to members of the two societies, contains information on Irish historical matters.

[4] Studies in Irish History, First Series, consists of seven volumes, vols. I–V edited by T. W. Moody, R. Dudley Edwards, and David B. Quinn, and VI–VII by T. W. Moody, R. Dudley Edwards, and J. C. Beckett. A second series of the *Studies* is edited by T. W. Moody, J. C. Beckett, and T. D. Williams.

[5] *The Irish Sword, Journal of the Military History Society of Ireland*, 1952——; *Reportorium Novum, Dublin Diocesan Historical Record*, 1955——; *Seanchas Ardmhacha, Journal of the Armagh Diocesan Historical Society*, 1954——; *Clogher Record*, 1953——; *Irish Theological Quarterly*, resumed 1951——. For a list of journals in which material on all periods of Irish history is published, see *Bibliography of British History: Tudor Period, 1485–1603*, ed. Conyers Read, 2d ed. (Oxford, 1959), pp. 478–479.

[6] In 1960, the *Proceedings* announced a *History of Irish Catholicism* to be published by the Committee.

[7] Only a few of the Commission's volumes can be noted here, but critical notices appear in *IHS*. See R. D. Edwards, "The Work of the Irish Manuscripts Commission," *Studies*, 26:481–488 (September 1937), and James Hogan, *The Irish Manuscripts Commission: Work in Progress* (Cork, 1954).

[8] The most recent catalogue is *Irish Manuscripts Commission: Catalogue of Publications Issued and in Preparation, 1928–1962* (Dublin, 1962). See also the periodical *Collectanea Hibernica*, 1958——, directed by the Franciscan Fathers, published yearly and devoted to the publication of sources.

mission also issues a journal, *Analecta Hibernica,* 1930——, containing documentary material unsuitable for separate publication, as well as information on its own proceedings and proposals. In assembling and organizing sources, notable work has been done by the National Library of Ireland, especially in making available in microfilm collections of Irish materials in foreign repositories.[9] Always, of course, account must be taken of the vast destruction of records, especially that of 1922.[10]

Irish history, at the moment, stands in need both of many more monographs on special subjects, and of new works of synthesis. The research of the last twenty-five years has, in many fields, led to revisions and reinterpretations which must be incorporated with older work. Despite few new books on some subjects, much more is now known, for example, on ecclesiastical history in the seventeenth century, on the era of Lord Strafford, on the seventeenth-century plantations, on the penal laws, on the rise of the Catholic middle class in the eighteenth century, on social and economic history in the earlier nineteenth century, on the era of Parnell. Irish historians are moving ahead to these new tasks of organization and synthesis, and, at a meeting of the Irish Historical Society in December 1962, a cooperative history of Ireland was projected, to be published in three volumes by 1970.[11] Some of the need for making

---

[9] The microfilm collection now contains something like 5,000,000 pages of material copied. Card catalogues controlling this material are being integrated with other files, the library's own holdings and others. Plans are under way to publish this consolidated catalogue in book form. Also, the National Library now has a card index to the first fifteen years of the *Freeman's Journal* (from 1763) and a catalogue in progress, in fact two-thirds completed, for a wide variety of Irish periodicals. Each article will be treated as a monograph and placed under the categories of name, place, subject, and date. These categories will also govern manuscript collections. See also *Analecta Hibernica,* no. 15 (1944) "Survey of Documents in Private Keeping," 1st ser., reports presented by Edward MacLysaght, and no. 20 (1958) "Survey of Documents in Private Keeping," 2d ser. by John Ainsworth and Edward MacLysaght.

[10] On Irish records see Margaret Griffith's articles, "Short Guide to the Public Record Office of Ireland," *IHS,* 8:45–58 (March 1952), and "The Irish Record Commission, 1810–1830," *ibid.,* 7:17–38 (March 1950). Also D. A. Chart, "The Public Record Office of Northern Ireland, 1924–1936," *ibid.,* 1:42–57 (March 1938). For an earlier survey see Herbert Wood, "The Public Records of Ireland before and after 1922," *TRHS,* 4th ser., 13 (1930), pp. 17–49.

[11] The history would be divided into thirteen periods to be covered in a three-volume work, the text in two volumes and reference material in a third. As soon as possible after 1970, the plan is to publish a series of volumes comparable to the *Oxford History of England* with each of the thirteen periods covered by a volume, with, again, an additional volume (a fourteenth) devoted to reference material. The suggested thirteen periods are: (1) to 800 (2) 800–1200 (3) 1200–1366 (4) 1366–1534 (5) 1534–1603 (6) 1603–1660 (7) 1660–1714 (8) 1714–1783 (9) 1783–1829 (10) 1829–1858 (11) 1858–1890 (12) 1890–1921 (13) 1921–1949. The general editors are T. W. Moody, T. D. Williams, and J. C. Beckett. For the most recent statement on this project, see *IHS,* 14 (September 1964), p. 176.

more widely available the results of recent research is being met by the
Dublin Historical Association which has been publishing short studies
on a number of significant subjects.[12] Irish historical writing itself needs
attention, and a study, or a collective work, devoted to the history and
historians of modern Ireland would be of the greatest value.[13]

A number of general histories and surveys of special subjects have appeared since 1940. The best of the general works is James C. Beckett's *A
Short History of Ireland,* Hutchinson University Library (1952; rev. ed.,
1958), notable for its clarity and fairness of judgment. A more popular
survey is Brian Inglis, *The Story of Ireland* (1956). Organized topically,
it concludes with a good account of Irish affairs since 1922. Edmund
Curtis' *History of Ireland,* first published in 1936, reached its sixth edition in 1950. Among special subjects nothing has replaced the older surveys in economic and ecclesiastical history.[14] One recent study, Alfred
G. Donaldson's *Some Comparative Aspects of Irish Law* (Durham, N. C.,
and London, 1957), contributes to the much neglected field of Irish constitutional history, and calls attention, in its second chapter, to the main
lines of Irish constitutional development.[15] For agricultural history,
John O'Donovan's widely praised study, *The Economic History of Livestock in Ireland* (Dublin and London, 1940), has broader implications
for Irish economic history than the title might suggest. Though intended
as surveys for the general reader, S. J. Knox's *Ireland's Debt to the
Huguenots* (Dublin, 1959), and John M. Barkley's *A Short History of
the Presbyterian Church in Ireland* (Belfast, 1959), throw light on the

[12] Four of these have appeared: Maureen Wall, *The Penal Laws, 1691–1760*
(Dundalk, 1961); J. G. Simms, *The Treaty of Limerick* (Dundalk, 1961); F. S. L.
Lyons, *Parnell* (Dundalk, 1963); J. H. Whyte, *The Tenant League and Irish
Politics in the Eighteen Fifties* (Dundalk, 1963). The series announces for 1964–
1965: K. B. Nowlan, *O'Connell and Young Ireland;* J. L. McCracken, *The Irish
Parliament in the Eighteenth Century;* David Thornley, *Irish Politics in the Eighteen-
Sixties and Seventies;* E. D. Steele, *The Irish Land Question in the Nineteenth
Century.*

[13] A few articles have appeared on history and historians. See F. X. Martin, "The
Writings of Eoin MacNeill," *IHS,* 6:44–62 (March 1948); T. W. Moody, "The
Writings of Edmund Curtis," *ibid.,* 3:393–400 (September 1943); Norman D.
Palmer, "Sir Robert Peel's 'Select Irish Library,'" *ibid.,* 6:101–113 (September
1948); Donald MacCartney, "The Writing of History in Ireland, 1800–1850," *ibid.,*
10:347–362 (September 1957); Walter D. Love, "Charles O'Conor of Belanagare
and Thomas Leland's 'Philosophical' History of Ireland," *ibid.,* 13:1–25 (March
1962).

[14] There is no satisfactory general work on ecclesiastical history. For economic
history there are the three surveys by George O'Brien which cover Irish economic
history from 1600 to the famine (1918–1921).

[15] Donaldson is also valuable for Ireland's role in the history of the British Commonwealth.

history of Irish Protestantism. Two collections of documents covering broad periods of history are now available: *Irish Historical Documents, 1172–1922* (1943), edited by Edmund Curtis and R. B. McDowell with an emphasis on constitutional and political history,[16] and James Carty's three-volume work, illustrated, which includes a wide variety of materials for the years 1607–1921.[17]

With the opening of the seventeenth century,[18] with the battle of Kinsale, with the "flight of the Earls," modern Irish history begins. The old Gaelic world has fallen, and the writ of English law runs throughout the country. Peculiar difficulties confront the student who tries to unravel, for this century, the threads of political or economic, cultural or religious history. All the great problems—plantation; the conflict of viewpoint and interest found in native Irish, old English, and new English; the Counter Reformation; the lingering Gaelic civilization; the British colonizing mentality—impinge on one another in intricate ways.[19] Despite the problems, much work needs doing and fresh books need writing on a century which sees the origins of modern Ireland. Unlike the nineteenth century, the seventeenth has not strongly attracted non-Irish scholars.

Colonization and land confiscation are central themes for the entire

[16] For comments on the selection see H. G. Richardson in *IHS*, 4:358–361 (September 1945); and A. G. in *Studies*, 32:579–581 (December 1943).

[17] I, *Ireland: From the Flight of the Earls to Grattan's Parliament, 1607–1782* (Dublin, 1949); II, *From Grattan's Parliament to the Great Famine, 1783–1850* (Dublin, 1949); and III, *From the Great Famine to the Treaty, 1851–1921* (Dublin, 1951). For geographical background see T. W. Freeman, *Ireland: Its Physical, Historical, Social, and Economic Geography* (1950), revised and republished as *Ireland: A General and Regional Geography* (1960).

[18] Work on Tudor Ireland is listed to January 1957 in Conyers Read, *Bibliography of British History: Tudor Period, 1485–1603*, pp. 478–518. See on the Irish section, review in *IHS*, 12:283–288 (March 1961). For special relevance as immediate seventeenth-century background see for constitutional history: T. W. Moody, "The Irish Parliament under Elizabeth and James I: A General Survey," *Proceedings, Royal Irish Academy*, 45 (1939), sect. C, pp. 41–81; and R. Dudley Edwards and T. W. Moody, "The History of Poynings' Law: Pt. I, 1494–1615," *IHS*, 2:415–424 (September 1941). For the military events preceding Kinsale see G. A. Hayes-McCoy, "Strategy and Tactics in Irish Warfare, 1593–1601," *ibid.*, 2:255–279 (March 1941); and Rev. John J. Silke, "Why Aguila Landed at Kinsale," *ibid.*, 13:236–245 (March 1963). Also G. A. Hayes-McCoy, "Gaelic Society in Ireland in the Late Sixteenth Century," *Historical Studies: IV, Papers Read to the Fifth Irish Conference of Historians* (1963).

[19] A new edition of the *Bibliography of British History: Stuart Period, 1603–1714*, ed. Godfrey Davies (Oxford, 1928) is in preparation. See *English Historical Documents, 1660–1714*, ed. Andrew Browning (1953). Part VIII on Ireland, pp. 701–783, contains a bibliography of older and more recent work. For criticism of the Irish section see *IHS*, 9:96–98 (March 1954).

century, causing as they do several revolutions in Irish affairs. Older historians have dealt with the subject, but not enough is known about the English and Scottish settlers, of the motives which made them come to Ireland, of the plantations themselves. For the earlier part of the century, there is one outstanding plantation history, T. W. Moody's *The Londonderry Plantation, 1609–1641: The City of London and the Plantation of Ulster* (Belfast, 1939), which throws fresh light on the Irish policies of the first two Stuarts, on their relations with London, and on the London companies in Ulster.[20] No comparable study, unfortunately, follows the history of the plantation after 1641. For the end of the century, one gap in the history of land confiscation has been authoritatively filled by J. G. Simms in *The Williamite Confiscation in Ireland, 1690–1703* (Studies in Irish History, VII, 1956). Setting out with new materials to solve the question left unanswered by W. F. T. Butler[21] regarding land ownership before and after the war of 1689–91, Simms concludes that Catholics owned considerably more land both before and after the Jacobite war than Butler thought. It was the operation of the penal laws which caused the later Catholic losses of land.[22]

No study of the Cromwellian land settlement has replaced Prendergast.[23] The Irish Manuscripts Commission has published *The Civil Survey* which has been edited in ten volumes with valuable introductory material by Robert C. Simington, whose long association with the former Quit Rent Office has given him an extraordinary knowledge of the various Irish plantations.[24] Three volumes of the *Books of Survey and Distribution* have also been published by the Irish Manuscripts

[20] See T. W. Moody, "Sir Thomas Phillips of Limavady, Servitor," *IHS*, 1:251–272 (March 1939), and "The Treatment of the Native Population under the Scheme for the Plantation of Ulster," *ibid.*, 1:59–63 (March 1938).

[21] *Confiscation in Irish History* (Dublin, 1917).

[22] See J. G. Simms: "Land Owned by Catholics in Ireland in 1688," *IHS*, 7:180–190 (March 1951); and "Williamite Peace Tactics, 1690–91," *ibid.*, 8:303–323 (September 1953).

[23] John P. Prendergast, *The Cromwellian Settlement of Ireland*, 2d ed. (1870). For the Cromwellian era see J. R. MacCormack, "The Irish Adventurers and the English Civil War," *IHS*, 10:21–58 (March 1956); John W. Blake, "Transportation from Ireland to America, 1653–1660," *ibid.*, 3:267–281 (March 1943). On military affairs see Hugh Hazlett, "The Recruitment and Organization of the Scottish Army in Ulster, 1642–9," in *Essays in British and Irish History in Honour of James Eadie Todd*, ed. H. A. Cronne, T. W. Moody, and D. B. Quinn (1949), and "The Financing of the British Armies in Ireland, 1641–49," *IHS*, 1:21–41 (March 1938).

[24] *The Civil Survey* (1654–6) ed. Robert C. Simington, 10 vols., Irish Manuscripts Commission (Dublin, 1931–61). Not all the records of the survey, which ironically Ireland owes to Cromwell, have survived. These ten volumes contain what remains.

Commission, again under the editorship of Simington.[25] These two famous collections of materials are a basic source for the economic and social history of seventeenth-century Ireland, and for the origins of the Anglo-Irish gentry and aristocracy of later centuries.[26] There is no work devoted to the viewpoints and attitudes of the colonizers.[27]

New works of historical narrative or political analysis are few, but for the period before 1641 there is Hugh Kearney's outstanding and original *Strafford in Ireland, 1633–41: A Study in Absolutism* (Manchester, Eng., 1959). Kearney's verdict on Strafford's Irish career differs from the favorable one which some English historians have presented. Strafford emerges as indeed an able administrator, but one who initiated no essentially new policies. Chapters on the sixteenth-century background, on finance, on church and state, on the Irish parliament of 1634, on economic policy, give Kearney's study something of the character of a general history of Ireland in the early seventeenth century. A career in sharp juxtaposition to Strafford's is that of Richard Boyle, Earl of Cork, and Lord Treasurer of Ireland. Terence Ranger's forthcoming biography of Boyle [28] should shed important light on this period, and already, in a long article, "Richard Boyle and the Making of an Irish Fortune, 1588–1614" (*IHS*, 10:257–297 [March 1957]), Ranger has studied Boyle's rise to power and the ways in which the crown had lost its opportunities in Ireland.[29] The political and religious involvement of Ireland with the

[25] Vol. I, *Roscommon*, vol. II, *Mayo*, ed. R. C. Simington (Dublin, 1949, 1956); vol. III, *Galway*, prepared for publication by B. MacGiolla Choille, intro. R. C. Simington (Dublin, 1962). The Books of Survey and Distribution for each county indicate the position as to landownership in every parish and barony prior and subsequent to the forfeitures under Cromwell and William III. See Rev. P. J. McLaughlin, "Surveys of Ireland in the Seventeenth Century," *Irish Ecclesiastical Record*, 73:129–139 (January–June 1950).

[26] See Sean O'Domhnaill, "The Maps of the Down Survey," *IHS*, 3:381–392 (September 1943); for the uses and value of this "Irish Domesday" in social and economic history see J. G. Simms, "The Civil Survey, 1654–6," *ibid.*, 9:253–263 (March 1955).

[27] For the sixteenth century, and for ideas behind plantation see David B. Quinn, "Ireland and Sixteenth Century European Expansion," *Historical Studies: I, Papers Read to the Second Irish Conference of Historians* (1958). Quinn suggests the significance of the plantation of Ireland in the wider context of comparative and, more especially, of Spanish colonial history. Also Howard M. Jones, "Origins of the Colonial Idea in England," *Proceedings of the American Philosophical Society*, 85 (1942), pp. 448–465.

[28] See Terence Ranger, 'Strafford in Ireland: A Reevaluation," *PP*, 19 (April 1961), pp. 26–45. The relevance of Strafford's Irish policies to the central issues of English politics is discussed.

[29] For further light on "Strafford's Ireland" see: J. P. Cooper "The Fortune of Thomas Wentworth, Earl of Strafford," *EcHR*, 2d ser., 11:227–248 (December

Puritan revolution is the subject of Thomas L. Coonan's *The Irish Catholic Confederacy and the Puritan Revolution* (New York, London, and Dublin, 1954), a work which fails to maintain objectivity toward the complicated and controversial history it covers. The Confederation of Kilkenny whose collapse opened the way for the Cromwellian conquest still awaits a definitive history, but the difficulties of studying it, as well as the history of which it is a part, have been brilliantly appraised by J. C. Beckett in "The Confederation of Kilkenny Reviewed," *Historical Studies: II, Papers Read to the Third Conference of Irish Historians* (1959). General historical works for the post-1660 period are lacking.[30]

Religious history is at every turn intimately involved with political history. For the early- and mid-seventeenth century, materials have been accumulating in the form of recently published documents and significant interpretive articles for the comprehensive history of the Counter Reformation which remains to be written. All the work done re-emphasizes the importance of looking not alone at London-Dublin, but at Ireland itself, and especially at Irish political and ecclesiastical relations with Europe. The Irish Manuscripts Commission has published a selection of the papers of Luke Wadding,[31] the Irish Franciscan, founder of the Irish College at Rome, and in 1949 issued the final volume of its edition of the *Rinuccini Memoirs*.[32] *Archivium Hibernicum*, the journal of the Catholic Record Society of Ireland, resumed publication in 1941 and has been printing important records of the Irish colleges in Europe. Some idea of the work being done and yet to be accomplished in Irish Counter Reformation history can be obtained from

---

1958); Victor Treadwell, "The Irish Court of Wards under James I," *IHS*, 12:1–27 (March 1960); C. R. Mayes, "The Early Stuarts and the Irish Peerage," *EHR*, 73:227–251 (April 1958); Hugh Kearney, "The Court of Wards and Liveries in Ireland 1622–1641," *Proceedings, Royal Irish Academy*, 57 (July 1955), sect. C, pp. 29–68, and "Richard Boyle, Ironmaster," *Journal of the Royal Society of Antiquaries of Ireland*, 83:156–162 (1953). On temporal and spiritual loyalties see, J. J. Silke, "Primate Lombard and James I," *Irish Theological Quarterly*, 22:124–149 (April 1955).

[30] For 1688–1714, an older unsatisfactory history is R. H. Murray's *Revolutionary Ireland and Its Settlement* (1911). On a projected bibliography of sources for the period 1685–1702 see J. G. Simms, *Analecta Hibernica*, no. 22, Irish Manuscripts Commission (Dublin, 1960), pp. 3–10.

[31] Brendan Jennings, ed., *Wadding Papers, 1614–1638*, Irish Manuscripts Commission (Dublin, 1953).

[32] Fr. Richardus O'Ferrall and Fr. Robertus O'Connell, *Commentarius Rinuccinianus De Sedis Apostolicae Legatione Ad Foederatos Hiberniae Catholicos Per Annos 1645–69*, ed. Fr. Stanislaus Kavanagh, O.M. Cap., vols. I–VI, Irish Manuscripts Commission (Dublin, 1932–49).

an excellent collective volume, *Father Luke Wadding: A Commemorative Volume,* edited by the Franciscan Fathers, Dun Mhuire, Killiney (Dublin, 1956). Of these studies, two especially contribute to the broader history of the period: Fr. Canice Mooney's "Was Wadding a Patriotic Irishman?" and R. Dudley Edwards' "Irish Catholics and the Puritan Revolution." [33] Professor Edwards also surveys English policy from 1603 to the Commonwealth in "Church and State in the Ireland of Michael O'Cleirigh" in *Miscellany of Historical and Linguistic Studies in Honour of Brother Michael O'Cleirigh, Chief of the Four Masters,* edited by Fr. Sylvester O'Brien (Dublin, 1944), and, more recently, discusses the impact of the Reformation and Counter Reformation on the traditional culture of Ireland, in "Ireland, Elizabeth I, and the Counter Reformation" in *Elizabethan Government and Society, Essays Presented to Sir John Neale,* edited by S. T. Bindoff, J. Hurstfield, and C. H. Williams (1961). Another work, valuable for Irish-European affairs is F. X. Martin's scholarly biographical study, *Friar Nugent: A Study of Francis Lavalin Nugent (1569–1635), Agent of the Counter Reformation* (Rome and London, 1962).[34] Hugh Kearney in "Ecclesiastical Politics and the Counter Reformation in Ireland, 1618–1648" (*Journal of Ecclesiastical History,* 11:202–212 [October 1960]) offers some historical continuities as explanations for the confusing divisions of the Kilkenny Period. Of the numerous valuable studies by the Rev. Patrick J. Corish,[35] one places in interesting juxtaposition the views on Irish affairs of two ecclesiastical writers, Anglo-Irish and Gaelic: "Two Contemporary Historians of the Confederation of Kilkenny: John Lynch and Richard O'Ferrall," (*IHS,* 8:217–236 [March 1953]). Rev. John Brady in "The Irish Colleges in Europe and the Counter Reformation" (*Proceedings of the Irish Catholic Historical Committee* [1957], pp. 1–8) suggests that

[33] On Archbishop Ussher see in this volume Fr. Aubrey Gwynn, "Archbishop Ussher and Father Brendan O'Connor." Also the Ussher commemorative essays in *Hermathena,* 88:3–80 (November 1956). For the Church of Ireland see F. R. Bolton, *The Caroline Tradition of the Church of Ireland* (1958).

[34] A more general work by F. X. Martin, *The Irish Capucins and the Counter Reformation, 1591–1641* has been completed, and is to be published. See also, Fr. Benignus Millet, *The Irish Franciscans, 1651–1655* (Rome, 1964).

[35] See Patrick J. Corish, "The Reorganization of the Irish Church, 1603–1641," *Proceedings, Irish Catholic Historical Committee* (1957), pp. 9–14. Also: "Rinuccini's Censure of 27 May, 1648," *Irish Theological Quarterly,* 18:322–337 (October 1951); "John Callaghan and the Controversies among the Irish in Paris," *ibid.,* 21:32–50 (January 1954); "The Crisis in Ireland in 1648: The Nuncio and the Supreme Council: Conclusions," *ibid.,* 22:231–257 (July 1955); "Bishop Nicholas French and the Second Ormond Peace, 1648–9," *IHS,* 6:83–100 (September 1948).

the colleges were the greatest force in the Catholic religious revival, and "forged close links with the continent which were only loosened by the French Revolution."

Economic and social history, in varying degrees, must contend with the paucity of records, and, apart from the studies on colonization and land confiscation, remains to be written.[36] One new social history, a genre rare in Irish historical work, examines the period after 1660: Edward MacLysaght, *Irish Life in the Seventeenth Century: After Cromwell* (2d ed., Cork, 1950). Scattered materials can be found in a number of local histories, but a work which would supersede or fill in the outlines of George O'Brien's economic history has yet to appear.[37] Mercantilism in its English-Irish aspects has been the subject of two interpretive articles by Hugh Kearney which suggest directions for further research. The first of these, "Mercantilism and Ireland, 1620–40," *Historical Studies, I, Papers Read to the Second Irish Conference of Historians* (1958), presents the view that "calculated Machiavellianism" was not always the explanation of the English Acts of Trade, and suggests that the background of each English act needs careful study. The second article, "The Political Background to English Mercantilism, 1695–1700" (*EcHR*, 2d ser., 11:484–496 [April 1959]), studies the Irish Woolen Act of 1699, and suggests the interests which played on government action. The very recent work of P. J. Bowden, *The Wool Trade in Tudor and Stuart England* (1962) contains material of interest to Irish historians. One aspect of the economic history of the century is the exploitation of the land and its resources by "new men," such as the Earl of Cork, a subject examined by Eileen McCracken in two original and interesting articles which illustrate what plantation and unregulated enterprise could do to reduce the area of Irish woodlands: "The Woodlands of Ireland circa 1600," *IHS*, 11:271–296 (September 1959), and "Charcoal Burning Ironworks in Seventeenth and Eighteenth Century Ireland" (*Ulster Journal of Archeology*, 3d ser., 20 [1957], pp. 123–138).

The Irish eighteenth century is only beginning to receive intensive scholarly attention.[38] The famous works of Froude and Lecky are still

---

[36] See in the bibliographical section of Hugh Kearney's *Strafford in Ireland* a discussion of the broader problems of Irish seventeenth-century economic history. See also P. L. Prendeville, "A Select Bibliography of Irish Economic History, Part II, 17th and 18th Centuries," *EcHR*, 3:402–416 (April 1932).

[37] *Economic History of Ireland in the Seventeenth Century* (Dublin, 1919).

[38] See D. L. Keir, "Froude and Lecky on Eighteenth Century Ireland," *Bulletin of the Irish Committee of Historical Sciences*, no. 14 (November 1941). Also R. B. McDowell, "Things to Be Done in Irish History: Eighteenth Century," *ibid.*, no. 21

useful and valuable, but many special studies are necessary before a more complete picture of the internal history of the country appears. Since the work of Sir Lewis Namier, there has been speculation about the writing of an Irish "structure of politics" [39] but only very recently has a scholarly study in the Namier tradition appeared: Edith M. Johnston, *Great Britain and Ireland 1760–1800: A Study in Political Administration* (Edinburgh and London, 1963). Although her study, based almost wholly on original sources, is concerned with the general history of the period, the main divisions of the book concern the administration, the electoral structure, and the parliament itself, and a bibliographical section brings together the scattered materials which have, in recent years, contributed to parliamentary history. Studies of administrative and parliamentary history for the earlier part of the century include valuable articles by J. L. McCracken, one of which is a most interesting investigation of "Irish Parliamentary Elections, 1727–1768" (*IHS*, 5:209–230 [March 1947]).[40] J. C. Beckett, in "The Irish Parliament in the Eighteenth Century," (*Proceedings of the Belfast Natural History and Philosophical Society*, 2d ser., 4 [Sessions, 1950–51, and 1954–55], pp. 17–37) emphasizes that despite the legislation of 1782 the Irish parliament was, at the end of the century, very much what it was at the beginning, and in "Anglo-Irish Constitutional Relations in the Later Eighteenth Century," (*IHS*, 14:20–38 [March 1964]) calls attention to the effects which the growth of Irish national sentiment and changed English attitudes to Irish affairs had on the character of constitutional relations. The long continuance of Pitt's ministry, Beckett notes, tended "to reproduce a system of Anglo-Irish constitutional relations not very dissimilar from that which had existed before 1782."

The period examined by Miss Johnston from the administrative side is looked at from the political and social angle by R. B. McDowell in *Irish Public Opinion, 1750–1800* (Studies in Irish History, I, 1944). Par-

---

(November 1942). *English Historical Documents, 1714–1783*, ed. D. B. Horn and Mary Ransome (1957), has an Irish section, valuable for bibliography, but inadequate for internal history. See also: L. W. Hanson, *Contemporary Printed Sources for British and Irish Economic History, 1701–1750* (Cambridge, Eng., 1963); and R. L. Munter, *Handlist of Irish Newspapers, 1685–1750*, Cambridge Bibliographical Society: Monograph no. 4 (1960).

[39] See David Large's review of Namier's *The Structure of Politics at the Accession of George III*, 2d ed. (1957), in *IHS*, 13:76–80 (March 1962).

[40] See J. L. McCracken, "The Conflict between the Irish Administration and Parliament, 1753–1756," *IHS*, 3:159–179 (September 1942), and his article, "The Irish Viceroyalty, 1760–1773," in *Essays in Honour of James Eadie Todd*, cited above n. 23.

tially based on pamphlets listed in twenty-two pages of bibliography, McDowell's study examines what Irishmen thought about the major issues and events of the period. Pitt's Commercial Propositions, a crucial issue not considered in McDowell's book, are extensively discussed in Vincent T. Harlow's *The Founding of the Second British Empire, 1763–1793*, I, *Discovery and Revolution* (1952).[41] Useful also, for Anglo-Irish political history is Thomas H. D. Mahoney's *Edmund Burke and Ireland* (Cambridge, Mass., 1960), the first satisfactory and scholarly study of Burke's relation to Irish affairs.

A subject of first importance for this century is the Catholic and Gaelic nation living under the penal laws. To understand the rise of the Catholic nation, the relaxation of the harsh persecuting laws, the survivals of an earlier Irish life and culture, and the character of the society, civil and ecclesiastical, which emerged from the penal era, further studies on regional differences, economic and social life, education, and the church are needed.[42] On the penal laws alone, a full history is yet to be written, but important research is being done. In *The Penal Laws, 1691–1760: Church and State from the Treaty of Limerick to the Accession of George III*,[43] Maureen Wall, writing on the ecclesiastical side of the penal legislation, summarizes the present state of knowledge on the laws and indicates how laxly they were enforced, their enforcement depending at any given time on political, rather than on religious, considerations. She concludes that the Catholic church in Ireland, by 1760, had more freedom to work out its destiny than in many countries where Catholicism was the state religion. Mrs. Wall's survey, based on her long research, is an invaluable addition to Irish eighteenth-century history. Robert E. Burns, in "The Irish Penal Code and Some of Its Historians" (*Review of Politics*, 21:276–299 [January 1959]), surveys interpretations of the code made by earlier historians and by more recent scholars, while in a second article, "The Irish Popery Laws: A Study of Eighteenth Century Legislation and Behavior" (*Review of Politics*, 24:485–508 [October 1962]), he puts forward some possible connections be-

[41] For policy and opinion on Ireland and the Empire, see Harlow's chapters, "The Irish Revolution as an Imperial Problem," and "Irish Independence and Imperial Unity." Also, a chapter, "The Imperial Problem of Ireland," in Richard Koebner, *Empire* (Cambridge, Eng., 1961). Koebner has analyzed the text of Grattan's speeches, as they were given, and as they appeared in the edition of 1822, edited by his son: "The Early Speeches of Henry Grattan," *BIHR*, 30:102–114 (May 1957).

[42] A common term for the suppressed nation, "hidden Ireland," comes from Daniel Corkery's *The Hidden Ireland: A Study of Gaelic Munster in the Eighteenth Century* (Dublin, 1925).

[43] See above, n. 12.

tween the psychological and environmental theories of John Locke and the Irish penal code, and suggests that the purpose of the laws was to "change a people." While the link, if there was one, would have been Locke's Irish friend, William Molyneux, Burns indicates that there is no positive evidence that Molyneux, or anyone else, applied the theories of Locke to the Irish situation.[44] J. G. Simms, in "Irish Catholics and the Parliamentary Franchise, 1692–1728" (*IHS*, 12:28–37 [March 1960]), discusses the voting rights of Catholics until their disfranchisement in 1728.[45]

Of the various contributions to the history of Irish Catholic life, one of the most revealing is Maureen Wall's article on "The Rise of a Catholic Middle Class in Eighteenth Century Ireland," *IHS*, 11:91–115 (September 1958), which discusses the part played by the Catholics in the commercial life of the country up to 1782, and suggests that the laws against them were modified to make their wealth available for the economic development of the country.[46] The history of the Irish Catholic exiles in Europe needs study, but a valuable basis for further work can be found in Richard Hayes's *Biographical Dictionary of Irishmen in France* (Dublin, 1949), which unfortunately neglects to give exact references to sources. More regional history is also necessary. A biographical work by Donal O'Sullivan, *Carolan: The Life, Times, and Music of an Irish Harper* (2 vols., 1958), reveals something of the "hidden Ireland" of Connacht, a province which is also the subject of an interesting article by J. G. Simms, "Connacht in the Eighteenth Century," *IHS*, 11:116–133 (September 1958). Eighteenth-century travelers who crossed the Shannon, notes Simms, had the sensation of entering another world.[47] Catho-

[44] See his "Thoughts on Converting the Irish, 1715," *Irish Ecclesiastical Record*, 98:142–144 (September 1962).

[45] See his "The Making of a Penal Law, 1703–4," *IHS*, 12:105–118 (September 1960). For some examples of the actual operation of the penal laws see two articles by Kevin McGrath: "John Garzia," *Irish Ecclesiastical Record*, 72:494–514 (December 1949), and "The Clergy of Dublin in 1695," *ibid.*, 74:193–200 (September 1950).

[46] See her "The Catholic Merchants, Manufacturers and Traders of Dublin, 1778–1782," *Reportorium Novum: Dublin Diocesan Historical Record*, II, no. 2 (1959–60), pp. 298–323. Also Mrs. Wall (under the name Maureen MacGeehin), "The Catholics of the Towns and the Quarterage Dispute in Eighteenth Century Ireland," *IHS*, 8:91–114 (September 1952).

[47] See J. G. Simms, "County Sligo in the Eighteenth Century," *Journal of the Royal Society of Antiquaries of Ireland*, 91 (1961), pp. 153–162. For essays on the social history of Gaelic Ireland see "The Big House" in Corkery's *Hidden Ireland*, and "The Gaelic Background" by Gerard Murphy in *Daniel O'Connell, Nine Centenary Essays*, ed. Michael Tierney (Dublin, 1949), pp. 1–24. For a literary

lic education has been the subject of a number of studies,[48] and in *The Sign of Dr. Hays' Head* (Dublin, 1958), Thomas Wall devotes some attention to eighteenth-century Catholic printers. Two noteworthy sources for Catholic history are now available: *The Minute Book of the Catholic Committee, 1773–1792*, edited by R. Dudley Edwards in *Archivium Hibernicum,* 9 (1942), pp. 3–172, and newspaper extracts published in *Archivium Hibernicum,* 16–20 (1951–57), Appendices, pp. 1–304, by Rev. John Brady as "Catholics and Catholicism in the Eighteenth Century Press." These reveal some of the social reality, as against the letter, of the penal laws.

For the dissenting sects, gaps in the work of Froude and Lecky have been filled by J. C. Beckett in *Protestant Dissent in Ireland, 1687–1780* (Studies in Irish History, II, 1948). It was not simply bigotry, as Lecky thought, Beckett contends, but rather fear, which made the established church so adamant towards full rights for Presbyterians. In 1689, and again in 1715, it was clear that they would defend the revolution settlement. The benefits to be derived from concessions were already certain, while the dangers of generosity to a powerful body were great.[49] There is a sizable older literature on the Ulster Scot and his migration to North America, not all of it scholarly or objective, and some of it dedicated to proving the superiority of the Ulsterman. Carl Bridenbaugh, in *Myths and Realities: Societies of the Colonial South* (Baton Rouge, La., 1952) finds no evidence to support the assertion that the experience in Ulster made the Lowland Scots better settlers, after the beginning stage, if indeed at all.[50] James G. Leyburn, in *The Scotch-Irish: A Social History* (Chapel Hill, N.C., 1962) devotes a section to the Scots in Ulster, and

study see R. A. Breatnach, "The End of a Tradition: A Survey of Eighteenth Century Gaelic Literature," *Studia Hibernica,* 1 (1961), pp. 128–150.

[48] For the origins of Maynooth see Maurice O'Connell, "The Political Background to the Establishment of Maynooth College," *Irish Ecclesiastical Record,* 85:325–334, 406–415 (May, June 1956); 86:1–16 (July 1956). Also J. D. Fitzpatrick, *Edmund Rice, Founder of the Brothers of the Christian Schools* (Dublin, 1945); R. B. Savage, *A Valiant Dublin Woman: The Story of St. George's Hill, 1766–1940* (Dublin, 1940); J. J. Walsh, *Nano Nangle and the Presentation Sisters* (Dublin, 1959). See the earlier, and excellent, M. G. Jones, *The Charity School Movement* (Cambridge, Eng., 1938), pt. II, ch. vii on Ireland.

[49] See J. C. Beckett, "The Government and the Church of Ireland under William III and Anne," *IHS,* 2:280–302 (March 1941). Also for religious life in Ulster, see David Stewart, *The Seceders in Ireland,* Presbyterian Historical Society (Belfast, 1950).

[50] See W. F. Dunaway, *The Scotch-Irish of Colonial Pennsylvania* (Chapel Hill, N.C., 1944); T. W. Moody's article in two parts, "The Ulster Scots in Colonial and Revolutionary America," *Studies,* 34:85–94, 211–221 (March and June 1945); E. R. R. Green, "The Scotch-Irish and the Coming of the Revolution in North Carolina," *IHS,* 7:77–86 (September 1950).

attempts to prove the importance of the Ulster experience as preparation for America.[51]

New works of narrative history are few, and have been concerned with the military and naval events at the end of the century. The best of these, Commander E. H. Stuart Jones's *An Invasion That Failed: The French Expedition to Ireland, 1796* (Oxford, 1950), contains material on French sea power after 1789, fresh detail on the expedition itself, and a sympathetic portrait of Wolfe Tone.[52] Irish history, of course, from the American Revolution to the Union, is rich in significant subjects, and its attraction for nineteenth-century nationalists is well known. If, indeed, these years did produce some greater sense of "the case of Ireland," they also saw, quite naturally, persisting conflict, class and religious division.[53] A fresh, comprehensive appraisal of Ireland in the "age of the democratic revolution" has yet to be written.[54] One obvious need is a new study on the United Irishmen.[55]

For both economic and social history the most significant work is Ken-

[51] Leyburn's work does not take note of Moody's *Londonderry Plantation,* nor of Beckett's *Protestant Dissent.*

[52] See Charles Dickson, *The Life of Michael Dwyer, with Some Account of His Companions* (Dublin, 1944); *The Wexford Rising in 1798: Its Causes, and Its Course* (Tralee, 1955); *Revolt in the North, Antrim and Down in 1798* (Dublin, 1960). Sir Henry McAnally, *The Irish Militia, 1793–1816: A Social and Military History* (Dublin and London, 1949); Jules Dechamps, *Les Iles Britanniques et la Révolution Française, 1789–1803* (Brussels, 1949); Richard Hayes, *The Last Invasion of Ireland: When Connacht Rose,* 2d ed. (Dublin, 1939). On the attempted rising of 1803 there is Helen Landreth, *The Pursuit of Robert Emmet* (Dublin, 1949). For a discussion of this work see a review in *IHS,* 7:303–305 (September 1951).

[53] Maurice O'Connell, *Irish Politics and Social Conflict in the Age of the American Revolution* (Philadelphia, 1965) appeared too late for discussion in this article. See his "Class Conflict in a Pre-Industrial Society: Dublin in 1780," *Duquesne Review,* 9:43–55 (fall 1963). See Robert E. Burns, "The Belfast Letters, the Irish Volunteers, 1778–9, and the Catholics," *Review of Politics,* 21:678–691 (October 1959), a discussion of the early history of the Volunteers with emphasis on their essential Protestantism. Also his "The Catholic Relief Act in Ireland, 1778," *Church History,* 32:181–204 (June 1963), and A. Paul Levack, "Edmund Burke, His Friends, and the Dawn of Catholic Emancipation," *Catholic Historical Review,* 37:385–414 (January 1952).

[54] For some generalizations see two articles by R. Dudley Edwards: "The European and American Background of O'Connell's Nationalism," *Irish Monthly,* 75:468–473 (November 1947), and "The American War of Independence and Irish Nationalism," *ibid.,* 509–20 (December 1947). On trade: Theresa O'Connor, "The Embargo on the Export of Irish Provisions, 1776–9," *IHS,* 2:3–11 (March 1940).

[55] See R. B. McDowell: "The Personnel of the Dublin Society of United Irishmen, 1791–4, with a List of Persons Known to Have Been Admitted as Members," *IHS,* 2:12–53 (March 1940), and "United Irish Plans of Parliamentary Reform," *ibid.,* 3:39–59 (March 1942). There is an earlier book by Rosamund Jacob, *The Rise of the United Irishmen, 1791–4* (1937). See review in *IHS,* 1:89–90 (March 1938). Also T. W. Moody, "The Political Ideas of the United Irishmen," *Ireland To-day,* 3:15–25 (January 1938).

neth H. Connell, *The Population of Ireland, 1750–1845* (Oxford, 1950). Revising traditional estimates of eighteenth-century population, Connell suggests that the seemingly spectacular rise of the 1780's had begun before that decade. Earlier marriages followed by increased fertility is a central explanation of population growth. The years after 1780 saw radical rearrangements in rural society of a nature to allow early marriage. Behind it all was the potato, nutritious and available. More extreme claims for the potato as a factor in Irish rural history are made in the remarkable work of a botanist, Redcliffe N. Salaman, *The History and Social Influence of the Potato* (Cambridge, Eng., 1949).[56] Only recently, William L. Langer, in "Europe's Initial Population Explosion," *AHR*, 69:1–17 (October 1963), discusses the broader European aspects of food and population problems raised in Connell's study and suggests the evolution of human diet and its social consequences as a vital subject for historical inquiry. Some general questions about the late eighteenth-century Irish economy are raised by Patrick Lynch and John Vaizey in *Guinness's Brewery in the Irish Economy, 1759–1876*, I (Cambridge, Eng., 1960),[57] the portrait of a business, based on the firm's records. The Union played no great role in the destruction of Ireland's economy, they contend; and Ireland had in these years not one economy but two, a rural, largely subsistence economy covering about three-fourths of the country, and a cash economy of the eastern seaboard area from Belfast to Cork, with outposts such as Limerick and Galway. This latter economy was linked closely to England's as the first was not.[58] These gen-

---

[56] See Dr. Salaman's shorter survey, *The Influence of the Potato on the Course of Irish History* (Dublin, 1943). K. H. Connell's review of the longer work, "Essays in Bibliography and Criticism: The History of the Potato," *EcHR*, 2d ser., 3:388–395 (no. 3, 1951), suggests that it was "tenurial relationships" which played a role in the domination of the potato.

[57] A second volume is to appear. See also Peter Mathias, *The Brewing Industry in England, 1700–1830* (Cambridge, Eng., 1959).

[58] For another business history see F. G. Hall, *The Bank of Ireland, 1783–1946: With an Architectural Chapter by C. P. Curran and Biographical Notes by Joseph Hone*, ed. George O'Brien (Dublin and Oxford, 1949). See also Frank Fetter, *The Irish Pound, 1797–1826* (1955). On monetary matters see in *Hermathena* a series of articles by Joseph Johnston: "Commercial Restriction and Monetary Deflation in 18th Century Ireland," 53:79–87 (May 1939); "Berkeley and the Abortive Bank Project of 1720–21," 54:110–119 (November 1939); "A Synopsis of Berkeley's Monetary Philosophy," 55:73–86 (May 1940); "Locke, Berkeley and Hume as Monetary Theorists," 56:77–83 (November 1940). There is no adequate study of Ireland in the British mercantile system, but see two articles by Francis G. James: "Irish Smuggling in the Eighteenth Century," *IHS*, 12:299–317 (September 1961), and "Irish Colonial Trade in the Eighteenth Century," *William and Mary Quarterly*, 3d ser., 20:574–584 (October 1963). James contends that Ireland's economic position in the old Empire was far more important than has been recognized.

eralizations re-emphasize the necessity for further investigation of the economic history of the years between 1780 and the Act of Union.

Constantia Maxwell's discussion of the social history of the country in *Country and Town in Ireland under the Georges* (rev. ed., Dundalk, 1949), must be supplemented by the works on the history of the Catholics mentioned above.[59] Georgian Dublin, which occupies a special place in the history of the Anglo-Irish ascendancy, is portrayed in Miss Maxwell's *Dublin under the Georges, 1714–1830* (rev. ed., 1956).[60] A notable study by Maurice Craig, *Dublin, 1660–1860* (Dublin and London, 1952), presents some, but not all, of the city's history and adds important architectural material. A shorter work, beautifully illustrated, is John Harvey, *Dublin, a Study in Environment* (1949).[61]

The Irish nineteenth century [62] has been very much "written," but much of the writing has been biased and unscholarly. The research and reflection of the past two decades have been putting into new perspective a fair number of controversial and passionately discussed historical subjects: the famine, the policies of British statesmen and Irish leaders, parliamentary policies, the role of the Catholic church, emigration, the struggle for land and higher education. Nationalism, one of the unifying themes, has been the subject of three significant, and quite different books which look at the century as a whole. Nicholas Mansergh's *Ireland in the Age of Reform and Revolution: A Commentary on Anglo-Irish Relations and Political Forces in Ireland, 1840–1921* (1940), is an original work, difficult to characterize briefly. Impartial, imaginative about intangibles, concerned with both economics and politics, Mansergh sees the Irish question as essentially "a problem in politics." [63] Eric Strauss, in his brilliant *Irish Nationalism and British Democracy* (New York and

[59] For social history of the lesser gentry see Elizabeth Bowen, *Bowen's Court* (New York, 1942). A history of her family from their seventeenth-century settlement, the work is sometimes evocative rather than strictly historical, but valuable.

[60] See her *The Stranger in Ireland: From the Reign of Elizabeth to the Great Famine* (1954), a collection of travelers' descriptions and opinions.

[61] A number of works deal with eighteenth-century Dublin institutions which have continued to the present day: Terence de Vere White, *The Story of the Royal Dublin Society* (Tralee, 1955); O'Donel T. D. Browne, *The Rotunda Hospital, 1745–1945* (Edinburgh, 1947); J. D. Widdess, *An Account of the Schools of Surgery, Royal College of Surgeons, Dublin, 1789–1948* (Edinburgh, 1949).

[62] Bibliographies are needed, but, for a limited period and confined to holdings in the National Library of Ireland, see two volumes by James Carty, *Bibliography of Irish History, 1912–1921* (Dublin, 1936), and *Bibliography of Irish History, 1870–1911* (Dublin, 1940). See P. L. Prendeville's earlier "A Select Bibliography of Irish Economic History, Part III, The Nineteenth Century," *EcHR*, 4:81–90 (October 1932).

[63] See his *Britain and Ireland*, rev. ed. (London and New York, 1946).

London, 1951), explains his work as a history of the "nexus" between Great Britain and Ireland. Economic interpretation dominates, but not unimaginatively so. P. S. O'Hegarty, a participant in the events described in the latter part of his work, *A History of Ireland under the Union, 1801 to 1922* (1952), has written neither an impartial history, nor indeed, the whole history of these years, but an important source for political nationalism, valuable for quotations from not readily available documents. Although literary works are outside the scope of this survey, historians of nationalism and of Irish society will find much to interest them in Thomas Flanagan's *The Irish Novelists, 1800–1850* (New York, 1959), which, in its introductory chapters, discusses the question of Irish identity.[64] Surveys on a number of special subjects antedate 1940,[65] but we do not yet have a parliamentary history nor a new history of the Catholic church although significant work in these fields has been done. Administrative history, long neglected, is now examined for the whole century by R. B. McDowell in *The Irish Administration, 1801–1914* (Studies in Irish History, 2d ser., II, 1964).[66] The remaking of the Catholic church in nineteenth-century Ireland, a subject of as much significance as repeal, the land agitation, or education, is receiving attention, and an American scholar Emmet Larkin, working on a history of the church for the entire century, sets out some of the problems involved in "Church and State in Ireland in the Nineteenth Century" (*Church History,* 31:294–306 [September 1962]).[67]

For the earlier part of the century, there have appeared a number of significant works in the broad field of economic and social history. Dr.

[64] For the half century covered by *The Irish Novelists* see the essays in *Social Life in Ireland, 1800–1845,* ed. R. B. McDowell (Dublin, 1957). Hubert Butler's "The Country House: The Life of the Gentry" suggests the possibilities of a subject on which little has been written.

[65] The still valuable surveys published prior to 1940: J. Dunsmore Clarkson's pioneering work, *Labour and Nationalism in Ireland* (New York, 1925); John E. Pomfret, *The Struggle for Land in Ireland, 1800–1923* (Princeton, N.J., 1930); Elizabeth R. Hooker, *Readjustments of Agricultural Tenure in Ireland* (Chapel Hill, N.C., 1938).

[66] See McDowell's articles "The Irish Executive in the Nineteenth Century," *IHS,* 9:264–280 (March 1955), and "The Irish Courts of Law, 1801–1914," *IHS,* 10:363–391 (September 1957).

[67] See Kennedy F. Roche, "The Relations of the Catholic Church and the State in England and Ireland, 1800–1852," *Historical Studies: III, Papers Read before the Fourth Irish Conference of Historians* (London and Cork, 1961); and two articles by J. H. Whyte: "The Influence of the Catholic Clergy on Elections in Nineteenth Century Ireland," *EHR,* 75:239–259 (April 1960), and "The Appointment of Catholic Bishops in Nineteenth Century Ireland," *Catholic Historical Review,* 48:12–32 (April 1962). See also, E. R. Norman, *The Catholic Church and Ireland in the Age of Rebellion, 1859–1873* (Ithaca, N.Y., 1965).

Connell's work on population, already noted, is essential background.[68] For the reality of an increasing population's way of life in a depressed economy there is Thomas W. Freeman, *Pre-Famine Ireland: A Study in Historical Geography* (Manchester, Eng., and New York, 1957), which studies the country as a whole, as well as its various regions. The unique developments in Northeastern Ulster are the subject of E. R. R. Green's *The Lagan Valley, 1800–1850: A Local History of the Industrial Revolution* (Studies in Irish History, III, 1949), which examines the eighteenth-century background, the rise of Belfast, and the lessons learned by the linen manufacturers from the short lived cotton industry. The work suggests, but does not answer, questions on the problem of capital for investment outside of Ulster.[69] British policy in relation to the economic problems of Ireland is approached in a new way by R. D. Collison Black in *Economic Thought and the Irish Question, 1817–1870* (Cambridge, Eng., 1960), a case study on the relations between economic theory and economic policy. Although recognizing the problems created by the different conditions of the two countries, the classical economists did not make a profound examination of the origin and character of that difference and sought solutions which would remodel Irish economy along the lines of the English. Students of the political history of the period who are concerned with "the condition of Ireland" question will be much indebted to Dr. Black's work.[70]

Of all works on Irish history in the last twenty-five years, the one which has, perhaps, received the widest scholarly attention is *The Great Famine: Studies in Irish History, 1845–1852*, edited by R. Dudley Edwards and T. Desmond Williams (Dublin, 1956, and New York, 1957).

[68] See K. H. Connell, "The Colonization of Waste Land in Ireland, 1780–1845," *EcHR*, 2d ser., 3:44–71 (no. 1, 1950). Connell takes issue with George O'Brien's view that there was little reclamation between the Union and the famine. See also his "Some Unsettled Problems in English and Irish Population History, 1750–1845," *IHS*, 7:225–234 (September 1951), and "The Potato in Ireland," *PP*, no. 23 (November 1962), pp. 57–71. The population discussion continues in Michael Drake, "Marriage and Population Growth in Ireland, 1750–1845," *EcHR*, 2d ser., 16:301–313 (December 1963).

[69] See also John J. Monaghan, "The Rise and Fall of the Belfast Cotton Industry," *IHS*, 3:1–17 (March 1942); and Ivor J. Herring, "Ulster Roads on the Eve of the Railway Age, c. 1800–1840," *IHS*, 2:160–188 (September 1940). Urban labor history for any part of Ireland has been neglected, but see Rachel O'Higgins, "Irish Trade Unions and Politics, 1830–1850," *Historical Journal*, 4:208–217 (no. 1, 1961), and her "The Irish Influence in the Chartist Movement," *PP*, 20 (November 1961), pp. 83–96.

[70] There are forty-three pages of bibliography. See also Dr. Black's *The Statistical and Social Inquiry Society of Ireland, Centenary Volume, 1847–1947* (Dublin, 1947).

Described by the editors as a contribution to an ultimate history of the famine, this collective work has been widely commended for its scholarship and objectivity. Introductory chapters examine Irish society in the forty years before the famine, and others discuss famine relief measures, medical history, emigration, the politics of the period, and the famine in Irish oral tradition. The editors' foreword, a contribution to Irish historiography, notes that their volume does not deal with the long term implications of the famine. A full economic and social history of post-famine Ireland awaits more specialized studies in Irish economic history for the late nineteenth and early twentieth centuries.[71] The most recent and moving work of Cecil Woodham-Smith, *The Great Hunger, Ireland, 1845–49* (London and New York, 1962), adds little to *The Great Famine,* but does present the story as a unified whole, and, for some matters, in much greater detail. On Charles Trevelyan, whose decisions were crucial in famine relief, and whose papers she has been the first to use, Mrs. Woodham-Smith makes some severe judgments.

Political history for the first half of the century would be much benefited by a full-scale study of the national movement, which has, perhaps, been seen too much in terms of Daniel O'Connell and his Young Ireland critics. A number of books have appeared, however, on the political and religious history of the period, and among these, the most widely useful is R. B. McDowell's *Public Opinion and Government Policy in Ireland, 1801–1846* (Studies in Irish History, V, 1952), a valuable guide to the politics and society of post-Union Ireland.[72] Brian Inglis, in *Freedom of*

---

[71] A few articles will indicate some of the lines of inquiry: Kenneth H. Connell, in "Peasant Marriage in Ireland: Its Structure and Development since the Famine," *EcHR,* 2d ser., 14:502–523 (April 1962), presents material, some of it obtained with the assistance of the Irish Folklore Commission, the implications of which he proposes to work out more fully. See also his "Land Legislation and Irish Social Life," *ibid.,* 2d ser., 11:1–7 (August 1958). S. H. Cousens, in "Emigration and Demographic Change in Ireland, 1851–1861," *ibid.,* 2d ser., 14:275–288 (December 1961), notes "considerable resistance" to emigration after the famine, a resistance he calls social and not economic. W. L. Burn in "Free Trade in Land: An Aspect of the Irish Question," *TRHS,* 4th ser., 31 (1949), pp. 61–74 discusses the Encumbered Estates Act and speculates on "what might have been" had something similar to the 1870 land legislation been enacted in 1849. More directly on land legislation itself see: Hugh Shearman, "State Aided Land Purchase under the Disestablishment Act of 1869," *IHS,* 4:58–80 (March 1944); and two articles by K. Buckley: "The Fixing of Rents by Agreement in County Galway, 1881–85," *ibid.,* 7:149–179 (March 1951), and "The Records of the Irish Land Commission as a Source of Historical Evidence," *ibid.,* 8:28–36 (March 1952). See Thomas P. O'Neill, "From Famine to Near Famine, 1845–1879," *Studia Hibernica,* 1 (1961), pp. 161–171. Also O. Robinson, "The London Companies as Progressive Landlords in Nineteenth Century Ireland," *EcHR,* 2d ser., 15:103–118 (August 1962).

[72] For the immediate post-Union years see Michael Roberts, *The Whig Party,*

the Press in Ireland, 1784–1841 (Studies in Irish History, VI, 1954), examines the changing relationship of government and press, but does not range far into peripheral history. James A. Reynolds, in *The Catholic Emancipation Crisis in Ireland, 1823–29* (New Haven, Conn., 1954), makes a study of the Catholic Association based partially on new materials. Fr. John Broderick has studied one aspect of the repeal movement in *The Holy See and the Irish Movement for Repeal of the Union with England, 1829–1847* (Rome, 1951).[73] No original major work has appeared on Young Ireland. Denis Gwynn's *Young Ireland and 1848* (Cork, 1949) makes extensive use of the Smith O'Brien papers, but adds less to the work of Gavan Duffy than one might have hoped. Gwynn's *O'Connell, Davis, and the Colleges Bill* (Cork, 1948) examines the controversy over Peel's educational plans for Ireland. T. W. Moody's *Thomas Davis, 1814–1845* (Dublin, 1945) is a short appreciation of the famous patriot.[74] On James Fintan Lalor, that original and different thinker who saw the uselessness of patriotic nationalism without fundamental land reform, there is Thomas P. O'Neill's biography in Gaelic,[75] as well as his article, "The Economic and Political Ideas of James Fintan Lalor," *Irish Ecclesiastical Record*, 74:398–409 (November 1950).

Peel and O'Connell, the two dominant public figures in Irish politics in this era, have received some attention. Norman Gash has published the first volume of a projected longer work, and in *Mr. Secretary Peel: The Life of Sir Robert Peel to 1830* (Cambridge, Mass., 1961), has given fresh appraisals of conditions in post-Union Ireland. An apologia, which

---

1807–1812 (1939), and Donald J. McDougall, "George III, Pitt, and the Irish Catholics, 1801–1805," *Catholic Historical Review*, 31:255–281 (October 1945). Also for the period to 1825, J. T. Ellis, *Cardinal Consalvi and Anglo-Papal Relations, 1814–1824* (Washington, D.C., 1942). G. I. T. Machin's *The Catholic Question in English Politics, 1820 to 1830* (Oxford, 1964) is the most recent study of the Catholic emancipation question.

[73] Of some interest for these years, Alexis de Tocqueville's *Journeys to England and Ireland* have been made available in a new edition and translation edited by J. P. Mayer (1958).

[74] For a review of the centenary writings on young Ireland see Kevin Nowlan, "Writings in Connection with the Thomas Davis and Young Ireland Centenary, 1945," *IHS*, 5:265–272 (March 1947). For the identification of *Nation* articles, see Kevin M. MacGrath, "Writers in the 'Nation,' 1842–45," *IHS*, 6:189–223 (March 1949). Also Randall Clarke, "The Relations between O'Connell and the Young Irelanders," *IHS*, 3:18–30 (March 1942). For a statement on the nationalism of Young Ireland see R. Dudley Edwards, "The Contribution of Young Ireland to the Irish National Idea" in *Feilscribhinn Torna: Essays Presented to Tadhg Ua Donnchadha*, ed. Seamus Pender (Cork, 1947). Also G. S. Kitson Clark, "The Romantic Element, 1830–50," *Studies in Social History: A Tribute to G. M. Trevelyan*, ed. J. H. Plumb (1955).

[75] *Fiontan O'Leathlobhair* (Dublin, 1962).

calls Peel's belated change of mind on Catholic emancipation "a political, not an intellectual conversion," will not resolve, for students of the period, all the difficulties of that elusive problem "Peel and Ireland." [76] On O'Connell, a commemorative volume, *Daniel O'Connell, Nine Centenary Essays,* edited by Michael Tierney (Dublin, 1949), contains estimates of his work and character, his fame and reputation, and covers the whole of his life. Denis Gwynn's biography, published originally in 1929, was revised and republished for the centenary.[77]

O'Connell's career in parliament suggests the importance of a work on the "structure of politics." Norman Gash, who gives some attention to Ireland in his *Politics in the Age of Peel: A Study in the Technique of Parliamentary Representation, 1830–1850* (1953), notes the lack of any "general and authoritative study" on the Irish political system in this period. Various articles, however, suggest the formidable difficulties of effective Irish parliamentary action in the earlier years of the century. In "Daniel O'Connell and the Repeal Party" (*IHS,* 11:297–316 [September 1959]), John H. Whyte argues that O'Connell had a clearer grasp of what could be attained in parliament than his less experienced Young Ireland critics, who were suggesting the kind of parliamentary action to be achieved only in the era of Parnell.[78] David Large, in "The House of Lords and Ireland in the Age of Peel, 1832–1850," *IHS,* 9:367–399 (September 1955), calls attention to the fact that in the eighteenth century the number of peers in the English house with a stake in Irish land was about one-eighth of the whole body, but by 1833 virtually one peer out of every four had a stake in Ireland through the ownership of land, and, for a majority of these, their economic interest was entirely centered on their Irish estates. A. H. Graham throws light on a famous episode in O'Connell's relations with the Whigs in "The Lichfield House Compact, 1835" (*IHS,* 12:209–225 [March 1961]), and concludes that the Compact, was a fact and not a myth, but not, as has been suggested, dishonorable to either side.[79] The years immediately after 1850 are examined by

[76] See Galen Broeker, "Robert Peel and the Peace Conservation Force," *JMH,* 33:363–373 (December 1961).

[77] *Daniel O'Connell,* revised Centenary edition (Cork and Oxford, 1947). Also Sean O'Faolain's *The King of the Beggars* (1938).

[78] See Sir Henry Blackall and J. H. Whyte, "Correspondence, O'Connell and the Repeal Party," *IHS,* 12:139–143 (September 1960).

[79] For a review of Repeal in its historical context see Kevin B. Nowlan, "The Meaning of Repeal in Irish History," *Historical Studies: IV, Papers Read to the Fifth Irish Conference of Historians* (1963). Dr. Nowlan's book *The Politics of Repeal: A Study in the Relations Between Great Britain and Ireland, 1841–1850* is in press. For some of the political pressures of the period, and English anti-

John H. Whyte in his excellent *The Independent Irish Party, 1850–9* (Oxford, 1958), in which he studies the efforts of the Irish Tenant League to obtain land legislation by supporting parliamentary representatives who would act as an "independent opposition," the failure of this attempt, and finally the influence of landlords and clergy on elections.

In the political history of Ireland between 1848 and 1870, Fenianism is a dominating theme,[80] but no scholarly and full history of the movement has been written, although a special aspect has been treated by Fr. William D'Arcy in *The Fenian Movement in the United States: 1858–1886* (Washington, D.C., 1947), based to some extent on the O'Mahony-Rossa papers. The most important addition to Fenian materials is *Devoy's Post-Bag, 1871–1928,* edited by William O'Brien and Desmond Ryan, introduction by P. S. O'Hegarty, I, *1871–1880* (Dublin, 1948) and II, *1880–1928* (Dublin, 1953). The unity of the collection derives from the fact that the letters which comprise it were written to John Devoy (1842–1928), a dominant figure in Irish politics in America for nearly fifty years. *Fenian Memories,* by Mark Ryan, edited by T. F. O'Sullivan (Dublin, 1945) adds to the small literature of Fenian memoirs. The career of Isaac Butt is the subject of some recent scholarship on Butt himself and on the parliamentary history which precedes Parnell. Terence de Vere White's oddly named *The Road of Excess* (Dublin, 1946) is a sympathetic biography of Butt, his failings, his distinction of mind, his evolving opinions.[81] Butt's later political career and the parliamentary history involved are analyzed in Lawrence Mc Caffrey's *Irish Federalism in the 1870's: A Study in Conservative Nationalism,* in *Transactions of the American Philosophical Society,* n.s., 52 (Philadelphia, 1962),[82] and even more recently in David Thornley's *Isaac Butt and Home Rule* (1964).

Catholic attitudes, see Gilbert Cahill, "Irish Catholicism and English Toryism," *Review of Politics,* 19:62–76 (January 1957), and "The Protestant Association and the Anti-Maynooth Agitation of 1845," *Catholic Historical Review,* 43:273–308 (October 1957).

[80] See *IHS,* 11 (September 1959), p. 337, regarding a projected *History of Ireland in the Age of Fenianism.* The present writer has seen no further notice of this. Desmond Ryan, long a student of Fenianism, has a statement on the position of Fenian history in *Bulletin of the Irish Committee of Historical Sciences,* no. 79 (June 1957). He is at work on a study of James Stephens. See his earlier *The Phoenix Flame: A Study of Fenianism and John Devoy* (1937).

[81] White's book is deficient in scholarly apparatus. Based on the Butt papers in the National Library, and on family papers, the book does not sufficiently discuss these collections. An edition of Butt's correspondence is needed.

[82] See L. J. McCaffrey, "Home Rule and the General Election of 1874 in Ireland," *IHS,* 9:190–212 (September 1954), and David Thornley, "The Irish Conservatives

Despite the absence of "Parnell papers" to smooth the historian's way, the Parnell era itself is a very well documented part of modern Irish history. Parnell himself, apart from his accomplishments, is remote and not easily analyzed, and the difficulties of a satisfactory biography are formidable. Curiously, no collection of his speeches has been made. Whatever evaluations lie ahead will, certainly, be much indebted to the significant work of these past few years. Conor Cruise O'Brien, in his brilliant and original *Parnell and His Party, 1880–1890* (Oxford, 1957), studies Parnell's party machine, its development, its membership, and its accomplishments, and argues that Parnell's goal was a self-governing Ireland living in harmony with Great Britain. His achievement, the uniting of the constitutional and revolutionary wings of the nationalist movement, often made this larger purpose of reconciliation unclear to his contemporaries. O'Brien's lucidly written pioneering study should interest the political scientist as well as the historian. Another study, of a quite different kind, F. S. L. Lyons' *The Fall of Parnell, 1890–91* (Studies in Irish History, 2d ser., I, 1960), covers the eleven months between the O'Shea divorce case and Parnell's death. Two introductory chapters on Parnell's life to 1890 are commendably clear on what contemporaries saw and knew, and on what later evidence has done to clarify the story of the divorce.[83] Lyons has set out his meticulous research in a beautifully written and sympathetic narrative. Articles on various aspects of Parnell's career and the history surrounding it are numerous, and concern his economic ideas, the attitude of the Roman Catholic hierarchy to his fall, and various problems of politics and opinion both in Great Britain and in Ireland.[84]

---

and Home Rule, 1869–1873," *IHS*, 11:200–222 (March 1959). Also Rev. Patrick J. Corish, "Cardinal Cullen and the National Association of Ireland," *Reportorium Novum*, III, no. 1 (1961–62), pp. 13–61, an article which calls attention to the fact that Fenianism has been overemphasized in the history of the 1860's. On the whole subject, see E. R. Norman, above n. 67.

[83] On the controversies surrounding Parnell, the work of Henry Harrison is crucial, and mostly written before 1940. But see his "Parnell's Vindication," *IHS*, 5:231–243 (March 1947), and in connection with this, *Joseph Chamberlain: A Political Memoir, 1890–92*, ed. C. H. D. Howard (1953).

[84] F. S. L. Lyons, "The Economic Ideas of Parnell," *Historical Studies: II, Papers Read to the Third Conference of Irish Historians* (1959); four articles by C. H. D. Howard, "Documents Relating to the Irish 'Central Board' Scheme, 1884–85," *IHS*, 8:237–263 (March 1953), "Joseph Chamberlain, Parnell, and the Irish 'Central Board' Scheme, 1884–85," *ibid.*, 8:324–361 (September 1953), "Joseph Chamberlain, W. H. O'Shea, and Parnell, 1884, 1891–92," *ibid.*, 13:33–38 (March 1962), and "The Parnell Manifesto of 21 November 1885 and the Schools Question," *EHR*, 62:42–51 (January 1947). David Thornley's "The Irish Home Rule Party and Parliamentary Obstruction, 1874–1887," *IHS*, 12:38–57 (March 1960), has some

Like Parnell, Michael Davitt has had no new adequate biography, but T. W. Moody, who has had access to Davitt family papers, has written a number of articles which suggest a larger work to come, and which give a sympathetic interpretation of Davitt's career. Of Moody's articles on Davitt, special note should be taken of "The New Departure in Irish Politics, 1878–79," *Essays in British and Irish History in Honour of James Eadie Todd,* edited by H. A. Cronne, T. W. Moody, and D. B. Quinn (1949).[85] Important also for the activities of Davitt and Parnell is Norman D. Palmer's *The Irish Land League Crisis* (New Haven, Conn., 1940) which, while concentrating on the years 1879–1881, devotes some preliminary chapters to a survey of agricultural developments in the preceding decades, and the working of the Land Act of 1870.[86] Conservative policies and attitudes, hitherto neglected, are studied for the Parnell era by Lewis P. Curtis, Jr., in *Coercion and Conciliation in Ireland, 1880–1892: A Study in Conservative Unionism* (Princeton, N.J., 1963). Examining the premises on which the conservative leaders opposed Home Rule, Curtis goes on to investigate their policies from 1885 to 1892, and the impact of the Irish question on conservative tactics and thought. The "complex structure" of the Unionist alliance does not form part of his work.[87]

---

observations on the broader historical effects of obstruction on the Westminster parliament. Also, T. W. Moody, "Parnell and the Galway Election of 1886," *ibid.,* 9:319–338 (March 1955); J. F. Glaser, "Parnell's Fall and the Non-Conformist Conscience," *ibid.,* 12:119–138 (September 1960); W. L. Arnstein, "Parnell and the Bradlaugh Case," *ibid.,* 13:212–235 (March 1963). See Emmet Larkin, "The Roman Catholic Hierarchy and the Fall of Parnell," *VS,* 4:315–336 (June 1961), and "Mounting the Counter-Attack: The Roman Catholic Hierarchy and the Destruction of Parnellism," *Review of Politics,* 25:157–182 (April 1963). Finally, for the Parnell era, note should be taken of a second edition, with a new introduction by M. R. D. Foot, of a famous work which surely belongs to Irish, as much as to English history: J. L. Hammond, *Gladstone and the Irish Nation* (1938; 2d ed., Hamden, Conn., 1964).

[85] See also, "Michael Davitt, 1846–1906: A Survey and An Appreciation," in three parts, *Studies,* 35:199–208, 325–334, 433–438 (June, September, and December 1946). Also, "Michael Davitt in Penal Servitude, 1870–1877," *ibid.,* 30:517–529 (December 1941), and 31:16–30 (March 1942); "Michael Davitt and the 'Pen' Letter," *IHS,* 4:224–253 (March 1945); "Michael Davitt and the British Labour Movement, 1882–1906," *TRHS,* 5th ser., 3 (1953), pp. 53–76.

[86] See also James J. Green, "American Catholics and the Irish Land League, 1879–1882," *Catholic Historical Review,* 35:19–42 (April 1949).

[87] For English reactions and the Irish issue as a force in making converts to conservatism see R. C. K. Ensor, "Some Political and Economic Interactions in Later Victorian England," *TRHS,* 4th ser., 31 (1949), pp. 17–28; and John Roach, "Liberalism and the Victorian Intelligentsia," *CHJ,* 13:58–81 (no. 1, 1957). On Chamberlain after 1886 see Peter Fraser, "The Liberal Unionist Alliance: Chamberlain, Hartington, and the Conservatives, 1886–1904," *EHR,* 77:53–75 (January 1962).

The period from Parnell's fall to 1922 has had no single comprehensive history devoted to it.[88] A recent collection of biographical essays edited by Conor Cruise O'Brien, *The Shaping of Modern Ireland* (Toronto, 1960), is a fresh and helpful introduction to the period, but suggests the need of a larger work which would assess all the forces and policies, Irish and British, creating the foundations of twentieth-century Ireland.[89] Parliamentary history prior to the third Home Rule crisis is the subject of F. S. L. Lyons' *The Irish Parliamentary Party, 1890–1910* (Studies in Irish History, IV, 1951), less a general history than a study of the inner workings of the party.[90] Now available are various selections of the writings of James Connolly, edited and published between 1944 and 1951,[91] and a biography, *The Life and Times of James Connolly*, by C. Desmond Greaves (1961). James Larkin's career is the subject of a new work by Emmet Larkin, which is not only a biography of the famous labour leader but also a valuable addition to Irish labour history, especially for the years before 1914.[92]

The role of Ulster in the Home Rule crisis suggests the need of examining its nineteenth-century history. In lieu of any single work, there are two volumes of very good essays, both edited by T. W. Moody and J. C. Beckett, *Ulster since 1800: A Political and Economic Survey* (1955), and *Ulster since 1800: A Social Survey* (2d ser., 1957). D. C. Savage in "The Origins of the Ulster Unionist Party, 1885–86," *IHS*, 12:185–208 (March 1961), points out that even in 1885, the Ulster leaders were prepared to resist, and, if constitutional action failed to stop Home Rule, had prepared a convention and a solemn covenant to declare Ulster's

[88] W. Alison Phillips' earlier work, *The Revolution in Ireland, 1906–1923* (New York, 1923), Unionist in viewpoint, covers some of this period and has a historical introduction.

[89] Redmond, Hyde, Griffith, Carson, and the young Yeats are a few of the figures discussed in this volume which also contains a chapter on the years 1891–1916 written by the editor. A number of works on the dramatic and literary aspects of the period, and necessary to an understanding of it, cannot be included here. See, for example, Alan Denson, ed., *Letters from A. E.* (1962).

[90] See F. S. L. Lyons, "The Irish Unionist Party and the Devolution Crisis of 1904–05," *IHS*, 6:1–22 (March 1948), and H. W. McCready, "Home Rule and the Liberal Party, 1899–1906," *IHS*, 13:316–348 (September 1963).

[91] *Socialism and Nationalism: A Selection from the Writings of James Connolly*, introduction and notes by Desmond Ryan (Dublin, 1948); *Labour and Easter Week: A Selection from the Writings of James Connolly*, ed. Desmond Ryan, introduction by William O'Brien (Dublin, 1949); *The Workers' Republic: A Selection from the Writings of James Connolly*, ed. Desmond Ryan, introduction by William McMullen (Dublin, 1951); also, *Labour in Ireland*, introduction by Robert Lynd (Dublin, 1917; reissued Dublin, 1944).

[92] *James Larkin Irish Labour Leader, 1876–1947* (1965).

hostility to an Irish parliament. John W. Boyle in "The Belfast Protestant Association and the Independent Orange Order, 1901–1910," *IHS*, 13:117–152 (September 1962), brings together some northern Irish labour history and the traditional politics of Protestant Ulster.[93] Strongly antipartitionist in viewpoint, Denis Gwynn has discussed some aspects of the history of the Home Rule Crisis in *The History of Partition, 1912–1925* (Dublin, 1950). Two works deal with the Curragh affair: A. P. Ryan, *Mutiny at the Curragh* (1956) and Sir James Fergusson, *The Curragh Incident* (1964).

Events from 1916 to the Treaty have produced a sizable amount of controversial writing, but Edgar Holt's *Protest in Arms, The Irish Troubles, 1916–1923* (1960) is a fair, interestingly written survey based on secondary sources.[94] The 1916 Rising itself has been the subject of a number of works,[95] but scholars will especially value an article on the role of Eoin MacNeill, which takes the form of notes and comments on two of MacNeill's memoranda and becomes, as well, an introduction to the literature on 1916: F. X. Martin, "Eoin MacNeill and the 1916 Rising," *IHS*, 12:226–271 (March 1961). Frank Pakenham's justly famous work on the Treaty [96] has not been superseded, but nowhere has the quality of these famous years been conveyed with such historical perspective, with such justice and sensitivity, as by W. Keith Hancock in "Saorstat Eireann," a chapter in his *Survey of British Commonwealth Affairs*.[97]

---

[93] See D. L. Armstrong, "Social and Economic Conditions in the Belfast Linen Industry, 1850–1900," *IHS*, 7:235–269 (September 1951). A collection of essays *Ulster under Home Rule*, ed. Thomas Wilson (Oxford, 1955) contains historical background.

[94] For one phase of the struggle see Richard Bennett, *The Black and Tans* (1959).

[95] See Desmond Ryan, *The Rising* (Dublin, 1949) and the critical review by Florence O'Donoghue which discusses the problems of writing on 1916: *IHS*, 6:303–306 (September 1949). Max Caulfield's *The Easter Rebellion* (New York, 1963) is less history than evocation.

[96] *Peace by Ordeal, An Account, from First Hand Sources, of the Negotiations and Signature of the Anglo-Irish Treaty of 1921* (1935; reissued, 1951). See Dorothy Macardle, *The Irish Republic, a Documented Chronicle* (1937; 4th ed. Dublin, 1951), valuable, but a pro-Republican work.

[97] *Survey of British Commonwealth Affairs*, I, *Problems of Nationality, 1918–1936* (1937). Several works on Ireland, concerned primarily with the post-1922 period, have introductory historical material: see Donal O'Sullivan, *The Irish Free State and Its Senate: A Study in Contemporary Politics* (1940); J. L. McCracken, *Representative Government in Ireland: A Study of Dail Eireann, 1919–1948* (1958); Terence de Vere White, *Kevin O'Higgins* (1948). For "external association" and the symbolism of the crown see "The Implications of Eire's Relationship with the British Commonwealth of Nations" in Nicholas Mansergh, *The Commonwealth and the Nations* (1948).

Irish higher education in the nineteenth and twentieth centuries has been the subject of two outstanding books: Fergal McGrath, *Newman's University: Idea and Reality* (Dublin, 1951), and T. W. Moody and J. C. Beckett, *Queen's Belfast, 1845–1949: The History of a University* (2 vols., 1959). To write fairly of Irish higher education, involved as it has been in bitter religious and political controversies, is no light task. Admirably written, these two works are contributions not merely to educational history, but to the general history of Ireland. Narrower in scope are two volumes on Trinity College: *A History of Trinity College, Dublin, 1591–1892,* by Constantia Maxwell (Dublin, 1946), and *A History of Trinity College, Dublin, 1892–1945,* by Kenneth C. Bailey (Dublin, 1947).[98]

Emigration has received broad and uneven attention. On the American side, the emphasis has been on the American experience; the causes for migration have been given less emphasis than the results, and studies have been directed less to the motherland left behind than to the receiving country. A survey of the problems of the study of European migration in the nineteenth and twentieth centuries, made by Frank Thistlethwaite at the Stockholm meeting of historians in 1960, is of some interest for Irish history. Thistlethwaite asks for an understanding of "the complete experience of migration from one society to another," and suggests that the questions raised by Marcus Hansen in 1927 have remained largely unanswered.[99]

Supplementing W. F. Adams' earlier survey of Irish emigration to

[98] On University College Dublin see *Struggle with Fortune, a Miscellany for the Centenary of the Catholic University of Ireland, 1854–1954* ed. Michael Tierney (Dublin, 1954). For Trinity College, see R. B. McDowell and D. A. Webb, "Trinity College in the Age of Revolution and Reform (1794–1831)," *Hermathena,* 72:3–19 (November 1948). On the years between Peel's Act and Newman's University see a series of articles by Mary Vale, "Origins of the Catholic University of Ireland, 1845–1854," *Irish Ecclesiastical Record,* 82:1–16, 152–162, 226–241 (July, September, and October 1954); also Rev. John Ahern, "The Plenary Synod of Thurles," *ibid.,* 75:385–403 (November 1951), and 78:1–20 (July 1952). For a brief general statement see T. W. Moody, "The Irish University Question in the Nineteenth Century," *History,* 43:90–109 (June 1958). For education below the university level, see John Jamieson, *The History of the Royal Belfast Academical Institution* (Belfast, 1959) and T. O. O'Raifeartaigh, "Mixed Education and the Synod of Ulster, 1831–1840," *IHS,* 9:281–299 (March 1955).

[99] Frank Thistlethwaite, "Migration from Europe in the Nineteenth and Twentieth Centuries," *Comité International des Sciences Historiques, XIe Congrès International des Sciences Historiques, Rapports, V, Histoire Contemporaine* (Uppsala, 1960), pp. 32–60. See Marcus Hansen, *The Atlantic Migration, 1607–1860* (Cambridge, Mass., 1940), and "The History of American Immigration as a Field for Research," *AHR,* 32:500–518 (April 1927).

North America,[100] a number of studies have appeared on emigration to America and to Great Britain. On the American side, the outstanding and well-known work, not entirely concerned with the Irish, by Oscar Handlin, *Boston's Immigrants, 1790–1865: A Study in Acculturation* (Cambridge, Mass., 1941) has been revised (1959) to include material to 1880. Two essays by Thomas N. Brown, valuable as well for the history of Irish nationalism, suggest that "complete experience of migration" mentioned by Thistlethwaite. The peasant in Ireland was not a nationalist, Brown argues. It was the loneliness and isolation of his American environment, the nostalgia for Ireland which made him one.[101] Apart from Arnold Schreier's *Ireland and the American Emigration, 1850–1900* (Minneapolis, Minn., 1958), little has been done on the effect of emigration on Ireland itself. Emigration into Scotland has been examined by James E. Handley in *The Irish in Scotland, 1798–1845* (Cork, 1943), and *The Irish in Modern Scotland* (Cork, 1947), two pioneering studies valuable both for Irish emigration and for the Industrial Revolution in Scotland. On England, John A. Jackson's *The Irish in Britain* (London and Cleveland, Ohio, 1963) is a work of historical sociology, containing material to the present time. It by no means exhausts the subject.[102] Finally, a recent solid study of the actual processes of emigration presents the view that the magnitude of emigration drove the British government forward towards regulations which arose not from theory but from the exigencies of a situation which had to be dealt with in new ways. In *A Pattern of Government Growth, 1800–1860: The Passenger Acts and Their Enforcement* (1961), Oliver MacDonagh suggests that Irish emigration set

[100] William F. Adams, *Ireland and Irish Emigration to the New World from 1815 to the Famine* (New Haven, Conn., 1932).

[101] "Nationalism and the Irish Peasant, 1800–1848," *Review of Politics*, 15:403–445 (October 1953), and "The Origins and Character of Irish American Nationalism," *ibid.*, 18:327–358 (July 1956).

[102] See Barbara Kerr, "Irish Seasonal Migration to Great Britain, 1800–1838," *IHS*, 3:365–380 (September 1943). For the United States the most recent study is William V. Shannon, *The American Irish* (New York, 1963)—written by a journalist who has based his study on the important relevant materials. Though brief on the Irish background, it carries the story forward to the third and fourth generations. See Carl Wittke, *The Irish in America* (Baton Rouge, La., 1956); George Potter, *To the Golden Door: The Story of the Irish in Ireland and America* (Boston, Mass., and Toronto, 1960). For some material on the Irish see James P. Shannon, *Catholic Colonization on the Western Frontier* (New Haven, Conn., 1957). Also, Richard J. Purcell, "The New York Commissioners of Emigration and Irish Immigrants, 1847–1860," *Studies*, 37:29–42 (March 1948), and Albon P. Man, Jr., "The Irish in New York in the Early Eighteen-Sixties, *IHS*, 7:87–108 (September 1950). A new sociological work contains material on the Irish in New York City: Nathan Glazer and Daniel Moynihan, *Beyond the Melting Pot* (Cambridge, Mass., 1963).

the pace, and it was to the Irish situation that the interference and regulation of the years 1815–1860 must be largely traced.[103]

Biographical [104] studies have appeared, but not in great numbers, a hardly surprising fact when so much of the history involved is being restudied. Despite a wealth of great subjects, fresh biographical work on the seventeenth century is almost nonexistent.[105] More work has been done for the eighteenth century, but there are many serious gaps. Of the large literature on Swift, a few books have a special historical interest. Louis Landa in *Swift and the Church of Ireland* (Oxford, 1954) examines Swift's clerical career, and Oliver Ferguson, in *Jonathan Swift and Ireland* (Urbana, Ill., 1962), writes a traditional historical introduction and provides sketches for the background of each of Swift's Irish works. Irving Ehrenpreis has published the first volume of a projected longer work, *Swift: The Man, His Works, and the Age*, I: *Mr. Swift and His Contemporaries* (1962). Berkeley has found a scholarly biographer in Arthur A. Luce, *The Life of George Berkeley, Bishop of Cloyne* (1949).[106] Desmond Clarke has written a short study on an important figure, *Thomas Prior, 1681–1751, Founder of the Royal Dublin Society* (Dublin, 1951), and another on an Ulsterman who became governor of North

---

[103] See Oliver MacDonagh's articles "The Poor Law, Emigration, and the Irish Question, 1830–1855," *Christus Rex*, 12:26–37 (1958); "The Irish Catholic Clergy and Emigration during the Great Famine," *IHS*, 5:287–302 (September 1947); "The Regulation of the Emigrant Traffic from the United Kingdom, 1842–55," *IHS*, 9:162–189 (September 1954). Also G. R. C. Keep, "Some Irish Opinion on Population and Emigration," *Irish Ecclesiastical Record*, 84:377–386 (November 1955).

[104] There is no multi-volume Dictionary of Irish Biography. J. S. Crone's *A Concise Dictionary of Irish Biography* (1928; new ed. Dublin, 1937), contains brief sketches, but no bibliographies. The files of *Studies* contain many articles on scholars, journalists, physicians, missionaries, scientists, architects, etc. Scholarly works on some of these careers would contribute to Ireland's social and intellectual history, and to a clearer picture of her place in the contemporary history of western Europe. Men like Sir Robert Kane, for instance, deserve wider attention than they have received. On Kane see D. O'Raghallaigh's brief, *Sir Robert Kane: A Pioneer in Science, Industry, and Commerce* (Cork, 1942), and T. S. Wheeler, "Sir Robert Kane, His Life and Work," *Studies*, 33:158–168, 316–330 (June and September 1944).

[105] See Eric Strauss, *Sir William Petty, Portrait of a Genius* (1954), a disappointing book from the author of *Irish Nationalism and British Democracy*. A number of books and articles have been written about the martyred Archbishop Oliver Plunkett: see Alice Curtayne, *The Trial of Oliver Plunkett* (1953); Deirdre Mathews, *Oliver of Armagh* (Dublin, 1961); Marie de Miserey, *Bienheureux Olivier Plunkett* (Tours, 1963) incorporates recent findings. For the earlier half of the century there is a very good and interesting study of a less well known figure by Donal Cregan: "An Irish Cavalier: Daniel O'Neill," *Studia Hibernica*, 3 (1963), pp. 60–100; 4 (1964), pp. 104–133; to be concluded.

[106] For Berkeley see a collection of essays in a commemorative issue of *Hermathena*, "Homage to George Berkeley, 1682–1753," 82:1–46 (November 1953).

Carolina, *Arthur Dobbs, Esq., 1689–1765* (1958). Burke's career and ideas have attracted many scholars, and aside from Mahoney's study one might note Francis P. Canavan, S.J., *The Political Reason of Edmund Burke* (Durham, N.C., 1960) which, in its opening chapters, calls attention to the possible influence on Burke's thought of his course of studies at Trinity College, Dublin.[107] Works on minor parliamentary members would be welcome, but even for the major ones, new books are few. Maurice Craig's *The Volunteer Earl* (1948), a study of the Earl of Charlemont, is a nicely executed portrait of an eighteenth-century traveler, art connoisseur, and builder, with less emphasis on his political career. Grattan's life will surely be restudied, but the most recent biography is Stephen Gwynn's *Henry Grattan and His Times* (Dublin, 1939). Mary McNeill's *The Life and Times of Mary Ann McCracken, 1770–1866, a Belfast Panorama* (Dublin, 1960) is not only an interesting life of the sister of Henry Joy McCracken, the United Irishman, but a portrait of late-eighteenth-century Belfast, changing after 1800 in economic life and opinion. In *The Desire to Please* (1943), Harold Nicolson has done a study of his ancestor, Hamilton Rowan, the United Irishman. Frank MacDermot's *Theobald Wolfe Tone* (1939) is the most recent good study of a demanding subject.

Good nineteenth-century biographical studies, aside from those already considered on O'Connell, Butt, and Parnell are few. James J. Auchmuty's *Sir Thomas Wyse, 1791–1862: The Life and Career of an Educator and Diplomat* (1939) contributes to the history of Irish education, one of Wyse's deepest interests. The two Young Irelanders, Charles Gavan Duffy and Thomas Davis, so linked in Irish history, have not found recent biographers. The difficulties of Duffy's "life in two hemispheres" are immense, and Davis' short life requires, probably, less a biography than a critical analysis of his opinions and influence. One Young Irelander's American career is the subject of Robert G. Athearn's *Thomas Francis Meagher: An Irish Revolutionary in America* (Boulder, Col., 1949). Another figure of the Repeal decade is studied by Patrick Rogers in *Father Theobald Mathew: Apostle of Temperance* (Dublin, 1943). Donald Read and Eric Glasgow's *Feargus O'Connor, Irishman and Chartist* (1961) is of some interest for Irish history. Father Peadar MacSuibhne, in *Paul Cullen and His Contemporaries, with Their Letters from 1820–1902* (3 vols., Naas, Leinster Leader, 1961–65), has presented some new materials on the Cardinal's life with an adulatory in-

[107] See Carl B. Cone, *Burke and the Nature of Politics* (Lexington, Ky., 1957).

troduction. It is not the critical biography that the career of Cardinal Cullen requires. A minor figure in Parnell's party, a Canadian, is the subject of a scholarly work by Margaret Banks, *Edward Blake, Irish Nationalist* (Toronto and London, 1957). Maev Sullivan's uncritical *No Man's Man* (Dublin, 1943) is an apologia for her father, T. M. Healy. Some interesting material on Irish legal history is to be found in V. T. H. Delany's *Christopher Palles, Lord Chief Baron of Her Majesty's Court of Exchequer in Ireland, 1874–1916* (Dublin, 1960). Margaret Digby's *Horace Plunkett: An Anglo-American Irishman* (Oxford, 1949) is a scholarly study based on diaries and private correspondence. Carson's career has been re-examined by H. Montgomery Hyde in *The Life of Lord Carson* (1953). Padraic Colum's *Ourselves Alone* (Dublin and New York, 1959), a sympathetic study of Arthur Griffith, and Rex Taylor's *Michael Collins* (1958) are also additions to the literature on revolutionary Ireland. Two volumes of "memoir" literature contribute to the Parnell era and after: Andrew J. Kettle, *Material for Victory*, edited by L. J. Kettle (Dublin, 1958), and John T. Horgan, *Parnell to Pearse* (Dublin, 1948). Horgan's work contains reflections and viewpoints of interest for the constitutional tradition in Irish politics.

Local history in Ireland as elsewhere is increasingly the concern of professional scholars. Only by extensive and careful studies of parishes, towns, regions, and families can generalizations be refined and modified.[108] A recent example of parish history which illuminates national history is Rev. Patrick Egan, *The Parish of Ballinasloe: Its History from the Earliest Times to the Present* (Dublin and London, 1960). Of several good local studies on Ulster, there is an especial historical interest attached to Gilbert Camblin's *The Town in Ulster* (Belfast, 1951) which discusses the town planning involved in the seventeenth-century plantation. Also to be noted for Ulster are W. R. Hutchison's *Tyrone Precinct: A History of the Plantation Settlement of Dungannon and Mountjoy to Modern Times* (Belfast, 1951), and Estyn Evans' *Mourne County* (Dundalk, 1951), an historical geography of South Down. A very recent work by M. W. Heslinga, a Dutch geographer, has implications for the

---

[108] Dermot Gleeson discusses the problem of local history in the preface of his *The Last Lords of Ormond* (1938). See also his "Problems of Irish Ecclesiastical History for the Local Historian," *Bulletin of the Irish Committee for the Historical Sciences,* no. 62 (September 1952). Also his last work, a collaborative effort with Fr. Aubrey Gwynn, *A History of the Diocese of Killaloe,* I (Dublin, 1962), pt. 1: *The Early Period* by Fr. Aubrey Gwynn, pts. 2–4: *The Middle Ages* by Dermot Gleeson. For a useful guide see Thomas P. O'Neill, *Sources of Irish Local History,* 1st ser. (Dublin, 1958).

historical controversies over the border: *The Irish Border as a Cultural Divide: A Contribution to the Study of Regionalism in the British Isles* (New York, 1962).[109] Again, William O'Sullivan's valuable *The Economic History of Cork City: From the Earliest Times to the Act of Union* (Cork, 1937) has significance for general economic history. M. D. O'Sullivan's *Old Galway: The History of a Norman Colony in Ireland* (Cambridge, Eng., 1942) carries the history of a famous city only through the seventeenth century. On family history one can do little more here than mention Edward MacLysaght's two recent valuable works: *Irish Families, Their Names, Arms and Origins* (Dublin, 1957) and *More Irish Families* (Dublin, 1960).[110] The history of the Irish language, is, of course, related to local history; to say this is not to be unmindful of the larger significance of this great subject for so many aspects of Irish history.[111]

The purpose of this survey has been to set out a record of accomplishment. At various points, it will have been apparent that another essay could have been written on work yet to be undertaken. For many subjects, although indeed much as been done, scholars still await the book which will replace the article or the unpublished thesis, and make new knowledge more widely accessible. To end on a negative note, however, would be to fail in judgment. Valuable books, the products of careful, objective scholarship, do exist where none were before. *Irish Historical Studies,* which continues to perform distinguished services for Irish historical scholarship, has recently completed its twenty-fifth year. On this side of the Atlantic, American scholars, working both in Irish literature and in Irish history, have recently founded a society to coordinate their

[109] On Belfast: Emrys Jones, *A Social Geography of Belfast* (1960). For eighteenth- and nineteenth-century urban history, R. W. M. Strain, *Belfast and Its Charitable Society: A Story of Urban Social Development* (London, New York, and Toronto, 1961). For early industry, E. R. R. Green, *The Industrial Archeology of County Down* (Belfast, 1963).

[110] There have been a number of important works on anthropology, natural history, landscape, and folklore of interest to the historian. See: Estyn Evans, *Irish Heritage* (Belfast, 1942); Conrad Arensberg, *The Irish Countryman* (New York, 1937); and Conrad Arensberg and Solon T. Kimball, *Family and Community in Ireland* (Cambridge, Mass., 1940); Robert L. Praeger, *The Way That I Went*, 3d ed. (Dublin, 1947); and Maire MacNeill, *The Festival of Lughnasa*, for the Irish Folklore Commission (Oxford, 1962). Two examinations of the Irish scene and character might be noted: Sean O'Faolain, *The Irish,* Penguin Books (Middlesex, 1947); and Arland Ussher, *The Face and Mind of Ireland* (1949).

[111] For the language see two surveys: Daniel Corkery, *The Fortunes of the Irish Language* (Dublin, 1954) and Desmond Ryan, *The Sword of Light: From the Four Masters to Douglas Hyde* (1939).

efforts.[112] The goal which Irish history shares with all other histories is understanding. As the twentieth century creates different perspectives on the parochial and national struggles of an earlier time, historians must continue to seek, with fresh questions and with whatever new knowledge may be available, the reasons why men acted as they did, and to try to understand the nature, at different times, of the whole society in which they lived. Irish history, surely, has moved to do these things.

[112] See John V. Kelleher, "Early Irish History and Pseudo-History," *Studia Hibernica*, 3 (1963), pp. 113–127 (Paper read at the Inaugural Meeting of the American Committee for Irish Studies, Chicago, December 1961).

The British Empire
and Commonwealth in
Recent Historiography

✧

PHILIP D. CURTIN

O F THE areas and subdivisions falling under
the heading "The History of Britain and the British Empire," the field of
Imperial history holds a position that is both unique and unenviable.
Other fields, like "Tudor and Stuart England," are fixed forever in time
and space. By contrast, the Empire is not only an ungainly beast, but one
that constantly changes its size and shape with the passing of the years.
Until the middle of the nineteenth century it was hardly recognized as a
proper field of historical study. And when, early in the twentieth century, it achieved both status and a reasonable following of students and
researchers, the Empire began to transform itself into the Commonwealth, and some segments even left the Commonwealth.[1]

The result has been a paradox. The importance of the field has been
increasingly recognized as its nature and scope have been constantly
changing. From the time of Seeley onward, Imperial history has come
into its own as the Europe-centered view of history has given way to a
broader view of "world" history. The rise of Russia and the United
States, the increased importance of the new non-Western nations, and
the relative decline of Europe have all contributed something. As Europe counted for less, the Empire counted for more, and a kind of peak
was reached in the 1930's when the Empire was still intact and at its
greatest extent. Then, all of it could be taken as the proper field for Imperial history, and an enormous field it was—inhabitants in the hun-

[Reprinted from *AHR*, 65:72–91 (October 1959).]

[1] Since the British Empire has been called just that during most of its history,
the term "Empire" or "Imperial" will be used here to mean both the present Commonwealth and the present dependent Empire.

dreds of millions, hundreds of different cultures and subcultures represented, plural societies of every conceivable kind, and scores of constitutional units to serve as the political framework for as many societies,
both large and small.

But with the war and the postwar period, the same wheel that
brought the Empire into prominence gave another turn. The newly-
important colonies became more important still. As growth enabled one
after another to read itself out of the dependent Empire and into the
Commonwealth, their historians tended to read themselves out of the
field of Imperial history. Canadians, New Zealanders, and Australians
more and more cultivated their own gardens of national history, while
Burmese and Sinhalese began talking about the "British period" of their
distinct past, just as Americans had long before relegated their membership in the British Empire to a special "colonial period" of American history. These tendencies, especially in the older Dominions, were by no
means new, but the "Balkanization" of Imperial history tended in the
postwar decade to dissolve the whole in favor of the parts.

Nor was this the only threat to Imperial history as a field of study.
While some Commonwealth historians moved toward the production of
"national" history of their own countries, others, in the Commonwealth
and elsewhere, began groping toward other, quite different, frames of
reference. In the new, mid-twentieth-century setting, each country
might make a specialty of the study of its own history, but it was clearly
impossible to organize historical study so that each nation received equal
weight. Yet the history of the non-European world in the modern period
had to be taken into account. The question was: what new frame of
organization was to emerge? So far, two strong possibilities have offered
themselves, and both have developed to some extent out of the existing
field of British Empire history.

On one hand historians became increasingly aware of other European
empires. The British Empire was not a unique structure, but only the
largest and latest of a whole species. This being the case, why not study
the species as a whole, rather than take one individual in isolation? Why
not look at "the expansion of Europe," rather than the expansion of British Europeans? Some universities—even Cambridge—added the new
rubric "the expansion of Europe." By using the new approach, the modern world outside of Europe could be considered comparatively by concentrating on the most important single factor in the history of any individual country—the impact of the West.

Other historians took a different view. If the British Empire was not a unique political structure, neither was European culture the only culture worthy of specialized study. The unifying factor was not the impact of Europe, but the original cultural setting of each region of the world. The proper unit of study was "regional history." South Asia, East Asia, Southeast Asia, the Moslem world, Africa south of the Sahara, and Latin America each seemed to be an individual cultural entity. Its history should be seen from within, and the impact of British or other European expansion should be considered as an external influence. This tendency of thought was marked in the United States by the proliferation of regional "institutes" in many of the major universities, each of them avowedly "interdisciplinary" in organization and heavily supported by the funds of the philanthropic foundations. In England, the School of Oriental and African Studies at London University has shared in the trend. Symptomatically, its "Professor of the History of the British Dominions in Asia" recently became simply "Professor of Oriental History."

Both the ecumenical and the local tendencies pose a considerable future threat to the status of Imperial history as a recognized field of study. Neither tide, however, has yet run strongly enough to damage this status beyond repair. In Britain, the relative decline of Europe throws some added emphasis to the history of the Empire. In America, Imperial history has been a growing field, though at times it has grown at the expense of domestic British history. It is in the members of the Commonwealth, oddly enough, that the whole Empire has lost ground as a field of historical study—mainly for the sake of increased national history.

If Imperial history continues to hold its own, it will be partly because of a new breadth and vitality in recent historical writing. Following tendencies common to all areas of the historians' craft, the content of Imperial history has been changing in the past two decades. New depth has come to a field that was once dominantly constitutional and political, through the addition of social, economic, and intellectual history. New breadth has come through the production of first-rate works of synthesis.

To some extent, these changes have come because the problem of Empire, as seen by British policy makers, has itself changed. Dropping back twenty years to 1938, the Empire seemed to be mainly a constitutional entity. The achievement of the Statute of Westminster, the Edward VIII crisis, the set of problems surrounding the partial nonfunctioning of the Government of India Act of 1935—all of these called forth discussion, centered on the question of what Britain should do about the Empire. Since Imperial action was initially legislative, constitutional, and administrative, these things attracted the first attention of policy makers. They also attracted historians. The groundwork of Imperial constitutional and administrative history had been laid earlier in the century by A. B. Keith, G. L. Beer, and H. T. Manning, among others. In the later 1930's, the important new work often centered on current problems. Kenneth Clinton Wheare's *Statute of Westminister and Dominion Status* (1938) and Robert MacGregor Dawson's *Development of Dominion Status* (1937) explored the origins of the new Commonwealth relation. Arthur B. Keith's *A Constitutional History of India, 1600–1935* (1936) looked for the background of the Government of India Act.

These works followed an older tradition of narrowly political and constitutional history. Valuable as they still are, they could hardly answer the problems of the time. Even as they were appearing, it was increasingly clear that India and Ireland would not easily follow the road to Dominion status taken by Canada two or three decades earlier. Lord Moyne's Commission in the West Indies and Lord Hailey's *An African Survey* [2] showed that things were not going well in the dependent Empire. A thicker and deeper kind of Imperial history was needed to give a new perspective, and this kind of history was provided by Sir Keith Hancock's *Survey of Commonwealth Affairs* (2 vols., 1937, 1942). It was a history of the Empire during the interwar decades, constitutional and political in basic emphasis, but it also showed how much of Imperial history had not been written by his predecessors. By giving a new direction and emphasis, Hancock did as much as any single historian to preserve the field of Imperial history from the threats of both localism and ecumenicalism.

The *Survey* first of all asked new questions. Historians had asked, "How has the Empire been run?" and by implication, "How should it be run?" These were proper questions for, say, 1920, but by 1939 new complications invalidated some of the old answers. Hancock began again by setting his study in a new framework, centered on the problem of the state in the modern world, and of political sovereignty in general. More than this, he showed by his treatment of discrete problems in various

[2] Subtitles have frequently been omitted in the interests of preserving the free flow of the narrative.

parts of the Empire that neither a merely local approach nor a merely Imperial approach could untangle the full complexity of the history.

This is not to say that the history of central policy dropped from the scene at the end of the 1930's. There was still important work of revision to be accomplished. Paul Knaplund's *James Stephen and the British Colonial System, 1813–1847* (Madison, Wis., 1953) completed the rehabilitation of Stephen's reputation. Robert L. Schuyler surveyed the transition from the first Empire to the second in *The Fall of the Old Colonial System* (New York, 1945). Other work followed the tradition of Hancock in dealing with the history of recent times. Nicholas Mansergh's *Survey of British Commonwealth Affairs: Problems of External Policy, 1931–1939* (1952), the series of "Commonwealth Papers" edited by Sir Keith himself, and, in a different way, the "Studies of Colonial Legislatures" edited by Margery Perham all carried on the work of filling in and giving depth to studies of the Imperial constitution.

A second influence tending to strengthen the field of Imperial history against the forces of localism was the writing of broad works of synthesis taking the whole Empire through a few decades. Charles M. Andrews' *Colonial Period of American History* (New Haven, Conn., 1934–37) went back over some of the ground covered earlier by Beer. Lawrence H. Gipson's *The British Empire before the American Revolution* (1936–56; New York, 1958———) took in the whole Empire, and not merely the thirteen colonies. Gipson's synthesis is followed by Vincent T. Harlow's *The Founding of the Second British Empire, 1763–1793* of which the first volume appeared in 1952. For the period after 1793, where Harlow will end, there are still no works of broad synthesis claiming to deal with the whole Empire. William P. Morrell's earlier *British Colonial Policy in the Age of Peel and Russell* (Oxford, 1930) is very nearly a work of synthesis, but it falls short by the fact that it is just what the title indicates—a study of colonial policy rather than a general history of the Empire. Much the same is true of Alexander Brady's admirable *Democracy in the Dominions* (Toronto, 1947). It deals with the comparative political development of the Dominions in the early twentieth century, but it is limited to the Dominions.

The lack of broad synthesis between Harlow's period and the present is not merely a matter of chance. Gipson's Empire and Harlow's Empire were relatively simple compared with the Empire of the later nineteenth century. Both Brady and Hancock were forced to take something less than the whole Empire as their field. Brady did it by leaving out the dependent Empire; Hancock did it dealing at one level with the general tendencies of "Commonwealth Affairs" and at another with specific problems in particular colonial areas. Both solutions are successful in meeting the authors' purpose, but the fact of having to resort to them underlines the problem of synthesis in more recent Imperial history.

The difficulty is reflected in text and reference works. The arrangement of the *Cambridge History of the British Empire* (8 vols. in 9, Cambridge, Eng., 1929–59) is typical of the way the Empire is presented to the student. Of the eight volumes, only the first three attempt to deal with the whole Empire, in three time segments broken at 1783 and 1870 and ending in 1921. The remaining five are, in fact, national volumes for the histories of the more important dominions, so much oriented toward purely national history that the two volumes for India are identical with Volumes V and VI of *The Cambridge History of India* (Cambridge, Eng., 1932–37). Recent textbooks have met the problem in much the same fashion. They are either mainly histories of central policy, like Eric Anderson Walker's *The British Empire, Its Structure and Spirit* (1943), or else a series of separate studies of the principal events in each important region of the Empire, as in Paul Knaplund's *The British Empire, 1815–1939* (1941) or Alfred L. Burt's *Evolution of the British Empire and Commonwealth, from the American Revolution* (Boston, Mass., 1956). If the result is a patchwork, the fault lies not so much with the authors as with the intractable nature of the material itself. Canadian political or economic history, for example, is not intelligible in isolation from events in the metropolis, and neither is Imperial policy intelligible in isolation from the domestic histories of the societies that made up the Empire. Simultaneous presentation of two or more strands of narrative, however, is technically almost impossible; while isolation of one strand for separate presentation does injustice to the complex realities of Imperial politics. This problem is one shared to some extent by all historical writing, but it is more severe where Imperial ties connected quite distinct societies to one another.

Recent historical writing in the Commonwealth and the emerging new states of the tropical world, however, has not been concerned so much with the problems of synthesis as with the development of distinct traditions of national history. Canadians, for example, were once more interested in the Empire and Commonwealth as a whole than they now are.

In the later nineteenth century they felt they belonged to the Empire—not in the sense of being a British possession, but in a sense of membership. This feeling is no longer as strong as it once was. They still cling to their British heritage as a way of achieving identity against their monster neighbor to the south, just as they cling to their "North-Americanness" as a way of achieving identity as against the mother country. But there are changes. The tie to Britain means something, but the tie to the Commonwealth (to say nothing of the dependent Empire) means less and less. For historians, even the old political tie means less since the 1930's, and Canadian writers have lost interest in the constitutional and political problems centered on the attainment of responsible government. Chester Martin's *Foundations of Canadian Nationhood* (Toronto, 1955) is a symptom of the shift. In 1929, Martin produced *Empire and Commonwealth* (Oxford), a series of six more or less connected essays on the development of Canada from the first Empire to the second Empire and on to the Commonwealth. He emphasized the achievement of political nationhood within a framework that was on the whole both Imperial and British. In the new work he finds more threads of Canadian nationhood in Canada itself and in its political expansion. He is more concerned with the individuality of the Canadian experience, and is little concerned with the similarities between that experience and the similar nation-building in the United States, or in the rest of the Commonwealth.

But even those Canadians who look for historical comparisons tend to look south of the long border rather than further south across the Pacific. As early as the 1920's, Canadian historians were applying Frederick Jackson Turner's "frontier thesis" to Canadian history.[3] But the "frontier thesis" was soon modified. Aside from the need of a growing nation to find its own identity, Canada was not simply a northern extension of the United States. One important line of modification came through the greater Canadian emphasis on the role of the metropolis in westward expansion. The important work of Harold Adams Innis in economic history stressed the transportation networks which provided a link between the metropolis and the frontier. The subject was further explored by Donald G. Creighton's *The Commerical Empire of the St. Lawrence, 1760–1850* (New Haven, Conn., 1937), in which the central theme was

[3] For a recent discussion of the frontier thesis in Canadian history, see J. M. S. Careless, "Frontierism, Metropolitanism, and Canadian History," *Canadian Historical Review*, 35:1–21 (March 1954).

the rivalry between Montreal and New York for the dominance of the Canadian (and American) West. Others, too, have taken up the role of the metropolis—the influence of London in Montreal, or Montreal's relations with satellites and rivals as diverse as St. Paul, Winnipeg, and Fort Churchill. The latest of the large-scale works on this theme are John S. Galbraith's *The Hudson's Bay Company as an Imperial Factor, 1821–1869* (Berkeley, Calif., 1957), stressing the metropolitan influence of London, and Marjorie W. Campbell's anti-Hudson Bay Company study of *The North West Company* (New York, 1957).

If "metropolitanism" has been one recent tendency of Canadian historiography, "Atlanticism" has been another. It is the belief that Canadian history must be seen in a wider framework than that of the national frontiers—that Canadian history makes sense without at the same time taking in the whole Empire or the whole European expansion. Yet it cannot be properly understood unless we look simultaneously at the economic and political history of the "Atlantic community" of Britain, Canada, and the United States. The "frontier thesis," with its recognition that Canadian and American pioneers were developing a continent in common, was one parent of this view. Arthur S. Morton's *A History of the Canadian West to 1870–71* (New York, 1939) was important here, and the point was made still more explicitly in Marcus Lee Hansen's *The Mingling of the Canadian and American Peoples* (New Haven, Conn., 1940). More recently both Joseph Kinsey Howard, with *Strange Empire: A Narrative of the Northwest* (New York, 1952), and Paul F. Sharp, with *Whoop-Up Country* (Minneapolis, Minn., 1955), have produced literate and important studies of the westward advance along the forty-ninth parallel. John Bartlett Brebner's *North Atlantic Triangle* (New York) followed in 1945, filling in the political and economic aspects of Canadian-American-British interrelations, and Gerald S. Graham's *Empire of the North Atlantic* (Toronto, 1950) used the Atlantic concept in a study of Empire and sea power during the eighteenth century.

It is a point of some interest that many have begun research into some smaller part of the Atlantic community and have later found themselves drawn into "Atlanticism" by the nature of the material itself. Brebner, for example, began to study Canadian-American relations alone and found that it could not be done intelligently without reference to Great Britain. More recently, Brinley Thomas began a study of migration patterns within the Commonwealth and found in the end that he had to add the United States—that the Commonwealth alone was not a useful unit for migration studies. The result was *Migration and Economic Growth: A Study of Great Britain and the Atlantic Economy* (Cambridge, Eng., 1954).

But the greater bulk of recent Canadian historical work lies outside the scope of both "metropolitanism" and "Atlanticism." Though a purely quantitative measurement is suspicious, some of the main lines can be seen in the lists of doctoral theses in progress announced annually in the *Canadian Historical Review*. A rough tabulation of the announcement for 1955 shows the following totals:

Economic History and Economic Policy	23
Local Political History	18
Foreign Relations	14
National Political History	8
Imperial History	8
Migration History	6
Intellectual and Cultural History	4
Biography	3
Other	4

As a measure of the change in historical interest, this list can be set against the pattern of the Canadian volume of the *Cambridge History of the British Empire,* published in 1930. Only four chapters in twenty-eight were devoted to economic or financial history. Only one was devoted to foreign relations—and then only if "Canada in the World War" can be considered as foreign relations. None was specifically concerned with immigrants or where they came from. In the 1955 list, the relative rise of economic history, and of provincial and local history is outstanding. The field of Canadian foreign relations, which hardly existed two decades ago, has in many ways replaced the interest in the Empire and Imperial affairs. Canadian scholars today are clearly more concerned than ever with the specifically Canadian past and with Canada's place in the world. They are much less interested in Canadian relations with the Commonwealth, as such, or even in Canadian relations with the mother country in particular.

The same pattern is reproduced in Australia and New Zealand, with the same lack of interest in the history of the Commonwealth as such, the same shift from political and constitutional to economic history and foreign relations, the same search for an identity. But there are also differences. "Canadianism" is not the same as "New Zealandism," and even Australia and New Zealand see themselves differently in the mirror of the past.[4]

In both countries, however, historiography has reflected the tendencies of thought in general. Both showed an early optimism about the future, a belief that they were creating a nation in a desired image. In Australia it was the image of material welfare, fair shares, and a nearly classless society. In New Zealand it was that of a newer and better England in the southern seas, leading a charmed life far from the ills of the Old World. The looming giant of the United States was absent. Europe was far away. If Asia seemed to loom at times, it, too, loomed at a distance. A great deal of early Australasian history was, following this belief, something of a success story. Settlers came, defeated hardships, and made a new life for themselves. Miners came looking for gold and ended by founding a democracy. If the Maori Wars were forgotten by most or covered over by pride in a later and more successful "native policy," so were the "bad old days" of convict settlement either forgotten or taken to have little influence on the new Australia that was emerging.

But the Australasian dreams were shaken by the depressions of the 1890's and the 1930's, by the wars of the 1910's and the 1940's. In the 1930's and even earlier there began a process of reassessment that has continued after the Second World War. As in Allen Curnow's "Unhistoric Story,"

> The Pilgrim dream pricked by a cold dawn died
> Among the chemical farmers, the fresh towns; among
> Miners, not husbandmen, who pierced the side
> Let the land's life, found like all who had so long
>
> > Bloodily or tenderly striven
> > To rearrange the given
> > It was something different, something
> > Nobody counted on.[5]

Historians embarked on the search for a new identity, and for an explanation of why it was "something different, something nobody counted

---

[4] See J. C. Beaglehole, "The Development of New Zealand Nationality," *Journal of World History*, 2:106–123 (no. 1, 1954), and R. M. Crawford, "The Australian National Character in Myth and Reality," *ibid.*, 2:704–727 (no. 3, 1955).

[5] *A Book of New Zealand Verse 1923–1950*, ed. Allen Curnow (Christchurch, 1951).

on." Some New Zealanders took up the background of the welfare state, like Leslie Lipson in the mildly disenchanted *Politics of Equality* (Chicago, 1948). The main emphasis of writing in New Zealand, however, was the reconstruction of New Zealand's past on a district-by-district basis. A survey of New Zealand historical writing from 1948 to 1955 lists no less than seventy-nine district histories, by far the largest category of historical writing for the period.[6] During the same years (leaving aside studies on the Second World War), not half a dozen works appeared in New Zealand on any aspect of Imperial history in any wider sense.

The course of recent historiography in Australia has been somewhat different. Australians have tended to paint on a somewhat larger canvas, and in addition to local history they have worked more with social, economic, and intellectual history at the state or national level. The social and economic emphasis is, in itself, a part of the pattern of Australian development. Just as the Australian tradition was one of social and economic equality, so have historians followed that tradition from the time of Timothy A. Coghlan's monumental *Labour and Industry in Australia*, which appeared in four volumes during the First World War (1918). It was continued by Stephen H. Roberts and Edward O. G. Shann during the interwar years and has continued even more persistently since then. The Australian slant toward social history is evident in the choice that Charles M. H. Clark and L. J. Pryor made of material for their *Select Documents in Australian History* (2 vols., Sydney, 1950, 1955), and in the more recent cooperative work edited by Gordon Greenwood, *Australia: A Social and Political History* (Sydney, 1955). As new works that are already "standard," these two set the canon of "received" Australian history for the postwar period.

New research has taken a similar direction. Noel G. Butlin, in particular, has been working on a general reinterpretation of economic history during the second half of the nineteenth century, which he presented tentatively at the Canberra History Conference in 1957. If Butlin's work represents "pure" economic history, other writers shade off toward social history on one hand and intellectual history on the other. Some thirty theses on phases of the Australian labor movement have been undertaken since the Second World War. On the borders of economic and intellectual history, John A. La Nauze's *Political Economy in Australia* (Melbourne, 1949) bridges the gap between the Australian economy

[6] *Historical Studies—Australia and New Zealand*, 7:112–117 November 1955).

and the "Australian mind." Here again there is support from an older Australian tradition of interest in the national character and national literature, an interest marked by a peak of interpretive achievement in Sir Keith Hancock's *Australia* (1930). More recently Raymond M. Crawford's essay *Australia* (New York, 1952), Vance Palmer's *Legend of the Nineties* (Melbourne, 1954), Sidney J. Baker's *Australian Language* (1945), and George Nadel's *Australia's Colonial Culture* (Cambridge, Mass., 1957) have followed the interest in intellectual history. A series of anthologies and studies of Australian literature also represent a part of the search for the essential Australian character.

Nor are Australian historians in agreement about the nature or the origins of "Australianness." Some, like Brian Fitzpatrick, find the center of Australian history in the class struggle—a struggle both within Australia and between Australian workers and British capitalists. Australian nationalism and even Australian nationality can be seen as a product of this struggle. Others find the core of the Australian ethos in the "outback" of the bush ranger, the bush ballad, shearers' unions, "mateship," and a frontier democracy where all were equal in a common struggle against an unfriendly nature. This interpretation, though similar to the American "frontier thesis," was not derived from Turner. Australian journalists, if not historians, had discovered the uses of the outback egalitarianism well before Turner, and it was not until Frederick Alexander's brief *Moving Frontiers* (Melbourne, 1947) that a serious effort was made in Australia to compare the American and Australian frontiers.

In addition to the "frontier" school of Australian history, there is also a "metropolitan" school. It is less developed than Canadian metropolitanism, but it stresses the rule of the capital cities and denies the frontier origins of Australian democracy. These writers emphasize the importation of British liberalism in the nineteenth century. They point to the role of the urban middle class in defeating the "squatters" in the political battles of the 1850's, and some even suggest that the "bush" legend was invented in Melbourne and Sydney for partisan political purposes—specifically, in order to identify Australian nationalism with collectivist political ideas. With this, the ethos of the outback becomes an ideology, and we have come full circle—back to the quasi-Marxian interpretation.

Historical writing in and about India and Pakistan has not followed a course essentially different from that followed in Australia, New Zealand, or Canada. There is the same lack of interest in the history of the whole Empire, the same concentration on new work in local and provincial history, the same search for a national identity. But Indian nationalism was different from Canadian or New Zealand nationalism. It was a movement of protest against foreign rule rather than merely a restless self-assertion within the framework of self-government. Indian historians before the First World War took one line while British historians of India took another. Indian historians featured repressive aspects of British rule, the sins of administration, and Indian rebellions against it. British historians, on the other hand, seemed to write a history of, for, and sometimes by the administration. Constitutional, political, and legal developments were given special importance. The administrative actions of the rulers were emphasized at the expense of the social consequences they produced among the ruled. Although there were exceptions to all these tendencies, the British raj was too often represented as the end of the long road of Indian history, rather than merely the latest of a series of epochs—and one that would also pass away in time.

With the arrival of independence, reassessment came from both sides. The British period was over, and historians could do their work better now that they had some idea of how the story would end. The old emphasis on the problems of administration still left some mark on British thought, but the end of responsibility brought a new perspective. Englishmen could now sit down to a final retrospect and ask, "How well did we do? Where did we do badly, and where were we at our best?" Within a half-dozen years two works of high quality and broad scope attacked these questions. Sir Percival Griffiths' *The British Impact on India* (1952) took up the problem in its institutional aspects. Philip Mason, writing under the pen name Philip Woodruff, produced *The Men Who Ruled India* (1953–54), which turned more to the personal side of the British raj. In spite of the excellence of these works, British historians have not finished their reassessment.

The same sort of broad reassessment is also being done from the Indian side, and it will surely continue for some decades more. Kavalam Madhava Panikkar's *Asia and Western Dominance* (1953) is one example, with a broad view stretching to all of Asia. In a narrower field, N. V. Sovani's two articles in the *Journal of World History* for 1954 are a dispassionate assessment of British rule, and mainly of its economic aspects.[7] Another example of the new objectivity is Surendra Nath Sen's

[7] N. V. Sovani, "British Impact on India before 1850–57," *Journal of World History*, 1:857–882 (no. 4, 1954), and "British Impact on India after 1850–57," *ibid.*, 2:77–105 (no. 1, 1954).

1857 (Delhi, 1957), a balanced history of the great Mutiny after a century during which many Indian historians wrote about it partly in the cause of Indian nationalism and only partly in the cause of scholarship.

Another kind of recent Indian historiography growing out of independence is the history of the nationalist movement. There have been biographies of Jinnah, Gandhi, Nehru, and Tilak, reflecting to a greater or less extent the kind of hagiography that dealt with Washington in the first generation after the American Revolution. Other work has been more general, dealing with some part of the movement as a whole. Aksayakumar Ramanlal Desai's *Social Background of Indian Nationalism* (Oxford, 1948), and "Minoo" Masani's *Communist Party of India* (1954) are among the increasing number of works in this class. In addition, Indian historians reflect the coming of independence in their concern with foreign policy. As in Canada, studies have begun to appear that trace Indian foreign policy back into the period when it was managed by British officials.

Along with the necessary reassessment and history of nationalism, there has been new and original work on the more distant past by both Indian and foreign historians. They have gone back over the fields covered earlier, clearing up, straightening out, and deepening the places where investigation has been shallow. Perhaps the most important general result of this work is to point out the extent to which the British raj was not a single organism. Instead, it was only a superstructure, covering, but not entirely obscuring, the vast variety of South Asian life. Here, as in Canada and Australia, the new movement toward economic and social history came into its own. Holden Furber's *John Company at Work* (Cambridge, Mass., 1948) did much to set the trend by emphasizing the commercial operations of the British East India Company rather than the more spectacular crimes and achievements of Clive and Hastings. It was followed by Sukumar Bhattacharya's *East India Company and the Economy of Bengal* (1954), dealing with the early eighteenth century. In 1956 Narendra Sinha published the first volume of his *Economic History of Bengal* (Calcutta), this one covering the period from Plassey to the Permanent Settlement, while Amales Tripathi brought out *Trade and Finance in the Bengal Presidency, 1793–1833* (Bombay). British historians have also turned to the social and economic history of India, as in the work of Kenneth Ballhatchet on *Social Policy and Social Change in Western India 1817–30* (Oxford, 1957). Taken together, these works represent two new tendencies of Indian historiography. Fol-

lowing the process of reassessing the British period, they have over-
turned once and for all the "black legend" of British financial policy that
Romesh Chandra Dutt developed during the struggle for independence.
But their more important contribution has been to shift the framework
of investigation from the whole of India to a single province. A great
deal more work of similar scope must be done before the outlines of Indian history in the British period can be called complete.

Recent trends in the historical writing about South Africa have been
somewhat different from those in other members of the Commonwealth.
South Africa's recent history has itself been different. Embittered relations between the English-speaking and the Afrikaans-speaking segments of the white community, the rise of the Nationalist party, and a
new awakening of the African majority have all had their influence on
historiography. The Afrikaners, to be sure, have looked for the historical
roots of their national identity, just as the Canadians or Australians have
done. This is no new development; but after Jan Smuts's passing the
Empire meant very little. The "double nationalism" of Empire and country, which was never very strong in the Afrikaner community, now began to disappear altogether. Afrikaans history not only ignored the "Imperial Factor" and concentrated on local events, it also returned to the
early and middle nineteenth century, to the period of the Great Trek
and its aftermath. The spread of white settlement into the interior took
on the proportions of an Afrikaner national epic. One might call this a
movement toward "frontierism," but it was not the same kind of frontier
as elsewhere. It was not the frontier of "mateship" or Clear-Grit radicalism, nor simply a conquest over nature or an unfriendly environment. It
was first of all the conquest of an alien and "barbarous" people who already held the land. Rather than looking to this frontier for the roots of
democratic institutions, the Afrikaners have been searching for a parochial tradition that could stand up against the outside influence of British liberalism. They have not only revived the republican traditions of
the Transvaal and the Orange Free State; some have even turned to the
former republics for traditions of nonparliamentary government and of
one-party rule.

English-speaking South Africans, British historians, and foreigners
have taken a different line. They, too, have tried to explain the present
by investigating the past. They, too, have asked, "How have things come
to be as they are?" Their difference with the Afrikaners lies in their interpretation of the present. Where one group sees mainly the rise and

triumph of the Afrikaner nation, the other sees mainly the rise of racial tension, the failure of liberalism, and the failure of the Empire. On the English-language side, there was once a period of self-congratulation over the liberal peace of Vereeniging and the formation of the Union, but it barely lasted into the 1920's. Later in the decade, W. M. Macmillan was already writing the history of nineteenth-century "native policy" with the implicit question, "Where did we fail?" The question was asked again in the earlier works of the Dutch-born Cornelis W. de Kiewiet. It was developed further in the detailed treatment of "The Settlers' Frontier in Southern Africa," in the final volume of Sir Keith Hancock's *Survey of British Commonwealth Affairs* (New York, 1942). De Kiewiet returned to the problem during the war and presented his interpretation in a general work, *A History of South Africa, Social and Economic* (Oxford, 1946). Some South African historians, like Arthur Keppel-Jones, have followed in the same tradition.

However different this tradition may be from that of the Afrikaners, it would be a mistake to think of it as anti-Boer history. These historians deplore the present condition of South Africa without blaming one segment or the other of the dominant minority. The failures may have come partly with the rise of a Boer nationalism, but they also came through the racial attitudes of the white (and originally English-speaking) trade-unions, through the peculiarities of South African economic growth, and through the failures of British liberalism itself. Hancock dealt with some of the failures of liberalism during the interwar years. G. B. Pyrah's *Imperial Policy and South Africa, 1902–1910* (Oxford, 1955) went back to the crucial period of the "transfer of power," when Liberal statesmen abdicated their responsibilities and turned South Africa over to the white minority in the name of Liberal principles. On the other side, Sheila Patterson's *The Last Trek* (1957) traces the development of the Afrikaner mentality from the nineteenth century, when the Boers were an "out-group" suffering under what they conceived as British oppression. She shows how much of the old attitude remains, even though the Afrikaners are now clearly the dominant minority in their own country. Gwendolen M. Carter's *Politics of Equality* (New York, 1958) fills in the political history of the last ten years with an evenhanded condemnation.

Amid the diversity of interpretation in recent South African history, it is worth noting that neither the English-speaking nor the Afrikaans-speaking historians have paid much attention to the history of the African peoples who make up the vast majority of the country. There is, however, a third tradition of South African historiography. Some writers, though rarely the professional historians, have made a beginning at investigating African history in the southern part of the continent. Much of the work in this field rests on a base of long standing. A. T. Bryant and J. Y. Gibson began publishing Zulu history and tradition early in this century. In 1931 F. H. Dutton translated Thomas Mofolo's classic *Shaka* into English from Sesuto (Oxford). More recently, Ernest A. Ritter, in *Shaka Zulu* (1955) tried to see Shaka as the Zulus saw him.

Although Zulu history has held a special fascination for Europeans, other regions have received increasing attention in recent decades. Heinrich Vedder's *Das alte Südwestafrika* (Berlin, 1934), an excellent reconstruction of tribal history and the history of the European conquest, was translated into English in 1938 under the title, *South West Africa in Early Times*. Isaac Schapera's *The Bantu-Speaking Tribes of South Africa* (1956) contains a great deal of history, though unhistorically presented. Within a smaller scope, G. Tylden's *Rise of the Basuto* (Cape Town, 1950) is a concise synthesis of the history of Basutoland from the Basuto point of view, and A. Sillery's *Sechele* (Oxford, 1954), is one of the best of a number of biographies of important African leaders. Most of these works deal with pre-European Africa, but there is also a history of Africans under European rule. Bengst G. M. Sundkler's *Bantu Prophets in South Africa* (1948) tells a great deal more about what happened to African culture in the twentieth century than the formal historical works usually do.

The fact that most of these authors were not professional historians is a symptom of the status of history north of the Limpopo as well. The early writers and collectors of history were (and still are, to a large extent) administrators, missionaries, or anthropologists. The professional historians seemed determined to leave the field of African history—as opposed to the history of European activity in Africa—to amateurs or to members of other disciplines. Some of the best of the older generation of historians, like Sir Reginald Coupland, held that there was no African history before the nineteenth century. This was certainly true before the First World War, in the sense that there was no body of historical knowledge about Africa. There were occasional works, like those of Raymond L. Buell, John W. Blake, Samuel Johnson, Edward W. Bovill, William W. Claridge, or Elizabeth Donnan's collection of slave-trade documents. But, in general, to find an adequate history of any part of Africa for any period was the exception rather than the rule.

Certain aspects of African history, however, were dealt with more thoroughly than others. Historians were especially interested in the diplomacy of imperialism and the relations between the European powers scrambling for Africa in the decades before 1900. But they were much less interested in the diplomacy between the Europeans and the African states, and they tended to recolor the map on the basis of European agreements, without bothering about the actual conquest of the country. Africa, in short, was treated as a large block of real estate, and the Africans were not thought sufficiently civilized to be treated as protagonists of history.

For the period after the European conquest, the principal interest of British scholars was administration and administrative history—an interest clearly derived from the British administrative responsibility for a large part of Africa. In this field they produced historical work of a high quality, much of which was summed up in the historical sections of Lord Hailey's *African Survey: A Study of Problems Arising in Africa South of the Sahara* (1938; rev. ed., 1957). The *Survey* and the work that went before it, however, were not historical in their basic purpose, and in the final presentation the historical material is treated merely as a background for contemporary administrative problems.

With the Second World War and the postwar period a new generation of historians appeared who took seriously the problem of writing African history. They found large areas untouched by previous research, and they found a preliminary job of removing old errors—beginning with the belief that there was no African history before the coming of the Europeans, and no purpose to writing the history of African activities even after that date. Though they still left most pre-European African history to the anthropologists, they did some of their most effective work in the period just before the European conquest, where European records are available.

For West Africa, K. Onwuka Dike's *Trade and Politics in the Niger Delta* (Oxford, 1956) struck a new balance in weighing the African and European aspects of Anglo-African relations, without at the same time trying to redress past errors by glorifying the African past for the sake of present nationalism. Saburi O. Biobaku's *The Egba and Their Neighbours* (Oxford, 1957) is the history of an African people, rather than a history of political and economic contact between Africans and Europeans, and it shows how much "straight" African history can be reconstructed from European archives. W. E. F. Ward's *History of the Gold*

Coast (1948) is based on oral tradition, while another step toward the reconsideration of African history is John D. Fage's *Atlas of African History* (1958), which gives full weight to African as well as European activity.

The Sudan has been another center of historical activity. The sum of the work of British and Sudanese alike is a fuller reconstruction of the history of the Sudan than of any part of tropical Africa except Ghana. Mekki Shibeika's *British Policy in the Sudan, 1882–1902* (1952) is an objective account of the Mahdiyya. For a later period, Saad ed din Fawzi's *The Labour Movement in the Sudan 1946–1955* (1957) is an important contribution to the history of African nationalism and the coming of independence, a field that is receiving increasing attention. Richard Hill's work on bibliography and biography provides reference tools not generally available for African history. Anthony J. Arkell has recently summarized the earlier history of the country in his *History of the Sudan to A.D. 1821* (1954), while John S. Trimingham provides another kind of basic summary, this time of religion, ethnography, and politics in his *Islam in the Sudan* (1949). With all this new work, however, there are still wide gaps, notably the virtually untouched period of the Egyptian occupation of 1821 to 1881.

Elsewhere in British tropical Africa historical work has been more scattered, and historians have tended to concentrate on the Imperial theme more than they have done in most of the Commonwealth. There have been important biographies of Sir Harry Johnston by Roland A. Oliver in 1957 and of Lord Lugard by Margery Perham in 1956. The missionary movement has been increasingly studied, first of all by Charles P. Groves in his multi-volume *The Planting of Christianity in Africa* (4 vols., 1948–58), which appeared from 1948 onward. Both Roland A. Oliver's *Missionary Factor in East Africa* (1952) and A. J. Hanna's *The Beginnings of Nyasaland and North-Eastern Rhodesia, 1859–1895* (Oxford, 1956) are important studies of the role of missionaries in the European conquest.

But in tropical Africa as in South Africa, some of the most important work—important, that is, for its impact on historical knowledge—is being done by researchers from other disciplines. Probably the most important change in the interpretation of African history in recent decades is the contribution of the American linguist Joseph H. Greenberg, whose *Studies in African Linguistic Classification* (New Haven, Conn., 1955) forced a complete reconsideration of the Hamite problem and effectively destroyed the old hypotheses about the movement of peoples and cultures in pre-European Africa. The anthropologists have recorded a great deal of tribal history which may sometime be useful, though at present it is scattered and uncoordinated. More important, they have contributed greatly to history in their studies of social change under the impact of European rule. Lloyd A. Fallers' *Bantu Bureaucracy* (Cambridge, Eng., 1957) can serve as an example of this work. Formally, it is a study of the Soga and the impact of European administration on the native political system, and the basic orientation is anthropological. At least 80 per cent of the work, however, is history in everything but name, and it is better history than many historians are now writing about Africa. Much the same might be said of Arnold L. Epstein's *Politics in an Urban African Community* (Manchester, Eng., 1958), which deals with the recent history of Northern Rhodesia, or of David E. Apter's *Gold Coast in Transition* (Princeton, N.J., 1955) for the transfer of power in Ghana. Whoever does the writing, it is clear that the history of British tropical Africa has been transformed and is still being transformed into a new body of knowledge, in which the recognized "history of Africa" as it existed in 1938 will form only a small part.

The history of other scattered parts of the dependent Empire has taken a course similar to that of African history. Like the history of the Empire as a whole, the prewar history of the dependent Empire was largely a history of British administration, put together from the official prints, memoirs, and the official records at the Public Record Office. These records are invaluable, of course, but they are not the only sources for Imperial history. They were, furthermore, gathered with a certain selectivity—by administrators and for purposes of administration. Sir Keith Hancock tells of having prepared in London a manuscript on the Maltese constitution. He later went to Malta with the intention of adding a little local color and filling in a few gaps, but he found from local experience that he had to tear up his draft and begin again.[8] Too many historians never made the trip at all, and their manuscripts ended in print rather than in the wastebasket. Fortunately, this sole dependence on London is passing, and with its passing a revision of the history of each of the smaller colonies is beginning, often with a broadening leaven of social and economic and intellectual history, and with some techniques borrowed from other social sciences.

These trends are actually those common to the history of central pol-

[8] Sir Keith Hancock, *Country and Calling* (1954), p. 156.

icy or to the history of any of the larger members of the Commonwealth. There is in the best new history of any part the realization that the history of the Empire cannot be written solely within the local or solely within the Imperial frame of reference. Neither the narrow local circle of vision nor the circle of vision of the metropolitan center—equally narrow, in its own way—is adequate. When two societies are connected politically and economically and intellectually as part of a single Empire, however amorphous, both societies must be considered simultaneously before the history of either can be made truly intelligible. In the long run, it is this fact, which Hancock recognized in the 1930's, that has kept Imperial history a viable unit of study in spite of the disruptive tendencies of fission and fusion.

This essay was first drafted in the summer of 1958. In the intervening years the historiography of British Empire history has changed even more rapidly than in the period 1938–1958 covered by the essay. Knowledge of the subject has expanded in many directions. New concerns with local history, with social, economic, and intellectual history, with the history of nonwestern societies, and with comparative history have changed our whole outlook. The result by 1965 is a body of knowledge far too large to serve as a useful area for historical specialization. When the core of British Empire history was political and constitutional history, normally viewed from the perspective of London, the individual historian could achieve a general competence. He might work effectively in the history of many different geographical areas. Today, this is no longer the case.

Regional specialization, which seemed a growing tendency in 1958, has now triumphed. The history of the British Empire in Africa is rapidly being annexed by African history. In 1958, courses in African history were offered by no more than a half dozen universities. Today there are at least fifty. The history of British India has gradually been absorbed into the broader history of South Asia. Regional specialization in the history of Southeast Asia has grown to annex Malaysia. By 1964, even the *American Historical Review* had responded to the changing patterns. New works on Australian history were reviewed under the heading, "Asia and the East" (though a conservative strain kept the listings of new articles under "The Commonwealth and Ireland").

The growth of regional specialization has been accompanied by a decline of interest in the field of history formally labeled "British Empire and Commonwealth." But this decline is only apparent. In effect, the scope of the subject is being redefined. The new tendency is to restrict "British Empire" to the study of central policy, Canada, Australia, and New Zealand. Interest in this narrower field of history has not declined, though it has not grown as rapidly as interest in Africa and Asia. Within the broader field of history covered by this essay, recent historical work has been in greater quantity and of higher quality than ever before. What has taken place in recent years is the inevitable fission of a growing body of knowledge. As it becomes too large and complex for convenience, new areas of specialization emerge.

THE AUTHORS OF THE ESSAYS

WILLIAM A. BULTMANN is Professor of British History at Ohio Wesleyan University

JOHN CLIVE is Professor of History and Literature at Harvard University

PHILIP D. CURTIN is Professor of History at the University of Wisconsin

PAUL H. HARDACRE is Professor of History at Vanderbilt University

MARGARET HASTINGS is Professor of History at Rutgers—the State University of New Jersey

J. JEAN HECHT is Research Associate at Columbia University

MAURICE LEE, JR., is Professor of History at the University of Illinois

BRYCE LYON is Professor of Medieval History at Brown University

HELEN F. MULVEY is Professor of History at Connecticut College for Women

ROGER W. PROUTY is Visiting Lecturer in History at the University of Massachusetts at Boston

LACEY BALDWIN SMITH is Professor of History at Northwestern University

ROBERT WALCOTT is Professor of History at the College of Wooster

HENRY R. WINKLER is Professor of History at Rutgers—the State University of New Jersey

PEREZ ZAGORIN is Professor of History at the University of Rochester

THE CONFERENCE ON BRITISH STUDIES

When after the war attendance at the annual meetings of the American Historical Association grew to mammoth proportions, scholars interested in British history formed the Conference on British Studies, with eastern, midwestern, and western sections, in order to maintain more intimate contact through smaller meetings, in spring and fall. The Conference circulates a newsletter, *The British Intelligencer,* and issues periodical surveys of "work in progress," the latest of which is *Current Research in British Studies by American and Canadian Scholars,* edited by Anthony H. Forbes and Marion J. Johnson (Marquette, Mich.: Northern Michigan University Press, 1964). The Conference has founded a scholarly periodical, *The Journal of British Studies,* published at Trinity College, Hartford, Connecticut, the first number of which appeared in 1961. The Conference also offers triennially a prize of $300 for the best first book in the field of English or Commonwealth history by an American or Canadian scholar. Past recipients have been Philip P. Poirier in 1960 and C. Warren Hollister in 1963. The Conference was incorporated under the laws of the State of New York in 1964.

Index of Authors Cited

❖